BACKYARD RACEHORSE

FOURTH EDITION

**Written by Janet Del Castillo
and Lois Schwartz**

Illustrated by Janet Del Castillo

COVER PHOTO BY ANGIE DRAPER

D0543427

Published by:
Prediction Publications & Productions
3708 Crystal Beach Road
Winter Haven, FL 33880

Library of Congress Catalog Card No. 93-086831
ISBN No. 1-884475-02-7

ii

ATTENTION

Anyone engaged in training horses, exposes himself to the inherent and associated risks of such actions, including possible personal injury. This manual suggests techniques for training racehorses, but in no way assures or represents that trying these techniques will not result in injury. When you partake in any activity with horses, you do so at your own risk. The authors and publishers disclaim all liability in connection with the use of the information provided in this manual. Seek professional instruction and supervision, before attempting new skills.

TABLE OF CONTENTS

You'll Like This!

**Flip through the bottom right-hand corner of the book
to see the horses gallop.**

ACKNOWLEDGMENTS

The following people have been a great source of information. I sincerely appreciate the time they have spent with me in person, on the telephone or through correspondence. Communication between those of us in the industry is of utmost importance if we hope to achieve our goal of being informed owners, trainers, and veterinarians.

Tom Ainslie, Writer, *The Racing Form*; Thomas L. Aronson, Racing Resource Group, Inc.; W. Ashbury, DVM, University of Florida, Gainesville, FL; Ann Cain, Mullica Hill, NJ; Albert A. Cirelli, Jr., Professor, University of Nevada; Pat Clark, Circle Resources, Mansfield, TX; Michael Conder, Melbourne, FL; Sharon Creigier, PhD, Prince Edward Island, Canada; Trevor Denman, Track Announcer at Del Mar, Hollywood Park, and Santa Anita, CA; Michael Dickenson, Fair Hill Training Center, Elkton, MD; C. Douglas Donn, General Manager, Gulfstream Racetrack, Miami, FL; C. Kenneth Dunn, President & General Manager, Calder Racetrack, Miami, FL; Gail Emerson, Equine Dental Technician; Cheryl Hall, DVM, Merced, CA; Sue Hengemuehle, DVM, Okemos, MI; Donna Harper, DVM, Las Lunas, NM; Carol Holden, Sporting Life Farm, Middleburg, VA; Heather and George Humphries, Leesburg, VA; Robert Jack, DVM, President, American Association of Equine Practitioners; Ruth B. James, DVM, Mills, WY; William E. Jones, DVM, PhD; Mary Ann and David Kent, Kent Arabian Farm, Grand Rapids, MN; Lennart Krook, DVM, PhD, Cornell University; Mary Lebrato, Rio Linda, CA; Michael Martin, President, Thoroughbred Horseman's Association, Inc.; C. Wayne McIlwraith, BVSc, PhD, Colorado State University; Mary D. Midkiff, Equestrian Resources; Robert M. Miller, DVM, Thousand Oaks, CA; Larry Moriarity, Master Equine Dentist; Ed Noble, DVM., Ocala, FL; Roy Poole, Jr., DVM, PhD, University of California at Davis; James Rooney, DVM, Professor, Veterinary Science, University of Kentucky; Scott Savin, President, Florida Horsemen's Benevolent & Protective Association; Sue Stover, DVM, University of California at Davis; Bill H. Walmsley, National President, Horsemen's Benevolent & Protective Association: Alistair Webb, BVSc, PhD, FRCVS, University of Florida, Gainesville, FL; Gerald Wessner, DVM, Tampa, FL; Greg Wisner, Thoroughbred Pedigree Consultant, Dallas, TX; Holly Wright, J & J Tack, Lakeland, FL.

Special Thanks To Mary Ann Chessman and Lee Schonberg for their help

ELLIE CROWDER- Thankyou!

Thankyou Kim Shelley for keeping the horses Galloping while I worked.

Walda- I owe you Big Time!

Sharing information is vital to our industry.

THANK YOU!   THANK YOU!   THANK YOU!

Sometimes I think I'm all alone and shouting against the wind. That is not so. I have a wonderful support system of family and friends who have encouraged me in my endeavors. To them I say, "Thank you." It is important that someone somewhere believes that what you are doing has value. These people, at various times of my highs and lows, have been there to give me the courage to carry on.

Mom and Jim -who were always ready to pitch in when the going got rough.

My children - Alex, Nando and Victoria - have certainly shared in the overall adventure . . . helping me acquire the knowledge and experience I have put in this manual. We are all better people, in spite of the struggle and hardship we have endured. Adversity builds character . . . isn't that so?

Barbara, Lucille, Marlene, Ubie and Walda - all have helped in their very special and unique ways. Special thanks to Matthew Mackay-Smith, DVM, Medical Consultant for *Equus Magazine*, for his comments and suggestions. Also to Carol Marusak, DMV who kindly advised us on medical issues. My appreciation of the endless patience and guidance of the Tampa Bay Downs Stewards, Dick Kinsey, Charles Miranda, and Dennis Lima, must also be mentioned.

A special thanks to Lois, my type "A" pain in the neck editor, who tries to keep me on the straight and narrow. Due to her efforts, this edition is more logical and readable.

This 4th Edition would have taken much longer on its journey to the press without the help of *Jacki Hanks* and *Mitzi Perry*. Many thanks to them both.

While speaking of editing, I must thank Taryl Elliot for the final fine combing of the text. And very special thanks to Marianne Chessman and Lee   for the wonderful job they did of reviewing and bringing little bloopers (and a few big ones) to our attention.

Charlie Carmac and his son, Andy, deserve much recognition for their kindness and help over the years at Tampa Bay Downs and the Miami tracks.

Many, many others, owners and trainers who put up with my unusual methods, track personnel, entry clerks, stewards, stall men, grooms . . . I've learned from all of them. Exchanging experiences and sharing ideas helps us all become better educated about horses and training.

Thanks to patient owners ... I wish their horses were faster!

I hope my manual is the beginning of an open forum to share hands-on knowledge and improve the welfare of the horse and the future of HORSERACING!

DEDICATION

This edition is dedicated in memory of my mother, Mary Griffin and her husband Jim, and Lois' husband, Eddie Schwartz. They were the source of happiness, inspiration and comfort to us both. We miss them deeply and wish to acknowledge the tremendous influence they had on our lives.

The other deep loss that must be mentioned is my sweet mare, First Prediction. She was my wonderful racehorse and is the horse that makes the cover of the book so beautiful.

A Word About the Fourth Edition

Much has happened in our personal lives and in the world of racing since we began working on this book ten years ago. The first edition appeared in a loose leaf notebook. We like to believe we have made much progress since then. We also believe that the research done by the scientific branch of our sport has shown enormous progress. That progress when used judiciously with a thorough understanding of its benefits and problems is priceless to all horsemen and women.

Saturday saw the running of the Preakness. Tears came to Lois' eyes as Funny Cide tore down the stretch. They were tears of joy for a horse owned by everyday people and trained by a long-standing trainer. May the winning streak carry on to the Belmont which will be run after this edition goes to press. Our hope is that our readers are inspired to believe that anyone can win these races if they happen to find a talented horse and treat it judiciously.

This edition includes some wonderful letters from our readers. These letters are delightful. We hope you enjoy them. Those of you who are dealing with your own horses will certainly relate to the problems these readers have encountered and solved. We love hearing from you and want to thank everyone who has written. We wish there was space for all your letters.

FOREWORD

Many factors went into the decision to write this manual. The first was the need for more communication with those outside the racehorse industry who were considering becoming a part of it. My intent is to have a friendly dialogue with people who share my love of horses. The first few chapters are very basic and maybe repetitious to those of you who are at home around horses. They are to help newcomers get a grasp on things. I hope to encourage all of you, especially the COMPETENT HORSEPERSON to consider racehorses. If you have competed in Rodeos, Hunter-Jumper Events, Horse Shows or other equine competitions, and trained your horse yourself, you may be experienced enough to train for racing. I hope this manual will teach you to adapt your own circumstances to train a useful racehorse. You may have your own property or keep your horse at a boarding stable. Either option can work.

I recall those days of innocence when we naively said, "Let's own racehorses!" The learning process was slow, painful and filled with disappointment. We started with mares and foals. It took a long time to get to the reality of the racetrack. Along the way, my family and I learned about fencing, animal feed, mare and foal care, and breaking and training. The responsibility of raising and caring for animals was a good discipline for us all. The animals always had to be taken care of first. Our plans had to fit around their schedule. The children were able to earn a little towards their college, while being a part of our side business. Tax-wise, this helped offset income from other sources. We read trade magazines and discovered that stakes horses won the big purses. We could always trace the blood lines of our backyard horses to some famous racehorse. They are all related, if you go back far enough.

The real trials and tribulations came when the horses had to go to the track and a trainer. There were so many hurdles to overcome before getting a horse in a race let alone the winner's circle. There was another complete language to learn at the track. Terms like, "break his maiden", or "fire the legs" or "blister the knees." What did it all mean? When I queried, I was assured I didn't need to worry my pretty little head about such things and was told, "Just send the check."

I was the liaison between the person who paid the bill (my husband) and the person who wanted the bills paid (the trainer). Explaining to my husband why the horse wasn't running or describing to him some new wonder they were performing to enable the horse to run was not easy. My husband was a very high-strung, volatile doctor who didn't want excuses. Today, 30 years later, I remember him closing the encyclopedia after reading that Thorough-bred horse racing is the Sport of the Kings and saying, "Well, we have breeding that goes back to Kentucky Derby winners on both sides. I want my horse trained for the Kentucky Derby. With good breeding and good blood there is no reason he can't win." He called the trainer and told him to train the horse for nothing less than the Triple Crown. After a few months, the trainer finally said, in exasperation, "Doctor, this horse can't even beat my pony horse. He's not fast enough to work yet." At that point, my husband decided the trainer hadn't enough faith in our horse. We found someone else who was willing to tell him what he wanted to hear.

Another thing I remember about our first trainer was his billing creativity. In the 1970's he was charging $35 per day in base costs. He then itemized and charged extra for bandages,

**Everything suggested in this manual worked for me!
Do what works for your circumstances?**

safety pins, electrolytes, as well as for legitimate items such as shoes and vet costs. In his own way, he got even for having to put up with a temperamental, difficult owner.

So we went to the races. The hardest part for us was having to face reality. After we invested $18,000 in the horse, he was going to have to run for a $3,500 claiming price. How could that be? The concept of someone claiming our horse, after all our sweat and money, was beyond comprehension. If you have been raised around the track you understand . . . outsiders and newcomers don't. We had to learn to "Put the horse where it can win." Unwillingly after a few humiliating races, we allowed the horse to be dropped to a level where he became a useful claimer . . . not the Triple Crown . . . but once in a while he helped to pay his board bill.

The illusion of racing and the reality of racing were so different that soon my husband refused to accept the collect calls from the trainer. He no longer wanted to hear the word "horse" spoken in his presence. Surreptitiously I had the horses shipped back to the farm to do what I could. About that time, my husband and I parted ways, for reasons that had nothing to do with horses, and I decided to give myself two years to see if I could train well enough to support the small farm.

At that point, I started looking for books on how to train racehorses. There were books that interviewed famous trainers, books about famous horses, one that had the routine of a known trainer, but nothing that worked in my situation. So, by luck, observation, and hard work, my own style of training evolved. I've done my homework, and in the following pages will share my knowledge and observations with you. I will continually stress that my way is not the only way. In fact this is one of the most important lessons for you to learn. There are many ways to "skin a cat." Open your mind. See how my suggestions relate to your circumstances. Don't be afraid to try your own ideas. But first and foremost, keep the welfare of the horse in mind.

Since Lois read the book and got hooked on racehorses, she has scattered some comments of her own through the book. She thinks that just because she has a hunter-jumper-dressage-cowhorse background, raised our foals to about twenty-four months and spends hours at the computer working on the book, she has the right to an opinion. As of this edition she is clinging to the sixties, riding gaited horses through the mountains of Tennessee and still kibitzing.

Whether you are training Appaloosas, Arabians, Paints, Quarter Horses or Thoroughbreds, a horse is a horse is a horse. Basic horse sense and training development are the same. The personalities of the various breeds differ. Thoroughbreds and Arabians are more hot blooded.

We all have been intimidated into believing the only place to train a horse is at the racetrack. Expensive for us . . . and unnatural for the horse. The joy of doing it yourself, in your own environment can be a major part of training. Your sense of accomplishment when the horse you trained wins will never be matched or forgotten. With this in mind, come with me and . . .

Let the games begin!

LET The GAMES BEGIN!

THE IMPOSSIBLE DREAM

TO BEGIN THE GREAT ADVENTURE . . .

THE IMPOSSIBLE DREAM
by Alex Del Castillo

I shouldered my sea bag and waved one last time at my ride as it disappeared over the hill. Home at last! I drank it all in with a thirst that was born from a long absence and made more acute by the rigors of Navy life. My steps carried me through the white pillars marking the entrance to our drive. Home was Rancho Del Castillo, all white board fence and lush green pasture and, of course, the horses. They were in large open paddocks along either side of the drive, trotting about with their ears perked up, placidly munching grass or fussing with a friend over the fence. Just doing horse things and being horses.

What looked to be an older two-year-old took notice of my presence, stuck his head through the top two boards and gazed at me expectantly. That earned him a pat on the neck and a rub behind the ears as I murmured in the low, soft tones that I had always used with our animals. As he nuzzled me in return, I found myself savoring the not unpleasant smell of a healthy horse. That may sound silly to someone who has never spent much time around the animals, or is so familiar with them that one stops noticing it. However, being on leave from the Navy, where cold metal, gray paint, hydraulic fluid and PineSol are the order of the day, a soft nuzzle and the scent of a horse's breath had the same effect as a home cooked meal. You have to understand, I feel pangs of sentiment whenever I catch a whiff of horse manure, even at a parade.

When I got to the house nobody was around. This was not unexpected as both my sister and brother had long since moved out and on to lives of their own. I had hoped to catch my mother between trips to the track, but instead only got a glimpse of her in the sharp white and red diesel pickup with a matching trailer as she pulled away from the barn and started on the oft traveled trek to Tampa or Calder, Hialeah, or Gulfstream in Miami. It was still relatively early and both sides of the two-horse trailer were occupied.

I considered what this meant with regards to when my mother might return. It was March, so her most likely destination was Tampa Bay Downs, then in season and an easy hour or so away. The early hour meant Mom probably intended to work at least one of her charges through the gates or get a timed work before the racing started at 1:00 PM. If neither horse were in a race that day, she could arrive at the track, work the horses, take care of any business on the backside and probably be home early in the afternoon. If she had a race, her return would be delayed.

Things had not always been so predictable. As a teenager I had spent my school weekends and summers, as had my siblings, helping Mom campaign our then meager retinue of cheap claimers. In those days that "crazy lady from Winter Haven" would show up at the receiving barn in a tired old Wagoneer and equally battle scarred red trailer. Old track hands would snicker as the harried red headed mother of three would direct her kids in the unloading of the horses from the trailer and then see to the transfer to stalls in the receiving barn. "You see", they would say, "she's got it all wrong. Race horses belong at the track, where they race; you can't ship in the day of the race and win". They would continue on about her other silly notions, but were tolerant, albeit condescending to this outsider. I noticed that many of these sage old experts had holes in their shoes.

In spite of the common wisdom, we did begin to win; nothing spectacular mind you, just enough to keep the bill collectors at bay. My mother's convictions, which fundamentally were based in the tenent that horses should be allowed to be horses, pure and simple, had begun to pay off. Early in the game she noticed that many horses kept at the track developed vices and personality problems. She always said a good racehorse need not be psychotic.

Training at home consisted of gallops through the adjacent orange groves, swimming in the lake and, perhaps, most importantly, spending most of the day in open paddocks as opposed to being cooped up in a stall all day and asked to go all out for one of the twenty-four hours. It was no wonder to me that horses kept at the track tended to be more high strung. A trip-wire psycho horse is not necessarily any faster than a sane one. I suspect many such horses expend themselves in antics before the race.

As time went on, my mother carved a respectable niche for herself and her methods. She was not alone in her philosophy of training, and people were starting to pay her to train horses for them. Her reputation was that of an honest trainer with somewhat of an unorthodox method. She shunned gimmicks and drugs, preferring to get many honest runs out of a healthy horse rather than race an unfit, injured horse maintained by painkillers or questionable surgeries. The key to her method was that of a sound foundation - her horses didn't start racing until they were fully developed and fit, somewhere around three years of age.

While it is true that three-year-olds race in the Kentucky Derby, many people don't realize how many youngsters are broken down and rendered unfit to race before their first win. It is only the exceptional and precocious that can be so successful at such an early age. Poor folks can't afford to pick the stars out of hundreds of horses. We have to do the best with what we've got. I shudder to think how many viable (not Derby winners, but horses that might have had respectable and profitable careers) horses have been squandered by having been pushed too hard, too soon. The fact that Mom is still in business without ever having to pay big bucks for "Blacktype" horses or stables of yearlings, proves the validity of her philosophy. It should also be noted that not one of the horses she instills with the aforementioned sound foundation has ever broken down at the track. This is no small feat.

As I write this, I gaze out to the back pasture. Down near the lake a small, unassuming gray mare munches on grass, now and then swishing her tail at the occasional fly. It occurs to me her story will help illustrate my remarks thus far, as well as bring me to the point of these ramblings. Paul Marriott (right, the hotel guy) donated what seemed to be an unpromising member of his extensive stable to the Florida Boys Ranch, where Mom was a volunteer, for use as they saw fit. The director of the facility realized that he could not afford to keep this animal and another filly, and offered them to us for $5000 "on the cuff". Although at the time against the ropes financially, my mother took them on credit.

Both fillies were entered into Mom's regimen, but it soon became apparent that one of them, although fit, didn't have what it takes to win races. The other, a little gray named First Prediction, after months of jaunts through the grove and swims through the lake, seemed ready to prove her worthiness at the racetrack. After a second and a third place showing at Tampa Bay, a trainer offered us $25,000.00 for the filly. Although the tenfold return was tempting, the resounding consensus of my sister, brother, and me was "Oh, Mom, don't sell the filly"! Though based on sentiment, that decision proved to be wise financially.

First Prediction, with her unremarkable size and tremendous stretch run, came to be

a leading Stakes filly in Florida. She was dubbed "The Iron Maiden" for her ability to run and consistently win as often as every eight to ten days or so. Of course, with every win the Boy's Ranch received a donation.

Now retired after some one hundred plus races and winnings of over $300,000, First Prediction is the embodiment of Mom's racing philosophy. Were it not for the unlikely chain of events and gut feeling, this horse would have been doomed to obscurity, profiting no one. How many other First Predictions are out there, needing only the individual training and sound foundation that big money owners and trainers don't give them?

You say, "Gee, well, that's a nice story, but I'm not a trainer and don't know much about racing, etc.". If you have bothered to read this far, I expect it is safe to assume you have some interest in horses. No doubt many of you compete in shows or the like. I did, but eventually lost interest in merely winning ribbons and trophies. I don't mean to disparage showing in any way; it builds horsemanship and allows one to be rewarded and recognized for his or her labors and efforts.

My point (I know, finally!) is that training Thoroughbred racehorses and campaigning them offers all of that and more. Nothing can compare to the thrill of the home stretch run. The horses giving it their all in the finish - necks outstretched, ears pinned back and hooves thundering. Jockeys clad in brightly colored silks, perched high and forward on their mounts cajole them for that last bit of speed as they vie for position. The noise of the crowd crescendos to a roar as people cheer their picks. Then on the outside of the pack you see it, your colors (there is no mistaking as no two designs are the same) on your jock, on your horse. The leaders are beginning to tire and your horse is inching past the pack, fourth, third, second, and now neck and neck with the leader. "GO, GO, GO!" you scream, flailing your arms, pounding on the person next to you who doesn't notice, caught up in the moment himself. Fifty feet to go, jockey and horse are one, and yes, did you see, they nose ahead and then finish! I can't do justice to that feeling. Your heart is in your mouth, there is just nothing like it, you have to experience it.

I don't mean to give anyone the idea that racing is all sweetness and light. There are tough breaks and lots of hard work to get through before you step in the winner's circle for the picture. Thing is, the effort that goes into training a racehorse at home is comparable to that of preparing a serious show horse. The rewards from racing, however, far exceed those of showing. I mean besides the emotional high, there is, of course, the money. Few horses conventionally trained ever win, much less show a profit. Most of our horses are of lackluster backgrounds, but have won at least once.

If you show or just keep a horse, why not give it a shot. The horse eats everyday whether you race it or show it or just ride it. Don't think you can race to pay the rent; but if you are lucky and work hard, anything you get is pure gravy. Just because you train your Thoroughbred to race doesn't preclude it from other endeavors if it just doesn't win. Many of my mother's horses have gone on to become very competent and fit hunter-jumpers after their racing days are over.

You may never win much, but that just sweetens it when you finally do step into that winner's circle. Besides, you never know, you might find your own First Prediction. We're still looking for another one.

Alex Del Castillo
U. S. Naval Academy   June, 1993
Annapolis Maryland

TO BEGIN
THE GREAT
ADVENTURE. . .

Owning a racehorse should be a pleasure. Saturday afternoon television flashes ecstatic owners winning thousands of dollars for a minute and half of work on the part of their horses. Some of the winners cost millions in a sale . . . others as little as $2,500. It looks easy. Go to a sale, buy a horse with your spare change, and win the Derby. Why not! These are not unreasonable goals. People on television do it all the time. However, when you get involved, you will learn that centuries of effort and experience are involved.

Keep in mind that the BEST expert advice and millions of dollars DO NOT GUARAN-TEE that the horse will make it to the races . . . let alone win a race. Perhaps this is why we all have a chance. The most obscure breeding may relate to great bloodlines and throw a winner. Around 40,000 foals are registered with the Jockey Club every year. Only a small percentage ever win a race.

This is not intended to discourage you, it is to prepare you for the reality of racing. An educated owner is a great asset to the racing industry.

Another goal of this manual is to help you avoid suffering the many humiliations I have endured over the years. A prime example is the day my mother came along on one of my first trips to the track. She was not a horseperson, but I was stuck, short of help and needed an extra set of hands.

I had two horses to work that morning. While I was cooling the first one, the other came back from the track. "Mom, finish walking this horse. I have to take care of the other one." The horse my mother took was on a very long lunge line, because I was also short of proper equipment. A few minutes later I checked to see how my mother was doing. To my horror, I saw she had tied one end of the lunge line to the bumper of my truck and 20 feet away the other end was connected to the horse . . . who at that moment was starting to graze. "Mom, quick, go to the horse's head!" Too late! As we watched, the horse took a few turns in a circle effectively wrapping the lunge line around his legs . . . more and more with each turn. Finding his legs restrained, he did what any Thoroughbred would do . . . he had a fit. He fought and struggled against the restraint of the lunge line until finally his own violent struggling threw him to the ground with a thump!

This whole, embarrassing, scenario did not go unnoticed by anyone within a thousand feet of the receiving barn . . . surely half the population of the backside. I stuck the horse I had into the nearest open stall and ran over to the struggling animal, who was flailing his legs to release them from the line which by now, was wrapped in a tight tangle around all

Owning a race horse should be a pleasure.

four legs. With the whole world watching, I cautiously freed the horse . . . trying to keep an impassive look on my face. "Ho hum, horses try to hang themselves on my bumper all the time."

"Mom", I said, "What possessed you to tie the horse that way? You never, ever tie a Thoroughbred . . . especially not with a lunge line!" "Goodness", Mom said, "I see cowboys tie their horses like that all the time on TV. I didn't know I shouldn't. Besides . . . my back was bothering me!" It took years to live down that terrible display of poor horse management. To this day, I blush when recalling the "Show" mother and I put on for the backside. Fortunately, the horse only suffered nylon rope burns and swollen legs . . . no broken bones, torn ligaments or other serious injuries.

There is a lesson or two to be learned here. One is never tie up a horse with enough rope to hang himself. The other might be to never take your mother to the backside. "Well", Mom said, "She doesn't ask me to help her anymore!"

In the following pages, I want to share with you the joys and anguishes of race horse ownership. Whether you begin as a breeder watching your own foals develop, or as an owner buying a prospect, a race horse will be one of the most challenging endeavors of your life. It comes with no promises and plenty of pitfalls.

The primary lesson is always have competent people with horse sense working around your animals.

The Horse...
Where to Get Him...
What to Look For!

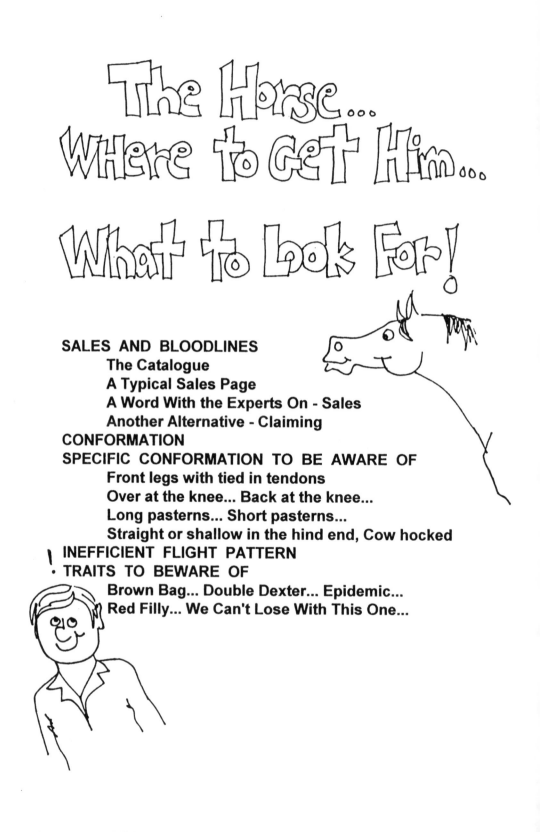

SALES AND BLOODLINES

Even when buying a horse for someone else, I am a bargain hunter. This doesn't mean I want the cheapest horse around, which can turn out to be very costly. It does mean I want the most horse for the money, whether the price is $5,000 or $50,000.

Before going to a sale, study the catalog. Generally there are anywhere from 100 to 1,000 horses listed in the catalog, depending on the size of the sale. The catalog tells you a great deal about each animal's history and family connections. It is not mystical.

Much more weight is given to the dam's (mother's) side of the family than to the sire's (father's). It is generally believed that the dam influences the talent of the offspring more than the sire, except when the sire is very dominant and all his offspring look like him, act like him, and have his build.

Many people put a lot of weight in black type. The animal whose name is written in black type is a winner of a stakes race (a race in which entry money was paid). This is considered the most difficult and prestigious type of race.

Any horse with black type on his page in the catalogue is considered more valuable. You must observe where the black type occurs; the closer the blood relation to the animal, the better.

When a horse has black type in the first paragraph, it generally means that the dam, a brother, or a sister has some running ability. If the black type appears in the second dam, you are into grandmothers, great aunts, and cousins. Black type in caps means winners. In small print it means placed or showed.

The catalogue page tells all about the sire and how successful his offspring have been. It will also give the sire's racing history.

Look for a dam who has run, and has had offspring who are runners. Such a horse can be very useful even if there is no black type.

So, first look for horses who have dams and sires who have run successfully, and then dams who have useful offspring who "last" and have run. Look for soundness and talent in a bloodline. If various offspring have made $20,000 or $30,000 dollars within a few years, they are useful horses. If they make that much in a year and have run for four or five years, better yet!

Go through the catalog and fold over the pages of horses that you like. Sometimes I'll like a particular sire because of characteristics I have seen in his offspring. For instance, "On to Glorys" have heart and are extremely strong boned and resilient. Certain bloodlines run well on a particular track. We all want success, so performance counts. Look for a horse suited to your situation. Remember that bad tempered sires tend to throw that characteristic.

Once you have identified the horses you like in the catalog, go to the barns and look at each one. Ask the handler to take the horse out and watch him walk, check his legs, and note your observations on his page in the catalog. If you are a novice, be sure to have a competent advisor you trust guide you

If you see a horse with a flaw you can't live with, put "no" by his name and don't consider him . . . even though he may appear to be a bargain in the heat of the bidding. Examine every horse ahead of time so you don't buy an unknown horse foolishly in the heat

Keep your cool in the heat of bidding!

of bidding. At that point it is too late to examine him properly. It could be that he is worth the money, but unless you have examined him thoroughly ahead of time, resist the urge to buy. They all look good under the lights in the auction ring. It is very deceiving.

Establish ahead of time your limit for each animal, taking into account bloodline, conformation, and your gut response to the animal. Now, with the catalog pages folded and notes on the horses, you sit down for the action. Wait until the bidding settles on a horse you like; and if it's in your budget, go for it.

If you buy a horse, go immediately to the barn and have a vet check him out. For about $600 the vet can take X-rays of joints, scope the horse, and look for any problems that would keep him from being a useful race horse. If the horse has a **paralyzed flap** or other listed problems, you may be able to return him to the seller. This examination must take place within a very short period of time, so do it at once. Depending on the sale rules, you may still have time to buy another horse. Read the front pages of the catalog for the sale rules and regulations.

When you buy privately, you still should have the horse vet examined and scoped before closing the deal. It is money well spent, to avoid loosing your time and money on a horse with built-in problems. A legitimate seller will allow such examinations. If you know nothing about conformation and how it relates to racing, find an astute person to help you.

The Catalog

To familiarize yourself with a catalogue, look at any Thoroughbred sales book. Beginning at the top there is a simple three-generation pedigree. Under that are the particulars on the sire of this individual - his race record and produce record, if any. The first dam is next. If her name is printed in bold, capital letters, she is a stakes winner. Her race record will be listed after her name, then, under her will be any foals of note she has produced along with their accomplishments.

The page will go on to highlight the second, third and in some cases fourth or fifth dams - depending on how far back the researchers had to go in the family history to find runners. At the very bottom will be any engagements this horse is nominated to, or if it's a broodmare, the stallion she was bred to and his particulars will be listed.

The catalogue page can probably provide the buyer with almost all of the information needed to make a buying decision, *if the looks and conformation of the horse are also suitable.* What must be kept in mind is that the more black type (stakes winners) on the page, the more expensive this individual is likely to be.

Most serious buyers go a step further and purchase what is commonly referred to as a buyer's guide. One is published for every sale. This takes the pedigree and produce record into much more detail. It will list things like what any siblings of this particular animal has sold for, if this individual has ever sold at auction, and if there are any upcoming improvements to the page. If it's a broodmare, it will list any foals sold at auction along with the stud fee of the stallion she is currently in foal to.

If purchasing a horse privately, no matter if it is a broodmare, weanling or yearling, this information is still accessible. Companies such as Jockey Club Information Systems and Brisnet have extensive databases that provide this information for a nominal fee.

 **Do not buy a horse until you know what to look for or have a competent trustworthy advisor!**

Typical Sales Page

Property of Ocala Stud Farms

Hip No.   Barn
40   **Chestnut Colt**   **4**

Half-brother to 8 winners, including Key Policy ($82,875). Out of sister to OUT THE WINDOW ($408,353, Laurance Armour H., etc.), Let Me In (dam of GUARDS UP, $150,825; CUT THE MUSIC, $131,377; HOW TO KNOW, $126,615), half-sister to Excluding (dam of TAIPO, $60,498).

Relatives —

The horse —

			Raise a Native
	Exclusive Native		Exclusive
Qui Native		Francis S.	
	Qui Blink		Winking Star

Chestnut Colt
April 26, 1989

			*Shannon II
	Clem		Impulsive
Clem's Ex (1967)		Shut Out	
	Exclusion		Bee Ann Mac

Father →

By **QUI NATIVE** (1974). Stakes winner. Sire of 9 crops of racing age, 135 foals, 102 starters, 72 winners of 313 races and earning $3,324,011 in N.A., including Native Mommy ($491,430, Mutual Savings Life Ladies H. [L] (FG, $60,000), etc.), Sheena Native ($393,782, Majorette H. [L] (LAD, $53,100), etc.), Exclusive Greer ($241,138, Pioneer H. [O], etc.), Native Drummer ($110,257, Forego S. (LAT, $12,058), etc.), stakes-placed Link [L] (3 wins to 3, 1991, $148,693), Qui Square [O] (8 wins, $107,205), etc.

1st dam

Mother →

CLEM'S EX, by Clem. Sister to **OUT THE WINDOW**. This is her 13th foal. Dam of 11 foals to race, 8 winners--

Half brothers and sisters {

Key Policy (c. by Diplomat Way). 6 wins, 4 to 7, $82,875.
His Ex (f. by True Colors). 8 wins, 2 to 8, placed at 9, 1990, $76,005.
Mischievous Saint (f. by Explodent). 5 wins, 2 to 5, $73,933. Producer.
Colorex (c. by True Colors). 5 wins, 2 to 6, 1991, $73,638.
Batchelorette (f. by On to Glory). 7 wins, 4 to 7, $56,230.
R. T. Saxon (c. by Royal Saxon). 6 wins, 4 to 6, $49,425.
Babblejack (c. by Sezyou). 9 wins, 3 to 5, 1991, $46,571.
Johnny Two Dance (c. by Pollux). 16 wins, 2 to 8, $45,637.

good!

2nd dam

Grandmother on Mother's side

EXCLUSION, by Shut Out. Placed at 3. Dam of 10 foals, 7 winners, incl.--
OUT THE WINDOW (c. by Clem). 22 wins, 2 to 7, $408,353, Laurance Armour H., Stars and Stripes H., Better Bee H. twice-once in ntr, etc. Sire.
Excluding. 2 wins at 3, $9,925. Dam **TAIPO** (c. by *Ballydonnell, $60,498).
Oui Madame. 18 wins, $53,448. Dam of **Oui Henry** (c. by Flag Raiser, $94,330, 3rd Hawthorne Juvenile S.-**G3**, etc.). Granddam of **WHITE MOMENT** (f. by Balance of Power, $51,440), **OUTOFAJOB** (c. by Marshua's Dancer, $30,880), **Whodatorsay** (f. by *Star Ice, $223,936), etc.
Let Me In. Dam of 10 winners, including--
GUARDS UP (c. by Cornish Prince). 7 wins, 2 to 5, $150,825, Jerome H.-**G2**, Keystone H., 2nd San Pasqual H.-**G2**, Leland Stanford H. Sire.
CUT THE MUSIC (c. by Stop the Music). 5 wins, $131,377, [Q], 3rd [Q].
HOW TO KNOW (c. by Green Ticket). 25 wins, 2 to 8, $126,615, Lakefront H., 3rd Thomas Edison H., Midwest Championship H.
Back Out. Dam of **Closed Corp** (c. by Affiliate, 5 wins, $88,002, 3rd [Q]).
RACE RECORD: Has not started.
Engagements: OBS Championship S., Florida Stallion S.
Registered Florida-bred. *←Fees have been paid for these Engagements!*

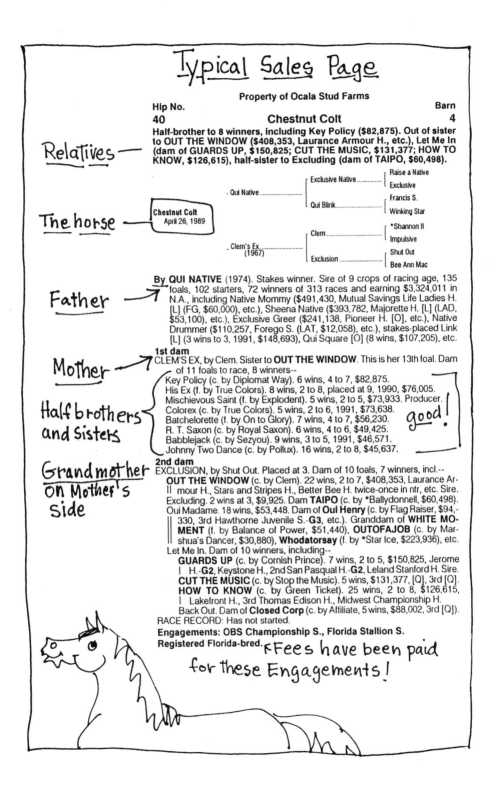

A Word With the Experts On -
SALES
by Melissa Sykes

The buying and selling of Thoroughbreds has become more than just something that breeders do to cull their stock. It has become big business. Horsemen and investors have been concentrating on making money rather than winning races for quite some time.

The various sales companies came about as a way for breeders to sell their excess stock. But with the price of bloodstock and the demand for animals rising in recent years, these same breeders have begun producing more and more horses specifically for the market place and not simply to race themselves. Sale companies have responded by tailoring individual sales for specific types of stock. For instance, beginning in late summer through early fall, sales featuring only yearlings are held. Fall and winter sales are referred to as 'mixed' with horses of all ages catalogues but the majority will be broodmares and weanlings. In spring and early summer, two-year-olds are offered at the various two-year-old in training sales across the country.

According to the Jockey Club the percentage of Thoroughbreds sold at auction each year has been steadily increasing. For instance, in 1990, 8,760 yearlings were sold representing 18% of the foal crop of 1989. Ten years later, that percentage had increased to 26%.

For those wanting to race and, possible, train your own horses, the sales are a good place to find exactly what you want. Breeding a mare and racing the resulting foal is a long-term commitment - and you can't predetermine the sex or conformation of the foal. At a sale, you can base your purchase on any criteria you design. For instance, if you live and race in New York, a two-turn turf horse might be the way to go. Or if you're based in Florida, those early two-year-old sprint races may be on your schedule. Whatever your goal, you can be sure that there is a horse at a sale that will fit the bill.

Before embarking on a horse-buying spree, you need to be familiar with the rules of the game. Keep in mind, what you see is not, necessarily, what you get. Every sale has its own set of rules. These rules are set out in the front of the sales catalogue, referred to as the Conditions of Sale. Read them very carefully. They explain, in detail, what constitutes a reason for not taking possession of an animal. Remember, this is the sale companies' business - they are in this to make money. And they don't make money if a horse is returned to the seller. So the 'rules' must be read and understood before you raise your hand and bid.

Many owners will attend the sale with an advisor of some sort. It may be their veterinarian, trainer or a bloodstock agent. Be sure this is someone with whom you feel comfortable and would trust to hold your wallet. This is exactly what they are doing. Agents make a commission on the horse, much like a Realtor. However, unlike real estate,

5

Look for a horse that fits together.

an agent can and often does represent both sides in a negotiation. His commission comes out of the selling price of the horse - and the buyer is the one paying it.

But this only applies to private purchases, you say. What does this have to do with buying at an auction? Yes, agents often broker private sales. But that doesn't mean the same thing isn't going on elsewhere. Let me give you a for instance: A potential owner engages an agent to buy a yearling on his behalf. He tells the agent that he has $45,000 to spend on said yearling. The agent will do one of two things.

One - he will find the owner of a few animals suitable for his purposes and worth the approximate budget. He will then bid in the ring and secure the animal for $45,000 give or take a few thousand. He will expect the owner to pay him 10% of the selling price for his services.

Two - he will find an animal worth quite a bit less than $45,000 and propose a partnership with the consignor. He finds out what the bottom selling price is for the horse, buys the animal on a handshake, bids the owner's $45,000 in the ring and pockets the difference. Oh, and he will still charge 10% of the selling price for his services. There are other variations of this scenario, but you get the picture.

Another interesting twist at the sales these days is the repository of x-rays. It used to be that if a buyer were interested in an animal, he'd have his veterinarian take x-rays of the knees, hocks, stifles and ankles looking for any irregularities. The vet would also perform and endoscopic examination of the horse's throat to check for breathing problems. It would not be unusual for some horses to be examined fifteen or twenty times. To avoid these excessive examinations the sale companies established the repository, - a central location where the consignor has provided these radiographs and endoscopic films.

The sale companies did not do this out of concern for the horses. With the repository in place, many auctions have ceased providing a bone warranty. This bone warranty was a protection for the buyer. If he was unable to have his own radiographs taken prior to bidding, he could have them taken after and return the horse if there were problems. Because of the backlash from buyers, most of the sale companies have reinstated the bone warranty even though they have kept the repository. Once again, read the conditions of sale to determine if the bone warranty applies.

Along with the repository has come the perceived need for a veterinarian to be involved in the buying of racehorses. Yes, a veterinarian can be an integral part of the buying decision. But, along with agents, the vet's motives should be questioned. A very well known farm manager from Kentucky wrote a letter to the editor of one of the Thoroughbred trade publications shining a light on this very subject. It seems veterinarians can and often do have a vested interest in whether or not a horse sells. This can hamper his subjectivity if you retain him to inspect an animal and he, in fact, is the seller. In a perfect world, he will inform you of the conflict and suggest you have someone else advise you. But we don't live in a perfect world do we?

There are a lot of good, reputable agents and veterinarians out there. Take your time and find one if you are not comfortable making the buying decision alone. The old adage 'buyer beware' was coined solely because of horse sales. Remember that.

The sale companies may have rules about consignors bidding on their own horses (also referred to as running them), but they are very loosely enforced.

Don't rush into buying a horse.

Another Alternative -
CLAIMING

Remember To check With the Lasix office!

MARY - the Stewards Secretary at Calder!

The following articles give excellent insight on the subject of claiming. Perhaps they illustrate why I find claiming races so distasteful. Although these races may be necessary to have "even racing fields", they have their pitfalls. Is it good for horses to be shuffled from barn to barn as they lose their form or become more and more sore? How would you like to be the owner of a horse that can't walk out of his stall the day after you claim him? Worse yet, what if he is ineligible to run because of his Lasix status?

The Danger of Claiming Horses on Lasix

Thanks to Mary Donato, Secretary to the Stewards at Calder for the following: "If you are planning to claim a horse, one of the most important things to do is ask the Lasix Office for a history of the horse. If you are not aware of his history you may claim a horse the is ineligible to run for a lengthy period of time or worse yet ineligible to run again period, because he has bled through Lasix more than once.

From the Handbook for Thoroughbred Owners of California

"Claiming is the means by which the majority of new owners enter the racing world. It's not only one of the least expensive ways to get into the game, but it's the quickest: in as little as two weeks, a new owner can have the chance to see his own horse race - and perhaps win - at his home track... and for as little as $4,000, plus tax and licensing.

Claiming is the ingenious American method for insuring a sense of parity among horses in any given race. The price at which a horse can be claimed is established as part of the entry qualifications for that race . Knowing the horse can be purchased by any other owner or trainer generally discourages owners from putting horses in a race where their quality is sure to make them winners. If they do, it will likely mean that their valuable, promising horse will be claimed, and - before the day is out - be the boast of someone else's stable.

The claiming game, popular as it is, is both complicated and fraught with interesting pitfalls - for new owners and experienced ones alike. There are many owners who have been enthusiastic claimers for years and have yet to turn a profit - but there is so

Your obligation is to understand the rules.

much to be gained, so much steady action, and so much still to be learned that they remain as game for the challenge as they were when they began, whether that was two years ago or twenty.

The claiming procedure is carefully regulated and involves a number of precise, prescribed steps. First, you will have spotted a horse you like or have a hunch about and who runs in claiming races within your price range. Before you act on your desire, however, you should find a trainer who either specializes in claiming, or at the very least is willing to work with you on the claiming process. It is not only practical to go in with a trainer at your side, but necessary: You cannot, by CHRB rules, receive your claimed horse without having a licensed trainer (or his/her designated handler) on hand to lead the horse away from the official Receiving Barn.

The practical reason to engage a trainer prior to claiming is that trainers see virtually every horse on the grounds during morning gallops and workouts. If your intended claim is not a horse they know, they can generally seek out from the myriad of backstretch

workers someone who knows something about the horse you fancy. The trainer will report back to you about what has been learned and knowledgeably turn you on to - or turn you away from - any given claiming candidate.

As a first-time claimer, you can actually start and finish the process of becoming a licensed thoroughbred racehorse owner, complete with a stable name and an account, on the same morning of the day on which the horse you wish to claim is racing (but do allow two or three hours).

Your first stop on that day, unless you have phoned ahead and received the forms by mail, is the office of the California Horse Racing Board (CHRB), usually located near the barn area. There you will be given 1.) an Application for License to own a thoroughbred race horse, 2.) a Supplement Application for License as Owner which indicates in what form you intend to do business - i.e., Sole Proprietorship, Partnership, Syndicate, Stable - and what name(s) will officially be used, and 3.) a form called the Personal Financial Statement.

Your next stop is the Stewards' Office, to obtain an Open Claim Certificate. This visit must be made by you in person. The Steward will need to be satisfied that you have engaged a licensed trainer to receive the horse, and that the trainer holds current Worker's Compensation Insurance. The Steward will review your financial statement... and may also ask you questions designed to determine if you realize the actual cost of owning and keeping a horse.

Once the Steward has signed your Open Claim Certificate, it must be presented to the CHRB office along with your completed application documents and a check for $250

Claiming is quick, but is it easy?

to cover your application for Open Claim License. You will not possess a license unless or until you successfully exercise the claim, since one of the qualifications for license is the actual ownership of a race horse.

Your final stop is the office of the Paymaster of Purses presiding at the track where you intend to make your claim. You, or your trainer, bearing a letter of authorization from you, must establish an account with funds sufficient to cover the cost of the horse you're after. Its claiming price will be listed in the Program on race day. Since you are not already an owner with an account, the Paymaster will prefer that you present a Cashier's check sufficient to cover your claim, and don't forget to add in sales's tax, which varies from venue to venue (call the Paymaster's office before having your check cut). Technically, you could pay by personal check, with a letter of guarantee from your bank, but there's the risk that the check and letter won't be accepted. A wire transfer from your bank is equally shaky, since the banks - in trading your money back and forth - may drop the ball and cost you the chance to execute your claim.

Once the Paymaster has established your account (it shouldn't take more than 15 minutes), he will hand back a brown Agreement to Claim card.

Now come a couple of tricky parts - unless your trainer is available to run this gauntlet for you: Get directions from the Stewards or Paymaster to the exact location of that track's claim-card BOX. Locations vary and can be obscure. Then, you will probably wait, poised, until almost the last instant - which is exactly 16 minutes before post time - to have your claim card time-stamped and placed in the official box. The reason? It's likely that your trainer will want to make an eagle-eye study of your horse during the 35-40 minute period when the mounts in the race are walked from their barns to the saddling ring. This is the trainer's last chance to pick up suspicious signs from the horse's action or behavior - a limp, a tired or stiff look, unusual sweating - anything that might suggest that the horse is not being risked in this claiming race, but dumped.

Though it's not usual, your trainer may advise dropping the Agreement to Claim card in the trash instead of in the box. The money in the Paymaster's office can be re-claimed, or left on account for your next try.

If your time-stamped claim card has been deposited in the box, you still don't know your chances of acquiring the horse in question. There is no way of finding out, before the finish of the race, how many others are also bidding for the claim.

When the race is over, you will go to the corner of the Winner's Circle where the official known as the Stewards' Aide holds the brown cards. If there is more than one card, they will be turned face down, and numbered on the back. Then, the shake. A bottle of peas, or numbered dice, is shaken, and one pea is drawn. The card-holder coinciding with the number receives a delivery slip to present at the receiving barn - and now owns the horse. Again, you can re-claim your money from the Paymaster

The Shake When more than one Claims the horse

Hope you get a raceable horse!

if you didn't get the horse, or you can leave it on account.

But wait - the claiming experience is far from over. Several possible surprises and questions are still to come. First, if you were the winning claimer, you owned the horse the instant it left the gate. If, after leaving the gate, it broke down, or came up lame, or didn't finish, you still own it. You may have drawn the pea and spent up to $100,000, plus tax, for an animal whose racing career is clearly finished - or worse, who has to be euthanized because of mortal injury suffered in the race. In the latter case, you will even be responsible for removing it from the track. The only sense in which you don't yet own the horse is if it finished in the money: the former owner, the one who entered the horse, gets any and all purse money your new horse earned in that race.

Finally, you will have to wait to actually take possession of your horse until it has gone to the Receiving Barn and been blood-tested for illegal drugs and excessive levels of legal drugs by the State Veterinarian. This may take an hour, or all afternoon.

If either the Racing Vet (who follows the horses from the saddling paddock through the race to the finish line), or the State Vet has spotted your horse as looking unsound, injured, or bleeding from the nose, it will be placed on the Vet's List," and you might not be permitted to enter it in a race in California for anywhere from a few days to six months. You - the new owner - will be responsible for the time and cost of getting the horse legally up to speed" before you can race it.

The ultimate test result in a claim will come in privately, the morning after the race, when your trainer tells you whether the horse woke up fit and healthy. If it didn't, you may

Claim Box

have been tricked into paying too much for too little. Actually, bluffed might be a more accurate term: as in poker, this is a fair part of the claiming game. Ninety percent of all racing horses will eventually turn up in a claiming race - and, as Mother said, you will have good days, and you will have bad ones. The most likely result will be a raceable horse.

You will be able to race your new horse as soon as it is rested - provided you raise it in class,hat is, enter it in a race at least 25% more expensive than the one you claimed it from. To race the horse at a lower claiming level- or to sell it, for the purpose of racing, to anyone else, you will have to wait 30 days. Otherwise, in a couple of weeks or so, you, as the new owner of your claimed horse - much like the owner of any sports franchise - will have your first track experience with the thrill of victory or the agony of defeat!"

**Anyone in horse racing is going for
"The Impossible Dream"!**

CONFORMATION

Many books discuss the conformation of horses. Some go into great detail about angles and relationships of degrees of slope of shoulder to length of leg, etc. Generally, form and function do go hand in hand, but I have seen some poorly conformed horses beat well built ones time and time again.

My uncle, a breeder of Quarter Horses, once said that good conformation doesn't get in the way of being a good runner. Indeed, good conformation has little to do with the innate gift of speed a horse may have. Poor conformation will perhaps hinder a horse from lasting long term, but he could have a world of speed.

Many trainers are frustrated by horses with high speed and crooked legs. Why? If you have a car with one bald tire and three good ones, you can probably go many miles with the bald tire as long as you don't go too fast. Zoom to ninety miles an hour and you may have a blow out. Racehorses are somewhat the same. As long as you don't redline the system, the horse will last. When you start racing and asking for high speed at a sustained distance, your weak "tires" may become a critical factor. When I started training, I used to gallop my horses six miles at an open gallop, and they flourished. Then, when pushed to high speed, the stresses on imperfect joints began to take a toll.

As a trainer, you must consider conformation carefully. Some flaws are easier to live with than others. There are horses so talented that they run faster than the average horse without redlining their systems. As your horse becomes progressively more competitive he will, by the nature of the sport, find himself in tougher races. As you win on one level and progress to another, you will find where your horse should be running; in claiming races, allowance races, or stakes.

Wise trainers with less than perfect horses try to keep them where they don't have to run too hard to win. Some horses are so honest and game that they will try no matter what. The trainer who is attentive and monitors the horse's legs can tell when a race has caused damage.

Now, let's talk more specifically about structure. We must judge those conformational faults we can live with and those we can't. **My judgments are based purely on personal experience and are by no means the only accepted opinions.**

My first choice among horses would be a **well balanced horse with very correct legs.** If both the sire and dam were stakes winners, their well built offspring should have an edge. Yet, we need to remember that if both parents were great, they could be a hard act to follow.

If our first choice is not affordable, what do we settle for?

A horse must fit together well. This sounds very unscientific, but as long as his parts seem to blend together, he can be useful. For example, I've seen many Quarter Horses bred and fed to have huge muscle mass. They look great at first glance. They have a burly chest and big hind quarters, but from the knees down the horse will have light cannon bones and small feet. This kind of horse will not stand up to racing, and I doubt that he will be able to do much performance work since his body mass and bone structure are so out of balance.

   **Look for a horse that fits together.**

At the other extreme, a light boned horse is useful only if legs and frame are in proportion. I had a mare so light framed she probably didn't weigh over 900 pounds. Her bones were like titanium. She was very correct and very tough. She never had any kind of leg problems. As a unit she worked great. She was a useful claimer who ran every ten days comfortably.

Northern Dancer was actually a small horse. Photos show he was a well balanced package on sturdy legs, though he did toe out. Such a horse is a joy to ride. They are even and solid in movement.

Some horses have unusually long backs and short legs. This type of horse is prone to sore backs since the span between the front and rear legs is long and less efficiently supported.

When you come across a huge two-year-old, remember **a big boned horse generally needs more time to develop.** The pressure on his joints is greater and he may gallop "heavier" and be harder on himself than a lighter horse. Just as with a gangly teenager, he must work harder to get his act together and to coordinate himself. He may take longer to find his stride. **Size does not guarantee speed or length of stride.**

If you see a Thoroughbred with large muscle mass like a Quarter Horse, he may genetically have more of a tendency to "fast twitch" muscles. He may be more efficient in sprints than in long races. There are many theories about fast twitch and slow twitch muscles, and whether training tends to encourage one type of muscle over the other. It is said that long gallops develop slow twitch, long distance muscle bunches; speed work develops fast twitch, quick responding muscle bunches. Since more than just muscle goes into developing a race horse, by training the horse with my methods you let the horse tell you whether he wants to run long or short, although genetics may be a more dominant factor than method of training. The other type of Thoroughbred commonly seen is lanky, with smooth slab-type muscles and

a svelte look. His muscle, even developed, will not be bulky. A trainer might suspect that he will develop into a distance horse. Of course, the bulky look can sometimes be created with steroids. (See Section on Medications.) All sorts of varieties come in between these types. I had a filly with a tremendous chest and no rear end. She has the lungs but no rear power. **Remember, all parts of the horse must fit together smoothly for the exceptional horse.** But, imperfect animals may find their own competitive level . . . and, in the right hands, do very nicely for a long time.

You should look for a horse with an intelligent eye, large nostrils and a good attitude. Usually a "kind eye" is an indication of a sound temperament and a manageable horse. See if you recognize "The Look of the Eagles". I know that sounds romantic, but . . .

**Anyone in horse racing is going for
"The Impossible Dream"!**

SPECIFIC CONFORMATION TO BE AWARE OF

Front legs with tied-in tendons

The horse may be light boned or heavy boned. However, if the tendon is tied-in behind the knee, it could be a point of weakness, when redlined. Of course, a good training foundation always helps. Look for solid short cannons with parallel lines when the horse is viewed from the side.

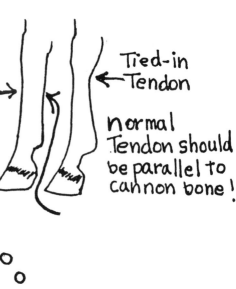

Over at the knee

I don't hold this against a horse, as it may improve with exercise. The horse can always improve with a good foundation. Many good runners have been over at the knee.

Back at the knee

This is a problem to avoid. It will cause pressure on knees and ankles. Even though exercise and fitness help, it is easy for this type of horse to tire and chip joints when redlined. Depending on the severity, he could be a very poor racing prospect. If you see this in a stallion who has not raced, don't breed to him. He probably couldn't hold up to racing himself. Why look for trouble?

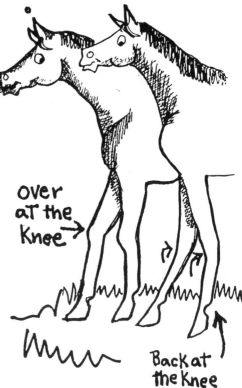

Legs don't have to be beautiful.

Long pasterns

Long pasterns become stronger with training. The horse will be comfortable to ride. The longer pasterns are like better shock absorbers. In racing you must make sure such a horse is very fit. When he starts to tire, his fetlocks will drop and he will have a tendency to run down on them when he is redlined. This means the fetlock hits the track surface, and the horse can get burns or open wounds. I have seen this type of horse being cooled out after a race, often having tremendous tissue damage in the fetlock area. You can prevent injury by putting on bandages with pads to protect his fetlocks. After a workout or two at the track, you'll be able to see if your horse has this tendency. If he does, always protect him. (See Section on Legs Bandages.)

Long Pasterns

Short upright pasterns

Horses with these come with their own set of problems. If the horse is upright, he will tend to pound and be choppy on his front end. As well as providing a more uncomfortable ride, this conformation puts a great deal of **stress on the joints.** The shoulder could become sore easily, especially if the horse is running on a hard track. He might have an edge on acceleration out of the gates and may be better in short races. He just **doesn't have good shock absorbers** and may run better on a heavy track or on a turf course. These surfaces are kinder to his joints.

Short upright Pasterns

‹Short›

Straight or shallow at the hind end

These horses seem weak in the rear. They tend to have stifle or hock problems.

Cow hocked

Unless it is severe, horses with this problem seem to be very agile and athletic and run just fine even though they wouldn't win any Conformation Classes. Keep an eye out for heat which may occur in this type hock.

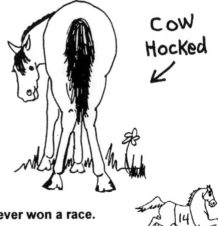

Cow Hocked

Beauty never won a race.

INEFFICIENT FLIGHT PATTERN

If you look at some horses from the rear, it appears that their flight pattern is very inefficient when they walk and trot. It looks as if they make a circle with their hoof, before they put it down for the next stride. A **toed-in** horse circles the foot to the outside, which is called **paddling**. A **toed-out** horse circles the foot to the inside, which is called **winging**.

I tended to eliminate these kinds of horses, because I thought the trait showed inefficiency of movement and weakness in conformation. Having been forced to train horses like this, I learned that **many horses look inefficient at a walk and trot, but at a gallop or run, the pattern was completely different.** The legs could be two solid pistons, straight in their flight pattern at high speed and very efficient at covering ground. So, don't lose hope even if your horse looks like he will trip over his own feet. When he grows and develops, he may be great. On the other hand, horses with slight deviations at a walk or trot may be very inefficient at a gallop.

Toe in   Toe Out

Watch !

Remember that horses have been bred for speed over the years. **Many crooked legged horses have tremendous speed. We must not eliminate horses just because of less than perfect angles. When we know they have weaknesses in their structure, we must give them time for the bone to mature and more preparation with long, slow gallops during their early training.**

Some horses seem to withstand and tolerate their conformational flaws. Others **show warning signs right from the beginning.** If you have a horse with a crooked knee that carries persistent heat in the knee after each work, you are being warned. **The horse is telling you he can't tolerate that level of stress.** If you continue to redline a horse in this situation, **he will break down before he runs.** Unfortunately, some trainers will drill to the point of breakdown, rather than tell the owner the horse won't stand up to training. Others will recommend surgery, injections, etc.

My own feeling is that if a late two-year-old or three-year-old **shows these problems in training,** especially my kind of training, **he is not a good racing candidate.** I advise owners to **get out now,** rather than spend another year of training and medical problems. They may **ruin the horse** anyway. Many horses can't stand up to the rigors of training and racing. If this is the case, find them a home where they can be useful as pets or riding horses. Telling owners not to put money into a certain horse has been one of my biggest problems. They don't want to hear this, and probably will find another trainer willing to try.

 **Many crooked legged horses have tremendous speed.**

TRAITS TO BEWARE OF

Horses are a lot like people. They have different personality traits, and just as **some people are hard headed, so are some animals.** If you perceive certain undesirable tendencies in your horse, don't continue training the animal. There are macho type people in this world, who believe they can straighten out a bad horse. However, some traits cannot be changed. They are in the animal and appear when you least expect them.

If you are new to training horses, it is not good to start out with high strung animals. I started with Quarter Horses. They are more tolerant of beginners. The mistakes you make during your learning process generally are not so crucial to an Appaloosa, Paint or Quarter Horse. Thoroughbreds can react so violently, when mishandled, that they may injure you or themselves.

For handling normal, non-quirky problems, Mark Rashid has written a wonderful book, *Considering the Horse*. It is a series of narratives about horses with behavioral problems. He may not deal with any of the specific problems you encounter, but his philosophy may help you find solutions to your problem horse. He opens the horse's mind to his readers and emphasizes the importance of horse sense

We want the nice guy!

Indolent

Scared

Feminine

The nice guy

Cranky

Look at the "eye" of the Horse!

Leave complex horses with difficult personalities to the professionals.

Brown Bag

He was raised here at the farm, out of my first wonderful mare. The horse was never mistreated and seemed quite normal. He was broken uneventfully, started the trail rides properly, and was no more difficult than any of the other animals I trained that year. When we started to do long, steady gallops, he would swerve left or right in a 90 degree turn. It didn't matter if there was a tree, a fence or any other obstacle, and there usually was.

Sometimes he would go days without doing this, and then suddenly do it again. We couldn't anticipate his behavior. It didn't seem to have any relationship with external stimuli, location on the route, or whether it was early or late in the gallop.

When he misbehaved, I would yank, shank and spank doing everything to let the horse know this was bad behavior. He seemed oblivious to the punishment.

One day, when the horse was about 30 months old and nearing track time, I was riding him. (I am large and heavy and hoped this would make it hard for him to pull his tricks.) He bolted, and much to my disbelief, ran smack into a 12 foot high irrigation pipe. I had pulled to the right and to the left, but to no avail. The horse ignored me and crashed into the pipe.

Lying on the ground with my left foot on his belly, to keep him from stepping on me, I thought, "That's it! Its too dangerous to train an unpredictable horse alone in the fields. This idiot needs the controlled environment of the track"

Hmmm- I Think I'll go That way!

A trainer at the track wanted him. I agreed to sell, but forewarned the trainer about the horse's bad habit. I explained in detail how the horse veered to the right or left without warning. The trainer said, "No problem."

Later, I asked the trainer how the horse was doing. "Galloping fine," said he. "Has he tried his sharp turns yet?", I asked. "Nope," said he. " Do you warn the rider before you put him on," I asked. "Do you tell him about the horse?" He said. "Hell, no, he'd be afraid to ride him. I don't say anything." A point well taken.

This information made me very uncomfortable. I am incapable of putting a rider on a horse that has a hang-up, without warning him. I constantly hear trainers saying, "That's the rider's problem. I don't want to give him ideas about the horse."

To make a long story short, the horse was put in his first race. Unfortunately, he got the number one hole. He broke out of the gates, hung a left into a rail and lost the race. The trainer sent him back to the gates, got him blinker-approved, and he won his second race. He's back at the track again this year and is still as erratic as ever. He has won some races, but he still hangs a left or right when you least expect it. You never know if he will run or bolt.

Interestingly enough, Brown Bag's sire has thrown various runners with the same tendency. It seems to be a genetic trait. Good luck if you try to change something like that!

 Its too dangerous to train an unpredictable horse alone in the field!

Double Dexter

Who could forget Double Dexter? While in the receiving barn she dug four-foot holes in the floor. I'll never forget walking up to her stall door and only seeing the tips of her ears, because she was standing in a pit. This filly was so erratic and nervous that no one believed she could possibly run after expending so much energy waiting for her race.

Many felt Double Dexter would be better off living at the track. Little did they know that she already had. For the month she spent there, she would gallop, fret and dig in her stall until she was exhausted. Then the ding-bat would fall asleep, rest, awaken, and start all over again. It was hard to keep weight on her.

Double Dexter was simply nervous and high strung. Interestingly enough, she was basically happy at the farm. She had her friends and held her weight.

She was a small but extremely plucky little filly with bones of titanium. Never sore out of a race, she had tremendous resiliency; but she could lose a race at the gate because she was so nervous.

Each year Double Dexter got progressively better. At five, she was almost manageable. If you drove in half an hour before the race and unloaded her to run, she didn't fret and went right to racing.

The stewards at Tampa Bay were good to me. They would let me arrive close to race time, for which I was very appreciative. This helped Double Dexter tremendously. She won two or three races each year at Tampa and did pay her way.

Double Dexter almost killed her owner in a trailer while being loaded. The horse lost control and overreacted hysterically to the tight quarters. She went into a frenzy and flung herself every way until she was cut loose. The owner was trapped inside the trailer with her and was almost crushed to death. Dexter "scooched" under the butt bar of the trailer to escape. Luckily, both owner and horse survived, but that episode gave me half of my gray hair.

One day someone offered $2,000 dollars for her and the owner said, "Sell." The last I heard, she was running in Puerto Rico. She was sound enough to run for many years when she was sold.

This kind of horse is very tricky to handle, and only good help should work around such a hyper animal. The horse is not being mean, just over-reactionary, but still can be dangerous. If you are not extremely competent, don't put yourself in a threatening situation by trying to handle an "impaired" animal. **Take heed . . . don't look for trouble . . . get a horse with a reasonable personality.**

Epidemic

There are probably people in Mountaineer Park who still remember Epidemic. He was a huge brute of a horse I bought as a maiden in October of his fourth year. In Florida,

Get a horse with a reasonable personality.

a horse must win a race before he is five or he can't run, so I knew I would have to work fast.

Epidemic was a powerful, broad-boned hunk of a horse. He looked like he lifted weights in his stall, he was so muscular. When galloping him in the grove, a ring bit meant nothing to him. Nor did the silly person on his back. It was like being on a runaway train when he took off. Realizing the danger, I told my son Alex (the 6'4", 240 pound son) that the horse needed some attitude adjustment.

Alex is basically gentle natured. He felt his sheer strength could handle anything this horse could try. Being 18, Alex knew bullets couldn't pierce his skin; so he condescendingly agreed to give Epidemic a spin in the grove.

Ten minutes later, the horse came galloping back, riderless. Five minutes after that, with pieces of tree protruding from his clothes, Alex came limping home. He mumbled about how the horse had no mouth, no feelings, and no response to anything.

So . . . I decided this horse would do better at the track.

Since he had run before, I took him to Miami and put him in a race. We threw the jock up on the horse's back in the beautiful paddock area of Hialeah. The horse started to trudge off, and to our amazement, he literally knocked over the groom, who fell with arms and legs flailing. Epidemic stumbled over him, walked through the flowers and into the fence of the paddock.

I scurried through the flowers, after the horse. The jock was still sitting on Epidemic's back in amazement. As he jumped off, he said, "I'm not riding this ox!" I was left to drag the horse back to the parade area.

I managed to find another jock, and the horse ran uneventfully, arriving 8th out of 10 horses. He did, at least, stay on the track when aimed in the right direction. Apparently, the only way to handle him was to run him.

When Tampa opened he had one month to break his maiden. Six days after the Miami race, he ran fifth. Five days later, he ran fourth. Four days later he was third. I reentered immediately and three days before the end of the year, on his last chance to win, he ran second.

A man from Mountaineer Park bought him for eight or nine hundred dollars and hauled him home. He won the first time out.

Later, I heard that they felt the horse had some kind of screw missing, though he could run. The owners got rid of him, because he would walk over people and things. He simply wasn't controllable. None of this surprised me. He was another good horse to get rid of, even at a loss.

The older we get and the more experience we have, the wiser we become. There are many challenges I have undertaken out of sheer ignorance. Since I survived the ordeals, they were learning experiences - not to be repeated.

For my son's version of his part in this story, don't miss Section *A Word With My Children, Alex.*

Leave complex horses with difficult personalities to the professionals.

Red Filly

This is the saga of one very difficult red filly. She was born by the light of a silvery moon. A perfect strong boned, beautifully formed red filly. Her sire, On To Glory, was the sire of my only really good horse and he was throwing runners here in Florida. For Jan and Rick Stanford, two seminar attendees, it was the first equine birth they had ever seen. They were awestruck by the miracle of birth and the resiliency of the newborn. "This horse will do great things" they predicted. That sounded good to me as I hadn't had a viable runner in ages.

I needed an allowance or stakes quality horse (Don't we all?) to justify my training program. So the dream began...this will be the one! Many readers will admit that they have the next Cigar frolicking out in the pasture. As a yearling red filly was hauled over to Lois' ranch where she would have large pastures and friends to run with.

At first Lois found her very intimidating. The filly would roll her eyes and overreact to every change, immediately injuring her legs while trying to charge through a solid wood fence when moved to a new pasture. Lois was ready to send her to a sale rather than risk handling such a troublesome animal, but bonding commenced with the leg-wound treatment. Soon Lois and her husband Eddie were partners in her ownership, along with my parents.

Though difficult to handle, the filly showed great intelligence. The problem there was that she would overreact to every situation apparently aware of all the bad things that could happen in her life. It became obvious with basic groundwork that the filly would fight everything - from surcingle to saddle to round-penning to bitting. Everything was a battle - although usually a short one. Boy we would say, "If she puts that same energy into running, she'll be some racehorse." The videos of her early training show a leaping, plunging, rearing animal more eager to fight than to go forward.

A dear friend, astute in the sales industry, suggested that I sell her since her bloodlines were good and she had perfect conformation. "No, no, this could be my big horse!" said I. "Hmmm...she's got a bad eye. She's going to be difficult." said my friend.

The time came to train and I went to the ranch with my nearly new, very sturdy four horse slant load trailer. Red Filly loaded perfectly and I secured her in the second slot from the front and closed and secured all the other panels As I started to drive away I heard great crashing and slamming noises. Since she was "bungeed" - tied on both sides and locked in surely she couldn't get loose and the rhythm of the road would soon soothe her.

The message is this: observe and learn from everything you do. Remember what works and forget what doesn't. Don't berate yourself if you made a wrong decision.

Ignore the "Monday Morning Quarterbacks". Just carry on.

As I drove slowly away from the barn, Lois raced up behind me in her car. "She's loose! She's loose in the trailer", she yelled over the roar of the diesel. I got out and saw that the panels were swaying and clanking and the filly was trying to turn around. I repositioned her and this time used two lead ropes to anchor her head. She must not learn that she could get loose and break the equipment. With more crashing and thudding, the truck again pulled onto the ranch road. The filly seem to be quieter as I accelerated... good... she's accepting the trip.

Lois on the other hand was standing at the barn watching our progress when suddenly the filly flew through the small window in the back door of the trailer. She landed gracefully, loped up to Lois unharmed and rested her head on Lois' chest saying, "See Mom, I didn't let them take me away."

Dumbfounded, Lois secured the filly in a stall and came racing after me yelling, "She's out. She's back at the barn." She had broken the shanks, sprung the panels and jumped out of the moving trailer through the little back window! Impossible, but it explained why there was no more noise emanating from the trailer.

Now I couldn't haul her home until the welder had installed new locks with pins making it impossible for any horse to spring the panels. My two old pony horses accompanied me on the next attempt to haul her home Mulliken was in the first space and his panel locked before red filly was loaded into the second stall. Big old Cherokee went in the third. Driving away there was some minor crashing and thumping for a few minutes. They boys ignored her and munched their hay contentedly. Meanwhile red filly jerked her head trying desperately to free herself - all to no avail.

It was the perfect time to run my list of errands. We went from place to place opening the windows at each stop. Filly was lathered. Her eyes bugging out for the first hour. Finally she got tired of the ruckus and decided to munch her hay if she couldn't get out of that darn box. During the six hour trip home she accepted the confinement. A very important lesson.

She had been saddled and round-penned for months with Mr. Blue Jeans at the ranch. Nevertheless, she reared, bucked and fought her riders before accepting them. Then came the gallops. She absolutely refused to leave the side of the pony horse. She would not go forward without one. No amount of kicking, arguing, cajoling or beating would get her to simply gallop forward willingly. If you are wondering why anyone would bother with such an animal, in retrospect so am I and so did many others including our farrier, Jim Sheridan.

After a terrible session trying to shoe her, he had a solution. He handed me the bill to which he had scotch taped a bullet with a note saying, "You know where to put this."

Some horses give new meaning to stubborn.

The bill hangs on my wall to this day. And yes, the bullet is still attached to it.

Meanwhile, we found that if we held her back and let the pony horse go ahead on the route, she would run hard to reach him. However, she continued to refuse to gallop alone and leaned on any animal at her side. My legs were bruised from digging my stirrup into her side, poking her and pushing her away. All of this only made her lean harder. We galloped her with another racehorse to no avail. She only galloped as fast as the horse next to her.

The track opened. We spent many trips pony-ing her outside on the track perimeter road until we felt we might be able to control her on the track. There were endless suggestions to give her something to settle her down and I did give extra vitamin B. However, I believed that if I could train her through her problems she would be a useful athlete. In the receiving barn, she would weave, fret and try to crash into the stall door. When a farm buddy left the barn to go out on the track, she tried to break out of the stall. I was persistent and gave her plenty of time to settle.

The gates were another nightmare. She was too nervous inside them and would try to squash the riders . On the track she would sort of breeze, but only in company and only as fast as the other horse. I had one big horse that bore out on the far turn at the track. I put the red filly on the outside and she held him in on the rail by just being herself. Eventually it came time to race. She wasn't fully fit but I had no horses to challenge her in the morning. As usual, I used races to get her in the groove.

She raced with a patient and strong jockey, always breaking beautifully. Once out she would latch on to the nearest horse and lean on him the whole way. We tried blinkers and different bits. Still she would lean on any horse that came along either side.

Oops!

Meanwhile we lost races because she quit in the stretch. Was she tired, have sore shins, muscle tear, or was it the roar of the crowd? Now she was having acupuncture for a possible muscle tear in her back. Then we tried ear plugs and muffs to reduce the crowd noise. In spite of herself, she was improving, quitting a little further out in each race.

Since she was nervous in the paddock, nervous in the post parade and nervous in the gates, the jockeys were telling me to give her something to "help" so that she could

Never tempt fate!

Jim Sheridan
Blacksmith
1 Bay GELD - $70.00
1 Red filly - $100.00
You know where you CAN put this!

concentrate more on running. The main "help" for calming a fractious horses seems to be SoluDeltaCortef, a steroid, which if used frequently, will cause negative effects long term on the overall structure of the horse.

Once you start using "stuff" when and how do you stop? I was determined to give her experience at the local track until she stopped fighting and maybe just run. After all, how many times do people take horses to horse shows to win ribbons and how many years did it take to get the blue one.

One fateful day, while in the gates, she heard the gate next to her bang, thought it was the start, reared straight up, whirled around and ended up facing backwards, ready to go, in the gates. Remarkably, she did not harm herself, but was scratched anyway.

Too much!

It took almost twenty races and two seasons to break this filly's maiden. Craig Faine was the jockey and he waited for the race before shipping up north. He had put up with so many of her shenanigans that he was determined to win on her. When she won it was in maiden special weight. That meant we got a bigger purse and better breeders' bonus for the win. On the way to that win she had dropped riders left and right, had propped in the middle of a work, crashed through the stall door and terrorized the backside. She also kicked incessantly in the trailer and cost me a fortune with ruined hind shoes.

It's a good thing that I owned part of the horse. Few owners would put up with the time and patience necessary to get this horse settled and useful. Though she made over $30,000.00 by that time, if the owners were paying day money, they would have barely broken even. The advantage of having a place to turn out the horse certainly helps with cost. We had waited on sore shins, coughs, muscle tears, bad breaks, flipping in the gates, a tear between the tendons and many other minor setbacks. However, we finally had a sound four-year-old starting to understand the racing business. Although she still had a miserable attitude around the barn and track (the glass was half empty, not half full), and she still tried to kick at us if we were careless, but she had become workmanlike and might eventually even like racing.

At that point we had to put her in where she could be competitive. The second time we put her in Claiming $10,000 she was gone! What a shock-coming home with the empty trailer! I did resent that someone else could take all of our blood sweat and tears and reap the benefits. She went to a lesser track in the North and won the next two times out as she was fit from Florida and sound. Many months later I heard that she was scratched at the gates (being sore and lame) at a very cheap track in the bottom claiming ranks. That made me sad-she had been a beautiful filly-even though difficult-and I grieved at her fall from grace.

Eventually we must retire our horses or run them where they can win. If you run them where they belong and they are on the board, they will be claimed. That is the most distasteful part of racing. Why can't we could run them in easier races without fear of losing them to claiming! That's life.

**Once you start using "stuff" when
and how do you stop?**

WE CAN'T LOSE WITH THIS HORSE!

Those fateful words, "We can't lose with this horse." came back to haunt me during the two years I tried to train the filly. I had a partnership with two wonderful owners who were patient, understanding, and who paid their bills promptly. They allowed me leeway in buying them horses and were interested participants in the training of their animals. I was given a limit of $25,000.00 to find them a promising horse in the two-year-old in training sale. It was the most they had ever committed. We all wanted a winner. The filly I found was light boned but balanced and fleet looking. Her pedigree was promising. She had eight half siblings that had won races and earned over $70,000, with three of them earning well over $100,000. The sire had made over $2,000,000. So confident we had covered all the bases, I uttered those fateful words when talking to the owners. After all, we had breeding, balance, soundness, and solid confirmation. And, of course, competent training.

We can't lose with this filly!

That's what she thinks!

The training started uneventfully. She had the usual turnout for two months to allow her to grow and chill-out from the sales prep. She showed early signs of a questionable attitude when asked to perform, but since she was still a teenager, I assumed that would pass with more training and maturity. At times shes balked in the route. Kim, my rider, would have her hands full getting the filly to do as she bid. Then the filly had a tendency to flip over when she got "hot". We were cautious and continually worked on that character flaw. She covered the ground with a low flowing stride - a real "daisy cutter" and tuned up to speed with ease. Being light framed, she showed no sign of heat or weakness in her bone.

Time came to breeze her at the training center and to start gate work. After a light gallop on the track she was taken to the gates where we wanted her to walk through. She fought Kim and was stubborn when asked to enter. Kim was persistent and eventually the filly went in and came out acceptably. The next time we came I had a veteran rider get on her as I felt she needed an experienced hand with the gate work. She was not cooperative and fought before finally succumbing and entering. We went home and had her go through our gates under various circumstances.

Though moody and petulant at times, she did perform. Tampa opened and we went to the track where, though nervous, she galloped strongly and with great speed. When sent to the gates the first time, the crew had her walk in. She was a little balky but did go in. They opened the gates, Kim kissed to her to leave and she refused to move. The gate crew tapped

Racehorse must want to run!

her lightly on the rear. She stood like a rock. They took the long whip and tickled her heels and then snapped it behind her. What horse, when confined, doesn't want to leave when given the opportunity?

To my amazement, she dug in her toes, leaned against the back gate and would not move. The crew shouted, banged, snapped the whip more aggressively, and finally lashed it on her hind legs. She never moved a muscle. Finally, they opened the back of the gate. Two men got behind her and pushed as hard as they could, trying to pry her out of the gates. The more they pushed, the more she leaned back against them. Others joined the foray until they finally tumbled her out the front of the gates. The Starter, Max, looked at me and said "Take her home. She doesn't want to be a racehorse!"

I was indignant. Who was he to tell me that just because this filly was a wee bit stubborn in the gates we were to quit training her. We had a large financial investment in this horse and I was sure I would work her out of this glitch in her training.

After months of work utilizing every trick in the book - eating in gates, standing in them for long periods, walking through innumerable times, being led in and out, front and back. Sometimes she was good. Sometimes she would fight going in. Other times she would refuse to leave. She would smash Kim against the sides or try to flip over backwards. There was no consistency or relationship between good training days and bad ones. It was impossible to know if she would break.

This Filly HAD ME pulling my Hair out!

I tried one more time at Tampa. After the unsuccessful session, Max said he didn't want to see that filly again. So I took her with me to Miami and talked to the starter there-explaining the saga. He agreed to give her a chance and after some cajoling, she broke acceptably and got her gate card!

I put her in a race as she had done various solid works. That first race I held my breath. The gates opened and she broke. She ran credibly, making a big run at the end. With a sigh of relief, I hoped we were over the problem.

With trepidation I entered her in Miami again for her second lifetime start. She was in the 9th hole that day, the last to load. She had on yellow blinkers. As I watched, the announcer said "They're all in". The doors flew open. A tight group of horses thundered out of the gates. None of them wore bright yellow blinkers. Those were on a dark horse still standing in the 9th hole. The announcer commented that

Listen to the experts.

the nine horse did not break and continued with the race call. As I watched, the gate crew tried to get the horse out of the gates. The jockey got off, they pulled her blinkers, and even tried to back her out. She refused to move. Finally they pulled the gates off of her. That was it. She was now a "non-starter". If she did that one more time she would be banned from the racing world.

When discussing this dilemma with other trainers, one said flatly "I can get her out. Give her to me for two weeks!" The owners agreed to send her to him at a training center with an on site gate crew. Two weeks later the trainer called and admitted he could not get consistency with her breaks. Two other trainers, using all their wiles, were equally unsuccessful.

The owners at last decided to breed her. Months later she came up barren and they were again enticed to try training. She was so talented and fast, maybe time off had improved her attitude. She banged herself so much fighting in the gates that she was again retired and has since had a foal.

I went back to Max the following year at Tampa and recounted her saga admitting that he was right. She didn't want to run, "When they don't want to run you might as well find them another job. Most horses, even the volatile, hot headed ones eventually learn how to work with us, if they want to run."

I had believed her "flaw" could be overcome. She certainly taught me a lesson and cost her owners a fortune. Lets hope the foal justifies all of the anguish.

Never again will you hear me say, "We can't lose with this one!"

Never Tempt Fate!

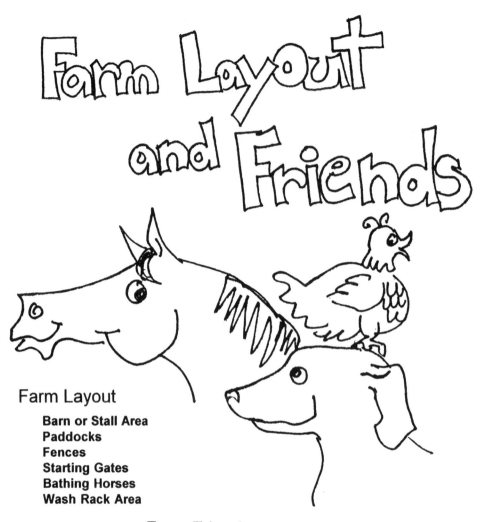

Farm Layout

Barn or Stall Area
Paddocks
Fences
Starting Gates
Bathing Horses
Wash Rack Area

Farm Friends

Chickens... Goats... Dogs
A Visit from the Vet... Coggins... Vaccinations
A Comment on Vaccinations
You and Your Vet... The Anatomy of a Horse
Two of the Most Common Equine Ailments
Some Less Common Equine Ailments
Deworming... Equine Dental Care
Teeth Determining Age... Alternative Therapies
To Medicate or Not To Medicate

FARM LAYOUT

Barn or Stall Area

The ideal situation would be nice large paddocks, each with its own large stall. You could turn the horse out for a portion of the day or confine him. This arrangement would work for anyone with one or two horses. For those of you with several horses, a row of stalls with common walls utilizes materials more efficiently. Remember clean stalls mean healthier feet and respiratory systems. Fresh circulating air means healthier respiratory systems.

My farm is small - only 13 acres. The logistics of having many horses of both sexes is challenging. I solve the problem by having two barns. One is for the females - the girls dorm. The other is for the boys. I do this to avoid crucial mistakes at turn out time. Sometimes you will have help that doesn't quite understand who you said to turn out. **A filly in heat next to a racing colt can cause damage to both. Avoid accidents.** Always try to keep paddocks and stalls for colts and fillies completely separate. Young horses remind me of teenagers, **constantly thinking of having a good time and procreating.**

Learn to read body language when working around animals. **Be aware of what they are saying to each other with their switching tails and squeals. You could be hurt if you're not paying attention.**

I prefer a large, airy pole barn with a very high roof. Florida has such mild winters that our stalls can be very open. My barn has four **stalls, each with its own small paddock.** The stalls are 14' x 14', nice and roomy. **The paddocks are 14' x 20', enough space for a horse to doze in the sun if he wants, or sleep out under the stars, which they seem to enjoy at certain times of year.** Best of all, usually they choose to drop their manure in the far corner of the outside paddock rather than dirty the sawdust in the stall. This not only helps save sawdust, but if your schedule gets hectic and you don't clean the stall-paddock area for a few days, it is not crucial, because the horses are not standing in manure. **All the horses that have been raised on my farm drop manure outside.** However, horses from the track tend to drop it in the stall. They had no choice.

Lois made the following comment about stalls: "As a child I thought we were doing horses such a favor to stall them, give them a home, and protection from inclement weather. Later, I realized that what seemed nice to me might not be so nice for a horse. Maybe they actually preferred being outdoors where they could roam freely. Perhaps the comforts of home did not offset being incarcerated. All too often, we tend to judge what an animal wants or needs from our own perspective. Try to think about the animal's natural life-style and how he will react physically and mentally to your ideas, before making decisions about his well being."

Even when the farm is full, **every horse must have a stall during the heat of the day. I also put the horse in the stall to reinforce rest a day or two before a race, always allowing him turnout time. The stall-paddocks are completely lined with conveyer belting. These are active racing horses; they like to roll on their backs and could get their legs caught in the rails.** Hot tape is secured to the top board

**Allow their formative years to be natural.
They will be more sensible and adaptable as they mature.**

so they don't lunge at each other too much. This arrangement is riskier than enclosing them in the box type stalls that are home to most racehorses. Horses are herd animals. They like to nuzzle and talk to each other. Socializing keeps them mentally healthy and allows them more tranquility long term. It helps avoid the vices so prevalent at the track. As horses mature, they are more adaptable to the race track environment.

The aisle in front of the four stalls was originally just hard packed dirt. It occurred to me to store the bedding sawdust there until it was needed in the stalls. Now **whole loads of sawdust are dumped in the aisle.** This provides about two feet of sawdust that settles into a nice base. The sawdust lasts two to four weeks. When cleaning stalls, **sawdust is easily raked from the aisle into the stalls.** This short cut is very convenient, keeps the sawdust dry and protected from the elements, and **has cut my stall cleaning time down to almost nothing.** When I see dirt under the sawdust, its time to order another load. **This simple adaptation has saved me energy, time, and money.**

All my feed and water buckets clip into a screw eye. They can be removed and scrubbed when necessary. Hay is put under the feed buckets so that any spilled grain falls on it. **I am completely opposed to hay nets or racks.** They can cause back problems. Horses are grazers, not browsers (though they can nibble leaves from trees). **Horses are built to eat off the ground. When they twist their heads to eat at shoulder level, they do not employ normal physical movements.** Ideally, both feed tub and hay should be on the ground. If your horse paws at the bucket on the ground, raise it and make the necessary adjustments. When a horse has a back problem, he is fed on the ground or with the bucket in a hole. As he eats, he is flexing and exercising his back without even realizing it. A rubber mat is placed on the ground under the tub. The hay ration is put on the mat. When the horse drops grain as he eats, it falls on the hay. Hopefully, the hay and mat will reduce the amount of dirt he ingests.

My partner, Lois, who kept our broodmares in pastures, fed on rough cement patio blocks in order to reduce sand intake. It also kept the horses from standing in the mud during rainy season. Later she noticed that it helped wear the horse's feet to a natural angle. Always be aware of the side effects of your innovations.

All paddocks and stalls must have ample water. If you want to monitor your horse's water intake or have problems with ice, use buckets. Otherwise automatic watering devices are very convenient. They can be easily installed with PVC and are real time savers.

Your own stable and paddock areas may vary considerably. Different geographic areas need different types of construction. Ask your land university or extension office for stall and barn recommendations. Then study your needs and make your barn as convenient and labor saving as possible!

Four stalls on either side of center aisle. Sawdust dumped in center aisle. Small paddocks behind stalls.

Paddocks

Some of my horses live in small sand paddocks which are not attached to their stalls. These paddocks have a shelter roof over one end and are approximately 20' x 36'. During the day, each horse gets to spend at least an hour in a large grassy pasture where they can run and frolic. The farm has four grassy pastures.

Rolls of old conveyer belt are useful for lining any small paddock. It discourages the biting of knees and lunging through the fence. The horses can run freely, frolic and rear. Horseplay is necessary and helpful. However, we don't want them hurt. Horses love to roll in close quarters - invariably next to the fence, because it's sandy and soft from their hooves tearing up the soil. They tend to roll into the fence and get their legs caught between the fence boards no matter how close or far apart the boards are spaced. This can cause scraping of tissue and lacerations on their legs. Using conveyer belt between boards has proven to be good protection. Those of us in racing are aware that **horses can inflict a great deal of damage on themselves just being horses.**

Every paddock must have water and a **red mineral block**. This is mandatory here in Florida due to the intense heat. The horse must be able to regulate his own salt intake as necessary. Each paddock has its own feed tub out of reach of neighboring horses. It is important that each horse eat his food at his own pace without harassment from his neighbors. Although we have noticed that a neighboring horse can induce a picky eater to finish his feed.

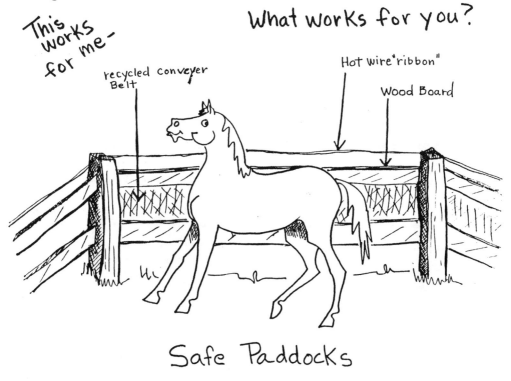

This works for me -

What works for you?

recycled conveyer Belt

Hot wire "ribbon"

Wood Board

Safe Paddocks

For safe paddocks, be sure that all nails or dangerous items are far from the inquisitive lips and bodies of your horses. Bored horses can get into trouble with anything in reach.

Fences

Good easily visible board fences are my first choice. Their main drawback is maintenance and the fact that they become brittle with age. When a horse, while frolicking or by accident, crashes into a board fence, there is a danger of him being impaled. In major Thoroughbred farms, miles of double fencing are utilized to keep horses from playing across the fences. It is an extra safety factor when fences are broken. Needless to say, it is expensive enough for most of us to put up board fences, let alone double fencing. There are new types of vinyl fencing. I have had no experience with them. They should be worth investigating.

Many types of wiring are being sold as fencing for horses. If you decide on **horse** wire fencing, use the woven type rather than soldered, which breaks and can cause injury. It is desirable to run a **wood sight board** on top for visibility. Do not use goat, pig or chicken wire type fencing. A horse can easily stomp his foot through this kind of wire and, in the process, tear his skin and tendons. For obvious reasons, **I am adamantly opposed to any kind of barbed-wire fencing.** However, if you must use it, make sure you mark it clearly with bright rags or tape fluttering every few feet so that the horses can see it. My vet friends say that barbed wire pays their mortgages.

I use electric tape across the top of all my paddocks. It helps separate animals that want to horseplay across the fence. They may clunk their heads together, but they respect the hot tape. I tried hot wire but found that it was a terrible danger when the electricity went off. The horses would fight and break the wire off the holders. The loose wire could easily tangle around a leg and sever a tendon. I solved this problem by wrapping the wire around each holder several times so that, if the wire did break, it would be less than eight feet long and less apt to tangle around delicate legs. Ribbon or tape is easily seen and will break rather than strangle or tighten. Hot tape can also be used temporarily until proper fencing is installed.

If you can afford the expense, you may want to consider vinyl fencing. It is very attractive, requires little maintenance and seems to be much safer than other types of fencing.

Michael Flynn the former Executive Director of the NY Breeder's Association reports that at his brood mare and stallion farm when they had wood fencing about 10 out of 300 horses would be stalled at any given time due to accidents incurred from the wooden fencing. After installing the vinyl fencing these injuries were eliminated.

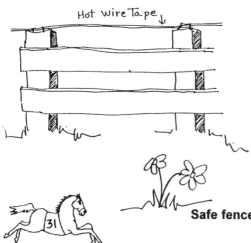

Hot wire Tape

Safe fences for safe turnout.

Starting Gates

Everyone feels that it's necessary to have a starting gate at the farm. Frankly, I think **gate work is one of the last things you worry about in training**. However, it is always a good idea to **encourage your horse to walk into small areas** and to learn that he doesn't have to fear such experiences.

Have the foresight to build the gates at the beginning of your training program. I have a two-stall pretend gate built of wood. (Use any materials you have around.) The sides are padded with rug, and **a guide board extends forward between the two stalls to encourage the horses not to veer when breaking.** At one time I had a barricade board across the front. Supposedly we could yank it open and hustle the horses out. Experience has taught me this isn't necessary. **You need stalls, open as shown to walk horses in, to stop them and back them out or to walk them through.** Eventually you can gallop them out. **Finishing touches of breaking out of the gate should be left for track training.** Gate crews are experts and need to have the horse work out with them. This is discussed more thoroughly in the Training Section.

My gates are positioned at the base of a hill. When the horse eventually learns to gallop out, he is going up hill, which will help strengthen his hind end. Some trainers believe that starting on a hill is very difficult on a young horse. Others believe training on hills is good for conditioning. Be judicious and make your own decisions based on how your animals handle the work.

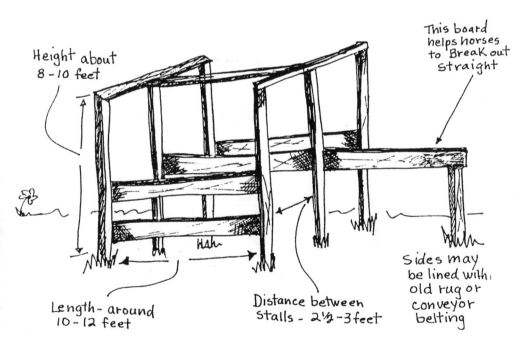

This board helps horses to Break out straight

Height about 8-10 feet

Length- around 10-12 feet

Distance between Stalls - 2½-3 feet

Sides may be lined with old rug or conveyor belting

"Pretend starting gates may be made out of PVC or leftover lumber.

Bathing Horses

Before you start bathing any horse, be sure to have everything you need at the head of the wash rack - shampoo, hoof pick, and a grooming box. Never leave a horse unattended while you run to look for something. **Always bathe the horse at your wash rack area**. In Florida, we bathe our horses very frequently. If they are not bathed every three or four days during the hot, rainy season, many horses develop rain rot or some other kind of skin itch. Being outside a great deal, they get caught in the rain. When the rain is over, they roll in the sand to dry off. The soil nurtures many bacteria. **By scrubbing our horses every three or four days, we kill the bacteria and cleanse the skin.** (Often Azium, a steroid, is given to horses to relieve skin itch. Isn't a little bleach and soap preferable?)

My shampoo recipe is quarter cup of bleach to a gallon of water with a squirt of Palmolive liquid or some other common household soap. (Buy it on sale.) If you prefer, you can use Betadine or any of the liniments with disinfectant qualities. I find that bleach disinfects the skin, and inhibits the cycle of itch, and have had good results over the years. When I am lax during the rainy season, the itch begins.

In Florida water temperature is not an issue. The warning against the use of cold water when cooling a horse seems to forget that cold water and ice are used for heat exhaustion. If the horse flinches at cold water, he is no different than the rest of us when cold water takes away his breath, hose him until the runoff water is cool. In very cold climates, you would probably want to use warm water and/or blanket horses until they dry. (See a Word With the Experts On Grooming in Backside Personnel.)

To bathe the horse prepare the soap, water and bleach in a two gallon container. Hose the horse very aggressively with a nozzle sprayer. **The skin should be drenched and stimulated by the hard hosing.** Dip a scrub brush in the solution and scrub the entire body with the mixture. Take the horse's tail and dip it completely in the bucket. The bleach is great for getting grime off the tail. If you rinse in a reasonable amount of time, it doesn't bleach the tail. Then, having first picked out the feet, dip the whole foot in the sudsy bleach solution. Scrub all the feet with the brush. Using the nozzle at medium pressure, spray all over the body and rinse out the soap and bleach. The dirt pours off and the skin is stimulated by the water massage. Be sure to remove **all** the soap and bleach. You do not want your horse's coat to dry out or become irritated.

After the bath, release the horse from the wash rack and while holding him on a loose shank try to hose water directly on his face. Be careful of his eyes and ears. You want him to become accustomed to the sensation of water or dirt hitting him head on. It prepares him for the sloppy water or mud that can be flying at him during the rigors of racing.

While bathing your horse, you can learn a great deal about him. **If he is sensitive to being scrubbed or rubbed in a particular area, try to determine if it is because he hurts or if he is just ticklish.** The clues he gives help you gauge his overall state of health. As you handle your horse, **you learn his idiosyncrasies. Learn to be tuned into how he reacts during baths and grooming.** The first thing most horses do when turned out after a bath is roll and get dirty again... a nice layer of dirt probably discourages flies. That's all right... at least you know he was clean!

You can handle a young horse alone with the proper layout.

Wash Rack Area

The wash rack area is one of the most important areas on your farm. At the track two people are usually needed to handle horses who can't be tied and are very nervous. Most of us must work alone, so it is essential that we design our layout efficiently. As you can see by the drawing, my wash rack consists of a large concrete slab approximately 14' x 14' covered with rubber matting. I have a sturdy round hitching pole supported by two sturdy posts. These can be wooden or steel pipe. Drawings of my wash rack are included. You can adapt your facilities according to your needs and availability of materials. Remember, **these are suggestions.** Certain points are essential. **The hitching pole must be round** so that the lead line slides easily when looped around it. This allows you to pull the lead line, forcing the horse to stand closer to the hitching pole. **You are also able to release him quickly if it becomes necessary. My principal wash rack is completely enclosed by fencing.** I use this rack with new and/or more fractious horses. **It is imperative that they be confined and learn good behavior during baths or treatments.**

After a few lessons the horse will learn that the hitching pole is not to be feared, and you will find yourself more comfortable bathing him. If he throws a fit, all he can do is fight and pull himself loose if you allow it. **He will still be confined by the perimeter fence** and the lead line will still be on him, making it easy to catch him again and loop the lead line around the hitching pole. Always close gates and be sure an area is safe before you handle a fractious horse. Before my wash rack was confined, if the horse got loose, he could gallop all over the place getting into trouble or harm.

Even alone, you can control his head while working on his back legs by looping a longer lead line or lunge line around the hitching pole. You hold it in one hand while you are at the rear of the horse using the other hand to wash his legs or whatever. If your shank is 20 feet long, you can teach the horse to move forward by looping the lead line around the hitching pole and tapping the horse from behind with a buggy whip. This way he learns that a tug on the head and a tap on the rear mean that he is to go forward.

If your horse has not been handled much, especially around his legs, loop the lead line around the hitching pole to control him while you rub his legs and body with the buggy whip. If he kicks to the touch of the whip, yank, shank and sharply say, "No!" After a few lessons, he learns that the whip is an aid not to be feared and stops kicking at it. Another way to accustom him to having his legs and body touched, is to hose him all over until he accepts and enjoys it.

ENCLOSED WASH RACK
Note how the lead shank
must be wrapped.

Rubber mats are placed over the concrete slab.
The poles are welded steel.

FARM FRIENDS

Chickens

Anyone who has come to my farm knows I can't discuss its layout without telling about my chickens.

This all began when my children joined the Four H Club. One of their many projects was proper chicken raising. When the project was completed, it was easier to turn the chickens loose, than worry about their feed and water. The chickens reverted to their clever, cagey ways in no time and soon took up residence in the hay barn at night. During the day they did "manure patrol duty". People even asked if I had trained them to seek out every pile of manure and very efficiently peck and scratch to break it down! Their work effectively broke up the piles in the pastures, thus helping control the fly problem.

The incessant raking on the part of the feathered stable help breaks up the fly cycle. **If a fly egg laid on manure is left undisturbed for 24 hours, another fly is added to the population.** If the egg is disturbed by rain or by a little crew of chickens pecking to get undigested grain, the egg does not hatch. **Breaking up manure also helps the process of pasture fertilization.**

There can be a danger of salmonella from chicken manure. Investigate the situation in your area to decide if the effect is worth the risk. Never allow the chickens to contaminate feed and water areas. Use your horse sense. Sometimes we can become overly cautious about the dangers in our environment. A healthy horse should be able to coexist with a certain amount of bacteria.

Horses learn to tolerate the chickens and even enjoy their flapping and noisy conversation. Actually, some become great friends.

Goats

Goats are a good, if somewhat odorous, companion for insecure horses. They are easy to keep, are allowed on the backside, and offer entertainment to both horse and barn help. If your horse is more tractable with such a companion, be sure to have the companion goat dehorned and neutered.

Horses enjoy good company too.

35

Dogs

Since we have discussed chickens, we should mention dogs. I have owned many dogs over the years and have found some to be dangerous around horses while others are nonthreatening.

Shepherds have an uncanny herding instinct. One shepherd we hand raised from four weeks knew from the beginning that he shouldn't bother the horses. As he matured, he seemed to look and see if there were any humans around. If he thought he was alone, he would slink toward a horse grazing in the field. The horse would immediately sense the dog, react nervously, and trot away. The dog was then in his glory! Once the horse started to run, the dog would joyously chase him, snapping at his rear legs. There was no way to break the dog of this habit. It was almost as if he said, "The devil makes me do it!" This became such a problem we had to get rid of him.

Rottweilers instinctively want to bite the rear end of the horse. This is very dangerous, especially if you happen to be riding a fractious two-year-old. It is even upsetting to an old steady animal. I won't have the breed, because you can't fight instinct!

The older I get, the more I try to eliminate trouble. Some dogs are jealous when you start handling your horses. They must be tied up before you begin your work. I no longer have that kind of patience. Too many horses have stomped on me when they sensed a threatening animal sneaking up behind them. One of my horses ended up in the swimming pool because a dog chased him into a frenzy.

It's good to have dogs around horses. It's good for them to learn to get along. Start with puppies whose parents you have met. I have had more luck with large dogs that have no herding instincts.

Through trial and error you will find what you can live with.

A Visit From the Vet

Jerry Wessner was kind enough to supply this information on vaccinations. Jerry graduated from the University of Pennsylvania Veterinary School in 1965. He was a practicing racetrack vet for many years. His help is appreciated.

Coggins Test

Every horse should have a Coggins Test. This test is named after Dr. Coggins who developed the test for detection of Swamp Fever or Equine Infectious Anemia (EIA). EIA is a viral disease transmitted from an infected horse through blood transfer. This transfer may occur by blood contaminated needles or syringes, mosquitoes, flies or any vector or means that allows EIA contaminated blood to come in contact with circulating blood in a healthy horse. Horses that contract EIA have the virus in the white blood cells for life.

Usually an infected horse will show intermittent fever, depression, progressive weakness, weight loss, edema, and either progressive or transitory anemia. The disease may incapacitate or kill horses with the anemia, or it may go quiescent and never cause anemia again. The quiescent stage is the most dangerous.

Before the Coggins Test, many horses were infected through insect vectors or multiple use of needles and syringes. The Coggins Test detects both the carrier and the infectious state. Most racing jurisdictions will not allow horses to race if they have a positive Coggins Test. The majority of states allow the infected horses to live if suitable quarantine facilities are built and quarantine measures adhered to. Most states prohibit the interstate shipment of positive Coggins horses. Although this disease will probably never be eliminated, economic losses of horses have decreased dramatically since the advent of testing was coupled with strict control measures. Some states require testing every six months, while others only require annual tests. Whatever your state requires, be thankful you will probably never see this disease.

Vaccinations

Vaccinations or immunizations are injections made up of either killed or modified live viruses or bacteria that do not cause disease in an animal, but offer protection or immunity, as if the horse has succumbed and recovered from the disease. Vaccinate your horse. It is cost effective.

The cost of a vaccination is far less than the cost of treating a disease.

Tetanus Toxoid

All horses should be vaccinated annually with Tetanus Toxoid. All the unvaccinated horse needs is a small non-draining wound or abscess in the foot or other part of the body and, if infected by the tetanus organism, the animal will have a very painful and expensive illness. Symptoms of tetanus are a stiff sawhorse appearance, rigid tail and flickering of eyelid over eyes when startled. Tetanus causes spasms and a great deal of pain. Inoculate during the first year and repeat in four weeks. Boosters must be given annually.

Botulism

Botulism is caused by the same family of bacteria that causes Tetanus. It is characterized by muscular weakness that leads to paralysis. Death ensues from paralysis of respiratory muscles. A minute amount of toxin can kill a horse, so beware and vaccinate. Inoculate during the first year and repeat in four weeks. Boosters must be given annually.

Potomac Horse Fever (PHF)

This is a disease that originated in Virginia and is caused by pleura pneumonia-like organisms (PPLO) which are very similar to organisms that cause Rocky Mountain Spotted Fever. PHF is characterized by severe diarrhea and sometimes laminitis (founder). Horses that have both diarrhea and laminitis are hard to save. An immunization is now available.

Encephalitis

Encephalitis means inflammation of the brain and coverings, or meningitis. This virus causes horses to be very ill. Since the brain is involved, CNS signs will be evident: blindness, blind staggers, convulsions, circling, head pressing and abnormal behavior. There is a trivalent vaccine currently available... Eastern, Western, and Venezuelan. It is almost 100% effective when given early enough.

Strangles

Strangles is a respiratory disease caused by a bacteria called Streptococcus Equi. This disease is somewhat spotty now, but if it does appear, your land and area will be contaminated for seven years. The disease is manifested by high fever and swelling and sometimes bursting of the submandibular lymph nodes. Symptoms are fever and large swollen glands under the jaw. Three vaccinations given seven to ten days apart the first year and then repeated annually are recommended.

Flu and Rhino

There are 35 viruses that can cause respiratory disease in the horse. These viruses offer no cross immunity. Theoretically, it is possible for a horse to be continually infected with 35 distinct respiratory viruses. Recovery from one would not offer any protection from the other diseases. The two main viruses are Flu and Rhino. Many two-year-olds at the racetrack seem to have chronic cough and respiratory disease. Discuss with your vet ways to prevent or control the Respiratory Disease Complex in young horses.

Equine Protozoa Melitis

EPM is a neurologic disease of horses, caused by a protozoan parasite called Sarcocystis neuroma. Exposure has been reported to be as high as 90% in the racehorse population. Exposure means that the horse has ingested the parasite, that it is in the horse's body. It does not mean that the parasite has invaded the nervous tissue yet. Many factors enter into a horse getting an active infection. The immune status of the horse probably is the most important. Stress is another important factor. Active infection can follow exposure

Remember an ounce of prevention is worth a pound of cure.

anywhere from two weeks to two years and is probably related to stress to the animal. Keep in mind that steroids lower the immune system and could leave your horse less able to resist active infection.

West Nile

It has become very apparent that West Nile is here to stay. There have been countless articles in this regard in equine periodicals. The good new is that the vaccine was finally approved by the FDA. The bad news is that it is not 100% effective, is expensive and for utmost protection should be given up to three or four times a year, depending on your location. It is strongly suggested in every article that prevention is crucial. Drain all standing water, cut bushes that grow along banks and use a repellent on your horse. Be sure to use one specifically designed for horses. There are several new products that have little or no toxicity. Screening stalls or in someway keeping horses in during peak mosquito feeding hours -dawn and dusk is another excellent idea. As are fans. A fan blowing on your horse will not only keep him comfortable, but will keep the mosquitoes away. They have difficulty flying in wind currents. Be very careful with the electric cords. They can be lethal if stepped on by a metal shoe or bitten by a bored horse looking for something to play with.

A Comment on Vaccinations

Be judicious and only vaccinate for those illnesses your horse may contract. Over vaccination may affect the immune system. Discuss your situation, travel plans, etc. with your vet before vaccinating. Horses on a farm do not need same coverage as horses on the road or at a larger facility. In areas with a high incidence of rabies, this vaccination should be discussed with your vet. Remember to use your common sense when making any decision pertaining to your horse's well being.

You and Your Vet

It is imperative to have a good working relationship with your veterinarian. Your participation in the relationship is vital. Vets have no respect for owners who only see their horses at six Sunday morning at which time they call the vet (who may have been up all night delivering a foal) in a state of panic about a wound or problem that is now six days old and either cannot be or is very difficult to treat. Another pet peeve is an owner who does not know the normal values for temperature, heart rate, respiration rate or the usual color of the gums. Learn to be observant so that when you do call the vet he knows that there is a real problem and that he can trust the information you provide. Normal values are:

Temperature - 99-101 F

Heart rate - 28-44 beats per minute

Respiratory rate - 8 - 20 breaths per minute

Capillary refill time - 1 - 2 seconds (To test this press your finger on the gum. A white spot will appear see how many seconds it takes to return to the same color as the surrounding gum)

Gums - should be nice and pink - paleness could indicate anemia or internal bleeding

Skin pinch for dehydration. It should refill promptly.

Trust must run in both directions.

The Anatomy of A Horse

Anatomy

Poll

Crest

Throat Latch

Back

Croup

Shoulder

Point of Hip

Chest

Barrel

Flank

Thigh

Chestnut

Knee

Elbow

Gaskin

Hock

Shins

Cannon Bone

Pastern bone

Fetlock Joint

ankles

Hoof

Coronet Band

Fetlock

Paralyzed flap

Sore
Back

Sore
Shoulder

SORE
STIFLES

SHOE
BOIL

HERNIA

Back
at KNEE
(WEAKNESS)

Hot
Hocks

Curb

BOWED
TENDON

QUARTER CRACK

Common Race Horse Problems

**Proven scientific medications are beneficial
when used judiciously.**

Two of the Most Common Equine Ailments

Time and experience will teach you what you can handle. There are many basic horse health books. Try to have good reference books. I strongly recommend *The Merck Veterinary Manual*, Published by Merck & Co., Inc., Rahway, N.J. and *How To Be Your Own Veterinarian (sometimes)*, by Ruth B. James, DVM, published by Alpine Press, Mills, WY. "Merck's" gives very technical information, whereas Dr. James gives wonderful hands-on advice.

Colic

This is the most common ailment you will encounter. It is abdominal pain from gastrointestinal, as well as non-gastrointestinal, causes. It may be a slight tummy ache or a life threatening blocked intestine. Aside from just appearing off the horse may not want to eat (a very important sign) and will turn his head and look at his stomach. As the pain increases, other signs are pawing, stomping, rolling gently or violently, kicking at the abdomen, decreased or absent manure output, distended abdomen, elevated heart and respiratory rate and white, blue, purple, or red mucous membranes. Call the vet immediately and follow his instructions.

Cuts

These are frequent and can be caused by barbed wire, splintered boards, tree branches, etc. If the wound is open and bleeding profusely, confine the animal and put pressure on the wound with a clean rag or cotton, holding the bandage in place with vet wrap if possible. Horse blood tends to coagulate quickly, so try and stop the bleeding and then call the vet. Don't panic.

If your horse has small nicks and scratches, remember aggressive hosing is the best treatment. If not already vaccinated a tetanus toxoid vaccination should also be given. If your horse has had a tetanus toxoid vaccination within the previous two to three weeks, administer a booster shot. Where there are many flies and heat, hose the scratches a few times a day. This will inhibit irritation to the skin caused by the drainage of serum from the wound.

When the legs are scraped or cut below the knee, the swelling or edema can be frightening. Light exercise (hand walking, free round penning at a jog, or turnout) will help alleviate the edema, as will aggressive hosing.

Some of the Less Common Equine Ailments

Refer to the Glossary for definitions of specific ailments and terms such as Anhidrosis (Non-sweater), Azoturia (Tie-up), Bean, Bleeder, Blister, Bog Spavin, Bone Spavin, Bowed Tendon, Bucked Shin, Capped Hock, Contracted Feet, Cord-up, Cracked Heels, Epiphysitis, EIA (Swamp Fever), Founder (Laminitis), Joint Capsule, Navicular

Consult a vet for any unusual symptoms.

Disease, Neurectomy, Nerved, Osselets, Osteochondrosis, Popped-A-Splint, Quarter Crack, Quittor, Rhinopneumonitis, Ring Bone, Roarer, Sesamoiditis, Shoe Boil, Speedy Cut, Splints, Superficial Flexor Tendon, Suspensory Ligaments, Thoroughpin, Thrush, and Wolf Teeth.

DIARRHEA

This can have many causes, and can be quite serious. It can develop into colitis (inflammation of the colon), which might lead to dehydration and toxic shock. Signs of colitis include fever, red to brown mucous membranes with prolonged capillary refill time, depression, colic, and increased output of watery, smelly diarrhea.

EYE INJURIES

These always require immediate attention from the veterinarian. Squinting, tearing, cloudy appearance of the cornea, narrowed pupil, and swelling are clinical signs that might be apparent in horse with an eye injury.

FRACTURES

Fractures have sudden onset and non-weight-bearing lameness. The limb is usually swollen unless the fractured bone is within the hoof.

LACERATIONS AND PUNCTURE WOUNDS

These are open wounds that generally constitute an emergency. Lacerations should be sutured within the first six to eight hours in order to maximize the chances of successful suture placement, hasten healing, and minimize scars. Puncture wounds - penetration by nails or other foreign bodies - can be quite serious, especially if they penetrate the hoof or joint capsule.

Wounds must be kept open to facilitate healing from inside out. After the wound is "set" hosing is essential. Start with a gentle water flow. Increase it very slowly. Regular "irrigation" or hosing will speed the healing process.

LAMINITIS/FOUNDER

See the Section on *Setbacks*. The Interview with farrier, Jim Sheridan, also discusses laminitis.

Typical Stance for Laminitis!

A Horse with Laminitis tries to get the Weight off his Toes! Usually on front end!

Horses are trouble looking for a place to happen.

Deworming

Your vet will suggest the best deworming program for your area. Keep in mind that your goal is to control parasites in your pasture as well as your horse. (Be sure to read about my Chickens.) Part of an article by Rupert P. Herd, MVSc, PhD, Department of Veterinary Preventive Medicine, College of Veterinary Medicine, Ohio State University is quoted below. See how up to date you are in equine parasite control.

12 Common Deworming Myths

"MYTH - Repeated deworming is the only effective method of worm control.
TRUTH -   Seasonal (spring/summer) strategic treatments are just as effective for adult horses as are year-round treatments. Twice-weekly removal of dung is even more effective than repeated deworming and greatly reduces reliance on chemical control.

MYTH - Tube deworming is more effective than paste deworming.
TRUTH - Paste deworming has proved to be highly effective in millions of horses worldwide, and it is easier, faster, and safer than tube deworming. Tube deworming is best replaced by crucial services such as monitoring parasite control with egg counts. -

MYTH - Qualitative fecal egg counts are just as good as quantitative fecal egg counts.
TRUTH -This is true in small-animal practice, in which you only need to know whether the animal is infected. In equine practice, you need to quantitatively measure the degree of pasture contamination, the presence of drug resistance, and the best interval between treatments.

MYTH -Fecal egg counts provide a measure of the severity of worm infection and the size of the worm load.
TRUTH - There is no correlation between the number of eggs passed in feces and the number of worms in the horse. Horses with severe larval cyathostomiasis commonly have low or nonexistent fecal egg counts because the larvae responsible have not reached the adult egg-laying state.

MYTH - The large strongyles are the most important worm pathogens in horses.
TRUTH - This is no longer true because there has been a dramatic drop in their prevalence in most horse-breeding regions since the advent of modern anthelmintics in the early 1960's. The modern drugs have been and still are effective against the large strongyles, with no indication of drug resistance occurring.

MYTH - Modern drugs are effective against all worm states, including hypobiotic and encysted cyathostomes.
TRUTH - No anthelmintics approved in the United States are effective against the encysted cyathostomes of horses. Even repeated high doses of modern anthelmintics have failed in the treatment of larval cyathostomiasis.

Your goal is to control parasites in your pastures as well as your horse.

MYTH - Rapid rotation of drugs every few months will prevent the development of drug resistance.
TRUTH - The common practice of rotating dewormers at every treatment or several times a year has been associated with the rapid spread of resistance in the United States. By contrast, there are no reports of resistance developing on farms that practice an annual rotation of drugs using only one dewormer each year.

MYTH - Horses can be treated every 30 to 60 days, year after year, without anthelmintic resistance developing.
TRUTH - The more frequently a dewormer is used, the faster resistance will develop. Overprotective treatment programs (e.g. 12 treatments per year) are not only unnecessary, but are counterproductive because they raise the risk of drug resistance and other drug-related problems.

MYTH - Treatments given according to set calendar months without regard for epidemiologic principles provide good parasite control.
TRUTH - Many of these treatments are given at the wrong time of year to prevent serious pasture contamination and do not prevent horses from ingesting large numbers of pasture larvae.

MYTH - Risk of reinfection decreases after a "killing frost."
TRUTH - Subzero temperatures and heavy snowfalls have little adverse effect on third-stage infective larvae on pasture, unless there has been alternate freezing and thawing. Infective larvae will generally survive on pastures of winter, but die off when temperatures rise in late spring.

MYTH - Harrowing pastures at any time of year provides good parasite control
TRUTH - Harrowing is beneficial during hot, dry periods when pasture larvae are exposed to sunlight and desiccation. Harrowing in damp, overcast conditions simply spreads viable larvae from roughs to lawns and heightens the risk for grazing horses.

MYTH - Pasture rotation is an effective method of parasite control.
TRUTH - This approach cannot be relied upon for good parasite control because of the prolonged survival of infective larvae for up to one year on pastures. It may even increase the risk of parasitism if weather conditions favor larval development at the time when horses are rotated to a fresh but contaminated pasture."

Deworm with your climate and your calendar.

Equine Dental Care

When a horse tries to bolt, swing his head or fight the bit, think teeth! They may be bothering him. A horse's mouth can be the source of a great deal of trouble if the trainer is not on his toes. Many problems in controlling a horse may be related to his teeth and mouth. For a while, one of my horses would bolt and run all over the track uncontrollably. I interpreted this behavior as fear and nervousness at the track and used a pony and various other devices trying to control him. The problem occurred when the jockey "took a hold" of him. It hurt his mouth. Had I thought about teeth, much time and effort could have been avoided solving his problem, because once his teeth were filed he was a different horse.

Many thanks to Larry Moriarity, Master Equine Dentist, for some of this information. Horses have two kinds of teeth. The incisors in front are commonly called nippers. The molars in back are commonly called grinders. The nippers were designed to enable the horse to obtain food when grazing. The grinders masticate food for digestion. Keep in mind that these teeth were designed for grazing, not eating out of a feed bucket. Many dental problems arise from eating feed.

The upper jaw is wider than the lower, causing the upper molars to grow downward and outward. The lower molars grow upward and inward, hence the molars do their work on a bevel. Due to the grinding of food, the enamel on the free sides of the molars receives no pressure, allowing the outside of the upper molars and the inner side of the lower molars to grow to sharp extended points. Filing the molars to make them even is called floating.

Floating can be performed either by your vet or by a farrier trained to do this. For more serious problems your vet should be able to recommend a good dentist. Most racetracks have resident dentists. Ask in the office for information about the track equine dentist.

Signs of teeth problems include lugging, slobbering, cribbing, bolting of grain, indigestion, colic, scouring, nervousness, cutting of the cheeks and tongue, a change in chewing habits, dribbling of feed, washing feed in the water bucket, and holding the head to one side when eating. If you notice weight loss, it could be caused by a dental problem. Your horse may not be grinding his food enough to digest it. You may also notice halitosis, swelling of the face, and refusal to eat hard grain.

According to our equine dentist, incisor deformity can result in malocclusion. Severe dental problems can lead to TMJ (Tempular Mandibular Joint - Migraine headaches). In such cases the atlas bone can become misaligned which can affect the entire skeleton. Another worst case scenario would be pockets of bacteria in the gums and cheeks caused by dental decay. The bloodstream carries these toxins to the liver and kidney for elimination. This causes stress to those organs and can eventually cause problems.

Avoid dental problems. Have your horse's teeth checked. Bad teeth may lead to various health and behavior problems.

Teeth - Determining Age

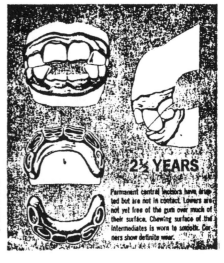

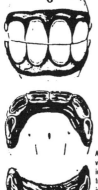

1 YEAR

All deciduous incisors (baby teeth) are visible. Centrals and intermediates are in contact. Chewing surface of the centrals show wear. Upper and lower corner incisors are not in contact. The dental star in the centrals and intermediates is a dark line on labial (lip) side of cup.

2½ YEARS

Permanent central incisors have erupted but are not in contact. Lowers are not yet free of the gum over much of their surface. Chewing surface of the intermediates is worn to smooth. Corners show definite wear.

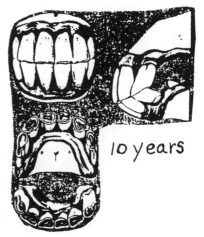

5 YEARS

Permanent dentition is complete. All teeth are in wear. Canine teeth have erupted completely. The centrals and intermediates show wear on the chewing surface ,but cups are still visible and are completely encircled by enamel. Corners are beginning to wear.

10 years

Teeth can help determine age.

Alternative Therapies
by Lois Schwartz

In the past ten years alternative therapies have come to the forefront in health care. They have also become a major market. They are hotly debated with nearly fanatical support on either side of each issue. Alternative therapies range from supplementation, acupuncture, chiropractic, magnets, massage, homeopathic, holistic, to animal communicators. What to do? First we must remember to "Do no harm". Next we must use our common sense and knowledge in selecting the time and situation in which one of these therapies might help.

Not being an authority, I would suggest that we stand back and take a very calm and logical look at things. My own conclusion is that these therapies have their place in the overall well-being and care of any animal and that they can be good preventive measures. However, we must use logic when deciding on their use for acute illness. Our health care providers and the wide range of medications they offer may be our best bet there. I personally do not believe that illnesses such as EPM or West Nile can be cured by magnets, massage or anything other than good proven medicine. Alternative measures may help the horse feel better, but they are not cures. The horse may even survive if they are used. However, I would chose to give my animals the most up-to-date care, probably at the closest top-notch clinic or university vet school, when faced with an acute illness.

It's reasonable to opt not to use unproven or questionable vaccines despite advertising designed to scare you into using them, Insisting on titers before vaccinating for things like rabies, encephalitis or tetanus on yearly schedules is also a viable alternative. However, it would be irresponsible to reject proven vaccines for life-threatening diseases in favor of options like homeopathic nosodes.

It important to understand the difference between fact and fiction - objective findings and unsubstantiated opinions. If your horse's bone scan shows a pelvic fracture, but your chiropractor claims that the horse has a cervical dislocation and an animal communicator tells you the horse wants you to move him to a different pasture, there should be no question as to which diagnosis you believe. The health of your horse is your responsibility. Don't subject it to the latest fashion.

This does not mean that alternative therapies should be discarded. Many of them are helpful and are being given serious consideration and are used by many vets. Use them judiciously.

As to finding competent people in these new fields, the American Veterinary Medical Association is attempting to recognize specific branches of alternative therapy for animals as well as certifying bodies for the practitioners. Contact them if in doubt.

My personal thoughts regarding these therapies and when they should be used follows:

Acupuncture is a therapy that we should consider. It has been used throughout Asia for centuries. The differences we see in its use reflect the differences between Eastern and Western philosophies. In the east acupuncture is used to maintain a good "chi" or energy flow. Although it is used for specific problems, its main purport is as a preventive. In our Western world, we want instant everything. Acupuncture may take time to balance the system and obtain the desired results. It is not a magic bullet.

The health of your horse is your responsibility.

There have been several articles written about massage. One insists that while massage may help humans, when we are massaged we are incumbent and relaxed. A horse on the other hand is standing with his muscles locked, thus making it difficult for massage to be beneficial. Nevertheless, if you observe a horse being massaged he usually looks relaxed and very comfortable. There is no way I can determine if the massage just feels good and makes the horse feel better or if it truly improves the underlying problem. Depending on the underlying problem, it may not matter. One also wonders if massage is involved when our horses rub and groom each other in the field.

My personal experience with magnets has been inconclusive. They have not seemed to help my back aches caused by crushed disks. On the other hand, many people believe they get considerable relief from inflammation and muscle spasm by applying a magnet with the proper polarity to the area. They certainly fall within the axiom, "Do no harm." So if your horse seems to respond, by all means use them. So far there is no evidence of benefit or harm in scientific research.

The holistic approach to overall well being makes all the sense in the world. An imbalance in one area manifests itself in another. By all means be sure of the source of any abnormality you notice in appearance, behavior or gait. You may be very surprised when you find out.

Homeopathy is another delicate issue to discuss. I have seen and heard of dramatic results. I have also seen and heard of disappointments. It is, however, another therapy that seems benign and possibly worth a try. Again I would be ready to jump in with conventional therapies in very acute circumstances.

Supplementations and nutraceuticals have become big business. Supplements that provide the proper vitamin and mineral balance are usually part of good feed. Others seem to help joint health. Some, I fear offer little improvement at great cost. Read your labels and every article you can regarding supplementation. We discuss them in the Section on Feeds and Supplementation.

Animal communicators are the thorniest issue of all. Some of us are more observant of a horse's behavior and some of us are more gifted in understanding horses than others. People who couple observation and understanding may be able to give you some insight regarding your horse, his behavior and his needs. However, I would be very skeptical of anyone asking me to hold a phone to my horse's ear and then giving me a diagnosis of his liver. But then skeptic is my middle name. You should observe, read and think until you reach your own logical conclusion. Remember common sense is the least common of the senses.

Even if your horse isn't the fittest, you want him to survive.

To Medicate or not to Medicate... That is the question.
The answer... Common Sense

by Lois Schwartz

There is no doubt that medical technology is here to stay and that we must be grateful that it is. It has vastly improved the life spans and the life quality for humans and animals. We owe many thanks to researchers and the medical community. However, before leaping on the technological bandwagon, let's apply some common sense to our medical problems and determine if we need modern technology or if the old fashioned way and mother nature are sufficient in certain situations.

No one wants to see an animal suffer, but does a little pain constitute suffering? Or is it there for a reason? The same holds true for swelling. Doesn't it increase circulation and carry out other physiological activities necessary for the healing process? Don't both these symptoms help the animal avoid further trauma to his lesion? If these symptoms exist for a reason, do we tend to over react to them and seek cures greater than the problem?

The case in point presented itself recently with a lame filly. I noticed the problem at her morning feeding and was checking the swelling when a vet happened to arrive on other ranch business and offered to take a look. Judging by the abrasions on her ankle we deducted that the filly had devised a way to wrap the board fence around her hind leg, although neither the fence nor the filly gave any clues as to where or how.

The vet saw no indication of bone damage and decided that x-ray was unnecessary. However, he prescribed the following:
1. Bute to kill the pain
2. Stalling her to avoid further trauma to the lesion
3. Massage with liniment for swelling
4. Azium in her feed to reduce the swelling and finally
5. Wrapping the legs to keep the swelling down.

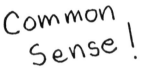

I thanked the vet for his concern and he continued on his way. Enter the horns of dilemma. I stood there pondering the situation, and asking myself why his recommendations would be better than Mother Nature. Remember I had not rushed to the phone to call him nor did either of us have time to discuss the pros and cons of the treatment. Also please understand I am not faulting the vet. His recommendations are standard protocol, prescribed every day. I also understand a vets dilemma of feeling obliged to offer something more sophisticated than just saying, "Throw her out in the field for a few days and call me if the swelling isn't gone by then." After all they have spent much time and money to obtain the knowledge we often need.

Nevertheless, let's look at these particular procedures and ask ourselves, "Why is this treatment necessary?" and "Exactly what is it doing for the horse?"
1. Bute to relieve pain. We all know that Bute relieves pain. However, like aspirin, it may cause serious side affects such as stomach ulceration. In the case of minor swelling, isn't the pain there for a reason? For severe pain, one would want to intercede and keep the horse comfortable.
2. Stall the horse. Well, if we are going to give him But to relieve his pain, we'd better stall

Proven scientific medications are beneficial when used judiciously.

him or he'll be racing around the pasture unaware of his injury and probably cause himself further injury in the process.

3. Liniment and massage. Couldn't agree more. Both of those increase circulation and enhance healing. However, between treatments, turn out also increases circulation, so why not leave the horse in his paddock? Be sure to check the label on that liniment and determine what's in it. If we don't understand the Latin names, let's look them up or call the producer and ask just what it is.

4. Azium in the feed. I have great respect for steroids when they are necessary. It is the same kind of respect I have for the ocean and the sea, one that calls for caution. If you are not aware of the side effects of steroids, read about them or ask your doctor or vet for information. Then ask yourself, "Are these potent medications necessary to relieve the swelling of minor injuries?"

5. Wrap the legs. Bandaging is another area which requires caution. Many animals have suffered severe injury due to improper bandaging. Again, "Why?" pops into mind. Why not just let the horse try and walk out of it.

 I finally opted to keep the horse in a small paddock. Hose the leg, because liniment on the abrasions would sting, and hosing is an excellent massage and also helps heal the abrasions. And last but not least - monitor, monitor monitor for any sign of more than the slight trauma I suspected. If after three days, there had been no improvement, I would have called the vet to discuss the situation. And yes, because I respect him, I would have explained what I did and why.

 The true culprit in this case was the lack of time. Had there been time to discuss his protocol, I am sure we would have avoided those Horns of Dilemma. After all, we had worked together for many years and respected each other. Later I did discuss my dilemma with him. He agreed that Mother Nature was indeed all that was necessary in this case and that he should have remembered my philosophy and prescribed "Her" in the first place. We actually had a good laugh. Our mutual respect thrives to this day.

Respect is the basis for good relationships.

EQUIPMENT

Equipment for Training
- Helmets
- Flak Jackets
- Leads (Shanks)
- Bridles
- Bits
- Reins
- Side Reins
- Martingales

and Yokes
- Saddles
- Whips

Equipment for the Track
- Blinkers
- Shadow Rolls
- Tongue Ties

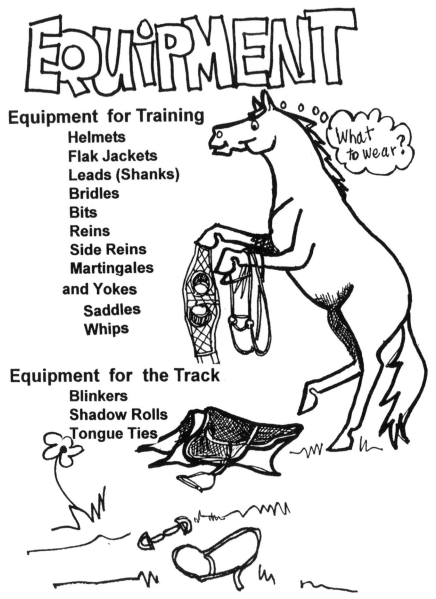

Check List for Trips to the Track

EQUIPMENT FOR TRAINING

This section will briefly cover basic equipment you will need in training an average racehorse with no known quirks or problems.

Helmets

Before you get on a horse, it is mandatory that you automatically put on your riding helmet. There are many varieties available. You may purchase them at tack shops and racetracks. I have a special fondness for the Jofa hockey helmet, because one saved my life. Lois was saved by a hard hat (and head). Any of the approved safety helmets you choose will be acceptable.

Flak Jacket

Flak jackets are protective vests that cover the torso. Most race tracks and training centers now require their use. They come in various levels of protection and generally fasten with adjustable velcro. Develop the habit of using them. They can be purchased at tack stores or from catalogues.

Leads (Shanks)

Whenever you handle a horse, use a 24" chain shank over the nose. Run the chain through the ring on the left side of the noseband up over the noseband and through the ring on the right side of the noseband. Continue under the chin to the ring on the left side located below the buckle. Be sure to leave the bottom strap of the halter between the chain and the horse's jaw. By passing the chain over the noseband and outside of the bottom strap you protect the nose and jaw. If the horse were to step on the shank his nose could be seriously injured by a chain placed directly on the bone structure. By running under the chin to the ring under the buckle, you avoid having the halter

Keep halter noseband between chain and nose bone

Keep bottom strap between chain and jaw bone!

slip up over the horse's right eye. It also has the nutcracker effect by completely wrapping around the horse's head. Never hurt the horse or yank on him unless his actions demand it. When his behavior is unacceptable, punish him immediately to swiftly teach him you won't put up with dangerous comportment.

Introduce new equipment at home.

Bridles

For the training stages, any style leather or nylon head stall with a nose band and chin strap will be suitable. When your horse is ready for the track, you may want to purchase some fancy racing tack.

Bits

Start training with a simple D snaffle. It is not too severe and allows decent control of the horse. A nose band will help teach the horse to keep his mouth shut and to keep his tongue under the bit.

D-Bit

ring bit

In the second stage of training, as the horse grows stronger and into more speed or shows a harder mouth, you may find you need more control. Get professional advice on more effective, stronger bits. Generally, it isn't necessary to go to severe bits. Sense how the horse likes to be ridden and decide what is most suitable for your horse. Be aware that each horse acts differently. Some like to lean against the bit . . . others like it barely in contact. Each horse will evolve his own way of going. NOTE: We never use shank bits with curb chains or straps as we want the horse to lean into the bit for balance when running - and don't want to punish the horse for doing that.

Reins

Use reins that do not slip through your fingers. When the horse is in a lather, slippery reins can be a real problem. Braided leather or rubber padded reins are good choices to help you keep steady contact with your horse's mouth, especially when you get into the Speed Phase of training. Leather or suede gloves also may be helpful.

Side Reins

If your horse has a tendency to throw his head out and run rather than tuck it in and give at the poll, he may need the extra help of "side reins". Various types are available in tack stores. I use less expensive bungee trailer ties that have snaps on both ends. Lois makes them with inexpensive rubber surgical tubing easily available at home improvement stores. All types are attached to the "D" of the bit at one end and either looped around the girth or fastened to a ring at the other. They should not be used in a stall or while leading or tacking a horse.

Putting Bungee "Type side reins reminds the youngsters to "give" at the poll - The side bungees may also help when galloping fractious 2 year olds -

The exercise is "isometric" and devel- a strong hind end

The horse should be turned out in the round pen and allowed time to realize that if he throws his head or tries to flip The horse must learn to go forward while tucking in over, the side rein bungees will inhibit his his head - This gives the rider more control ability to do so. Safety is paramount when working with fractious animals and having these flexible side reins allows the horse to teach himself how to go forward with his head tucked in. If you touch your chin to your chest you

Avoid excessive equipment.

will feel a pull down your back. By teaching the young horse to run against the bit and to carry his head down in the aerobic phase of training, you will get more out of his works. His back will develop more strength and he will have to use his hind quarters more. It is almost an isometric type of training.

Although they are not designed to be used while riding, if he is a "flipper", a horse that would rather throw himself over than go forward, the bungees can be used while galloping, usually with a looser head set. Be careful, horses have been known to flip even while wearing them. Use your judgement as to your horse's tolerance of them and to the head set that will work best for him.

After a girl riding at my farm had her pelvis broken when the flipper landed on top of her, we pulled the side reins so tight the filly's lower lip was almost touching her chest. We made her go forward from the ground and taught her to gallop almost in place with her head set that tightly. This was necessary, because she could easily have killed someone. Once she learned to go forward with her head set that way we cautiously started riding her, using a pony to block her while she was mounted. The pony accompanied her until she was more co-operative. Then we let out the side reins slowly until she held her head nicely and gave at the poll.

By using side reins until the horse is reliable, you have an extra safety factor if the horse is fractious. It is easy to lose your balance and yank your reins. If this happens, the side reins will remain consistent, keeping the head down and generally inhibiting the horse's ability to go over backwards. Some of you may have seen horses able to flip over when their chin was almost touching their chests - it is possible. However, if the side reins are connected low on the girth they should help control the horse early in training.

Under no conditions should the reins be too tight. That will be counter productive. As the horse becomes more compliant, ease out the reins and give him more head. When we graduate into running and breezing we will want to allow him to carry his head comfortably where he can breathe his best. Remember many races are won by a nose. This tool should only be used to help you control the horse. It aids both his mental and physical development.

Martingales and Yokes

Use a set of "rings" or a running martingale in the early stages of training. It discourages a horse when he tosses his head or rears. It also teaches him to "give at the poll" when you rein in, rather than allowing him to stick out his nose and try to fight. Martingales should not be used at the track for speed works or races.

At the track the riders like a yoke on every horse they gallop or breeze. They use it for security if the horse is fractious. If he bucks or

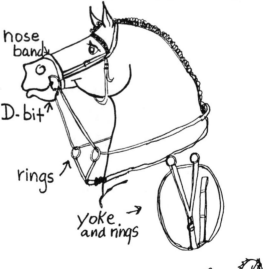

nose band

D-bit

rings

yoke and rings

Keep equipment clean and in good repair.

54

rears they can use the yoke for balance - it keeps them from pulling him over or yanking the mouth. It also keeps the girth in place.

Saddles

The saddle should be placed about two fingers' width behind the shoulder blades. When you are breaking your horse, you will have to decide what to put on his back. Either a western or english saddle is suit-able. When you free roundpen, a western saddle is good to accustom the horse to something flopping around on his back. When I start riding, I go to an english exercise saddle, because it has nothing more than a "tree" type structure covered by leather with stirrups attached to it. It allows me to feel how the horse is moving. Since I recommend long stirrups at this stage, the early riding style is almost like being bareback with stirrups.

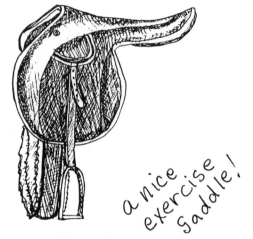

a nice exercise saddle!

Use any saddle you possess for Phase I training. When you begin Phase II training, a western saddle may be too structured for you, the horse, and the style of riding you will be doing. I recommend you buy an exercise saddle at this point, so the horse will not be inhibited and can move easily.

Washable nylon girths with elastic between the girth and buckles on both sides covered with fleece are easy to clean and don't rot if you wash them frequently or live in a very humid area. Leather girths mold or rot quickly unless they are oiled frequently. Frequent oiling is a lot of work for the do-it-yourselfer.

My preference in stirrup leathers is the type with nylon stitched between two pieces of leather. When the leather frays you know it is time to replace them. If you use the plain nylon "leathers" you will see substantial fraying as a warning before they break.

Always use a good thick pad between the saddle and the horse. If you are riding a number of horses, use a clean saddle cloth of washable cotton under the saddle pad of each horse to avoid the sweat and bacteria being carried from one horse to another. Although training saddles are lightweight and will not be on the horse for hours and hours at a time, remember that many back problems are caused by poorly fitting saddles. Be sure the saddle fits your horse and is properly placed on his back.

Whips

You or your rider should always take a riding crop or whip when riding young horses. This is to accustom them to it as a **training aid**. The jockey is **expected to carry a whip and use it as needed** in the race. If the horse has not been accustomed to it at home, valuable time may be lost while teaching him about it at the racetrack.

Good quality equipment is a wise investment.

EQUIPMENT FOR THE TRACK

Specific problems tend to show up when you begin training at the track. Then depending on how your horse behaves, you will have to decide whether to use blinkers, more complex bits, tongue ties, etc. **Your trainer and rider will be able to tell you what equipment will help solve specific problems.** Always analyze whether the horse needs a change in equipment, or whether something you are doing is causing problems in his behavior.

Some trainers use all sorts of equipment "just in case", right from the beginning. Much of the equipment may hinder the horse rather than help him. This can be confusing to the animal. Add one item at a time, and observe his behavior after each addition. Always introduce new equipment at the farm in a familiar environment. Then try it at the track.

If your horse is racing, be aware that any change of equipment, such as blinkers, must be declared when entering the horse in a race. The less equipment necessary to do the job, the less chance for confusion or mistakes.

Blinkers

Blinkers are used to make the horse concentrate on his business. They keep him from veering or bolting. They are also used on timid horses who don't want to pass others or on horses who are distracted by the crowd.

A colt who is more interested in the horse next to him than the race may need blinkers. The jockey might say the colt is "hanging". It means he doesn't want to pass the horse next to him. Blinkers may stop that behavior. Sometimes blinkers will cover one eye leaving the other open. Sometimes half blinkers are used. There are endless blinker configurations. Trainers will try anything to get a good run out of the horse! Remember Gate Dancer? He had blinkers with ear muffs attached so he wouldn't hear the crowd. Don't laugh, he won a lot of races that way!

Shadow Rolls

Shadow rolls may be used to encourage a horse to drop his head. He must lower it to see over the lambswool covering on the nose band. The lambswool band also blocks the horse from seeing his shadow and shying at it.

Tongue Ties

If you notice your horse continuously fussing with his tongue over the bit, under the bit, and around the bit, and you know his teeth are not bothering him, he may need a tongue tie. We use tongue ties for a variety of reasons. Primarily to maintain the tongue in its proper position. Some very nervous horses will curl the tongue behind the bit during a race hampering their ability to take in sufficient air. Other horses will have a tongue that is too long for their mouth, making it necessary to accommodate it for them. If the horse has a loose palate tying the tongue may help keep the soft palate in its proper position. At times the rider feels the horse is not breathing properly and will recommend trying a tongue tie. You may even hear the trainer say, "I don't know what his problems is. Let's try a tongue tie."

Try to have 2 complete sets of tack so that your truck is always RACETRACK Ready!

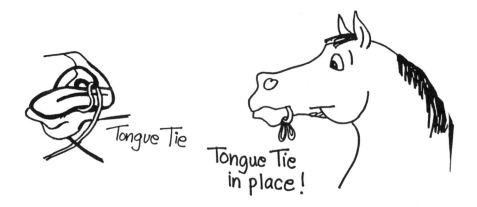

Tongue Tie

Tongue Tie
in place!

Tongue ties can be made of a variety of materials. You can purchase a ready made tongue tie at the tack shop, or you can make one out of soft cotton flannel pieces an inch and a half or two inches wide by about 18" long. The leg of nylon pantie hose also makes a good tongue tie. One trainer I knew used the wide rubber bands.

A word of caution. When I see a horse with his tongue tied and hanging out turning blue, I wonder how that can help him run a race. Be careful to tie the tongue tight enough to keep it in position but loose enough to allow circulation. If a horse drools excessively, it may indicate his tongue is tied too tightly. Have a seasoned trainer teach you how to tie the tongue.

Keep it simple.

CHECK LIST FOR TRIPS TO THE TRACK

If you can afford it, you may want to keep your trailer permanently stocked with doubles of all items you will need to ship-in and run! It can save you last minute confusion.

Equipment
Saddle with girth, stirrups, and pads (for morning works)
Halters, lead ropes
Boots, leg wrap
Cool out blanket (if weather requires)
Bridles with bits, reins, and yoke and "rings"
Blinkers
Buggy whip and lunge line
Helmet and flak jacket
Tongue ties

Grooming box
Brushes, curry combs, scraper to remove water after bath, hoof pick, scissors, shampoo, detangler, Vicks for the nose, a clean rag to wipe nostrils, and some cleaning rags.

Medicine Chest
Electrolytes, Bute, DMSO, thermometer, bandages, liniment, standing bandages, vet wrap, poultice.

Barn needs
Feed, hay, bags, buckets, hooks, muck bucket, pitchfork, folding chair, copy of *Back Yard Racehorse - Fourth Edition.*

Papers
Your license, for each horse a Coggins, Health Certificate, brand inspection paper (where required) and any other papers required by your track.

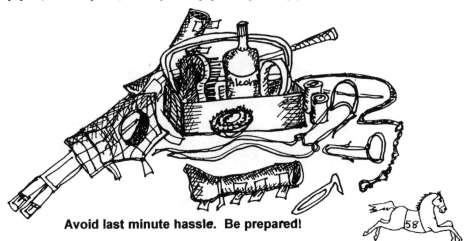

Avoid last minute hassle. Be prepared!

FEEDS and SUPPLEMENTS

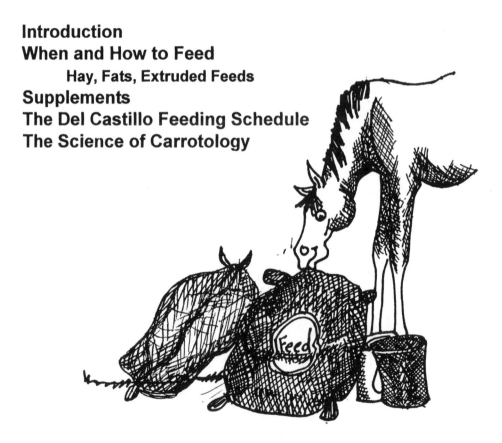

FEEDS AND SUPPLEMENTS - Introduction

In different parts of the world, you see people eating different basic foods as their mainstay. Whether it is potatoes, rice, wheat, or corn, supplemented with meat, fish, or combined proteins, there is a tremendous diversity of diets.

When it comes to feeding horses, you will find an equal diversity of opinions. Owners have come to me with charts, scales and very intricate instructions on how their dear little horse must be fed. They assure me that they have calculated exactly how much he needs because he burns X amount of calories per work. I marvel at their precision . . . how do they know so precisely ?

The first step with any diet is to make sure there is an adequate supply of calories and protein, then balance minerals and look for vitamin deficiencies.

It is extremely impractical to have different feeding menus on large farms. (The exception being a horse with a specific problem.) The more complicated the feeding program, the more opportunity for mistakes and accidents. Too many steps may confuse your help and even yourself when in a rush.

All of my animals receive the same basic feed mixture. Everyone on the farm is fed a 12 percent sweet feed mixed locally that has more corn than oats. Pound for pound, corn is much higher in energy than oats. University studies have shown that corn converts most efficiently into glycogen, which fuels cells during anaerobic stress. The amount of feed given to each horse varies depending on his size and level of training. Don't miss the articles in the back of the book on Osteochondrosis and its relationship to overfeeding.

Every animal gets free choice hay, usually fertilized coastal, orchard, Colorado, or other good green **grass** hay, which is also about 10 percent protein, and is locally grown. My basic feed measurement for Thoroughbreds - yearlings, two-year-olds and up - is about four quarts of the mix twice a day. Yearlings and two-year-olds need food to build and grow. The more mature horses are easing into racing and need to replace fuel that is burned. Quarter Horses are easy keepers. They seem to need less than half as much feed as the Thoroughbreds. When a new horse arrives, until he adjusts to the feed, he is given a third of the usual amount, gradually increasing it to the four quarts, twice a day.

Corn converts most efficiently into glycogen, which fuels cells during anaerobic stress.

Any change in type, amount or frequency of feeding must be done gradually to avoid digestive upset which may lead to colic and/or laminitis. (Remember everything goes to the feet.)

Observe who finishes and who leaves feed. Once your horses are stabilized within your feeding program, augment the feed if an animal looks too thin. Cut it back or increase exercise if he's too heavy. Some large racing horses need as much as eight quarts twice a day.

Since each metabolism is unique, it is imperative that you understand what kind of "keeper" your horse is. Personality can be a major factor in feed consumption, sending the charts right out the window. Is the horse high strung or laid back? What's his genetic background? Some bloodlines are historically easy to maintain and others are more difficult. There may be other influences too subtle for us perceive.

Sometimes, horses appear high strung because they are given high protein feed which is not burned off with a reasonable training program. Fifteen minutes out of the stall doesn't burn many calories.

My training program requires horses to be turned out every day for a few hours. If they are being overfed, they can run and frolic to burn off their excess energy. The point is, although charts may say a horse needs so many pounds for so much work, it is really a very subjective figure. Look at your horse . . . is he carrying enough weight or does he look drawn?

Horses in the interval training program, where they are worked every four days and galloped miles in between, develop muscles with a "hard" look. When I was following the interval training program, my horses looked drawn and overtrained. The program was drilling out their speed and brilliance. When a horse's muscle gets too hard a look in the interval training method, it is not usually because of lack of feed. Mine were eating huge and frightening amounts! The look stems from overtraining. It is important that you learn to tell the difference between overtraining and underfeeding. If your horse is eating huge amounts of feed, is on a good worming schedule and still looks ribby, it may be that you are overworking the animal. The problem can be frequent high speed works without time off for the animal to rebuild in between these stresses. This is especially hard on young animals.

Two, three, and four-year-olds are really very much like teenagers. A tremendous amount of food energy goes into building bone, muscle and tissue. Just as teenagers get big hands and feet and skinny bodies before they fill out, horses go through adolescent growth spurts.

Good feed, good training and lots of turnout during this growing period are imperative. At five, a horse is considered mature in bone and body. If we race judiciously as they grow and develop, and allow time for rebuilding between races, we are forming a useful, strong animal that can last many years!

An excess of anything can be dangerous!
Learn to know your animal and feed accordingly.

WHEN AND HOW TO FEED

Did you notice that I mentioned giving grain twice a day? In the old days, while innocently imitating track procedures, I got up in the dark and woke up the horses to feed them. When they galloped two hours later, I worried that it might be too close to a heavy meal. Eventually, it occurred to me that I had breakfast when my work was done, so the horses could do the same.

Now, I get up at dawn, (the actual time varies greatly from summer to winter) give all the horses hay, and turn out those who go from stalls to paddocks. **The animals loosen up in the paddocks, frolic, and socialize while I pick out the stalls.** After their ride, round penning, or swim, they go back to their turnout paddocks until feed time. They can still nibble on the hay that was given at dawn. At ten AM in the winter or nine AM in the summer, they are given their grain and supplements along with enough hay to last all day. Depending on their schedule, they are stalled during the day and turned out at night in the summer - vice versa in the winter. They are fed hay and grain again at dusk.

During the hot summer days, they are fed in the cool of the evening. In the winter, they are fed while there is enough light to visually observe how they look, before they are tucked in for the night.

This schedule makes sense, because animals are sensitive to earth rhythms, whereas we tend to be more tied to the clock. If you work and must arrange your horses around your schedule, that is fine. Animals are adaptable and can live with many different situations. **The most useful animals are those that aren't ruffled by unpredictable circumstances.** Races and traveling schedules will break up their routine soon enough.

The racetrack routine is very restricting. The track is only open until ten o'clock for works and training. All the horses must be finished by then. Doing most of the training at the farm, you are able to adapt the training program to suit your life-style and schedule. You can have horses and another life, too.

Once a week, all of my horses were given four quarts of bran well saturated with water and perhaps a squirt of corn oil. Then the use of bran fell into disfavor. Now studies are again recommending the use of bran. It seems that these studies have shown that bran does not interfere with the absorption of phosphorus after all.

We are happy to be back on our bran routine, which to avoid confusion, is always feeding bran on Sunday morning. No supplements or other products are added. Some horses are like children when confronted with healthy food. They say, "Yuk . . . bran again." Others devour the bran. Still others try to hold out, only finally choking it down when there is no hope of real feed. Those who refuse to finish get it stirred into their night grain.

We live in an area where horses can ingest a great deal of sand when grazing on short grass. The bran seems to control the problem of sand colic. Keeping fresh, properly cured hay in front of them also helps with this problem.

Animals are sensitive to earth rhythms.

Hay

Speaking of hay. . . a few comments. People rave about alfalfa for horses. Alfalfa is very high in protein, about 18 percent. For me, this is too rich to combine with the high protein grain the animals are being fed. A lower percentage of protein in their roughage is preferable. If needed, I might give a one-inch flake of alfalfa once a day as a treat! In our effort to provide the most nutritious feed, we forget that the animal might find it comforting to eat a lower quality hay all day long, instead of a small amount of high protein hay for a short period.

Hay is one of the best defences against sand colic. Be sure to use a coarse hay. Be cautious of hay that is too fine textured. A good quality grassy hay such as orchard, timothy, or meadow grass mix with a slight amount of alfalfa is a good choice.

When buying hay pull a sample from deep in the bale to be sure that there is no sign of mold or excessive dust. Clover may cause your horse to slobber. This is believed to be caused by a mold on the clover. Although not apparently a health problem, it is messy. One would think the horse would need to increase his water intake to offset the loss.

Munching on hay or grazing is very soothing for horses. It allows them to fulfill their desire to chew and graze which fulfills a very basic drive that is millions of years old. After quickly consuming high protein pellets that fill their nutritional needs, they may start chewing on boards, doors and other surfaces out of boredom. Work with the animals' intrinsic needs. Remember, they are grazers.

If you are feeding your horse too much protein, his manure will be more like cow manure - soggy and wet possibly with a heavy pungent odor. To remedy this, give more hay and less high protein grain. You'll see the difference!

Here are some general comments about feed. A 12 percent sweet feed mix should be available from a reputable local feed mill or company that mixes feed for your area. Read the guaranteed analysis. It should tell the crude protein, fat, fiber, etc. Trace minerals and vitamins should be mentioned. Ingredients such as folic acid, selenite, etc., either occur naturally in the feed or are added to the mix. This is mentioned so that you don't go overboard with supplements. When the horse is racing and you feel he needs help, you may want to add a little more of this and that, but too much supplement is dangerous.

Feed companies have nutritionists design their feed. They have done intensive studies as to the nutritional needs of horses. Follow their instructions as to the amounts of feeds for specific weights and exercise regimes. They also recommend how much hay or free choice pasture should supplement the grain. 14 to 16% protein feeds are invariably high calorie. Studies indicate that it is the rapid growth rate stimulated by the high calorie intake not the

Overfeeding can cause bone weakness.

protein that may be a factor in DOD (developmental orthopedic disease. Horse Journal Jan 02

Doctors Krook and Maylin have stressed in their book, *Race Horses at Risk*, that **many breakdowns are attributed to abusive overfeeding and supplementing to push early growth.** This has resulted in animals with improperly developed bone. Cysts of cartilage form in the bone, which weaken its overall strength. The bone caves in when put under the stress of racing. This type of breakdown happens time and time again.

It is disheartening to think that a healthy looking animal can have serious internal faults. If you want to know more about this subject, read the book. It is an eye opener. *The Merck Veterinary Manual, Seventh Edition*" has the following comment on treatment of Osteochondrosis "...In addition to surgical considerations, nutritional imbalances must be corrected, and toxic elements eliminated. **Overfeeding of high-energy feeds is a common error.** Exercise must be regulated . . ." Be very careful not to overfeed. High protein and low exercise can lead to Osteochondrosis.

For questions about feed and problems to be aware of in your area, call your local extension office or nearest agricultural university.

My whole philosophy is this: Remember the natural life-style of the animal and try to keep him in a way that allows him to be a horse.

FAT

Some trainers, thinking that their horse needs more feed (when really he may be overtrained), will add pure corn oil or other kinds of fats to the feed. There are horses that may be unable to metabolize excessive fat and may develop pockets or globules of fat which constrict major vessels. This in turn may cause impairment of blood flow.

However, recent studies suggest that for high strung horses oil (corn, soy, or olive), may be a good way to increase weight without making the horse hotter. Keep in mind that large quantities of oil may reduce the horse's ability to absorb nutrients, due to the oil coating the intestines. It is also important to consider the increased calorie intake and balance it with a calorie reduction elsewhere in the diet.

Observation in the field indicates that when fat is used as part of the total dietary energy source it will provide a more concentrated supply of energy and that horses need time to adjust to fat utilization - sometimes up to three weeks. Remember fat in the diet will provide more energy, so total daily feed intake must be decreased if the work level and body condition are to remain the same. If you plan to top-dressing fat or oil on feed do so with a small amount and increase that gradually, keeping an eye on eating behavior and general well-being. Also remember that supplementation of fats or oils requires a reassment of the total dietary nutrient balance, especially for young, growing horses which receive exercise.

Animals are sensitive to earth rhythms.

Extruded Feeds

Extruded horse feeds are created using a process in which ground grains are cooked under pressure and moist heat, then exposed to cooler air so they "pop" like a kernel of corn... because this process creates a feed that is about twice as large and half as dense as a "loose" grain mix or pellets made with the same ingredients, it takes most horses longer to eat it. Slower eating means horses have more "chew time", which can help satisfy their grazing urge and discourage them from snacking on the barn and fences. They'll be less likely to bolt their food and put themselves at risk for choke and colic.

It's suspected... that a horse which eats extruded feed retains more water in its cecum, which can reduce the risk of impaction colic and help prevent dehydration in stressful situations... there is good evidence the overall digestibility of extruded feeds is higher than that of plain grains, sweet feeds, or pellets.

CHECK with Your Local Extension Office for Nutrictionneeds in Your Area!

A local Feed Mill should have the proper mix for your area.
It should be fresher than feed shipped in from far away.
Check with the nearest Agricultural University for Specific Nutrictional needs in your area!

Your role as a trainer is to know when enough is enough.

SUPPLEMENTS

This subject could be debated forever. There are testimonials for all kinds of products. It is easy to fall into the vitamin and health food syndrome. True health food fanatics live restricted lives that revolve around strange diets. Some of us think "Death is better than eating that stuff!"

Go back to Mother Nature. Horses are grazers. They meander constantly to get a bite of grass here, a few seed heads there, a lovely salad over yonder all courtesy of their environment. I am instinctively frightened by the amount of grain we give these horses. They would have grazed for many, many hours, burning many, many calories to encounter that much protein in the wild. We stress our animals in ways that are not natural (sustained high speed, with weight on their back), so we assume that we must compensate.

Overall we have improved their life-style in relation to the dangers of the wild. However, we stress their metabolism, especially if they are honest. I tell my horses that nothing in life is free and that they must perform for me in exchange for the comforts they are given.

The amount of weight a horse loses in a race is amazing. **The one minute and twelve seconds of racing can take so much out of the animal that he needs days to recuperate.** This is where supplements may be necessary. After being over stressed, the horse needs help to rebuild. A horse may be dehydrated for a few days after a hard race. In Florida, during the severe summer heat, this is especially true. I give a handful of electrolytes for a few days after the race, always checking his skin to see how he is doing. To judge how the horse is rehydrating, pinch the skin on his neck and see how long it takes to snap back

Don't try to fool Mother Nature.

to normal from the pinch. The longer it takes the more dehydrated he is. **Remember that electrolytes are also assimilated from a good diet and a salt mineral block.**

The time a horse needs to rebuild himself is the best barometer of his overall ability to withstand the rigors of racing. I am opposed to jugging a horse after a race to speed his recovery. Jugging means having the veterinarian give the horse a solution of electrolytes and IV fluids intravenously. Many trainers administer jugs several days before an event to insure maximum performance. The composition of the medication solution allows the body to utilize what it needs and eliminate what's not needed. If there are deficiencies in a diet, this may help. However, I generally prefer to balance his needs with oral supplements. The whole structure of the horse is stressed in a hard race... the bone, muscle, and soft tissue. By jugging the horse you make him feel better than he really is. It is better to allow the horse to mope around for a few days - self imposed rest. **His body tells him he needs rest, and that in itself will make him rest. When he is recharged, he'll tell you by frolicking when you turn him out.** Most horses I've trained show a definite pattern. If they have tried hard and raced honestly, they are a tad off their feed that night. They might be slightly off for another day or so. By the fourth or fifth day it seems that their own endorphins make them feel high off the race. They are on their way to rebuilding. When turned out they frolic and cavort. Light free round penning and maybe one flying open gallop and they are ready to race again on the tenth day.

After a few races or hard works, you begin to discern between a robust horse that needs and wants to race frequently and a horse that is hard on himself in a race. Unlike many humans who can push themselves and come back stronger, when a horse is pushed too much, he is capable of doing himself real damage. When he has an adrenaline rush, he is capable of running on a fractured leg or doing other equally harmful things to himself. The rider on the horse urging him to go faster and faster may make the horse overexert.

The cost of training a horse at the track is so high that owners put too much emphasis on the horse's daily behavior. If he has one bad day or is slightly off his feed, there is a tendency to over react. "Call the vet . . . we're losing time." At home you can be more relaxed about allowing him rebuild-days and giving him time off. **We all have bad days. Horses are no exception.** They are not machines! Blood tests and X-rays for every minor bump get to be very expensive. At home you have another great advantage over the track; you can constantly observe and monitor your animal.

If your horse's gums aren't pink and healthy, check with your veterinarian. See if your horse is wormy. Have a CBC and blood chemistry run, if there is a problem. In a well fit and conditioned horse, the gums will flush up pink very quickly during exercise, indicating an efficient cardiovascular system. When horses swim, they curl their upper lip making it easy to assess how long it takes them to go from light pink gums to rich strong pink, as they exercise. It's a good gauge of their cardiovascular efficiency.

Time has been taken here to discuss the above because **there is a tendency to over supplement and overdose the horse.** A huge amount of money is spent on feed and joint supplements. Observe what works. Read the literature and judge whether it makes sense. If a talented horse is kept happy and healthy, he will run. If it makes you feel good, give your

  Horses are grazers.

horse a pinch of this and a squirt of that. Try not to overdo. The kidneys will have to work overtime to filter the excess additives out of his system. One simple all around vitamin once a day should be adequate for his needs. Anything above and beyond that should be studied for real value and cost If you chose to supplement, be sure that what you use does not alter the overall balance of his feed. Before adding supplements check your labels for the vitamins and minerals already included in the feed you are using. Only supplement what is needed.

A new product on the market appears to have remarkable results in preventing and even treating bone related injuries. Souther Equine Brand BIO-Si provides a bio-available source of silicon, which when fed to horses seems to strengthen the bone, prevent OCD lesions and speed healing after surgery. I had a horse with soft and persistently weak bone. I tried this supplement and it seemed to help. After giving time and the supplement the horse is able to withstand the training regime. If you have a similar problem you may want to look into this product. In this instance I am caught between trying not to make a testimonial and yet sharing with you information about products that may be beneficial to your horse's health.

Another supplement you may want to consider is some sort of sand removal if you live in a sandy area. We have come across a product that does seem to help with sand colic. It is Equisyl Advantage, a psyllium-based product, that is fed daily. Lois knows a veterinarian who while performing a necropsy was astonished to find no sand in the gut of the horse - a local Florida horse.

WHAT GOODIES Do we have?

Keep the feed Tasty!

No magic powders will help a horse without talent.

Del Castillo's Feeding Schedule

Dawn Turn out horses to individual

paddocks (after feeling and checking legs!)
Give Hay * note whether or not all grain was eaten!

9 or 10AM Grain and Hay
and Vitamins!
Tuck back in stall - all (all feed
morning work done! supplements are
added at this feeding)

Afternoon - Turn out for
an hour or so ··· depending
Sometimes I gallop, round pen or swim
in the afternoon - depending on schedule

½ hour before Dark Hay and Grain -

Tuck Horses in for night

Hay 3 Times a day
Grain 2 Times a day
Bran - Sunday A.M.

THE SCIENCE OF CARROTOLOGY

You are probably wondering, "What the heck is carrotology?" Early in my endeavors with horses and racing, a friend came to visit. She loved horses. She knew nothing about training , but was an expert in nurturing. For years, Claire has returned and taught the horses how to eat carrots. Yes, they sometimes need to learn this important skill. Claire's husband, George, is a sharp handicapper from way back. He also comes to see what the horses have to say. Sometimes Claire will come in and tell me, "You know, Aly says his shin is bothering him!", or share some other observation. I dutifully go out and check the animal to find that she is instinctively right.

Over the years, she has befriended all of the horses on the farm. She does have her favorites - she brought gourmet carrots to First Prediction. She shares her carrots, kindness, and advice with all the horses. They all know Claire and George by sight, and nicker to them when they arrive.

It is very special for the animals to have someone who does nothing but love and care for them. When I had quite a few horses, I assigned girl riders to specific horses so that they would take a personal interest in them.

You will be warned time and time again not to fall in love with your horses. This is business - be pragmatic! You must realistically appraise the ability of the animals you are training, but **that does not preclude caring and loving them.** Some animals are so honest and noble that one can't help but admire them. **There is nothing wrong with having feelings. It might help the racing industry tremendously to have more feeling and caring individuals involved.** All horses should have a support group like George and Claire. Find some "Grandparents" for your horses.

George and Claire

Give your horse a kiss on the nose. Let him know you care!

LEGS BANDAGES SHOEING

LEGS, BANDAGES, AND SHOEING - Introduction

Walking down the backside shedrow is like walking along a horse hospital ward. Nearly every horse has some kind of bandage, poultice, plastic wrap or scabby paint on his legs.

Years ago, I was bewildered by terms like blistering, firing, poulticing. They were a foreign language to me, but all the trainers and grooms seemed to know what they were talking about. With time and experience, I learned that was not necessarily so.

My opinion of firing and blistering is mentioned in other chapters. Briefly, the theory is to insult the area with a chemical or physical burn, causing the body to supply blood to the injured area and to create scar tissue. Doesn't the actual problem do that? Don't fractures, bucked shins, and other injuries cause swelling, heat, and therefore increased blood supply to the injured area while the body is trying to heal?

In any case, I'm told a good blister (i.e., huge swelling and scabbing of skin caused by a caustic agent) will straighten things right up. Some trainers recommend training during the healing process. Others may stall the horses. There are many theories, but not much concrete evidence that any of this voodoo is more valid than rest and massage. Doesn't massage also stimulate heat and blood flow? Think about the animal's problem from a competent horseman's point of view and see if the solution your trainer or track vet suggests makes sense. An experienced veterinarian who knows horses . . . not just racehorses . . . can give you an answer. Racetrack veterinarians are very good at keeping compromised horses going. Is that your goal? If you explain your philosophy to the racetrack veterinarian, he can advise you accordingly.

Bandages give support if needed.

There are reasons for using bandages. They are good support for an animal trying to defend his injured leg. He puts so much weight on his good leg that it can stock up from the added stress. Under those conditions, both legs should be bandaged. A horse that has a cut or wound should be bandaged and medicated for a few days to get the healing started. Then begin gentle irrigation (hosing) to encourage blood flow to the area. This helps the body form new scabs, which will enhance the healing process and allow the wound to heal from the inside. A wound that scabs over and heals on the outside may leave a pocket of infection inside. When the wound is set and no longer oozing or fragile, usually after three or four days, the area should be exposed to air.

Horses that are forced to stand in their stalls most of the day tend to stock up. Standing bandages are put on them to keep the filling down. Wouldn't **walking them twice a day or turning them out be preferable to having them bandaged all the time?**

There are a few things to remember about bandages:

Never leave them on while the horse is turned out. As he moves, they can slip and bow a tendon from the constriction or come loose and tangle.

Never leave a bandage on for twenty-four hours without rewrapping it.

Never put a bandaged horse in a van and assume that he will be checked. Send the horse with a groom or don't wrap his legs.

Most importantly - don't fool yourself into thinking your horse has healed from an injury because his leg is tight after removing the bandages. Leave him unbandaged with free movement in order to properly assess his recovery.

TRAINERS GET A FALSE SENSE OF SECURITY WHEN BANDAGES SUPPRESS SWELLING. SUPPRESSED SWELLING DOES NOT MEAN HEALING HAS TAKEN PLACE OVERNIGHT!

**Bandages have their place...
be sensible when you use them.**

BANDAGING AND LEG SUPPORT FOR RACING

Support wraps such as Vetwrap are used all over the country. Some trainers I highly respect use them on all four legs of every horse, in every race. This can be expensive, about ten dollars a race, and dangerous if the groom is not completely competent. Many a horse has been injured by incorrectly applied bandages. Unless I know that a horse has a tendency to hurt himself or get into trouble, I don't wrap him.

Once in a while, a horse will get into a scuffle coming out of the gates or in the heat of the race. Vetwrap would protect tendons that might be cut or injured in such instances. Statistically, the chances of such injury are slim. If you are a super cautious person or your horse tends to hurt himself, be safe rather than sorry. Don't forget that damage may also be caused by incorrectly wrapped bandages. Always supervise the wrapping or do it yourself.

"Polos" are the soft cushioned bandages, in bright colors, seen on horses during their early morning workouts. They protect the animal from hitting himself during the workout, but are never used for races.

There are new bandages on the market every day. Like supplements, they promise miracle results. Some are supposed to keep a horse from bowing . . . hard to believe. There are many variations on the theme of support and strength. Some tests suggest a decrease in leg concussion with particular types of wraps. They could be very beneficial to a horse with tendencies toward leg problems. Wraps may also decrease the amount of damage done if a horse does break down in a race. At times you might want to wrap a horse for racing. Let your horse sense tell you when to do so. **If you have a horse that is compromised or has bad ankles, by all means give him the extra support if you choose to race him.** It might be helpful under racing conditions.

**Always use your own judgment and
horse sense.**

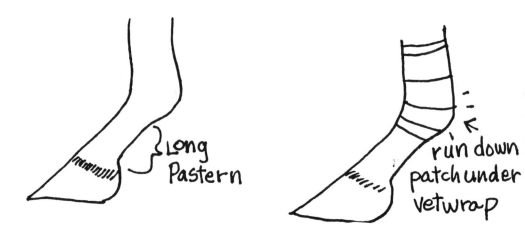

SOLUTIONS FOR SPECIFIC LEG PROBLEMS

Horses with long pasterns have a tendency to run down during a race, even with the best conditioning. As fatigue sets in, the fetlock drops lower and lower. Eventually, it can hit the track, causing a burn or worse injury. Trainers try to avoid this problem by using rundown patches. Rundown patches are pieces of material that are placed at the point of impact and wrapped with Vetwrap. Patches of plastic, rubber, or leather are available for the same purpose.

If your horse comes back from a work at the track with a burn on his fetlocks . . . on either the front or rear leg or legs . . . make sure he has protection the next time he goes to the track - after he has healed. **Don't allow the burn to become a chronic problem.** It could hamper the animal's desire to run.

A protector made from a motorcycle inner tube has worked on some of my animals. Motorcycle inner tubes being smaller than automobile inner tubes and larger than bicycle inner tubes are just right for protector material. I have created various types of leg, heel, and fetlock protectors using them. Someone showed me one of the styles, and the others have been devised as the need arose. They can be left on the horse all the time. After a few minutes of stomping their feet, the horse forgets them and accepts them as a second skin.

Illustrations on how to make them are included. They work very well for some horses and eliminate hitting problems in certain cases. Horses can be raced wearing these protectors.

Avoid initiating chronic problems.

Style 1　Style 2　Style 3

Style #1 - Protects the fetlock area from rundown . . . either front or back legs. You might wrap Vetwrap over it in a race, so it doesn't twist around. This style is useful to protect the hind hooves from hitting the front ankles if your horse has that tendency.

Style #2 - Protects the balls or heels of the front feet. You might have a horse that consistently catches himself while galloping and running. Make sure his feet are well balanced, the toes aren't too long, and try this.

Style #3 - Protects the front of the rear ankles and coronet band from being hit by the front feet. A horse that brings his rear legs up and under, interfering with his front action, will show hitting and cuts around the coronet band and ankles. One rear hoof may also hit the other in this area. If you see persistent random cuts around the rear ankles and coronet band, try this design.

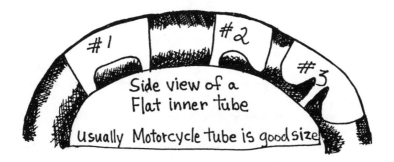

#1　#2　#3
Side view of a
Flat inner tube
Usually Motorcycle tube is good size

Protect your horse if necessary.

SHOEING

To shoe or not to shoe. The question is easy for me. I never use shoes until the horse is nearly ready for track works. But, this is Florida, where, if the horse is well trimmed, he has little use for shoes. Initially, I thought shoeing was necessary. Then I wondered why? I tried not shoeing and found it was much better for the majority of horses. However, if his white line is splitting or he has a specific need, shoeing should be considered. Remember the old adage "no foot, no horse"? About 90% of all lameness problems are caused by foot problems. Good, healthy feet are the basis of any performance. Like good tires to a car.

Keep horses in training on a good trimming schedule. Use a simple trim. The line of the pastern should continue straight through the hoof. You take each foot individually and trim or shoe to its own characteristics. Some very simple drawings are included that encourage you to consider the horse, not an abstract angle someone has deemed as the perfect angle. Horse's feet are as individual as our own. Horses may have skinny "muley" feet, very shallow and platter- like feet, a great hoof wall, or weak hoof wall. Some are white (the "lore" being a white foot is a soft foot) and some are dark.

Feed supplements may help strengthen the hoof wall. Biotin with methionine is deemed helpful. Making sure your horse has all his trace minerals is a must. A clean dry stall is also essential. Check the old shoe of your horse if he's living in a stall or at the track. If you see erosion on the shoe where its sits on the hoof (usually by the nail hole), it is caused by ammonia from urine. This means the stall is not being kept clean and dry.

Have your horse jog barefoot on the road to see the natural wear down pattern of his hooves. A little concussion is good for the bones. It seems to be tradition to put training plates on the front of the horses and sometimes all the way around. If your area is rocky or hard, or your horse is chipping, by all means protect the hoof. **If all is well, don't rush into it.**

If the horse is crooked legged, shoeing can help his performance dramatically. If he hits himself when he runs - his front foot cutting his ankle, etc. - various shoes must be tried until the right combination is found.

As a new owner, do you know that your horse's shoes might cost more than yours, and that he needs a new set every six weeks? This is generally an extra expense on your monthly training bill and may run from $40 to $80 dollars or more, depending on your location and the complexity of the job.

I have wanted to start some of my young horses racing barefoot. However, the stewards tend to be somewhat inflexible. They say a horse that starts barefoot will have to race the entire meet barefoot. With that option, it was better to use shoes than risk putting my animals at a disadvantage.

Decide when to put on shoes after a gallop or two at the racetrack. Our local track is heavy and sand covered. Therefore, I have the farrier file down the toe grabs or put on a rim shoe. **Toe grabs can cause problems, especially on hard, unforgiving surfaces.** If your track is very hard and you have toe grabs protruding, the way the horse breaks over is changed. Recent studies indicate that toe grabs may increase the risk of catastrophic

Many, many foot problems are started in the name of good training.

suspensory injuries. Also, our farrier has noted a high incidence of bucked shins with toe grabs.

Aluminum racing plates are generally used for racing. They are light weight and easy for the farrier to shape. If you turn your horse out with plates on, he'll sometimes catch himself while frolicking . . . the toe of the hind foot "grabs" the heel of the front foot. That's the price I'm willing to pay for his peace of mind. Make your farrier aware of this. Having him make sure that the shoe doesn't hang over the heel of the foot will help. Bell boots, on the front, might help too.

Trainers at some tracks change the shoes if the track turns sloppy, or use one kind of shoe for turf and another for dirt. Changing shoes too frequently is not good for the wall of the hoof. **At some racetracks, you must get permission from the stewards to change the style of the shoe.** This is because the shoe style can impair or improve the horse's performance. One trainer I knew used heavy, thick steel shoes on his horse for all training and working. When race time came, he changed the shoes to light weight aluminum and the horse felt much more agile. His performance improved with the change. At today's major tracks, the trainer probably couldn't get away with such tactics.

Horses with hoof problems may need more frequent sessions and special treatments. There are many new products and innovative styles of shoes. It is important that your trainer be experienced enough to separate a gimmick or fad style of shoeing from a therapeutic, innovative device. Usually there will be university studies on innovations and rational testing to show the usefulness. Ask the trainer what the shoe is doing and see if it makes sense to you. If it sounds like witchcraft . . . draw your own conclusions.

My horses rarely have foot problems. I believe a great many problems are started by the enforced inactivity of an animal. Walking, grazing, and moving are integral parts of being a horse. Being overfed and forced to stand in a tiny stall all day and then asked to run guts out is sure to set up the horse for problems. The dark moist environment of a stall allows thrush and fungus to thrive. The Section on Bathing explains about dipping the feet in diluted bleach water or scrubbing the frog with a mixture of soap and bleach. This practice is a tremendous help in controlling fungal problems as are stalls with an outside paddock where the horse may choose to drop manure. Clean stalls are a major contribution to healthy feet.

The combination of poor shoeing, lack of legitimate exercise, standing all day and overeating puts great pressure on the feet. Combine this with infrequent shoeing, coercing a long toe and no heel, and you will probably make a complete mess of the horse's feet and possibly cause laminitis.

Right

WRong

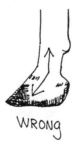
WRONg

Toe grabs on a hard surface may change the break over action

If you have specific problems, speak with the experts and read, read, read.

Many horses that have lived at the track for years before coming to my farm have very deformed feet. A horse that had been on the track for three straight years was sent to me suffering from persistent abscesses in his feet. They apparently tried to cure the abscesses with shoeing. This was a huge, beautiful, seventeen hand horse. He arrived with bar shoes. His feet were falling out of them. The feet wanted to grow larger than the shoes permitted. He was the equivalent of a Chinese woman with bound feet.

It was obvious that his feet were bothering him. The heels were so contorted and contracted they couldn't breath. When a horse moves, it is necessary for the hoof to flex. There was no way the hooves on this horse could flex with bar shoes. They were nailed in position. His heels were malformed and "contracted." His frog and hoof shape were completely distorted. When I told the owner he had been improperly shod, he commented that he had paid over $2,000 for shoeing in the last year or two.

The most important thing I did for this horse was pull off his shoes and have him constantly turned out and moving in deep sand. The sand was kind to his feet, and the movement allowed blood supply to reach the feet. After about eight months, the heels had started to relax and we could clean them without too much trouble. The abscesses had formed in the folds of the heels, surely due to the filth trapped there. Aggressive hosing helped stimulate blood flow and clean the area.

The same adage used for physicians applies to trainers. "Above all, do no harm!". There are many good books about shoeing. Make it a point to read some.

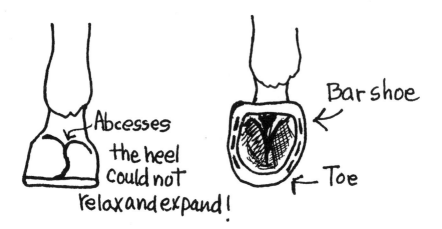

The basic principal of hoof repair is simple. Do whatever it takes to allow the foot to land flat and fly true. If one part of the hoof strikes the ground before the rest, trim away the "long" area or build up the short side with a degree pad.

Natural feet for natural gait.

The Effect of Hoof Angles on Joints

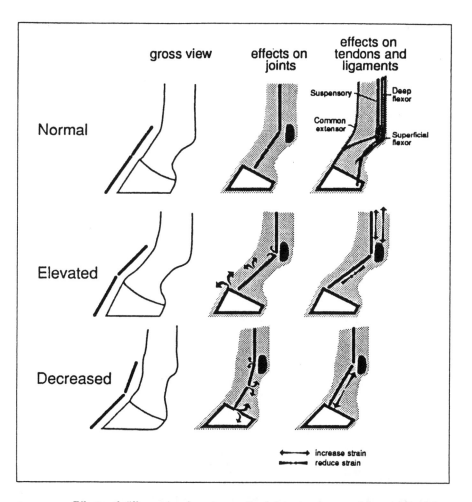

Effects of different hoof angles on the joints, tendons and ligaments of the lower forelimb. Increasing hoof angle flexes the two lower joints of the phalanges and slightly extends the third joint, while decreasing the hoof angle has the opposite effect on these joints. Lowering the heel increases tension on the deep digital flexor tendon, while elevating the heel decreases tension on this tendon and increases tension on the superficial digital flexor tendon and suspensory ligament.

Drawings appear in *Legs, Bandages, and Shoeing.* from *Hoof Balance and Lameness: Improper Toe Length, Hoof Angle, and Mediolateral Balance,* by Olin Balch, DVCM, PhD, Karl White, DVM, Doug Butler, PhD, CJF, FWCF and Sarah Metcalf, DVM, from the *Compendium of Continuing Education, Practical Veterinarian 17 610: 1276-1283, 1995.* Reproduced with permission.

The following debunking of some "Footlore" was published in *Equus Magazine*, 1995, Issue 219, (Reprinted with permission of Fleet Street Publishing Corporation) in *A Hoof-care Primer*, by Emily Kirby and Celia Strain. The article is well worth reading and keeping in your files.

Footlore and Truth

"Footlore - If horses' feet aren't cleaned out at least once daily, they will become diseased.
Truth - For horses confined to quarters with mucky footing, frequent cleaning may well be necessary, but horses living on clean earth probably enjoy some protection from the mudpack that remains undisturbed in their feet.

Footlore - Hoof length and angle can be manipulated to improve a horse's speed or performance.
Truth - Quite the contrary is true. Any shoeing manipulation that unbalances the foot or alters its natural flight pattern serves only to introduce awkwardness and undue stress into a performance. The shoeing changes that *do* improve speed and way of going are those that return balance and efficiency to the stride.

Footlore - White feet are weaker than dark feet.
Truth - The pigment granules injected into the horse as it grows from the coronet do make a dark hoof wall slightly more brittle and resistant to abrasion, but unpigmented horn is not inherently weaker. If this were the case, a striped hoof would alternate between strong and weak areas depending upon the color."

This shows how the hoof should → fall when well balanced !

The essential goals of hoof management . . . are maximum efficiency of movement and minimum risk of unsoundness.

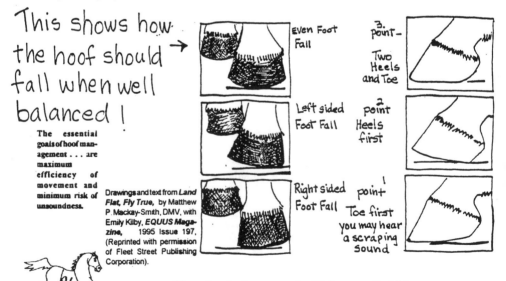

Drawings and text from *Land Flat, Fly True*, by Matthew P. Mackay-Smith, DMV, with Emily Kilby, *EQUUS Magazine*, 1995 Issue 197, (Reprinted with permission of Fleet Street Publishing Corporation).

Even Foot Fall

Left sided Foot Fall

Right sided Foot Fall

3. point - Two Heels and Toe

2 point Heels first

point Toe first you may hear a scraping sound

Shoe for balance and efficiency of stride.

THE DUCK FOOT

In Florida we sometimes use the term "duck foot" for the way many horses' feet start to look after years of shoeing with the mistaken belief that a longer toe will allow the horse to have a longer stride. The theory is that the long toe forces a horse to throw his foot out further, enhancing the length of his stride. (Obviously. If he doesn't fling the toe forward, he'll fall over it.) Making the toe longer puts more pressure on the tendons. Look at the mechanics. Isn't this is a perfect set up for bowing tendons?

With all the stress we put on the horse, let's not do more damage by fooling with the natural angle of the hoof. Long toes, high speed, and hard surfaces are a perfect combination for breakdown. Stand back and look at your horse while he is standing on a level surface. Have him trimmed to follow the healthy logical angle that keeps the hoof and pastern on the same line, as shown below. Thoroughbreds tend to have very little heel, so usually we are working on toes and maintaining whatever heel we have.

Equus Magazine, 1991, Issue 170, contained a very clear article on hoof angles entitled ***Balanced Hooves***, by Barbara Robbins. You can obtain this article by calling Fleet Street Publishing at 1 (301) 977-3900). The logic of good shoeing is discussed.

When in doubt... use your horse sense.

What is a Quarter Crack?

In simple words, a quarter crack is a split in the hoof wall. It is found in the back quarter of the hoof, hence their name. These are often called "sand cracks. However, sand cracks include toe cracks, bar cracks and heel cracks. The front feet are affected more often, because they bear more weight.

The depth of cracks varies. They can be so deep into the sensitive laminae that blood appears. This opens the door to serious infection. Puss, heat and/or lameness may be present in severe cases. However, these are not likely in superficial cracks unless they are left treated.

Usually cracks will begin at the bottom of the hoof wall, on a bearing surface. It is vital to stop it before it reaches the coronet band, although cracks can start there and progress downward. Remember that hooves grow slowly, about nine months to totally replace themselves. So don't expect an instant cure.

Sand Cracks are found in the Toe, the bar and the heel

Trauma may cause a quarter crack at the cornet band

Quarter Cracks are at the back quarter of the hoof (They are a "sand crack!")

front

flares may cause Quarter Cracks

Usually cracks start at the bottom and run upwards to the coronet band.

A wound induced crack may begin at the top and continue down.

Never leave a quarter crack untreated.

A Word With the Experts On -
INTERVIEW WITH FARRIER
Jim Sheridan

What drives a farrier?

Usually, its handed down from father to son, in my case through several genera-tions. Others do it for love of horses and the outdoors, working independently, and of course the money.

What changes have you seen in your 40 years experience?

There seems to be little change in equipment, tools (I still use some of my grandfather's), or basic techniques. What has changed are the types of shoes made, and especially the education and research into hoof problems. It has become a science. We appreciate all this new information.

What do you think of the newer techniques?

Many of them have greatly enhanced our ability to help a sore horse. Time has disproved others. I wouldn't jump into something simply because it is the "latest" thing.

What do you recommend for founder (laminitis)?

Years ago for founder we lowered the heels and made an acrylic packing to put pressure on the sole. Later they began resecturing the front of the hoof from the toe up to relieve pressure on the foot. They put a heart bar on to put pressure on the frog so that the coffin bone was supported back to its original position. No matter which way you go, pressure on the sole for support is vital.

What do you suggest to avoid and treat cracks and abscesses?

To avoid them you must be aware that both very wet and/or very dry conditions can cause cracks. Also if the feet get too long due to improper or infrequent trimming, cracks can appear. Treatment is usually to cut out the crack and treat it with a weak iodine solution. They can also be sealed with a product like "Tough Stuff" or repaired with an acrylic filler. Unless they are very severe, there is no need to modify the training program for cracks. Sometimes we have to suture them with pins and wire to let the hoof regrow. Those are the most sever cases of quarter crack.

Abscesses form when moisture, sand and bacteria penetrate a crack or there is a severe sole bruise or injury. If an abscess develops, there will be heat in the hoof due to the infection smouldering within the hoof. The abscess must be cut out to relieve pressure and pain. At times your farrier may want to have to the foot x-rayed to locate the abscess. This is better than digging around until you hit it.

After the abscess has been cut out, the foot must be kept clean and dry. People often pack the foot with icthammol and wrap it, using a boot or duct tape to keep it in place. However, even so it is very difficult to keep sand and moisture out of the wound. Soaking is not recommended. It allows more moisture into the wound and further fermentation within the foot. I think a sealing product like "Tough Stuff" or one of the new acrylic fillers do a better job of keeping the wound clean and dry.

Schedule routine foot care for your horse

For anything less than very severe abscesses you would not have to stall your horse. You can continue your training program after proper treatment and there is no sign of lameness.

What do you think of angles for trimming?

For race or pleasure horses I use my eye to determine an angle as natural as possible from the pastern to the ground. If you don't have much experience checking the angle may be a good idea. Gaited horse people often want specific angles to attain certain breakovers and a better gait. However, in race horses we want a natural break-over. I avoid cutting heel unless it is absolutely necessary as in the case of a very high heel and short toe. Some horses with laminitis tend to grow a lot of heel which you have to keep down.

What do you think of long toes?

They create a lot of problems because they put unnecessary pressure on the tendons and ligaments and prevent the foot from breaking-over correctly. They also have a tendency to make the horse trip.

Why do you change shoes for the turf?

Most tracks don't allow you to run with toe grabs, blocks, turn downs, and in some tracks not even rim shoes because they dig up the grass. Usually people train on the dirt track with toe grabs and change shoes for a turf race. Each track has its own rules as to which shoes are allowed on their turf.

What do you think of toe grabs?

High toe grabs in young horses can cause a lot of problems. Any toe grab can cause bucked shins. Years ago I found that on young horses bucked shins could often be prevented by switching to a Queens Plate, a shoe with a built-in toe grab level with the shoe. On tracks where the horse needs more traction, block heels or toe grabs are used in the rear. Recent studies shows toe grab related breakdown. Even before that if a trainer wanted toe grabs, I preferred the low toe, especially on a hard track.

High Toe Grabs may cause sore shins!

Learn to recognize a healthy foot.

What do you think of cutting the bars of the hoof?

I never cut the bars out. They are a support mechanism and keep the heels from contracting. If they get too high, they should be trimmed so they don't hit the ground first. They should be level with the wall at the heel allowing the heel of the shoe to bear the weight of the bar at that point. The frog should be trimmed very little so that it is level with the ground surface of the wall at the heels. They are an extension of the hoof wall and provide more weight baring surface.

What can owners or trainers do to make the farrier's life easier?

They can train their horses to behave and pickup their feet without a struggle. These are thousand pound animals, not pets. Don't baby them. Teach them respect and manners. They are quick as cats. In spite of their experience and knowledge of horses, many a farrier has been severely hurt and even disabled by an ill behaved horse.

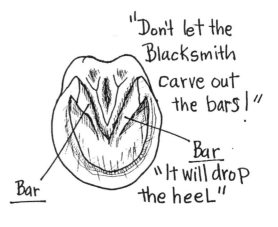

Gary Ladd agrees with Jim and had me draw this!

"Don't let the Blacksmith carve out the bars!"

Bar

"It will drop the heel"

Bar

According to Pat Parelli, farriers should charge extra for horses that take extra time to shoe. Remember a farrier's time is money. Be there when he arrives and have your animals ready. It is appreciated when the horses are fairly clean, but please, please, please not wet.

It is also important for owners to understand how important it is to have a routine schedule for trimming and shoeing. If a foot is left uncared for, it is harder on the farrier and the horse to correct problems that have developed.

The owner should also learn what comprises a good job or a mediocre job. Only that way can he demand the best quality work for the horse. Often owners or trainers want a horse shoed in a specific way. If that is not the way the farrier usually does it, the farrier should remember who is paying the bill and accommodate that person. I often hear people saying their farrier won't do this or that. I only dissent if I believe that what is being asked will compromise the horse.

To help diagnose a lameness problem, an owner should learn when the feet look healthy and when they are hurting. He can look for cracks and sole bruises and observe if the horse is standing on the toe or heel, holding his foot up or spending excess time lying down. Usually if there hoof problem, there is a temperature difference. It may be necessary to hold both feet simultaneously to determine a temperature difference. If an owner suspects a foot problem, he may want to call the farrier first. Farriers have experience and can

No foot - no horse.

test the foot for tenderness. If he feels the problem is not in the foot, the farrier will have you call the vet. Remember to mention any lameness to your farrier. He may be able to diagnose the source.

Can the farrier's input help in the training and racing process? Sometimes for a horse that is hitting or not travelling right trainers ask us for suggestions regarding change of, or correction of shoes. Trainers don't usually ask for our input, although it could be helpful to them.

First of all he must learn his trade from a reputable experienced farrier. I don't recommend the six-week schools as they tend to turn out people with little training. You just can't learn everything that fast. We used to spend three to five years as apprentices on the track. It takes hard work, dedication and experience to do the job right. Also farriers must be sober, friendly, professional and on time. The biggest gripe owners have is a tardy farrier or one who doesn't call to cancel an appointment. Of course, this goes two ways.

How do you qualify to be a farrier?

On the track usually you serve a three to five year apprenticeship with a journeyman. You can also go to a horseshoing school. After your apprenticeship, you take a union exam and/or a state exam. To work at the track you must be licensed. You have to pass the state exam to obtain a license. Off the track there are other organizations that give exams.

What are your best and worst memories?

The best thing is to work on a horse that is compromised and crippled and make him sound. It will take time and patience, but it is very rewarding.

Worst was finding the bottom of a glass beer bottle overgrown in a horse's foot. It took me hours to cut and pull out all the pieces. Eventually I had to use needle nosed pliers for the small slivers. I treated foot continuously for several months until it was sound only to have the horse drown in a swimming pool after few weeks later.

What would be on your wish list of things to change?

I wish we knew more about the delicate internal mechanisms of the hoof, what causes the problems and how we could correct them.

Laughing he said, "I wish somebody would take the aggressive tendencies out of horses and give them smaller feet."

Jim says, "Remember, everything goes to the feet."

Speaking of Farriers...

We want to share a little episode that took place on the farm last week. Janet was headed to Miami to run four horses. Two new horses needed shoes and since her regular farrier was away, she called a fellow who had been recommended, although she had not previously used him. He had promised to come on Wednesday, but called to cancel to Thursday. Janet had already scheduled an important appointment for Thursday and was distressed when the new farrier appeared with four or five friends as she was ready to leave. She stayed long enough to watch him put shoes on one horse and then dashed off to the appointment having left complete instructions and a backup person with the farrier.

Much to her horror she found on her return that the farrier had "tranked" (tranquilized) the second horse because it kicked. Now consider the following:

1. The horse was "tranked" without her permission or even knowledge,
2. The horse had been fidgety but never to the point of needing such treatment,
3. The farrier knew the horse was going to Miami to run the next day and claimed that the stuff he used was untraceable.

Angry does not begin to describe Janet when she discovered the goings on. Obviously after the fellows left. She had to scratch the horse, and call the owner to explain the situation. Was this a lesson in humility. Possibly, however certainly it was a lesson about the everyday practices of some horsemen.

Understand that the friends who came with the farrier were all horsemen. You would think that at least one of them could handle a fractious horse. Certainly one of them should have been capable of properly using a shank or twitch before opting for a tranquilizer.

However, whatever we think. There are a couple of lessons here:

1. First never leave a horse with people you do not know, even if you have discussed what you want done and leave a backup person, you are open to mistakes.
2. Teach your horse ground manners. It will save you time and trouble. (This horse was fractious, but not dangerous.)

A set of tools and needles do not a farrier make.

A Word With the Experts On -
RACEHORSES AT RISK
by Melissa F. Sykes

It's a typical scene. A Thoroughbred is having his feet trimmed and shoes put on. There's a box full of racing plates in the back of the farrier's truck – all shapes and sizes. There are rim shoes, flat shoes, heart bar shoes. There are toe grabs, stickers and turn downs. No matter what the racing surface or track condition, there's a special shoe designed just for the occasion.

But, according to recent studies conducted by researchers at the University of California (UC), some of these special shoes are causing more harm than good to the animals wearing them.

Over a two year period, the research team, lead by Albert Kane, DVM. of the Veterinary Orthopedic Research Laboratory at UC, performed postmortems on over 200 racehorses that died at a facility under the jurisdiction of the California Horse Racing Board (CHRB). The study's goal was to identify causes of catastrophic injury associated with shoeing so that recommendations could be made for the prevention of such injuries.

A direct correlation between the use of toe grabs and catastrophic injury was found. A traction device, toe grabs are attached to the bottom of the horse shoe and come in three heights: low (4 mm), regular (6 mm) and high (8 mm). (It should be noted that the use of toe grabs is illegal on many racetracks.)

"If we look at the most common type of catastrophic injury, suspensory apparatus failure, the odds are six times greater for an animal wearing low toe grabs" versus the one shod without toe grabs, said Kane. "And the higher the toe grab, the greater the risk." For instance, the risk increases to 16 times greater with regular toe grabs over no toe grab.

"The use of toe grabs may provide too much traction. So much, in fact, that it actually stops the hoof more suddenly than it wants," increasing the added force to the lower limb. "Under more natural conditions, the horse's hoof slides a little while landing and taking off," explained Kane. "This is a normal part of the gate cycle and may help to dissipate some of the shock to the lower limb. Toe grabs may decrease the ability of the hoof to slide as it lands and takes off resulting in increased forces acting on the lower leg."

The use of toe grabs may also affect the geometry of the hoof as it makes contact with the ground and the angles of the joints as they support the load of the horse. By raising the toe, it may create a decreased functional hoof angle similar to the long toe - low heel conformation.

"On the bright side," said Kane, "rim shoes were associated with a decrease in injury." The odds of suspensory apparatus failure with rims was 2/3 lower than without rims.

And while no studies have been done on horses racing without shoes, it is an option at Florida tracks. "It's very rare to have a horse running barefoot," said John Kelly, a

Which shoe will win the race?

paddock blacksmith at Calder Racecourse. A horse racing without shoes "Sometimes has a bruise and they want to run him any way."

A solution to the traction question, which is staring us right in the face, is that "we don't appreciate how much traction a flat shoe gives us. It increases the amount of cup in the foot and the crease (that indentation where the nails go) will pick up sand. And sand on sand gives traction," said Kane.

Kane and UC have just received a grant from Grayson-Jockey Club to follow up their postmortem studies on live racehorses. The team will be documenting shoeing related risks of nonfatal musculoskeletal injury and lameness in Thoroughbreds and how hoof conformation contributes to the risk of injury.

According to research member, Dr. Susan Stover, "We'll follow our test horses and look at how they are affected by little things (i.e. nonfatal) such as tendon swellings, joint swellings, bucked shins and if these injuries are related to shoeing and hoof conformation."

The team is hoping to document what many horsemen have come to realize, that the way a horse's hoof is shaped has a direct bearing on his soundness and performance.

A common belief thirty years ago was that a horse whose foot was shaped such that the toe was long and the heel was low would increase the length of his stride by delaying break over. (Break over is the point during a horse's stride when the heel is raised and the toe is just about to leave the ground.)

"It has been demonstrated that this doesn't have any effect on stride length," said Dr. Pat Colahan, Associate Professor at the University of Florida. "The correct view is that it increases the strain on legs. It is not an appropriate way of trimming."

Whether appropriate or not, horses in Florida tend to have this look. Ocala horsewoman Susie Hart explained what owners in the South must contend with. "Because of the wet ground, especially in Florida, it's easy to get that pinched heel and long toe" it's how the horse's feet grow under these conditions.

Although it is only a theory, Kane also believes environment is a big factor in hoof problems. "If you look at the wild horses in places like Nevada - their feet are hard as rocks. But, take that mustang with the very upright, healthy foot, take him back to some place like Virginia and put him out in those wet fields. He'll develop the long toe - low heel."

The key, Kane, Colahan and Hart agree, is to define the horse's individual hoof angle and to maintain that angle.

According to Colahan "If you draw a line straight through the pastern and foot, it should equal the slope of the shoulder." These angles will vary from horse to horse, but, for a typical Thoroughbred the angle should fall between 50 and 55 degrees. "You have very little influence over the angle of the pastern - it's conformation." Trying to alter that angle in an adult animal usually results in a deformed foot.

For conformational correctness and soundness Colohan recommends you start looking at very young foals - over two weeks and less than two months. "Any conformational defect below the cannon bone (i.e. toeing in, toeing out) has to be corrected before that foal is 60 days old. Those growth plates are closed by four months of age."

It all comes down to your farrier. "If you have a good farrier, your horse's feet will look good."

A competent farrier is essential for good feet.

Hauling and Shipping

HAULING AND SHIPPING - Introduction

When you are going to do your own hauling , you must be aware of the many pitfalls along the road. I have trucked over 500,000 miles and have learned a few things along the way.

First and foremost ... maintain your equipment and check your lugs before leaving.

Make sure your truck or hauling vehicle is large enough and strong enough for the load. Be sure your hitch is properly attached to the frame of the vehicle. **Make sure your hitch dealer is reputable and installs the recommended size hitch for the weight involved.** There are charts indicating the proper ratio of hauling vehicle wheel base to trailer length. **Never exceed the recommended limits.** In the old days, vehicles had real bumpers. Some hitches were attached to the bumper. Very bad, because the bumper was only attached to the car by bolts. For heavy duty hauling, a variety of hitches attached to the frame of the vehicle by bolts or welding are available.

When hauling a four-horse, bumper-hitch trailer with one or two horses, never put both horses in the rear of the trailer. **Always put more weight on the tongue to avoid fishtailing.** If you have ever experienced the horror of fishtailing, you know the sheer terror of having no control whatsoever over your vehicle. It is a hard way to learn about weight distribution. If you are hauling a two-horse trailer with one horse in it, put the horse on the left. No, not so you can look at him in your mirror, though that's an added benefit, but because on two lane roads it keeps the trailer more stable when there is no shoulder on the right. The horse's weight could cause the trailer to pull and slide off the right side. **Think stability!**

Always have rubber mats on the floor of the trailer. A little bedding on top not only gives the horses stability, it makes manure removal easier. You don't want your horse struggling to keep his balance because of poor footing. Horses seem to prefer having something to prop themselves against while traveling.

My horses seem to travel better when they have bars or walls to brace against. If you watch a lone horse rolling by you in a stock trailer, you'll notice that even though he has the whole trailer, he'll be braced against one side and corner to balance himself. If you are hauling one horse, put up the center bar to give him some support. Think about it. If you were standing in the middle of a trailer rolling down the highway, and had no use of your arms, how would you maintain your balance? Maybe by wedging yourself against something? **Any dividers between horses should have rug or rubber padding all the way down to the floor.** My very expensive trailer did not have this. Once a horse stepped on the coronet band of his neighbor. You cannot afford this kind of injury.. It is primarily a problem in trailers where horses travel side by side. In a slant load trailer the horses are staggered and do not seem to step on each other. Examine your trailer and install the necessary safeguards.

Bungee trailer ties are available in any tack shop. Snap one end to the side ring of the halter and one to the trailer. They allow the horse movement but stretch and pull the horse's head back to where it should be. Be sure they have a quick-release snap on one end.

Keeping hay in front of the horse can allow dust and hay particles to circulate in the breeze and enter the horse's airways. Try feeding hay at rest stops. Lois has found that many horses are reluctant to drink and that feeding them a few carrots provides some moisture and also helps sustain gut motility.

Keep your trailer clean and in good repair

Stress can predispose horses to disease, particularly respiratory disease when associated with shipping. The quality of air that the animal breaths during transport can affect the lungs. Gases, such as ammonia, carbon monoxide, and hydrocarbons, can impair the horse's ability to clear the lungs, hence setting the stage for illness.

If you are traveling in hot country, remember how much heat a horse's body creates. Always keep the windows and vents open but your horse's head **inside** the trailer. Have you ever seen very closed-in trailers with no air circulation, rolling down the road in the summer? Did you wonder if the owners opened the trailer to find a horse with heat stroke? In hot weather keep the trailer open for breezes. If your windows are in the front of the trailer, make sure your horse is tied loosely enough to move his head out of the wind, if he wants. Never tie him so tightly that he can't drop his head, cough, sneeze and generally make himself comfortable. He can get a crick in his neck or back if he must carry his head in an awkward position.

The question of whether horses are better off facing front or back is often discussed. Sharon Cregier, PhD, in her book, *Alleviating Surface Transit Stress on Horses,* University Micro Films, Ann Arbor, MI, strongly recommends having horses face backward in transit. Although rear facing trailers are difficult to find, some believe that horses travel better in them. You may want to investigate this option when buying new equipment.

My horses seem to like the equipment I have. Horses are pretty adaptable. They even stand sideways in some vans. The fashion in new vans and trailers seems to be at an angle, a slant load, which is okay, too. Don't worry unless you have a problem with a particular horse.

Regarding types of trailer, bumper hitch versus gooseneck, there is little doubt that goosenecks are more stable. A truck with dually tires is also more stable. You can even feel the difference as a passenger. This is especially apparent on curves and hills.

Recently I was shocked when I decided to use my two- horse bumper pull trailer for a trip to Miami. My rational was that since it was so much lighter than the gooseneck, it would be more fuel efficient. To my horror, in these days of excessive fuel prices, I used more fuel with the two-horse than I used with the five-horse gooseneck.. The only explanation I can imagine is windflow. The small trailer must have been less aerodynamic than the gooseneck.

Accustom yourself to cleaning manure and bedding if you overnight. And be sure the to hose your trailer after trips. Urine corrodes aluminium to the point of destruction. "White rust", a white powdery buildup on aluminum indicates corrosion. Without proper cleaning, you may have to replace the floor in as little as four years. When you remove mats for thorough cleaning, be sure they are dry before putting them back.

As long as the horse has good air circulation, and is not too hot or too cold, he should be all right.

A FEW SUGGESTIONS FROM AN EXPERIENCED HAULER

When my teenaged sons were entrusted with the horses and equipment, they were told, **"Drive as if you have no brakes!"** Of course, this was a typical worried mother, forced to depend on the reliability of a seventeen year old. (My God, how could I?) But, actually, that is very good advice. **You must never think, even if you have super electric brakes, that you can haul a trailer with a horse in it driving the way you drive a car.** Zooming up to lights and having to stop quickly just won't do with a horse in the back. He'll be sitting beside you before you know it. Remember, his body mass is high. If you throw it around, it can be very unstablizing to the towing vehicle, and very hard on the horse.

If you drive as if you have no brakes, you'll shift cautiously up to speed, and try to coast down when coming to stop lights, downshifting if you have a manual transmission. This is better on your equipment and the horse. No sudden jerks to start and no hard braking to stop.

When you get into the vehicle to haul, take a moment to think. **Under no circumstances feel pressured or rushed.** If you are running late, accept that you will arrive late, and let it go. There is nothing more horrible than a trailer wreck with live animals.

Initially, I found hauling very perturbing. Driving my horses and children down the turnpike in torrential rainstorms, or trying to stay on a tiny two-lane road with giant semitrailers breathing down my neck and having no place to pull over, was terrifying. I would imagine a horrible twisted wreck featuring my trailer in a mangled mess. It was necessary to make a conscious effort to block that image out of my mind and imagine myself arriving safely at the racetrack. When you get in your vehicle and are ready to start your trip, stop; close your eyes and image yourself arriving safely at your destination. Take a deep breath, remind yourself not to hurry and have a good trip! Over the years, I have had to force myself to concentrate on this kind of positive imagery. Don't disregard the dangers. Control them as best you can by driving safely and soberly with proper equipment.

It is impossible to avoid the summer thunderstorms in Florida. Go slowly and cautiously when you're caught in inclement weather. You can listen to good tapes or books on tape for amusement. In the North, plan your racing and track training to coincide with the good weather. You probably don't want to be hauling on icy roads or in snow storms. Plan to train at home or lay up in the bad weather and run when the snow and ice is gone. **Work with the environment, not against it.** On long trips it is handy to have a copy of the *Overnight Stabling Directory* in case you need to find a place to layover. Check the Bibliography for ordering information.

Cell phones seem to be replacing CB radios. Either is a big help when you are traveling in unfamiliar areas. Truckers give good advice on routes, traffic and conditions via the CB. Either is essential if you are broken down on the side of the road. Yes, this does happen to all of us, even with the best of care.

In my twenty years of shipping into races, a race was never missed due to hauling problems. Being a female, and training from the farm, I was acutely aware of how bad it would be to miss a race because of an equipment breakdown. There have been close calls, such as

Drive as if you have no brakes!

the time due to burnt out bearings, a wheel fell off the four-horse trailer in the middle of the cane fields at ten o'clock at night. Luckily, a trailer repairman made the mistake of answering his phone at eleven PM. He gave in to my pleas and worked on the axle, with the three horses in the van. We were back on the road by two AM. The horses made the races in plenty of time. (We had to make the races. One of the horses was owned by a syndicate of five lawyers. All they needed was some kind of silly excuse such as a wheel falling off. . . Ha!)

Both of my trucks are capable of hauling either trailer at all times. You don't have to have backup equipment if you are only training for yourself. **If you are a professional, you must have backup… the worst possible things happen at the worst possible times.**

One of my trucks broke down three hours into the Miami trip. A call home and the other was on its way. Fortunately, I have great kids and wonderful neighbors willing to help me in a pinch. Another time, an engine, 5,000 miles beyond the 50,000 mile warranty, blew because of a faulty water pump. (On some diesels, this is a common occurrence every 50,000 miles.) Rather than arranging a tow home, I had the truck and horses towed to the racetrack 100 miles away. The time to worry about the truck was after the race . . . the horses came first.

Never, never, never unload a horse on the side of the road! If the horse is having a fit in the trailer, that's where he will have to have it. It would be worse to unload him and risk having him get away from you. He might run into the traffic and cause havoc. No matter what, keep the horse in the trailer until you are in a farm where you can unload safely.

Years ago, I kept Rompun, a tranquilizer, in my glove compartment for emergencies. There are very stringent rules about needles on the backside of the racetrack and I was afraid of entering the racetrack with anything like that. I have discussed this problem at length with the track vets, but found no solution. I just haul and pray. If you have problems with a hysterical horse, go to the nearest policeman, police station or fire station. They will help you find a vet in emergency circumstances.

Never feed a horse heavy grain before a trip. Give him hay along the way. If it is a long trip, give him a handful of grain every now and then so he doesn't think he is being starved to death. Always offer water when you stop. Generally, on a three-to-six hour trip, you'll only need to stop for gas and water once. Feed your horse when he is settled at the track, the night before the race.

I go to Miami the night before the race, because the trip is five- to-six hours. The trip to Tampa is an hour and a half, so we go the day of the race. Birmingham is 12 hours away. On that trip, we stop for water, but never unload.

When shipping in to the track, it is handy to carry two water buckets and one feed bucket for each horse unless you are staying at or near the track. You only need one bucket of each if you are staying close enough to the track to check and water them frequently. In hot weather, they drink a lot of water and need two buckets of water in front of them. Take feed portions tied in plastic bags and already mixed with vitamins, etc., and a couple of bales of hay.

Have a complete set of equipment is on hand so that you are prepared at the track. A complete set of racing equipment (bridles, blinkers, etc.) is kept hanging on hooks in the back seat of my truck. An exercise saddle with extra girths and saddlecloths also lives permanently in my truck. Everything is ready to use. There is a complete grooming kit with brushes, tape, alcohol, and Vicks for the nose, tongue ties, and various little items. A separate set of

Will yourself to arrive alive.!

equipment is kept at the farm. **If you don't own enough equipment for two full sets, make an equipment list. Check it twice before you leave to be sure you are prepared at the receiving barn.**

Have all the paperwork necessary to get through the stable gates: Coggins, health certificate, and registration papers. Try to be respectful and courteous to track personnel. This is not always an easy task, especially if you have been braving storms, bad traffic or crazy horses. When you get to the receiving barn, unload your horse as efficiently as possible. My routine is down to a science. It takes me fifteen minutes to unload, feed, tuck in four horses for the night, and hose out the trailer. Always clean the trailer. Ants are attracted to manure. They taught me the hard way to hose out the trailer immediately upon arrival.

Once at Calder, after a long day at the races, my four horses were loaded one by one in the big trailer. I was so eager to get on the road back home, that the swarm of red ants devouring manure went unnoticed. In the darkness the night before, I had failed to completely remove the manure. While pulling out of Calder, I heard a great deal of kicking and stomping in the trailer. I knew better than to ignore it, and pulled over. The horses were in a frenzy because ants were crawling up their legs and stinging them. I immediately returned to the receiving barn, unloaded all four horses, scrubbed and hosed them and the trailer. An hour later we departed again and arrived home very late that night.

When you embark on your travels, be calm, cool, and collected. Keep a few rousing tapes in your truck. *This Land Is Your Land, This Land Is My Land* is a great song to sing as you cruise across beautiful expanses of open countryside on your way to the track. Visitors accompanying me in the truck grumble about my off key singing and archaic music, but that's okay. It keeps me going. *Michael, Row Your Boat Ashore* always gets my blood pumping. It can keep me awake for an extra ten miles at the end of a long haul. Friends tell stories about trips from hell when referring to escapades where they were trapped for six hours in my truck enduring a gamut of music, from *If I Had A Hammer* to Tschaikowsky's *1812 Overture*. (Played loudly, the cannons sound like they are being shot from the back seat . . . guaranteed to wake you up if you are drowsy). These friends also complain about getting grease or a little dirt on their clothes when they help me load the horses. What are good friends for but to share exciting times; so what if they get a little sweaty or dirty along the way?

**Think of the fun you and your friends will
have when you all begin your
GREAT ADVENTURE!**

EQUIPMENT FOR HORSES BEING HAULED

Various types of wrapping and bandaging exist for horses during travel. Personally, I prefer the neophrene boots that cover the leg from below the knee to over the hoof. They attach with velcro, fit nicely, and protect the coronet band as well as the lower leg. Using fleece and bandages is very time consuming if you ship frequently. You can put the shipping boots on in a few minutes and be ready to go. I use boots on the front legs only. Horses tend to fuss and kick, trying to get them off their hind legs. (That's my excuse . . . if you prefer, put them on all four legs.) The boots cost around $65 dollars a set, and are worth the investment. They can be washed and wear well.

Beware, many horses have what are called "bandage bows". Bandages can slip or be put on too tightly and cause damage to the tendon. On a long trip, **someone must continuously check the wraps or the horse is better off without them**. One of the worst stories is about a trainer who wrapped his horses' tails so they wouldn't be rubbed raw on the trip. The van hauling the horses from Florida to the North broke down for several days. The horses were given food and water and were cared for, but no one thought about the tail wraps. When the horses arrived and the wraps were taken off their tails, it was too late. The blood supply had been inhibited. The horses lost their tails and the trainer lost his job. He surely never expected such a delay. Be very suspicious of wrapping for any period of time, unless there is a medical reason. Don't create problems. If the trip is long, some trainers pull the shoes and leave the horses barefoot. Be sure your horse has competent supervision when he travels. Shipping boots, bell boots and leg wraps all contribute to the safety and comfort of the animal if they are competently utilized.

Happy Trails!

PREPARE TO HAUL HORSES

Have the <u>correct equipment</u> for the job!

Have your <u>vehicles well maintained</u>!

Have the trailer <u>well padded and safe</u>!

Have <u>good air circulation</u> for the horses!

<u>Drive as if you have no brakes!</u>

NEVER DRIVE UNDER STRESS OR IN A RUSH!

Be prepared. Have <u>plenty of gas</u>!

Have your horses' <u>travelling papers in hand</u>!

Read the map!

Commercial Hauling

You may at some point need to ship your horses with a commercial shipper. There are many well known shippers in the business as well as some smaller qualified outfits that do this on a regular basis and have vast experience. It is sometimes possible to find one or two open slots in a large shipment of horses destined to the area you need. Speak with several shippers to see if such an arrangement is possible. It can cost effective for you.

When speaking to the shipper there are some questions you need to ask and you need straight answers to them. Such questions would be:

1. Their experience as well as the experience of the driver and grooms doing the specific trip.
2. A written estimate of charges, both expected and unexpected.
3. The timing of scheduled stops and where these occur.
4. Would the horses be unloaded and if so for how long?
5. How would emergencies either illness of an animal or accident (God forbid) be handled?
6. Is the company insured and do they insure the safe arrival of the animal itself?
7. Are they DOT registered?
8. Would the horses be transferred to another carrier for some reason and if so which carrier and why?
9. How many animals would be in the vehicle, how many drivers (if it is a several day trip) and how many grooms?

Be sure that you feel comfortable with all the answers.

If it is a long trip that you are not personally supervising, leg or tail wraps are not recommended. **Never use shipping or any bandages during shipping unless you are absolutely sure that are properly applied and will be taken off and properly reapplied every 12 hours.** Be sure your hauler is reliable and has reliable help.

Do your home work.

A Little Comic Relief!

This is a comic strip I did when my children were young - Mullikin is still our pony horse!

Meet Mullikin Stu-

A FEW SUGGESTIONS ON LOADING

I have just come in from struggling with a horse that was not taught to load when she was young. Perhaps this is the best time to discuss loading techniques. **You must have obedient horses that load with no problem under all conditions in order to successfully train off the farm.** The ideal way to teach a horse to load is when he is very young and you can shove him around. Teach him to eat in the trailer. Take a bucket of feed and have him follow you in or put mama horse in the trailer to eat. He will easily learn not to fear the DARK BOX.

Horses purchased at sales usually have not had much experience in loading. You may need ten strong men and a vet with a tranquilizer to get the animal into a small trailer. When you get him home, the first thing to do is teach him to load. If you have time, try leaving your trailer in the pasture. At feeding time, put the horse's food in the trailer. Begin with feed on the ramp. Move it further inside each day for a week or two until he is comfortable eating inside the trailer on his own. Then practice loading him at random times without enticement.

Unfortunately, I seem to receive horses that have been allowed to run free for two years, pulled in, run through the sale with the help of mood altering drugs, and then sent to me as the fuzzy haze from the drug wears off. By this time they are frightened of their new environment and react appropriately.

In such a situation where they must be loaded immediately, it is good to have two, or preferably three, strong men. **Begin with no prejudice about the horse.** I actually act as if I expect the animal to docilely enter the trailer with a slight tug on the shank. Have the trailer parked and attached to the truck in an enclosed field. If the animal gets loose, he will not be able to go far. The ramp should be easy to step onto and at a gentle angle. My first trailer did not have a ramp. The horse had to step up and into it. If your trailer doesn't have a ramp, don't worry. He can learn to step into it.

Horses apparently perceive the ramp as a bottomless pit. Their general reaction is, "Oh, boy, I'm not stepping on that!" They throw up their heads and pull back hard - horse body language for "No!" Have a shank with a chain on the horse for these lessons. Put the chain is over the nose, as described under "Shank" in "Equipment for Training". At this point, yank sharply on the shank and let him know you won't permit negative behavior (pulling back and refusing to do as you bid).

Use a twenty foot shank with a 24" chain when loading. If a horse pulls it out of your hands, you can still grab it fast. Be very vocal with naughty horses. Say, "No!" sharply. If

Teach loading early!

the horse continues to pull back, I'm of the school that says, "You want to pull back, then go back!" Yank, and if he continues to back up, continue to yank sharply on the chain. At this point it is probably better to put the chain over the gum, under the lip. (This seems to be an acupuncture point. Pressure on the gum may influence his behavior positively.) You don't want to do any damage, but you want this animal to respect you when you say, "No!"

A Horse that rears is a Terrible Danger!

The minute he stops pulling back, praise him and gently lead him forward. If he balks and pulls his head back again, yank (a quick sharp pull). It is imperative not to allow the horse to get in the habit of pulling back and rearing to fight you. You must be firm about unac- ceptable behavior. **A horse that rears is a terrible danger.** When he stops pulling back, your helper can tap him on the rump to encourage the horse to go forward. When he does, he is praised and there is no pressure on his head. Never yank on the horse unfairly or in unfounded anger. It must always be clear that punishment is for negative behavior, not because you are having a temper tantrum.

It may take just five minutes or a couple of hours for the horse to realize that if he goes with you there is no pain, and when he fights you he is punished. When you get back to the ramp, and he still refuses to step on, go inside the trailer and guide and control his head while the two strong helpers lock hands behind his tail and literally shove the horse inside. Once he is in, close the doors quickly. Praise him and feed him. You can take him for a short ride. Then open the door and back him out, allowing him to turn his head to see where he is going. Walk him around for a minute and ask him to go back on the trailer. If he refuses, go back to step one and shank and yank until he is willing to obey. Usually, the fight is not as long or as difficult the second time.

This system usually works. Remember, **if you are going to start the loading process, plan to spend the whole day, if necessary, until you get the horse in the trailer**. If you give up before he is in, **you'll have double the trouble next time**. You may have the same situation getting him into water to swim, generally you will have a big fight the first time, then a few mini fights, then it gets easier, until the horse discovers that the trailer or the water isn't so bad after all.

Whenever it was time to work with a difficult horse, he was told, **it's the trailer or DIE**. Hopefully, he would get the message early, before we were both exhausted. The best time for loading lessons was when my sons, the six foot three cowboy type and the six foot four wrestler, were handy. One horse, Street Beat, knew how to load when he came to me. He was not afraid of the trailer. But he had a "Maybe I will, maybe I won't!" attitude. The horse pulled his trick one day in Miami, when it was time to load up and start the long trip home. Since

Never start a lesson you can't finish.

I usually handled loading myself, I didn't expect a problem. He balked and became difficult. He acted like a horse's ass, backing into cars and doing all sorts of dangerous things. He seemed to know that I couldn't punish him there. Finally, several strong men had to help me load him. I made up my mind he wouldn't pull that on me again.

The next afternoon, I called my son out and we began **THE GREAT STRUGGLE.** It was June in Florida. The humidity was easily equal to the temperature of 101 degrees. We started the loading process and the horse balked. We did my "if you want to back up, back up" routine. He backed all the way to the fence before he would stop and come forward. My son, Nando, was driving him from behind. Every time the horse got near the ramp, he would balk. Again and again, we struggled. After an hour and a half, my son, the horse and I were standing there panting glowering at each other. The sweat was pouring off of us in buckets. Nando said, "Mom, do you think he could die in this heat?" I figured the horse was at least as sturdy as we were . . . and we weren't dead yet. I said, "Nando, I don't think so . . . but if he is going to die, he is going to die in the trailer!" Street Beat must have heard me, or decided that today we were not to give up. He acquiesced, strolled into the trailer, and never balked again.

There is a mental game going on here. Horses are animals. If they can dominate you, they will. **You must dominate them mentally and convince them that you are physically dominant also.** You may need to use equipment to prove your point. Use what you must, but always be fair to the animal. **Many times they are legitimately frightened** . . . other times they remind me of my children between fourteen and twenty one . . . **stubborn and willing to test you every way they can!**

Horses respect those who command respect.

YANK & SHANK

In today's world "Yank and Shank" have become politically unacceptable. Although, I totally agree with Imprinting and the milder forms of training, Thoroughbreds in training are unpredictable and can easily harm you. Therefore, it is imperative for your own safety that you impose good manners. When a racehorse bursts from his stall full of energy, you must give him some space, but you may need a chain over his nose or lip to be able to control him and save yourself and your horse from bodily harm. Use of the chain or punishment must be just and quick. Scars on a horses nose are just as unacceptable as an injured handler. Steady pressure on a chain will lose the battle. A quick tug or some jiggling of the chain will get his attention and is far more effective.

Jiggling a chain placed over the gum or nose without exerting pressure is especially effective if you need him to stand still for a farrier or veterinarian. It is also better than tranquilizing him for every little thing - especially on race day when you can not tranquilize him. Remember to stand on the same side as the person treating him. This gives your horse room to move away from both of you.

We must gain trust of the horse by treating him kindly and fairly and being consistent in our own behavior.

The milder methods of training are wonderful, but require much ground work. Imprinting is excellent, but don't spoil that cute little foal forgetting that he will soon weigh over 1,000 pounds and can be very dangerous, knock you over, step on you etc. Any training must include discipline.

On large farms with many handlers and grooms, it is virtually impossible to impose imprinting and hours of ground work. At the track, it is even less possible. However, remember that the better your horse behaves the kinder he will be treated by others - especially at the track where he must behave.

by Lois Schwartz

Keep halter noseband between chain and nose bone

Be Kind But firm!

Keep bottom strap between chain and jaw bone!

What ever you do, you must impose discipline.

A Word With the Experts On -
A practical View of Horse Training Philosophies

by J.P. Giacomini

Can I Tell It Like It Is?

"Many innovative trainers promote increased kindness first, then suggest a new approach to the training of horses. Their literature usually describes OTHER trainers' methods as brutal excess while equating the practice of discipline with egomania, lack of compassion or the downright absence of moral righteousness.... the occasional brutality so violently criticized is not the mark of a wicked character, but rather a consequence of frustration combined with a lack of knowledge.

As a result of this pressure, we are seeing an unfortunately growing laxity and horse owners are too often getting hurt by their "beloved" horses. Eventually the approach backfires and drastic measures are used as a last resort to control the "renegades" (before the fatal trip to the slaughter house). Candid vets often admit that they have to use sedatives when performing routine procedures, because amateur-owned horses are becoming increasingly dangerous to handle and many owners do not tolerate even a modicum of lifesaving discipline applied to their brat. When horses were exclusively used as working tools, advocating increased kindness was a priority, but when they are, for the most part, becoming pets, a little discipline could go a long way towards increasing everybody's safety.

I suggest that a no-tolerance attitude for misbehavior or laziness, insistence on tangible results, love and encouragement, are all equal parts of the educational equation. Could we promote THAT idea in a complacent world too busy being indignant against a perception of excessive authority to realize which of the two excesses (permissiveness or toughness) creates the greater danger? Unconditional love is great but love-that-insists-on-good-behavior works better! It also implies that humans practice self-discipline and become competent owners."

Excerpts from an article in "Southeast Equine Monthly" Feb. 22, 2003. For more information and JP articles, visit JP at www.equus.net or call Tel. 281-992-2229. This article may not be copies in any form without permission. Send reprint inquiries or request complete list of articles. Email address: jp@equus.net.

Teach Respect!

"Tough love" goes a long way!

SUGGESTIONS ON LOADING

Don't start unless you have the <u>time to finish</u> the job!

Assume the horse will cooperate!

<u>Praise</u> and <u>Reward</u> him when he obeys!

<u>Punish</u> him when he is bad.

"Yank and shank" if necessary!

Get him in the trailer, <u>feed</u> him, <u>pet</u> him, <u>praise</u> him.

Unload him.

Reload him.

Have a helper behind the horse to drive him forward.

Training Aids

Treadmills

Chart Keeping

Swimming

Heart Rate Monitor and Interval Training

Hot Walkers   **Exercise Machines**

TREADMILLS

My experience with treadmills is limited. According to what one reads, they are very useful for gathering data on heart function and general physical conditioning. Much information has been compiled about exercise physiology by having horses train on a treadmill. They have also been used to study horses with paralyzed flaps. It has been possible to film the actual flap movement during aerobic and anaerobic exercise. This information has enabled the veterinary community to understand how the flap actually works. Treadmills are also used to study blood chemistry while the animal is actually performing. In cold and snowy areas, when there are no other alternatives, they can be useful to keep horses exercised. A certain amount of muscle development can be maintained using a treadmill.

However, be leery of using a treadmill for fitness training a racehorse. When a horse is taken out and ridden, he develops various sets of muscles. He also learns skills for coping with the environment mentally and physically. **All the hours in the world on a treadmill will not help a horse walk out boldly in a field, or not be frightened by a covey of quail, a rabbit scampering, or a dog showing an interest in him. Nor will it develop the muscle and balance necessary to carry a rider while performing.** All elements must be dealt with in training. This means taking the young horse out and having him learn from experience.

Show people use the treadmill to develop certain muscles. Since our goal is to develop a useful, strong, resilient horse, real galloping is our best tool. Try to combine logic and common sense with scientific knowledge. A great deal of damage can be inflicted utilizing mechanical aids that are supposed to help. Think of a horse galloping on a treadmill. Can the breakover of the hoof be the same as on a natural surface? This alone could change his gait and put unnatural stress on the joints. Under certain conditions, the treadmill might be useful. A real gallop is preferable in my opinion.

**Use your common sense.
Choose what will work for you!**

JUNE — 2004 *should be Large enough to do whole month →*

	1	2	3	4	5	6	7	8	9	10
Pregnant mare	Trim			Bathe				Ⓑ Bathe	W	Bathe
Mineral Gold	Raced - calder, shoes when Reset	quiet - Better Turned out	Better	Bounc- ing Happy	R.P. good Feels	Swim Hard gallop Happy here	W	W		Enter for Race? Race? Miami?
2 yr old Colt	R. Pen		trim Swim R. Pen	Ride 3 miles ① Legs OK	R.P. No saddle Ride 3 Miles Legs good	No Filling Legs good	W	Ride 3 miles Better	out	R. Pen ② Ride
2 yr old Filly	Runny Nose Paper green cough mucus!		No clear- ing -	Mucus NO cough	No cough	R.P. No feels cough good	R.P. Trail Ride 3 miles easy!	W	good!! No cough 3 miles	Bounc- ing Trail ride 3 miles Clear!

④ Filly Has Bad cold + cough - green Mucus - put Vics - cleaned nose - Turned out in small pen - not near any other Horses - a little off feed!

Put any notes or special Treatments here - identify what was done - why

Very hot - horses in 10AM-4PM - Out at night! MANY Baths!

① He is silly - Looks at everything - Ovck reacts - very skitteris h!

⑤ cut wash

W = wormed with ivermectin on June 10th

③ watch out - itch starting on Back - Bathe after each Rain!

② acting better - goofy 1st mile but then settle in - some galloping and trotting!

Your charts will show Trends!

USE Color to Highlight!

CHART KEEPING

Charts are vital. You must write down all your observations. When you return from handling your horse, write down whether he was lethargic, pissy, or extremely bright, etc. A pattern will emerge indicating how your horse reacts to his training. **Your observations tell you how durable he will be and how frequently he can race.**

Since you are galloping or working every third or fourth day, your comments will tell a great deal about how he is responding physiologically to the insult and stress. Your comments will provide a base line reference as to the level of filling the horse has after work . . . slight amount on front and back . . . just a little in one joint only (beware). **Note any and every change.**

Write down Everything!

Your horse might have needed five days to rebuild from the first few three mile gallops. As you monitor, you might find he starts recuperating after three or four days. As his body becomes more efficient and competent with the training, he may soon recover the next day. Some light fillies are tuckered out for five or six days after a race. They only need to be turned out with a kiss on the nose and some nurturing between races. These are examples of the type of information you should put on the chart.

A sample of one of my charts is included. I use a large size poster board and line up the days of the month across it. Any comments that don't fit into the squares are put down below. Write down any work done on the horses; teeth, shoes, worming, etc. Different treatments may be highlighted with different colors.

Although these charts get pretty messy, they enable you to review past years and see how the horse evolved. You can see if there were signs early on that were missed. The chart shows this because notes about filling and heat are carefully kept. Your notes will show that some horses are consistently off their feed for a day or two after a work or race. You will note that others bolt out of the stall, leaping and carrying on the day after the race. Put it all down, and train accordingly. Be very, very specific in your observations about eating, attitude, soreness, edema, or heat. Knowledge about your animals is the key to keeping them sound and happy.

Good trainers are observant trainers!

SWIMMING

Swimming is excellent. It takes all the weight off the horse's joints and makes him feel good. Just mulching in the water is therapeutic. However, swimming should not be used instead of galloping to train a healthy horse. Galloping prepares a horse to be a runner.

Swimming is good for an injured horse, under certain circumstances. When a horse is recovering from bone trauma and the injury is still too compromised to allow him to be turned out to frolic and feel good, **swimming will help him get his blood circulating without the bone concussion** that would cause more injury. Having an injured horse jog in the water is good, too. The water deflects the concussion of the hoof striking the ground and the horse begins using his muscles sooner than he would in complete confinement. It's excellent also if the horse has had a temporary strain.

However, if your horse has open, festering wounds, it may be better to allow some degree of healing before you have him swim. These wounds should be hosed on a daily basis. Use your own judgement, as to the severity of the wound, in relationship to water. Salt water might be helpful. Avoid swimming "bleeders". It stresses their lungs so intensely, they may start bleeding immediately.

Horses that have foundered will get great relief walking, floating and moving around in the water. If the founder is severe, this might be the only relief they get from the pain. When First Prediction foundered, we put her on a 20 foot shank and let her float, while we sat on the dock reading or contemplating life. Doubtless, this water therapy helped her recover from the severe founder.

Use swimming the same way you use free roundpenning. It keeps a horse supple and allows cardiovascular exercise between gallops. It is especially useful in the summer, when it is a convenient way to cool the horses.

Between races, when a horse is "dead fit" and competing, he could swim every other day and be free roundpenned on alternate days. This keeps the horse fresh for races and relieves any soreness from the last race. If you have an old class horse with lots of aches and pains, swimming is probably good for him between races. This kind of horse needs to be kept healthy and comfortable. The races keep him fit. **He only needs recovery time after the races to rebuild from the trauma.** Used this way, swimming is a good maintenance tool.

 Never use swimming as the only form of exercise.

The horse must always be turned out and allowed to move. Some farms religiously swim horses. They take them from the stalls, walk them to the pool or lake, swim them and put them back in the stall. This is not good. The horses' bodies are only developing swim movement patterns. Their bodies must also develop regular running patterns. They also need concussion to the bone to maintain its strength, integrity, and development. Therefore, **galloping, interspersed with free roundpenning and swimming is the recommended exercise program.**

If you don't have access to water, don't worry. Fortunately, my farm is on a lake. Our wooden dock was lined with conveyer belting in areas that might be dangerous. A floating dock was attached at the end of the stationary dock. To swim a horse, a shank is put on, and he is forced to swim around me while I stand on the floating dock. Some people swim horses out of small boats. I have no experience with this. If you have easy access to a body of water, enjoy it.

Swimming can be used as a treat for the horses, as a therapy for injuries, as a part of the training program, but never as their only source of exercise.

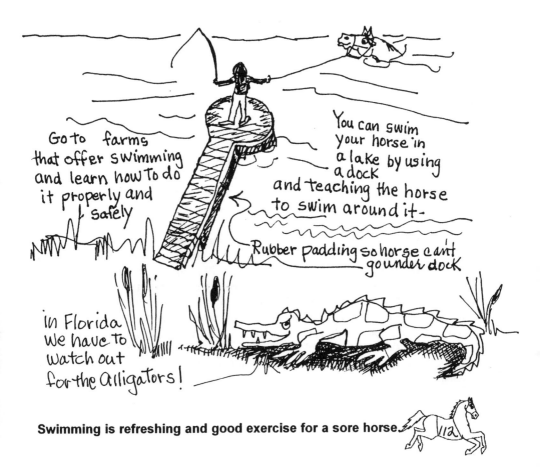

Go to farms that offer swimming and learn how to do it properly and safely

You can swim your horse in a lake by using a dock and teaching the horse to swim around it.

Rubber padding so horse can't go under dock

In Florida we have to watch out for the alligators!

Swimming is refreshing and good exercise for a sore horse.

HEART RATE MONITOR AND INTERVAL TRAINING

Early in my training endeavors, I read everything possible and attended seminars. One seminar, held in Philadelphia, was on sports medicine. Tom Ivers was the main speaker. He was teaching "Interval Training". At that time, his program touted workouts every fourth day and miles of galloping on the other days. The horse was never given time off to rebuild. As a beginner, I thought it sounded like a good program. I used the heart rate monitor, but allowed for track "variations". My horses were galloping in heavy sand and hills. His were galloping on a flat predictable surface.

The interval training method encourages long slow miles, up to a point, and then many speed works within the galloping program. It contains very specific instructions on how to build up speed. The program emphasizes high tech monitoring and is quite structured. It depends on equipment which separates the trainer from his animal. **The trainer may focus on interpreting the numbers and ignore the physical signs the animal is showing.** The program is very aggressive, physically, for young animals. It requires many miles of galloping on a daily basis at the track. It is also very demanding for the trainers and exercise people. **Too grueling for man and beast**.

I was able to do the speed intervals with the proper distance, follow the spiking of the heart rate in full speed, observe how long it took to recover, etc. The most important information the heart rate monitor told me was that my training route certainly did "fit" the horses. Their recovery from sustained high heart rate was well within the recommendations. They were working harder and going slightly slower than they would on the racetrack, because they were carrying more weight and galloping in heavy sand. That was fine with me. Pure speed could be honed at the track. The monitor taught me they were cardiovascularly fit.

However, we must keep in mind that we are training a complete body, not just the heart and lungs. My horses lost tremendous amounts of weight, even though they consumed huge quantities of feed. They also developed swelling in the fetlocks if they did the recommended speed works and gallops. If they rested a day or two, they came back with a better attitude and were much fresher. During the third stage of Ivers' program, they seemed to be over drilled and would go off their feed. **The problem with the program stems from demanding too much speed too frequently.** This holds for racing, also.

In the third stage of interval training, you are asked to give tremendous amounts of feed and gallop many, many miles. I believe my methods are kinder to the horse and trainer. At that time, Tom said that a horse in his program will be doing five-eighths of a mile with faster and faster works, honing into five furlongs in a minute two, a

Never over-train.

minute one, a minute, fifty nine seconds, etc. There are horses that, on their best day, with the best training in the world, can't deliver five eighths of a mile in a minute flat, or a minute one or two, etc. If his training were that consistent, every horse Tom put through the program would become a champion. There are many basically untalented horses that show good conformation, heart rate, etc. Unfortunately or fortunately, talent and other undefined qualities come into the picture .

Before trying Tom's methods, my horses were galloping about ten miles a day, and I'm not light. I have never been under 160 lbs. (God, what an admission!) I had been a recreation director, and felt drilling and pushing, etc., would work on horses as well as it did on humans. This was a mistake. **Horses and humans do not develop equivalently.** One of the most important differences is that **the horse has a built-in overdrive system.**

According to *A Marvel of Design* by Karen Kopp Du Teil, *EQUUS Magazine,* 1992, Issue 180, (Reprinted with permission of Fleet Street Publishing Corporation)

"the equine spleen stores an emergency supply of red blood cells, amount-ing to a third or more of the body's total supply. When the horse gets excited, his adrenal glands release adrenaline , the "fight or flight" hormone, which tells the spleen to contract and release its reinforcement troops into the blood stream. The horse is unique in that his innate built-in "fight or flight" ability has been honed through the centuries. When he needs a surge of power, his spleen kicks in and he is given an extra shot of red blood cells. This in turn can increase his oxygen intake nearly 35 times from rest to run. By comparison, human athletes are highly trained to develop their oxygen delivery capacity. At the height of their training, they can only increase their oxygen intake about 10 times. **Therefore, the horse is a natural runner and his training is to enable him to sustain his gift of speed.**"

Based on my observations from galloping my own horses for about 25 years, I do not believe that works or races every four days, with miles of galloping in between, make the horse faster. It may make him stronger or more fit, but it wears down his brilliance of speed in the process. **He doesn't have time to rebuild from the trauma of an honest work or race to replenish red blood cells and release fatigue toxins.**

When I had sets of four or six horses, they were "insulted" (stressed), and then rested and allowed two to four rebuild-days to rest and recuperate, depending on the phase of training. As explained in the training chapters, **the rest days are vital for the rebuilding process.** Turnout and free roundpenning are my way of allowing them free but loosening up time.

Tom Ivers' interval training is highly intense; and remember, we're working with animals that have brains, personalities, various likes, dislikes, and tendencies. None fit into the heavy training schedule completely. **Controlling to the second every work on a given day is asking a lot from horse and rider.**

I hate to tell you some of my predicaments, while trying to read the heart rate monitor strapped to my thigh, control the horse and keep the electronic leads underneath the girth, where they would give an accurate reading. It must have looked hilarious. We barely

The horse's "fight or flight" ability has been honed through the centuries.

missed the trees many times when I was concentrating on the numbers instead of the horse. Now the monitors have been greatly improved and are very user friendly.

Tom says each horse is slightly different and that his training should be adjusted accordingly. I agree. There are many ways to train. **The monitoring did help me assess and understand the horse's cardiovascular system.** Usually the horse's physical signs provide the same information, if you know how to interpret them. **The horse's attitude and body will indicate to you his readiness to do another round.** Horses brought up with a solid incremental foundation ease very nicely into speed logically and naturally. Let them tell you what they are physically able to do.

The heart rate monitor is a good device to measure an individual's recovery time. It teaches you about cardiovascular function. You can train quite well without it. There are subtle changes going on in the horse that don't register on the monitor until it is too late, such as fractures, etc.

Another thing I learned with the heart rate monitor was that on extremely hot days, after the exercise, the horses would continue panting although the monitor showed the heart rate was back to normal. Why? The horses were trying to cool off. The panting was lowering their body heat.

A group of horses that I had trained following Tom's methods were sent to Chicago. They were two and a half years old and were honed, not an ounce of fat on them from miles of galloping. When they arrived in Chicago, the track trainer was upset. He felt they looked gaunt. (The stress of the trip probably made them a little dehydrated.) I told him to allow them a few days to recover from the trip and to gallop them. He followed the instructions, then called and said, "They certainly are the most fit horses I've ever received." I learned that having a horse that honed was not appreciated. I had done three times as much work as any other trainer, and the track trainers weren't really happy. The trainer told the owner the horses needed more weight (fat) before he would continue training.

All the galloping in the world does not make a horse run faster than he is able to run. Therefore, it is imperative that as a trainer, **we seek the way to allow the horse to develop his own natural speed without breaking him down.** Our main job is to do no harm along the way.

My overall view of interval training as taught by Tom Ivers in *The Fit Race Horse* is that it is entirely too much work, too much stress on the limbs, and too much feed being passed through the horse. I understand that Tom has recently modified the program giving it more flexibility.

Although I don't agree with all of Tom's methods, there is a great deal of extremely valuable information for both owners and trainers in his books. They are fun to read and were invaluable to me. My program evolved from a combination of training programs and experiences. It is incremental and track training interspersed with rest, common sense, and hands-on monitoring

Hot Walkers

Hotwalkers are seen at the backside of every race track. They are a labor saving device that eliminates the necessity of hiring help to walk and cool out the horses. The hotwalker usually has four arms and looks like a giant umbrella clothes line. Horses are connected to it by their halters and learn how to follow the arms around the circle at various speeds. The most common is at a walk.

The risk of using these devices must be balanced with the service rendered. Fractious horses come bounding out of their stalls and are attached to the arms. They buck, rear and carry on-wanting to roll and dip their heads and loosen their backs. They can be so rambunctious that there is danger of crushing the vertebra behind their ears as they pull and yank against the halter connected to the unyielding arm.

Though the machines are more stable these days, they have been known to topple over allowing horses to escape and gallop off over the backside. It is remarkable to see how some smart horses have adapted to this machine and are able to fly around the tether and bucking and kicking with joy while still safely attached.

I much prefer free turnout, but many trainers must use them and do so successfully with no complaints.

Hotwalkers — popular
on the Backside of the
Race Track

Do hot walkers provide real exercise?

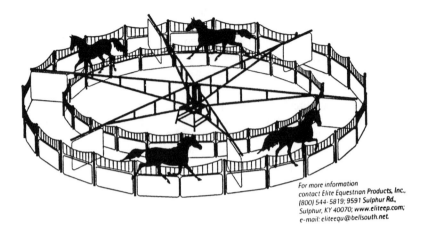

For more information
contact Elite Equestrian Products, Inc.,
(800) 544-5819; 9591 Sulphur Rd.,
Sulphur, KY 40070; www.eliteep.com;
e-mail: eliteequ@bellsouth.net.

Exercise Machines

There various styles, the Exerciser, European Exerciser, Equiciser, Eurociser, and more. The concept is similar for all of them. The apparatus is comparable to an enclosed hotwalker.

With this machine, the horses are allowed to be loose inside compartments that rotate around an enclosed circle. See drawing. The rotation speed can be regulated and the horses may safely trot or slow gallop for a period of time.

For breaking babies, tack can be worn, including side reins, and they can learn to go forward and accept equipment accepting a rider. I hope a company will soon make a saddle pad that can safely carry about 100 pounds of lead. On days when a rider is unavailable or when a young horse needs work, the lead pad and this machine may be a viable solution for small trainers with young horses. A certain amount of foundation can be achieved with this device although a real rider is best whenever possible. The animal must be able to cope with the outside world.

I think it can be very useful both on the backside and at farms. It is a safe way to do basic slow exercise for racing horses. They have freedom of movement, can buck, kick, drop their heads, snort and clear out their lungs in a safe environment. It can be used to maintain a racing horse that needs light exercise between races.

As the cost of labor escalates and good help becomes harder and harder to find, we must look for ways to do most of our work singlehandedly. If properly used, this machine may be a solution. It is very appealing and while I don't have one myself, various friends do and are satisfied with it.

Find a safe way to exercise your horses.

A Little more Comic Relief from Mullikin

BASIC TRAINING

WEANLINGS TO EIGHTEEN MONTHS - GROUNDWORK

YEARLINGS - EIGHTEEN TO TWENTY- FOUR MONTHS

TWO-YEAR-OLDS - AT TWENTY-FOUR MONTHS

GOALS OF BASIC TRAINING

MR. BLUEJEANS

WEANLINGS TO EIGHTEEN MONTHS - GROUNDWORK

If you are raising your own foals, a good book to read about handling them from birth is Dr. Miller's *IMPRINT TRAINING OF THE NEWBORN FOAL* If you have bred your own horses and have some youngsters out in the field, here are a few tips that might help them develop into better racehorses. If you have a big field, chase the youngsters or throw dirt at them to encourage them to run the perimeter of the field in a group. You can observe a lot about their personalities, learn which are dominant and which are not. By encouraging them to run, you have also already started the process of disciplined galloping.

When handling weanlings, make a special effort to teach them to lead like young ladies and gentlemen. Have them walk in and out of places like trailers and accept being tied. The drawing in the Wash Rack Section shows you how horses should be tied in order to allow you to control them . . . or let them loose if they are in a panic. Our foals were raised on a cattle ranch. At birth they were in a paddock next to a landing strip. They soon became accustomed to the noise of airplanes. The landing strip was also used for culling, cutting, and working cattle. Although this was a lot of commotion for the foals, they adapted very well. As weanlings Lois began taking them for walks. She started by taking them a few steps from their paddock and slowly encouraged them to walk around the barns and machinery. We felt that this gentle exposure to the world enabled them to accept the bustle of the track. A word of warning: Be extremely careful if you decide to walk your weanlings. Their size makes them easy to control, but you do not want to hurt them or teach them to be afraid of strange places and sounds. Also beware of permitting cute antics which could become dangerous antics later on. You must teach confidence and discipline.

It's good to teach weanlings to stand at attention and be confined while still very young. You can save a lot of tough training time by teaching them that it's natural for you to lean on them, rub your hands up and down their legs, lift their feet, and generally hang all over them. All of this ground work accustoms them to being handled, which eventually becomes second nature to them. If you have a trailer, this is a good time to feed them in it once in a while and take them for a ride. An easy way to teach them to lead and come forward when you pull on the halter is to put them in as safe 12' x 12' stall and fasten them to an eye bolt in the wall with a bungee for trailers. Be sure the bungee has a quick release snap on either the wall or halter end. The youngsters will soon learn that pulling back puts pressure on their poll and that coming forward and standing quietly releases that pressure. There will be some scrambling, pulling and fighting. However, they learn quickly and the small stall prevents them from stretching back too far. Be sure to stay close at hand in case you are needed.

Even as weanlings horses can learn voice commands, such as "NO!" for negative behavior. Don't expect too much more from them . . . they're just babies. Horses are animals God designed to be grazing or constantly moving. Try to keep them as close to their natural behavior and environment as possible.

Providing a natural environment is the foundation of my training. Horses are natural herd animals. They like to be together, to jostle each other, to scratch each other on the back, and to horseplay. Eventually, it will become necessary to isolate them in their stalls. We want to put that off as long as possible.

Let them learn as many social interaction skills as possible.

YEARLINGS - EIGHTEEN TO TWENTY-FOUR MONTHS

Before we start, I want to remind you that your goal is to develop a strong horse that will be able to run for years. You are not preparing your horse to run as a two-year-old. You will begin his career later. If he has talent he can run for many years.

Start yearlings with what I call free round-penning. Free round-penning is done in a rather large corral or small paddock without putting a lunge line on the horse. With a long whip, encourage the animal to gallop around the perimeter. Ask him to gallop steadily two to five minutes at a time, alternating directions. By doing this once a day, or once every couple of days, you **encourage their bodies to learn the discipline of galloping at a sustained speed for an extended period of time**. Even as yearlings, we want them **to start developing their racing muscles**. By nature, horses like to frolic. They stop and start, run in spurts, and whirl around. By imposing just a little bit of discipline on that natural activity, you encourage development of the galloping muscles. In addition, you can begin to establish a few halter training points. After their gallop, they should be taught manners; how to walk, stop and back up on a lead. Always be sure to handle and rub their entire body.

Only free round-pen. Lunging young horses in tight circles puts excess torque on green bone and can cause sore muscles and bone problems. People spend thousands of dollars breeding the best horses for potential speed, then inhibit their natural ability with counterproductive training.

To free round-pen, use an area at least 100' x 100'. Smaller circles are too tight. Use as large an area as you want. At the ranch, we use a paddock about 100' x 160' (Lois needs the exercise). If the paddock is too large, the horse will outsmart you and stand in a corner, unless you chase him. Makes me wonder, "Who is round-penning whom?" But maybe you need the exercise too.

Initially, your yearlings can be free round-penned in a group of the same sex. When they get older, they should be worked separately, because they frolic wildly and will kick each other. **There is a danger in galloping horses together at any age**. By the same token, **it teaches them to handle other bodies in close proximity**. Even if they get bumped or bruised, they have a good six to ten months to heal. It is important for them to learn to gallop and carry themselves together in a group. Many people will disagree on this point, but I believe in the school of hard knocks. **In my experience the more interaction the horse is exposed to when young, especially socially, the better adjusted he will be when he goes to the racetrack.**

When Thoroughbreds are what we term "hothoused" and prepped for sale, they are separated from their friends and not allowed to play with anyone or be turned out. I remember buying a yearling at a sale. I brought him home and put him in a medium size paddock that had a four-board fence. A horse was on the other side of the fence. When the new horse arrived, he was turned loose. He looked around in amazement. As the neighboring horse came over to say, "Hello", the yearling took one look at him, turned around, crashed through the four-board fence and galloped down the road. He was terrified of seeing another animal coming toward him.

Don't rush! You want your horse to last many years.

Fields are a safe place for your horses if the fences are good and strong. The animals will get to know their environment. The general consensus seems to be that, when a horse is up for sale, nicks and scratches will detract from his overall value. Therefore, the poor yearling is kept in isolation to keep him pretty. In addition, yearlings are given all the food they want to fatten them up. This is where many future problems commence. A diet too rich in protein and calcium can start bone problems that appear later! Presented groomed and polished, these yearlings certainly look very beautiful for the sale.

About November or December in the yearling year, it's time to tack. Begin with the headstall and bit - no reins. Leave it on for several hours at a time for a couple of days until he eats and drinks normally with the bit in his mouth. Be sure it fits properly or he will work his tongue over it. Also be sure there is nothing in his stall-paddock area that he can hang himself on. Wearing the bit for a few days teaches the horse to accommodate the bit in his mouth. Eventually it will become second nature to him.

Now he graduates to a surcingle. Begin in a small paddock. Let him wear the surcingle for a couple of days, when he is turned out in the paddock. You can use a pad with the surcingle for more comfort. After he is accustomed to the surcingle, add reins to the headstall. Pass them through the rings on the surcingle, buckle them on top, and free round-pen. Avoid restraining the head with the reins. Leave them very loose.

When our student accepts this equipment, he graduates to a saddle. Put the saddle on in the stall at feeding time or when he is in a paddock for a few hours. When he is fully accustomed to the tack, he can be free round-penned.

My preference is to start with a western saddle, without any stirrups but with the floppy fenders. This rig weighs a good 30 to 40 pounds. When the fenders flop, the horse probably will buck initially, but he will get used to it.

Next put on the snaffle bridle again. This time run the reins through the hole in the pommel and over the saddle horn and free round-pen.

Some trainers like to "bit-up" a horse using the lunge line. They make the horse gallop in either direction with the surcingle and bridle "setting his head". My feelings are that a horse should not be forced to carry his head any tighter than is comfortable for him. Therefore, I do not lunge in this fashion. Racehorses should not have their natural movements restricted this early in the training process, especially their head movement. They should learn to carry their heads naturally.

Frolicing is Fun !

Observe your horse's natural way of going.

In some areas, shoes aren't necessary for young horses. Keep hooves well trimmed at a natural angle. Remember that the natural angle is the angle where the hoof continues on a straight line through the angle of the pastern. (See Section on Shoeing.) A competent farrier can help you. If the horse has a particular problem with his feet, or has splitting hooves, use protective front plates. If you have a rocky soil or hard surfaces and must use shoes, by all means do so. I personally try to avoid shoes until the last possible minute.

Late in the yearling year, you should not be doing enough work to strain your horse. You are free round-penning him only 15 to 30 minutes every third day at most and giving him time to rebuild. "No pain, no gain," is a saying that is true to a certain degree with young horses, but it is better to wait an extra day than to rush them. If you follow the every third or fourth day training schedule and turnout, you provide two or three rebuild-days to evaluate the effect of the training on his body.

You must be very thorough in your evaluation. Feel his tendons, sesamoid bones, suspensory ligaments, knees and ankle joints. The day after you free round-pen him, it is very important that you observe whether your horse has a tendency to be congested in his lower leg near the ankle and whether he is carrying fluid in the tendon sheaths. If he does, it is the reaction to the stress you have given him. Don't worry. After a day or two of rest, it should go away and his legs should be tight. When his legs no longer show filling and his skin is nice and firm around the tendons, usually by the third day, you can resume training.

A late yearling with no weight on his back should not show any kind of physiological change in the front legs. Swelling may commence later, as you start more aggressive training with weight on his back.

Many trainers tend to be too aggressive and demand too much, too soon. Remember, the horse does not need to be fully developed for racing until his third year. You want to develop him to bring out his full potential. Day by day you demand a little more and allow him to come back stronger. This is a very logical and easy process, if you have patience and do not force him physically or mentally. Don't ask him to gallop or behave too long. At this point he has a short attention span and you do not want to push beyond it.

Young horses have a short attention span!

Always praise and leave your training on a positive note.

Free Roundpen with Saddle and Bridle

Until your horse is about 24 months old, he only needs to be free round-penned every third or fourth day with rest and turnout time for rebuilding in between. Have him gallop a good steady, level gallop five to ten minutes in either direction. After the training he received as a weanling, he should be used to having his feet cleaned, being bathed, groomed and loaded into a trailer. Now your horse has learned to respect the bridle. He has gotten bucks and kicks out of his system and accepts a certain amount of restriction with the bridle and saddle. Be sure you always use good equipment. It would be a bad lesson for him to learn that he could buck off a saddle and potentially the person on it.

As your horse approaches 24 months, you will have to consider whether or not to geld him. To be or not to be is the question. We all nurture the dream of finding the super horse who will win races, stand at stud, and be a famous sire. In reality these horses are few and far between, and the market is full of good sires. So you must be realistic and decide if you want the hassle of handling and keeping a stallion. According to Dr. Rick Archer, "Gelding is the ultimate attitude adjustment. When attitude gets in the way of training, at any age, its time to geld. Geldings stay sounder, race longer, are easier to train and nicer to be around. "

After gelding, remember that irrigation (hosing the area with cold water) is essential after the surgery. It should be combined with some light work such as round-penning to avoid a buildup of scar tissue. Some trainers chose this post gelding period as the ideal time to saddle and ride a young horse. He's not as likely to pitch a fit and buck

If you do decide to geld, you might be interested in an article Lois ran across about castrating cattle. The article mentioned that testosterone is the inhibiting agent in the body's production of growth hormones. Consequently, animals that are castrated very young never close or solidify the growth areas on the long bones. They continue growing, which is why they may be taller. Therefore, their muscles also become longer and more svelte, and the animal may look slightly feminine when compared to the non-castrated animal. This article raised several questions in our minds. We wonder if horses respond similarly to castration. If they do, would having an open growth area be a source of weakness in the legs of a racehorse? We are seeking answers to these questions and encourage you to do the same. We will share our findings with you via the Newsletter, as soon as possible. One conclusion we reached was to allow our colts to be at least 24 months before gelding.

Another interesting consideration regarding gelding is mentioned by Ruth B. James, DVM, in her book *How To Be Your Own Veterinarian (sometimes)*. She suggests that a good time to begin riding your horse is immediately after he is gelded. He will need 30 to 60 minutes of exercise daily to avoid inflammation and aid the healing process. Rather than free round-pen him, start riding. His discomfort may keep him from trying to send you into orbit.

Free roundpen and turnout!

TWO-YEAR-OLDS - AT TWENTY-FOUR MONTHS

As your horse is nearing 24 months, there is a certain escalation in his training. It is a natural progressive evolution that allows the horse to graduate to carrying weight on his back. If you just got your horse, and he has had no training, give yourself a month or two for teaching him the ground work discussed in the Yearling Section.

Remember there are many wonderful systems of training. If you have one that works for you, use it. My suggestions are for those who really don't know how to begin. **You must have strong riding and training experience if you plan to train your own horse. Do not attempt to train if you are not an extremely competent horseperson.**

A two-year-old can carry a pretty large person. I was intimidated by an article that said no one over 90 lbs should ride racehorses in training. I weighed substantially more. I have found, through experience, that a young horse can carry a lot of weight . . . if it isn't for too prolonged a period of time . . . or too fast. If you weigh 150 to 160 lbs, you can start riding your horse when he is between 24 and 28 months.

Before you mount your horse it is **imperative that you put on your safety helmet.** This cannot be overemphasized. There are many different helmet styles. Any reputable tack shop sells them for sale.

When you mount your horse, remember to make all movements very clear. Be very patient with him. Try to think like the horse. Never punish him for something he fears. If he is disobedient on purpose, say, "No!" and punish him firmly.

With young colts in particular, I look them in the eye, say, "No!", and shake my finger. I observe whether or not they tend to be respectful. If not, I brandish a whip. You must be very careful not to accept negative behavior in a two-year-old. They are like teenagers. They will try anything and everything until you draw the line. **It is much easier to draw lines before they get bigger, stronger, and smarter.** Their respect for you has to start now! Rewards work wonders at this stage. You will be surprised to see what your horse will do for a reward.

Since you are starting to ride, everything you do with the horse is crucial. Every movement you make must be very clear. He must not take advantage of you in any way, shape or form. Start to ride your horse for 15 minutes every other day, for the first month. Riding every day, or even every third day, is acceptable. The frequency is not crucial, at this point.

During the first month, ride him in a large pasture. Teach him to stop, turn around and back up. You might try some figure eights, at a trot. Use any solid basic training method. Jim Lyons, Pat Parelli and others have excellent methods for breaking horses. Basically, get him to understand all of your commands and to respect you. After a month or two, when you feel he is cooperating, you can walk, trot, canter, and do figure eights. Then you can begin

Do not allow bad habits to commence.

Trail Riding. (Phase I)

Teach Respect!

Positive imaging is very handy, when riding a two-year-old. Horses are somewhat psychic. If you are riding a two-year-old, and you see a piece of paper blowing in the wind or a cloth flopping in the wind, your natural instinct is to think, "Oh, my God, he is going to shy." What you do instead, is think very positively and "image" your horse obeying you and going by that blowing cloth or paper. Put an image in your mind, and **mentally will the horse** to go right by whatever it is that frightens him. **You give him the courage to do it.** If you tense up and expect him to shy, he will fulfill your expectation, because that is the message you have transmitted. It is a real challenge and exercise of mind over matter for you to override your natural fear of the horse acting up, when logically he might. You must will him, with a tremendous mental power and body language, to go on and through whatever is frightening him. He must obey your commands and do what you command.

My daughter had a horse named Mullikin Stu. She wanted to jump with him, but he had her over a barrel, because she was afraid he would balk at the jump. She would get on the horse thinking," He's going to balk, he's going to refuse to jump." Mullikin sensed her anxiety. He'd come up to the jump and refuse it, because it was the message he received. It took a lot of work to encourage my daughter to believe that this horse was going to jump over the fence. When she reached a fence, she learned to whack him on the behind while thinking, "YOU WILL GO OVER THIS FENCE." Mullikin obeyed the command and they had no further problems. You must achieve this attitude with your horse. It may take several days to make your positive image a reality.

The importance of being mentally positive and powerful, when you are teaching horses, cannot be overemphasized. It has nothing to do with body size. The smallest jockey can handle the largest horse. It has to do with a knack and finesse in handling the animal.

Be aware that your mental attitude is quickly transmitted to and adopted by your horse. If you are angry, sad, annoyed, or upset, the horse will sense and reflect or react to your mood. This can commence a vicious circle. It sets the stage for negative behavior, an unproductive training session, or worse yet a setback in your training.

There is a great deal of equipment out there to help you. I must admit to always using a lead rope with a chain over the nose on my horses. Before you jump to any conclusions, you are welcome to come and see that none of my horses have a ridge of scar tissue from chain abuse. It is seldom necessary to shank a horse hard, but when it is necessary, I can if the chain is there. Most of the time, my horses are docile and completely willing to cooperate. Very early in their training, they learned the ground rules. They must obey me, they must go where I tell them to go, and they must follow where I lead.

Teach respect gently, but firmly.

One of the most important things for you to learn at this point in training is regular **daily monitoring of legs**. You will be asked to make this a nearly religious habit throughout all phases of training. My daily monitoring pattern for two-year-olds, when they begin to be ridden, is as follows:

The first day, before you ride him familiarize yourself with his legs by running your hands around the knees, down the front of the cannon bone and around the ankle. Then go to the back of the knee and run your hand down the back of his leg. Learn how your horse feels. His tendons and the skin over them should feel very tight. You should not feel any edema, pockets of fluid, or sponginess. You should be able to cup your hand under the fetlock and feel very firm bone and tissue. This is a two-year-old, who should have no infirmities, swelling, or problems. When you ride him, which is only for about 15 or 20 minutes, your goal is to get him to obey you at a walk, trot, stop, etc.

The next day, in the morning, particularly if he is stalled up during the night, you must monitor his legs again. Run your hands over the knees, the cannon, the shins, down the back of the tendon and cup around the fetlock. On the day after you start riding your horse, or sometime within the first month, you may notice a little edema where you cup your hand under the fetlock or around the ankle joint. **It is normal to have some filling the day after you exercise your horse.** All you do is feel it and say, "Okay, he has some edema." and note it on his chart. Don't ride him, just turn him out. He needs rebuild-time. The next day bring him in and monitor his legs again. The edema should be down, or almost down. It should certainly be less than the previous day. **You are learning how to monitor your horse's response to the training stress you are giving him.** Usually, by the third day the edema is gone and his legs are nice and tight. **This tells you his body is adapting to the "insult" you are giving to his system.** "No pain, no gain." This animal will become strong and gradually adjust to carrying weight without damaging himself physiologically.

Often when people find edema the day after a horse has been ridden, they want to put on leg bandages. **Do not put bandages on two-year-olds when they have edema that is related to new work.** Monitor the situation. Within three days the edema should be gone and you can ride him again. Stress him again, by riding him 15 or 20 minutes. Don't

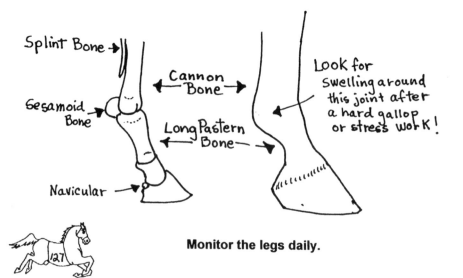

Monitor the legs daily.

worry if he has edema again the next day. **You will find that the horse will slowly and surely adapt to the work he is doing.** As he becomes accustomed to the work, increase the time you are riding him - just don't overdo it.

A certain amount of fluid retention around the sesamoid bones, where you cup the fetlock is perfectly normal, in front and rear legs. The filling should be equal in the two front leg joints, but not necessarily equal to the filling in the two rear legs. It is only mild congestion in either set of legs and is nothing to fear. **Frequently, you will find more congestion in the front legs.**

The horse's legs should not be congested in the first month. As you progressively increase training, you will increase tissue insult. **As long as you do not ride the horse until after the edema is down, you will not harm your horse.** The physiological change that you see and feel in the legs is a perfectly normal adaptation to the incremental stress of race training. If the horse only gets acute edema in one leg, or shows acute lameness or soreness, you are dealing with a different problem and should address it, as it is a potential lameness.

For this preliminary Basic Training, work on having your horse obey commands while you ride him. He must be controlled. You must be able to stop him and to turn him. Don't leave your confined area until you both understand the basics.

Long before a horse is obviously Lame he may have filling and heat in the joint! Learn to read EARLY SIGNS

Feel the Knees, Ankles and Tendons every day Observe them before training and after Training

Now you graduate to the Trail Riding Phase.

GOALS BASIC TRAINING

Have horse comfortable being
handled, bathed, led, and saddled.

Feed in the trailer at times.
Hopefully, he will enter
the trailer quietly.

After he is 18 to 24 months,
<u>free roundpen</u> in a large area
every <u>third</u> or <u>fourth</u> day.
Do about five minutes in each
direction at a gallop - or until
he gets into a good sweat.

<u>FEEL AND MONITOR JOINTS!</u>

Establish what is
"<u>Normal</u>"
for your horse!

Keep young animals <u>outside</u> and
running <u>free</u> as much as possible.

MR. BLUEJEANS

This Section is for the "over the hill" trainers who can no longer ride their own two-year-olds. At 50- something, I must find ways to get the job done without injuring my body. I no longer ride two-year-olds. Since my children are grown and gone, good help is sometimes hard to find. It has been necessary to evolve a way of preparing the 22-month-old yearlings for riding without getting hurt. Saddling them with a 60 pound western saddle and free round-penning them every third day is a good beginning. From the ground I can teach them to go forward, stop

Mister Blue Jeans

and turn. As they progress, it is possible to find riders willing to work on weekends. For the midweek training session, Mr. Bluejeans rides the western saddle. Mr. Bluejeans is easy to come by and to work with. You take an old pair of sturdy bluejeans, tie or sew each leg at the bottom and fill them with sand. When they are full, tie the waist and bingo - a midweek rider. Be careful. Don't develop a hernia trying to lift this 80 pound load of sand onto the saddle. You'll find a way.

Once Mr. Bluejeans is mounted, you tie his legs to the stirrup flaps and his waist to the horn. Then off he goes. The horse is now free round-penned with at least 140 lbs of weight on his back. Twenty minutes of galloping with Mr. Bluejeans' weight flopping around, gives the horse's structure the weight-bearing stimulation it needs. The horse also learns to accept weight without fighting a live rider.

Be innovative. Seek solutions. A friend of mine had saddle pads made to carry lead weights. He put weight on his horses that way. I had a funny experience that I must share with you. Some of my horses were tolerating Mr. Bluejeans, but when faced with a rider in the saddle who towered over them became extremely agitated. A visit to the local Triple X shop solved the problem via a life sized blowup boy toy. (A blowup dummy.) To make this creature more tolerable (mostly to myself) it was dressed in boots, jeans, floppy shirt, and hat.

A kerchief over the mouth completed the costume. We walked the "dummy" up to the horse, quickly swung him onto the saddle and bungied him in place. The horse was then turned out in a small paddock until he settled and learned not to fear the contraption on his back. This episode gave new meaning to creativity. I believe we saved time and possible injuries. You don't have to order all of your equipment from a fancy catalogue. Always bear in mind the goals you want to achieve. Then find a way to achieve them within your budget, in spite of less than ideal circumstances.

Innovation can solve many problems.

THE THREE PHASES

OF

INCREMENTAL

TRAINING

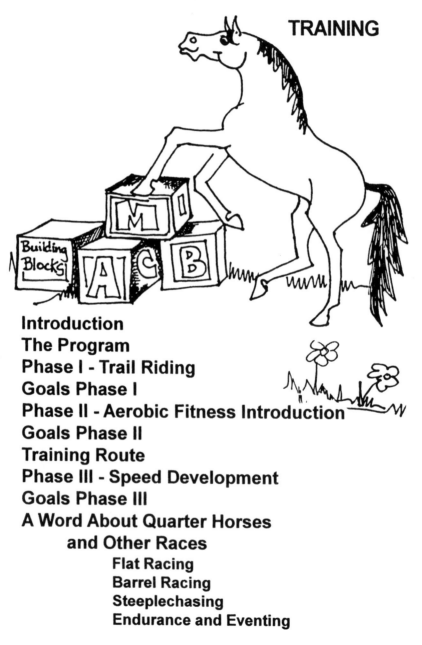

THE THREE PHASES OF INCREMENTAL TRAINING - Introduction

You have a green-broke two-year-old, at this point. He has been worked in a relatively enclosed area. For a month or two he's been taught manners. He should have learned to stop, back up, do circles at a walk, trot, canter, and do figure-eights at a trot. **Now you're ready to embark on an eight-to-ten month journey to make a racehorse out of him.**

It is imperative that you understand your Training Program. **You only saddle and ride your horse every third or fourth day. The other days are "rebuild-days". These are days that the horse is not saddled. He is primarily turned out.** However, you may want to swim, roundpen, teach loading, or reinforce any other lessons your horse needs. **These "rebuild-days" are vital, even when he is racing. This is his rest time, the time he needs to recover and rebuild.**

To better understand the concept of incremental foundation training, think about blisters on your own hands. If you are not accustomed to hard work (maybe you spend your days at the office) and then decide to do some gardening one day, using the shovel usually creates blisters on your palms. You can only do so much before the pain of the blisters tells you the tissue can't take any more trauma. You call it a day. A few days later you notice that calluses have started to form where there were blisters. Your hands are tougher and you can return to your task. If you gradually increase the time you work with the shovel, always allowing your hands to heal between sessions, you soon have tough hands with hard calluses that are able to handle heavy labor.

This training program uses the same process. **A young healthy horse is given incremental stresses to judiciously "challenge" his body.** It is the equivalent of callusing or toughening the joints and sinews of his structure. If you don't stop shoveling when your blisters start to form, you begin to destroy the tissue and ruin your hands.

With horses, if you continue training and pounding a horse that is showing a reaction to the stresses on his body (slight filling in the joints), you begin to destroy the tissue and joints. **Never overstress the body in the process of toughening.** That is why monitoring the joints is so important. You observe how the body is adapting to the increase of stresses on it. Horses that never show a reaction to the stresses can continue with training. Horses that develop inflammation need time for their "blisters" to heal before the training continues.

Under no conditions should you medicate or wrap a horse that shows this normal response to the stresses on his body. He only needs to be turned out and allowed movement until he is ready to go again.

Think of the calluses on your hands. They were blisters until they became the tough hard skin that could tolerate heavy work. **No physical reaction . . . no adaptation to more work!**

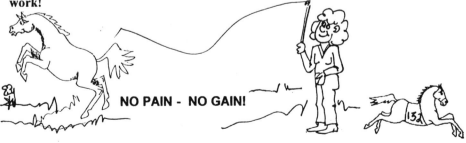

NO PAIN - NO GAIN!

To achieve this incremental foundation building, the training is divided into three Phases. Each Phase has its own logical goals, but is flexible, in terms of time, to allow for individualization.

In Phases I and II, from 24 to about 30 months, you are going to deal with going three miles at a walk and trot with some galloping. **You will progressively increase the galloping every third or fourth day, until your horse can do a solid three miles in a relaxed gallop.** This will take about six months and is the goal in Phase II. You will have ridden over various terrains, up and down hills, and included many left and right turns. **Your horse will have learned natural lead-changing, and will have developed superb balance and surefootedness.** His mental attitude will be excellent and keen because he has been turned out and is "horse-happy." **At no time during this period, have we asked your horse for speed.** At no point during these four to six months does he need to see the racetrack.

In Phase III, between approximately 30 to 34 months, (sooner if your horse has handled Phases I and II with no physical or mental problems) you develop speed in your athlete. **Speed is where redlining and danger begin.** It is the last thing you request.

Start this training process riding with full weight in the middle of the back. As the horse becomes more fit, begin to ask for more speed within the distance. Finally, at the track, take off the weight. **Your horse has learned to carry heavy weight a long distance. Now, he hones into high speed, short distance, and light weight.** My goal is to develop a very tough resilient animal. When you get to the track, the horse thinks, "Gee, this rider only weighs 100 lbs, I have been carrying about 175 lbs over hill and dale and through sand. Here the track is flat and smooth. This is a piece of cake." He should be able to continue training and running soundly at whatever achievement level his conformation and genetic gifts allow. This is the most you can ask of any horse.

Never pull back or stop a horse that is shying or Propping! He will feel confined and become more frightened.

Always push young Horse FORWARD - Even when Frightened!

Give your horse the courage to go forward.

The Program

Day 1 ride the horse -

2 Turnout
3 Turnout
4 Ride Horse
5 Turnout
6 Turnout
7 Turnout

sample
weekly
exercise
program

Day 8 Ride horse
follow day 2 - 8 again

Turnout is a kind of cross Training for a horse!

Work hard, Rest and Recover

Work hard again

**The horse is fresh
and sound on each
exercise day!**

**He <u>recovers</u> and <u>rests</u>
on rebuild-days !**

**He <u>progressively</u>
builds <u>stamina</u>
with each ride!**

**As a horse becomes fitter
in second and third Phases,
he may need 4 or 5 rebuild-days
between Breezes.**

I can do That!

**He must <u>recover</u>
and <u>rebuild</u> from
the <u>stress</u>.**

**His legs and attitude
tell you when he is
ready to stress again.**

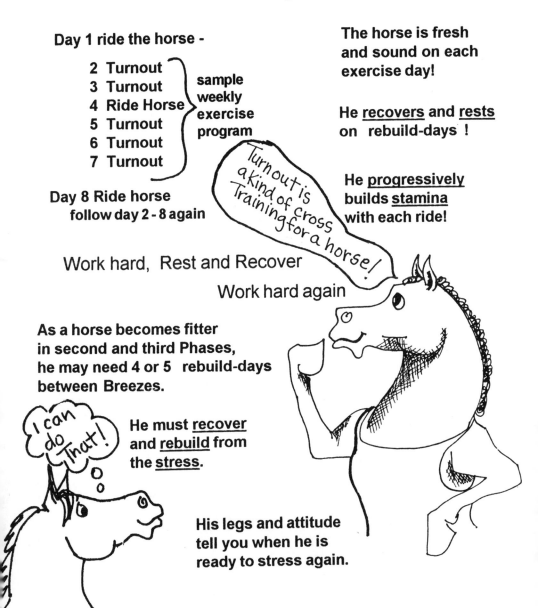

PHASE I - TRAIL RIDING

You are ready for Phase I when Basic Training has been completed. Basic usually takes a month or two. Your horse will go forward easily, walk, trot, canter, stop, backup, and do figure eights. Now, at about 24 months, (his age may vary depending on the horse and circumstances) you start trail rides and establish your route. Find a route that will cover a minimum of three miles. I prefer five miles to allow for warm-up and cool-down.

Only ride every third day. The other days are rebuild-days. When you do put a saddle on your horse's back, he should go at least three miles. Over the next two to four months, speed is gradually increased from walking, to trotting to a light gallop.

Your first goal is to get through three miles on your horse. At first, this may take an hour or two, depending on you, your horse, and his attitude. As he goes out on the trail, he will shy, look around, react to every little distraction and generally be silly. Remember, he is young. Everything is new and frightening until he learns more about the big world out there. **Ask a friend with an older, steady horse to ride with you. The older horse will help calm the younger one.** If necessary, you can put a lead shank on your future racehorse, and let your friend lead or "pony" him down the trail.

The first few times you traverse your route, it will seem to take forever. Carry a riding crop and tap him on the rear to make him go forward (the same way you would if you were on the ground). Do not over react and get angry with the horse at this point. His wariness is natural. Don't start fighting a horse who is not being mean. He's just cautious and insecure. **You must give him the courage and confidence to go forward.**

At the beginning, wear your stirrups long. **Your legs help control the horse and help you defend yourself when he shies and acts like the two-year-old he is.**

Sit flat on the horse's back **with your body straight and your weight in the center of his back.** You can use either an english or a western saddle. Let him learn to carry your full weight.

If you have exposed your horse to a variety of trails and terrains, the groomed track should be easy

At this early stage, do not make an issue of elements that frighten him. For example, if he encounters a water puddle and refuses to cross it, let him go around it . Then approach it from the other direction and encourage him to step into it. However, if the situation threatens to become a knock down, drag out fight, it's much wiser to gracefully avoid the conflict for the day. **Get him to like going three miles, without major problems or major fights.**

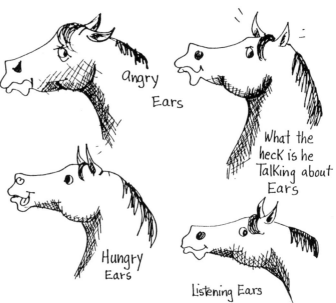

After you feel he is more or less confident with the surroundings, start being more firm with him. **Start helping him overcome unreasonable fears.** Try to see how he perceives the environment. Have a comfortable, relaxed, trail ride (nearly an oxymoron on a two-year-old). Usually, after four or five rides on the same route, the horse will begin to relax.

The horse's ears are his Barometer . When you first started riding him, were his ears so tense that they looked like they could snap off? The ears warn you about his fear; they let you know what looks strange and should alert you to the propping and wheeling that young horses are prone to do.

When the horse is relaxed on the route, start asking him to gallop. Don't force things, just "cluck" or "kiss" and encourage him to go forward willingly. At first he will gallop in spurts, then he'll drop back to a walk as he tires. That's fine. When you think he has caught his breath or has rested a little, encourage a trot or gallop again. Just kiss to **urge forward motion.** Then drop back to a trot or walk. Then kiss to gallop again.

Your first goal is to get through three miles. Your second is to get through three miles with as much trotting and gentle galloping as your mount can tolerate comfortably. Never push for speed. A nice, light, relaxed gallop will do. At some point, usually after a month or so, you'll find you cover your three miles mostly trotting and galloping. Now you must try to bridge the trotting to all galloping. Again, always allow the horse to drop back to a trot when he wants. **He will willingly gallop further as he adjusts and becomes fitter and stronger.**

You'll find that when you start galloping, some horses will dip their heads... be ready for a buck. When this happens, sit very far back in your saddle, yank up his head and urge him forward with your heels. He must have his head down to buck. Make him lift it and gallop out instead.

Never stress him or ask too much.

136

Remember you only saddle and ride your horse every third day. The other days are rebuild-days when he is turned out. You may free roundpen him on the rebuild-days, but its not necessary. Your horse's bone is very green and young at this point. Don't push him. He will over stress himself easily if you're not tuned in and sensitive to what is good for him.

If your horse doesn't eat the night after you've done the three miles, you have over stressed him. Wait until his appetite returns, before you stress him again. Monitor his body frequently, as discussed in the previous Section. Be especially religious about the leg monitoring and make sure any ankle or knee congestion is down before you stress him again. The day after you ride, early in the morning before he has moved enough to reduce inflammation, is the best time to see how his body is tolerating the stress. It is normal to find edema or congestion around the ankles, both front and rear. If the horse has been turned out loose in his stall paddock overnight, any filling caused by the previous day's stress should spontaneously be down by morning.

Make a habit of monitoring his legs daily to see how long it takes him to rebound from stress and note it in his chart. You will see a pattern. Remember, ankle congestion after rides is a sign that you have stressed tissue and tendon, and that they are reacting and rebuilding to tolerate the stress. If your horse becomes lame or has heat or more swelling on one leg than the other, you must address the problem. This could indicate a muscle strain or pulled tendon, which requires therapeutic rest. Always remember to observe your horse as he moves freely in the paddock. Notice if he seems sore, lame, or stiff. He should walk out of the soreness from his work within a day or two, and be ready to ride again. If he doesn't seem quite right after three days, give him another day off. You have plenty of time. **The horse needs time to grow and time to just be a horse. If you rush him, you will regret it.**

Another aspect of training deals with starting gates. Diagrams of pretend starting gates are included in the Section on Farm Layout. Ride him up to the gate and stop him. Let him look. Ride him through the gate. Do nothing more. Every time you go out, which is every third or fourth day, if he is calm and you have his attention, ride up to the gate, stop, walk in, stop, and walk him out. Don't ask for any speed. One of your goals for the 28th month is to get your horse comfortable with the gates. Have him walk into the gate, stop, back out, stop, walk in, stop, and walk out of the gate. No speed. No jumping. You only want the horse to be familiar and completely relaxed around the gates.

If you have gates for two or three horses, it is better. You can walk them all in, stand them all together and walk them out. They may get a little nervous. Do not let them get frightened or upset when they walk into the gates. This is a very important and crucial time. It will become part of their routine. In Phase II, when the horse has more sense and miles under him, you may try the "stand in gate, gallop out routine". Right now, don't worry. The trainer at the track will teach him to break out of real gates with other horses.

In this first phase, you're teaching your horse to go forward for a sustained period, to obey, to learn about the big world, to go over various terrains, to go on uneven footing, and to carry weight for a sustained period in the middle of his back. By the end of Phase I, your horse should be able to go three miles at a slow, perhaps slightly erratic, gallop and recover a normal breathing rate, after a period of cool-down, before reaching the barn.

You are now ready for the Aerobic Phase.

GOALS - PHASE I

Trail Riding

By the end of Phase I, your horse should be able to be ridden a <u>minimum</u> of <u>three miles</u>.

He should be able to gallop more or less - <u>three full miles</u> - <u>even if erratically</u>.

He should be <u>recovered</u> and <u>breathing normally</u> when he returns to the barn.

He should be ridden <u>only</u> every <u>third</u> or <u>forth</u> day the other days are <u>"rebuild days"</u> for turnout and rest.

Ideally he should be 25 - 27 months of age.
(if broken at 24 months)

Continually check legs - charting congestion - if any.

Do not ride him until his legs are <u>normal</u> and <u>recovered</u> from his previous ride.

Encourage
<u>Confidence</u>
<u>Steadiness</u>
and <u>Sense!</u>

As you enter **Phase II training, your horse should be able to get through three miles at a gallop.** Perhaps he gallops erratically, but he does it. Now, you will work toward **Aerobic Efficiency.** You will begin to gallop three miles at a steady open pace, only slowing down for sharp turns or steep inclines. You are teaching him to gallop and turn at the same time, trying to help him get his legs under himself.

Remember, as a rider you are trying to go with the animal. While sitting flat on his back, not up high in stirrups, look for a comfortable settling in on the horse's part. He should recognize that he has a three mile trip in front of him. You want to help him get through this in a workmanlike fashion. The horse may be a little aggressive the first mile or so. Relax and steady him. You have lots of time.

His ears should start to relax as you progress in aerobic work. He should be familiar with the route and, as he becomes more comfortable, there should be a steady rhythm to his gallops. His head and neck should flow and rock without tension. His ears should flop forward and back as his head goes up and down.

Get the horse to do three miles aerobically. This means he is breathing "within" himself. Hopefully, you will start hearing a relaxed fluttering sound in his nostrils as he gallops. This shows good relaxation, and implies the horse understands he is going to gallop for awhile. The noise is similar to that made by gently closing your mouth and expelling air in a "Burrrrr" or "Purrrrr" sound. Your lips will tickle a little if you're doing it right. I make this noise, when I am galloping the horses. Remarkably, it encourages them to do the same. They mimic the sound.

Horses that fight and are not relaxed will breathe differently. They make a firmer and more determined noise. You must work making this type horse relax. Often, the horse will fret and fuss in the first mile, begin to relax and settle in during the second, and finally even out and concentrate to finish the third.

Developing a fit, aerobic horse takes about three months. You should still ride no more frequently than every third day. He needs his rebuild-days. **If he seems dull, has persistent congestion in his joints, or has any other problem, wait until the fourth or fifth day.** Always turn him out every day. Free roundpen him on the third or fourth day until you feel he can do three miles again. There should be steady improvement in strength, ability, and agility as he progresses. However, **there will be a ride or two that make you think you've gone backwards, instead of forward. Don't get upset! It's only natural.**

Keep your exercise chart current. When you get off the horse, record all your impressions. The horse is dull today, bright, sore, cantankerous, he did not eat, etc. Make notes about your horse's personality, attitude, and physical response. Later on, these notes will help you evolve a training program that suits your horse.

Fillies tend to overdo. They try to give too much and have a tendency to be off their feed after a gallop. Some will need more time off between exercises.

If you stable your horse at night, you will notice in the morning when you turn him out that the day after his exercise he is more sedate than other days. Usually by the third or

Don't rush. You have plenty of time.

fourth day he will bound out. Some horses are so stout they can use another mile beyond the basic three. If they're holding up structurally and they want to keep galloping, let them go another mile. It's good for them to come home tired, **not overtired, or anxious, but relaxed.**

During this more or less three month period, **you are looking for long, steady, relaxed gallops and a good mental attitude.** There should be an evolution to a strong

three miles, with an eventual mile warm-up in front, and a mile cool-down after. The horse should not be breathing hard when he gets back to the barn. As he becomes more efficient, he will go the three miles in less time. You can **encourage the horse to pick up the rate of his gallop as he progresses.** Encourage more efficiency of movement in the gallop by collecting his head and urging him steadily forward. He should not be shying or hesitating, but galloping forward smoothly and steadily . **AT THIS POINT, NEVER LOOK FOR HIGH SPEED.**

Try to gallop in company. If you have a pleasure horse, a friend or spouse can ride him beside you. This will steady your horse. Soon, your horse will leave them behind, as he learns to gallop relaxed and with a ground-eating stride. (Lois says, "If your horse can't beat the pony horse, retire him now") If you and a friend are doing the same program, it is a great experience for the two of you to gallop side by side. Take turns going in front and behind each other . . . bumping each other. Learning to pass horses and learning to listen to the rider are important lessons for youngsters. Teaching your horse maneuverability will help him be agile when he goes to the track. This is a good time to experience dirt in the face, and some of the other indignities of a race.

Continue going to the pretend gates. Stand inside, back out, go forward, and gallop out from a flatfooted stance. If there are two riders and two horses, all the better. Remember, no speed . . . just gallop out side by side. It may be better to do this after your long gallops when the horses are settled. Hustling them out of the gates will make them **too high, too soon. Gallop them out quietly encouraging them to go straight.**

By now you have both become more confident in your route and in the horse's ability to handle it. You will now find that you have more contact with your horse's mouth. As you increase your speed you want to increase control, or "steering". You'll lean with him around curves and pick him up if he starts carrying his head too low. You'll start guiding more with the reins. At the end of Phase II you will want to start pushing him into the bit more.

Racehorses are helped and held together by the jockey's control of the head via bit contact. Horses evolve their own way of going. Some like to pull and have you hold them. Others gallop kindly with a loose rein. **When you "pick up the bit" and take a tight hold, they know it's time to start going faster.** You and your horse learn how to get along together to achieve your goals. The horse must obey and respond to your guidance. In turn, you learn what he likes. You develop together.

You must always have control.

Keep your eye on his ears. Remember they are a barometer of how he is handling the training you have given him. When he was younger and less experienced, his ears were straight up and forward, looking with trepidation at all the new sights. The ears were his radar. Now his ears should be relaxed, showing a more confident animal.

In the 28-to-30-something month period of training, you **start to stall your horse for a least part of the day** in order to help him adjust to being in the stall, and to protect him from burning up too much energy. **You want him to direct and concentrate his energy into his gallops.** Find a routine you are comfortable with and stall him either all night or all day. He will learn to be in a stall and act like a good boy. Remember, at the end of his training period, when he is 30 to 36 months old, he will have to go to the track. If he stays there, he will probably be confined in a stall for 23 hours a day. This is a very hard adjustment for horses who have never been asked to be in a stall at all. If you want a horse to be a racehorse, he must spend time at the racetrack, unless you are able to race off the farm!

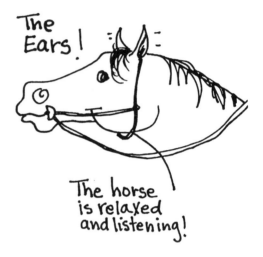

The Ears!

The horse is relaxed and listening!

You may need more equipment now. Your horse probably began with a D snaffle bit and nose band. You can graduate up to all levels of control with your equipment. Equipment should be added as individual horses present individual problems.

Continue to reinforce trailer loading and unloading. We discussed loading and taking him for little rides when he was a weanling. This is important for the horse. When he actually starts being hauled, it shouldn't be traumatic. He should enjoy it. My horses have been good haulers. They didn't necessarily start out that way, but they became seasoned, happy, travelers.

At the end of Phase II you should have achieved the following goals: The horse has developed an ability to go longer distances more efficiently, with a gradual stacking of stress to the system. There has been a slow progressive building of strong bone, tendon and aerobic air. There has been good healthy mental growth and a desire to run without fear or pain. He is galloping a strong steady three mile gallop with a mile warm up and a mile jog cool down.

If you are an extremely competent rider, you and your horse are ready for SPEED!

GOALS PHASE II

Aerobic Fitness

By the end of this Phase, your horse should <u>gallop</u> a <u>steady, strong three miles</u> with one mile <u>warm-up</u> and at least one mile <u>cool-down</u>.

Gallops should get <u>progressively stronger</u> and <u>faster</u> as he grows more <u>mature</u> (but <u>not redline full speed</u>).

He should be <u>relaxed</u> and <u>breathing rhythmically</u>. He should <u>cool out</u> by the times he is <u>back</u> to the barn. He should have been <u>ridden</u> at least <u>half and hour</u>, even though the real gallop doesn't take that long.

<u>Trail ride</u> and enjoy the scenery while <u>he cools with a rider on his back</u>. <u>Carrying weight</u> in the <u>middle</u> of <u>his back strengthens</u> his <u>whole structure</u>!

<u>Ride only</u> every <u>third</u> or <u>fourth day</u>. The others are "rebuild-days".

Constantly <u>monitor legs</u> and <u>joints</u> for <u>filling</u> and <u>heat</u>!

Hopefully he is still <u>turned out</u> for at <u>least</u> a <u>few hours</u>.

No riding with a rider until his <u>structure</u> is <u>normal</u> from last <u>gallop</u>!

(or all day or all night)

He should be <u>stalled</u> for a portion of the day or night to <u>accustom</u> him to <u>partial stall life</u>!

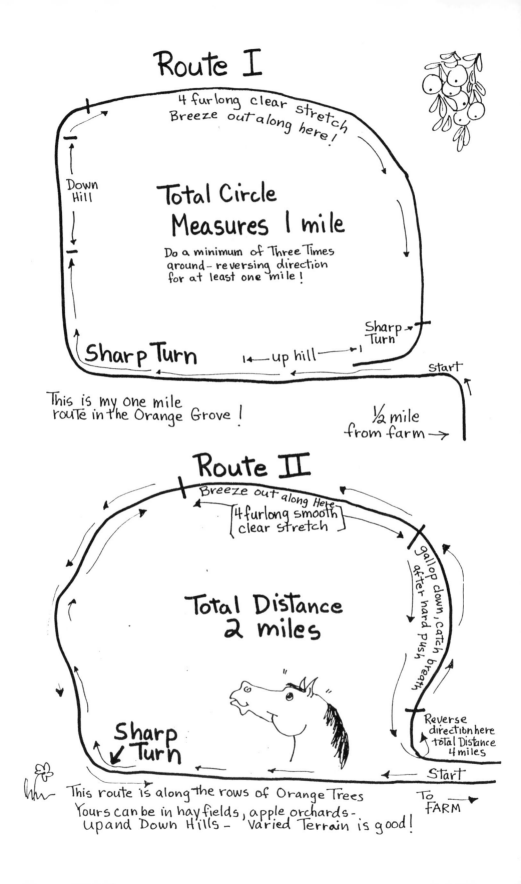

Route I

4 furlong clear stretch
Breeze out along here!

Down Hill

Total Circle
Measures 1 mile

Do a minimum of Three Times
around - reversing direction
for at least one mile!

Sharp Turn

up hill

Sharp Turn

Start

This is my one mile
route in the Orange Grove!

½ mile
from farm →

Route II

Breeze out along Here
4 furlong smooth
clear stretch

Total Distance
2 miles

gallop down, catch breath
after hard push

Reverse
direction here
total Distance
4 miles

Sharp
Turn

Start

This route is along the rows of Orange Trees
Yours can be in hay fields, apple orchards -
Up and Down Hills - Varied Terrain is good!

To
FARM

PHASE III - SPEED DEVELOPMENT - BREEZING

Early in my training days, I wondered, "What's the best way to train a racehorse? How do you make the transition from a fairly fit useful horse to a racehorse? What are the methods?" I searched for answers in training manuals and trainers' notes, but no one seemed to explain the **transition from gallops to speed in a safe, logical manner**.

First of all, you must remember, **SPEED KILLS**. A horse can gallop six miles over hill and dale, jump 20 fences and come out feeling fine. But if he hasn't been properly prepared, ask him to go full speed for six furlongs to a mile and you will encounter many problems.

As I mentioned before, compare speed stress in a horse to a car with everything mechanically perfect, except a bald tire. You might be able to go forever at 50 mph but try to go 90 and the tire will blow! The horse's weakest point (legs, heart, or lungs) is equivalent to the bald tire when you go to sheer speed.

Phase III explains the transition to speed. In Phase II, you have developed a sound, fit horse able to do reasonable work for a sustained distance. Now we want to hone his speed.

If you are not an extremely skillful, strong and confident rider, or your terrain is dangerous (due to cars, roads, steep inclines, sharp turns, dogs, etc.) and you don't have a few straightaways on your route, now is the time to send your horse to the track with a trainer or start shipping-in for morning works.

Speed in a horse is the equivalent of all-out sprinting in the human athlete. Anaerobic muscular fitness is required. This involves developing and conditioning the "fast twitch" muscles. These muscles operate under conditions of high lactic acid production, for very short periods, producing an oxygen debt. This muscular conditioning is best done gradually, by asking the horse to extend into bursts of full speed, followed by aerobic recoveries.

Fast twitch muscles are activated, developed and physiologically primed by speed bursts. In a relatively short time, the horse can be honed to a fine-tuned, powerful sprinting machine. **The previous months of slower gallops provide the necessary structural and cardiovascular basis for this transition.** After building bone, joint, and lung fitness, you turn to speed gallops, called "breezes", to achieve peak muscle fitness.

Once you start breezes and are kissing or clucking to the horse and letting him extend out, you can get in trouble. When a horse tastes speed, you open Pandora's Box. If at any point along the way, you cannot control the horse, STOP RIGHT THERE! Send him to the track. It is very dangerous not to be in control of a horse that is starting to run full speed, particularly on uneven terrain. Speed makes horses both stronger and stronger willed. This is good for the racehorse, but is dangerous when tearing through trees.

What's the best way to train a racehorse?

To transition into the actual development of Speed, you take your Phase II horse who gallops steadily for three to five miles, and **allow him to breeze along the safest portions of the route.**

My galloping route runs through an orange grove. (See Route I drawings.) It is a circular route, approximately one mile long, with very sharp curves on two sides and a long, straight stretch that provides a four-furlong (one half mile) breeze area. Your route could be through wooded trails, be more hilly, involve flat desert, or be a 100 acre pasture. Adapt your route to provide safe breezing for your horse.

My route consists of multiple laps around a circular route. There is about a mile ride to get to and return from the route. The first mile of the route is done at an open full gallop. The second mile, I **kiss to the horse and let him extend or breeze in the safe part of the mile, if he wants to.** The third mile, I let him do what he wants, not pushing him or asking him for more. If you are fortunate enough to have safe three-to-four furlong sections in your training route, and you feel competent in what you are doing, you can kiss to him and have him breeze in these sections, if he is willing. Remember, you always go three to five miles, but kiss to him only in the second mile of the route. Allow him to ease into full speed. Never, never whip or push the horse to run. **Let him breeze in a natural manner.** Let the horse "come back to you" after the breeze. Never pull him up sharply. Let him develop without having his natural desire to stretch out impaired. Make sure you have room to do this. Only ride him every fourth or fifth day. On his rebuild-days between breezes, turn him out in the pasture or free roundpen him. During the first month or two of Phase III, allow him to breeze slightly every time you ride him.

As you progress with speed work, the secret is to **let the horse extend out to his own capabilities.** You don't want to push him to the edge too soon. **Remember, fillies may try to run too hard, too soon.** You must be cautious about how much you allow the animal to do. This is where the art of training enters. If you are at all insecure about how much to allow your horse to do, or if you are not tuned in to how much your horse can handle, it's time to turn the horse over to a racetrack trainer.

Do not over train!

At this point in training, **the horse expects to gallop at least three miles, no matter what.** Horses adapt differently to speed stress. Some will be finished by the third mile and return to the barn at a walk or trot. Let them slow down when they want. Never push them. Others, even when tired, will maintain a gallop and try to extend out more on the breezing stretches in their route. It depends on the personality and ability of the horse.

If you find that your horse wants to go fast for the first mile, but slows down the second mile, even though you kiss to him, do not force him to do the third mile. The horse is probably trying to tell you that, by nature, he is going to be a sprinter. He is going to run early and then get pooped out. Hone into building his speed in two miles. Two miles at your best route speed should give him enough foundation to finish a 6 or 7 furlong race at top speed when he goes to the track.

On the other hand, if your horse cruises the first mile, hits the second mile fast when you kiss to him, then slows down some before running a very strong third mile, you probably have a distance horse. He will need a certain amount of time to gear-up to full speed. This type of horse will need ample warm up time before a race.

As you go into this last phase of fitness, **you should be using an english or exercise saddle, because it is lighter.** You will notice, as you start to gallop or breeze out, that you naturally tend to lean a little bit forward, stand up in your stirrups, and put your weight over the horse's withers. **When the horse levels into high speed galloping, it helps him if you are slightly up off the saddle and not sitting on his back.** At this point, it is better to shorten your stirrups a little. Shortening the stirrups, does not mean shorten them to jockey length, just to a length that makes you comfortable, so you can lift your weight and rock on top of the horse, rather than remain sitting flat on his back when he goes into his breezes. In other words, you **evolve from sitting flat on the back to a more forward seat, with the concept of trying to hinder the horse as little as possible with your weight.** Your goal is to keep your center of balance over his center of balance. Hang onto the mane or yoke until you get the hang of it,

If you can imagine walking along carrying a loosely tied knapsack which bounces and flops every time you start to run, you can understand what a horse feels with a loose rider going thump, thump, thump on his back. You want to be in as tight a position and in as tight a package as possible. **Leaning forward and standing slightly, in the stirrups, as you allow him to rock under you and extend out, is a very natural, wonderful feeling.** You should grow and ease into this . . . just as the horse is growing and easing into his breezes. Between the breezes, you still sit flat on his back. You have already developed his muscles to carry your full weight. When he goes to the track he will be ridden by a jockey who is substantially lighter than most of the people doing this training. **When the horse graduates to a lightweight person, for a shorter distance, on a faster surface, he will have great power and endurance.** At that point, the logic behind the program comes together beautifully.

During these last few months of training, you have to key in to what your horse wants and is capable of doing.

Mane and Rein in each hand!

As you progress in the speed work, you will notice that your horse is no longer carrying his head in a relaxed manner. He is now leaning more against the bit. You will have to take a tighter hold on him. You want the horse to respond to your signals and believe me, you want his mouth to get somewhat harder and firmer at this point. Always use two hands. Grab a handful of mane, hold the horse very firmly with **mane and rein in each hand**.

The more you extend into speed, the firmer the contact you need with his mouth. I equate it to a tighter and well connected steering wheel. When you are driving a car slowly you can have a rather relaxed hold, with a certain amount of play in the wheel. **When you are going at a high speed in a car or on a horse, you must have complete control.**

Encourage the horse to lean against the bit. Have very firm contact with him as he is breezing out. This will help him when he goes to the racetrack. Contact with a racehorse's mouth is very different than what you may be accustomed to in dressage or jumping. The jockey maintains the horse's balance by encouraging him to lean against the bit. Jockeys often "take a cross" on the horse's neck. (The right rein goes over the neck to the left hand and the left rein goes over the neck to the right hand. This way the jockey can keep a firm contact on the bit and yet brace himself against the neck.)

Watch the ears as your horse rolls into breezes. When he tries to run harder, he will concentrate more. Instead of having his ears "scoping" and looking at things on the trail, he will now have them cocked back listening to his rider and eventually straining with all of his body to run his hardest. His ears will be flattened, not as in anger, but showing the concentration necessary to run hard, carry his rider over the terrain and obey him! Observe horses in the stretch during a race. Most are concentrating and have their ears back. When a trainer says his winning horse galloped across the finish line with his ears perked up, he means that his horse didn't have to work hard to win the race.

Any time your horse misbehaves give him a sharp whack. Use the whip to guide and discipline him. You don't beat him, unless he deserves to be beaten. **The horse should experience the whip as an aid to discipline...not as punishment.** Always have your

The art of training is sensing how much your horse can do without harming himself.

whip handy. If he goes into his gallop and wants to buck rather than gallop like a gentleman, crack him and say "No" in a very firm voice. Also, yank his head up and urge him forward with your heels. Let him know that negative behavior is not acceptable.

As long as there is a good turnout pasture for the horse on his rebuild-days when he isn't working, he can exercise on his own. If you want to ride your horse on the rebuild-days, or if you don't have a proper place to turn him out, very specifically ride him on a different route and direction where you never, ever gallop. Take him for a nice trail ride of some kind. The point is, that when you do a particular route, a horse learns exactly where he is allowed into speed. **You must change the pattern on rebuild-days or you will fight him the whole way.** If you insist on riding him on these rebuild-days, you don't want to fight him or confuse him,

Do not over train. This cannot be over emphasized. Be very careful to never over work the horse. If you ride the horse any more frequently than every fourth or fifth day, or push him too hard, he will start loosing weight. **The minute you hit the higher speeds, excess fat will start melting off him.** If you work him too much, he will come back trembling and highly agitated. He might have loose, watery manure. You must use your skills as a trainer now. Look at your horse very carefully. He might seem dehydrated the day after a speed work. Always monitor his legs and write your comments in his chart. Remember, if there is any kind of swelling, edema or heat, you must turn the horse out, swim him, free roundpen him, or walk him. **Do not ride the horse until all swelling has completely disappeared. By not wrapping his legs and by observing him carefully every day, you will perceive how much recovery time your horse needs.** Each day his structure will toughen as he adapts to the work.

If you feel that the horse has strained something, twisted a leg, has different kinds of swelling, or has a pull and is not evenly stocked up, check with your vet. You might have to do some bandaging.

Practice gates – preferably angled up a hill !

Start targeting dates for taking your horse to the track.

As you progressively hone into more speed, you start to stress every fiber of the horse's body. It is believed that it takes at least four days for a horse to recuperate from a hard anaerobic push. **He will need more rest, free movement, and time to recuperate and rebuild between breezes** as he bridges to high speed. You will eventually back off his breezes to every fifth day, then every sixth day, with turnout and free round-penning in between on his rebuild-days. As **he gets fitter, he will start thinking speed.** If he begins to get speed-crazy, look for a trainer. Make your target date for the racetrack.

Remember, no more long slow gallops. **You are now flying through three miles.** Your horse is anticipating the run. You are probably doing the equivalent of a two minute mile, with speed spurts on your three mile route. You are only slowing enough to turn safely and maintain control of the animal. My mare needed two full miles to gallop down, after she did her hardest push in the third mile. Never inhibit the horse if he wants to continue to gallop down, even if it takes three miles.

Let the horse come back to you! He is working out the lactic acid build up from the oxygen debt created by a hard gallop! SLOW GALLOPS IN BETWEEN ARE NOW CONTRAINDICATED. From here on out, **we are honing for speed with open gallops easing into breezes.**

All racehorses are considered three-year-olds in January, regardless of the month of their birth. Since I do not race the horse until he is nearly three, I try to hone the horse into race condition by the time the track opens near me. You should be doing the same thing.

The horse tells you how much he can do
But you must learn how to <u>Listen</u>!
How he eats – how he acts –
How he responds to increments of <u>Stress</u> in Training –
This is how the horse <u>tells</u> You!

Try to be race ready by the opening day of the meet.

GOALS - PHASE III

Speed Development - Breezing

Start <u>speed spurts</u> within Three mile route.

> <u>Always ask</u> for <u>speed</u> in <u>second mile.</u>
> <u>Repeat</u> in <u>third mile if horse wants.</u>

Horse may eventually <u>want to run hard</u> at the same spot in <u>first mile</u> - that's okay -
But always <u>ask</u> for <u>speed</u> in <u>second mile.</u>
Soon you have <u>three stretches</u> with <u>speed spurts within three miles.</u>
You <u>slow</u> for <u>turns</u> and <u>uneven</u> areas -
<u>Now</u> your horse tells you how he wants to run.
<u>Early</u> speed - <u>Late</u> speed - <u>Steady</u> speed.

Discuss with a Trainer when your horse should go to the track.

> Your horse should only be ridden
> every fourth or fifth day.
> The other days are rebuild-days.

He is now starting to go <u>full speed</u> for the <u>spurts</u> in the <u>three mile route.</u> He needs <u>REBUILDING - RECOVERY</u> time.

Always have free choice hay - good grain and <u>augment feed</u> if he looks "<u>sucked-up</u>". On rebuild-days - <u>TURN OUT</u> and <u>OBSERVE MOVEMENT</u>. He may be <u>quiet</u> the day following a gallop - He may be <u>bounding</u> and <u>full</u> of <u>energy</u> by third or fourth day. FREE ROUNDPEN horse if he <u>feels great</u> and its not time for gallop!

AIM for TRACK!

Start <u>BREEZES</u> at track about every seven days with <u>free roundpenning</u> in between!

MONITOR LEGS

Adjust this schedule to what <u>you perceive</u> as <u>appropriate</u> for <u>your horse</u> and <u>terrain!</u>

A WORD ABOUT QUARTER HORSES AND OTHER RACES

Those of you who are training Quarter Horses often ask how this program fits your needs. You must understand that the *Backyard Racehorse* incremental foundation training prepares any horse for his future performance. When you monitor the legs, you can see when the horse has been stressed too hard and how much he can tolerate. The younger he is, the longer it takes for congestion to go down after he has been stressed too hard. Don't be surprised if it takes four or five days for his legs to get tight again. It takes as long as it takes. A horse can start racing at two if his body has shown you that it can tolerate the work. If he can't, give him time.

Flat Racing

Follow the program in the Trail Riding and Aerobic Phases as stated. The main difference appears in the Speed Phase. The Thoroughbred program is aimed at developing speed for several furlongs. A Quarter Horse race will be about as long as the short speed spurts in the Thoroughbred gallops. Since you do not have to develop distance speed, you may not want to do more than one or two speed spurts. You can graduate to the track as soon as your horse is galloping aerobically with little or no effort.

When you transition to the track, have the rider warm up your horse with at least a mile gallop and breeze him out of the gates. If he breaks well, don't keep returning to the gates. **Always be sure your horse "comes back to the rider" and fully gallops down after a breeze or race** to eliminate the lactic acid from his system and avoid tie-up.

Once he breezes out straight and knows to run hard - put him in a race. **Instruct the jockey to warm him up well before the race** - at least a mile - and to allow him to gallop down as far as necessary afterwards. Almost any horse can breeze or work two or three furlongs.

Your goal is to enable him to tolerate the wear and tear on his body from the stress of weekly races (no works between races). To achieve that goal **you give him a solid foundation and turn him out for a few hours every day between races to rebuild.** Of course, if he has wrenched something in a race, he will probably need more time.

 Quarter horse races are pure speed.

Barrel Racing

Those of you who are into Barrel Racing are probably saying, "How does any of this apply to me?" The incremental foundation training is essential for your racing too. You want a sound horse that will last.

Most of you will be training at home and shipping-in for your event. That in itself will help you have a sound horse. If you are not conscientious about your training and only ride your horse to race him, please read the Section on Bleeding. Are you pushing your horse in the same manner? Barrel racing horses are also know to bleed. Think about their training and ask yourself if the horse had enough foundation.

Those of you who must keep your horse at a training center should try to ride at least twice a week. Be sure your horse gets plenty of turnout time on the days you don't ride.

Barrel racing horses usually start a little older and race for many years. That is fine. Take as much time as you need. They need plenty of time to develop bone that will withstand the torque on their legs when they race. Because of that torque and the stress to the legs and lungs, you must give your horse a very solid incremental foundation if you want him to be sound and to last.

I cannot overemphasize the importance of monitoring legs and allowing the horse to have rebuild-days. Since you are not redlining your horse, he will not need as much rebuild time as the Thoroughbred program suggests. You must evaluate just how much he needs.

My suggestion is that you follow the Basic Training. Elaborate on it to achieve your goals of bending and flexing the horse. Use what ever training method you prefer. You will probably continue that training through your Trail Riding and Aerobic Phases, since it is more complex than the Basic Training needed by a Thoroughbred.

Although you spend much time working circles etc. in an arena, by taking your horse out and exposing him to a trail gallop route with plenty of bends and turns, you will teach him natural lead changing, balance, to keep his feet under himself, and to gallop freely. It will provide a pleasant break to the training for both horse and rider adding a needed dimension to your training.

Continue with the Aerobic Phase until you get a steady two-to-three mile gallop with good aerobic efficiency. This will give plenty of stamina for the short runs around barrels, should help avoid any future bleeding problems, and will develop good strong legs. The concussion provided by galloping is vital for building bone and strong legs.

You can virtually skip the Speed Phase. It would only make the horse hot, teach him to lean into the bit, and make him difficult to handle. Your only real speed spurt is the dash after last barrel. Any fit horse can handle that. Speed training for it would be counterproductive.

Be sure to use your horse sense as you adapt this program to your needs.
Many thanks to Holly Wright for her help with this topic.

Everything suggested in this manual worked for me!
What can <u>you</u> do that works for you?

Steeplechasing

We could take a hint from the steeplechasers. The following article is taken from the program for The Little Everglades Steeplechase, Dade City, FL - March 10, 2002

"Steeplechase Horses

All steeplechasers are Thoroughbreds whose lineage must be proven with official Jockey Club registration papers. Horses can begin their steeplechase careers at age 3.

Most steeplechasers competed or still compete on the flat. The ideal steeplechaser has speed, stamina, smarts and enough athletic ability to run and jump at the same time. In general steeplechase horses are larger than their flat counterparts, but size is not a rule. Big horses tend to have more stamina, which is important. Also, horses trained for steeplechasing develop larger muscles across their backs - to help with the jumping.

The best jumpers clear the fences in one long stride - much like a human hurdler humps in track and field events.

Almost all steeplechase trainers are based on private farms, where horses enjoy the outdoors while also exercising and working toward their next racing date.

It is not unusual to see a steeplechase horse compete until age 10 and beyond. At age 13, Ninepins won a Grade I Stakes at Saratoga in 2000.

Steeplechase horses typically run six to ten times a year. The season features no racing in January and February, plus a light summer schedule - assuring horses of lengthy vacations. Most "down time" is spent outdoors in fields. A steeplechase horse in the off-season is often dirty, hairy - and happy.

After their steeplechase careers end, horses often become foxhunters, show horses or simply pleasure rides for their owners or trainers. Hall of Famers Flatterer and Zaccio found "second Lives" as a dressage horse and a foxhunter, respectively.

Endurance and Eventing

Those of you who are already into endurance races should find this program especially beneficial. You do miles and miles of trotting and galloping to achieve the needed stamina. A two day rest period would be especially beneficial to allow your horse time to rebuild from those long works.

Steeplechase horses last for years.

Useful Restraints

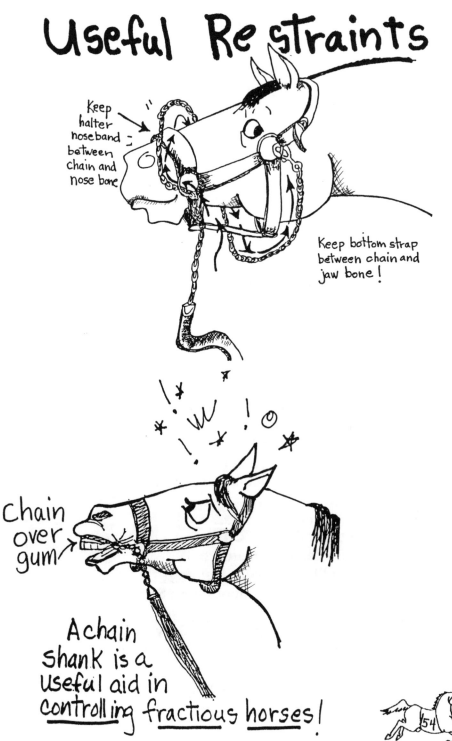

Keep halter noseband between chain and nose bone

Keep bottom strap between chain and jaw bone!

chain over gum →

A chain shank is a useful aid in <u>controlling</u> fractious <u>horses</u>!

54

THE TRANSITION - FARM TO RACETRACK -
Introduction

First, congratulations! If you have gotten this far, you have achieved a great deal. You have a horse that you have been nurturing and developing into a running machine. He should like to run and should be chomping at the bit at the threshold of pure speed for a prolonged distance. **How do you bridge from the speed spurts you have been doing within your three-to-five mile route to a speed machine?**

I am going to discuss two ways of handling the transition from farm to racetrack. Although the basic training theory is the same, the life-style of the horse is different. Therefore, I will repeat each step of training for each option so that there will be no misunderstanding as to how the horse is handled.

The first option is presented to those of you who live close enough to the track to haul your horse in and have found an astute trainer willing to work with you.

A Cooperative Track Trainer is worth His Weight in Gold! !

The second option is for those of you who must keep your horse at the track. You want the trainer to understand what your horse is ready for and how to cope with him on the rebuild-days when he should not be tracked.

Ideally, the first option is preferable. It is the best for you and the horse. I realize that it is not always possible for you to keep the horse at home and ship-in. There are many *Backyard Racehorse* advocates. Contact each other when you are working with the logistics of track training and need some help. Cooperation between people with the same mind set works . . . even though we frequently feel we can do things better by ourselves.

I am continuously increasing the list of trainers and farms that work with my program. This list can be obtained through the *Backyard Racehorse Forum*. **As the Forum grows, we will network our information and have a solid base of Backyard Trainers.** You can reach us at backyardracehorseforum.com.

Backyard Racehorse Forum is a network for Backyard Owners and Trainers.

FIRST OPTION - WEEKEND HAULERS

If you live in the North, you should plan to start your horse on the track in the spring. It's no fun to be hauling or aggressively riding in cold, dangerous weather. Always accommodate your training schedule to the weather. Training in snowy country will be more erratic than in warmer climates. Those of you who live where weather is not a factor, can aim to breeze your horse at the track in November or December of the two-year-old year. If you are in the last phase of training and ride every fifth or sixth day and free round-pen in between, the horse will be ready to go to the track.

Here in Florida, I have my horses ready when the track opens in December. Northern horses will be a little older when they first visit the racetrack, as they will be in their three-year-old year. This is fine. You want your horse to last, so you give him growing time. You are not in a rush. You want your horse to run as a three, four and five-year-old. **You forego the early two-year-old money and the early two-year-old breakdown.**

When your horse is doing three aggressive breezes within the three mile route, he can go to the track. It is time to begin the official breezes and works. **To work and to breeze are specific track terms** which are almost interchangeable . . . but a breeze is slightly less aggressive than a work. A work should be challenging but not as hard as the ultimate test, the race. **To breeze the horse means to let him run as fast as he can,** kissing to him and encouraging him, **but not hitting him.** He should be a tad under his absolute top speed. **To work the horse means to ask and "drive" or hit him.** A trainer will have his horse work with another horse in a pretend race. Many horses are redlined in their works and are tuckered out for the race. If it looks like the rider is asking for everything the horse has, that is a hard work. An honest willing horse will give you everything he has even in a breeze. He is eager to please unless he has had a bad experience while running. Then he may hold back and refuse to try at all. That is why **I like the animal to grow into his or her speed.**

Works are done at the track. At **such high speed it is dangerous to try a work at home. You may be breezing your horse at home as long as you have safe, clear stretches on your route.** Works are generally picked up by the official track clocker. He can tell when a rider is "setting" a horse down and will "pick him up at the poles" and time the speed of the horse for each furlong. Some trainers don't want the clocker to pick up the time. They try to sneak a horse in very early when it is dark or the track is very busy. It doesn't usually work. The clockers in Florida are astute. They can recognize a horse by the way it goes and they don't miss many works. The clocker then asks the rider the name of the horse as he heads back to the barn. If the rider or trainer purposely gives the wrong name, he can be fined. The clocker turns in the sheet of timed works to the office. The times are then printed in the *Daily Racing Form* so the public has access to the information. **You need at least two official works in order to start your horse the first time.** This requirement may vary from state to state. Check the regulations in your area.

The track trainer will tell you the ground rules at his track. You need guidance with the logistics . . . what time you can arrive to work out in the morning . . . how long you can

**When your horse is ready for the track
let him go!**

stay in the receiving barn . . . whether he has an open stall that you can use over night and so on.

You must establish your relationship with the track trainer. Most of them are used to having complete control of the horse and charging you day money. A track trainer willing to work with you as a ship-in is invaluable. As a ship-in, you interrupt the trainer's schedule. But, if you are willing to pay, the trainer will find the time to work with you. You can offer him a flat fee for the mornings he works with you. He will coordinate getting a rider and will help you with any logistical problems that arise. If he is interested and willing to run your horse, negotiate his piece of the purse. A good trainer's cooperation will help you greatly. Listen to him, learn all you can from him. Hopefully, he will establish a good working relationship with you. You can't even get into the backside of the racetrack without the trainer signing in you and your horse. He carries insurance and is responsible for your horse while he is at the track. The trainer's overhead is high. Take this into consideration when negotiating the relationship.

You now have a trainer who has agreed to work with you and your horse is ready to go. The first time your horse visits the track, it should be a getting acquainted trip. Your trainer should arrange for a rider who can spend plenty of time with your horse. Pay the rider double the going rate and he will take the extra time necessary to familiarize your horse with all the new experiences at the track.

As the rider takes a few turns around the shedrow, your horse will see the everyday hustle and bustle. With his stirrups long, the rider should then take the horse to the track and jog him the wrong direction on the outer rail for the circumference of the track. During the ride your horse will see horses galloping by. All he is expected to do is look around at everything. If the horse becomes agitated or nervous during this first mile, have him do another one. He needs to become comfortable with his new surroundings.

Fractious horses may need a pony for the first trip or two on the track. Your trainer can make whatever arrangements you need. When your horse has

How much water does your horse Drink after a Work?

Real communication is a meeting of the minds.

completed the jog in an acceptable manner without being ponied, the rider should turn the horse around to the right direction, and do a collected gallop the full mile of the track. If the horse gallops well, and the rider finds him capable, the rider will kiss to him and allow him to "breeze down the lane" (Home Stretch) during this full-mile gallop.

Stress to the rider that he must not pull up the horse sharply after the finish line. He must let the horse gallop out as far as he wants to go. If the horse wants to gallop out another full mile, so be it. The horse will slow down on his own when he is tired and "come back to the rider" (*Backyard Racehorse* term for allowing the horse to slow down when he is ready . . . we should have been doing this all along in our buildup gallops.)

The way your horse handles this first trip tells you if he is fit if he is not too green about the new environment. Some horses are so busy looking around they don't apply themselves to the run at all. Your horse should want to run since you have been galloping him a strong three miles. This first session should have allowed the horse to expend enough energy to slightly stress his system. When he returns to the barn, watch how long it takes for him to get his breath back, and observe how he drinks water while he is cooling down. If he only takes a few sips, you probably didn't stress him much. If he sticks his head in the bucket and tries to guzzle the water, you know he wasn't fit enough for the work he did and might be over stressed. According to an article in the August 2002 issue of the *Horse Journal,* "...Giving cold water does not cause founder or colic, although it may cause temporary discomfort... but your horse will prefer, and should have, cool rather than warm water after work on a hot day."

Never be afraid to ask why things are done if they don't make sense. Be strong enough to do what you know is right - even if others think you are nuts. A good example is the simple task of keeping a hot horse moving after a work or race. Sometimes they come into the barn breathing so heavily they're almost shaking. The grooms, set on ritual, stop the horse, take off the bridle and bathe him before giving him a few rounds to settle down, catch his breath and start to relax.

I've seen horses tie-up with this kind of routine. Yet, the grooms think I'm crazy when I walk my horse around with the bridle on until I feel he's settled enough to take it off. There is little time for the animal to adjust from high speed on the track to static slow walking around the barn. Some believe this causes lactic acid buildup in muscles. The further your barn is from the track on the backside, the better for your horse's cooling out process.

There are many rituals on the track that go against everything we know about exercise physiology and preparing a sound fit racehorse. Transfer all your common sense horse knowledge to the track. Your horses will be better for it.

It is common for the horse to **cord-up** with his first works. Actually, anytime he tries too hard and is not fit enough, this can happen. **Cording-up** means that his back muscles are

Continue to turn out and monitor.

over strained. As you cool him out after the breeze or work, you will see a tightness along his back. Ask your trainer or groom to show you what to look for so that you understand. Make sure you note in the chart that he **corded-up. Do not increase** the distance of his breeze until he returns with a normal back. As far as treatment goes . . . I cannot overemphasize rebuild-days with turnout and movement until he is bright and bounding again. I have never had to give medications for cording-up. I allow rest and then try again!

Listen to the rider. He may say the horse tired fast or was very strong and didn't seem tired at all by the experience. Remember what the rider says, and when you get home dutifully note the information on the horse's chart.

Monitor his legs the next morning, as you have done throughout this program. It should not surprise you if you find some congestion around the ankles. It is a very typical reaction the first time the horse is on a hard surface. Observe everything about your horse . . . how he eats . . . what his attitude is . . . how his limbs look. Turn him out as you usually do and record everything. On each successive rebuild-day, observe, check, and note. By the fourth rebuild-day, he should be eating normally and his legs should be fine. If they are not, let him rest until they are.   By this time, he should be feeling good and want to frolic. The stress of this work should have triggered his endorphins and he should be rebounding and feeling high.

During this time, free round-penning for 15 or 20 minutes to get him in a good sweat should be enough on the rebuild-days.

Six or seven days later, go back to the track. Have the rider jog the horse or walk him the wrong direction around the track again... the full mile so he can again see everything. **Then have him turn the horse around at the finish line and let him gallop strongly and openly a full mile, breezing him down the lane. He must allow the horse to continue past the finish line until he slows down and "comes back to the rider."** We are trying to bridge the speed spurts from Phase III into solid five and six furlong works.

Horses should never be pulled up hard after the finish line when they are really rolling. Pulling up hard is very dangerous. It causes a great deal of tying-up,

**The rider can give you a candid opinion
of your horse's behavior.**

because the body doesn't have time to eliminate the lactic acid in a normal fashion. Always permit the horse to keep moving until he settles down.

Think about an Olympic Sprinter. When he crosses the finish line, he doesn't just stop. He jogs beyond the finish line and continues to move to avoid severe leg cramps. A similar phenomenon happens to your horse when he does a hard push. Lactic acid builds up in his muscles due to oxygen debt.

This introduction to the track is very logical. **It teaches your horse that he will always be asked to run down the lane.** He learns **that the finish line never changes but that the starting gates do.** (The gates are moved around the track so that no matter where the race starts, **it always finishes in the same place . . . in front of the grandstand.) You learn how fit your horse is by how far beyond the finish line he carries out the work.** You see whether he really needs a lot of warm-up before a race by observing whether he is running faster in his work or breeze down the lane or whether he runs early and is tired by the time he hits the home stretch. The pattern of an early run or a late run will begin to emerge.

The rider will tell you if your horse is stronger after the finish line and wants to run long, or whether he wants to run early and not be rated. The track trainer's observations are very important to you.

After this second trip to the racetrack, you repeat the same routine as after the first trip. If all goes well, consider sending your horse to the gates on the third trip. You can begin to get him used to the process. The first time send him to the gates after he has done his breezes. He should be tired and easier to handle. He can also be cooling down as he walks from the track to the gates. The crew will have the rider stand the horse in the gates and then gallop or walk him out. It will depend on what the horse is capable of doing. After a few lessons, the horse should be ready to break from the gates. Now you can have him do an easy mile gallop. Then take him to the gates to break and breeze. This will enable you to get timed works as well as the gate card.

When the Starter (head of the gate crew) thinks the horse breaks well, he will give you a gate card. Put your confidence in the gate crew and heed their advice. They have had tremendous experience and will know how to handle your horse.

One thing to watch for at the gate! Some jockeys just hold the reins. When the horse leaps out, the jockey may try to maintain his balance with the reins. The bit **jerks the horse's mouth** just when we are trying to teach him to break efficiently. If the poorly trained jockey does this a few times, the horse will learn to connect leaping out of the gate with a hard yank on his mouth. Soon, even if the jockey doesn't yank, the horse will throw his head up in anticipation of the yank. This will distract him and he will not break efficiently. Tell the jockey to **hang on to mane and rein** when breaking. A pull on the mane in no way inhibits the horse's head or keeps him from breaking properly. Watch your exercise boy or jockey at the gates. **Don't allow bad habits!**

As you progress you will see a change in the horse. He will start anticipating the track and the breezing. **Have him learn to put his energy into the gallop at the track if he gets overanxious.** By the third or fourth trip, when the horse knows what the racetrack

**You should now have a gate card and
be doing fairly tight works.**

After a few trips to the Track, shins may get sore!

is all about, it is probably not necessary to do the mile jog the wrong way. **Tell the rider to back up to the wire (go the wrong direction around the track to the finish line), turn around and immediately go into a strong gallop and breeze four furlongs down the lane.** Have him permit the horse to gallop out as previously explained. If the horse comes out of the four furlong breeze well and recovers well, on the next trip ask for five furlongs. If he does this well, have him breeze out of the gates the next trip. If he handles each challenge well, continue to increase the distance and/or speed until you get a good five or six furlong in a time acceptable to race. The trainer will tell you about times and conditions on the track. He will tell you about your horse's work as compared to others at the track.

To get an idea of whether your horse is breezing or working viably, look at the clocker's sheet or racing form on the date you last worked your horse. Compare your horse's time and distance to the other horses on the list. If your horse is two seconds slower than average, he needs to be tighter. Work the same distance next week and see if he can go faster. If he improves, step up his distance.

At this point, you have shipped-in to the track once a week for approximately six to eight weeks, and free round-penned for 15 to 20 minutes every third or fourth day at home. **Do not turn out your horse the day before a race or a work.** Stall him that day and night. It will give him an edge.

Do you have your gate card? A gate card is the official permission from the Starter, stating that your horse has been schooled and has broken from the gate in an acceptable manner.

If your horse's shins are going to be sore, they may start now. Don't get upset if they do. Look at the Section on Bucked Shins and proceed from there. Remember,

Watch how he recovers before challenging him again.

bucked shins are a common set back, not the end of the world. This is why the farm is so much better than the track. You have time to allow the judicious healing of Bucked Shins. **Treat them cautiously. When they improve, continue training.**

Once you have a strong five furlong work, with a strong gallop after the finish line, look for a race. Many trainers like to work a horse until he's perfect before they enter him in a race. Not me. **I use the first four races as part of the training process. I consider them the last four works.** Accept that it may take about four races for the horse to learn to break well, run straight and begin the concentration necessary to become a useful racehorse.

After four races, the horse should be well, fit and running as honestly as he can. You will have to judge whether he got a good break and had a good position before you can determine what kind of horse he is. There is some fine tuning that goes on at this point. Your trainer will help you with these things. He might feel that the horse needs blinkers. Many trainers put them on automatically. I personally wait to see if they are needed. Let the horse go with as little equipment as possible. **Aids like blinkers, stronger bits, and tongue ties should be used only when necessary.** Rely on the advice of your track trainer - if the advice makes sense to you. If it doesn't make sense, question it. Ask why he recommends things and try to think from the horse's point of view. Always try to help your horse. Read the Section on Setbacks.

Remember to **continue monitoring your horse.** See how he is the day after works and races. Monitor his legs, see how he's eating, observe his attitude and write it all down in his chart.

 Know your horse.

TRACK BREEZES

The first time or two, go the wrong direction a full mile to give the horse time to see all activity before galloping. Have the rider use long stirrups!

Beginning at <u>finish line</u> (after wrong direction mile), gallop horse in right direction.

At top of <u>Stretch</u>, kiss to horse and <u>Breeze</u> to <u>finish line!</u>
Let horse continue Breeze and <u>Come Back</u> to rider.
> (This way you don't inhibit a fit horse from getting the exercise he needs!)

He may <u>Breeze</u> a <u>furlong</u> or <u>two beyond finish line</u>
keep timing and see where the horse slows down.

OBSERVE:
> Where horse tires -
> How long it takes to cool -
> How much water he drinks
> -

Next Trip to Track

Begin the same - Then Breeze 3 furlongs from finish line.
Let horse continue Breeze beyond finish line (if he can).

Each Successive Work or Breeze

Extend the length of Breeze and/or Tighten the Speed.

Only go <u>further - faster</u> if horse is <u>healthy</u> and <u>sound!</u>

A little more...
a little faster!

a little fitter!

Typical Chart Notes
Trip #1 Breezed 2 furlongs in 24
Trip #2 Breezed 3 furlongs in 39
Trip #3 Breezed 3 furlongs in 37
Trip #4 Breezed 4 furlongs in 52
Trip #5 Breezed 4 furlongs in 50
(Continue until you have 6 furlongs in 1:18 or so.)

RULES OF THE TRACK -

TRAFFIC PATTERNS WHEN GALLOPING
WHO MAY GALLOP ON THE TRACK?

Many people are not aware that there are rules and regulations as to who may gallop on the race track and how they earn the right to gallop.
Some trainers, if they have their trainer's license, may ride their own horses at the track. The best preparation for galloping at the track is to gain experience galloping at training farms. Usually with the guidance of the trainer at a large farm, a rider can learn to adjust his style to the riding necessary at the track. Breaking babies and graduating to riding them is good prep work for an aspiring exercise rider. I always like to get riders that have had a strong hunter jumper or event riding background. This kind of experience gives the riders confidence and their knowledge and horsemanship is usually extensive.

Training farms want reliable skilled riders who can give FORWARD MOTION AND BOLDNESS to the young horses. If the rider is competent, the farm may take him to the racetrack to do the early gallops. After the horse is familiar with the track activity and heavier traffic, the trainer usually asks a jockey to breeze the young horse.

All early "getting to know the track" experience is better done with the exercise rider. He or she may be heavier, and have more time than a working jockey. He can teach the horse the manners of the track and take the extra time to straighten out quirks and bad habits before the trainer asks the jockey to do the faster speed works. If the exercise rider is not on your payroll, he usually gets a flat fee for getting on a horse. If you are asking him to take more time with your horse than average, make sure you pay him extra. He earns according to how many horses he ride.

If you are training and galloping your own horses on the farm, it is important to learn how the horses must transition from farm work to track work. If you have been galloping in a field, on a clay road, etc., anywhere but on a training track, you probably have a good trail horse who is sensible in relation to his environment. He has a good basic foundation in going over different surfaces but has not had speed work. He might tuck his head in and give at the poll. Once he has learned the basic training and hopefully has achieved a level of aerobic work, it is time to encourage him to extend out and gallop with speed. In most instances this must be done at a training track or a racetrack.

Speed has the rail!

Skilled riders make a horse go forward.

A time or two on the track is necessary for the horse to learn the pattern… how and where to run. The first few times he is on the track, he may not realize the rail is his point of reference. The horse must learn how to run and hold his position in relation to the inner rail. Activity at the track is rather ritualistic. It is important that you as the rider or the trainer, know the rules and customs at the racetrack.

When going on to a racetrack, there is usually a gap for entering and another for leaving it. It is important to be aware of the location of the gates and the hours they are working in the morning. If the entrance in is near where the horses break, the traffic and speed works may be zooming by your green horse when he is getting accustomed to the track. It is good experience for him to handle the activity and listen to the rider. Remember that the finish line always stays the same and the starting gates move around to accommodate the different distances of the races. Therefor you always want your horse to have a strong kick down the lane to the finish line. From the very beginning, have him used to breezing or working his fastest at that part of the track. Horses are creatures of habit and can learn useful patterns that will help them in the heat of the race.

Because you are shipping in, it is doubly important to make the practices consistent and the experiences positive. When galloping on the track, speed always has the rail. Slower horses should be in the middle and outside. Faster horses will pass on the inside and generally their riders will shout and warn you if you are blocking them. If your horse shows insecurity his first time or two with all the action, then it would be good to have him accompanied with a pony horse. Going backwards on the outside rail at a walk or jog is customary and a good idea so the horse may look around. If he handles that well, turn him around and have him gallop in the right direction (to the left). Try to imprint the habit of running the hardest from the top of the stretch to the finish line… that is how the race is won! To take the horse to the gates, the approach is important. Depending on where the gates are in the morning, the horse may gallop around the track to them in the right direction or the rider may "back him up to the gates" by going at a walk or trot on the outside rail in the opposite direction. A rider may have trouble pulling up a horse that has galloped the right way to the gates. It is important to know how controllable your horse is and work with his personality.

If you are shipping in, you want to teach as much as possible while your horse is there. After a breeze, the horse may go to the gates and stand and trot out the first few visits at the track. As he is learning the patterns for running he is also learning how to break from the gates. It is good to have him gain the gate experience over a period of time. Don't just

Make the track experience positive.

go to the track, breeze or work the horse then, when he is fast enough, start thinking about the gates... the track training should combine all of lessons necessary for winning races. Most jockeys and exercise riders allow the horse to look around when he first enters the track. The intelligent horses quickly learn patterns and like to see what's going on before they are rushed to their work. When leaving the track, the rider stops, turns the horse around to face the track before leaving through the exit gap. This is so the animal doesn't learn to dash out the minute he knows he is going back to the barn.

An important role of the out rider is catching loose horses, helping control fractious horses, and in general, being there for any emergency on the track. That's just what they do in the morning. In the afternoon the outrider is the spiffy looking person leading the post parade in front of the grandstand. He is usually dressed in a red hunting jacket or vest with white pants and black boots. He is again there to help the riders with unruly horses. When the horses break from the gates, he is ready to control any problems. After the race is over and the horses fly by the finish line, you'll see the out rider on the other side of the track to catch the horses that don't want to stop for their riders. The out riders learn which horses are problems and they are ready for them. The outrider is in constant contact with the Stewards and security via radio-telephone. After a race a jockey can make any claims of interference or objections about the race to the outrider who then transmits it to the Stewards. As a trainer, I have found the out riders to be a tremendous source of advice and help on the track. They have a huge responsibility and must be skilled and reliable horsemen. If you are just beginning your on-track riding experience, learn from these experts!

If you as a rider, have not had track experience, don't assume you know everything. Gain experience on training farms or with patient trainers at the track. You might start out ponying for your trainer and that way you help him and learn at the same time. There is nothing like apprenticing with a knowledgeable person. Work for free and try to understand why certain routines are used... don't think you know it all... respect what is done... and then see how it fits into your goals and aspirations in the racing industry.

When you get to the real race track, introduce yourself and be open to any advice the outriders may give you. Remember - he is your best friend when you're on a runaway horse!

Pony horses are a big help until your horse is comfortable on the Track!

ADVICE FROM THE OUTRIDERS:

LEARN THE "RULES OF THE ROAD" AT THE TRACK

LEARN HOW TO ENTER AND LEAVE THE TRACK PROPERLY

SPEED ALWAYS HAS THE INSIDE RAIL

NEVER PULL UP IN THE MIDDLE OF THE TRACK OR IN FRONT OF HORSES - VEER TO THE OUTSIDE AND SLOW DOWN

BEFORE YOU MAY GALLOP ON THE TRACK - YOU MUST BE APPROVED BY THE OUTRIDERS AND STEWARDS

APPROVED HELMETS AND SAFETY VESTS ARE REQUIRED.

The "Outrider" is like the Traffic Cop

Experts give the expert advice.

Cowboys on the Race Track -
the Rough Riders of the Backside

The day I saw Todd Reynolds in the kitchen of Tampa Bay Downs, he was trying to decide which knee was more in need of his only knee brace. He is 34 years old and ready to hang up his spurs. For years Todd has been one of the "cowboys" on the backside. Trainer Ron Jerdee recommended him when I was having a problem with a horse. The horse wouldn't gallop out and I was getting over the hill and not able to argue with the stout gelding. "Todd can ride anything - and he's kind to them. - he doesn't get onto them unless they are really trying to be bad.!"

I left the horse with Todd for some work. That's what he does. He takes horses that aren't fitting into the program and tries understand and solve their problem. Some horses have "stage fright" when going onto the track. Instead of getting progressively better with each trip in, they get worse. In that case, it may be better for the horse to spend some time at the track.

Todd has worked with problem horses for years. He is also the outrider at the track. He is a real horse trainer who likes to train roping horses. The thoroughbreds are tough. He says it takes 6 Advil to get him moving in the morning. He has decided to stick roping horses. I was sorry to hear that as Todd knows his business. But anyone dealing with horses will reach a point where it's time to call it quits. Todd doesn't bounce back like he used to, so its time.. He's still riding but is a little more selective.

If you want to find the "cowboys" on the backside of a track, the best person to ask is the outrider. He sits out there all morning watching the different riders handle their mounts. He knows the good riders, the bad riders, and the great riders - the ones who manage to get difficult horses to comply and obey in spite of themselves.

Lance Cronk is another true race tracker. His dad was a trainer. So Lance grew up with horses. He's been riding saddle broncs for fifteen years (says bareback broncs, which he used to rider are too hard on the body). He has handles problem horses like a horse whisperer. He works with them from the ground first to make sure there is some communication before he rides them.

One filly had been through three other colt breakers before she came to him. She was "beat up pretty bad" and it took him a long time to make friends. She had been knocked around and it took him days to get close enough to her head to put on the bridle. Since Lance also makes and repairs saddles, he was able to fashion a special bridle for her. He made a four foot strap to go around her head. Then he would ease it up from behind the neck to finally buckle the headstall to the bit. He had to add straps to the bit that hung down so he could attach a shank to the straps. She wasn't letting anyone near her! He then started slowly taught her to trust him.

She is doing well and has been sent back to the trainer with the suggestion that a girl handle her . Lance feels that girls can be kinder. He also suggested that the same girl handle her all the time to build confidence and security. He sounds like a horse psychiatrist doesn't he? Lance feels most horses aren't born bad, they're just mishandled. People let them get

Horses aren't born bad, they're mishandled.

into bad habits. He says you have to "outsmart" them or "out stout" them". His other motto is, "Never start a battle you can't finish." He doesn't like to see an animal beaten, but recognizes that they must be out ridden. Otherwise they learn that they can do what they want. Many horsemen aren't good enough to outride tough horses. That's when we need the cowboys like Lance. He likes the horses and loves what he is doing.

If you're standing at the rail at Tampa in the morning, you can't miss Pete Cimini. He is larger than most of the riders out there. His leggings are adorned with a skull and crossbones. He's called "spider man" because his legs long, but he like his stirrups short. He exudes confidence on every horse he rides. Those rough horses have to think twice before trying to drop him. Horses that he considers tough prop and wheel. They gallop along as good as gold, then suddenly stop dead and heel fast. That can drop the best of riders. The jockeys don't like to ride that kind of horse and they can't afford to be hurt trying to straighten them out. Pete can save the day with "non-compliant" horses, . Trainers pay him double the going rate to ride them. He is worth every cent. He is still going strong and seems to relish the challenge. Pete rides in the morning and works the gates in the afternoon. He is the outrider at in Delaware Park.

Cindy Patrick is the best female cowboy I know. Even the male chauvinists on the backside say she is one tough lady. The problem is you'll never be able to get her on your horses because she runs her own stable with her husband, Gary Patrick. We all need a Cindy in our barn. How did Gary get so lucky? I'm told she gets up, makes him breakfast, changes the baby, goes out and tacks up 8 horses and loads them in the trailer Then she and Gary haul over to Tampa to work them. They are often in the receiving barn early. While I'm waiting for the riders to come out and get on my four horses. Cindy gallops, cools and waters EIGHT horses. All before the break! (I'm lucky to get two out!) Oh yes, Gary is there, and he does pitch in to cool a horse or two. I asked him what he contributes and he looked at me wisely and said, "I'm thinking all the times. Thinking - that's work too!" They are very successful as a team.

Cowboy
Pete

He
rides
the
Tough ones!

Leave difficult horses to the cowboys,

RACE DAY
from Handbook for Thoroughbred Owners of California

Not many people, in the course of their lives, get to experience the "highs" of anticipation, expectation and sheer glamour that this day provides for the thoroughbred racehorse owner. Depending on the size of your stable, furthermore, this is a thrill that recurs every few days to few weeks. Whether your horse wins, finishes in the money, or simply runs a good race, the experience of this day, for a horseman, is LIVING.

Your trainer and the barn staff will be intensely living the excitement along with you, from the moment they awaken. The horse, if it has raced before, will soon know "what day it is"; unusual things happen.

First, the racer will get a "light" breakfast at about daybreak - and the trainer will check to see if he or she "ate up," that is, felt fit and finished all the feed. The trainer will take the horse's temperature, just to make sure nothing is amiss. At some early hour, the Official (State) Veterinarian will be by for a pre-race examination.

The vet will run experienced hands down the horse's forelegs, checking for signs of swelling or heat. He will ask the groom to walk the horse back and forth, to check for soreness or "favoring" (and in some cases, will ask to see the horse briefly trotted or jogged right there at the barn). Finally, he will check the tattoo on inside of the thoroughbred's upper lip and make sure it matches the official Jockey Club Registration number assigned to the horse's name.

At some point in the morning, the horse may be walked - or perhaps jogged or galloped on the track for a few minutes - for a warm-up. (Horses are never "worked" on race day.) After that, and a bath, the horse will be muzzled to keep it from any further eating. Like all professional athletes, it will do better in competition on a light stomach.

If the horse is a known "bleeder," the trainer's vet will come by about 4 hours before race time and inject it with no more than 5 ccs of diuretic - Lasix and/ or Premarin. This is a completely legal drug (in proper doses) which will lower the horse's blood pressure and reduce the risk of bleeding from the small, thin-walled capillaries of its nose, throat and lungs under the stress of hard running.

The only other kind of medication permitted in a horse's bloodstream on race day is a small quantity of one of four "legal" anti-inflammatories - usually phenylbutazone, or "bute" - which will be indicated in The Racing Form with a capital "B" in the horse's running lines (though all the anti-inflammatories are indicated with a "B"). Some trainers, in addition, will have the horse stand in a foreleg ice-bath for up to 90 minutes to relieve any nagging discomfort that might distract it from running its best race.

This information applies to California tracks.
Check your track's information before you arrive

Now is when the trainer and assistant trainer -and the owner, if you have been at the barn that morning - go to change into more formal wear for the festivities ahead.

An hour or less before the designated race time, your trainer will receive the "20 minute call," summoning your horse to the Receiving Barn for a final "walk-by" witnessed by the Official Veterinarian. The Horseshoe Inspector will check to see that your horse's shoes are legal (i.e., "stickers" are sometimes not permitted) and in good condition. An official called the Horse Identifier will again verify the horse's lip tattoo, as well as its color and markings, against its file - a Jockey Club Registration certificate and photographs.

After that, your trainer, the trainer's assistant, your horse and its handler will go to the saddling paddock, where it will come under the watchful jurisdiction of the Racing Veterinarian. At this point, the Paddock Judge will check and note the gear your trainer has brought for your horse.

There are a half-dozen or more bits which may be used to curb a horse's tendency to drift in or out. A tongue-tie is used to be sure the horse's tongue won't obstruct its air passage. Blinkers, hood-goggles, and even earmuffs are part of racing equipment for many horses: they may keep a flighty or fractious horse's mind on the race. But the use - or decision not to use - of any of these devices must be cleared with the Paddock Judge prior to the race (and in the case of blinkers, prior to the issuance of the Overnights). Finally, the jockeys' valets bring out their saddles and help the trainers secure this scant but crucial gear onto the horses.

When the official preparation is over, your trainer finishes with a ritual as old and as beautiful as horse racing itself. For all those who say racing is "just a business," they should witness this moment of highly personal contact, filled with hope, that sends these wondrous athletes into competition: a pat on the neck, sometimes even a kiss, and a few special words whispered in the horse's ear comprise a racing "pep-talk" in a private language. As an owner, these are moments you won't want to miss.

Once in the walking ring, the trainer will often introduce you to your jockey, and then discuss with the jockey what kind of race the horse wants to run or is likely to run. Every eye in the pack of spectators near the saddling paddock will at some point be on your horse, your trainer and you. Up in the stands, fans will be watching to see the horse's "mood," and overlays and underlays to the "morning line" will take place largely as a result of what the fans witness in the walking ring.

Unless your horse is in the first race of the day, you (as the owner) will already have been seated for the race and will now return to your table or box.

At all the major California tracks, the racing associations (by contract with TOC) provide owners of horses racing that day with free admission to the track and usually free Clubhouse or Turf Club seating for the owners' party. The "perks" for such occasions vary in generosity from track to track, and from race to race.

Enjoy the festivities.

At least one day in advance of your horse's race (or as soon as the "Overnights" are published), please remember to contact the track's Owner Liaison and arrange for the complimentary services entitled you. The Liaisons can also help you find suitable accommodations and transportation if you are coming in from out of town for the race. Should you experience any delay or difficulty in making these arrangements, contact the TOC Owners' Liaison at that track for prompt assistance [see Appendices for names and numbers].

Once the trumpet and the post parade and the loading into the gate have been accomplished, the race - from the words "And away they go!" - is likely to become a mighty adrenaline blur (not to mention a surrealistic time-warp) for any devoted owner. Nevertheless, should you see on the monitor or through your binoculars anything that looks like interference (bumping by another horse, or another jockey's whip hitting your horse), you are free to go to any of the Stewards' Hot Lines (or "Quick Lines") and register a protest. Obviously, it's a sound practice to find out where these phones are before the race, since all protests affecting horses "in the money" will necessarily take place in a matter of minutes, if not seconds, after the finish of the race.

Though there is a group of at least three Stewards carefully watching every race - and though they generally have Patrol Judges with walkie-talkies stationed at the 1 / 8th pole, the 3 / 8ths pole and the finish line - any trainer, owner, or riding jockey can still "claim foul" and request a hold on the posting of "Official" results until the Stewards have re-run and studied the race tape to carefully judge the consequences and magnitude of the complaint.

Once the "official" result has been posted, however, the outcome of the race - barring positive drug tests or legitimate contests regarding ownership - will stand, and the purses will be distributed accordingly.

Your horse may win - by a nose, by a length, or by a mile. Don't hesitate! Start down to the Winner's Circle, bringing along whomever you want to help you celebrate, and savor every step. The track photographer will be there to record the scene of your trainer and jockey on and around your winning steed, and you beaming close by. The track's racing association will make available to you (yes, for a price) not only these "winning" photos, but often a videotape of the race, and even a copy of the breathtaking "photo finish," if there was one. You should frame these pictures: you have earned these moments.

(If your horse came in Place or Show, you can also request videotapes of the race to make the purse you have collected even sweeter.)

No matter how your horse finished (provided it was not injured) you will have had a great day... a day that few others on the planet, and only a few score in history, can truly appreciate.

Many thanks to the *Handbook for Thoroughbred Owners of California* for this excerpt.

Congratulations!

Have a great day!

A Word With the Experts On -
Shipping-In - Race/Work and Go.

by Charles M. Bownds

Ship-ins need to understand how the receiving barn functions both for working in the morning and racing in the afternoon. I raced off the farm when I lived in Houston, TX and raced in Louisiana and later when I managed a farm in New Jersey near Blairstown and raced all over the east coast.

The first rule is: **Have your papers ready and current.** This includes health certificate, coggins and, where required, brand inspection papers Having these papers will save you and the track personnel time. Keep them in your vehicle!! You will be upset if you are turned away because your paper work is not in order. Your twelve hour drive means nothing if you arrive without YOUR paper work! The second rule is: Call the Race Office to be sure you can ship in to work and get your stall assignment. The race office will help you. Be courteous to them!

Other rules include such things as having all necessary equipment. Make sure you have water buckets and feed tubs for each horse. To avoid buying extra feed tubs and save space in your trailer use water buckets for feed tubs when you are away from home. You should have a travel box with screw eyes, extra snaps, halters, lead shanks, brushes, hoof picks, etc. Not all racetrack receiving barns have gates. If not, you must have webbing stall gates and any gear needed to confine your horse.

Be sure to have your own muck bucket, pitch fork, rake and broom. DO NOT expect the racetrack to provide you with these items. This year at Tampa Bay Downs some of the ship-ins did not bring the basics such as feed tubs, water buckets etc. for their horses. They expected the racetrack to furnish everything and were furious when that didn't happen.

"Proper" barn ettiquette is turning to the left when you come out of your stall. When leading your horse, continue with the flow of traffic in that direction. If you have to stop while leading your horse, call out, "Hold back!" or tell anyone who might be in harm's way to watch out. Ettiquette includes working with your horse in the stall. Never take a horse out of the stall and cross tie him in the shed row.

Be courteuos to your fellow horsemen. If you are unsure of anything ASK! People will be happy to help you, if you ask. Another problem is litter. It is amazing what has been found in stalls. Receiving barns are not garbage dumps. Do not leave trash such as leg wraps, packaging, coke cans, food, or anything else on the ground or in the stall. Pick up your trash and dispose of it in the proper place. Never dump ice water in the stall. Such behavior will make it very difficult to get a stall next time you need one. You must also be cognizant of time restraints if you shipin to work and go. Be sure to vacate your stall on time and be on your way before the afternoon race ship-ins arrive.

If you have a bedding preference, inform the stallman. He will tell you if there is alternate bedding such as shavings or straw. In California shredded paper and moss are sometimes available. The stallman is there to help you. Talk to him and the folks in the race office. They can't help you if they don't know what you need. If you are not sure of where to go and what to do, you can make a dry run, before your first trip. It is a good time to look around and ask questions.

Best of luck to you. We'll see you at the races.

If a man does not keep pace with his companions, perhaps it is because he hears a different drummer. Let him step to the music which he hears, however measured or far away.

Great Moment in History: From his backyard at Walden Pond, Thoreau becomes the inspiration for GHANDI, MARTIN LUTHER KING JR. AND JANET DEL CASTILLO.

This is a drawing by Pierre Bellocq, the son of "PEB" the cartoonist for the racing form. Pierre and his brother Remi are both talented artists and horsemen.

Pierre and Martine Bellocq have helped when I ship in To Miami - 5 hours away - They have been so Kind - the trips home are long when I don't win (most of the time) Pierre gave this to me on one Trip!

Race Day Grooms

As a ship-in, your needs for a groom are different than the trainers at the track. You will need a groom to "run" your horse. He will take the horse from the receiving barn to the paddock and saddling area. While the trainer saddles the horse for the race with the valet, the groom holds him and then leads him around the walking ring while the trainer, jockey and owner confer about the strategy of the race. The groom holds the horse while the trainer "legs up" the rider and then the groom leads the horse to the track.

After the race the trainer and groom meet the jockey and horse at the finish line. The trainer observes the condition of the horse and listens to the jockey's comments while the groom takes the horse back to the receiving barn and cools him out. Many ship in trainers arrive with their own help to "run" their horses. I certainly did early on. My children helped by being my grooms. Since they have grown up and have lives of their own, I use track help.

You will be lucky if you can get a groom as reliable as Dave Tucker, who has run all of my horses at Tampa for the last few years. He knows my routine and I can go to the front side and have lunch like a real person, knowing that my horse will arrive prepared and ready for his race.

When I arrive to park my trailer and unload my horse, Dave is waiting and helps carry my gear and settle the horse in his assigned stall in the receiving barn. He arranges the tack box by the stall and hangs the equipment the horse will use by the stall door. We review the day's entries - the race the horse will be in, his equipment and whether I want him hosed off various times on the way to the track (I take advantage of the hoses provided along the way to the track. This helps keep the horse feeling fresh in spite of the Florida heat.)

Dave usually "runs" various horses from the receiving barn and stays with them while the vet comes around to check them before the race. Most racetracks expect your horse to be with a handler while in the receiving barn so it is good to have a regular reliable person like Dave.

When I am ready to head home, Dave has the equipment back in my trailer with the bridle and blinkers rinsed and hung properly in the tack compartment. He has made my days at the track much more comfortable, even though I haul my own horse there. With good help you can really enjoy racing!

Grooms for ship-ins can cost as little as $10 or $15 if you do most of the work. Usually I pay between $30 and $50 per horse depending on whether he goes to the spit box or not. Check the going rates at the track and pay accordingly. You don't want to be suckered by anyone but you don't want to underpay either.

When a groom runs two or three horses in a day, he may make more than the trainer.

A Word With the Experts On -
THE PROFESSIONAL GROOM
by Ted Landers

One of the most important occupations on the racetrack and farm is that of the professional groom. A "professional" in any field is defined as: engaged in, or worthy of the standards of a profession. The ultimate success of any racing stable depends on the men and women who are employed as professional grooms. They are truly the unsung heroes of horse racing. The groom as caretaker is directly responsible for the daily care of the horse under the supervision of the trainer. The basic, fundamental quality of a good groom is his or her love for horses.

This fondness for horses is what makes the required hard work and long hours tolerable, even enjoyable. Without this love and compassion for the animals, a groom quickly becomes unproductive, careless, and irritable with the horses. Trainers do not want an employee who does not care what happens to the horses and does the minimum amount of work necessary to continue drawing a paycheck. They would much rather hire a person who respects and appreciates the horses.

A good groom should exhibit the following characteristics:
*possess a genuine love for the horses.
*take pride in the work as well as the overall appearance and condition of the horses.
*be punctual, trustworthy, and maintain a neat, clean appearance during the working hours.
*never smoke or drink alcoholic beverages around the stable during working hours.
*communicate with both horses and fellow workers in a quiet, pleasant voice.
*refrain from using offensive language around the stable during working hours.
* be willing to work long hours if circumstances require it.
*keep the trainer or assistant trainer informed of any changes in the well-being of the horses.

A person who possesses all of these characteristics will do much to promote the physical condition and attitude of a horse, making the trainer's (and the groom's) job easier and more rewarding. It is highly unlikely that the trainer will experience much success with a horse that is constantly nervous and irritable due to its handlers. However, if a horse is healthy and content, a trainer can expect that horse to perform at its peak on the racetrack.

A good groom should make a sincere effort to understand each horse in his or her care. Good communication is the key to a successful relationship between the groom and the horse. Most of the problems which a groom encounters can be avoided with a little background knowledge about how horses think and react to their environments. Understanding why a horse acts a certain way will help the groom decide how to react in an appropriate and professional manner. An inexperienced horse person may make the mistake of trying to impose human behavior on horses. This misunderstanding is not only useless, it can sometimes be dangerous. Horses are noble creatures, but their behavior is not

 A good groom is a tremendous asset.

based on the same logic or instincts as human behavior. The average adult horse has the approximate intelligence of a three-year-old child. Therefore, a good handler should be just as patient with a horse as he or she would be with a young child.

Like humans, horses vary in mentality and personality. They have many moods and individual reactions to situations which they encounter every day. They are also creatures of habit and become very upset, both emotionally and physically, if their daily routines are changed. Horses have very long memories, especially for experiences of pain or fear. A domesticated horse's long memory for bad experiences can be quite exasperating for a trainer because it can result in bad habits.

In fact, almost every bad habit a horse has acquired can be traced to a human being. A good groom should always respond to a horse's behavior with calm, gentle understanding. The duties of the professional groom consist of many skills and tasks. It is the basic duty of every groom to provide for the well-being of every horse trusted in their care. The groom should notify the trainer or assistant trainer of any changes in the horse's personality or physical health.

The basic skills of a professional groom include the following:

GROOMING - There are various methods of grooming horses, but whatever system is used, it should be efficient. The following grooming method is used successfully by many professional grooms at the racetrack and farm. Gently wipe the horse's entire body with a *rub rag* to remove dust and visible soil. With the *rubber curry comb* used in a circular motion bring the ground-in soil, dead and loose hair as well as dandruff to the surface of the body. Utilize the rubber curry comb on the body excluding the legs and head. The rubber curry comb may be irritable to some horses in these areas. With the *soft body brush* and the *stiff dandy brush* whisk away the soil, hair and dandruff brought to the surface of the body coat by the rubber curry comb. With the *stiff dandy brush* be sure to brush the mane and tail to remove bedding and debris. After grooming the body with the rubber curry comb and brushes the final step is to rub the entire body with the *rub rag* to bring out a glossy shine to the coat. It is the duty of every groom to properly care for the horse's feet on a daily basis. This includes using a *hoof pick* to remove manure and soil from the bottom of the feet. The feet are also washed with warm water and a sponge, and dried with a clean towel. All grooming tools should be cleaned with hot water, soap and a mild disinfectant on a daily basis.

CLEANING STALLS (MUCKING) - The goal of cleaning a horse's stall is to remove the soiled bedding and replace it with clean dry bedding material. Stalls may be bedded with either straw, wood shavings, sawdust or peat moss. The choice of bedding depends on cost, availability and personal preference of the trainer. The bedding should be deep enough to provide comfort to the horse and to keep the horse as clean as possible.

The groom is required to completely clean the stall once a day. This is usually done in the morning when the horse is out on the track for exercise or walking around the barn. In the afternoon the groom is required to simply *"freshen -up"* the stall by removing the visible piles of manure and urine as well as giving the horse fresh water and hay. The groom must transport the manure and soiled bedding to a manure pit or designated area outside the barn. The groom may use a *wheelbarrow, muck basket* or a *muck sack* to remove the soiled bedding from the barn.

A good groom has many skills.

Racetrack officials provide for the removal of the manure from these designated areas throughout the backstretch. Normally a groom is required to care for at least three horses therefore they may be required to clean three stalls on a daily basis. They may also be asked to assist other grooms in cleaning stalls especially if a horse is scheduled to race. They may be asked to pitch-in when another groom is off or on vacation, out of town with a horse or simply out sick.

TACKING - Preparing a horse properly for exercise or a race requires a certain amount of skill and attention to detail. Not only must the groom know how to put on the horse's tack, he or she must be able to fit each article correctly to the horse, so that the equipment is effective and safe. Tack usually consists of a saddle and bridle and may include a running martingale, blinkers, and a noseband . The groom who knows the exercise schedule knows what equipment each horse needs. While it is normally the trainer's responsibility to make sure the horse is properly turned out for a race, it is the groom's job to see that the horse is correctly equipped for exercise. Poorly-fitted tack can cause a horse to perform badly. The stable supplies its employees with the necessary saddle and bridle. It would be unusual to have a saddle and bridle for each individual horse in the stable. In a stable that has a large number of horses it is not uncommon for the horses to go out to the track in sets. Each set may consist of 2 -10 horses depending on the total number of horses in the stable. Therefore it is not uncommon for the groom to wait and use the tack from a horse in an earlier set. Tack varies depending on the type of exercise a horse will be performing. For example, if a horse is scheduled for a fast breeze, a running martingale may be eliminated from the usual equipment and blinkers may be added.

The groom is in charge of tacking up the horse when the trainer has scheduled the horse to go to the track for exercise. Tack up the horse with all of the equipment prescribed by the trainer, including a tongue tie and any track bandages which may be required. Then, if the rider is not ready, the groom will walk the horse around the shedrow until the rider is ready to mount. When the horse returns from the track after exercise, the groom is required to remove the tack and bandages from the horse.

WASHING THE RACEHORSE

During its racing career, a racehorse must be washed on a daily basis, and the groom is responsible for this task. Usually, the groom has an assistant who holds the horse during the washing process.

There are several reasons for washing a horse:
. to maintain the health of the skin.
. to remove dirt and sweat.
. to reduce body temperature to normal after exercising or racing.

It should be understood that while bathing makes the horse clean, nothing replaces good grooming to get a horse's coat healthy and glossy. Bathing should always compliment grooming as part of maintaining the overall health and appearance of the horse.

Now that racing is a year-round activity, sometimes the racehorse must be washed in cold temperatures. During the winter, or whenever the weather is unusually cold and windy, the horse should be washed indoors if possible. Some barns are equipped with special indoor wash stalls with hot and cold running water. If such facilities are not available, an empty stall may be converted to a wash stall. A heat lamp installed overhead

Good grooming makes a horse shine.

in the stall keeps the horse from getting a chill and aids the stall floor to dry quickly.

If there is no wash stall or no extra stall, and you must wash the horse in its own stall, remove most or all of the bedding before beginning. Be sure to use a minimal amount of water so the floor does not become flooded. When you are finished washing the horse, remove any wet bedding and lay down dry bedding to ensure a fresh, comfortable bed for the horse. The entire washing time should be about 10 minutes and drying time should be about one hour. Obviously, in cold weather it would be better to wash and dry the horse as quickly as possible to avoid any drafts or chill which may cause the horse to become ill.

MISCELLANEOUS DUTIES

Other important duties that are required by the groom on a daily basis include the following:

FEEDING - The groom plays an important role in the feeding process, making sure that the horse's food and water is fresh, that the horses are fed at the same time every day, and that each horse finishes its feed satisfactory.

BANDAGING - There does not have to be anything wrong for a groom to wrap the horse's legs with bandages. Bandages may be used for several different reasons besides medical treatment, including protection and support. The trainer supplies all the bandages for the horses in each groom's care. The groom is responsible for applying the bandages for exercise while the trainer or assistant trainer is responsible for this task when racing. Each groom is responsible for washing and rolling their bandages.

TRANSIT PREPARATION - One of the most important tasks for a groom is preparing a horse for shipping. Shipping horses from racetrack to racetrack, and from farm to farm occurs daily all over the world. The common modes of shipping horses include by airplane, van , or trailer. Horses are prone to injury during shipping, particularly when they are being loaded and unloaded from the transport vehicle. Long trips can also make horses vulnerable to illness. Therefore, it is the duty of the groom to properly prepare horses for shipping so as to avoid illness and injury. The trainer may require some or all of the following equipment:

*shipping boots or bandages on all four legs to protect legs and feet
* head bumper (poll guard) to protect the poll area of the head
* halter wrap to prevent chaffing on the face
* tail wrap to protect the tail hairs during transit
* blanket to prevent a chill during transit
* hay net filled with grass hay to allow the horse to eat during transit

This article tells us about an IDEAL Groom!

HEALTH - A good groom should know each horse well enough to recognize if it is acting abnormally. Careful daily observation of equine behavior is the best way to stay alert to each horse's condition. Under the direction of the trainer and veterinarian the groom may be required to administer medication and treat wounds on a daily basis. The groom should make note of bowel movements, urination, appetite, body wounds ,and the presence of heat on the legs and feet. The groom should also know how to check the horse's vital signs (pulse, temperature and respiration) and verify that all is normal. It is the groom's job to report any early warning signs of problems to their superiors.

A good groom knows his horses.

CLEANING EQUIPMENT - Many trainers have their grooms remove and clean the halters and leather shanks after the morning training and grooming sessions are over. The grooms clean the leather halters and shanks with a leather conditioner and cleaner and polish the brass with a metal polish. After cleaning, the halters and shanks are hung neatly outside each horse's stall door.

After the early morning feed is completed the feed tubs are removed and cleaned thoroughly with clean water. The water buckets are removed from the stall and cleaned as well. During this period the groom may also clean the grooming tools, bandages, saddle cloths, girth covers, stall webbings, wall boxes and storage boxes. Usually the exercise riders will clean the tack including saddles, bridles, martingales, nosebands and breast plates.

CLEANING THE SHEATH AND UDDER - Every professional groom is required to clean the sheath of the male horse and the udder of the female horse on a regular basis. Both these areas are neglected by some caretakers due to the unpleasantness associated with this task. Both the sheath and udder are subject to the accumulation of dead skin, soil and natural body secretions commonly called smegma.

A dirty sheath or udder becomes evident in one or more of the following ways:

  * physical examinations of the sheath ,penis, or udder
  *constant tail rubbing due to itching
  * spraying of urine (male horse only) instead of a steady stream
  *attempts to bite at the sheath or udder

Cleaning the sheath of the male or the udder of the female is a task which should be performed, on average, every two to three months, although the sheath and udder should be checked at least once a month for cleanliness. Cleaning these areas can be included as part of the grooming process or can be done while washing the horse.

Most horses do not like to be touched in these sensitive areas. However the groom can make the experience tolerable for the horse by using warm water, a mild soap, and a clean soft sponge. It is also recommended that the groom wear latex or rubber gloves when cleaning the sheath or udder, for hygiene purposes.

BLANKETING - Blanketing the racehorse is generally the groom's responsibility. There are three basic reasons for blanketing a horse:

  *to keep the horse warm and dry in inclement weather
  * to prevent a chill and to absorb moisture from the body after bathing
  .   *to keep the muscles warm and supple

It is important for the groom to keep the horse's blankets clean and neat. A blanket that is folded and stored properly lends a neat appearance to the stable.

BRAIDING - Braiding the mane and tail is a skill which all professional grooms should master. Although difficult to learn it can be mastered with a reasonable amount of practice. There are several reasons for braiding the mane. One reason is to train an unruly mane to lie flat against the neck on the off side. Another reason to braid the mane is for appearance. A braided tail is sometimes referred to a *"mud knot"*. A mud knot prevents the tail of a running horse from becoming laden with mud when the horse runs on a wet and sloppy racetrack. Putting the tail up in a braid makes it easier for the groom to clean after a race or workout in such conditions.

Cleanliness is a must.

CLEANING THE SHEDROW

It is the duty of the groom to rake the shedrow and sweep in front of the stalls. This makes the entire stable appear neat and tidy. Raking and sweeping is usually done after the morning training hours and at the end of the day.

A GROOM'S DAILY SCHEDULE

A groom rarely has the luxury of sleeping in. Some trainers require their employees to report to work at 5: 30 AM seven day a week, but allow them two or three afternoons off per week, depending on the work load and racing schedule. Fortunately, the majority of trainers allow the workers in their employ at least one full day off per week. But not every racing stable starts its day this early. Much depends on the region of the country you are in. Trainers have various reasons for implementing their time schedule, including season of the year, climate, location of the track, and access to the racetrack facilities.

5:30 AM.

Remove the feed tubs from each stall. Clean the feed tubs and hang them outside the stall to be ready for the midday feeding. Remove any stable bandages or night sheets from the horses. Then take each horse's temperature.

Grooming

Groom each horse thoroughly and clean the feet. Check the training schedule for the horses.

Tacking

Then tack up the horse with the equipment and bandages prescribed by the trainer. The first set of horses may go to the track for exercise as early as 6:00 AM.

6:00 AM.

If horse is ready before the rider arrives then walk the horse around the shedrow until the rider is ready. Give the rider a leg up onto the horse and lead the horse around the barn until the rider give the OK to release the horse.

Mucking

Prepare the wash buckets and washing materials for the daily bath. After the horse has left the barn begin mucking out the empty stalls. Clean water buckets and fill with clean fresh water. Fill hay rack or nets with fresh hay.

Untacking

When the horses return from the track, bring each one inside its stall and remove the tack and bandages.

Cooling Out

Thoroughly wash and cool down each horse. After each horse is dry and is returned to its stall, groom it and clean the feet. Wash and pack the feet with mud at this time, if required.

Bandaging

Apply any necessary liniment or poultice to the legs. Then wrap the stable bandages on the legs as specified by the trainer.

10:00 AM.

When all the horses in your care have completed their morning routines, remove the halters so each horse is loose in the stall. Clean the halters and shanks and hang them outside the appropriate stalls.

The groom has a long day!
Establish a schedule.

Cleaning

Clean the brushes and wash dirty bandages, saddle cloths, rub rags and girth covers. After washing hang or set everything out to dry. Rake and sweep the shedrow in front of the stalls occupied by the horses in your care.

10:30 or 11:00 AM.

It is again time to feed the horses. Top off the water buckets with fresh water, then make sure the horses have enough hay. Place the feed tubs with the midday meal inside the appropriate stalls. Remove the feed tubs as the horses finish feeding. Rinse out the tubs and hang them outside the stalls to be ready for the evening feeding.

Break Time

If you are finished feeding and none of your horses are scheduled to race that day, you need not return to the barn until 2:00 or 3:00 P.M.

2:00 or 3:00 P.M.

When you return in the afternoon take the temperatures of all the horses in your care.

Stall Maintenance

Sift through each stall and remove any visible piles of manure and urine-soaked bedding. Clean the water buckets thoroughly and place them back in the stalls with fresh clean water. Be sure to add hay if necessary.

4:00 P.M.

Feeding

The feed is placed in the tubs and given to each horse for the final evening meal.

Cleaning

Rake and sweep the shedrow area. Begin rolling the clean dry bandages and folding all laundry from the morning training session. When the horses are finished eating, remove the feed tubs and clean them thoroughly. After cleaning the feed tubs hang them outside the stalls to dry.

5:00 or 6:00 P.M.

Your day is usually complete

Note: The length of each workday for the groom varies with the type of training that is scheduled each day. *The sequence of events described herein does not include racing.* If the horse is scheduled to race, the groom must accompany the horse at all times. It is not uncommon for a groom to finish all of his or her duties very late on a race night.

There is much more involved in the care of a racehorse than just "grooming". Trainers will attest to the fact that each racehorse is an individual and requires "customized" care. Good grooms that stand the test of time are valuable assets to trainers and owners, and will be rewarded. But the best reward, as any groom will admit, is walking into the barn each morning and being greeted by enthusiastic knickers, and leaving at night to the sound of horses peacefully munching their hay.

Ted has written an excellent book on grooming. You may purchase it by contacting him at 516-352-2544 or on-line at hosstcher@aol.com.

Professional Grooming and Care of the Race Horse By Ted Landers

Horse Care

Read! Learn!

Your horse is an individual. Give him individual attention.

THE EBB AND FLOW OF DAILY TRAINING

When I first got into this business I wondered, "What makes a horse a race horse?" I tried to find books that would give me an idea of the day-to-day training of a young horse. There were few to guide me. The 2001-2002 meet at Tampa was one of my most challenging. I had various never-been-started two -year-olds that needed gate cards and transition to the race track experience. To give you an idea of how real training goes, I am going to take you through some of these horses to show you how and when they evolved into race horses or were retired as they were unable to pay their way.

Since a majority of these were client horses, (more than I have had in years), I was eager to find out if they were worth the day money an owner pays to have a horse in training. Frankly it is not cost effective to own a $5,000 claimer. Even if he were to win every two or three months it is hard for the horse to pay his way. Then if he is a solid on the board type of horse, he will be claimed at that price. That is why my program works for OWNER-Trainers. Day money is not an issue as you can turn the horse out when he needs it and his costs, if you are doing the training, are no more than a pleasure-show horse.

Day money - what a non hands-on owner pays every day of the horse's life with a trainer (except when horse is on a lay-up farm) can be from $30 to $150. That adds up fast. When you add the vet bills that usually accompany a racetrack horse, possibly another $1,000.00 (more at the larger tracks), you can see why owners are in a rush to get their horses into races in hopes of making some money. (The medication for ulcers is a prime example. Ulcers can be caused in part by stress and the daily administration the latest medication can cost about $1,300.00 a month. And it is often prescribed "indefinitely". Ulcers can also be cured by two months of turn-out. Which would you choose?)

Therefore my goal by the end of the Tampa meet was to have the horses racing in order to evaluate their talent. If they couldn't compete at Tampa, would they be useful at other tracks - maybe in easier company - or should the owner sell his horse at that point and look for a more talented one?

Tampa Bay Downs opens for racing in December each year. I try to buy two-year-olds in training at the Ocala sales in April or June. Although much pressure and stress is put on young horses to prepare them for the sale, I always hope that I can find a diamond in the rough. I prefer buying a horse for less than ten thousand that can run and earn twenty or better, than buying one for twenty thousand or more that ends up running at five thousand.

Since realistically, most horses have average talent, even when they cost a lot, I look for horses that have runners in their background and appear to move well. At the Ocala Breeders Sale, as a horse enters the ring, a video is run showing his breeze. You can see his movement and if he has a flowing gait. Being a bargain hunter, I try to look at each animal before he enters the ring. However, I miss some and the video is a great help. I have bought more than one horse based on a split second analysis of his video breeze. A horse that is unsound as defined in the Sales Catalog may be turned back within 24 hours of purchase. That minimizes the risk slightly.

Most horses will end up as claimers!

What makes a horse a race horse?

Any horses purchased in a sale are generally turned out for a month or two to make sure that medications are eliminated and soreness has time to resolve itself before training begins on the farm.

Training a horse that has already been broken and is galloping is a modified Second Phase as described in that chapter. Ridden only twice a week, when ridden they must go at least the three miles up and down the hills at my farm and be able to achieve the goals of Phase Two before going to the track or training center for breezes.

Let's follow some of these horses from sale or private farm to race track and you can see how varied each animal's development is.

Shrimp Tempura

This is a filly that I purchased in the June sale at OBS. She was slightly built with a "goose rump" and was back at the knee. Generally back at the knee horses are not wanted, as they are predisposed to breakdown. That is generally true, but I have seen some straighten out with slow progressive training.

She had worked well in the morning and moved very smoothly. When the bidding stalled at $3,800, I bid $4,000 and brought her home. She was very nervous and jumpy. So I pulled her shoes and turned her out, my usual routine with horses that come out of a two-year-old sale. As she became acclimated to the farm, she was bathed, taught to load, and walked around the training route.

In mid July, we started trail riding her. Remember she came out of a sale where she had been pushed to breeze fast while very young. She needed time to relax and flush any medications out of her system. My notes in her chart follow:

July 2001
7/15 Trimmed.
7/17 Ridden around fields - seems sensible.
7/ 19 Ridden around route - very willing and kind!

For the rest of July she was ridden every three days. Her legs were checked and she never had any filling, so we continued. Each time she was ridden (a minimum of three miles), the rider asked for a little more galloping. She was not going a solid hard three miles, but she did more galloping and less trotting each time the saddle was put on and always did the full route. Her rider was sitting in the middle of her back for at least 40 minutes each time. This is how the horses develop a strong back. My route is a half mile perimeter "route" with hills and fairly sharp turns. We can do a pretty aggressive gallop on the short straight-aways but must slow down for the turns. We can't do full speed, but can build a pretty solid foundation with the heavy sand and the hills. The horse runs in both directions to learn to lead change and to use both sides of the body. Most horses show a preference for one lead or the other-just as humans are right handed or left handed. But they have to learn to go both ways.

Shrimp was Back at Knee

Steady improvement is your goal.

August 2001

8/1 I sold her to a client. Galloped at farm.

8/4 Galloped at farm.

8/7 Filly was lame on right front. We watched and by third day she seemed to be improving. She continued to be turned out and observed every day. (No bute or other medication was given, as she appeared to just need time.) Was lame until the 12th.

8/13 Excellent gallop. No lameness. Good. The next day, no filling.

8/18 Filly ridden full three miles. Almost solid gallops.

She went every three days until end of month.

September 2001

9/3 Galloped at farm

9/5 Galloped in company slowly at farm-bumping and changing position with other horse.

9/7 Full strong gallop for three miles then went into pretend farm gates and galloped out.

9/10 Stronger gallop. Again out of gates.

9/15 Stronger gallop. Again out of gates.

9/18 Vet came out and did a "Caslick" on all the fillies. This is minor surgery to correct pneumovagina (windsucking) that involves suturing the upper vulvar lips together.

9/19 Galloped in company slowly at farm.

9/22 Galloped strongly 3 full miles with mile warm up and mile warm down

9/25 We went to Ocala Breeders Sales (OBS) training center and had the filly breeze out in company after doing a slow introductory walk and trot around the course the first time.

9/29 Back to OBS where, after a mile warm up gallop so she could look around, the filly breezed in company. She did 2 furlongs in 24 seconds and three in 36. Very nice for her first effort with us! She shows great sense and a willingness to cooperate.

October 2001

10/7 Back to OBS. We had the filly back up on the track, do a mile slow gallop to look around and then she breezed with another horse. Shrimp did 12, 24, 36, 50 and galloped out well. Excellent the next day out of work. No filling. So I know we can continue and ask for more. Turned out every day for an hour or two between the gallops

10/13 Back to OBS Same routine. Easy first mile gallop and then at the half mile pole breeze. She did 4 furlong in 51. Could be the track was heavier that day or lack of company had her go slower. Each time we go to OBS we have the horses go and stand and then break out of the gates.

10/17 Front training shoes put on.

10/20 OBS Breezed out gates in company. I told the rider to let her go as far as she could. She wasn't timed. We were more interested in teaching her to break out of gates well.

Monitor legs and watch for filling.

10/27 OBS. Broke out of gates. Filly was getting a little fractious behind the gates. I walked her in circles to get her under control. She is becoming anticipatory about running. She is young and it is important to let her become comfortable with the gates. Her youth and willingness to run are making her excited. We work on having her become more calm and relaxed behind the gates.

November 2001

11/3 OBS. Broke out gates and breezed 5-6 furlongs. We tried a tongue tie as she played with her tongue last time. She had a slow start and I didn't get a time.

11/10 OBS. Broke straight out of the gates and breezed 6 furlongs in 1:18. Note that she only had turn out in between these works. She needs time to recover from speed pushes.

11/17 Tampa Bay Downs. First work on real race track. 3 in 36, 4 in 51, and breezed out five furlongs.

11/23 TBD Breezed 5 furlongs in 1:03

11/26 Horse dentist worked on teeth.

December 2001

12/3 TBD Filly goes to gates, breaks out and breezes 5 furlongs in 1:04. Gets gate card!

12/11 TBD Filly breezes out gates with real jockey.

12/12 Filly gets complete set of shoes.

12/17 Filly is tattooed. Thank goodness her markings are correct. She is now race ready.

12/18 First race. One mile on the turf. Normally I would start a little shorter but since she got in turf race, I decide to go with it to see how she handles the surface. I am not confident that she can run a solid mile. The morning of race her rear shoes changed as they have toe grabs which are not allowed on the turf. To our great surprise and joy she ran third in her first race-by 3 lengths from winner!
I enter her again for another turf race and she doesn't get in.

12/27 she is breezed at farm.

January 2002

(I had 22 horses in training at this time)

1/1 Filly is in a flat mile MSW on the Turf at Tampa Bay Downs (TBD). She started the year right by winning!

1/9 Galloped at the farm

1/12 Owner was so excited about the win that he put her into a stake race at Tampa. It was on the dirt and short. I didn't think she would handle that distance as she likes to roll into it. When the horses broke from the gate, she ended up last by many on the backside and then made a huge move at the top of the stretch and passed three horses. A really a good move all things considered.

1/18 Galloped filly at farm

Always allow recovery time.

1/22 Galloped at farm

1/26 Turf race 1 1/16 at Tampa ran a very good third!

February 2002

2/1 Galloped at farm

2/5 Flat mile race on Turf at Tampa Ran fifth. Went very wide to pass horses

2/12 Galloped at farm. (These gallops are now very efficient and strong. Rider is barely able to slow filly for the turns. She goes a steady solid three to four miles. This is all we do to keep her fit for races.)

2/16 She ran a mile 1/16 allowance race on the dirt. Ran second.

2/18 Wormed at farm.

2/23 The filly was again entered in the second stake in the series at Tampa. Again on the dirt and going 7 furlongs in the slop. She was knocked hard coming out of the gates. She did not handle the track at all well and hated the slop in her face. She beat one horse.

March 2002

3/2 Galloped strongly at farm.

3/4 New shoes. This time outer rims all the way around. They are allowed on the turf at Tampa and can help on the dirt as well. This avoids changing shoes every time the race is taken off the turf.

3/10 One mile race at Tampa against the boys on the turf. We try to keep fillies running with fillies but it is so hard to get into turf races that I took the chance. She was checked in the traffic and didn't run well.

3/19 Another turf race at Tampa 1 1/16 mile. The filly ran a game second. Note that she did no gallops between races. Just turned-out. She is a slight filly. Too much galloping will wear her down. She is maintaining her fitness and weight with this minimal training.

April 2002

4/2, 4/5 and 4/9 Filly was galloped on farm. We are beginning to have real problems getting into turf races.

4/14 In desperation I hauled filly down to Gulfstream in Miami to get a turf race. She is against tough highly bred horses and runs fifth by 6 lengths from winner.

At least we got a race. She needs races to maintain her level of fitness! (A little drama on race day. An hour before the race I was told that rim shoes were not acceptable on Gulfstream turf and needed to be changed or be scratched! I had a terrible time finding a farrier at two in the afternoon to do the job. It cost double, but that was better than losing the whole 500 mile trip and being scratched. Remember to always check the

Shrimp loves the Turf!

Be emotionally prepared for setbacks.

shoe rules at each track. The type of shoe allowed on turf varies from track to track.

4/22 and 4/29 Filly is ridden at farm. Can't get into races. I believe in running when horse is right and waiting when he is not. It is very frustrating to try and enter and be excluded time and again!

4/23 Filly is wormed. She is galloped every few days to end of month.

May 2002

5/2 Filly is in the perfect turf race at Tampa and is picked to win. She has the leading rider. We have great hopes. She broke, ran in the back of the pack as usual and when asked to finish strongly showed nothing! We were devastated until we had her scoped after the race and found she had mucus in her lungs and was put on medications.

June and July 2002

The Tampa meet is over. I try to get some turf races in Miami. They are all taken off due to all the summer rains.

7/2 We get a 7 ½ turf race at Calder. She ran 3rd closing strongly and losing by 4 lengths.

It is a five hundred mile round trip for the Miami races. It made more sense to try the circuit around Delaware. I am told there are many tracks that have turf. We hauled up in early August and settled in at a friend's farm twenty minutes from the race track. Only to find that the area is having a drought. In the month and a half stay, she got in one turf race. In that race the jockey in front fell off his horse and we had to check and go wide, ending up near last. Very disappointed, we came back to Florida and tried racing at Calder in September.

September - December 2002

9/8 We ran in a 6 ½ furlong dirt race to tune her up. She was 6th by 9 lengths and no factor. Good out of race.

We kept entering turf races and were constantly excluded or the race was taken off the turf. In desperation my owner asked to put her in a small stake on the turf so that she might at least get on the grass.

9/22 Hyperactive Stake 44k Calder Race Course. Filly was a real long shot with a rider who had never ridden in this country, but it was worth a try and to our pleasure she ran 2nd, 4 lengths from the winner.

9/29 We entered another turf race, it was taken off. She ran 6th by 12 lengths. Although she did not like dirt and slop, we ran her anyway, because it was a long haul down, she was sound and needed the work.

10/11 Back to Calder in an NW2 on the turf. She run her race, made the big move at end, but was checked in the stretch finishing 5th by 6 lengths.

11/2 We entered a 45k turf stake at Calder with a "real" rider (leading rider who had not been on her). In our opinion he never tried to move her and quit mid-stretch instead of trying. She was 12th out of 12. Very big disappointment.

11/9 Back to Calder with an aggressive top rider in The Good Intentions Stake for 38k . She improved to run 3rd in that stake. Was shod that day at the track.

Gallops at farm with no luck in getting in races. We keep trying and eventually find a race.

Finding the right race is another challenge.

12/2 Calder Turf NW2 ran 3rd. Was good out of race.

A few days later we noticed lameness. Perhaps hot nail-abscess? The shoes were pulled. The farrier tried to find an abscess. She was tender but nothing was found. Eventually an abscess popped out at cornet band. The lameness is over.

12/10 Wormed.

January 2003

1/1 A New Year! Filly was round penned. She had been off since abscess. Only turned out and allowed to play at will.

1/6 Filly is galloped at farm

1/9 Filly galloped at farm no shoes.

1/12 Went to TBD She breezed easy. Five furlongs in 1:05

1/20 Filly galloped at farm-good and strong.

1/25 We finally get into a turf race at Gulfstream.

It was really too long a race after the lay off but I wanted to use it as a prep. At a mile and 3/8 on the turf, it was the longest I had ever run a horse. I told the jockey to let her go easy as far as she could. All things considered she did well. She beat two horses, never quit and did not shame us. Most importantly she was excellent out of race.

We are aiming the filly for Turf races at Gulfstream but it is difficult to get in and when we do we know we will be against the finest horses on the East coast.

This filly is just beginning her career and I hope to run her for various years. Keep an eye out for her. She has already made about $50,000. She is at least paying her way and appears to be sound and happy.

Winnie

She was a home bred filly of a client. We started breaking her in April 2001. Before that she had been round penned, been tacked, and learned to load. She was so explosive that my regular rider couldn't get on her. Although she was used to the saddle and bridle, when the rider would try to mount, she went crazy. With hard headed horses I call in the "cowboy", a bull rider who loves to ride bucking horses. He is very gentle but can ride down a bucker until it learns it can't drop the rider. Winnie was ridden twice a week by the cowboy until she learned to go forward and co-operated. Interestingly as she became more rideable, she showed a tendency to tie up; even after a short ride. She was a heavily muscled quarter

horse type filly. During her training program we tried various remedies to help her.

May 2001

The first half of this month the cowboy rode filly every three days. By mid May my regular rider, Kim, was able to start her around the route. Only every third day. She was given a couple of hours of turnout on off days. Kim rode her a minimum of three miles. She tried to gallop a mile or so until filly was tired. She

If you need a strong rider, get one!

was allowed to walk then until she recovered. Then she galloped again until she could do the three mile gallop. She was ridden at least half an hour each time and would walk through the pretend gates at the end of each ride.

June - August 2001

Winnie was ridden twice a week. By the end of June she could gallop fairly consistently for the full three miles.

The goal in July was to get more consistent, faster and smoother on turns in route. Flying lead changes were finally accomplished in this month. Previously she had slowed to a trot around tight turns. Now she was learning how to use her body and sustain the gallop. On July 29, we loaded her in trailer and hauled two hours over to OBS We had the cowboy ride her around a racetrack for first time. She was very green and somewhat rattled but managed to get around the oval trotting, looking at things, and dodging the scary stuff. She then galloped a mile very erratically. She was relaxing by the end of it. She loaded into the trailer and traveled back home well where she was turned out again.

August in Florida is very hot. She was ridden twice a week through the month-early in the morning. She was improving mentally When possible, she was galloped with company . She learned to be bumped and change positions on the route

September 2001

On the first day of the month we hauled back to Ocala. We had the filly stand in the gates and gallop out. We also closed the gates, let her stand in them and hand opened them to let her come out. On the 8th we went back to OBS again. She wasn't ridden in between as she had looked a little sucked up. Given the FL heat and humidity, she didn't need to be overstressed. She was turned out every day for two hours. On this trip to the track she galloped a mile in company, walked to catch her breath, then slow galloped into a 2 furlong breeze down the lane (to the finish line). She tended to be intimidated when she came alongside other horses. Decided to try short blinkers next time to keep her concentrated on her business, not the other horse. She trailered back home very well.

9/8 She looked better after this trip. She galloped in company on route at farm. The morning after every gallop or visit to the track her legs were monitored for filling. If filling that appeared the day after the work is gone, in one or two days, training can continue.

9/16 OBS again. This time filly did a slow first mile. In the second mile she was asked to breeze 3 furlongs down the lane. The rider was told to kiss to her, but it was stressed that he let her continue her breeze beyond finish line if she was so inclined. We loaded and went home. She has become an excellent traveler and seemed to enjoy the trips.

9/17 Her shins are very tender. Since she was very crooked on her front end, it was not surprising to have some strain as she eased into speed. At this point it was necessary to allow time to rebuild the calcium over her shins

For bucked shins -
rest is best.

making them tough enough to accommodate her own intrinsic speed. My own regime for bucked shins is followed. At the end of September she is still sore.

9/18 The vet came to do "Caslicks" on all the fillies. (See Glossary)

The rest of month was spent in "bucked shins" mode.

October 2001

10/4 Filly seemed ready again. She did an easy three miles on the farm route.

10/9 She was galloped again and seemed ready to go back to serious work.

10/12 She looked good.

10/16 She did a slow gallop the first mile followed by her first official breeze in the second mile. She went 12, 25, and 39 seconds for the three furlongs down the lane. We noticed she stayed on the left lead. We wanted to see a lead change at the top of the stretch - to the right. Apparently she hadn't mastered it yet. She went and stood in gates.

10/19 We put on front shoes and just turned her out a few days.

10/24 We went back to OBS. This time she was "backed-up" (walked or jogged about half a mile the wrong way around the track.) Then she was turned around, and galloped slowly to finish line. At that point she was asked to do a two minute clip around the track followed by a three furlong breeze down the stretch which was carried out beyond finish line. So she accomplished tightening the speed in front of the breeze and carrying on beyond the finish line. She did this in company.

10/31 We went back to OBS and did a mile gallop in company. Then the horses went to gates and broke without a bell. They breezed from gates as far as they could go. They didn't break sharply and were not timed.

November 2001

11/7 Having only been turned out at home, we went back to OBS. She went to the gates after a mile gallop. She broke crooked, veering sharply coming out and breezed four furlongs. No time caught as the break was poor.

11/14 Back to OBS, again no gallop in between. Those shins needed to set. She was turned out and allowed to frolic on her own. This day she has a good strong breeze out of gates. No time caught but she shows a willingness to run.

Tampa Bay Downs is now open and then the horses can train on the real surface.

11/17 TBD The filly galloped a mile looking around because there is more traffic on this a good mile gallop, she was allowed to trot and then go into a second mile with a breeze down the lane. She did three furlongs in 36 seconds. Looks promising!

Promises, promises...

11/23 Back to TBD no gallop at farm. Winnie galloped a mile breezing four
furlongs at end in 51 seconds. Good. She was off her feed for a few days
after that we waited until she was bright and tearing around the pasture.

December 2001

12/2 TBD to breeze. She did an easy breeze. No time taken.

12/7 Filly galloped on farm and tied-up after barely starting. This was confusing. She knew the route and looked completely calm at the start. Then after a turn or two she is tight in rear and in stress. We put her on magnesium and lite salt, cut back the grain and added fat (soy bean oil) to her feed. With tie-up there could be muscle damage so it is important that she be turned out to walk out of soreness. Before long she seemed ready to go again.

12/13 TBD. She breezed out gates four furlongs in 52. No tie up.

12/17 TBD. She breezed out the gates four furlongs in 52. A slight improvement. No tie-up.

12/24 TBD to the gates. She broke slowly and had to be hustled. No improvement here.

12/31 TBD broke in company well. Breezed five furlongs. Improved off last break. I arranged to have her tattooed. Her marking didn't match papers. So we had to pay fifty dollars to resend papers and another fifty dollars to retake photos. To make matters worse, a horse can't run until the corrected papers are returned.

January 2002

1/4 to TBD Winnie breezes out the gates with real jockey (previously an exercise rider was paid to get on her). A real jockey is put on when the horse is close to running. The goal is for the jockey to do the last work or two so he is familiar with horse.

1/8 TBD. Another breeze. Notice that the breezes are closer together as the horse shows it can take the work.

At this point the filly was coming out of breezes with cold tight legs and was not off her feed.

1/14 TBD. Breezes out gates-five furlongs in 1:06-slow.

1/16 TBD. To break with bell at gates. No breeze, just a gallop.

1/26 TBD to break with blinkers on. Filly breezed out gates with blinkers in 1:04. Maybe we are getting close to a race.

1/23 She got a full set of shoes.

There may be physical reasons for poor times.

1/28 Back to Tampa for another breeze, 5 in 1:04. The filly is tattooed.

February 2002

The filly was off her feed after that last work until 2/5.

2/7 Back to Tampa. She worked sluggishly and returns coughing! A day later she had fever and was put on penicillin. For the rest of February she was on medication fighting a cough and snotty nose. So much for starting her!

March 2002

The best laid plans. Winnie was developing so well until the cold and nagging cough came.

3/5 She seemed better and galloped well at the farm with no cough.

3/8 She was galloped again at farm and was not pushed. After about a mile she shortened her stride and tied-up again! We were still following the magnesium, salt prescribed after the last tie-up and were adding a little baking soda to her feed as well..

3/11 I told Kim to let her do whatever she wanted-even if it meant walking. She went out to the route and within half a mile tied up. What frustration!

3/14 She was sent out again on my route and got around it with no problem.

3/16 She went out again and was fine.

3/18 She did the route at the farm and seemed back to her old self.

3/20 She went to TBD galloped and breezed 3 in 39 and galloped out. No problems.

3/25 Back to TBD 2 minute licked into a 3 furlong breeze and did 3 in 39 with no tie-up.

3/28 She worked five furlongs in 1:06 at TBD and got new shoes.

April 2002

4/5 TBD Filly 2 minute licked for a mile and then breezed 3 in 40 seconds. That was slow. I expected a sharper work.

4/9 Galloped at farm.

4/11 Breezed out gates at TBD a slow 1:06 I had recently scoped other horses that had been working at Tampa, because their speed should have been sharper. Several were found to have mucus in their lungs, but had no outward signs of infection, fever, mucus in their nostrils or cough. Decided to scope Winnie too.

4/16 The vet found that she also had the mucus coating her lungs. No wonder she couldn't run faster. She had appeared to have healed from her previous cough which had been treated with penicillin. This time she was put on a stronger medication (for seven days) and continued gallops at farm.

4/22 Ridden easy at farm and was fine.

4/24 Ridden at farm and tied-up after short gallop! What frustration! Since it was a mild tie-up and a race was coming up, I decided that I had to try her before the end of the meet. She had never tied-up at the track. I entered her to run.

4/28 First race at TBD. She was entered in a field of twelve, was good in the paddock and ran credibly, fifth out of 12 horses, and seemed very bright

Keep them where they belong.

and sound after the race. Unfortunately the meet at Tampa was winding down and I couldn't get her into another race. A friend, one of my "proteges" convinced me to haul her to River Downs where he had a farm about an hour away from the track.

May 2002

Filly was turned out a few hours every day.

5/9 We loaded horses up at 6 AM Thursday, May 9, and arrived at the farm Friday May 10 at 6AM. I don't know about the horses but I was beat. All the horses had stalls under a huge old barn and were turned out 2 hours a day.

5/12 We chased the filly around a large grassy paddock for 20 minutes.

5/14 Winnie was entered in 5 furlong race. It was her first time over the River Downs surface and it was pouring. She was tight and nervous and didn't run well. The jockey thought she was too tense.

She went back to farm and was round penned every third day in a large paddock until she had a good sweat and was breathing deeply. There are no riders on this farm but I felt the filly was fit from Tampa and just needed to run.

June 2002

6/1 River Downs six furlong race-$5000 claiming. We hauled her in from the farm and hoped that she would be more comfortable on this trip. The weather was good and maybe she had time to think this racing business wasn't so bad as she ran a very good race and ended up second.

 She had three more races in June

6/7 River Downs six furlong race-$7500. Claiming. We upped her in company as she showed a little talent and we didn't want to lose her so early in her career. She ran another good race and ended third. Back to the farm and 2 hour turn out and 20 minute round penning every third day-no rider while we searched for a race.

6/13 We got too high on her and did two things that cost us. We put her in Maiden Special weight (tougher competition) and changed distance to a mile. Jockey said she just didn't seem to fire. It could have been that she had to try so hard in higher company that she couldn't or the race distance may have been a factor. My plan was to keep running them so that when the right race came, they would be fit. We put the poor performance to the jump in quality.

6/21 A one mile $5,000 claimer came up. We entered. In that race she broke well and was competitive until the top of the stretch where she propped and finished last. The jockey had no explanation.

Winnie was put in various races, trying to find her spot for the following two months. She never seemed to be able to make any money. She was retired .She was a complete loss financially and I hope will make someone a decent pleasure horse.

Hidden Glory This is a horse that I bred with Lois. We nurtured and trained him. We protected his maiden condition by running him in MSW or high claiming with hope of breaking his maiden in MSW with a higher purse. Since we were the breeders we could earn

**A sound horse that has no racing talent can
make a good pleasure horse.**

breaking his maiden in MSW with a higher purse. Since we were the breeders we could earn the extra bonus when he won. On the 49th try at the age of five, Hidden Glory finally won- in a MSW race at Tampa. He had earned around $35,000 as a maiden bringing in enough money to allow us to keep trying with him. The breeder's bonus was almost $2,000 which justified running him "over his head" all that time. Many trainers were critical of my refusal to "drop him to the bottom so he could win". Had I run him in $5,000 maiden claiming races I believe he might have won earlier and easier. However, the purse would have been around $3,000, (as compared to $8,000 in MSW) and he would surely have been claimed early on. After all our work and sweat we might have realized $10,000 or $12,000 in total. Granted we took two years to win, we did it at our meet in our state with very little overhead and therefore did realize a slight profit. He was off every summer as Calder was too tough for him and a very expensive trip.

In Sept. of 2001, he was galloped to tune him up for Tampa. He was an older trained horse and you can see what we did to get him fit for racing. At the end of the previous season at Tampa he had apparently strained his right ankle. Though the x-ray showed no bone chip, he healed with a larger "scar-tissued" ankle that was eventually hard and cold. When he trained we had to monitor the ankle. If he had heat or edema, we waited until it was hard and cold again. We evolved a routine of a gallop when he was right and turnout in between.

To prepare him for the Tampa meet, (a good example of bringing back an older horse).

September - December 2001

9/10 easy gallop. Heat in ankle for a few days, but the ankle was hard-no filling or mushiness.

9/19 Easy gallop at farm as ankle was cold, hard and tight.

10/2 Ridden on farm long and slow.

10/10 Ridden on farm. Seemed acutely lame afterwards. We watched for a few days. He popped an abscess on 10/20.

10/15 Wormed

10/25 Ridden on farm.

11/5 Gallop on farm (feet trimmed... no shoes yet)

11/11 Gallop on trail ride in the forest. He loved it!

11/18 TBD. Breezed in 1:04. A useful work-good enough to look for a race.

11/28 Ridden on farm.

12/ 12 Strong open gallop at farm.

12/18 Enter to run for 6 furlong race@ $12,500 Claiming Non-winners of 2 (NW2). Ran in the middle of pack.

12/27 In for 1 mile and 1/16 @ 12,500 NW2 ran in front for 6 furlongs and tired.

January 2002

1/1 A $10,000 6 furlong NW2. Ran well. Was 6th by 7 lengths from winner.

1/12 A $12,500 NW2. He ran 6th by 14 lengths maybe too high a price to run?

1/14 Wormed

1/22 A $7,500 NW2. A mile and 1/16. He ran 5th by 5 1/2 lengths. The drop in price helped. He ran wide in both turns. It was a solid effort... need a

Are you beginning to see why patience is a virtue?

little racing luck

1/2 7 A $10,000 NW2. A mile. He ran a good race. He was 4th 3 lengths from winner.

2/14 A 6 furlong race for NW2 @ $10,000. He ran 8th by 9 lengths too short, and a bad post position.

Couldn't get in to races as Tampa was very competitive at that point

2/18 wormed

2/22 galloped at farm-couldn't get in race

3/1 galloped on farm

3/12 NW2 @ $5,000 for 7 furlongs. He was 6th by 6 lengths

3/19 NW2 @ $7,500 for 6 furlongs. He was 8th by 9 lengths

3/29 NW2 @ $5,000 for 7 furlongs. He was 2nd by 3 lengths

4/7 NW2@ $7,500 for 6 furlongs he was 4th by 15 lengths.

4/22 NW2 @ $10,500 for 6 furlongs. He was 4th by 8 lengths and the race went in 1:11, which is pretty fast for Tampa. We hadn't been able to get him in a cheaper race.

4/30 NW2 @ $10,000 for 7 furlongs. He was 5th by 17 lengths

At this point I was frustrated-Tampa was tougher than ever and it was not possible to put the horse where he needed to be in distance and price. I had to take what I could get. Fortunately, he was coming out of the races sound and fit. One of my "students", Greg, asked if I wanted to go to River Downs and ship-in off his farm. It seemed worth the effort. I agreed to haul some of my horses up with his filly, help him set up his farm and get him going with his own program. Glory was on the same kind of routine up there - turn out and races. He did win two races and was on the board various times. With no more effort than you would have with a show horse you could run your horse in a similar fashion.

The rest of Glory's story. He was claimed at Hoosier for $5,000.00 in his 80th race. He had never run on medications. I was sorry to see him put on Lasix shortly after that. He did not run well and soon was in for $3,500 claiming. He ran poorly there too. Then I noticed they took him off Lasix and he ran second at $3,500. We didn't see him in the form after that. The track closed. Greg then called the trainer who had him and purchased him back.

We will have to see how he is next season. He is back to his routine-turn out, gallop and races. That is our goal - to have a horse we race and keep happy in between races. Notice that the horse was racing fit without going to the track for breezes. We used races instead of breezes. Of course I had hoped he would win. However, he was kept over his head for fear of losing him, which can be self-defeating. Unfortunately, I like my horses and though it cost me in statistics as a trainer, he was ready to go at River and paid his way there before he was claimed.

Did Lasix "help" this horse

HOW CAN YOU GET ANY CLIENTS WITH SUCH TERRIBLE RACING STATS?

I have the worst stats as a trainer for starts vs. winning and being on the board. Many have asked if I am independently wealthy or have a sugar daddy. How else can I continue with so many starts and so few wins. Let me explain this once and for all. My goal as a trainer is to do the best for my owners and their horses. My job is to get them to the races soundly and evaluate their ability to earn money as soon as possible. While I will never run a horse I know is compromised or hurting or under painkilling medications, I will run a horse to give him experience or get him fit for his race.

I live in Florida. My efforts are timed to the weather and the opening of the racetrack in my area. The horses are purchased or sent to me around April of their two year old year.

You can't outsmart Mother Nature, so we start the breaking and galloping just as described in other chapters. The aim is to start racing in Tampa in December of the two-year-old year. They are generally ready for breezes at Tampa in November when the backside opens. Usually a month of breezes and gate work will set them up to start. My rule is to put them in a race, preferably at five or six furlongs, if they have their gate card and can breeze five furlongs comfortably in 1:04. The problem is that I have many three-year-old fillies and colts by the following January and the track only allows one horse to start per trainer if the entries are full. That means it is hard to get races for all the horses with the same eligibility. There is also the problem of the owners. They don't want their hopeful to start at the bottom in claiming. They might get claimed in that first race, or so they think. They don't want to lose their horse, at least not until they are convinced that he can't run fast enough to make any money. I start the horses whereever possible, but usually higher than the bottom claiming tag. Short races are best with the aim of putting them into longer ones as they become more seasoned or show a preference for a particular distance.

As mentioned in a previous chapter, the first four races are like the last four works with any other trainer. Most trainers will hone in during the morning to have an idea where the horse should run. They try to protect their statistics by putting them in as cheap as possible and hope for a win or place. While the fact is that most horses will end up running at the bottom for a tag, there is the chance that they need a few races to learn what is going on. Horses that ship-in need extra experience.

If the horses are sound, races help the owner get an idea of the horses' value. By the fourth race we should have a real idea of where the horse can win and at what price. If they show little ability and have no excuses in the races, I recommend selling the horse to owner trainers who can afford to run them without the concern of day money. If the horse isn't fast enough for that, we can offer a sound horse to the hunter-jumper, dressage or polo people.

Starting the season with ten untried two-year-olds means forty starts before we see where the horse can run viably. After some five months of training bills, it is time to unload them or win somewhere.

You can't outsmart Mother Nature.

Some trainers feel you "break their heart" by putting them in over their head. With maiden races I don't agree. My system allows them to get the experience they need without fear of break down, since medications are never used. There is also less expense, since the horses run on food and water and they are ready to go again in ten days.

Have you ever noticed that certain horses, even non racing horses, have a desire to be out in front? Trail riding, herding cows, or even in the field there are strong personalities that want to lead? We call that "heart" and love to see it in a race horse. That horse will always try. You see his talent and speed early, because he tries every time he is asked to breeze. Others need to learn to run. They may have tons of talent but are afraid to pass horses or be competitive in a group situation. No amount of morning works with one or two horses will prepare that horse for the challenge of many thundering horses in a race situation. Only experience will help them learn to handle the stress of running. They will either become better with each race or become more nervous. With perseverance your timid but fast horse may learn to run comfortably in a group. The first four maiden races teach me more about the horse and his ability than two or three more months of early morning works.

By the end of the Tampa meet, most of my horses have run various times. If they haven't won, those that show promise should be ready to win at less competitive tracks against cheaper company.

For the owner and the horse, Tampa has been the proving grounds to see if continuing the training will pay off. By running the horses as soon as they are fit and sound, the owner can make decisions about his investment. If the horse can only win cheap it may not be cost effective to ship him to other tracks. Probably only two or three of the group should continue in racing. However, if they can be retired sound for another job and have not cost the owner too much, it is the best I can do. No one can make a horse run faster than he can. Most are simply not fast enough.

Claiming is a way to get in fast and make good statistics if you have the personality for it. Astute trainers look for a horse early in his career that shows promise. They claim him and try to move him up, if he is talented and not ready to break down. If the horse turns out to be sore or compromised, the trainer will want to get out fast trying to win in the process. His owner may have claimed the horse at $25,000.00. Then the trainer may want to put him back in at $10,000.00, looking for the win and hoping to lose the horse.

If the horse doesn't win, isn't claimed and can't run, owner is out his investment. Or the horse wins for $10,000.00 and is claimed. The trainer gets the win on his stats, the owner gets the purse reducing his loss. What happens to the horse? Who knows? He can be shuffled from stable to stable with any number of problems that his current trainer doesn't want to know about. Some trainers may have every joint injected allowing the horse to look sound enough to be put back in a race as soon as possible.

Many trainers have no interest in the horse's problems. They just want to get him into the next race. There are so many "designer drugs" out that it is very hard to pinpoint problems short term. Horses that gallop sore in the morning can seem very sound the day of the race due to the miracles of modern medicine. There are many short term fixes that result in a horse's breakdown later.

 Perseverance will pay off.

For that reason, I don't claim horses. I am uncomfortable taking horses without knowing their true soundness and medication history. Most claimers are running on various medications that I won't use. Therefore I am not a good trainer for claimed horses.

The business of claiming is not cost effective if you try to rest and heal a horse with problems. It may work for those who are willing to "help" it get back in the next race before it goes bad. The saying is "Don't be the last one to own the horse."

This part of the business is very distasteful to me. In bottom races at every track you will see horses that have earned over $100,000.00 running for a $3,000 or $4,000 tag. The race times might be very competitive as, when the horse is "right", he can run his race. The fact is, it may be his last race, depending on how many times his joints have been injected or his bow wrapped. Track costs force owners and trainers to take the short term fix - get him in one more race and hope he makes money before he breaks down.

That is not the way I operate, so my statistics are terrible. The horsemen who read this book and like their horses, will have the same problem. However, we are good for the industry and if enough of us win and justify the expenses, we might start a new trend. One of these days this patience will pay off. It did before. We all want a BIG horse! We can't afford to buy it when it shows talent, so we must develop it. The problem is that most horses are not talented enough to win and justify their expenses.

On a small scale I start each racing season with six or seven two-going-on-three-year-olds that must learn everything. It is like having a group of teenagers that must learn all the rules the hard way. When we finally get them to work with us and run a few races, we find that most will not be fast enough. The next year we start all over again with a new group. That is the burden I bear. There is a saying in the racing business, "No one commits suicide with an untried two-year-old in the barn!" Truer words were never spoken. We have hope each year with every new group... maybe THIS one will be THE ONE!

Training is a learning experience.

SECOND OPTION - TO THE TRACK TO STAY

Not everyone should consider training their own racehorse when it is time to go to the track. The racetrack is another world, **a whole new set of rules.** Trainers at the track are very adept at entering horses and appraising chances for a particular horse in a particular field. An honest trainer will tell you if he agrees with your methods and ideas or not. You must find a trainer who shares your philosophy. Then allow him or her to call the shots.

When a horse that has been trained by the methods in this manual is sent to the track to stay, the transition can be hard. The horse is feeling good and has been allowed to run and frolic for a few hours every day. **In the racetrack routine, his every movement is restricted.** The amount of time he is ridden and exercised is decreased, and he has no turnout.

When I first started training, my horses went to the track after having undergone a more aggressive training schedule. They had been galloped five to ten miles everyday. When I turned them over to the trainer, the first thing he said was, "What's wrong with these horses? They just stand there. They're so quiet." I, of course, was offended. My "children" were just being good. I had turned them out every day and galloped them hard. When they went into a stall they were tired and well mannered.

A week later I came back to the track. As I walked by my sweet horses in their stalls, they lunged at me or anyone else who happened by. They were like all the other unhappy, bored horses who are not allowed to frolic. They were full of pent-up energy they couldn't release.

Bad habits can develop in horses who live at the track. These habits evolve over a period of time because the animal can't cope. He is not allowed normal living and is bored, nervous, frustrated, in pain, or all of the above.

When you go down a typical shedrow at the track you'll see animals bite at you, lunge at you and weave back and forth. Others are cribbers. They bite the stall door or feed bucket, and suck air in through their mouths. **These traits are manifestations of the frustration of being in an unnatural environment.** They help to alleviate the horse's boredom. **Most of these vices disappear when the horse is living at home and turned out.** However, some horses are high strung and are always nervous.

My horses soon became cranky like all stalled horses. Then they began having a great deal of trouble with tie-ups. I asked the trainer what the horses were doing. He told me they were being sent to the track to gallop one mile. As they came back, they all seemed to have tie-up problems. **Tie-up is manifested by a shortness of stride, generally in the rear, and in severe cases the inability to walk. The horse may paw the ground with his front feet and have spasms in his rump muscles. Trembling, sweating and obvious stress accompany these symptoms.**

After galloping one mile my horses were being pulled up, turned around and brought back to the barn. The problem was obvious to me. They were used to galloping five to ten miles. A one mile gallop was like a warm-up to them. No wonder they were tied-up.

If you find a trainer willing to listen to how you want your horse started at the track, he is worth his weight in gold.

They were full of energy, had a one mile warm-up . . . and were told, "That's it." They surely headed back to the barn bouncing and full of desire to run, with fuel pumped into their system that had not been burned.

Tie-up is a phenomenon that was seen a great deal in the last century. At that time horses were worked everyday but Sunday. On Sunday they didn't move. Their metabolism had to adjust to the different Sunday routine. When they went to work on Monday, their muscles had "locked". To avoid this problem feed was adjusted and the horses had some kind of exercise on Sunday.

When my horses had the problem at the track, it was because they had been over trained. **They were too fit and had too much of the wrong kind of work. I was galloping them too long and making it more difficult for them to adjust to the confinement of the track.** So, I took them all home and developed the program that I am teaching you.

No matter how it is approached, **it is difficult for horses to adjust to being stalled 23 hours a day. The younger they are the more difficult it is.** They want to bound out of the stall in the morning. This intimidates the groom and he will over shank the horse unless he is really tuned in and realizes the horse just feels great. You don't want your horse to be punished because he feels good. You can only hope your trainer has good help. These are things for you to be aware of that should be discussed with your trainer.

When the trainer takes your horse on the track for the first time, he must allow the rider to ride with longer stirrups than usual. He should have the rider take the horse in the wrong direction, completing the circumference of the track while allowing the horse to walk, jog, and look at everything. If the horse is nervous and over-reacting, have him ponied. Do a second mile while trying to relax and accustom him to the activity around him. Since the horse has had a lot of under-saddle experience and mental growth with you, he should not be too over-reactive.

Young Horses can find Confinement Difficult !

Don't fool yourself into thinking your horse is fine if you have been <u>M</u>as<u>k</u>ing <u>S</u>y<u>mp</u>to<u>ms</u> with <u>Medications</u>

When the horse has settled down, have the rider turn him around and gallop the full mile in a relaxed manner, allowing the horse to breeze down the lane and gallop out as far as he wants after the finish line. If this means going a whole extra mile, assure the rider and trainer that it is all right.

Always allow the horse to "come back" to the rider. It is very important for the horse to be allowed to gallop and slow down when he wants. If he doesn't get comfortably tired, you'll have an animal that builds up energy. He will start fighting the rider. Your horse will be fit. He just needs speed honing. He does not need miles of drilling, slow gallops or hobby horsing. He does need to become accustomed to the track routine. Assure your trainer that the horse must return tired or he will escalate his energy level.

For the next three days, the rebuild-days, your horse should not go to the track. **Continual trips to the track on a daily basis and the stacking of stress to the bone, common in conventional training, tend to break down young horses.** Ask the trainer to have someone hack the horse around the backside of the track for half an hour instead of going to the track.. **If there is no other choice on the rebuild- days, have him ponied for a least a mile or have him walked to the gates to stand in them.** At some tracks, a paddock may be rented and you can turn the horse out to frolic for a least an hour a day. **Again, I stress that daily pounding on unnatural surfaces eventually breaks down a young horse. In allowing your horse time to rebuild in between the track gallops or works, you keep him from many track breakdowns.** Many horses in conventional training do not survive the training process.

If a horse can't survive the training process, there must be something wrong with the process.

Why is training causing breakdown during a young horse's development? **Standing for 23 hours, which inhibits blood circulation, followed by running hard is the scenario which makes horses more prone to breakdown.** Your trainer may not like to hear your methods. They interfere with established routine and demand more from his help. But you want a healthy situation for your horse. **It is your goal, as an owner, to have the trainer get the best for and from your horse. You and your track trainer can reach compromises that suit you and the horse.**

You are into your fifth day at the track. On the first day, the horse breezed out after a mile or two jogging in the wrong direction to see everything. Then, hopefully, he had two or three rebuild-days without track pounding after his session on the track. If all was well, he could have been walked to the gates to stand and gallop out on those off days. If he did, he will only need a few more visits to the gates before you start incorporating every fourth day breezes with breezing out of the gates.

Now you must give the trainer some leeway with your horse. He may do every fourth or fifth day breezes. As the horse tightens and becomes more efficient and honest, he may need more time in between breezes and works to recover and rebuild.

Rebuild-day recovery time should be equivalent to an hour or more of turnout, or some kind of off track trail riding or ponying, no pounding, but lots of movement. Have him taken a couple of times around the track the wrong way, if you have no other alternative. The idea is movement without hard pounding. After four to six weeks of training at the track, you should get a handle on the horse. **He'll be trying harder down the lane and be more willing to quit after the finish line, as the works lengthen to racing distance.**

At this point, **if there is swelling, sore shins or lameness, do not give Bute and continue training. Allow the horse to rest and recuperate from soreness. Tell**

Don't get into the habit of ignoring pain on young sound horses by masking it.

the trainer you don't want jugs. You don't want Bute every night and you don't want pain-masking medication. If there is pain, it is for a reason. A young three-year-old should not have pain. If he does, he should be allowed to walk out of his soreness. I am not opposed to helping an older horse, who has soreness and stiffness, and needs Bute to run.

If pain killers are used the trainer cannot observe what is brewing in the young horse. In traditional training, if the pounding on the track surface causes soreness and filling, the trainer may give Bute, poultice, and wrap. This inhibits swelling. The next day it is impossible to determine the true status of the legs. The horse is sent out again and the process is repeated. **The horse's problems are masked by wrapping, poulticing, and medication.** When the horse goes bad, everyone is so sorry and no one can imagine why this happened with such up-to-date care. This is where overuse of systemic corticosteroids may begin.

You can now understand why I prefer shipping in. **It is life at the track that wears horses down - too little work - too much speed - at too young an age.** The horse stacks the stress of trauma from the track surface and over a period of time problems appear. **Turn-outs and free galloping are very important parts of training - especially for young adolescent animals.**

IF YOU CAN KEEP HIS TIME ON THE TRACK DOWN TO LEGITIMATE GALLOPS, BREEZES OR WORKS, YOU WILL DEFEND YOUR HORSE FROM MANY OF THE TRACK BREAKDOWNS. EXTRA TIME FOR GROWTH AND REBUILDING IS IMPORTANT.

Remember, these are the equivalent of the horse's teen years. **You want him to survive training and grow into a useful mature horse.** Beware of trainers who want to use a lot of medications on your horse. The horse should be sound, healthy and young enough to handle the work without chemical support.

At this point in training, you should read and follow the instructions given to weekend haulers. Let the trainer work or breeze the horse every five or six days depending on how the horse holds up. **When the horse is fit enough to go a strong five furlong work and gallops out strongly, put him in a race.** This is a difficult request for the trainer who values his starts-versus-wins track statistics. There is nothing like a race to find out whether or not the horse wants to be a runner. After four races, you should be able to tell if he is a cost-effective race horse. These are my suggestions. Your trainer may have a different approach. Respect and listen to him. He may want the horse tighter and ready to win the first time out.

If your horse appears to be trying hard in the races and has no legitimate excuse for losing, his best is probably not enough to justify the expense of the racetrack. Try not to be pulled into putting more and more into a horse that doesn't have the talent. It is not cost-effective. If he doesn't have racing talent, you still have a sound horse for another endeavor where he may have talent. If you are training at home, the expenses are not as great and you can afford to be more patient.

**Remember you can't give a horse talent
he doesn't possess.**

A MESSAGE TO FARM OWNERS AND MANAGERS

Today, horse farms are struggling to survive. They face major problems with labor and Workman's Compensation. If you understand the concept of the training presented in this manual, you will realize there are many ways to continue training at the farm and cut down the costs of riders by two thirds. **If a twice-a-week riding program is initiated, the labor and stress of getting out, galloping, bathing, and leg wrapping young animals every day is eliminated.** At the same time you will find that your horse develops progressively, at the rate that his structure can tolerate. You are training horses while listening to their individual responses to the stress put to them. Many tune up more quickly than anticipated . . . they show no filling with each progressive gallop, and therefore can continue right on to the races.

Since you are turning them out on the rebuild-days, there is no need to wrap and paint legs; they will adjust to the work load. **Be sure you or your employee monitors and charts any filling and waits until it is down before galloping the horse again.**

It costs you less to handle horses this way, and they are in real training. They are growing, developing and thinking. You will be pleasantly surprised at how little expense there will be to treat and medicate these animals. You're not overstressing them so they have strength to resist major infections. Again, the free movement and being outside a good portion of the day, in itself, will improve the animals' life style.

Whether or not you race off the farm will be a decision that you and your owner make. Obviously, I prefer it. Keep in mind, once your horses learn the track rules and routine, they really don't have to be cooped up at the track between races. Some may need a gallop or speed work between races (every horse is different). Depending on your location, you should be able to handle the logistics. **Horses living at the track only get about fifteen minutes actually on the track on any given morning.** You could arrange for riders at the farm to do more and develop them better with the twice-a-week schedule and rebuild time in between. Most track personnel cooperate with ship-ins. You may schedule your trips to the track so that you, too, only go once a week to work horses or combine a work in the morning with a race in the afternoon.

Turn out is a very important part of TRACK TRAINING - It allows rebuilding from the Track pounding between Works and Races !

**Sensible work and good rest
keep people and horses fresh.**

Standing in a stall for 23 hours out of every day, does not develop a _resilient_ _athlete_

A MESSAGE TO TRACK TRAINERS

We have chosen a difficult but rewarding business. I hope that as you read my program you will keep and open mind and try to find ways to adapt some of the ideas into your routine. Many times as you train, you find you are having to treat problems that are created by track circumstances.

A problem my horses have had only at the track, for example, is cracked heels. At some tracks, the dirt has stones or bits of shell in it. When the horse gallops on this surface every day, he can develop chronic cuts and bruising. Some tracks put chemicals on the surface for winter racing. These chemicals cause burns and chronic problems when horses must train on the surface every day. Washing fetlocks, pasterns, and heels with castile soap and rubbing them with bag balm or other lotions to help the injured tissue is very time consuming and work-intensive. These problems slow down training.

One track was famous for making horses sore in the shoulders and stifles. Trainers had no choice but to use the track and contend with muscle soreness. On the other hand, my horses would run or work and go home. They were usually sore the day after the work and fine by the second or third day. They walked and grazed while healing on their rebuild-days. They went into races feeling good and could take it easy until the next race or work. It was not necessary to give any kind of medication, because the horses were always bucking, kicking, and feeling good by the third or fourth day. By noting their activity on a chart, patterns would emerge indicating how much time each horse needed before he was ready to run again.

If you ship-in and gallop or work them on the track and then take them home, they can be turned out to heal between visits to the track. **The routine I suggest allows them to recover from the experience and be healed in time for the next race or work.**

Please be open to working with owners who want to be somewhat involved and ship-in horses for training. This can be a source of more horses to actively race in your stable and opens the door of our sport to more people who will help fill races.

Everyone gains from a compromise.

THE RELATIONSHIP BETWEEN
VETS, OWNERS AND TRAINERS

As you read this manual, do not misinterpret my feelings about veterinarians, owners, and trainers. In my desire to educate you, **the worst possible scenario is used when presenting cases**. My goal is for you to make your own informed decision as to how you want your horse treated. Your expectations about how your horse will perform must be tempered by the reality of his talent and soundness.

The trainer's role is to develop the horse to his personal best. Most trainers have the horse's welfare at heart. Their work is very challenging. Many trainers must move from track to track, depending on the season. They must pack their belongings and find a new place to live every three to six months unless they are lucky enough to have their own farm near tracks that are open year round. Their logistics and financial problems are great.

Compound that with the challenges of training young horses every year . . . horses that will have their own normal setbacks as they grow into useful animals. Every time there is a problem or slow down with the horse (which is to be expected), the trainer must call the owner with the Bad News. Most trainers, myself included, find this to be one of the most difficult aspects of training. **We don't like to deliver bad news.** We don't like the fact that the horse is showing problems or weaknesses and we don't want to stop him. Yet we must do what we perceive is best for the owner and the animal. How I dreaded the silence on the other end of the line when I said, "His shins are sore.", "He has a cough.", or "He needs time." I am aware that the owner is thinking of the per diem costs while the horse rests.

IT IS VERY IMPORTANT THAT THE OWNER AND TRAINER HAVE A MUTUAL RESPECT AND TRUST. Each must understand the philosophy of the other. The owner must believe that the trainer is doing an adequate job, and the trainer must understand the owner's intent in owning a racehorse. For example, many owners tie the hands of the trainer when they won't allow him to run the horse in a particular race. The owner generally thinks his horse is worth much more than the claiming price. It simply doesn't matter how much the horse cost or how much you have invested in him. He must run where he can win, where he can justify the training bills. Statistically, it is going to be a lot less than his cost. So trainers have the unpleasant task of having to tell the owner that his $20,000 dollar investment should start running at $5,000 if any money is to be made. It is possible that the horse will work his way up the ladder, but the start must be realistic. This is one of the many problems between owners and trainers. **We all want the Big Horse, and when the horse is mediocre or less there is disappointment on all sides.** The reality is that few horses will justify their cost. However, a good one can pay for many if we can only find him!

The other really unpleasant task trainers have is reporting to the owner that the horse didn't win. An excuse is expected. Many times the horse has run a good race, but just wasn't fast enough to win. What can a trainer say? The horse was outrun. If the owner is at the track, he can see for himself. That can make it easier . . . or more difficult . . . depending on the sportsmanship of the owner.

Trainers want to win . Each time they run a horse, they hope it will win, even if the

**Your expectations must be tempered by the reality
of the horse's talent and soundness.**

form clearly shows there are more talented horses in the race. It does happen, and when it does the bettors mumble about how the trainer must have set that one up. They don't realize we're just as surprised as they are. The bettor is convinced that the trainer had a large bet on the horse and "made a score". It does happen, but not as often as you think.

My racing career began as an owner. I knew nothing about racing or the track. I loved my horses and wanted them to win, just like in the movies. An owner expects the trainers to know everything about the horse. That may eventually be true, but at first, the trainer is learning. Each horse is different. His idiosyncrasies must be observed through trial and error. The trainer must decide on the distance of the race, the equipment, and the style of riding that suits the horse. He learns this as the horse progresses. As frustrating as it is, owners must be patient and understand that the horse tells his trainer things with each race. Some of his perceptions about a horse may be incorrect and he will have to go back to the drawing board. **Eventually, the horse, trainer, and owner should evolve an understanding that will be beneficial to all.**

A major problem is an owner who pushes the trainer and demands action when the trainer feels the horse isn't ready. This can be disastrous. Mutual respect and communication will alleviate this problem. An educated owner is much easier to deal with. Since owners are paying the bills, they should be kept as informed as they want to be. Some owners don't want or need frequent updates. Others want to be very involved. Matching the trainer's style to the owner's expectations is an important part of good rapport.

Owners are paying the bills. It is their right to know how their horse is handled. They may be in racing because they love to go to the backside and walk their own horse or bring him carrots. They may only want to be in the winner's circle. **Seek out your own kind of trainer. Look for mutual benefit.**

Owners, please remember a trainer can do everything right and your horse can still have problems or not be a runner. If this happens, don't blame the trainer. The possibility

Trainer   Owner   Vet

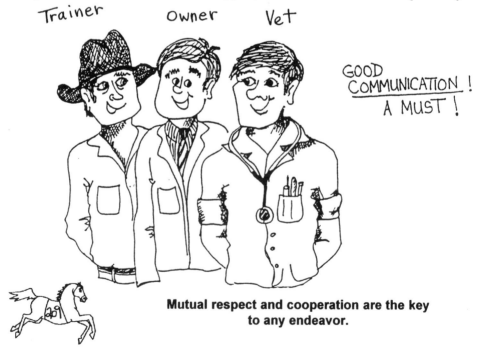

GOOD
COMMUNICATION !
A MUST !

**Mutual respect and cooperation are the key
to any endeavor.**

of winning is slim. Be fair and understanding. Something may happen to the animal after much hard work on the part of the trainer . If so, don't bad mouth him. Be fair, **there is a great deal of luck involved in training**. High strung, honed animals can be difficult to handle. The horse can be his own worst enemy. Just rolling in his stall, he can injure himself for life. These things happen even with the best of care!

Trainers have expenses like everyone else. Don't get a horse unless you understand what the projected costs will be. Don't expect your winnings to pay for training. **Figure out how far you can go with no economic compensation and discuss that with the trainer. He can tell you how realistic your goals are.** Always be prepared for the worst case scenario . . . then you'll be pleasantly surprised when things turn out better. . . Hopefully with my methods, your horse will not suffer as much breakdown as is typical. Also it should not take as long to establish his ability and usefulness at the track.

The veterinarian who practices at the racetrack has special challenges. He knows and generally keeps up to date on the best therapy for the horses. He is aware that sometimes rest and turning the horse out are easy, rational solutions to many problems. But the vet can only recommend such solutions. When a vet tells an owner, "Just give him some time and turnout.", the owner almost feels cheated. His reply may be , "Don't you have some kind of miracle drug that will cure him? Off time costs money." Then the vet must admit that there are medications, and will often explain the side effects. After that, if the trainer and/or owner insist, the vet must try the next best treatment, usually some sort of medication. Next time you have a problem, ask the vet if rest and turnout would do the trick. If your horse has talent, you may be money ahead in the long run. Dr. Green (the pasture) is one of the greatest cures of all.

The fact is that racing is a business in which horses are expected to produce. Financial pressures cannot be ignored. Veterinarians can advise various treatments to help a horse run better and without pain. Much of the therapy is very good. A great deal of the medication is therapeutic and helpful. Tell your trainer and vet what you are willing to pay for, what kind of treatment you want for your horse, and whether or not you are open to allowing time and rest to be a part of the game plan. Veterinary medicine has made great contributions to the racing industry. Many horses have had successful surgeries allowing them to be useful and capable of earning on the racetrack. **Trust and a clarification of the owner's philosophy are necessary to avoid misunderstandings.**

Whether to operate or not, weighing the economic impact in relation to the horse's earning power, can only be decided when all the facts are presented. Removal of spurs and chips may return a horse to a very competitive level with little trauma and expense in relation to overall cost and time lost. My suggestion is to get various opinions and information on any problem in order to make informed decisions. Veterinarians work with trainers but are generally happy to discuss and explain cases and options with owners. As an owner, be clear about your decisions and what kind of vet bills you are willing to pay. If you don't want your horse to run on painkillers and steroids, make it clear! It may save your horse's soundness if you chose competent training over medications that mask problems!

If you are reading this manual, I hope it is because you want to be an informed owner and/or trainer. Communication and knowledge are the key to successful relationships between the owners, trainers, and veterinarians. Each person has a very important role to play with the horse and the racing industry.

By working together we can strengthen our positive impact on the sport of horse racing.

The Business of Training

PARTNERSHIPS, SYNDICATES AND DEALS

A SAMPLE CONTRACT

TAX CONSIDERATIONS

INSURANCE

The Money Side of horses!

A WORD WITH THE EXPERT ON -
SYNDICATES, PARTNERSHIPS
AND VARIATIONS

WHERE ARE THE LITTLE OWNERS
AND TRAINERS AT THE BIG RACES?

PARTNERSHIPS, SYNDICATES, AND DEALS

The Agony and the Ecstasy

Some friends formed a syndicate, went to the sales, bought a fairly expensive horse and started the process of racing their GREAT HOPE. First I got weekly reports about how the filly was doing everything right, how she loved to gallop and was doing very impressive works. Then she had some predictable setbacks. After sore shins, coughs, inconsistent works, and problems in the gate, the trainer picked a date and said the horse would start. How exciting! What anticipation! The friends called me. They had already planned the next race, a little stake, that she could go in after her first out and, of course, first win. They told me they had the leading rider and he was very high on the filly. She went off favorite, the owners convinced she would smoke the field. She did run a very viable race but finished second. This is not bad for a first race. The jockey, however, was now a bum that did not pressure the filly in the stretch . . . "If he had, she would have won . . . he fell asleep in the stretch!" I suggested they buy the tape and watch the reruns. They did and saw the jockey really rode as well as could be expected. The horse simply tired. She would probably be fine and tighter for the next race.

When a horse loses, owners seek excuses . . . some reason why he didn't win. The main reason most of the time is that the horse was outrun. Good horses will win in spite of difficulties, bad breaks, being boxed in, too wide, etc. They win in adversity. Cheap horses barely win, even when everything goes just right. They are the claimers that fill the bottom races. As an owner, be judicious. See what really happens in the race and learn about your horse.

As a trainer, I get the horse to the first race to see what he does and how he comes out of it. Then I eliminate the excuses that might have caused him to lose. If he broke poorly, more gate work. If he hits himself, farrier work and leg wraps. If he shied or seemed to hang, blinkers. If he was uncontrollable, different equipment. Each new piece of information gleaned from the jockey after the race and observed by me must be interpreted in terms of the performance of the horse. When we finally get a fair race from a fit horse with no interference or problems, we know what we have. If he was running high, you can always drop him. If he was at the bottom, maybe he can win through his conditions.

Deals

In an ideal world, all owners have plenty of money and trainers don't have to make deals. Not so in the real world. The economic situation is such that we have had to become creative in our endeavors. Trainers may make a 60-40 or 50-50 split or whatever you both agree on. Half interest in the horse may be given to the trainer or a percentage of earnings, etc. It is important to define what expenses are paid by whom before splitting the earnings.

A friend suffered a perfect example of this problem. The deal was 40-60. My friend retained ownership of the horse and 40 percent of his earnings. She was paying 100 percent of all extra expenses such as ponies, vets and shoeing. She was surprised to find the trainer deducted his 10 percent earnings fee off the top before factoring the 40-60 figure. She also found that he had given highly questionable and unauthorized treatments and medications to

Good rapport between owner and trainer is essential.

the horse. He told the track bookkeeper that he had access to her account and obtained the earnings checks. Much after the fact, my friend found that from the $47,000 her horse earned, she was given a total of $7,000. It was a hard lesson to learn.

When you make a deal, spell out everything: Who pays for shoes, ponies, treatments, feed, hauling, and vet bills. I recommend to all trainers that with any deal, the actual cost of feed, bedding, etc. must be paid or the trainer can loose money as well as his time and effort! The percentages of ownership may be written on the horse's papers. All contingencies should be spelled out.

I have lost money on the majority of my deals. This is usually because I get untried horses and must spend time in developing them, only to find they don't have talent. Chances of having a winner are slim, but we all pursue the dream of the horse who can bail us out.

If you own a useful, performing animal, trainers will be more willing to make a deal. A formed, talented horse is a joy to train.

A trainer came to our area looking for horses. He called the owners of solid allowance horses and offered to train them free of charge. The current trainer of one of these horses heard about the call and gleefully told me how he had "punched the daylights out" of the pushy newcomer.

Owners, Trainers, and Deals

Always clarify the monetary arrangement with your trainer. It is imperative that costs be set on the training of your horse and that you understand the best and worst possible scenarios. An excellent sample of an Owner/Trainer Agreement was published by *The Thoroughbred Owner*, the official publication of The National Association of Thoroughbred Owners (NATO) in their Fall Edition of 1995, and is included on the following pages. I suggest two small additions. Under the heading "Compensation" it should be understood that often the trainer only receives 10 percent of the win purse. Some ask and get 10 percent of all earnings . . . second, third and fourth place. Clarify what your trainer expects to get from the earnings of the horse. Nothing is automatic unless defined as such. Modify the terms as you and your Trainer see fit. Write down the details and sign the document.

I would also suggest clarifying exactly what the Day Money covers in your Agreement. A common practice is for the owner to pay day money, for example, a base price

A Trainer's role is to develop the Personal Best of each horse WITHOUT breaking him down in the process!

of $30 a day. This should cover feed, usual supplements, bedding, and daily maintenance of the horse. Vet bills, shoeing and special feeds or equipment will cost extra. One of my first trainers charged me for safety pins and cotton used to wrap the horses legs. He also charged extra for electrolytes and salt. Since I was already paying $35 a day in the early '80s, this kind of bookkeeping was abusive.

At most tracks, the trainer doesn't pay for the stalls or the upkeep of track. If he is at a training center or at his own farm, he will have that extra overhead. Depending on your arrangement with him, he may or may not charge for hauling from farm to track or from track to track. I knew one trainer who had no trailer and no place to train his horses where they were stabled. Four or five days a week he charged his owner $30 to haul the horse to gallop at the track. Needless to say, this doubled the training bill and that owner, quite upset, changed trainers upon receipt of the first bill. Clarification can avoid misunderstandings.

A trainer should have the tools of his trade. He should have saddles, a variety of bridles and other necessary equipment to conduct his business. If your trainer wants you to pay for buckets, stall guards, and other items that should be general expense items, be cautious. Owners should pay for special equipment pertinent to their horse such as a set of blinkers with a particular cut to them or an unusual bit.

Costs above the day rate may be charged for extra services. Pony horses, used a couple of times a week to take your horse to the track, might be listed as an added charge. Having your horse's hair clipped when coming from a cold climate to a hot climate could cost $30 or $40 dollars. If a trainer has his own pony and his own set of clippers, he may provide those and other services at no extra charge.

Above the initial day rate, your bill will include the vet charges. Some trainers go overboard with vets. They pull blood continually, have ultrasound treatments, laser treatments, Jugs (fluids put in IV), and a plethora of other medications. X-rays are taken frequently. (Remember . . . if it shows on the X-ray, the damage has already been done). Some owners love this technology and are willing to pay for it. Make your philosophy clear. Be sure your trainer understands how you want your horse treated. Communication and mutual trust is important for both parties. Vet charges have been known to cost as much as or more than training fees. A horse needing that degree of medical support perhaps should not be at the track. (See Drugs and Medications Section.)

It is not unusual to have extra costs on race day. Disposable leg wraps, such as Vetwrap, cost about $2 a leg. There are all kinds of "natural" herbs, sold in one-dose tubes, that your trainer might use. An oral paste composed of natural ingredients is preferable to an injection if it is used to help the horse. It depends on whether or not the trainer gets the results he wants. In any case, these little tubes cost from $4 to $10 each. There may also be a hauling fee on race day from one track to another or from the farm to the track. Most trainers are trying to do a competent job and are aware of the costs. If you have good rapport with your trainer, he will keep you up to date, and you should have no major surprises.

Clarify monetary arrangements.
Write down the details and sign the document.

MODEL TRAINING CONTRACT

THIS AGREEMENT, made and entered into as of the__day of____, 20__, by and between:
_____, hereafter referred to as "trainer," and_____, here after referred to as "owner."

Trainer fully warrants that he/she has been, and is, duly licensed, in good standing and is unknowingly of any pending investigations or rulings which might interfere with his/her future ability to perform his professional duties, in any jurisdiction in which trainer may employ his trade.

Owner fully warrants that he/she is duly licensed, and is the sole representative of any and all entries having financial or legal interests in the horse(s) covered by this agreement.

In consideration of the covenants and agreements herein set forth, the parties agree as follows:

1. Owner employs the trainer to train the following named thoroughbred horse(s):

    _____
    _____
    _____
    _____

2. Trainer shall bear the responsibility for procuring and compensating:

    A. A capable and adequate staff for the care of (all) the horse(s) in his charge;
    B. All equipment, such as pitchforks, grooming equipment, etc.., all expendables, such as feed and general medicine, i.e., liniments, poultices, etc.., which are necessary for the general maintenance of horse(s).

3. Trainer shall also obtain, keep in service, and make available on demand, proof of workers compensation, and general liability insurance, sufficient to indemnify owner from liability of claims, demands, damages and defense cost arising from training and/or racing the horse(s) in the care of trainer, whether resulting from negligence of trainer, his agents, employees, or otherwise.

4. Owner shall bear the responsibility for any and all equipment, services, and supplements necessary for, and peculiar to, the specific needs of his horse(s). This would include charges for veterinary care, blacksmithing, shipping and specialized equipment, which are outside of normal needs of general maintenance of the other horses in the stable, provided the specific extraordinary expense has been authorized by owner and not required in any emergency circumstance.

Put it in writing.

5. Owner agrees to compensate trainer in amount of $_____ per day, per horse, and in the event that any purse money is awarded Owner, Owner agrees further agrees to fully compensate Trainer an amount equal to___% of such award, and Owner agrees to fully reimburse Trainer for any expense previously approved or authorized by Owner, that is incurred by Trainer in the interest of Owner and that is not covered in section 2,3, or 4 of this agreement.

6. The term of this agreement shall be for one year, beginning as of the day first above written unless terminated in writing by either party. Either party may hereto my cancel this agreement on___days written notice. Should this agreement be terminated for any reason, Owner shall bear the responsibility for removal of horse(s) from the care of the trainer within 48 hours of effective date.

7. Should either party breach the terms of this agreement and a civil action be instituted as a result thereof, it is agreed and understood that any and all attorney's fees and cost associated with the civil action shall be the responsibility of, and shall be borne by, the non-prevailing party.

8. This agreement is to be construed in accordance wit the laws of the state of_____, and any disputes arising under the terms of this agreement are to be brought in the county of_____, as the parties hereto submit to the jurisdiction of the courts of the state of _____.

Dated as of the day first above written.

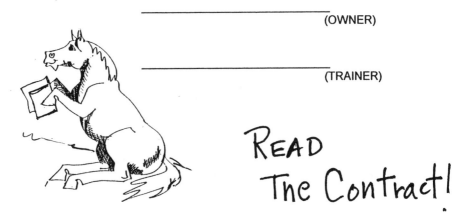

_____
(OWNER)

_____
(TRAINER)

READ
The Contract!

Our special thanks to D. Barry Stilz, of Kinkead & Stilz Attorneys at Law, PLLC, 301 East Main Street, Suite 800, Lexington, KY 40507, for this information. You may contact Mr. Stilz at 859-296-2300

Cover all your bases.

Insurance

As a new owner you will have to assess the need to insure your horse. This will depend on your consideration of insurance premium costs versus the cost of a possible catastrophe. You will also have to decide whether to insure for mortality only or if you want to include medical/surgical coverage. Remember that in the case of serious illness you may not have the option of euthanasia until certain medical or surgical procedures have been completed. Aside from the more common policies there are policies for permanent disability, live foal, and stallion fertility.

Above all, given the litigious society in which we live, you must be sure that you have sufficient personal liability in case your horse injures another horse or person, or their property.

If you decide to insure, inquire around about various insurance companies, how they handled claims, if a rep was available at odd hours of the day and night, how long it took to pay the claim and how much paper work was required. Be sure to check the guaranteed renewal of the policy as well as the exclusions section.

Be aware that if you insure a horse for $20,000 and then run him in a $5,000 claimer, you will only be paid the $5,000 for the loss. Conversely if your horse is insured for $20,000 and wins a $100,000 stakes (you should be so lucky) you are paid the $20,000 for the loss. Therefore, it is important to review your policies and change them according to your horse's current value.

It is best to deal with a company that specializes in equine insurance. That way you will be dealing with people who understand the business of horses. You should always check the A. M.. Best Financial Rating of the company - available at www.ambest.com. When you do take out a policy be sure to keep a copy of your horse's papers and his bill of sale with the policy and claims forms in case you need them in a hurry.

Remember that you must be completely truthful when filling the application. Not only is it a felony in some places to give incorrect information, but you could nullify the policy. Be assured that the insurance company will be in touch with your vet regarding previous illnesses, or reasons of death.

Lois lost two wonderful Tennessee Walkers to lightening last summer. Although the insurance did not eases her grief, it did enable her to purchase another horse.

Tax Considerations For

Pleasure Horse Owners

You must approach owning a race horse as a business. This requires keeping good records of all expenses and income. You may be able to deduct cost of your race horse from your taxes, including the expenses of your "pony horse" (which also may be your endurance or trail horse), trailer, truck, etc. Be sure to consult your tax accountant. He can help with deductions for capital items such as your barn, fences etc. according to the percentage of their use in your race operation.

This program is especially attractive to pleasure horsemen, because it allows them to participate in racing with the goal of making money (unlike pleasure horse riding) and be able to legitimately deduct expenses along the way.

Keep good records!

Where Are the "Little" Owners and Trainers at the Big Races?
or Its Hard to Say No to Major Money!

Have you ever wondered why the big races generally fill up with well known famous trainers entering world class horses? How do Wayne Lukas and some of the other brand name trainers always end up with top contenders for the major stakes? Do they have such tremendous luck that though 40,000 horses a year are registered as Thoroughbreds, the very highly talented animals fall into their hands?

It is difficult for the layman to understand the statistics against having Breeder's Cup quality horses one year, let alone various years. There are, of course, owners who are so fantastically wealthy that they own hundreds of royally bred mares to produce talented offspring. That kind of owner is buying the best to breed to the best in hopes of the best. He is using sheer numbers to help get that runner.

Owners with huge farms and hundreds of horses have "bought more tickets to the lottery". They have hedged their bets with astute breeding, excellent farm management and the best advice money can buy. Even with many new foals each year and hundreds being sent to tracks all over the country, the owner can find himself without the "GOOD ONE." It is then that he might put out the word that he is looking for a promising Stakes Horse and is willing to pay for it. When the two-year-olds start to run, the talent appears. When a young horse starts to look good and beats a few top contenders at major tracks, the offers pour in to the owner. Thunder Gulch was picked-up and purchased while already running.

The previous owner probably thought he was getting a good deal, selling him for $160,000 when he had been originally bought out of the training sale for much less. The big-name trainer with the wealthy client gets a promising young star. Many of the horses purchased that way are never heard of again, but the good buy - like Thunder Gulch - becomes a legend. It is the ability of prominent trainers to purchase the promising horses that allows them to stay on the top. The horse can come from anywhere. Larry the Legend was an example of that.

It becomes a self-fulfilling prophesy that the top trainers will get moneyed owners willing to give them the financial strength to buy the best. Meanwhile what about the rest of us? The little two-horse stables, the owner-trainers breeding their own foals that we hang on to far too long because we love them and don't want to risk losing them until we know what we have. Do we ever get to the big league? LUCK plays a huge part in this business. Let's say we have the luck to breed or acquire a talented horse. My own experience, on a smaller level, is typical of what happens. By default I got a filly that no one wanted for $2,500 on the cuff. She would not have sold in a sale for $1,500 that year based on her breeding and looks.

I trained her along with five other horses that season, and when I put her on the track, she had a real piece of speed that she generally put on at the end of a race. As this filly raced and became a more adept at running and winning, many offers were made to me. The first

Can the little guy have a great horse?

was $25,000 then $35,000 and then $125,000 and on up. The only basis for the offers was her ability to beat the other horses in the field.

Each time another offer reached me, I was surprised. My friends told me to take the money and run. As we all know, these horses can "go bad" at any time and each race may be the last. I was having such a wonderful time hauling the filly down to the track, running her, and hauling her back home, almost always with a check, that I had no pressure to sell. The filly was paying off the farm, buying the truck, putting the kids through school, and giving us all many thrills to be racing with Wayne Lucas, Woody Stephens and others.

The last offer I was given for the $2,500 "throw away" filly was $500,000. I turned it down without a thought because at that point I would have sold my lovely daughter before I would have sold the filly. She was part of our lives and we all knew that she would never be happy anywhere else. Even when she became severely ill and almost died from a virus shortly after that I had no regrets. Many have said, "Don't you wish you had taken that money?" You could be living off the interest!" I have to say, I would do it the same way again.

We got so much out of our experience with the filly that money can't buy. The lessons she taught us and the joy she gave us can't be measured. Now I see you old "hard hearts" rolling your eyes and thinking you might do it differently. Fine! Horse are much more than a meal ticket for some of us. Call it an affinity, a fatal attraction, a disease, but we do not always make choices for rational reasons. By the way, the filly, First Prediction ran for five seasons and made over three hundred thousand. Though the illness set her back a few years to start breeding, she had a weanling filly that we are dreaming about.

Back to the point, most trainers and owners will sell, take a profit and be very happy when an offer is made for their promising horse. Then, of course, there it is in the leading trainer's barn and once again people think only the super wealthy can afford horses and only the major trainers know how to train a Stakes horse!

Please understand that major trainers either have their choice of the best bred horses off their owner's farm or they get to buy the best at the select sales for top dollar. Some trainers have fifty, a hundred or even two hundred horses in training. They are constantly looking for the talent that can keep them on top. Even with the "numbers" edges, there are years that they don't get a good one. The racing public is harsh and can be very hard on well-known trainers. We must all realize that the trainer can only work with whatever talent his horses have. Just as with any major sport, the best coach in the world can't make the untalented talented. However, the good trainer could keep talented horses running for years. We could have older horses that could become sports heroes. In a business where so much can happen, even when you try to do everything right and protect your charges, it is a master who keeps his horses running into their forth or fifth years.

If you keep your "real job" and own and train horses on the side, maybe you'll have the luck of a talented one! And then you can keep and run him so that you, the little guy, can go to the BIG RACES!

Don't give up your day job.

A Word With the Expert On -
SYNDICATES, PARTNERSHIPS AND VARIATIONS!

by Scott Wells, Ruidoso, NM

One of the most positive trends in horse racing in recent years has been the increase in the number of racing partnerships. For a number of reasons, these partnerships (and they can be extremely varied in their makeup) lend themselves to enjoyment of the sport at its very best.

Most notably, from a business standpoint, it is far better to own part of a good horse than it is to own all of a mediocre one. Basically, good horses cost about the same to maintain as "cheap" horses. The differences are that they: (1) usually cost a good deal more to acquire, and (2) have the potential of earning substantial income. Many owners who in the past attempted to operate on a middle-class budget while searching for a rags-to-riches horse have realized that there are usually more rags than riches in that approach. However, armed with their hard-earned lessons, and hopefully having experienced at least a taste of the thrills of winning, they now take a more intelligent approach to the sport by joining forces with friends.

That leads to another of the benefits of group ownership: fun with friends. I have trained for some very diverse groups who, though they may have had little in common otherwise, did share one thing. They had a terrific time racing their horses. Some were high-dollar players who wanted to be participants in every major decision. Other partnerships were compromised mainly of fun-loving race fans who chipped in, bought a couple of horses, and merely wanted to know in advance when the horses would race. Most groups fall somewhere between those two extremes. With proper preparation and proper guidance, along with the patience and perseverance which is obligatory, nearly any group can experience joyous, unforgettable days (or nights) at the races.

However, the best thing about racing partnerships is that the participants, by combining their resources, are able to purchase a better racing prospect. Recent racing lore is replete with stories of successful partnerships whose relatively modest investments have bought them ownership of stakes winning horses. Almost without exception, these successful partnerships are typified by: (1) a capable, honest, highly-communicative trainer, and (2) a written agreement which names one partner as the main liaison between the trainer and the group.

In the past, many owners approached racing with the attitude that racing is the Sport of Kings and they intended to be kingly. These days, they realize that the phrases "strength in numbers" and "the more the merrier" have their place in today's racing climate.

A good partnership can provide fun and benefits for all.

Medications

AT THE RACETRACK

MEDICATIONS AT THE RACETRACK - Introduction

My opinions here may cause me some trouble. Perhaps this section should be called "Ethics in Racing: Medications, when to use, when not to use." I must share a little background information with you here. My father worked for the Federal Government, the Bureau of Narcotics, while I was growing up in San Francisco. The "evil" of drugs was indoctrinated in me at a very young age. Perhaps this early training has made me more reactionary than most when certain options are offered to get a few more races out of a horse.

I am constantly interested in the cause and effect of whatever is being done to the animals. I was married to a physician for 18 years and have great respect for the tremendous benefits science and medicine have provided for us.

The problem in racing is the attempt to "fool Mother Nature", when often rest and time off from the pounding and speed will alleviate a problem before it becomes chronic or irreversible. At the track, the trainer is reluctant to stop a horse for a slight problem close to racing time. So he asks the vet for something to "help" the horse get through the race. "You know Doc, he's been training so good. Our race is next Tuesday and now he has this heat in his tendon." Red Alert! Now is not the time to stress that tendon by running the horse.

Many trainers don't or can't stop at this point. There is tremendous pressure from the owner who doesn't want another darn excuse. The owner may even insinuate he will look for another trainer. The trainer, in desperation, looks for a quick fix which unfortunately may "fix" the horse for the rest of his career. The horse runs with chemical help and strong bandages, and bows his tendon. Now he is compromised for life. The trainer shakes his head and tells the owner, "What a shame. He was doing just fine until that misstep on the track. Just bad luck . . . but, hey, there's another sale coming up and we'll throw this horse out for a year and see how he does next year." This scenario is simplistic, but such skits are being played all too frequently at the track.

In similar situations, I have felt pushed into a corner. What to do? Use chemical help for a few more races to indulge an owner, or lose the owner and watch the horse run well for a few more races with another trainer. Afterwards, the horse is never seen again since you can only "go to the well" so many times.

The following story is typical of the problems trainers have. At the end of a meet at Tampa, my friend told me he had a three-year-old filly he was sending to the killers unless he could find someone who wanted her. She had won a few races and was very game. "She's got a knee," he said, without elaboration. I knew better than to ask if cortisone had been injected in her knee, or how often she was injected until he couldn't get anything more out of her. I looked at her . . . she had powerful hind quarters and was a muscular horse. Her knee looked "rough" but not puffy and full of fluid, though it was hot to touch. (Cortisone can eliminate heat and swelling, leaving the horse to think his joint is healthy even when it isn't.)

Be aware of cause and effect.

I agreed to pay $250 for her and decided to throw her out to pasture for the summer and see how she was in the fall.

Since she was running at $3,500 claiming races when she was right, she was certainly not worth spending any money on, even for X-rays. Surgery wasn't feasible, because she probably had joint deterioration from the cortisone at this point.

It wouldn't cost too much to carry her. If she wasn't lame next season, I'd try galloping her. I loaded her and took her home.

A friend from the track heard about my purchase and asked to buy half of her for $125 and agreed to help pay her upkeep. This was fine with me. Trainers become horse poor very quickly. It was great to have someone to help pay for feed.

In the fall, she started training (my third and fourth day ride) and she tuned right up.

She showed nervousness in the gates and had to be hauled back many times since she was left at the gate a few times.

She would become slightly lame out of the race, walk out of it, and be ready eight or ten days later. She was given Bute before the race but that was the extent of her medication. She had been on the Bleeders List, but I took her off as no signs of bleeding appeared and the Lasix seemed to do more harm than help. After an injection of Lasix, she would break into a sweat, have runny diarrhea and start urinating. She was running with a hard knocking gang of fillies and mares and did run viably in most of her races, once we solved the gate problem. To our great joy and astonishment she won a very game race where she was left in the gates, last out of 12 horses. She did a tremendous stretch run and won by a nose. What joy!

Her next race was a lackluster performance. The jockey got off, and said, "You know she's not pushing off her left leg the way she used to. I think her knee is starting to bother her again". In view of that, I turned to my partner and said, "It's time to give her away." "Wait a minute," he said, " You know there are ways to keep her going." Enter the horns of dilemma. The money would be useful. By injecting the knee with cortisone, the mare would feel no pain and could continue running with the illusion of a sound joint. I knew we could get a few more races out of her before the ultimate breakdown. Just thinking about this, my own knees and ankles started to hurt. As close as I have been to financial ruin, I have not been able to condemn a horse to this kind of finish. I realized, in this case, the decision was not mine alone to make. My partner accused me of being naive. Ridiculous, since I knew as well as anyone various ways to keep the horse running. Unfortunately, I was also aware of the consequences of those methods. I said, "Listen, if you want, I'll give you my half of the horse. Take her to another trainer, camouflage the pain and have her run full speed with a compromised knee."

Will your horse run on reality or camouflage?
Its your choice.

"Are you willing to be responsible for the injury that might result to a jockey, or the damage to the horse?" I asked. "If that's what you want, my half is yours. I can't even sell her the way she is. My choice would be to give her to a good home."

He looked at me. This was heresy. Something not too many smart trainers would admit is that **what you do today can cause breakdown tomorrow**. This is never presented as a cause and effect situation to owners. It is difficult for trainers to inform an owner that the horse could be incapacitated by trying to get a few more races. But, that is exactly what happens. Some trainers cleverly wash their hands of the responsibility. They just say they will "help" the horse feel better. The vet does his part by indulging the trainer and doing what the trainer wants. The vet might caution the trainer that when certain drugs are given, the horse should rest. The reality could be if the medication can't be traced and the horse can move, he will run. This is a great way for everyone involved to avoid responsibility when the inevitable happens. They can all commiserate about the bad luck - the "misstep".

Back to the filly and my predicament. My partner got my message and agreed to give the horse away. She is now herding cattle in Central Florida.

I will not train a horse that I know is in pain. Nor will I train a horse that is unaware of the pain he has. If the owner feels otherwise, the horse goes to another trainer. But I prefer losing an owner to the fear of someone being harmed or the horse breaking down. Obviously, I have lost owners and am not considered a sharp trainer when I refuse to use the "best" medical science has to offer. I'm in this business for the long run. I spend the time necessary to properly prepare the horse to run. That extra three to six months in the training program is costly, but worth it if the horse has talent.

This is why we need **new people in the business who can do much of the early work themselves**. Their horses will hold up better, and if they don't have talent, they will have another life as a hunter or riding horse. **Horses are not disposable items.** I will not turn them over quickly in search of the good one. Now I train a few a year hoping they will pay off, but recognizing the odds against it. I am happy and I can live with myself.

Back to medications. **Anytime you give a horse a painkiller so he can run, you are in trouble. Pain is a warning sign.** Being over fifty, I have a lot of aches and pains. I know that aspirin helps when my bones ache. Bute is probably the same for horses, helpful for slight problems. This doesn't mean mega doses. Some trainers say, "I love running that track; there are no limits on Bute." Too much of anything can be dangerous. **Vets see many horses with ulcerated stomachs caused by Bute abuse.**

One filly suddenly died on me two weeks after arriving on my farm from the track. The necropsy disclosed purple discolorations on the wall of the stomach . . . ulcers . . . where large amounts of Bute had eaten away the lining. Other horses on long-term Bute develop anemia or other blood disorders.

Many people don't worry about this, because the horses go to the killers when they're finished at the track anyway. Again, I can't knowingly set up animals for a short life. But in the racing business, where the owners pay a lot of money and want quick results, some trainers push horses until they produce or break down. There are always more horses coming along. Wouldn't it be more cost effective to rest the horse a few days and race many years?

Should a horse that is unaware of his pain be forced to run?

Beware any time a trainer says to you, "He had a little filling in his left ankle, but he isn't lame." Next comes, "I don't understand. He never took a lame step." Could be true, but if you are astute, the horse generally tells you that problems are coming. He gets filling or heat in a leg, favors it, paws and digs holes in his stall, or he stands and holds his feet in a particular way to alleviate pain. The way he walks out after he has been stationary tells you something. Observe the signs. Figure out the reason for his actions. Don't simply mask the signs with drugs and carry on. **When the horse is off, turn him out every day and observe. When he starts frolicking and feeling sound, go back to galloping. No vet bills** and, if you are observant, **you should not have catastrophic breakdowns.** This is the basis of my methods.

Race day, for most owners, is very expensive. The vet gives most horses a "cocktail" the day of the race. Usually it consists of a combination of vitamins (B-12 or multi-vitamins), and possibly various kinds of corticosteroids such as Azium or Vetalog that are supposed to help with inflammation. If allowed, nervous horses may be given SoluDeltaCortef. This is supposed to help a hyper horse. It is also a steroid. Many trainers swear by these injections. I now avoid their use and only capitulated in the past under duress from an owner. At the time, I didn't realize they were corticosteroids. I have never seen them produce dramatic results on my horses. But then, my horses were always sound. One hyper filly dropped her head when given SoluDeltaCortef and almost snoozed in the gate. She didn't run well half asleep. On the other hand, Lois had a broodmare down from undetermined causes, probably acute shock and colic triggered by an abscess. When given a shot of SoluDeltaCortef, she literally arose from the dead like Lazarus. The therapeutic value was obvious. The vet still calls her the "Miracle Mare". Every medication affects every horse differently. Do your homework and make your own informed decisions.

What to DO? HOW To Help!

Certain medications definitely make a dramatic difference on sore horses. Banamine is sometimes used a few days before a race. One owner claimed a horse from a very aggressive leading trainer ... famous for how hard he was on a horse. Indeed, the horse won the race the day we claimed him, and I went to the spit box to pick him up. As he cooled out after the race he got progressively more lame. By the time I took him to my barn, he could scarcely walk, he was in such pain. When the owner came back to admire his horse, I said, "Watch," and led him out. The horse was very sore. The owner agreed that I should take the horse home, turn him out and observe how well he walked out of his stiffness.

At home he was turned out in a grassy paddock. It should have been heaven to a horse just off the track. Most animals frolic and trot around from the sheer joy of being able to roll and have free movement after the confinement of track life. This horse just stood in the middle of the pasture and didn't move. When he did walk, it was very painfully. I watched him for days, waiting to see any desire on his part to move without being prodded. He never had any. I called a friend who worked in the barn where the horse had been claimed and asked

**Observe the symptoms and figure them out.
Don't simply mask them and carry on.**

if there was anything they did with this horse to get him to train. He said that the horse never went to the track without Bute every night. I tried it and he at least moved, but did not appear to be free of pain. He still seemed quite sore when he galloped.

Another phone call revealed that if I wanted a good gallop, he would need to have 10ccs of Banamine . . . a non-steroidal antiinflammatory drug. It acts like a super Bute and is a potent pain killer. The vet who treated the horse at the track advised me to give this medication two days before running or working him. This horse could only move with Bute. He could not move at all without help. I was so uncomfortable with the situation that I tried swimming him, but there was no way he could perform without the medications. He would go into races walking sound but come out lame. We had the vet try to pin point the problem but were never successful. The owner tried acupuncture and massage without much luck. He wanted to see his horse run.

It became more and more frustrating. I hated using medications, but knew he couldn't move without them. I was acutely aware that the owner figured since he claimed the horse when he won, why couldn't he win with me? The vet tried injecting stifles which seemed to make matters worse. At the same time, the owner decided to send the horse to Maryland. He became very sore on the trip as standing in a van right after getting his stifles injected is contraindicated. The owner and trainer both complained about his condition when he arrived. In hind sight, he was probably crashing from the medications used to keep him going as long as he did. I had no way of knowing the horse was going through substance withdrawal. I vowed never to accommodate an owner against my own principles. Trying for results because the owner spent money and wanted action with the horse, not lay up, was not my game. After the trip, this horse was laid up for six months and then started to run without much success. Horses trained my way don't have these problems. They run frequently, and I don't ache because I'm asking a sore horse to run.

I can't leave this subject without mentioning anabolic steroids. A friend of mine, an orthopedic surgeon, has seen the results of using these kinds of steroids on human athletes. He sees a lot of tearing of the muscle insertion on the bone, because a muscle that develops beyond the size it is meant to be is too powerful for the connective framework. It is like putting a huge engine on a small chassis. Nature has devised a beautiful balance with form and function. If larger muscle were needed, stronger insertion ligaments and tendons would develop, along with the framework.

We come along and hyper develop one component (the muscle) while disregarding the rest of the system. This is very dangerous. **Many horses are on anabolic steroids.** These drugs are not illegal. They tend to create very "pissy" personalities. Fillies appear to be in a permanent "PMS" syndrome. Anabolic steroids can make some horses dangerously aggressive! It is questionable if anabolic steroids do enable a horse to run faster. There is no proof that larger muscle mass enhances intrinsic speed. Many gifted runners are not heavily muscled. Imagine the stress on a system when anabolic steroids which increase muscle are coupled with corticosteroids which weaken tendons and ligaments. Heart, lungs, conformation and every other component must blend together to have a great horse.

Try to run and win the right way.

My lovely mare ran four years without any kind of chemical enhancement. **She ran on solid training against some super stars.** She came back again and again and was clean legged. **If you have a talented horse, you can run without all the junk.** If the horse isn't talented, nothing will help. Since most of you are doing proper training with good foundation, remember my mare. She was born with a little more speed than average and she ran and won. No cheap shot, no gimmicks.

Try to run and win the right way. You will feel good about what you are doing with your animals. I've had many other horses not nearly as talented as First Prediction, but they ran persistently for years because they had time to grow and develop.

Why do we have more **BREAKDOWN** and **BLEEDING** in racing today?
Could it be because of the <u>Potent Medications</u> that give the Horse,
the Trainer and the Owner the <u>ILLUSION</u> of <u>SOUNDNESS?</u>

You decide!

 **Medications don't cure a lack of talent.**

THE INFORMED OWNER

These opinions are very personal and are approached cautiously. Experience has taught me that most owners have no idea of exactly how their horse is being trained. They are often intimidated by the backside environment and terminology, a very dangerous and costly position.

This Section describes the purchase of a horse and the typical training routine at the racetrack. When your horse goes to the track, what I describe may or may not happen to your horse.

If your horse was purchased at a two-year-old-in-training sale, he was "cautiously" trained to breeze two furlongs. Many farms break their horses at 18 months and teach them to walk, trot, slow gallop and do figure eights. Depending on the date of the sale, the horse will be turned back out or begin his training, galloping every day or so. If his training begins, he will usually gallop no more than a mile and will be kept in a stall.

Think of what it might do physiologically to a young animal, with green unformed bone, when he is confined in a 12' x 12' stall for as much as twenty-three and a half hours a day. Is this a natural way to raise an athlete?

If your horse came from a farm where he was turned out most of the time during early training, he has a big advantage over the typical racehorse. When you drive through farm country, you see rolling hills with mares and foals grazing in pastures. Unfortunately, once horses go into training or sales preparation, many are stalled. Sales people don't want the horse to get any scratches or injuries that might make him look less attractive in the sale ring. They believe there is risk of injury if the horse is allowed to frolic and zoom around the pasture. Farm managers feel an obligation to protect the animals from such "dangers".

Short-term the horse is coddled and protected. Long-term, he is not learning to be comfortable with other animals. He is missing the natural exercise and growth necessary to be a resilient racehorse.

On large farms, when breaking yearlings and two-year-olds, long-term tranquilizing drugs are sometimes used to make them docile. The breaking process is easier and less time consuming. Many believe this is the only way to break and train fractious Thoroughbreds. I am not comfortable with this idea. The well adjusted, well trained horse will cope better with the racing environment if he has been allowed to develop and learn normally.

A day or two before the sale when these horses are asked to breeze for the first time, usually at the sale site, they will be pushed to get a good timed work. This is when many buck their shins. If the horse you want has bucked shins, buy him, but allow him time to rebuild, grow, and develop. It is too early to ask him to run fast, especially with so little foundation. Don't let him go directly to the racetrack. (See the Sections on Two-year-olds, and Bucked Shins.)

Most horses bought at a two-year-olds-in-training sales are sent directly to the track. They are confined in their stalls, only let out once a day to learn to gallop on the real track. Galloping on the real track allows speed that could never be attained on your farm, speed that is unnecessary, in fact harmful, so early. Since they are not allowed to move naturally, this kind of training starts making them sore. They are only getting a mile or two a day, but they

**Should an athlete be confined to a stall
23 to 24 hours a day?**

get it every day. Because they are running intensely on the track surface everyday, with virtually no real warm up or cool-down, the soreness compounds. These sore horses are given medication to allow them to continue training. Usually it is Bute every night.

No two-year-old should be medicated for that kind of soreness. It is much better to rest him and observe the soreness. When it disappears, continue his training. If asked to run without the needed rebuild-time, rest, and gentle movement required to adjust to their work load, these undamaged horses will become damaged.

At the track as the animal becomes more muscularly fit, he is able to go faster. This may be when bone chips start to appear. Then you have green bone, with chips, running on a hard surface. Sometimes the trainer will X-ray and allow the horse to continue training, if he feels the chip won't interfere with the speed. In this case, the horse can only continue with the help of painkillers, corticosteroids and wraps. So, the trainer wraps, gives support therapy, and continues training until the horse is injured. Any two-year-old that needs supportive medication and leg wraps is being over-trained.

The usual training will continue to be one or two miles daily, interspersed with a day or so of walking around the shedrow or on the hotwalker. As a new owner, I vividly recall going to the racetrack for the first time. I saw this type of training and asked if this was all they did. I actually said, "15 to 45 minutes out of the stall and you charge $35 a day. No afternoon exercise?"

Some trainers, sensitive to their animals, see the problems coming and allow turnout time back at the farm. Others capitulate, pressured by the owner who wants his horse running until he wins or breaks down.

The breakdown inevitably comes when the vet tries to "help" the horse continue training. He has to tell the trainer that there are medications that will enable the horse to continue running short term, but that they will be damaging long term. Corticosteroids in the joints alleviate symptoms. In conventional training even when the horse is sore, training continues. The horse runs unaware of the damage he is doing to himself, because he feels no pain.

As owners, you should know how to read the vet bills you receive from the track. They may tell you more about how your horse is doing than your weekly talks with the trainer, If you see X-rays on the bill, Red alert! Immediately ask why they were taken . If your trainer says, "Well, he was a little lame" or "There is some heat in . . ." a particular area, tell him to **stop the horse until physical signs are gone.**

Often the X-ray shows nothing, and the trainer continues training. He may not realize that some kinds of damage don't show up in an X-ray until it is too late. By continuing his training program, he compounds the damage.

Once a filly was sent to me from the track who supposedly had bucked shins. They had continued training her and she had won a race, but the trainer told the owner that she just didn't want to be a racehorse. When I looked at the horse, she had very rough looking shins. I had her X-rayed before we went home.

When we got home, I noticed that she didn't want to take her left lead and that she was slightly lame. Later, the vet called with the results of her X-rays. She showed a very clear crack on her cannon in the vicinity of the rough shin. Previous X-rays had not shown the

Allow rest and rebuild-time.
Observe soreness.

crack, though the horse certainly had physical signs of problems more serious than bucked shins. The lesson here is never ignore your own observations. X-rays and tests only help with diagnosis.

This filly was in training, lame and even won a race. Because the X-rays didn't show a break, she was pushed until damage could be seen. Had she been stopped a few days, when the shin problem started and allowed to heal, she may not have needed six to nine months of rest to heal a fracture. The fact is that there must have been some physical sign in her leg to trigger this X-ray. Until a physical sign disappears, whether the X-ray shows a problem or not, the horse should be turned out and rested. If the horse needs pain relief while he recuperates, by all means keep him comfortable. Do not resume his training program until the medication has been suspended and the horse has no further physical signs. Please be observant with your animals. This program is designed to teach you how to recognize problems.

The background on what might happen at the track should help you to understand that keeping the horse out and loose most of the time in his formative growth period, will allow him to withstand the track pounding. Many breakdowns in young horses could be avoided with a variation in the training regime.

The series of events that lead to the breakdown can sometimes be charted by reading between the lines of vet bills. Some vet bills from a leading trainer are included. They were received by a friend, when her horse was under the trainer's care at a major racetrack. The filly ran in stakes and was a fairly decent allowance horse. She was sent to this trainer by another trainer who told the owner the mare was fine except for a windpuff on her left front.

We will walk through this bill and pretend we are "Columbo". Let's see if we can reconstruct the scenario of the final breakdown of this filly.

Learn to recognize problems early on.

VET BILLS FROM A LEADING TRAINER

THE FOLLOWING VET BILLS ARE FROM AN ACTUAL LEADING TRAINER AT A MAJOR TRACK

TRAINING THROUGHOUT THE EIGHT MONTHS IS $45 a day. .. vet bills, shoes, and ponies are all extra.

The horse was at the track a total of eight months. I am going to walk you through those months. This filly had placed in a Stakes and was a solid Allowance horse. She definitely had ability.

Month One

Upon arriving at the track, the horse was seen by the vet.

1/4	Wormed
1/5	X-ray left ankle
1/6	Tube oil
1/8	CBC Blood Chemistry

TOTAL VET COSTS $155

We see the trainer observed something as he had the left ankle X-rayed. The oiling of the horse on day six suggests perhaps a colic. A CBC would not be unusual for a new horse coming into a trainer's barn. There are no further vet bills this month. Perhaps the horse is getting used to the track.

Month Two

2/13	Electrolyte Vitamin JUG
2/13	Banamine Injection
2/14	Adequan Injection
2/15	Pre-Race Treatment
2/15	Pre-Race Injection

HORSE RACED ON 2/15

2/15	Post-Race Endoscopic Exam
2/19	Liver and Vitamin Injection
2/20	Bronchial Injection
2/21	Bronchial Injection
2/21	Inject Right and Left Stifles
2/22	Bronchial Injection
2/23	Electrolyte Vitamin JUG
2/23	Banamine Injection

Let's use a little logic.

2/24	Adequan Injection
2/25	Pre-Race Injection
2/25	Pre-Race Treatment

HORSE RACED ON 2/25

Electrolyte jug - IV fluids mixed with electrolytes and vitamins and perhaps other additives. Expensive and unnecessary.

Banamine - A very POTENT PAINKILLER! Lame and sore horses under the influence of this medication appear sound. That definitely means pain was masked! Notice Banamine was given two days before every single race that this horse ran! If administered less than forty-eight hours before the race, it might show up in the drug test!

Adequan i.m., Luitpold Pharmaceuticals, Inc., Shirley, NY. - According to the product insert, "Adequan . . . diminishes or reverses the processes which result in loss of cartilaginous mucopolysaccharides . . . by stimulating synovial membrane activity . . . and increasing synovial fluid viscosity in traumatized equine carpal joints."

Pre-Race Treatment - Perhaps an inhalant of some type to open the lungs.

Pre-Race Injection - Probably a mixture of corticosteroids or pain killers, such as SoluDeltaCortef, ACTH, Adenosine, Meticorten, and Prednisone.

Liver and Iron Injections - Maybe the horse had a low blood count.

Bronchial Injections - Throughout the horse's time at the track, she is given this medication the three days preceding every race. No one can give me a clear answer as to what it is. It might be a medication from Canada called Clenbuteral (a steroidlike product) that has been used as a lung medication and is now illegal.

Injection of right and left stifles - This tells us that the horse is going sore in her stifles. (Horses indicate soreness in the stifles when they are short strided in the rear legs. They may also have trouble backing up or turning in small circles.) Although the problem may be in the front legs, we see the manifestation in the rear, because the horse compensates by shifting weight to the hind legs. Usually, the stifles are injected with a caustic substance, possibly an iodine type product that causes scar tissue to form in the area. This is called an "internal blister". The track this horse runs on is noted for causing soreness. Stopping this horse and allowing her soreness to heal would be preferable to medicating. The best cure for sore stifles is turnout, long trots and slow gallops on a kind surface.

The Post Race endoscopic exam suggests that the horse quit in the race and didn't run well. The trainer was looking to see if she bled.

THE VET BILLS THIS MONTH WERE $435.
TRAINING CONTINUES AT $45 PER DAY.

BEWARE WHEN YOU SEE INJECTIONS IN JOINTS ON YOUR VET BILL!

Month Three

3/1	Wormed
3/1	Flu Rhino Vaccine
3/8	Bronchial Injection
3/9	Bronchial Injection
3/10	Bronchial Injection
3/12	Electrolyte Vitamin Jug
3/12	Banamine Injection
3/13	Adequan Injection
3/14	Pre-Race Injection
3/14	Pre-Race Treatment

HORSE RACED 3/14

3/14	Another scoping . . . perhaps bleeding after this race?
3/22	Bronchial Injection
3/22	Equipoise Injection
3/22	Injection of Right and Left Stifles . . . again
3/24	Electrolyte Vitamin Jug
3/24	Banamine Injection
3/26	Pre-Race Injection
3/26	Pre-Race Treatment

HORSE RACED 3/26

3/29	Bronchial Injection
3/30	Bronchial Injection

Equipoise may be used to increase appitite and Agression!

anabolic steroids increase muscle mass — could make muscle

BARN GYM

too BULKY

The new injection this month is Equipoise, an anabolic steroid, which increases muscle mass. This is the same (banned) medication that caused such problems when used by the Olympic Athletes. Generally anabolic steroids are those that enhance muscle mass. You'll hear of weight lifters and runners using them. Corticosteroids are injected intra-articularly to alleviate symptoms of damaged joints. They are used systemically (injected intramuscularly) to alleviate swelling and pain. They are a short-term fix for sore horses.

Note that the horse has had her stifles injected again. They are bothering her, but she may not know it in a race, as all the medication she is given masks the problem. She'll be sore when the medications wear off!

She was scoped again. They must be expecting her to bleed. It is just a matter of time with all of these drugs.

TOTAL VET BILLS $400

Month Four

4/1	Electrolyte Vitamin Jug
4/1	Banamine Injection
4/2	Adequan Injection
4/2	Injection - right and left ankles
4/3	Pre-Race Injection
4/3	Pre-Race Treatment

HORSE RACED 4/3

4/8	Electrolyte Vitamin Jug
4/8	Banamine Injection
4/10	Pre-Race Injection
4/10	Pre-Race Treatment

HORSE RACED AND WON 4/10

4/21	Bronchial Injection
4/22	Bronchial Injection
4/24	Electrolyte Vitamin Jug
4/24	Banamine Injection
4/29	Bronchial Injection
4/30	Bronchial Injection
4/31	Electrolyte Vitamin Jug
4/31	Banamine Injection

Injection of Ankles!

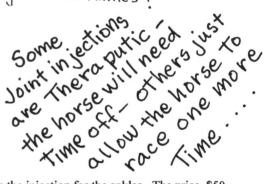

Some Joint injections are Theraputic - the horse will need time off - others just allow the horse to race one more Time....

The worst thing we see this month is the injection for the ankles. The price, $50, tells us it may have been cortisone, the first step toward the destruction of the ankles. Remember, cortisone is used for pain. When prescribed for human use, people are instructed not use or stress the injured joint. Horses are injected and asked to run hard, starting the cycle of destruction described in Drs. Krook and Maylin's Book, *Race Horses at Risk.*

(The exception seems to be using hyaluronic acid, a substance that is similar to joint fluid. It seems to cushion rough joints and enhance healing. **Horses should always rest after these injections!**)

The rest of the medications are as previously explained. In spite of all the chemicals, the horse does win! Many of these medications are not necessary. However, some definitely "help" the horse run. Others, of course, are destroying the horse because she is able to run when she should really be resting and healing. Continuing with the animal in this manner is counterproductive long term. **As an owner, it is up to you to decide how you want your horse to be handled.** Look for a trainer who has time to work more closely with you and time to get to know your horse rather than load him with medication. Trainers who have small stables might have that kind of time. (This is not to condemn leading trainers. Trainers with large stables simply have less time to work with interested, involved owners.)

THE VET BILL FOR THE FOURTH MONTH IS $377

Month Five

5/2	Pre-Race Injection
5/2	Pre-Race Treatment

HORSE RACED 5/2

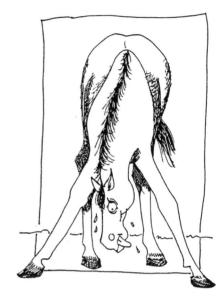

5/6	Encephalitis Vaccine
5/19	Bronchial Injection
5/20	Bronchial Injection
5/21	Banamine Injection
5/22	Adequan Injection
5/23	Lasix Injection
5/23	Pre-Race Injection
5/23	Pre-Race Treatment

HORSE RACED 5/23

5/25	Bronchial Injection
5/26	Bronchial Injection
5/27	Electrolyte Vitamin Jug
5/27	Banamine Injection
5/28	Adequan Injection
5/29	Lasix Injection
5/29	Pre-Race Injection
5/29	Pre-Race Treatment

HORSE RACED 5/29

This month the filly is put on Lasix. One more stress to an already stressed system. She did win another race this month. With all of the medications and then Lasix, it is admirable that the filly manages to finish races . . . let alone win one. This filly has been put in claiming races since her first start with this trainer. She has been progressively dropped in class with each subsequent race.

THE VET BILLS WERE $435 THIS MONTH

Be careful with Lasix in extreme HEAT !

Who can afford this?

Month Six

6/2	Bronchial Injection
6/3	Bronchial Injection
6/3	Injection - right and left hocks
6/4	Bronchial Injection
6/9	Electrolyte Vitamin Jug
6/9	Banamine Injection
6/10	Adequan Injection
6/11	Lasix Injection
6/11	Pre-Race Injection
6/11	Pre-Race Treatment

HORSE RACED 6/11

6/15	Bronchial Injection
6/16	Bronchial Injection
6/19	Electrolyte Vitamin Jug
6/19	Banamine Injection
6/20	Adequan Injection
6/21	Pre-Race Injection
6/21	Pre-Race Treatment
6/21	Lasix Injection

HORSE RACED 6/21

6/28	Bronchial Treatment
6/29	Bronchial Treatment
6/30	Bronchial Treatment

In one of the races, the filly ran second. We see that this month the hocks have been injected, probably with cortisone. Now she has been treated for sore stifles, sore ankles, and sore hocks. She still runs because she has "heart" and is not aware of her deterioration.

THE VET BILLS FOR THIS MONTH ARE $342

injection of Hocks!

Everything's sore but her heart.

Month Seven

7/1	Electrolyte Vitamin Jug
7/1	Banamine Injection
7/2	Adequan Injection
7/3	Lasix Injection
7/3	Pre-Race Injection
7/3	Pre-Race Treatment

HORSE RACED AND WON! 7/3

7/12	Bronchial Injection
7/13	Bronchial Injection
7/14	Electrolyte Vitamin Jug
7/14	Banamine Injection
7/15	Adequan Injection
7/16	Pre-Race Injection
7/16	Pre-Race Treatment
7/16	Lasix Injection

HORSE RACED AND WON! 7/16

7/17	Dewormed
7/25	Bronchial Injection
7/26	Bronchial Injection
7/27	Bronchial Injection
7/28	Bronchial Injection

Lasix! Bronchial Injections! Banamine! ADEQUAN!

This month the horse has won two races. Incidentally, one purse in one of the races was taken back three months later. The DRUG TEST CAME BACK POSITIVE! Perhaps the buildup of so many medications finally showed through in spite of the fact that the horse was on Lasix, a drug that may mask test results. The trainer's comment when he found out, was, "I don't understand. I gave her the same stuff I give all my horses!"

I will agree with that. Sometimes the vet bills of other horses in his barn were on the same page as those of this filly. I could see that every horse got the same stuff. The filly had been progressively dropped in price with each race and that is how she was able to win.

<u>**TOTAL VET BILLS FOR THIS MONTH ARE $420**</u>

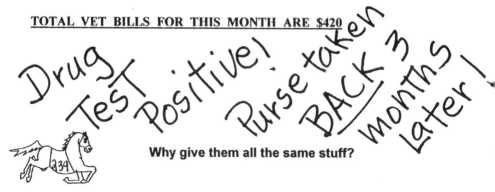

Drug Test Positive! Purse taken BACK 3 months later!

Why give them all the same stuff?

Month Eight

8/1	Bronchial Injection
8/2	Bronchial Injection
8/3	Bronchial Injection
8/4	Bronchial Injection
8/5	Adequan Injection
8/6	Pre-Race Injection
8/6	Pre-Race Treatment
8/6	Estro IV (Premarin - used for bleeders)
8/6	Lasix Injection

HORSE RACED HER LAST RACE 8/6

8/7	Eye Medication
8/13	Ultra Sound Tendon

Did you notice something different in this bill? The horse has been given Bronchial Injections for a more persistent period of time. I suspect she had a massive lung infection resulting from the bleeding. The medications may have suppressed this temporarily enabling her to run until the medication could no longer mask the damage to her lungs. These injections could be Clenbuteral, a lung medication, or Prednisone, a steroid that is used a great deal in lung disease. The latter has many side effects, one of which is aggression. It is used very cautiously in humans, as the illusion of well-being can fool you into thinking that your lungs are well.

At this point, the horse has an accumulation of problems manifesting themselves. The bronchial injections may help get one more race. Since this trainer certainly knows the signs of distress, he took a final shot. The Estro IV (estrogen - a female hormone) also implies that there might be a problem with her breathing and/or her lungs.

I'm not sure the horse even finished the race. I saw her five months after that last race and her ankles were still swollen and deformed. She had bowed the left front tendon down low and who knows what other damage had been done. It looked like the suspensory ligaments might also have been torn bilaterally. Unfortunately, there was so much disfigurement it was hard to tell. With time the ankles should start healing, but they will never be sound.

Had this horse been handled differently, she could have run for years. She did not have a bad step or bad luck at the track. **This is a text book case of abuse and poor management . . . all done in the name of Horse Training by a leading trainer.** This owner actually paid $45 a day to have a decent, talented horse ruined. He also paid enormous vet bills. Her bow may eventually heal, but she will never run again. She is only four years old. My recommendation to the owner was to breed her, if possible. (Steroids are known to cause fertility problems in horses. In the four years she has been retired, she has yet been able to conceive.)

As I reviewed this horse's history, I felt ill. Seeing the progressive use of medications, there is no doubt as to the outcome. I hope you question what is being done to your horse . . . and then maybe he will have a chance for a lengthy career!

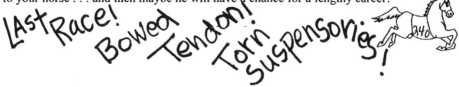

ANOTHER REAL VET BILL

This bill reflects a pattern of disintegration I have seen many times over the years in horses sent to me from the track because their performance seemed to be "tailing off". Observing them, I began to feel that I was running a "Betty Ford Clinic" for horses. This particular horse, NJ, arrived at my farm in December. The owner had called and asked if I would be willing to take it. The trainer had said there was nothing wrong with the horse. He had just tailed off. His form deteriorated with each race after he won his maiden race.

This horse, a colt, had been purchased in the March Two-Year-Olds-In-Training Sale and had gone directly from that sale to the racetrack. So, at the ripe old age of 24 months, NJ (the colt) found himself at the track. Keep in mind he was probably stalled and in training from the age of 18 to 20 months.

When he arrived, he really didn't look too bad. His joints weren't swollen or loggy appearing. It was obvious they had been fired, but he looked reasonably sound. He was very well balanced and proportioned. His legs didn't turn in or out. His conformation was correct. He was turned out in a small paddock. He didn't move when turned loose. He stood in the paddock and showed little interest in his surroundings. At the time this was attributed to the fact he might have been given a tranquillizer.

Upon my request, the owner sent me a copy of the vet bills so that I could try to reconstruct his experience and performance at the track. Let me share the bill with you.

Month One

3/3	Fecal Exam	
3/14	Tying-up Powder	
3/24	Firing of Shins	
3/24	Kling Bag	
3/24	Tetanus Toxoid Vaccination	
3/24	Firing Paint	
3/29	Kling Bag	

We may surmise from the treatment that the horse was put into training, had a tying-up problem, and was given a powder for it. He then bucked his shins. The trainer wanted to keep him going, had him fired and kept him at the racetrack. It appears that he was probably walked and hosed until his shins were better as there are no bills for April. Remember, this is a 25 month old animal, confined to a twelve by twelve stall and walked once or twice a day for maybe half an hour.

Month Three

5/9	Electrolytes and Vitamins
5/27	Fecal Exam

Since there are no other bills for April and May, we may assume that NJ is training uneventfully, probably galloping a mile to a mile and a half with gradual increments of speed at the end of the gallops every few days. He may have gone to the gates on occasion. The actual time he spent on the track would have been about 15 minutes a day.

They call 15 minutes a day exercise?

Month Four
HORSE RACED 6/7

6/20	Electrolytes and Vitamins
6/23	Bute
6/23	Meticorten
6/24	ACTH
6/24	Adenosine

HORSE RACED 6/24

These bills seemed tame compared to the bills we just examined. But why would a young healthy horse need painkillers and steroids every time he ran? Meticorten is a corticosteroid. **Meticorten and ACTH are very potent anti-inflammatory medications.** ACTH is an adrenocortcotropic hormone. It stimulates the adrenal glands to boost production of their own steroids. If they are boosted too often, the natural adrenal glands can become exhausted and stop production. They are effective in treating chronic inflammation but have potential side effects that can leave horses seriously crippled. This combination of medications was the pattern throughout NJ's time at the track. It appeared that the trainer and vet were giving these medications just in case, since there were no X-rays or other signs of joint problems.

THE VET BILLS FOR JUNE WERE $130

Month Five

7/11	Meticorten
7/11	Bute
7/12	Adenosine
7/12	ACTH

HORSE RACED 7/12

7/16	Electrolytes and Vitamins
7/22	Bute
7/22	Meticorten
7/23	ACTH
7/23	Adenosine

HORSE RACED 7/23

At least no Lasix or other breathing medications have been given.

THE VET BILLS FOR JULY WERE $136

Why is it that so many horses do not last more than one season?

Month Six

8/22	Electrolytes and Vitamins
8/22	Equipoise
8/27	Bute and Meticorten
8/28	ACTH
8/28	Adenosine

He's a colt!

HORSE RACED 8/28

I didn't like seeing that he was given Equipoise (an anabolic steroid) usually contraindicated in colts. He might have been off his feed, depressed or unaggressive.

THE VET BILLS FOR AUGUST WERE $113

The vet bills were identical for August, September, October and November. He raced an average of twice a month in October and won his maiden race. He ran poorly after that. He arrived at my farm in December. I told the owner the horse was quite depressed and moving very slowly. He was probably body sore and needed time to heal. He had a little heat in his left knee, but showed no lameness at this time. The vet came out and checked the left cannon bone to rule out fracture from the bucked shins. The X-ray showed no fracture, and at the time the vet noted that he not was lame.

In the middle of January the vet had to return. The horse had begun to show lameness. He was only being turned out and fed. He moved very little but appeared to be in pain and manifested much more heat and swelling in all the joints. He looked very poor. I now wondered if he had chips in joints, as his overall movement had deteriorated. The vet again checked the horse, noting that he was lame in both front legs. The knees and ankles were X-rayed to check for chips. The X-rays showed no bony lesions and rest was recommended.

It was at this point that I started calling vets asking questions about the medications used on the horse. I was told that ACTH suppresses the normal function of the adrenal glands when used long term with corticosteroids, and that two to three treatments a month in the horse's formative growth period was excessive. I also learned these medications could explain why the horse was so depressed and why he showed no colt-like interest in any other animal. It could take months for his adrenal glands to start functioning again.

Please understand that I do not claim to be a PhD in Pharmacology or Veterinary Science. However, I felt the need to try to understand the basics of this very complex field. Some may accuse me of over simplification. The information I gleaned from veterinarians and pharmacologists is shared with you concisely and in layman's terms, because it is vital that we have a basic understanding of the contents of medications given to our horses.

During my inquiries, I saw the following article, *Good Steroids, Bad Steroids*, by Laura Hillenbrand in *EQUUS Magazine*, 1991, Issue 166 (Reprinted with permission of Fleet Street Publishing Corporation). I feel it is worthy of our attention and have included part of it for you. "Corticosteroids . . . synthetically replicate the basic structure of the hormone cortisol, which regulates many functions within the body, including reducing inflammation . . . Some forms have up to **700 times the suppressive power of natural cortisol**. Corticosteroids have proved to be the least expensive, fastest acting, and most effective anti-inflammatory medications ever used in veterinary practice."

Imagine 700 times the power of nature.

Inflammation is a part of the healing process. When you inhibit inflammation, you are also inhibiting healing. Inflammation is also a sign that there is a problem. If ignored and suppressed, you enable the damage to continue. The article further states, "Along with the benefits, these substances carry potential side effects that can leave horses permanently, or even fatally, crippled . . . all forms of corticosteroid administration carry potentially harmful side effects. Repeated use of these drugs has been shown to handicap the adrenal gland, causing a drop in levels of several other key hormones as well as cortisol and creating hormonal imbalance . . . because they suppress the immune system and the inflammatory healing reaction, the drugs may also leave a horse vulnerable to undiscovered infection. **The greatest risk in corticosteroid therapy,** however, involves the possibility that the medication will so prevent the body's protective and restorative mechanisms that progressive structural damage occurs. This can happen in two basic ways. First, **corticosteroids can thwart or delay healing to such a degree that supporting capacity is never restored to injured tendons and ligaments, and essential structures such as the cartilage cushions between bones within joints are not regenerated.** Cartilage, which is naturally worn away with use, is slow to heal. **In horses repeatedly given corticosteroids** (especially when the drug is injected intra-articularly), **not only does the natural replacement of old cartilage stop, but the current wear greatly accelerates.** Eventually, **the cartilage is completely worn away and bone rubs against bone, leaving the joint crippled.** Secondly, the pain relief provided by corticosteroids, while doing nothing to cure injuries or inflammatory conditions, can **encourage a horse to use a damaged limb as if it were sound**, unknowingly risking catastrophe with each stride . . . all experts agree that high, frequent doses of the drug can inflict serious damage."

The article does suggest circumstances when the drug could be helpful. Usually it is given short term in small , locally targeted doses. This information is shared with you because, at first glance, the medications NJ received are not alarming. They were only given when he raced. However, I soon realized that NJ was going through a "drying out" or withdrawal from the medications he had been given. He was now a mere 30 months old but moved and acted like a 30 year old.

Although he was fed and consumed enormous quantities of grain and hay, he lost weight and muscle tone and looked like the kind of horse the Humane Society would fine me for starving. He was self destructing in front of my eyes. By early March the horse was looking worse. I took him to the University of Florida Veterinary Teaching Hospital. They examined and X-rayed him and listened to his history. Their diagnosis was Degenerative Joint Disease. It was possible that the cartilage was completely worn down and could not regenerate, there was so much damage. They had no idea whether he could ever be useful racing again or even sound. At this point, the horse was 33 months of age and had been physically on the track only six months.

After much discussion with vets, he was given four injections of Adequan* and then the oral equivalent Flexfree. (*GAG-Glycosaminoglycan - It allegedly helps cartilage growth, but only if the cartilage has not been totally destroyed).

In early May, NJ had acute swelling in his hind legs. I thought he might be going into renal shutdown or some other kind of metabolic problem. He was hauled back to the vet.

"Along with the benefits, corticosteroids carry potential side effects that can leave horses permanently or even fatally crippled."

The vet found the blood tests to be normal. After that, NJ seemed to recover somewhat. He started to develop a little muscle tone and began light exercise in July. He was subsequently sold to a person that understood he might never be sound.

The point is, this vet bill didn't appear to be excessive and the horse didn't appear to be in bad shape. **Only after he had withdrawal from the medications did his real state of health become apparent.** Why start this process? Train with common sense and leave medications for sick horses . . . not young healthy horses that only need time. Horses treated this way may never make it to a second season of racing. Many horses with similar histories have been unable to return to racing.

One day I ran into this horse's trainer at the track. He asked me about the horse. I told him how the horse had seemed okay when he arrived, but had gone bad in about two to three weeks. The trainer rolled his eyes heavenward, kissed his fingers and said, "Thank You, Jesus!! Can you believe it? While I have the horses, they're fine and then two to three weeks later with others . . . they go bad! And you know what? I know why they are so good with me! It's the medicine! I know what to use . . . thank you God for such good stuff!" This man truly didn't equate the medicine to the disintegration of the horses. He believed the medicine helped them. The fact that anyone can be so ignorant about the cause and effect frightens me. This is a horse trainer. He makes a living in the racing industry and he has not figured out why his horses only last one season.

So many of us are not aware of what is in medications we are giving our horses. I was not aware that SoluDeltaCortef*, Prednisone*, Vetalog*, Azium*, and Meticorten* are all corticosteroids. Since various medications are given persistently over long periods of time, it is not surprising that so many horses suffer the weakening of bone, suppression of normal hormonal function, and the lowering of the immune system. Minor colds and flues that normal horses should recover from in a week persist in these horses. Steroids suppress the symptoms and the horse keeps going. Then when lung problems do show up, they are more acute, because the horse has continued to perform when not well. Clenbuteral*, another steroid-like medication, again enables the horse to perform when he has lung problems and should be resting. Is there any wonder that there is more bleeding today? Horses are running with a false sense of health because of the potent qualities of the medications they are given.

Look at the list of brand names for medications and the explanation of what they are and what they do. Study your vet bills. Know what your horse is taking. "Something to make him feel good at the gate" is not an explanation.

Train with common sense. Leave medications for sick horses not young healthy horses that only need time.

ONE MORE VET BILL...
WOULD YOU WANT THIS DONE TO YOUR HORSE?

The horse in this story is a 24 month-old filly sold in a two-year-olds in-training sale in April. The filly was beautifully conformed . . . she had no "weak tires". She breezed in her "sales work" two furlongs in 22 seconds. Obviously she was a filly with the gift of speed. She was shipped to her trainer and immediately went into training. Her owners told the trainer not to medicate her. The following bills tell the rest of the story.

Month One

5/19	Bute IV 2 GM
5/24	Bute IV 2 GM
5/25	Bute IV 2 GM
5/29	Bute IV 2 GM

Why were injections of Bute given directly into the vein? The trainer convinced the owners that it was so the horse wouldn't get an overdose . . . he had problems when tablets were given in the feed. My own thoughts . . . There is always a risk of infection when injecting . . . especially into the vein. The thought of giving a sound young filly bute just to do early training is offensive.

Month Two

6/2	Bute IV 2 GM
6/7	Bute IV 2 GM
6/8	Bute IV 2 GM
6/11	Bute IV 2 GM
6/18	Bute IV 2 GM plus ACTH 40 MG
6/19	Bute IV 2 GM
6/20	Bute IV 2 GM
6/21	Bute IV 2 GM
6/30	Bute IV 2 GM

In the month of June, a period of early training, this filly has been persistently injected. I wonder about the pattern of the Bute. Is there a limit on the amount of Bute that may be used in that racing area? Remember, ACTH stimulates adrenal gland production. When used with frequency, the horse's own adrenal glands will stop functioning.

Could there be something wrong with a training process that breaks down so many horses before they ever start to race?

Month Three

7/3	Bute IV 2 GM
7/4	Bute IV 2 GM plus a Flucort Injection
7/7	Bute IV 2 GM

HORSE RACED   **7/8 - Showed promise.**

7/12	Bute IV 2 GM
7/23	Bute IV 2 GM
7/26	Bute IV 2 GM
7/27	Flucort injection
7/28	Bute IV 2 GM

HORSE RACED AND WON MAIDEN RACE 7/29

7/31	Bute IV 2 GM

Now we have a horse on persistent Bute. Any pain or swelling will be masked with so much Bute in the system. Be aware that long term use of Bute is hard on all organs including the stomach. Horses may develop ulcers or perforated stomach at a very young age because of so much medication. Flucort is a potent corticosteroid that has lasting side effects. This supposedly healthy young animal has had 12 injections this month . . . to run in two races.

Month Four

8/2	Bute IV 2 GM and ACTH 50 MG
8/5	Bute IV 2 GM
8/7	Bute IV 2 GM
8/8	Bute IV 2 GM
8/13	Bute IV 2 GM
8/14	Flucort Injection

HORSE RACED AND WON 8/15

8/15	Bute Injection 2 GM
8/16	Bute Injection 2 GM
8/27	Bute Injection 2 GM plus ACTH 40 MG and Vitamin E and Selenium Injections
8/31	Bute Injection 2 GM

The pattern continues . . . Bute, Steroids, and ACTH, twice this month. The vitamin E might be for possible tie-up.

You can't enhance the gift of speed.

Month Five

9/1	Bute injection 2 GM
9/2	Bute injection 2 GM
9/3	Flucort injection

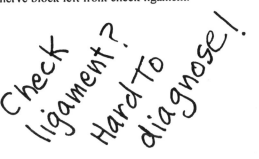

HORSE RACED AND WON 9/4

9/4	Bute IV 2 GM post race
9/14	Bute IV 2 GM
9/15	Bute IV 2 GM
9/18	Bute IV 2 GM and a nerve block left front check ligament.
9/19	Bute IV 2 GM
9/22	Bute IV 2 GM
9/23	Flucort Injection

HORSE RACED - POORLY 9/23

9/24	Bute IV 2 GM
9/29	Bute IV 2 GM
9/30	CBC blood analysis

Check ligament? Hard to diagnose!

We see the usual Bute used here, but there is also a danger sign. Why did they try to block the left front leg? Usually, when lameness has been diagnosed in a particular leg, but not the particular area, the vet will block different points and work his way up the leg. If the hoof is blocked and the lameness persists, the vet blocks the next joint higher until he reaches a point where the horse shows no sign of lameness. If a horse is not given systemic medications that reduce inflammation and heat, it is easier to determine that you are training too hard **BEFORE THE PROBLEM BEGINS**. In view of the Bute and steroids in this horse's system, it would be very difficult to find the cause of a problem. A diagnosis of check ligament usually means that they can't find out what the problem is. In this case, they blamed the lameness on check ligament. One thing sure, this horse has a real problem. Are you surprised?

Month Six

10/4	Endoscopic Exam, EIPH Negative - clean.
10/12	Bute Injection 2 GM - CBC blood analysis serum.
10/14	Trimethoprim Sulfa 100- Treats pneumocystis carinae pneumonia and urinary tract infections, Endoscopic Exam EIPH Negative - clean.
10/15	Bute Injection 2 GM
10/18	Bute Injection 2 GM
10/19	Bute Injection 2 GM
10/21	Bute Injection 2 GM

Stop before you develop a problem.

| 10/22 | Flucort Injection |
| 10/23 | Bute Injection 2 GM - A nonsteroidal anti-inflammatory |

HORSE RACED - POORLY 10/24

| 10/24 | Coggins Test |

In this month it is quite clear that things are going wrong. They keep looking for bleeding. Probably to explain the poor performance. They have run blood tests and given other medications . . . trying to figure out the problem. Could it be the obvious? This animal was trained with no regard to how she was responding to the normal stresses of the gallops. The blatant use of Bute shows that. The persistent use of the corticosteroids which have a long-term cumulative effect could finally no longer keep her problems masked. It is very possible that the trainer felt he was "helping" this horse throughout the program. It is possible that he believes it is inevitable that all horses go bad and it is just a question of how many races we can get out of them before the ultimate crash.

This is the fallacy that must be changed. Horses can race for years! However, during the training process, the trainer must allow the horse to heal from the stress to his body as he grows more efficient. It has been said that the anaerobic fitness in a horse can be brought to optimum capacity in three months. I believe that is true. **But the fact is that the structure of the horse may not be mature enough, soon enough, to sustain his natural speed.** That is why we have "90 day wonders". They can run early but their structure will be pulled apart as pressure is put on green bone and improperly prepared tendons and ligaments. The whole picture must be taken into account. **If you push the horse too fast, he will not last in his career.** Look at the patterns of most modern day horses. They run brilliantly and consistently for a series of races, then they have breakdowns that sideline them for months, years or forever.

Owners must decide what they want. They must allow the trainers to train judiciously and not pressure them, or risk the consequences. By sharing these vet bills, it is hoped that owners will educate themselves as to what they are paying for in terms of real training and what is legitimate medical support.

The filly's last vet bill shows X-rays on November 3. At that point the owners, after seeing two lackluster races and the glint gone from the filly's eye, decided to give her rest and then aim her for a stake a few months later.

The vet exam at the farm reported a dull, depressed animal with little appetite, very quiet and unresponsive for a young Thoroughbred. Lame on the left front. Heat and puffiness in fetlocks. The animal was rested months until soreness appeared to be gone. She was put into light training and as she progressed, seemed to go sore when pressured with any speed. She was reviewed by a Vet University hospital and found to have a broken bone in the foot. This filly was retired as a three year old.

I wonder what kind of horse she might have been if she had been handled differently. She probably would not have won the early stakes that she did win because she would have started racing later. But she might have been around to race usefully for many seasons. She did have the gift of speed!

At 30 months of age, having spent six months at the racetrack, this horse was permanently ruined. Interestingly, endurance horses, jumpers, three-day eventers, dressage, and even barrel racing horses are still competing up to 18 and 20 years of age. What is their secret?

STANDARD OPERATING PROCEDURE FOR A TWENTY-TWO-MONTH-OLD?

       I recently purchased a two-year-old in training filly at the Ocala Breeders Sales company. They have a repository that catalogues all medications given to the horses in training. As a buyer, one may go and see the list of medications given to the horse the week prior to the sale. Who knows what she was given prior to that. This filly was twenty two months of age. She had worked a very fast time (ten and change for one furlong).

       She was consigned to a top agent who always gets high dollar for his horses. The following is the list of medications she received the week prior to her sale. Under "reason for medication", SOP appeared on almost every line. Standard operating procedure - That indicates that every horse they have is treated this way - just in case. The sales consignors' duty is to get the horse looking good enough and fast enough to earn a high bid.

4/17	Ace, 2cc, Dantrium, Bute, Banamine IV 10cc
4/18	Bute
4/19	Bute, Datrium, Banamine IV 10cc
4/22	Bute
4/23	Bute, Banamine IV10cc
4/24	Bute
4/25	Bute, Banamine IV 10cc

       After arriving to the farm, she was fine for a few days and then became lame and carried heat in her knee. She also seemed depressed. A week later she blossomed into a full body fungal infection. Since my sale horses are always turned out for several months rest before any training starts, she will have time to heal and recover from the aggressive training she received to get a good price in the auction ring.

       Once again, be aware that horses prepped for sales are in training early and may have preexisting problems long before they start if they are on the "fast track".

If you start on the "fast track", you may end on no track.

COMMON MEDICATIONS:
THEIR USES AT THE RACETRACK

Pre-Race "Feel Good" Medications
ACTH - Adrenocorticotropic hormone
Adenosine
Azium (Dexamethasone) - a corticosteroid
Testosterone - an anabolic steroid
Triple A (a combination of Azium, ACTH
    and Adenosine)
Vitamin B-12
Vetalog (betamethasone)

Muscle Soreness
Adenosine
Azium (Dexamethasone) - a corticosteroid
E-SE - Vitamin E and Selenium
Lactonase
Prednisone (Prednisolone) a corticosteroid
Robaxin (Methocarbamol) muscle relaxant
Theelan - a estrone sulfate
Datrium (dantrolene sodium)

Pain Medication
Aspirin
Azium (Dexamethasone) - a corticosteroid
Banamine (Flunixon megulamine) a NSAID
Bute - Butazoladine (Phenyl Butazone) - a
        NSAID
Betamethasone - a corticosteroid (Betavet
        Soluspan)
DepoMedrol - (methylprednisone) a corticoster-
oid
DMSO
Prednisone (Prednisolone) a corticosteroid

Circulation
Aspirin
DMSO

Joint Soreness
Legend (hyaluronate sodium)
Conquer (hyaluronate sodium)
Adequan (polysulfated glycosaminoglycan)

Anti-inflammatory
Azium (Dexamethasone) -
    a corticosteroid
Bute - Butazoladine (Phenyl
    Butazone) a NSAID
Banamine - (Flunixon meglu-
    lamine) a NSAID
DMSO
Flucort - a corticosteroid
Meticorten - a corticosteroid
Prednisone (Prednisolone) a
    corticosteroid
Vetalog - a corticosteroid

Respiratory Problems
A-H Injections or granules
Antihistamine Injestions
Azium (Dexamethasone) -
    a corticosteroid
Clenbuteral
DMSO
Glycopyrrolate
Prednisone (Prednisolone) a
    corticosteroid

Calm Down Medication
Calcium and Vitamin B-12
SoluDeltaCortef - a corticosteroid

Bleeder Medication
Amicar
Estro IV - estrogen
Salix (formerly Lasix) - a diuretic
Naquasone a - diuretic
Intal (intratracheal)
Kentucky Red (potassium iodide)

Some of these medications are long-acting steroids. Others are simply vitamin mixtures. Others are mood-elevating drugs. Still others are potent pain killers. This is not a complete list. It is to familiarize you with names you will encounter frequently on the backside.

COMMON MEDICATIONS:
WHAT THEY ARE AND WHAT THEY DO

I strongly believe that we need to know what medications do for and to our horses. Given that belief and my lack of formal training in pharmacology, I have relied heavily on help and information provided by veterinarian friends and reference books for the next two Sections. *How to be Your Own Veterinarian (sometimes)*, by Ruth B. James has been widely quoted. She provides excellent information in layman's terms as to what each type of medication is and the potential side effects. Any bold type within the quoted material has been inserted at my discretion to highlight important information. Other heavily quoted sources are *The Merck Veterinary Manual, Seventh Edition, The Compendium of Veterinary Products, First Edition,* and *The Complete Guide to Prescription & Nonprescription DRUGS, 1995.*

I hope you will read these Sections with an open mind. A mind that is open to asking questions and seeking answers when things don't make sense. In order to simplify reading, registered trademark names are provided for some of the medications referred to in the text. Those products without trademark names are generic names or do not appear in the *Compendium of Veterinary Products, First Edition.* All references to the medications are the compilation of information provided by professionals. My interpretation of the material is presented to you in layman's terminology. The cause and effect observations in this entire Section are based on my hands-on experience and are not to be construed as scientific evidence. These medications are extremely beneficial if used therapeutically. They must be used in accordance with the recommendations of the manufacturing company. If you have doubts about their use, refer to the product insert and your vet.

Anabolic Steroids (Commonly used are: Equipoise - Testosterone, Winstol - Stanozolol, Deca-Durabolin)

The following information is taken from *How to be Your Own Veterinarian, (sometimes)* by Ruth B. James, DVM.

"Anabolic steroids are drugs which are produced in the body to allow the young animal to grow normally. Synthetic versions of the same thing have been thought to make young horses grow larger and faster for show or racing purposes. They have also been thought to stimulate the animal's appetite and make him put on more muscle faster than he would otherwise--a lot like fattening a beef for slaughter . . .

The major problem with these wonder drugs is their side effects, most of which are reproductive in nature. Fillies may become masculinized. Abnormal sexual behavior is also seen. The animals may mount other mares and act aggressively toward them.. They rarely come into heat. If they do, the heat is brief and infertile.

Stud colts are also affected reproductively. They have low sperm counts, lowered sperm quality, and smaller than normal testicles. In

If you wonder what it is, ask!

some cases, they may become completely infertile. Sexual activity was not enhanced by these drugs in the controlled studies . . ."

The Merck Veterinary Manual, 7th Edition lists the following potential side effects:

"Epiphyseal plate closure leading to stunted growth; decreased bone strength; and **reduced tensile strength of tendons**; . . ."

Corticosteroids (Commonly used corticosteroids or steroid-like medications are: Clenbuterol, Vetalog, Azium - Dexamethasone, Triple A, Prednisone- Prednisolone, Vetalog - Betamethasone, Depo-Medrol, Flucort, Meticorten, SoluDeltaCortef, Betavet, Soluspan.)

The following pages are directly quoted from *How to be Your Own Veterinarian (sometimes)*, by Ruth B. James. Many thanks to her for presenting this information so well and for allowing it to be used here.

"Corticosteroids' is the general name given to a group of hormones manufactured by the adrenal glands (which are found near the kidneys). These chemicals are produced by the body in response to stress. When normally produced, they help the animal to adapt to his surroundings. As manufactured chemicals administered by the veterinarian or owner, these drugs may help the animal to overcome insults to his body. Improperly used, they can render the animal helpless to defend himself against disease.

Horse owners and veterinarians often refer to this class of drugs as "steroids" or "cortisones". Both terms are shorter and simpler than saying "corticosteroids."

WHAT CORTICOSTEROIDS DO - AND DON'T DO

These drugs help to reduce inflammation and the body's responses to it. They often give considerable relief to acute problems. They may or may not help chronic problems by temporarily reducing inflammation and allowing the body to heal itself.

Steroids affect nearly every system of the body to a greater or lesser extent. They work on the brain, giving an increased tolerance to pain and often true pain relief. They give the animal a sense of well-being and help him to feel better. They also stimulate the appetite. Steroids increase acid production in the stomach; this may be harmful in horses who are not eating. They reduce mucus secretion in the intestinal lining causing decreased lubrication and digestion.

Steroids stimulate potassium loss from the circulatory system which may cause muscular weakness. They help maintain blood pressure and avoid fluid loss. This aids in shock by keeping fluid from leaking from the capillaries and helps keep the blood pressure normal. This fluid retention may allow the feet and legs to swell (a condition called edema).

Steroids increase blood flow to the kidneys and stimulate red blood cell production. On the other hand, they depress the lymph nodes which produce

If you wonder what it does, ask.

white blood cells; they also slow the movement of these cells. White blood cells act as garbage men in the body and literally "gobble up" bacteria in an infection, rendering them harmless and disposing of them. **Thus, the fact that steroids slow down these cells may aid the spread of infections.**

Steroids lead to decreased antibody response. For this reason, they are used in human transplants to help keep the body from rejecting the transplanted organ. **This is definitely NOT a desired response in the face of an infection - we need to let the body have all the help it can.. Administration of steroids, especially without accompanying antibiotics, may leave the animal susceptible to disease or allow the spread of bacteria which are already present.**

Steroids affect muscles by increasing protein breakdown. If used for long periods of time, they **may decrease the animal's muscle mass and strength. They also decrease the growth of cells called fibroblasts. These cells form the major part of cartilage and scar tissue and help to heal wounds. By both these methods, steroids may significantly slow growth in young animals. Steroids also interfere with the formation of new bone. Recent studies at Cornell University have pointed to long-term steroid use as causing extensive skeletal damage in growing horses and ponies.**

Steroids reduce mucus secretion in the lining of the respiratory system. Mucus helps trap bacteria and viruses that are inhaled and helps keep them from getting to the lungs and causing infection. Less mucus can leave the animal more susceptible to respiratory disease.

Steroids do not actually cure any disease except adrenal insufficiency. Adrenal insufficiency is a lack of production of hormones by the adrenal glands; it is extremely rare in the horse. Steroids may also help specifically in "autoimmune diseases" where the body "becomes allergic" to itself.

In using steroids, we must balance the good effects against the bad. For example, we do not normally use these drugs with broken bones as they retard healing. If, however, the animal is in severe shock, it is better to use them on a short-term basis and save his life; he can't heal if he doesn't survive the initial shock. **Cortisones are also valuable with horses suffering from endotoxin shock, such as that occurring in salmonellosis.**

Steroids should be used at the site of the problem whenever possible, rather than put into the body as a whole. For instance, injection directly into a joint may cause less long-term damage than giving the whole horse enough to reduce the pain in that particular joint. An ointment may be a much better treatment than an injection of one of these drugs for a skin problem.. This usage gives much better results at the site of the problem while reducing the change of side effects.

Steroids help to relieve symptoms of arthritis and allergies, but do NOT cure these problems. The conditions usually reappear when administration is stopped. In addition, **long-term administration of cortisones**

Learn how medications interact.

may lead to destruction of joint cartilage and permanent damage to the joint surfaces, leading to incurable lameness. Poor injection technique into a joint may lead to loss of the animal through infectious arthritis in that joint. If the steroids are accidentally injected into the tissues around the joint, they may induce bone formation in the soft tissues. This progresses over a period of several months and may lead to lameness. **To help avoid damage within the joint after a steroid injection, it is of the utmost importance to rest the animal for an adequate period of time after the injection is given.** Because they slow down cellular growth, steroids may significantly retard the healing of damaged joints.

Cortisone administration is often accompanied by antibiotics to help prevent the spread of infection. These products are especially valuable when used together to treat pneumonia.

Steroids are used in ointments to help treat allergic and inflammatory skin problems. They may also be used in eye ointments. In this form, they are used on healed corneal ulcers to eliminate the blood vessels which grow out onto the cornea during the healing process. These blood vessels may eventually cause blindness if they are not removed.

IMPORTANT: Ointments containing steroids should NOT be used on eye problems without consulting your veterinarian. Using one of these products on a fresh ulcer, cut or scrape may result in rapid spread of the lesion and loss of that eye.

Where should you use corticosteroid drugs? They are valuable for animals who are in severe shock and may help to save the animal's life. They are helpful whether the shock is endotoxin shock due to salmonellosis or is shock from blood loss or severe pain because of an injury.

Full doses of corticosteroid drugs should not be given with phenylbutazone, but partial doses of both drugs together may be more beneficial than either given alone. Give an adequate amount of the drug to do the job., as recommended on the label of the product you are using or as directed by your veterinarian. Harmful effects are most frequently seen with smaller amounts given over long periods of time; this type of treatment should be avoided.

NOTE: Other than using this type drug to treat shock, steroids should only be given on the advice of your veterinarian.

NOTE: There are some conditions in which steroids should NOT be used. They should not be given to horses with kidney disease, rickets, or osteoporosis (weakening of the bone). They should not be given to animals with infections that are not controlled by antibiotics, nor to those with surgical or slow-healing wounds or broken bones. **They should not be given to horses under four years of age because they may severely retard bone growth.**

They should not be used with septic arthritis (arthritis with infection in the joint, such as joint ill in foals). They are of little or no value in chronic lameness with extensive bony changes, such as ringbone.

Administration of cortisones to horses in the last third of pregnancy may cause abortion or premature labor. This may be followed by foaling problems,

Learn the side effects of what you use.

death of the foal, retained placenta metritis, or all of these. Steroids should not be used in horses with viral diseases or tuberculosis. They should not be given to animals who are being shown or raced, as they are illegal and may show up in blood or urine tests.

Steroids are frequently sold in combination with penicillin/strepto-mycin products. The combined products should not be used where you DO need a steroid, as they are not generally in high enough concentration in these combinations to do any real good. Using both the penicillin/streptomycin and the steroid separately allows you to use adequate, therapeutic dosages of each. Using one of these combination drugs where the steroid portion is NOT needed may lead to complications as listed above."

The following information is quoted from *The Merck Veterinary Encyclopedia, Seventh Edition:*

"Dexamethasone and betamethasone . . . are 30-35 times as potent as cortisol as anti-inflammatory agents . . . (With) cortisol and other glucocorticoids intestinal **absorption of calcium is decreased while renal excretion is increased** . . . These effects, in combination promote the mobilization of calcium from bone, and **bone strength is thereby reduced** . . . Side effects: Compounds with mineralo-corticoid activity such as prednisolone and prednisone, tend to cause retention of sodium and water, hence, edema . . . Side effects relating to glucocorticoid actions include . . . muscle wasting and delayed wound healing. Altered calcium metabolism can, with prolonged treatment, lead to osteoporosis and bone fractures. Reduced GI motility, thinning of the gastric mucosa, and reduced mucus production may arise, but glucocorticoids are rarely ulcerogenic. Nevertheless, . . . steroids may potentiate the ulcerogenicity caused by some NSAID . . . **Repeated injections or long-acting preparations may induce degenerative changes in cartilage (steroid arthropathy)."**

Recent studies are showing that steroids should not be used for laminitis, as the reduce the blood flow to the foot, which would cause further damage to an area already deprived of its blood flow.

DMSO

Another direct quote from Dr. James.

"This drug is really in a class by itself. The technical name for it is dimethyl sulfoxide. It is currently manufactured by Diamond Laboratories (Des Moines, IA 50317). This is a medical-grade product containing 90% DMSO. It comes either as a liquid or an ointment. Other DMSO is on the market, sold by feed stores and roadside stands. This is usually only 50 to 70% pure and may contain unknown contaminants. This less pure form is the one used as a paint thinner and solvent and should be avoided for animal or human use.

DMSO is recommended by the manufacturer and licensed by the Food and Drug Administration to reduce acute swelling due to trauma. At the present time, DMSO is the only product known which will carry other products through the skin. Cosmetic adds notwithstanding, the skin is a very efficient barrier

Use medications only for their intended use.

against most substances. DMSO can be mixed with antibiotics, corticosteroids, and other drugs to allow them to be carried through the skin. For this reason it is very important to clip the hair off the area you are treating. Then wash the skin carefully (several times) with an antiseptic soap (such as pHisohex, Winthrop Laboratories, New York, NY 10016) and water. Dry the water off and rinse the area with alcohol. Allow it to dry. Then go ahead and apply your DMSO mixture.

Because DMSO tends to absorb water, it should be kept in a tightly closed container. Otherwise, the next time you use it, you may find that it has absorbed enough water from the air to be more water than DMSO. When adding other substances to it, a convenient way to mix them is in a clean glass fruit jar with a wide mouth. This allows you to use a paintbrush to apply the mixture to the animal's skin. Use only natural-bristle paintbrushes. Over a period of time, the DMSO may dissolve both plastic bottles and nylon paintbrushes. If you are applying DMSO with your hands, use rubber or disposable plastic gloves to keep it off your skin. If you get some on your skin, you may experience an unpleasant, garlic-like taste in your mouth. This means that the drug has penetrated your skin and is circulating in your bloodstream.

DMSO is often mixed with nitrofurazone solution and a corticosteroid to paint on bowed tendons, bog spavins, which have just occurred due to overuse, and similar problems. Some people tout the drug as a cure-all for whatever ails your horse. It's not THAT great, but does have some use in reducing acute swellings. It is used to help reduce hematomas, sertomas, and other noninfectious problems where the skin is not broken. It is also useful when drugs, such as phenylbutazone (which must be given intravenously), have been deposited in the tissues outside the jugular vein. Used twice a day for several days, it may help to reduce the tissue irritation and reduce the chance that sloughing will occur from the phenylbutazone .This drug should not be used on open wounds. DMSO should never be applied after blisters or similar drugs have been put on the skin, as it will carry them right into the tissues, causing a severe reaction."

We have seen article lately that report reduced tendon strength with the daily use of DMSO. Be sure to read everything you can to keep abreast of the latest developments.

Nonsteroidal Antiinflammatory Agents (Commonly used are: Aspirin, Bute - Robaxin - Skelaxin - Paraflex Butazolidine, Banamine - Flunixin meglumine, Equiproxen - Naproxin)

Once again let's turn to Dr. James:

"This is the name given to a class of anti-inflationary drugs which are not related to cortisone. One of the best known of these drugs is aspirin. **Aspirin** - Mallinckrodt, Inc., Paris, KY, can be used in horses. As with the same drug in people, it is relative safe and has few side effects, especially when compared to other painkilling drugs. Horse aspirin are huge pills, in keeping with the size of the beasts we're using them on.

Medications may not be as innocuous as you think.

Phenylbutazone is the generic name of the drug most commonly used to reduce pain in horses. Its best-known brand name is **Butazolidine**, other wise known as **"bute"**- Wellcome Animal Health Division, Burroughs Wellcome Co., Kansas City. This drug reduces inflammation in a manner similar to aspirin and can help to lower fever. It is used to help reduce the pain in animals who have arthritis and helps to relieve pain due to colic.

The injectable form of phenylbutazone MUST be given intravenously and it can cause a severe reaction if some gets outside of the vein. If enough is placed outside the vein, a large area of tissue may slough from the animal's neck, or an abscess may form. Tablets are available. They should be crushed and fed with grain. A paste form similar to paste wormer is available also from Wellcome Animal Health Division.

Full doses of "bute" should not be given with full doses of corticosteroids. These drugs have similar actions and may have adverse side effects when used together at full dosage; partial dosages of each given together are permissible.

Horses should usually not be treated more than five consecutive days with "bute" because of the possibility of side effects. The most severe of these is a blood disorder called aplastic anemia. This disorder lessens the number and quality of red blood cells available to the animal. In the most sever cases, the body may not resume normal production of these cells and the animal may become severely ill. Other side effects include digestive upsets and liver problems. The later may show up as icterus (a yellowing of the membranes of the eyes and mouth).

Drugs such as "bute" and other antiinflammatory agents (new ones appear frequently) are valuable for keeping animals with chronic problems in use, when it is used sparingly and only as needed. Flunixin meglumine (**Banamine**, Schering Coorp., Kenilworth, NJ 07033) is another of these.

Naproxin (**Equiproxen**, Diamond Laboratories, Inc., DesMoines, IA 50317) is a relatively new anti-inflammatory agent. It comes in packets of powder which are given to the horse with his grain and can be used in much the same manner as phenylbutazone.

One good example of use for these drugs is a roping horse with ringbone who was used in high-school rodeos. There is no treatment for the ringbone. The horse was 15 years old and it would be easy to tell the people to put him down. But why waste the animal's years of training and experience and the fine disposition which made him a champion? Better instead to have the owner give him "bute" paste before the weekend rodeos and rest and coddle the old fellow in between. In this manner, they may get several more years of usage without causing the animal excessive pain.

If a horse is being kept on a nonsteroidal anti-inflammatory agent for a long period of time, or is given the drug in intervals, as with the horse mentioned above, it is often worth trying more than one of these drugs. One may work much better than another for a given animal. Also, it may be helpful to alternate between them to keep the animal from building a tolerance to the medication and to keep side effects at a minimum.

Be aware of side effects.

A Few Other Medications You Should Be Familiar With -

Sulfa Drugs

The following information is again taken from Dr. James.

"Sulfas were the first class of drugs able to attack and retard the growth of bacteria. This effect allowed the body to overcome the bacteria and survive the infection. Sulfa drugs were developed around the turn of the century and came into widespread use shortly afterward, saving the lives of many people. Sulfas were extensively used on animals until antibiotics were discovered and put into common usage. Sulfa drugs are still occasionally used, either as injections (which must be given intravenously because the solution is irritating) or in eye and other ointments. They are also used in the form of a sulfa-urea solution which is very effective for removing debris from the surface of old, contaminated wounds (see Wound Medications)."

Calcium and Vitamin B

Calcium is an antihypocalcemic dietary replacement. Sometimes it is given with vitamin B on race day as a calm down medication in horses. If used with diuretics such as Lasix, there is increased calcium ratio in the blood due to water reduction. If used with Bute, there is decreased pain relief.

Intal

An antiasthmatic, anti-inflammatory (non-steroidal). It is used for bleeding in horses and blocks histamine release from most cells. If used with cortisone drugs, there is a reduced cortisone effect.

Lasix

A diuretic (loop) antihypertensive. It is used for bleeding in horses. It decreases fluid retention by eliminating sodium and water from the body. If used with cortisones, there can be an increased potassium loss. The following is quoted from an article Dr. Sue Hengemuhle wrote for the **Backyard Racehorse Newsletter**, "Countless scientific studies have shown that furosemide (Lasix) effectively reduces pulmonary hemorrhage in horses with EIPH (bleeders). When phenylbutazone is given with Lasix, the pulmonary artery pressure rises back up to the values seen prior to giving the Lasix and bute; it's as if you never gave Lasix if you give bute with it."

Please note that Lasix for equine use is now being labeled as SALIX. Do not confuse it with the herb known as salix alba, better known as willow an early form of aspirin. At this time we do not know if racing forms will change the "L" which indicated a horse on Lasix to an "S".

Be sure to see *A Word With the Experts On - Lasix* later in this section. The subject is also covered under *Bleeders* in *Setbacks.*

Glycopyrrolate

Is used for respiratory problems in horses. According to **The Complete Guide to Prescription and Nonprescription DRUGS, 1995**; "It blocks nerve impulses at para-sympathetic nerve endings, preventing smoother (involuntary) muscle contractions."

Be familiar with what you use.

These are muscle relaxants and block the body's pain messages to the brain. In humans they are used as adjunctive treatment to rest, analgesics, and physical therapy for muscle spasms.

Hyaluronic Acid - Legend and Conquer

The Merck Veterinary Manual, Seventh Edition continues: "Hyaluronic acid is a normal constituent of connective tissue matrix and synovial fluid... Excellent clinical responses have been reported following the intra-articular injection of sodium hyaluronate in equine joint disease... although there are no serious side effects, local swelling has been described in some horses."

Recent studies on hyaluronic acid are very positive. It contains naturally occurring compounds found in joints and seems to have the cushioning and lubricating effects on them. They conclude that while HA injections in the joint are beneficial for acute inflammation in high performance horses there is danger of infection from improper techniques. Therefore, oral dosage of Legend is recommended. An added benefit is that Legend is less expensive. Conquer is injected. Both are very effective.

Adequan/PSGAGs

Adequan (Luitpold Pharmaceuticals) is a polysulfated glycosaminoglycan or PSGAG. Glycosaminoglycans are natural components of joint cartilage. Adequan contains extra sulfur molecules and also seems to have a cushioning effect in joints. Studies are not clear on exactly how these medications benefit joints, but they seem to show better results with intramuscular applications. There are also no clear results on efficacy.

Magnesium

Administration of magnesium has been shown to have potent vasodilating effects. It opens up peripheral blood vessels as well as circulation to the heart. The use of magnesium deserves further study, since it is certainly a safe alternative and virtually free of side effects.

Theelan

This is estrone sulfate which is related to estrogen. It is often used in stifle soreness. It may work by relaxing ligaments. We have found no studies that prove that.

Dantrium - dantrolene sodium

Use of this medication has been noted recently. It may be used for tie-up. It's use is prescribed for hypermetabolism of skeletal muscles.

Kentucky Red - potassium iodide

This is used for bleeders and probably produces a coagulating effect.

New medications appear every day. Some, such as **Marquis** for EPM, are of great benefit to the equine community. Be sure that what is prescribed for your horse is being used therapeutically not to mask symptoms in order to race him.

Help me!

EPM is Hard To diagnose!

Be grateful to the folks who do the research.

IMPORTANT NOTE: Giving painkillers, such as phenylbutazone, or drugs such as corticosteroids to relieve an animal's pain is NOT a substitute for finding out what is actually wrong with the animal. Using these drugs in this manner is as smart as putting a band-aid on a broken leg and hoping that it will heal. If the animal does not respond to rest and the passage of a little time, consult your veterinarian for an accurate diagnosis."

The Merck Veterinary Manual, Seventh Edition had the following information on NSAIDs;

"Their low solubility . . . delays absorption. *In vitro* studies with phenylbuta- zone, meclofenamate, and flunixin have shown that these drugs bind to hay and this may explain why peak concentrations in plasma can be delayed for up to 18 hours in horses . . . Side Effects: The most common side effect is irritation and possibly ulceration of the GI mucosa. All NSAIDs exert this action to varying degrees . . . **With toxic doses of phenylbutazone (only moderately greater than therapeutic doses),** ulceration in horses has been sufficiently severe to cause hemoconcentra- tion and death from hypovolemic shock."

Although bute is a first choice for anti-inflammatory therapy, remember studies have shown some of the following side affects with long term use:

intestinal tract ulceration
kidney damage
depressed motility in the large bowel, possibly causing impactions.
depressed bone healing
depressed cartilage cell formation, which means it may not be beneficial in the treatment of arthritis.

All of this may tend to make our heads spin. However, it does not mean you should object if your veterinarian recommends bute, just be aware that it is a prescription drug. And although it is sitting in your medicine chest, always check with your vet before using it on your own. It is our responsibility to stay informed of the research being done and to be aware of what medications do to our horses.

Try to see why the Horse hurts – How can he Heal?.

 Remember, horses can't tell us how they feel and may employ very physical ways of communicating with us.

A Word About the Current Buzz on the Backside

The "Electro Shock" Machine

The latest buzz on the backside is about the "electro shock" machine. I heard through the grapevine that there was this wonderful machine that would take away the pain of lameness with no trace in testing. Upon further investigation I found that a few studies had been done on various species and that in some instances the electro shock appeared to bruise the nerves and therefore create an analgesic (numbing) effect. In an effort to understand what all this really meant, I researched the basic info on this machine.

In the article written by Mary Beth Whitcomb, DVM, (in Veterinary Practice News) she states

"Extracorporeal shock wave therapy (ESWT) is rapidly gaining popularity in the equine performance horse industry in the United States. Shock wave therapy (also referred to as acoustic shock wave therapy) is being used to treat many orthopedic disorders in the performance horse, ranging from suspensory ligament injuries in show horses to stress fractures in racehorses. Shock wave therapy is thought stimulate bone and bone soft tissue interfaces, especially origins and insertions of tendons and ligaments. Horses treated with shock wave therapy can potentially return to competition sooner than those treated with traditional rehabilitation programs. The increasing demand for shock wave therapy is due to this potential for speed healing, improved recovery rates, and reduced costs with lay-up and rehabilitation".

Is speed healing our goal?

That is what they think. What it will do remains to be proven with proper testing under controlled circumstances.

That is a far cry from the comments on the backside where unlicensed people have obtained various different types of these machines and have been allegedly experimenting with their numbing effects on lameness.

It has been stated that when a vet administers this treatment to a horse, he must notify the racing officials that the treatment is five to seven days before the race. If non vets are using this on the farm and closer to racing day it may be a real issue in terms of safety to the horse and rider. Inhibiting the transfer of pain does not mean healing has taken place and in fact, the sound waves may cause micro fractures.

To continue with Dr. Whitcomb's article,

"Each treatment consists of delivering several pulses to the affect area. Depending on the energy level, shock waves are thought to stimulate bone formation, remove calcifications and treat enthesiopathies (bone/ligament, bone/tendon interfaces). The osteoinductive response has the potential to speed healing of stress fractures and enthesiopathies (bone/ligament, bone/tendon interfaces). ESWT is also thought to have a nociceptive effect. The modulation of pain is certainly beneficial when treating osteoarthritic disorders, such as ring bone and bone spavin where there is no risk to a rider. However, caution should be used when treating stress fractures in racehorse where a significant improvement in pain and lameness may prompt a premature return to the racetrack. This carries the potential for injury to an exercise rider or jockey".

She continues,

"Further research is imperative in understanding the benefits of ESWT in treatment of equine musculoskeletal injuries. The precise mechanism of action of ESWT on bone, ligament and tendon remains unknown. Objective clinical data and research is also lacking on the effectiveness and clinical outcome of equine shock wave cases. The use of this modality on current clinical cases presented to veterinary hospitals assists in recognizing potential benefits in treating specific disorders; however, good scientific data is necessary to objectively evaluate its effectiveness, both in the short and long term."

The treatment used by the university for bone problems at the moment is just one session and then a reevaluation three and six months later. It is too soon to know much, but I would be wary if offered this treatment for my horse unless I understood the real benefit and risk associated with it. Certainly it should be done with the supervision of a veterinarian.

hmmm...

ALWAYS Consult your Vet!

Let's do it the safe way.

EPO

A track acquaintance slithered up to me and whispered that he had heard about some really good stuff that made the horses run like they were being shot out of a cannon. "Man," he said "this stuff is really expensive and they use it on cancer patients, but it makes a horse feel real good and run faster than he ever has before!"

My usual skepticism reared its ugly head. My suspicious mind said that use of anything that changes a horse overnight can not be good for his health. The medicine he referred to may be EPO (erythropoietin or epogen) . In racing there has been controversy about these products and various states are trying to establish testing procedures to detect them as they do alter the performance of the horse.

Various articles were appearing at that time in human and equine sports magazines about "blood doping" in sports competition.

The following was taken from the position stand of the American College of Sports Medicin by Sawaka MN, et al:

"Blood doping is associated with risks that can be serious and impair athletic performance. These known risks are amplified by improper medical controls as well as the interaction between dehydration with exercise and environmental stress. Finally, the medical risks associated with blood doping have been estimated from carefully controlled research studies, and the medically unsupervised use of blood doping will increase these risks. It is the position of the American College of Sports Medicine that any blood doping procedure used in an attempt to improve athletic performance is unethical, unfair and exposes the athlete to unwarranted and potentially serious health risks."

Guezennec CY, writes "The use of doping is linked with the history of sports. Doping abuse escalated until the mid 60s when government and sports authorities

"Blood doping used in an attempt to enhance performance is unethical."

responded with anti doping laws and drug testing. Today the details of substances detected in controls give a good indication on the importance of doping use. Three classes of pharmaceuticals account for most of the positive controls. They are anabolic steroids, stimulants and narcotics. Their use can be related with the goal of the athletes. Anabolic steroids are mainly used in sports such as body building or weight lifting in order to develop strength. Stimulants are used in sports where speed favors performance. All the products that enhance blood oxygen transportation are used in endurance sports, their efficacy is not scientifically demonstrated, but their use does result in real risks. Several studies have evidenced the medical problems resulting from prolonged doping. Doping control is impaired by the fact that many products now used, e.g. EPO or rhGH, are not detectable.

While rHu - EPO is a godsend in medical practice, its use as a performance enhancing drug by athletes in endurance sports is an unethical and potentially dangerous procedure."

The previous information was made in reference to human sports. Unfortunately the race track is quick to utilize any performance enhancing "products".

We have been aware of the illegal use of anabolic steroids, stimulants and narcotics for years, However, the use of genetic engineering and cancer drugs that change the basic blood chemistry of the horse is very upsetting. When a horse is claimed that has been on these programs the trainers have had to become chemists in order to get the horse's system back into balance.

Canada is faced with a problem of horses dying shortly after they are claimed. These deaths occur more in the harness horse industry than in the thoroughbred and are currently under study. A pattern is beginning to emerge and I expect to see more information about this in the near future. For those of us in the business, this means that we must be aware of all the elements out there.

The following article, #4228, appeared in *the HORSE:*

Without Definitive Test, Battling EPO Use Big Challenge

by: Tom LaMarra - 3/14/03

"Officials said the classification of erythropoietins — the blood-doping agent commonly known as EPO — as a prohibited practice has curbed its use in some jurisdictions but a definitive test for the substance is a must if any regulation is to have teeth. Medication was just one of the topics discussed during the initial

Remember - a truly talented horse is hard to find.

sessions of the joint meeting of the Thoroughbred Racing Association, Harness Tracks of America, and Racetracks of Canada March 13 in Hollywood Beach, Fla. But the subject spilled over into another arena when regulators were called key to any successful enforcement policy. "Until there is a definite positive test, there is very little that can be done," said Lonny Powell, president of the Association of Racing Commissioners International, the organization that adopted the prohibited-practice model for substances that can't be tested on race day. "Prohibited practices have been adopted by many jurisdictions, and that has been a beacon of light."

Currently, there is a test for EPO antibodies. It has produced "positives" in Louisiana, New York, and Texas, but because it's not definitive, participants can only be warned and then monitored. Dr. Ken McKeever, the Rutgers University physiologist who is working with Dr. George Maylin of Cornell University to develop the test, said the evidence is strong even without the test. "A horse shouldn't produce an antibody unless it is exposed to that drug," McKeever said. McKeever suggested out-of-competition testing, which has been considered by some jurisdictions but not implemented because of logistic and legal concerns, would be effective for blood-doping agents and other substances.

Dr. Scot Waterman, executive director of the Racing Medication and Testing Consortium said testing at times other than race day has been discussed as part of the group's proposed national policy for uniform medication and testing. "We're trying to figure out the most equitable way of approaching it to protect due process," Waterman said. "We need to be able to define exactly what we're testing for ... it's not going to be a crapshoot looking for all kinds of therapeutic medications."

McKeever said New Jersey and New York are considering another approach: classify use of EPO as an equine health problem to facilitate out-of-competition testing. That way, a horse might be scratched before it races, and post-race testing wouldn't be an issue. Dr. Michael Weaver, director of veterinary services for the Canadian Pari-Mutuel Agency, said even though Canada has a uniform national drug-testing program, it has the "same serious problem with detecting new and difficult drugs. We're just as concerned with EPO as anyone else. We're just not sure how big a problem it is in Canada. He did say the drug's classification as a prohibited practice has "slowed trade" in the country."

I find it disheartening to think that these edges are being taken to win. If we continue raising performance levels via synthetic methods, the nature of the animal and the industry changes. We will all have to dope and medicate every horse in order to compete. Aside from the financial cost, the medical risk to these beautiful animals is enormous. Horses today don't last or start nearly as often as they used to. Certainly part of the reason is because we are "using them up" with methods that go against their nature. Our decisions must be based on what is good for the jockey, the horse and the industry.

We can keep a good one running for years if we respect for the nature of the animal.

A Word With the Experts On -
THE DOPE ON LASIX

by Melissa Sykes

Current thinking on the causes of EIPH subscribes to the theory that, during strenuous exercise, increased pulmonary pressure in the lungs causes the capillaries to burst. Blood then crosses the thin membrane into the air sacs.

Furosemide (commonly marketed under the trade name Lasix) has been shown to reduce this pulmonary pressure. That is the justification given for bleeders being treated with injections of Lasix before racing.

As researchers at the University of Pennsylvania's New Bolton Center reported in 1998, however: "The pressure change produced by the administration of furosemide may not be of sufficient magnitude to reduce pressure within the capillaries to a level where hemorrhage resulting from rupture of the capillaries would be prevented."

In other words, Lasix does reduce the pressure in the lungs, but not significantly enough to stop bleeding completely, according to the New Bolton study.

Why, then, do so many horses race on Lasix if the drug is not a surefire bleeding deterrent? The scientific community has known for some time that furosemide also acts as a diuretic. The diuretic effect reduces the horse's body weight, thereby lightening his load as he runs around the track.

The New Bolton Center study went on to say that "changes in performance noted following furosemide administration to bleeders may be due to reduction in body weight, rather than significant alteration of the bleeding status of the horse."

This year, researchers at Ohio State University came under attack when they published a study labeling furosemide as a "performance-enhancing" medication. Led by Kenneth W. Hinchcliff, BVSC, PhD, DACVIM, researchers analyzed the race records of a total of 22,589 Thoroughbreds racing on dirt surfaces in the United States and Canada between June 28 and July 13, 1997. The results, based on statistical analysis, confirmed that horses receiving furosemide raced faster, earned more money and were more likely to win or finish in the top three positions than were horses who were not treated.

The American Association of Equine Practitioners (AAEP) released a statement calling the OSU study flawed, because horses not administered furosemide were not examined to determine if they had, in fact, bled. (The AAEP maintains that nearly 100% of the racehorse population experiences EIPH.)

"I agree that we don't know which horses bled," responded Hinchcliff. "The strength of our study is the large number of horses involved. There is a strong association with Lasix administration and performance."

Hinchcliff's assertion likely would be supported by most experienced racing bettors. Ask any gambler what's the best bet in horse racing, and he'll likely tell you to always bet a horse using Lasix for the first time.

Unfortunately, no research has shown a complete absence of blood from the trachea, post race, as a result of furosemide administration to bleeders. It is assumed, since the horse performs better on Lasix, that the bleeding has been alleviated or at least reduced. But, that begs the question: When does EIPH impact performance?

Studies provide new information every day.

At this year's Breeders' Cup, only eight horses ran without the benefit of Lasix. Of those, only two were in the money – Docksider (3rd) in the Mile, and Royal Anthem (2nd) in the Turf. This year's Turf winner, Daylami, ran on Lasix for only the second time in his career, the first time being in the 1998 Man 'O War Stakes at Belmont. He won that race. All of his other races took place in Europe where race day medications are prohibited.

For a horse to be put on a US racetrack's bleeders' list - and therefore be eligible for furosemide treatment - blood must be evident either from the nostrils or through endoscopic examination of the trachea. However, there is no standard by which to judge the amount or origin of blood that needs to be present for the animal to be considered a bleeder.

When Lasix began to be used on bleeders, horses had to be examined by the racetrack veterinarian to confirm the incidence of bleeding. Nowadays, in many jurisdictions, the regulatory vets rely on the private practitioners treating these animals to confirm bleeding. This procedure, at best, reduces the workload of the track vet; at worse, it is a clear conflict of interest.

Prevention

Dr. W. Robert Cook, Professor of Surgery Emeritus at Tufts University and author of *Speed in the Racehorse: The Airflow Factors* feels racehorses can be better served by prevention than by treatment.

"We should be talking about prevention. You don't need any treatment for bleeders – just rest," he said.

Cook believes EIPH and the buildup of pressure in the lungs is caused most often by upper airway obstruction – not overexertion. This obstruction is so common in today's training methods that we don't even consider them a factor when it comes to performance.

Cook cites the following as causes of inspiratory obstruction and resistance:

1. The presence of a rider. A rider's weight on the thorax limits the natural elevation of the forehand during the hind leg weight-bearing phase of the gallop. Because of this, the horse has to breathe in against abnormal resistance from the weight on its diaphragm.

2. A tight girth. This renders the chest more rigid and less easily expanded to admit air. The horse has to work harder to breathe in.

3. Poll flexion. Anything short of full extension of the poll constitutes an obstruction of the airway at the throat.

4. Use of a bit. This causes tongue movement, followed by dorsal displacement of the soft palate and obstruction of the throat.

5. Use of a tongue-tie. This effort to reduce tongue movement simply adds to the horse's discomfort and neurological confusion. Tongue-ties stimulate digestive reflexes, which are diametrically opposed to the 'flight' reflexes necessary in racing.

6. Defects of conformation. Narrow air passages at any point in the upper airway may obstruct breathing. Deformities of the windpipe, for example, are extremely common in the Thoroughbred, according to Cook.

An ounce of prevention is worth a pound of cure.

7. Diseases of the upper airway. All such diseases obstruct inspiration. An example is 'roaring' or recurrent laryngeal neuropathy, a common inherited disease of Thoroughbreds and draft horses.

"It follows from this evidence," Cook said, "that it is not so much 'exercise' as "inspiratory difficulty' that triggers bleeding."

Joseph C. O'Dea, DVM, former president of the AAEP and author of *The Racing Imperative* recently wrote a guest commentary for the *Thoroughbred Times*. In his piece, O'Dea confirmed some of Cook's theories.

"Most observant racetrack practitioners recognize that bleeding is most frequently caused by anatomical obstruction and/or more often inflammation with resistant swelling in the upper air passages and the reduction in the size of the air passage space," wrote O'Dea. "Sometimes the degree of swelling is very minimal."

O'Dea also lambasted the prevalent use of Lasix in treating EIPH: "It is my perception that Lasix diminishes performance in as many or more horses than it enhances and in the long run reduces consistency and the percentage of winning favorites. Lasix does not level the playing field. Lasix tilts the playing field but you never know in which direction."

Bleeding in racehorses is not a disease, it is a symptom, according to Cook. And using furosemide to treat EIPH will not have a positive effect on bleeding until the cause of the bleeding is determined and remedied.

Horsemen who use Lasix as a means of keeping horses on the racetrack are buying the pound of cure instead of the ounce of prevention. That is unfortunate, but masking a symptom is easier than determining the cause of the problem.

Be sure to read the article on **Bleeding** by Mellisa Sykes. It appears in *Setbacks*.

Studies have shown -
Lasix does <u>not</u> stop
Bleeding!

See Bill Heller's
Book -
<u>Run</u> <u>Baby</u> <u>Run</u>!

Bleeding may be a symptom not a disease.

A Word With the Experts On -
CLENBUTEROL USE IN THE RACEHORSE

by Melissa Sykes

Much has been reported lately about the use/misuse of clenbuterol in the Thoroughbred. A Class 3 drug, clenbuterol is a bronchodilator used to treat respiratory ailments in the horse.

At this year's in-training sales, some horses were allowed to breeze on the drug while others had a 72-hour withdrawal. Many in the industry believe that clenbuterol both protects the lungs of those youngsters being asked to breeze in the under tack shows and that it acts as a performance enhancer.

According to the latest research, both of these assumptions are emphatically wrong.

Researchers Kenneth McKeever, Ph.D. and Charles Kearns of the animal sciences department at Rutgers University delivered the results of their studies on the effect clenbuterol has on the equine at this year's American College of Sports Medicine's annual meeting.

In separate studies, they examined how long-term use of clenbuterol affected body mass vs. muscle mass and exercise performance.

In body composition, nutrients are taken in and partitioned into either fat or muscle. The goal in conditioning an athlete is to decrease the fat and increase the muscle. Referred to as repartitioning, clenbuterol has this effect on the equine body in a short amount of time.

"We are seeing pretty dramatic changes in that horse in the first two weeks" of beginning the clenbuterol treatment, said McKeever.

Horses with larger muscle mass perform better. "It's not a coincidence that your body remodels with whatever stress you're going to put on it," explained Kearns.

The use of clenbuterol has an additive effect. "Clenbuterol is working to increase muscle mass."

When given clenbuterol long term, the body produces more fast twitch muscle fibers. These are the types of muscles found in sprinters. But, these muscles are added at the expense of slow twitch muscle fibers.

"It increases those (muscle fibers) that you would want a sprinter to have, which would seem like a good thing. But if you can't supply the energy (provided by slow twitch muscles), then they cannot sustain that work rate," Kearns explained.

"You would predict that clenbuterol would have a tremendous impact on performance. If this (creating more fast twitch muscle fibers) was all clenbuterol did, it would be a good thing," said Kearns. "But this isn't all it does.

In one study, McKeever and Kearns took 23 Standardbred mares and separated them into four groups: 1. Horses on clenbuterol plus exercise; 2. Horses received clenbuterol (no exercise); 3. Horses exercised only; and 4. Control group – no clenbuterol, no exercise.

The mares were subjected to an incremental exercise test to determine heart rate and respiratory recovery times. Researchers also looked at VO2 max – maximal oxygen

Use or mis-use?

consumption. This is when the animal is performing at its peak, converting oxygen to energy.

In the groups receiving clenbuterol, whether in conjunction with exercise or not, it took them as long or longer to return to normal heart and respiratory rates as the unfit control group.

"We wanted to see how training benefited the cardiovascular system," said McKeever. "In the exercise only group, everything came down much faster than the two groups receiving clenbuterol. We would have expected to see a benefit with clenbuterol and exercise, but didn't. The clenbuterol cancelled out the exercise."

Another decrease shown in this testing was in blood plasma volume. The horse needs this extra fluid during exercise for sweating and regulating the body's internal temperature. With horses on clenbuterol and exercising, blood plasma volume was decreased by 10%.

"Using clenbuterol in conjunction with Lasix (a diuretic commonly used for EIPH), you are dehydrating your animal to dangerous levels," Kearns said. "You are also forcing the kidneys to work harder. These are health risks that (trainers and veterinarians) should start thinking about."

And as for oxygen consumption, horses in the study that were exercised without clenbuterol significantly increased their VO2 max while those on clenbuterol with or without exercise "demonstrated significant decreases in VO2 max."

"Chronic administration of therapeutic levels of clenbuterol significantly decreased aerobic performance and the ability to recover from exercise."

Kearns noted the side effects of clenbuterol use – many of which Thoroughbred trainers may want to avoid. "Horses receiving clenbuterol exhibited increased heart rate, sweating, irritability, shakes and hives."

Other studies coming out of Australia indicate that clenbuterol may have a detrimental effect on the heart. "Researchers have observed an increase in collagen in the heart," said Kearns. "The heart can't stretch and has to work harder. They've also observed changes in the capillaries around the heart – the distance the oxygen has to travel is longer." Again, making the heart work harder.

In a related study from a researcher in Japan, 9-week-old male rats were given clenbuterol for four weeks, then withdrawn over a four week period. Bone lengths, density and muscle mass was measured. The femurs (thigh bones) of rats receiving clenbuterol quit growing during the administration of the drug. Although growth resumed once the drug was withdrawn, this bone became stunted in relation to the rest of the body and did not make up the lost growth.

McKeever and Kearns began to see significant changes in their animals after only two weeks of clenbuterol treatment. According to the FDA, clenbuterol should only be used for thirty days.

In the pari-mutuel industry thresholds and withdrawal times for clenbuterol vary from state to state. But, the repartitioning effect of clenbuterol stays with the horse much longer than many of the withdrawal guidelines.

"Stopping (clenbuterol treatment) 72-hours prior to race if the horse has been on it for at least two weeks is not going to affect the outcome," said Kearns.

Withdrawal is no fun for your horse.

In horses suffering from COPD, the administration of clenbuterol will help open the airways. But those airways can only open so far. In normal horses, the use of clenbuterol will not increase the airway diameter.

"If a horse is healthy," explained Ed Robinson, Matilda Wilson professor in the large animal clinical sciences at Michigan State University, "then the air passages are not constricted" and the use of clenbuterol does not help the breathing.

"The exercising horse releases adrenaline, they will release enough to do naturally what any little bit of clenbuterol would do."

As for protecting the lungs of those sale horses, Robinson points out that clenbuterol has no anti-inflammatory properties. "And there is no evidence of it stopping the incidence of EIPH. The drug is designed to open up the air passages of horses with asthma."

"In animals with COPD, it may return that animal to its original capability," said McKeever. "But (trainers) are way off the mark if they think it's going to help the normal horse. In young horses, especially, chronic use of clenbuterol is not going to help and they may end up with a horse that cannot perform as well as it did before."

Clenbuterol is for asthma.

ASK THE VET

Dr. Sue

We cannot leave the subject of medications without sharing this letter from one of our readers with you. This letter points out how important it is to question the vet bills and understand how your horse is being trained. If you're in this business for the long term, you must learn what really helps your horses run and what sets them up for break down or disease.

Dear BYRH:

I have a two-year-old colt in training at our local track and noticed charges for dexamethasone about every two weeks on the veterinary portion of my training bill. I haven't been able to ask the track vet about this medication because he is so busy, so I asked my physician about it when I was in for a check up. He said that he didn't know about horses, but in people, long term corticosteroid therapy could cause severe health problems. When I asked my trainer about this, he said that all his two-year-olds get this medication because it helps them train better. He gets very irritated when I ask too many questions, as if I am questioning his training techniques, which I'm not – I just want to learn and understand more about my colts training. What do you think about dexamethasone?   M.L.C Chicago

Dear M.L.C,

Your physician is correct in his concern regarding long term corticosteroid therapy in horses. The drug, dexamethasone is a synthetic analog of the naturally occurring corticosteroid, corisol, which is produced in and released from adrenaline glands. The amount released is controlled by other hormones, released from the hypothalamus and pituitary gland. This is known as a feed back loop. The animal's system is stimulated to release corisol and other corticosteroids when stressed, and they have a profound anti-inflammatory effect, as well as having an effect on protein, carbohydrate and lipid metabolism, and water/electrolyte balance. Synthetic corticosteroids, such as dexamethasone, have been designed to maximize anti-inflammatory properties and some are as much as 700 times more potent than corisol, but they have equally potent effects on protein and carbohydrate metabolism. The net effect is the destruction of fat stores and muscle mass which is broken down and re-synthesized into blood glucose (blood sugar) and glycogen (the storage from glucose which is stored in the liver.)

Corticosteroids may also reduce bone mass (causing osteoporosis), and may cause thinning of the skin and hair loss. The anti-inflammatory effects of corticosteroids are associated with a profound suppression of the immune system. When corticosteroids are giving systemically (either by oral or intra-muscular injection) they promptly suppress heat, pain, swelling, and loss of function associated with injury. On the surface, that sounds good, until you realize that those are the body's natural responses to injury and are part of the healing process. Corticosterioids caused delayed healing, which is why many veterinary surgeons won't operate on animals that have recently been injected with them unless it's a life or death situation. The use of synthetic corticosterioids may also short circuit the hypothalamic-pituitary-adrenaline gland feed back loop, and the net result is that the adrenaline glands may atrophy (shrink in size and lose their ability to produce corisol and and other corticosteroids).

Does it really help them train better?

When treatment with the synthetic corticosteroids is discontinued, the animal may have already lost the ability to produce natural corticosteroids from the adrenalines, which is essential for normal function and well- being of the animal. In a study conducted in 1983, a single intra-muscular dose of dexamethasone giving at the dosage of .02 milligrams per pound body weight caused adrenaline suppression within 12 hours post-injection, and normal adrenaline function did not resume until several days later.

I don't mean to give the impression the corticosteroids should never be used; they do have legitimate uses in the treatment of some injuries, but should be used judiciously and with rest, since healing is delayed. The potent anti-inflammatory properties or corticosteroids can mask an active problem and set an animal up for breakdown that may have been prevented had the injury been protected and treated.

You should consider asking your trainer and veterinarian why your colt started receiving dexamethasone treatment. If it is, in fact, a routine practice in your trainer's stable (i.e. no problem existed when he started treatment) you should consult with them to determine if the colt can be taken off the medication. If a problem did exist, you should know what it is, how it was diagnosed, and what rehabilitative therapy was recommended by the veterinarian. If a problem exists that has not been diagnosed yet, your money may be better spent on diagnostics (x-ray, ultrasound, etc,..) to find and fix the underlying problem, rather than using medication to mask the pain and inflammation of an active injury.

Doctor Sue Hengemuehle

Dr. Sue Hengemuehle is a veterinarian on staff with the Department of Animal Science at Michigan State University. She owns a private equine practice in Okemos, Michigan.

Find and fix the underlying problem.

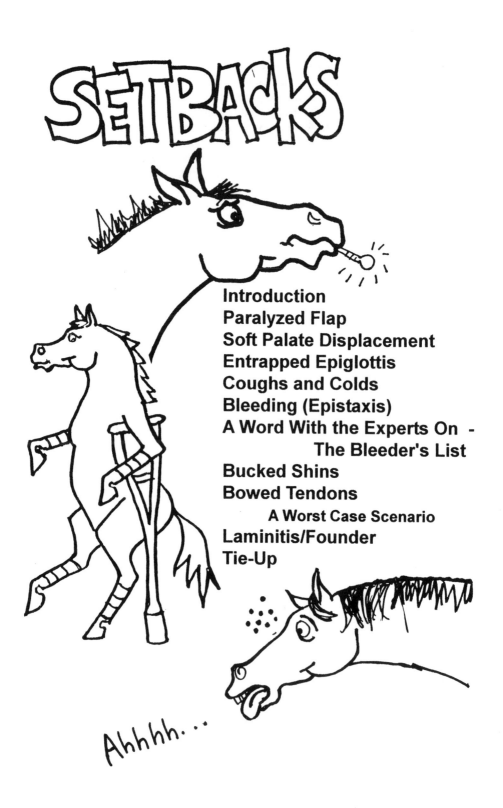

SETBACKS

Ahhhh...

SETBACKS - Introduction

Every owner enters into the joy of owning a racehorse with the illusion that the horse will start training, run faster and faster, and win lots of races. Unfortunately, it rarely ever happens this way.

Training a horse to be a sound racehorse is very much like raising children. You put in a lot of foundation, survive the childhood diseases, and the personality conflicts, before you arrive at a whole and complete person. Most of the time, with a horse, we don't know whether training is cost effective until we see how fast the horse can run. Sometimes we find we have spent too much money and effort on a slow horse.

No trainer can guarantee anything. In fact, it seems to challenge the fates if the trainer is foolish enough to say something like, "This horse is going to be a big winner." Disillusioned owners have told me many stories, even accusing their trainers of lying to them about horses. More than likely, the trainer was completely sincere. **He believed the horse he recommended for $20,000 would win back his cost, although statistically most horses will not pay their way, let alone their initial cost.**

If it were easy, trainers wouldn't have to work so hard and get up so early. A very clever trainer I knew told me my problem was not educating my owners properly. "Just tell them it's like owning a boat," he said. "The owner doesn't expect his boat to make him money. He has it for the pleasure it gives him." This might sound good, until you realize a boat doesn't humiliate an owner by running last in front of friends who have bet the boat very heavily.

Most of my owners are self-made men, the kind that can't relate to paying $20,000 for a horse, putting another $6,000 into training and being told the horse might be able to win in a field of $2,500 claimers. Who could relate to that, anyway? But, many times it is the scenario. It is possible **that the horse may be very useful at that level and steadily bring in enough money to justify his expenses.**

The joy of seeing your horse win at any level is a great experience. Of course, if the horse starts making money at a given level, he may be claimed. Other astute trainers or owners see that he is useful. They pick him up and make money from all your hard work. Nobody ever said life was fair.

I share this with you because many owners tell me they had bad luck . . . their horse got a cough . . . bucked his shins . . . popped a splint . . . Lord knows when he will run. This really isn't bad luck. It is very typical of a young horse going through normal experiences on his way to becoming a real racehorse. Just as our children experience coughs and ear aches in the process of growing up, **horses must encounter and overcome minor setbacks.**

Down time is expensive to owners paying $45 a day or more for training. Often the trainer, aware of the owner's attitude, feels pressured to continue training too soon when faced with a setback.

If the horse gets a cold at the track, he will probably be treated with antibiotics. Infections can bounce back and fourth in the shedrow . . . especially among young horses. This is another reason I encourage waiting to take horses to the track until they are more mature and have a higher resistance level. Coughs, colds and minor lameness are not as

Setbacks are part of developing a mature racehorse.

crucial at home as they are at the track. At home the horse has more space. Germs are less concentrated. It is easier to allow more time to recover when you're not paying expensive day money. Many times a few days or a week of turnout will allow the horse to fight the common cold or cough.

The following pages describe common and predictable setbacks, and how to treat them. Remember, my way is not the only way. These are solutions that work for me.

Until you have more experience, many of you will want to confer with a vet about these problems. *Lameness in Horses,* by O. R. Adams and *Equine Medicine and Surgery,* by American Veterinary Publications were my "bibles" when faced with a setback. *How To Be Your Own Veterinarian (sometimes),* by Ruth B. James is an excellent book on just what it says. An excellent book on anatomy is *Color Atlas of Veterinary Anatomy,* published by J .B. Lippincott Company, Gower Medical Publishing.

PARALYZED FLAP

A paralyzed flap is a big setback for the horse. If you suspect this problem, your veterinarian will slip an endoscope into the horse's nose to see whether or not the horse has Laryngeal Hemiplegia (Paralyzed Flap). The endoscope is a long flexible tube with a tiny camera at the end. The camera projects pictures of the throat onto a screen as it is moved around the area. It is best to have this procedure done between 20 minutes to an hour after work on a treadmill, the track, or your route at home. It is important to see these pictures while the horse is still breathing hard from his work.

Lazy or Paralyzed Flap

Healthy resting larynx

Healthy exercising larynx. Both sides are open!

Left laryngeal hemiplegia. One side is not open!

Do your homework, constantly learn from experience. Never be afraid to ask questions if something doesn't make common sense to you.

Simply put, because of a malfunctioning opening, the horse is unable to take in the air he needs, especially when he is under stress. This is a very frustrating problem and is most dramatic for racehorses.

Many times you don't know your horse has this problem until you finally redline him. During a hard work, a young horse in training, may make a "roaring noise" or stop running hard for no apparent reason. A vet exam will confirm whether he has a lazy or paralyzed flap. Lazy flap is an early sign of paralyzed flap. A lazy flap is slow to open and close. Eventually it becomes paralyzed.

There is a surgical procedure to correct this condition. I have not had very positive results with it. In an informal survey of trainers, few felt it was worth the effort or cost. Unless your horse shows real talent, don't invest time and money in the procedure. Before making any decisions, go to a large veterinary center where many of these procedures are performed and talk with experts in the field. As in all medical procedures, methods are improved every day.

SOFT PALATE DISPLACEMENT

This breathing problem occurs when a horse is running and displaces his soft palate, therefore impeding his airflow. Sometimes tying his tongue will help. Sometimes surgery is recommended. As always discuss such a procedure with a reliable vet before making any decisions. (See Bag of Tricks and Equipment for Racing.)

ENTRAPPED EPIGLOTTIS

This is yet another variation on breathing-related problems which impede air flow. In this case the horse must be scoped for diagnosis. I understand that a very minor surgery can remedy this problem. Be sure to investigate all medical and surgical procedures thoroughly before making your decision as to treatment.

Wait - this goes up your nose - Not your mouth!

It is very frustrating when you find a horse with potential who suffers from any of these problems... it's all part of being in the business.

COUGHS AND COLDS

When you start working your horse and you notice he coughs deeply in an unusual way or is breathing funny, it may be a cough or a cold. There might be colored mucus, yellow or green, draining from his nose. Stop working him immediately! Turn him out unless the weather is cold and inclement, or he becomes nervous when he is out. If you must stall him, make sure he is walked or turned out briefly each day. He needs movement to help him cough and drain the mucus.

Never leave a horse in a stall 24 hours without some kind of exercise, even if he is ill. His legs can stock up and other problems can occur if you don't stir up his blood. Ten minutes of hand walking twice a day will help.

Three days . . . that is my magic number. If the horse doesn't show improvement in three days, call the vet. Of course, if he has a high fever, is in acute stress or looks severely ill, call the vet immediately. **Consult the vet before using any cough remedies or medications. Many have substances that must <u>not</u> be used within so many days of racing.**

Don't load a horse with antibiotics for minor illnesses. Use your common sense. Remember your first child. The pediatrician was called incessantly until you learned to relax and not over react. After you handle enough horses, you'll learn not to over react.

Allow your horse rest and turnout until he no longer coughs or breathes funny. Then try free round-penning him. If he starts coughing persistently, he needs more rest. If he coughs a few minutes and then seems all right, continue the free round-penning.

If your horse is stalled at the track in the winter, it is possible that the air he is breathing in his stall is more harmful than the cold air outside. Urine odors and germs get trapped in tightly closed barns. The horses toss all kinds of viruses back and forth among themselves. It is possible that chronic low-grade respiratory infections may be a cause of bleeding. Single stalls with a half door open to the outside are better for horses as fresh air can circulate through the stall.

Horses have ciliated epithelial cells in their nasal passages and upper airways. These cells are responsible for trapping dust, mold spores and other debris prior to their entry to the lungs. Drs. Jackson and Pagan of Kentucky Equine Research believe the ammonia from urine and manure in enclosed stalls damages these cells, leaving the horse more susceptible to molds and other pathogens.

Remember, if your horse has been given the various systemic steroids which are so popular now, his immune system will be very weak and he will be susceptible to any kind of virus. Meticorten, Vetalog, Prednisone, Prednisolone and Azium are all **steroids that will lower his immune system.** Don't use them as short cuts to racing young horses!

Horses seem to have fewer respiratory problems when kept outside under good shelter as opposed to poorly ventilated barns.

BLEEDING (EPISTAXIS)
EXERCISE-INDUCED PULMONARY HEMORRHAGE

Before I talk about bleeders, I want to share a story with you. Thirty years ago I lived in a small tropical village in Colombia, South America. Although I had always loved horses, I knew very little about them. On weekends, the local vaqueros and campesinos would come galloping into the village to have fun and raise cain. They rode their criollo horses . . . pretty little animals with fine Arab heads. The village was small. They would gallop back and forth along the main street, showing off and drinking, knowing that the young women in the town were peeking out of their windows to watch the antics. The cowboys would race up and down the street, spurring their horses to a wild gallop, yanking them to a halt, then whirling and racing off in the other direction. Often, a horse would collapse and sometimes die. Bright red blood would gush from his nostrils when he keeled over. At the time, although I had no understanding of equine exercise induced pulmonary hemorrhage, it was obvious to me that the horses were run to death.

You must understand that these horses were work animals. Their primary function was to provide transportation. The vaqueros constantly rode among the cattle looking for animals with wounds, cuts, or for a new calf with a fresh umbilical cord. Such an abrasion would provide access for the screw fly. In their saddle bags, the vaqueros always carried a bottle of "McDougal", a creosote based medication that kills the screw fly larvae that infest wounds and abrasions. The horses were ridden up and down the narrow trails through the Andes mountains between the farms and town. These horses often doubled as pack animals carrying supplies up and produce, often coffee, down. They were not prepared for speed. Galloping was not a part of their daily lives.

Today there is endless discussion as to what causes bleeding. I can't help but think that one of the main reasons could be simply pushing a horse beyond his physical ability. Human athletes, when pushed beyond their limit, may show breakthrough bleeding in the lungs. Another reason could be the lack of preparation for the work asked of them.

Long before I saw these problems at the track, I saw horses overworked and bleeding. Could it be that obvious . . . more stress than the system can handle? Should we look for ways to teach a horse to run . . . but not run beyond what his structure can tolerate? Since horses can run themselves to death, are we setting them up to do more damage when we give them steroids and other medications that may enable them to run in spite of physical limitations and lack of conditioning?

There are many theories about bleeding and what causes it, but there are no proven answers. Typically, your horse is running, and in the middle of the race or in the stretch, he throws his head up and stops running well. His big moves and hard drives stop and he just gallops in. By the time he gets to the finish line, the horse might manifest bleeding by having blood pour out of his nostrils spattering all over his body. This is not a pleasant sight. The track vet and stewards make official notice of it and put him on the Bleeders List.

Bleeding might manifest itself with no visible problem . . . no blood . . . no throwing the head up. Your horse just fades and gallops in leaving you to scratch your head as you go back to the barn wondering what went wrong. Then after you walk him a few rounds and let

**Until you have a bleeding problem,
you're not really even aware of what it means.**

him drop his head to graze, you notice a trickle of blood coming from his nostrils. He too is a bleeder.

Some horses gush, others show a trickle and some bleed so little you don't know it until you've seen them race a few times fading in the drive. In desperation, you ask to have the horse scoped to eliminate the possibility of bleeding.

When you have your horse scoped, the vet will meet you at the barn after the race or work. The horse must have been stressed enough to trigger the bleeding. The vet will examine the horse with an endoscope to see if there is any bleeding that hasn't worked its way up and out yet. If the vet verifies that there is bleeding, he will send you to the State Vet, who will observe the horse and put him on the Bleeders List. (All of the rules mentioned apply to Florida tracks. Check the regulations in your racing jurisdiction!)

If your horse is put on the Bleeders List, it means that he must not run for two weeks and may be given Lasix four hours before his next race.

Once your horse is on the Lasix List, it is announced in the program and your horse must be on the grounds at least four hours before the race to have the Lasix administered by a vet. If your horse is observed bleeding through the Lasix, he will be ruled off for six months. If he continues to bleed, he will not be allowed to run. Some trainers, who fear the horse will bleed through the Lasix, instruct their grooms to keep the horse's head high after the race. The groom will lead the horse off the track with the horse's head resting on his shoulder so that blood does not drip in front of the officials.

Studies suggest that use of Lasix may improve any horse's performance, whether he's a bleeder or not. When Lasix is given, a horse tends to run better the first time back. The betting public likes knowing about Lasix administration. They think, "If the horse was moving well before he started to bleed, he might move really well with Lasix." There is also a belief that if a horse is on Lasix, other drugs can be given and the test results will be clouded, making it possible to administer illegal or unproven substances under the cloud of confusion.

I personally am very uncomfortable with a bleeder. If you have to give Lasix, be acutely aware of the diuretic effect it has on the horse's metabolism. I believe it is very dangerous to use Lasix, especially in heat and humidity. One hot afternoon at Calder, two Lasix horses dropped dead in the same race.

Think about the effect of Lasix, a powerful diuretic, on the horse's system. Four hours before a race you take away his water bucket and give him a shot of Lasix. Soon he starts urinating. Some horses react to the medication with trembling.

Water is Taken away from Lasix Horses 4 Hours before Race!

Others pass a loose stool. They all lose fluid. The theory is that Lasix lessens the pressure against the capillary walls by lowering the volume of fluid. In effect, the same amount of red blood cells are being circulated through the system, but with less fluid. Maybe, because the blood volume is less, they don't bleed as easily?

What is really going on physiologically? When you are running a horse in severe heat with chemically induced fluid loss and he is redlining his system, how can he lower his temperature with sweat if his fluid volume is already low? Does this combination of stresses (heat, severe exercise, fatigue and lack of water volume) cause an imbalance in his electrolytes which can cause irregular heart beat, heart attack and death? An electrolyte imbalance can cause heart attacks.

I don't have any answers, but I do think Lasix must be used cautiously, and not too frequently. You must allow the horse time to recuperate from its effects. A Lasix horse needs supplemental help with electrolytes and plenty of time to recover.

According to a study done by New Bolton Clinic and the University of Pennsylvania that Bill Heller cites in his book *Run Baby Run*, Lasix does not prevent bleeding. So when your trainer or vet says you are cruel not to "help" the horse, remind them that Lasix does not "help" prevent bleeding, although it may have other effects on the horse.

My horses, trained with the incremental stacking of stress (over the time period recommended), don't seem to bleed. I don't think this is coincidental. It is thought that bleeding does relate to speed work. We don't usually see it in horses doing long slow gallops. Bleeding has been observed in Quarter Horses who were flat racing and barrel racing. Early studies indicated a higher percentage of bleeders than among Thoroughbreds. Quarter Horses are not given much racing foundation since they are asked to run only short distances. Are they being asked to do too much without incremental preparation?

There are many theories to consider. Does it have something to do with the fragility of capillaries? Where does respiratory illness fit in? Could previous bouts of severe coughs or flu leave scar tissue that eventually tears and bleeds when the lungs are redlined? Is it the stress of the race, redlining the structure, that causes bleeding? Is it asking a horse, who has not been gradually brought up to the point of fitness necessary for the race, to run too hard, too soon? We must keep all of these possibilities in mind and train judiciously. Horses are very honest, and capable of giving much more than is physically safe for them. Fillies are always in danger of giving too much. If you work them too hard, too soon, you can ruin them for life. A horse should rise to the occasion and ease comfortably into running his best for a sustained distance. Some horses are overachievers and try too hard for their own good. They may bleed because the constantly give 110 percent and harm themselves in the process.

The effort of going into pure speed without incremental preparation could trigger a bleeding problem. To me, it is like flooring the engine of your car without a good, gradual warm-up. Sudden, pure speed is hard on a cold engine. It's even harder on an unfit horse's lungs and structure.

Be aware that there are also additives that can affect this problem. A situation that comes to mind is a filly that was sent to my farm to swim. She had undergone knee surgery. At that time MSM, a powder form of DMSO, was being touted as a great thing to speed up the healing of joints. The theory was that DMSO opened the blood flow to the capillaries;

Bleeding is a very complex subject.
If your horse has the problem, call the nearest university
or speak with a good vet and try to determine
what might help.

and the increased blood supply induced quicker healing (more good blood in, more damaged material out). I was told to give specified amounts of MSM to this filly, twice a day.

At the same time, a friend was suffering from chronically aching knees. The owner of the filly suggested that my friend take a spoonful of the same stuff two or three times a day. Everybody was talking about DMSO. My friend was in such chronic pain that he tried it. He jokingly commented that aside from an inexplicable desire to snort, whinny, and paw, he felt relief in his knees. Soon, he started having uncontrollable nose bleeds. They were so bad he had to be taken to the hospital to have his nose packed. Back home, he wondered if the nosebleeds were related to the DMSO. He stopped taking the powder and the nosebleeds stopped. He started taking the powder again and the nosebleeds resumed. Obviously this was not a medically controlled experiment, but I stored the information in the back of my mind.

Finally, the mare was sent to the track. I was told that upon her arrival, DMSO was administrated intravenously by a vet. Now the mare had been given powdered DMSO, DMSO IV, and knowing the racetrack, they were probably painting her knees with DMSO too. The horse started to run and she bled. She was put on Lasix. When she ran again, she bled through the Lasix, they had to take her home.

I told the owner about my friend's observations and asked him if he thought there could be any connection. He asked his vet and reported back to me that the vet said, "No. No relationship whatsoever."

I personally believe horses are given far too many substances that try to fool Mother Nature. Why not just keep your horse healthy, exercise him properly and give him time to rebuild from the extreme stress of a race?

Various vets have suggested that a horse might have a slight amount of bleeding when trying his hardest. They go on to say, if the horse is given time to heal from the intense race or work, there isn't a chronic problem. **They believe the problem starts when a horse has no time to rebuild.** Racetrack routine encourages works and or races every five days or so. What happens if the lungs are healing and the horse is dosed with steroids and mood enhancers, and then worked or raced five days after his last bleeding episode? More damage in the lungs, and retarded healing?

Then, because he's a bleeder, he's given Lasix, Bute and a plethora of steroids on the day of the next race. Now he's running with medications that may enhance his performance while tearing apart his lungs. Any emphysema sufferer will tell you how much Prednisone, an adrenal corticosteroid, helps his breathing and mental attitude. He'll also tell you that his **symptoms** are relieved and he feels very aggressive. These are good qualities for a race horse, but **no**

The two most important things a trainer should learn are how to develop natural talent and how to avoid breaking down the horse before discovering the lack of it.

healing has taken place. The discomfort is gone, but the **damage** is still there!

After a horse runs several times with these medications, the damage catches up with him. It's not just using Lasix. It's Lasix plus all the steroids and painkillers that cause such damage!

There are many concoctions on the market to help control bleeding. Some have a basis in diet, some are homeopathic, some naturally lower blood pressure, some like rutin, help coagulation and some are complete feed programs.

It is far easier not to have to deal with bleeding at all. **The point is that most racetrack ailments are related to pushing a horse beyond his abilities.** If you begin with a sound horse and follow the incremental training program, maybe your horse won't bleed.

Before we leave the subject of bleeders, I want to tell you about two horses I had in my barn. One was a lovely, large, honest gelding. This horse showed ability and had speed and courage, but could not carry the speed far enough to win. He lacked the capacity to deliver enough oxygen to carry his speed for the distance. He tried hard every time he ran, but seemed to always fade in the lane. Since he was very fit and had come off of a good foundation program, I knew it wasn't lack of conditioning. He tried hard in the race, and was off his feed a day or so after the race, which told me he was giving what he could. He had been scoped and the vet declared him clean.

I informed the owners that he just didn't have what he needed to be a racehorse. However, he was so lovely, I felt he would have a good second career as a jumper or in the show ring.

The owners wanted to try "helping" him. He was sent to a leading trainer's barn in another state and put on the medication routine there, which included Lasix and all the legal chemical enhancements available. He bled through the Lasix and was ruled off the track. He never won a race. He didn't run any better than he had with me and without the medications. The owners spent thousands of dollars more and ended up with a compromised horse.

The other horse was an owner's "home bred" with very little racing blood in his pedigree. After a few works, I told the owners I didn't want to start this horse, because he showed no ability. They knew I didn't use medications or enhancements, so they gave the horse to another trainer who tried to "put speed" into him by beating him out of the gates every day. He tried so hard that within a week of this routine, after a two furlong work he was bleeding.

"Aha!" said the owners. "That's the problem! Let's put him on Lasix." They did. The horse started bleeding through the Lasix and developed a terrible lung infection. They tried to treat it for a while at the track, but finally he was so sick he had to be taken home. His lungs are probably ruined for life and he still doesn't have the natural ability to be a racehorse.

It is difficult for owners to accept and understand the concept of talent. They think maybe if you hit him harder or train him more aggressively, he will improve. Instead, such treatment may cause an honest horse to over exert and break down. The two most important things a trainer should learn are how to develop natural talent and how to avoid breaking down the horse before discovering the lack of it.

To learn more about Lasix be sure to get Bill Heller's book, *Run Baby Run.* It will help you understand a very complex subject.

**As far as helping a bleeder goes, do your homework.
There is new knowledge available everyday.
Someday someone will have an answer.**

A Word With the Experts On -
THE BLEEDER'S LIST

by Melissa Sykes

Bleeding from the horse's lungs, commonly referred to as exercise induced pulmonary hemorrhage (EIPH), affects nearly 100% of the racehorse population according to the American Association of Equine Practitioners. Such bleeding in the racehorse has been observed for more than 300 years. One of the first documented cases was a horse named Bleeding Childers, who was foaled around 1716. Retired to stud, his name was changed to Bartletts Childers. As the great-grandsire of Eclipse, his name will be found in almost all of the pedigrees of American Thoroughbreds.

Horses that bled from the nose were easily identifiable, but only within the last twenty years (with the invention of the endoscope) has evidence emerged that the blood comes from the lungs and not the nose.

EIPH is thought to have occurred when evidence of hemorrhage into an airway is found by endocsopic examination after exercise. While experts know it occurs, there is a division within the medical community on what actually causes the bleeding.

Many researchers feel that "EIPH in the horse is a normal response of horses to strenuous exercise," said Dr. Howard H. Erickson, professor of physiology at Kansas State University. Strenuous exercise, the reasoning goes, causes high pulmonary vascular pressures that can in turn cause leakage of red blood cells into the lung tissue and air spaces.

In the lung, there is a very thin barrier separating air from blood. This barrier is made up of two layers. The first is the lining of the air sac, the second the capillary membrane. The difference between the pressure in the air sac of the lung and the pressure in the pulmonary capillaries is what causes bleeding.

And here begins the division of thought.

Environment

Air pollution in the environment has been put forth as a cause of EIPH.

"But racehorses in New Zealand, Australia and the Bahamas are kept out in the fresh air and still bleed," countered W. Robert Cook, FRCVS, PhD. and author of "Speed in the Racehorse: The Airflow Factors." Environment and air quality may contribute to the severity of EIPH, but it is not the root of the problem.

Genetics

Many in the scientific community believe that it is normal for the horse to bleed because it has been bred for racing and has developed an extraordinarily high capillary pressure. Since evidence exists that Bleeding Childers could have passed this defective gene to his offspring, it seems natural to assume that Eclipse could have also.

In addition, man has been breeding the Thoroughbred through the years in a quest for a perfect athlete. Part of that search for perfection demands the presence of an elite cardiovascular system.

But bleeding has been documented breeds other than Thoroughbreds. Quarter Horses and Standardbreds both have shown incidences of bleeding. Since both these

What really causes bleeding?

breeds originate from the Thoroughbred, it could be argued that genetics may still play an important role.

On the other hand, how can bleeding in draft horses during pulling competitions be explained?

"The presence of blood in the air sacs of the lungs is not normal for the Thoroughbred or any other mammal," said Cook. "It may be common, but it is not physiological. Bleeding in the racehorse is not a physiological response to fast exercise and an acceptable feature of racing."

Small Airway Disease

Upon endoscopic examination of a horse's lungs, evidence of bleeding is confirmed by the presence of lesions. These lesions are thought to be caused by any number of diseases that would obstruct the airway. Diseases such as bronchitis (COPD) or pneumonia will constrict the airway upon expiration (exhaling) and lead to lesions. One of the symptoms of small airway disease is coughing, since the obstruction is being met upon expiration.

Lesions resulting from small airway disease tend to be patchy, with no definitive pattern. They often will only affect one lung and they usually are distributed forward and downward in either one or both lungs (i.e. closest to the head).

In horses suffering from EIPH, however, coughing is rare and the lesions in the lungs "are distributed upwards and tailwards," Cook said. "More particularly, they are curiously symmetrical – both lungs are affected to the same degree at similar sights."

Cook feels that this is evidence that the airway obstruction is occurring upon inspiration (inhaling) rather than expiration.

Impact Initiated Wave

Professor Bob Schroter of Great Britain presented a new theory as to the cause of bleeding at an EIPH workshop in Japan in 1998. Schroter suggested that there is an impulsive force when the front leg makes contact with the ground in the running horse that is, in turn, transmitted as a wave through the lung. This wave causes damage to the lung, resulting in a progressive lesion involving edema and hemorrhage.

However, the landing on the front legs occurs during expiration, when the resultant lesions would be sporadic, not symmetrical, as documented in EIPH.

Asphyxia

"I think that we are all in agreement that blood comes from the pulmonary capillaries," said Cook. "Horses bleed because of a higher pressure of the blood side of the air/blood barrier. "

Cook disagrees with his colleagues, however, in believing hat this pressure is not caused by the positive pressure on the blood side of the barrier, but, rather from the negative pressure on the air side that is sucking blood corpuscles out of the lung.

The horse is trying to take air in, but there is some type of obstruction. And, if such is the case, the obstruction, in order to have the identical effect on both lungs, must be occurring at the juncture where the lungs attach to the windpipe or above.

"Lung lesions identical to those of EIPH occur in the standing horse if the airway is obstructed," Cook explained. "It is not exercise but asphyxia that is the trigger mechanism common to all occurrences of pulmonary bleeding."

Cook feels that if a standing horse with an airway obstruction has the same lesions as the horse that is exercising, it is the airway obstruction that causes the negative pressure in the lungs.

You can't run if you can't breathe.

Since man first domesticated the equine, various forms of suffocation have dictated his control over the horse. This is particularly evident in the racehorse.

Horses on the track are usually taught only the bare fundamentals of what is expected of them. Stop, go, turn left, turn right and they are taught through the use of the bridle, bit and reins. Leg cues and a loose rein virtually are unheard of. The Thoroughbred is controlled through what is kindly referred to as 'rating'.

The extent of rating can be equated with the amount of bow in a horse's neck. As the rider asks his mount for more speed, he "lets out the reins a notch or two." As he asks the horse to steady or slow a bit, he pulls the reins back in.

This give and take on the reins directly impacts the set of the head. And it's the headset or flexing of the poll that Cook believes causes the upper airway obstruction that leads to bleeding.

This argument falls in line with observations of the occurrence of EIPH at the racetrack. Horses are much more likely to bleed during their morning works (i.e. when the rider is rating them based on a clock in his head) than during a race (when less rating is needed because of running in a 'pack' or behind other horses).

"We haven't paid enough attention to what we're doing to a horse by means of poll flexion," Cook said. "It is so common, we tend to over look it as a source of damage to the lungs."

Cook feels his theory is consistent with all of the known facts about bleeding:
1. It affects nearly 100% of racehorses;
2. It's geographically widespread (appearing under conditions of air pollution and fresh air); and
3. It occurs in many breeds and many types of equine activities.

Furthermore, Cook's theory is the only one that explains the placement and symmetrical nature of the lesions in the lungs. It is this that separates his theory from the others.

"Lesions characteristic of EIPH can be produced by the accidental obstruction of the upper airway of a horse at rest or at exercise," he said. "None of the other theories are supported by this crucial experimental reproduction of the lesions."

In addition to rating, upper airway obstruction can be caused by slight tongue movement in response to a tongue tie or the bit. Cook has linked tongue movement and swallowing to narrowing of the airway in the throat and to dorsal displacement of the soft palate, both of which negatively impact inspiration.

"Though I have tried hard to refute this hypothesis, I have failed," Cook said.

Cook is the first to admit that bleeding is multifactorial, but only in the sense that there can be any number of ways in which the upper airway can be obstructed. The bleeding in and of itself is not the disease; it is merely the symptom.

"If you review the literature on bleeding, one sees that there has been a vast amount of interest in the topic of 'treatment' but relatively little in the question of cause," he said. "But how can you successfully treat any disease without a firm understanding of its cause?"

Be sure to read Melissa's article on Lasix in the Section *Common Medications: What They Are and What They Do.*

Now you see why it only looks easy.

BUCKED SHINS

If the worst problem your horse has is Bucked Shins, consider yourself lucky. If handled properly, they are a minor setback along the way to a mature racehorse. They can occur at any age when the bone is challenged, although they are more common in young horses.

The general consensus of opinion is that Bucked Shins are a tearing of the periosteum sheath caused by concussion and speed, and are generally found in immature horses. They can be considered a series of micro fractures. They usually occur when speed on a firm surface "insults" the bone. They can easily become a saucer fracture if not handled properly.

When the horses on my farm ran on a kind surface, even putting on speed, they didn't have shin problems. When they started racetrack works, after about three works spaced seven days apart, the horses would get sore or bucked shins. Since by this time the horse is getting anaerobically fit, working five to six furlongs, **I believe the stress of high speed at a sustained distance on a firm surface can cause Bucked Shins or soreness.**

If your horse has sore shins, he will be touchy when you run your hand down the front of the cannon bone. If the shins are really bucked, after two or three days, you will see a little knot or swelling on the front of the leg. If it is severe, the horse may stop in the middle of the track work and walk back in obvious distress. Then if you even point at the shin, the horse will pick it up quickly and very clearly tell you that it hurts. Sometimes it is not apparent that a horse has bucked his shins until 2 or 3 days after the work. Frequently, I have felt a horse worked well and had come out of the work fine. Then two or three days later, during his daily monitoring when I think he's out of the woods, much to my surprise he manifests sore or bucked shins.

Remember that horses with saucer fractures usually have had bucked shins. By avoiding this problem, catastrophic injuries may be vastly reduced.

If the shins become extremely sore, have them X-rayed to rule out a true fracture. If there is no fracture, follow your vet's advice, which will probably be poultice and rest. He may suggest "cooling the shins out and firing" them. This is a thermal cautery. Heat is applied to a series of needles that are pressed onto the front of the cannon bone. It reminds me of putting gun powder on a wound to sterilize it.

Many trainers and vets swear by the method. I almost had it done to one of my horses, but at the last minute I declined because it made no common sense to me. They say, "Well, cooling the shins out and firing them forces you to rest the horse. He is so inflamed that you couldn't possibly train him until the swelling and reaction subside." This is a poor reason to administer the procedure. Must a horse be incapacitated in order to rest him? Some horses rebuck even with this treatment. So what is gained?

Bucked shins are a minor setback if handled judiciously.

Chemical blistering is also a common remedy for sore shins. A very caustic solution is rubbed or painted on the horse's shins or completely around the front cannon bones. This causes a reaction like a terrible chemical burn. The legs swell up tremendously. The trainer then "works" on the legs until they come back to "normal", at which point he starts training again. Many trainers feel the blister and resulting scar tissue "toughen" the shins.

Over the years, I have found a solution that works for me. When your horse comes back from a work with sore or bucked shins, continue monitoring his legs every day and turn him out every day . . . all day if possible. To monitor him, gently and lightly run your hand down the front of the shin. His reaction to your touch tells you how sore he is. If the horse has been X-rayed and has no fractures, don't give him Bute. Observe how he walks and moves daily.

If he is really inflamed, by all means poultice him, but don't wrap the shin with more than two turns of cellophane. That's all - no standing bandages! Be careful with the cellophane. It can be put on so tightly in so many layers that it cooks the skin. After wrapping the horse's shins, turn him out. The next morning pull off the cellophane wrap and let the poultice dry and flake off. The following day hose until the poultice is entirely removed. Repeat the process if you feel it will help. Depending on the severity of the inflammation, your horse should not be as touchy on the shins after five days. At this point you should be able to tap the front of the shin with your finger. Learn how quickly he yanks his leg back in response your touch. He should gradually become more tolerant of the tapping. Always monitor his shins no matter how you think he is feeling, and write your observations on his chart.

When your horse seems better and is moving freely on his own in the paddock, gently free round-pen him at a light gallop. If the surface is hard, he may show a little soreness. Monitor his shins the day after the round-penning by running your hand down the front of the cannon bone or tapping along it with your finger. You must do this every day and continue to note his reactions on the chart. If he is more sore, let him rest for two or three days before you free roundpen him again. If he is less sore, gently free roundpen him. When he is not sore, go back to training.

Work him again no sooner than 14 days from the first day of soreness. If he comes back sore, repeat the process from the beginning. He should heal more quickly this time because he is now starting to strengthen his bone and is laying more bone density on the front of the cannon bone. You are trying to encourage new tissue to be laid across the bone. While you don't want to push the horse to overdo and fracture the bone, you do want to "judiciously insult" the bone. You will get a feel for this as you go along. You must monitor your horse every day and refer to your notes on his chart to maintain a good point of reference.

Never work him at the track more frequently than every ten days when he has had sore shins, even if he is not sore after five days. It takes ten days to replace the calcium lost in a hard work at the track. By allowing a certain amount of healing and not confining or stopping the horse, his body can repair, rebuild and toughen the shins. It may take two to six months for your horse to come out of the works or races without being sore. If he shows no soreness when you run your hand down the cannon ten days after his last soreness, put him in a race or work him. If your horse is racing at this time, make sure he isn't sore going into the race. Don't give Bute and fool yourself into thinking he is not sore when he is.

 It's very frustrating when you find a horse with potential who suffers from any of these problems . . . it's all part of being in the business.

BUCKED SHINS

X-ray horse to determine
no fractures.

Sore shins usually appear after 3rd or 4th
speed breeze at the track - caused by
high speed at sustained distance on a
hard surface!

Horse will be <u>very touchy</u> when
you go <u>near shins!</u> <u>Check
severity of soreness everyday!</u>

<u>Give rebuild time.</u>
<u>Turn horse out!</u>
After 5 days or so, <u>he should
be able</u> to <u>free roundpen.</u>

a "bump"
might appear
2 days or so
after Speed
Work

Shin

<u>Don't give Bute!</u>
His soreness keeps him from hurting himself.

<u>Check Shins</u> on <u>6th day</u>.
If <u>more sore, leave alone</u> another 2 or 3 days.
If <u>less sore, free roundpen</u> again.

Each day that he is <u>less sore</u>
than the <u>previous</u> day, free
<u>roundpen again</u> until you go
back to a <u>strong fast gallop</u>
with rider.

<u>Work</u> horse at track no
sooner than <u>14 days</u>
from <u>1st day</u> of <u>soreness.</u>

He may be <u>sore again</u> after work -
turn out, free roundpen,
and gallop again when <u>not sore</u>.

You are working through "BUCKED SHINS"!

A Worst Case Scenario

I share the following story to emphasize the importance of you and your trainer thoroughly understanding each other and understanding the methods to be used on your horse. Often the trainer will agree, only to decide later that what you want is either too much trouble, or is not in the best interest of your horse. (According to his methods.)

A friend was leaving the country for a vacation and after much research selected a training center that she believed would care for her horse as she wanted. The center had irrigated paddocks for turn out and a half mile track. She had been told that the trainer was easy to work with. She explained her methods to him. He assured her that there was no problem. He had trained that way before.

Because the trainer was leaving on vacation, she wrote out her program and underscored that the horse was not to be pushed. She wanted him worked at the speed he chose, light gallop or trot, for 3 miles every third day. The remainder of the time he was to be turned out in a paddock. The exercise rider rode the horse beautifully the day she went to observer him. Before she left, she asked that the horse needed to be shod immediately, because he tended to grow foot very quickly. She was assured that all would be well during her absence, and she left.

Ten days into her trip she called for a progress report and was informed that the horse was being stalled. "Why?" she asked. "Because he frolics, runs, and bucks in the paddock. Besides, the trainer only trains from the stall and he trains every day." she was told.

She immediately Faxed instructions to the trainer to either follow her program or stop training immediately and turn the horse out. At this point she became very anxious, but was headed into the African bush and further communication was impossible for 14 days, at which time she boarded a plane and headed home.

She was gone a total of 28 days and returned home to find the horse had only been shod the day before, had been worked every day, had been kept in a stall, had been exercised on the hot walker instead of turn out, and that he had bowed a tendon.

In hindsight it is easy to say that she should have left the horse in a field somewhere. However, she did her homework, was convinced she was dealing with reliable people, and left very clear, detailed written instructions.

 **Real communication is a meeting of the minds!**

BOWED TENDONS

There is no such thing as a "Little Bit Bowed". As many trainers are fond of saying, "It's like being a little bit pregnant . . . you are or you aren't"

Bowed tendons are devastating for a racehorse. Whatever his ability, it is forever impaired by bowed tendons. It is good money thrown after bad to try and bring back a horse with a bow. Unless he is exceptional and can run somewhere cheaper, and still win, the trials and tribulations involved aren't worth the cost. Generally the horse will improve and give you hope. He will train well and then in the last work before the race (in traditional methods), or in the first race back he will rebow.

Believe it or not, most of this anguish can be avoided if you are tuned into your horse and follow my advice about monitoring his legs, turnout and rest between works. I have been training and/or breaking and prepping my own horses, since the late seventies. I recognize that a horse really can have a misstep or bad luck in a twist or fall and indeed bow a tendon. But that is the exception rather than the rule. There are many bowed tendons on the racetrack due to the lack of incremental training. Others are due to horses being wrapped and medicated so much that you can't tell if a tendon is "cooking" or beginning to go. I can't overemphasize the value of the solid incremental training and the extra time allowed in the process of development and how important progressive building is to the long term, overall structural integrity of a racehorse.

Some horses may be conformationally set up to have tendon problems. They may be very weak structurally with thin, weedy tendons, and/or tied in tendons, long cannon bones, or exceedingly long pasterns . . . all of which predispose such horses to breakdown when redlined. This kind of horse should be trained cautiously for racing. He is not a good candidate for the rigors of the track.

Even wonderfully built, strong tendoned, short cannoned horses can break down. Look in the stallion catalogs . . . time and again you see bowed tendons. Almost 90% of the time they are bowed on the left leg. These are horses with great breeding and wonderful bone. How did it happen? The training process on the track. It's almost a text book case study on how to break down a horse. Start with a strong, good feeling animal with green, unformed bone and tendon. Shoe him incorrectly, give him a long toe and no heel. Put him in a 12' x 12' stall. Overfeed him and give him too many vitamins. Don't let him out but once a day for 15 minutes to run like heck for a brief mile or so. Then walk him half and hour (even worse walk him on a hot walker) and put him back in the stall. (Did you ever notice how a horse walks head up with his back concave on the hot walker? Shouldn't he be able to lower his head and stretch his neck in order to flex and relax his back?)

Ask anyone who knows anything about exercise physiology if any but super unusual horses can tolerate this kind of treatment. Of course, we have tendon breakdown . . . the animal is willing to give more than he has been properly prepared for, and he is willing to run beyond his structure. Add in all of the chemical enhancements used in the name of good training and you'll see a complete program of breakdown. It is so predictable that I am appalled no one has truly tried to change this cycle of destruction. Believe me, I love racing. I want it to succeed, and I want us to act more responsibly on behalf of these magnificent animals.

Stop training!
Allow rest!

It is simple to avoid bowed tendons. Monitor your horse's legs every morning. **When you perceive any heat or swelling in the tendon area,** back off training. In this case ice and support wrap for a day or two may be indicated. Check with your vet. He may recommend an ultra sound. Always have him ultrasound both legs to establish a point of reference. **Never give medications that mask the symptoms and fool you into thinking it has improved.** Give time and support. Read the warning signs. Interestingly, studies have shown that stopping the insult before real damage is done may lead to full recovery. Make sure the tendon is completely back to normal before continuing training. Healing takes as long as it takes. **You must wait on this problem or ruin the horse!** Unfortunately the tendon is usually bowed before most people catch it, then it is too late. They can only retire the horse and learn.

Ask to see the work/exercise chart for your horse when you go to the stable, or ask to have a copy sent to you with your monthly bill.

Bowed Tendons turn thick and Firm later - The first sign of problems will be <u>heat</u> and <u>swelling</u>! <u>Do</u>n't <u>Keep Training</u>! Allow Rest!

You have no control over a bow caused by poor conformation or a bad move. You do have control over a tendon that is starting to have slight heat or filling - IF YOU WAIT!

LAMINITIS/ Founder

Laminitis or Founder is probably one of the most feared problems of all horsemen. There is an old saying, "Everything goes to the feet." The truth of this cannot be over emphasized. All husbandry practices should be carefully reviewed if this problem occurs, especially if it occurs in more than one animal in your barn. Over feeding is a common cause of laminitis which can be easily controlled. Rapid change in feed which causes digestive upset is another cause that can be easily controlled by switching feeds slowly. Sudden access to fresh grass can cause "grass founder" and again is easily controlled.

Other possible causes are illness, surgery, fever, stress, over feeding, lack of exercise, improper foot care, trailer stress, even thrush from dirty stalls can evolve into laminitis. In other words any stress or shock to the system could trigger laminitis. It is a symptom arising from multiple causes, just as fever or nausea can arise from multiple causes in humans.

Aside from the well known causes of laminitis, recent research indicates that corticosteroids can cause laminitis and make it worse if used as treatment. This may be due to the fact that they affect the action of insulin and also because they are vasoconstrictors. The last thing we want to do is further restrict circulation in a foot with laminitis. Please be sure to read the comments on Corticosteroids in the "Medications at the Racetrack Section, Common Medications, What They Are and What They Do" .

After or during recuperation from a leg injury, a horse can develop laminitis from the stress of standing with extra weight on his "good" leg. For this reason wrapping both the injured leg and the leg that will take the extra weight is suggested.

If you notice your horse standing on his toes or if he looks like he is walking on eggs, check his feet for heat immediately and contact your vet or farrier.

Understand that laminitis results from a lack of blood flow to the foot which causes inflammation. In the worst cases the bone and foot wall can actually separate. This allows the coffin bone to rotate and possibly penetrate the sole. This is very painful and often unnecessary, since many causes of laminitis can be easily prevented.

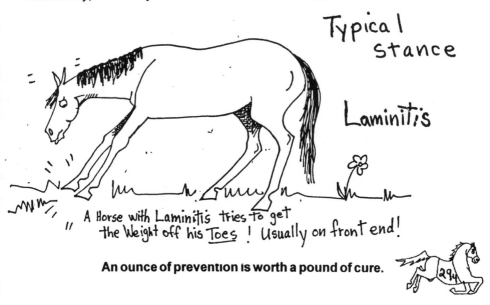

Typical Stance

Laminitis

A Horse with Laminitis tries to get the Weight off his Toes ! Usually on front end!

An ounce of prevention is worth a pound of cure.

TIE-UP

Recent research on tie-up has cast new light on the problem. Although there does not seem to be a single definite cause, the following excerpts from recent articles are very

An article in the April 2002 issue of *the Horse* defines tie-up as follows:

"Tying-up is a muscle disorder with many possible causes. Clinical signs include stiffness and muscle soreness. The muscles will feel firm to the touch, and the horse's urine might appear brown."

We have long believed that tied-up is the result of lactic acid build-up during exercise. Since lactic acid is a normal by-product of exercise and is usually handled efficiently by the body, more research is being done to investigate other causes. Causes may include such things as: cramping, electrolyte imbalance, energy metabolism abnormalities, imbalance of selenium and/or vitamin E, energy metabolism imbalances, vitamin B deficiency, and viral infections.

.   I have noticed more tie-up in fillies. It often seems to have been caused by emotional stress. I have no idea if there is any research on this phenomenon, but various people have mentioned seeing fillies tie-up when under stress.

Although there is much new information as to causes, the old traditional remedies still seem to work. Try adding bicarbonate of soda to the feed of horse prone to tie-up. Salt and electrolytes may also be recommended, but always check with your vet before administering a remedy. Also if the problem becomes more frequent and serious, you had best discuss it with your vet.

   **Will we ever know what causes tie-up?**

A Trainer can't make an Untalented horse have Talent! BUT! He can help a Talented Horse run for MANY YEARS!

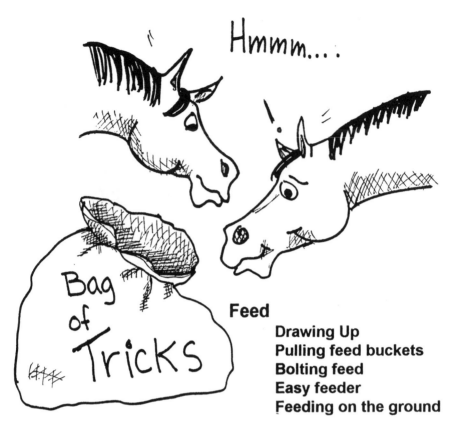

Hmmm....

Bag of Tricks

Feed
- Drawing Up
- Pulling feed buckets
- Bolting feed
- Easy feeder
- Feeding on the ground

Health
- Girth gall
- Loose palate
- Ring on hoof
- Sore stifles

Behavior
- Introducing new horses
- Little friends
- Galloping in company
- Racing Company
- Vicks in the nose
- Loading
- Unloading
- Handling hot and high horses
- Cooling hot horses in hot weather
- Kicking and striking in the stall
- Rolling

That's A good Idea!

Equipment
- Introducing new equipment
- Tongue ties

Expect the Unexpected

SOLUTIONS TO VARIOUS AND SUNDRY PROBLEMS WITH HORSES AND TRAINING

Tricks

Feed
Drawing Up on Race Day
Many trainers take away the food and water from a horse on race day. Immediately the horse knows he is in for it . . .he is going to race. I try to change as little as possible on race day. The horses have their usual feed at their usual time . . . (9 or 10 AM) and their normal hay. Sometimes I remove the water half and hour before getting him ready; but really, horses don't guzzle food or water before a race. There is a terrible old wives tale that says allowing the horse to have hay causes bleeding. It is completely unfounded. If you don't want them gorging on hay before the race, pull it out a few hours before post time. I have never had problems with horses who munch contentedly on race day.

Pulling Feed Buckets an Hour After They Are Given
Horses are grazers who nibble all day in the wild. When I feed in the morning, the more aggressive horses gobble it all down fast. I prefer that they take their time and munch all day. They have been conditioned at the track to eat fast before their food is removed. Eating fast is not a good habit for the horses. It is much better to allow them eat slowly and throughout the day. My horses usually finish their morning ration by noon. Since they have free choice hay, they continue snacking throughout the afternoon.

Bolting Down Food
Horses who have lived on the track sometimes bolt down their food. It is nice to see a hungry horse attack his food with gusto, but eating too fast can be harmful and interfere with proper digestion. To slow him down, you can put LARGE smooth rocks in his feed bucket. He will have to work around them to get his feed. Be sure they are too large for him to bite into. You don't want broken teeth.

Easy Feeder
When feeding hay and grain in small paddocks, Ron Vlaming of Saugus, CA, recommends using a 50 gallon plastic drum. He lays it on its side and cuts an opening about 18" x 18" longways on the side. He then fastens it to the fence and bingo a feeder that eliminates hay from blowing away and keeps hay and grain off the ground.

Devise ways to ease your work.

Feeding on the ground

A wise vet once told Nancy Crone of Matinsville, IN, that feeding grain on the ground (in a container if possible) forces the horse to masticate in a way that helps clear the head and sinuses. The grinding of grain is more beneficial than hay, because it causes the most effective drainage. Thanks for sharing, Nancy.

Health

Girth Gall

When sores start to form where the girth is placed on the horse, plastic wrap or cellophane wrapped a few times around the girth may help. (Change girth covers if training several horses, in order to avoid passing on skin diseases and bacteria!) With every third or fourth day training, girth gall is less of a problem.

Bit with SealTex Wrapped on it To hold down a Loose or soft palate problem. A figure eight is used To keep mouth closed!

Loose Palate Problem

The horse makes a "funny noise" while running. Between the vet, the rider, and the trainer, a loose palate is diagnosed. This means that the palate displaces itself while the horse is running. Sometimes wrapping Sealtex (a rubbery bandage) around the bit will create a kind of mass that holds the horse's palate in place. Usually a figure eight or a "dropped" nose band is used to keep the horse's mouth closed. When this little trick works, surgery may not be necessary. It also eliminates the necessity of a tongue tie.

Ring on Hoof

When buying a horse, particularly a young one, always look at the wall of the hoof. It can tell much recent history of the horse. Good hooves have very firm and smooth sides. Various ring like indentations are not so good. The rings can represent a very high fever, sickness, stress, or an extreme change in feed. For example: in the yearling or two-year-old sales, you'll commonly see one ring about half an inch down from the coronet band. It probably occurred when the horse was pulled in off of the field to be fattened and coddled for the sale. An acute change in the horse's life-style took place. He was stalled and his feed was augmented without allowing him the normal movement and exercise he previously enjoyed.

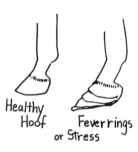

Healthy Hoof

Fever rings or Stress

This type of hoof is a very common at sales. Since the hoof grows about 1/4 to 1/2 inch a month, depending on the season, feed, environment, and genetic background, you can estimate when the horse was confined. Most sale horses need to be turned out for a month or two after you purchase them. Don't eliminate a horse for a few rings. Do be aware of probable cause. A horse with many, many rings has probably foundered and should be avoided as a race prospect.

Every trade has its tricks.

Sore Stifles/Locked Stifles

Fit horses confined to a stall may have a temporary loss of control in the stifle. In his article *Unlocking Sticky Stifles, EQUUS Magazine,* 1992, Issue 180, (Reprinted with permission of Fleet Street Publishing Corporation) Matthew Mackay-Smith, DVM, Medical Editor, has the following to say about this problem:

"Stall confinement of fit horses, particularly heavily muscled ones, and especially those tending to overstraight hind legs, may lead to the temporary loss of control of the patella (knee cap) in the stifle so that it "locks up." Usually this is painless, but it looks alarming because the horse can't flex the affected leg(s), and hops about struggling to get a leg forward. Sometimes, the horse's reaction bruises the joint or strains it, causing lameness.

A recent review of stifle surgeries found that convalescence is often longer than anticipated, and the stifle(s) may become arthritic several years later. Thus, there is some reluctance among veterinarians to perform the surgery unless it is unavoidable.

If a horse starts locking his patella(s) after a rest, and was never known to do so before, then continuous turnout in a large paddock or pasture and progressive exercise to build muscle tone are usually sufficient to cure the problem. If there is recurrence in a horse who has done it before or who has had a lifelong tendency to "lock" one or both stifles, more strenuous calisthenics (working up hills, pulling a log) may be necessary to keep the stifles smoothly flexing."

Behavior

New Horses at the Farm

Allow any new horse time to adjust to a new home. Let him become secure in his environment. He will learn quickly where to get his food and water and meets his friends over the fence. Don't attempt to train until you feel he is comfortable in his new surroundings. This usually takes three or four days. After he becomes familiar with his area, he'll run back to his secure home . . . his stall or paddock . . . if he gets loose. That is another good reason to allow him to have his own particular stall or paddock. Don't move him to a different one every night.

Little Friends

Some horses are very insecure. They may do well with a little goat, miniature horse or some other animal. You'll see many such friends in the stalls with the animals at the track. In the receiving barn at one track, I saw two full grown horses in one stall. One was obviously a Thoroughbred and the other a huge grade horse. The owner, a woman, explained to me that the mare was a bundle of nerves. She could run but was so nervous before the race that she would fret her energy away. When they tried having her pasture mate come along, she was much better. A good trainer does what he can to get the best performance from the horse. Sometimes you find yourself looking pretty silly. But that's okay. How did the horse run?

Galloping in Company

Try to have friends ride with you on occasion, so they can gallop along side, in front, and behind you. This accustoms your horse to galloping with other animals. Have the other rider bump you and lean against you and your horse. Let your horse learn that this touching is no big deal.

Always try to keep your horse relaxed.

Vicks in the Nose

Colts and fillies are very sensitive to odors . . . particularly of each other. To eliminate the danger of them thinking distracting thoughts, rub Vicks or any strong menthol based salve into the nostrils before racing and hauling your horses. It seems to kill their sense of smell for a while. Vicks is always used for works and race days to help clear the nasal passages. Horses eventually connect Vicks in the nose with a race. (Some states do not allow Vicks on race day. Be sure to check the regulations in your jurisdiction.)

Racing Company

There is a saying on the backside, "Keep yourself in the best company and your horses in the worst." It means put your horses in the easiest races you can find. The softer the competition, the better the chances of winning!

Loading Horses

When loading, once the horse is in, immediately close the back door or ramp so that he can't decide to back out while you are still fumbling with the butt bar. The butt bar and other things can be taken care of when the horse is well confined by the closed ramp or door.

Unloading Horses

Don't open the back trailer door or ramp until someone is holding the shank at the horse's head . . . ready to back him out. Often, the horse will see the door open behind him and start backing out while still tied up. Then he throws a fit when he finds he is still tied.

Handling Hot and High Horses

Never try to make a hot or an excited horse stand still. It is much easier and better for him to keep moving. It distracts him from his fear and works off the lactic acid buildup after a heavy work. It also works with the animal's natural instinct to move. Let's face it, we are not strong enough to hold a horse if he really wants to move. Let him think it was his idea. If you fight him, he will get even more excited fighting you.

The Shying Problem

Lucy Yahari, of Brooksville, FL, has had success by tieing empty plastic milk jugs partially filled with gravel on strings that are attached to the stall ceiling. The string length should allow the jugs to hang about ear level. When the horse moves around, the jugs will rattle and bump the ears. Soon the horse becomes desensitized and learns to tolerate the bumps and noise. Good idea Lucy.

Kicking or Striking at People in Stalls

Dog collars with small lengths of chains attached can be buckled above the horse's knees or hocks to discourage persistent striking or kicking while in the stalls. When the horse kicks or strikes, the chains slap against his legs, teaching him not to misbehave. (Idea from Donna Harper, DVM)

Cooling Hot Horses in Hot Weather

When cooling my horses after a work or a race in the terrible heat of the summer, I hose and hose them every turn around the barn to drop their temperature and cool them. It's so hot and humid some days in Florida that the horses never dry off. They maintain a constant sweat. By hosing all over the body each time you walk them around the shedrow, you help them lower their body temperature. They cool out much more efficiently. You can feel the body heat drop, as the cool water flows over the animal. We hose and put them in the stall wet with a fan blowing on them. (See *Bathing* in the Section *FARM LAYOUT.*)

Devise a solution to your problem.

At home, after a hard gallop in the summer, their tack is pulled at the lakefront. They are taken into the lake to cool off. The lake water is so tepid, it does not shock them. It is important to keep them moving if they are still breathing hard. It took about 40 minutes to cool them, before I started using the "lake" method. Now it takes about 10 minutes, plus another 10 minutes for floating and fooling around. They come out of the water feeling refreshed and relaxed. Since swimming is impossible at the track, there we walk and hose, walk and hose

Rolling

Even if he's not in a paddock or pen, a horse loves to roll - especially after his bath. If you can find a sandy area or a pile of sawdust somewhere around the backside it would be great to let him roll there before putting him back in his stall. Rolling helps him straighten out and stretch his back. It also allows him to scratch areas he can't reach. It is very therapeutic and healthy for him!

Rolling helps Horses stretch and scratch their Backs!

Equipment

Introducing New or Different Equipment

When trying new equipment, don't spring it on the horse the day of the race. Have him get used to it in the comfort of his stall or paddock. Blinkers, for example, are a very strange piece of equipment for the horse. When the horse wears them for the first time, he usually tries to back out of them. He seems to think that if he backs up, he'll be able to see. Eventually, he accepts that something mystical is not allowing him to see properly and settles down. If you put them on for a few hours while the horse is in his own paddock, he won't try to run through a fence he can't see. In their confusion horses who have gotten loose with blinkers on have been known to crash into things.

It is easier for an animal to learn the limitations of new equipment in his own territory. When breaking two-year-olds, they wear a head stall with a D bit all day. They must eat with the bit on and endure it for hours. They learn how to keep it comfortable in their mouths and don't fret when confronted with a complete bridle for the real training. Bandages, bell boots, vet wrap . . . all should be presented to the animal first in his own environment under non-stressful conditions.

Tongue Tie

Tongue Tie in place!

Tongue Ties

Panty hose can be cut and made into very comfortable tongue ties. An idea from Jess Cloud.

There is a solution for every problem.

EXPECT THE UNEXPECTED . . .
HORSES are UNPREDICTABLE

In handling young untrained horses, there is always an element of risk. As I have mentioned previously, I use Thoroughbreds in the example of the worst possible scenario. They can be the most volatile, high strung, over reactionary animals in the horse family.

One Easter Sunday stands out in my mind . . . I share it with you to **make you aware of the kind of risks you could encounter when working with horses.**

The horses were loaded and I was ready to head for the track. I had left Alex, my oldest son who was home for Easter with some Navy buddies, in charge of taking the saddles off some two-year-olds that were in the "getting used to the saddle" phase of training. Each horse was strolling around his paddock wearing the new equipment.

One particularly flighty filly caught my eye, and I decided to supervise her unsaddling as she was hypersensitive to being handled. I stopped the truck, jumped out and called Alex. Six foot four, two hundred and twenty pounds, Alex has always been very calm and kind around the horses . . . a steadying influence.

We both entered the small paddock, walking slowly toward the filly. I waited as Alex went quietly toward her head. She saw him coming and stood apprehensively. He spoke reassuringly to her. She seemed to be fine . . . then suddenly she whirled around and nailed Alex squarely, right under the chest with both rear hooves.

Alex stopped . . . turned around, took three steps, dropped to his knees and keeled over backwards . . . laying still as death. I ran to him. Only the whites of his eyes were visible. He was not breathing and had no pulse. "Alex," I shouted. "Wake up!" Dropping to my knees, I grasped him around the waist and shook him. It was like shaking a lifeless rag doll . . . his arms flopped and his head lolled back. No response . . . none. "My God," I thought, "My son. He's dead. He stopped breathing. He can't die . . . not like this . . . not here in this dirty corral." Such thoughts flashed through my mind as I tried pumping his chest and breathing life into him.

"Quick," I shouted to his friends who came running. "Call 9ll." I continued the CPR (Cardio Vascular Resuscitation) pumping and pounding with rhythm on his chest . . . sitting him up . . . jiggling him . . . anything to restore life. He had no pulse, no respiration. "Please God, don't let him die!"

I vowed that I would never, ever have anything to do with horses, if my son died. Other thoughts flashed inexplicably through my mind, as I mentally pleaded with Alex to respond while I continued the CPR. Suddenly, he started trembling and shaking all over - a convulsion. Paramount in my mind was a sick mare I tended once that convulsed and then died. In a panic, I kept working on him. Finally his eyes fluttered . . . he looked at me . . .

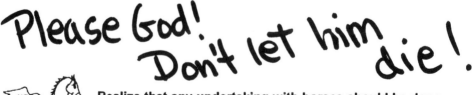

Realize that any undertaking with horses should be done with caution and care.

he recognized me. "Gosh," he said, "That was strange!" On my knees, I hugged and held Alex. He seem embarrassed . . . this huge hunk of a man being cradled in my arms like a baby. "Are you all right? Are you all right?," I kept asking while silently praying that his mind and intellect would be intact. There had been no pulse or heartbeat for what seemed like an eternity. It was probably only a few minutes.

He knew the day, the time, his name, and answered my questions coherently . . . albeit sheepishly. "How strange", he recounted, "I was there, somewhere, and I felt I had to do something. I couldn't remember what it was. Then it occurred to me . . . I had to breathe . . . that was it . . . I started, and there you were!"

I was just coming to the realization that my son was not dead . . . that he was okay . . . thank God, when I looked up and remembered that the truck was still running and the horses in the trailer were fretting and stomping. I had horses entered in two races in Tampa Bay Downs that Easter Sunday. Alex assured me that he was fine. I insisted that he go to the emergency room. He promised me that his friends would take him and insisted that I should not miss the races because of him. CPR certainly saved his life. I encourage all of you to learn how to use it. You never know . . . you may save someone's life!

I headed down the road and marvelled at how much we can appreciate life when faced with the threat of death. The horses ran miserably, but that was secondary to the fact that my first born was still alive and well!

Learn CPR !!

Be Prepared !

Be Cautious!

Just another day at the farm!

Useful Information and Track Terminology

INSIGHT INTO THE FRONTSIDE AND THE BACKSIDE

Before ever owning a racehorse, I had only been to the racetrack once in my life. I never bet, and my first day at the track was spent admiring the beautiful horses, the color, and pageantry of the races. I knew nothing about races, bettors or the politics that go into racing and nothing about the logistics on the backside.

The following information should help the uninitiated familiarize themselves without undergoing some of the painful lessons that come from learning along the way.

The BACKSIDE is the stable area of the racetrack. The FRONTSIDE includes the grandstand and clubhouse. It is where patrons go to see the races and bet. The following information describes the role of some of the people you will deal with at the track. Much of the information has been taken from the *Appaloosa Club Racing Handbook*

Depending on the layout of the track, certain offices are on the backside, within easy access of trainers. The RACING OFFICE is where trainers handle all the business of entering horses and filing ownership papers, turning in Coggins, etc.

Owning a racehorse should be a pleasure. Saturday afternoon television flashes ecstatic owners winning thousands of dollars for a minute and half of work on the part of their horses. Some of the winners cost millions in a sale . . . others as little as $2,500. It looks easy. Go to a sale, buy a horse with your spare change, and win the Derby. Why not! These are not unreasonable goals. People on television do it all the time. It looks easy? However, when you get involved, you will learn that centuries of effort and experience are involved.

Keep in mind that the BEST expert advice and millions of dollars DO NOT GUARANTEE that the horse will make it to the races . . . let alone win a race. Perhaps this is why we all have a chance. The most obscure breeding may relate to great bloodlines and throw a winner. Around 40,000 foals are registered with the Jockey Club every year. Only a small percentage ever win a race.

This is not intended to discourage you, it is to prepare you for the reality of racing. An educated owner is a great asset to the racing industry.

If you believe that nothing of value comes easily, you are ready to be a racehorse owner.

Condition Book Page

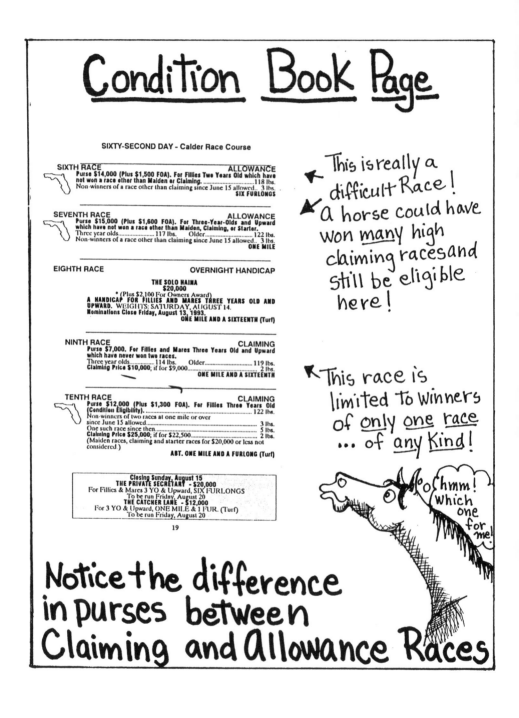

SIXTY-SECOND DAY - Calder Race Course

SIXTH RACE — **ALLOWANCE**
Purse $14,000 (Plus $1,500 FOA). For Fillies Two Years Old which have not won a race other than Maiden or Claiming. ....118 lbs.
Non-winners of a race other than claiming since June 15 allowed.. 3 lbs.
SIX FURLONGS

SEVENTH RACE — **ALLOWANCE**
Purse $15,000 (Plus $1,600 FOA). For Three-Year-Olds and Upward which have not won a race other than Maiden, Claiming, or Starter.
Three year olds......................117 lbs.   Older............................122 lbs.
Non-winners of a race other than claiming since June 15 allowed.. 3 lbs.
ONE MILE

EIGHTH RACE — **OVERNIGHT HANDICAP**
THE SOLO HAINA
$20,000
* (Plus $2,100 For Owners Award)
A HANDICAP FOR FILLIES AND MARES THREE YEARS OLD AND UPWARD. WEIGHTS: SATURDAY, AUGUST 14.
Nominations Close Friday, August 13, 1993.
ONE MILE AND A SIXTEENTH (Turf)

NINTH RACE — **CLAIMING**
Purse $7,000. For Fillies and Mares Three Years Old and Upward which have never won two races.
Three year olds...............114 lbs.   Older............................119 lbs.
Claiming Price $10,000; if for $9,000..........................2 lbs.
ONE MILE AND A SIXTEENTH

TENTH RACE — **CLAIMING**
Purse $12,000 (Plus $1,300 FOA). For Fillies Three Years Old (Condition Eligibility)...................................122 lbs.
Non-winners of two races at one mile or over
since June 15 allowed...3 lbs.
One such race since then...5 lbs.
Claiming Price $25,000; if for $22,500..........................2 lbs.
(Maiden races, claiming and starter races for $20,000 or less not considered.)
ABT. ONE MILE AND A FURLONG (Turf)

Closing Sunday, August 15
THE PRIVATE SECRETARY - $20,000
For Fillies & Mares 3 YO & Upward, SIX FURLONGS
To be run Friday, August 20
THE CATCHER LANE - $12,000
For 3 YO & Upward, ONE MILE & 1 FUR. (Turf)
To be run Friday, August 20

19

This is really a difficult Race! A horse could have won __many__ high claiming races and still be eligible here!

This race is limited to winners of __only__ __one race__ ... of __any__ kind!

ohmm! which one for me!

Notice the difference in purses between Claiming and Allowance Races

TRACK PUBLICATIONS

The Condition Book

Tracks conducting a live meet put out their Condition Book about every two weeks. It lists all of the races the track hopes to fill for that time period. Usually 8 to 14 different races are offered each day. Those attracting most entries are run. Some tracks write extra races every day to accommodate fluctuations in the equine population at any given time. The goal of the Racing Secretary is to have competitive fields for the betting public.

The purse for the race will tell you much about the difficulty of the race. Higher purses usually mean tougher races. Also note that longer races are more difficult, and will pay more than the same race over a shorter distance.

Many trainers moan and groan when owners learn about the Condition Book. Owners overestimate the potential of their horse. They want him running in allowance races with big purses and tough competition. Trainers, on the other hand, want to put the horse with the easiest company. They want him to win and gain confidence as he begins his career. Trainers want to work the horse up the ladder and make purses as he rises to his level of competence. The saying on the backside is "Keep yourself in the best company and your horses in the worst company." An owner who paid $40,000 dollars or so to get a horse to his first race, has nightmares when the trainer wants to run the horse for a $12,000 claiming tag. Much communication is necessary for both parties to be comfortable.

The maiden race and the non-winners of one and the non-winners of two races are going to be the easiest races the horse runs. Depending on whether the horse is running in claiming or in allowance races, soft spots may be found by reading the conditions of a race very carefully.

In the section on types of races, the differences between NW (non-winners) of two races lifetime allowance versus NW (non-winners) of two races other than claiming or maiden is described. If a horse is a NW of two races other than claiming or maiden, he probably has broken his maiden and may have won many claiming races. On the other hand, a NW of two races lifetime has only won one race. Big difference. Purses and competition may vary greatly even though they sound similar. Learning the subtleties of the *Condition Book* is a great help.

Trainers have a name for owners who decide they should choose the races for the horse: "Owners from hell". One of my owners fit the category. He would call me and inform that he had entered his horse in thus and such a race . . . without even asking me about the horse's condition. Maybe the horse hadn't recovered from his last race. Maybe he wasn't quite right. Maybe he was off his feed. When the owner was told that the horse wasn't ready or the race didn't suit him, he would say, "Well, if it really won't do you can scratch tomorrow."

Scratching a horse frivolously is not good policy. As a trainer, you can get a reputation for entering and scratching. You can also be "stuck" in a race, when the field is short and your horse is needed for the race to go. If you are stuck, you must have a vet scratch (meaning a vet must state that your horse has a physical reason for not being able to run). Depending on the ground rules at the track, a vet scratch may put you on the vet's list for 14 days. Then you might miss the race you really need. Be aware of all of the repercussions ahead of time. The racing office is trying to fill races in a competent manner. Don't waste their time with games.

The Condition Book is the trainer's bible.

A condition book has the ground rules of the track that publishes it. These rules may differ from those at other tracks. To avoid costly errors, make a point of reviewing the track's rules before you head for the track.

The Daily Racing Form

This is the Bible for the veteran racegoers and owners. Each day after the entries are drawn for the next day's races, the information goes to the Racing form.

The Form includes the past performances on each horse racing that day, along with post position, distance and other pertinent information. It tells the horses' latest workouts, provides charts of races, and covers current racing news.

Some tracks supply their own daily programs with the essential information (horse's name and breeding, post position, distance, jockey, weight, owner, trainer, etc.). At tracks where past performance lines are not printed in the program, the spectator can find the information on each horse in the *Daily Racing Form*.

Equibase Company

Equibase Company was formed to establish and maintain an accurate and reliable industry-owned central data base of historical racing records, Full-scale operation of Equibase began on January 1, 1991. The company is a partnership between the Thoroughbred Racing Associations of North America (TRA) and The Jockey Club. Speed pace and class ratings have now been added to the basic past performance information, and Equibase has become the dominant provider of information to handicapping services, thereby playing a major role in the expanded availability and affordability of such service. The Equibase performance database continues to grow, and now contains some 3 million starts, representing every race track in North America as well as most major foreign races. With the re-engineering of computer systems, major priorities continue to remain operational improvements in efficiency, and timeliness and accuracy of information.

The Overnight

The "overnight" is the sheet supplied every entry day afternoon by the Racing Office. It shows which races will be used and who got in. The First priority of the Racing Office is to fill the original races listed in the Condition Book. Then they try to fill the "substitute races" listed for that day. If these are not filled the Office goes to "extra races". You can find the "extra races" listed on the previous day's "overnight".

Be aware that the number of the race in the Condition Book does not correspond to its number on the card.

The note in the bottom of the box for each race on the overnight will say something like "10- 1 exc" or "10-16 exc" or 10-4alt-5 exc" tells you much about the race and your possibility of entering that particular race or a similar race on another date. The first number tells you how many horses are in the body of the race. The second number either tells you how many were excluded in that or if the number is followed by "alt" the number of horses on the alternate list. If there are scratches in the body of the race, the horses listed as alternates must be ready to race according to their position on the list.

The overnight also has reminders for the Closing date Stakes or overnight handicaps. There also may be messages from management to horsemen regarding rules regulations and activities.

 You can find the answers if you look in the right place.

1st RACE ($3) P/Pot
PURSE $8,700(INCLUDES $800 FOA)
F&M 4 & UP MAIDEN/CLAIMING $7,500-$6,500 — 6 FUR

#	Horse	Claim		Jockey	Wt
1	KEEP YOUR EYE ON ME	$7,500	E66	Flores R	Martino, R	120
2	RUCKUS LADY	$7,500		Feine C	Hall,	120
3	WIN M ALL MERNA(L)	$7,500	R83	Escobar M	Artz, D	120
4	BITY ROSE(L)	$6,500	E30	Henry W	Wirth, K	118
5	BEE ON TRACK	$7,500	E50	Garcia L	Griffith, G	120
6	GO PUR LAI(L)	$6,500	E85	Serrano A	Monahan II, R	118
7	BRIEF KISS(L)	$5,500	R89	Delgado J	Deannelllo, G	118
8	SALLY TIL(L)	$7,500	R81	Pompell T	Shank, R	120
9	BUGA LU GIRL(L)	$7,500	R84	Bernal O	Naylor, A	120
10	ROAN TO RUN(L)	$7,500	R84	Yang C	Pittman, D	120
11	OUT OF RULES(L)	$6,500	R87	Yang C	Thomas, M	118
12	OLDSMAR	$7,500	R87	Mendez E	Hodge, M	···110

Blinkers Off: GO PUR LAI

— 12-7exc —

2nd RACE (2) P/Pot
PURSE $10,200(INCLUDES $800 FOA)
F 3 YO MAIDEN CLAIMING $12,500 $10,500 — 6 FUR

#	Horse	Claim		Jockey	Wt
1	BLAZING BUCKEROO	$10,500	F41	Serrano A	Clark, E	118
2	SHORT ON CHANGE	$12,500	E2	Russell W	Meese, M	120
3	SUGAR LIPS	$12,500	E60	Escobar M	Pequelte, I	120
4	SMART ALIX(L)	$10,500	R83	Burningham J	Miller, R	118
5	BONUS MOVE(L)	$12,500	R82	Judice J	Proctor, T	120
6	RELAUNCH THE FEVER(L)	$12,500	R82	Pompell T	Pittman, D	120
7	DAYLIGHT DIVA	$12,500	E8	Bernal A	Bernhart, W	120
8	BISHOP'S GATE(L)	$12,500	R82	Gunn R	Zele Jr, M	120
9	DILIGENT GAL(L)	$10,500	R49	Yang C	Nelson, P	118
10	DANCING CREEK(L)	$12,500	R82	Delgado J	Scace, L	118

Blinkers On: BONUS MOVE

— 10-12exc —

3rd RACE ($1) P/Pot
PURSE $7,000
F&M 4 & UP CLAIMING $5,000-$4,500 — 7 FUR

#	Horse	Claim		Jockey	Wt
1	BEST BF(L)	$5,000	R90	Warner T	Botkins, D	118
2	PRETTY EXCITING TO(L)	$5,000	R77	Russell W	Hall, C	118
3	PER DEM(L)	$5,000	R88	Delgado J	Griffith, G	122
4	SERBIA(L)	$5,000	R78	Love L	Pace, P	···111
5	AIR OF EXCELLENCE(L)	$5,000	R87	Mendez E	Sostie, I	···112
6	TIME TO IN(L)	$4,500	R89	Yang C	Guclardo, K	118
7	MISTING(L)	$5,000	R81	Pompell T	Rice, D	122
8	ENDLESS POSIBILITY(L)	$5,000	R81	Pompell T	Seltrecht, J	118
9	GINGER SPIN(L)	$5,000	R82	Escobar M	Behrens, R	118
10	RED HOT SWORD(L)	$5,000	R77	Codilla A	Behrens, R	118

— 10-8exc —

4th RACE (7) P/Pot
PURSE $16,500(INCLUDES $1,500 FOA)
F&M 4 & UP — 1M & 1/16(TURF)

#	Horse			Jockey	Wt
1	SUCH A BREEZE(L)	tSpc	Codilla A	Kuwik, G	120
2	FATHER'S AIR CARGO	E49	Sanchez C	Delcastillo, J	120
3	SILVER RUCKUS(L)	E49	Bernal O	Wheeler,	120
4	MECKANENDA(L)	E22	Walsh M	Amoroso Jr, L	120
5	COOL GAZE	E14	Burningham J	Sargent, W	120
6	A LOT TA FUR FOR THE RUN	E37	Feine C	Gutierrez, R	120
7	LEISURELY KIM(L)	tSpc	Judice J	Block, C	120
8	SKY RAVENAL(L)	tSpc	Garcia L	O'Connell, K	120
9	OUTFLANKER'S STAR	tSpc	Mendez E	Sebreth, O	···110
10	AUGUST MOON DANCER(L)	tR42	Delgado J	Berkelhammer, B	120

ALTERNATES

11	HANNA SENESCH(L)	E49	Buckley III P	Ferraro, M	120
12	CATTACHE	E60	Russell W	Lyons, A	120
13	BUCK'S HUNNY(L)	E82	Pompell T	Skillington, T	120
14	MISS WHITNEY(L)	R82	Escobar M	Artz, D	120

Blinkers Off: CATTACHE

— 10-4alt-17exc —

5th RACE (4) P/Pot
PURSE $17,500(INCLUDES $1,500 FOA)
3 YO ALLOWANCE OPTIONAL CLAIMING $25,000 $20,000 — 1M & 1/16

#	Horse	Claim		Jockey	Wt
1	CAT IN THE COUNTRY(L)	$25,000	R91	Henry W	Clark, E	118
2	MAUVAIS DUDE(L)	$25,000	R87	Mendez E	Cantion-Bybolz, O	112
3	WHISKEY'S AGENDA(L)		R82	Yang C	Tamargo, R	122
4	I'M NOT ACTING(L)		R90	Escobar M	Paquelle, I	118
5	FINE RESULTS(L)		R26	Judice J	Proctor, T	118
6	JIMBO(L)		R91	Bernal O	Smith, J	118
7	SAMMIE SO SAH(L)		E21	Delgado J	Meneles, B	118

Blinkers On: FINE RESULTS

— 7 —

6th RACE (5) P/Pot
PURSE $10,200(INCLUDES $800 FOA)
4 & UP CLAIMING $7,500-$6,500 — 1M & 1/16

#	Horse	Claim		Jockey	Wt
1	DIG THIS COYOTE(L)	$6,500	R87	Russell W	Coyote, J	118
2	MANNY MANNY(L)	$6,500	R89	Pacheco E	Rosas-Cannesa, W	118
3	AYR THREE MILES(L)	$7,500	R83	Escobar M	Cheek, S	118
4	MARION CO CAT(L)	$7,500	R90	Yang C	Cook, D	118
5	CRYPTO SIRISHDAMS(L)	$6,500	R90	Burningham J	Schio, J	118
6	JOE CAN I QUIT(L)	$7,500	R90	Delgado J	O'Connell, K	118
7	MECKE'S MONEY(L)	$7,500	R90	Bernal O	De Amello, G	118
8	FIVE BUCKS(L)	$7,500	R83	Judice J	Anderson, J	118
9	LUCKY MAN REALITY(L)	$7,500	R88	Holassie R	Jordan, M	118
10	SPANISH GROOM(L)	$7,500	R89	Garcia L	Murray, M	118

— 10 —

7th RACE (X5) P/Pot
PURSE $7,000
4 & UP CLAIMING $5,000-$4,500 — 6 FUR

#	Horse	Claim		Jockey	Wt
1	PATTON POSER(L)	$5,000	R91	Delgado J	Carey, C	120
2	WESTERN COLONY(L)	$5,000		Mendez E	Tamargo, R	···108
3	CAPTAIN CARBY(L)	$5,000	R87	Buckley III P	Amodia, T	120
4	WHAT A RACKET(L)	$5,000	E60	Judice J	Giglio, M	118
5	CLOSE NUF TO PERFECT(L)	$5,000	R92	Escobar M	Artz, D	118
6	SAM S MIKI(L)	$5,000	R90	Burningham J	Coyote, J	118
7	CAP'N ANGELA(L)	$5,000	R74	Flores R	Martino, R	118
8	WELL DUN FERDINAND(L)	$5,000	R82	Yang C	Seltrecht, J	120
9	WEST OF MCGUIRE(L)	$5,000	R84	Bernal O	Hall, C	120
10	GREAT GENTLEMAN(L)	$5,000	E95	Maragh A	Hurlak, D	118
11	POLISH TOY(L)	$5,000		Serrano A	Collazo, H	118

— 11 —

8th RACE (10) P/Pot
PURSE $17,500(INCLUDES $1,500 FOA)
F&M 4 & UP ALLOWANCE — 1M & 1/16(TURF)

9th RACE (12) P/Pot
PURSE $9,100
4 & UP CLAIMING $5,000 $4,500 — 1M & 1/16

#	Horse	Claim		Jockey	Wt
1	CHIN CHIN(L)	$5,000	R81	Delgado J	Behrens, R	120
2	STARSHIP RAINBOW(L)	$5,000	R91	Judice J	Kull, C	120
3	TOP SENOR(L)	$5,000	R83	Escobar M	Reedy, W	120
4	WOLF AND HAWK(L)	$5,000	R89	Mera J	Pace, P	120
5	RICH FLIGHT(L)	$5,000	R83	Garcia L	O'Connell, K	118
6	BRANCH CHIEF(L)	$5,000	R87	Hengon W	Wheeler,	120
7	PLAY FOR SARATOGA(L)	$5,000	S70	Buckley III P	Ferraro, M	118
8	VIBRADO (UNV)(L)	$5,000	R87	Bernal O	Gutierrez, A	118
9	TIME ON THE RUN(L)	$4,500	R80	Yang C	Guclardo, K	118
10	BANKER JASON(L)	$5,000	R89	Russell W	Hall, C	118

— 10-5exc —

10th RACE (11) P/Pot
$50,000 GUARANTEED
3 & UP STAKE — ABOUT 1 1/8 (TURF)

THE COLUMBIA STAKES

#	Horse			Jockey	Wt
1	PEGS HALO(L)		R87	Garcia L	O'Connell, K	117
2	MARQUETTE(L)		E89	Cabassa A	Morb, M	117
3	GUARDIAN OF THE GATE(L)		E66	Pompell T	Rice, D	123
4	RACK EM UP(L)		E89	Bernal O	Camilo, J	117
5	BOLDLY CLEVER(L)		R85	Delgado J	Rountree, C	117
6	TOTAL ANILATION(L)		R89	Yang C	Cheek, S	117
7	ADMIRAL LANCE(L)		E56	Escobar M	Little,	119
8	DELL PLACE(L)		R87	Judice J	Proctor, T	117
9	POLISH REALITY(L)		R93	Buckley III P	Tamargo, R	117
10	ATIBA		R90	Burningham J	Mackaben, B	117

— 10 —

11th RACE (3) P/Pot
PURSE $17,000(INCLUDES $1,500 FOA)
F 3 YO ALLOWANCE — 5 1/2 FUR

#	Horse			Jockey	Wt
1	SWISS DOVE(L)		R87	Pompell T	Griffith, G	118
2	FLEET QUEEN(L)		R83	Feine C	Knipe, D	118
3	JABALSKI PRINCESS(L)		R72	Judice J	Hyatt, F	120
4	SHELBY'S ANGEL(L)		R38	Yang C	Cooper, C	120
5	SPLENDO MIDNIGHT(L)		R82	Garcia L	O'Connell, K	122
6	CRUZAN MIDNIGHT(L)		R87	Escobar M	Artz, D	120
7	TOUR IN STYLE(L)		R93	Burningham J	Meese, M	118
8	CLEVER MISS TRIXIE(L)		R88	Delgado J	Quick, W	118
9	RAINBOW ROSE		R88	Buckley III P	Tackett, B	122
10	PINK PARFAIT(L)		R90	Mendez E	Clardullo Jr, R	···108

— 10 —

12th RACE (X1) P/Pot
PURSE $19,700(INCLUDES $1,500 FOA)
F&M 3 & UP ALLOWANCE — 6 FUR (TURF)

#	Horse			Jockey	Wt
1	EVA'S PROSPECTOR(L)		tSpc	Escobar M	Artz, D	115
2	TAKE A LOOK(L)		tR88	Pompell T	Rice, D	119
3	JUST ONE ROSE(L)		tS92	Delgado J	Durrell, W	119
4	AWOL(L)		tR80	Judice J	Everman,	121
5	DIABLOS ANGEL EYES(L)		tS68	Mendez E	Clardullo Jr, R	···109
6	BEAUTIFUL DREAM GIRL(L)		E30	Buckley III P	Wheeler,	119
7	LARRY'S BOUNCE(L)		tR80	Bernal O	Camilo, J	117
8	OZILDA'S NANCY LEE(L)		tR90	Garcia L	O'Connell, K	117
9	MEGAN'S CRACKER(L)		tS92	Yang C	Mello, E	119
10	SHESA NATURAL ACTOR			Flores R	Fuller Jr, R	119

ALTERNATES

| 11 | CAUGHT A SLEW(L) | | tR88 | Sanchez C | Roberts, S | 119 |

— 10-1alt —

13th RACE (1) P/Pot
PURSE $16,000(INCLUDES $1,500 FOA)
3 YO MAIDEN — 7 FUR

#	Horse			Jockey	Wt
1	SUN COMMANDER		R81	Yang C	Clark, E	120
2	MR. ROCKY T(L)		R82	Burningham J	Sargent, W	120
3	SPECTACULAR CRISIS(L)		R59	Escobar M	Haydel, C	120
4	WHISPER BRIGHTLY(L)		E84	Bernal O	Collazo, H	120
5	ZERO DEGREES(L)		R84	Judice J	Rountree, C	120
6	SHAM B THE MAN(L)		R85	Mendez E	McAllister,	···120
7	SWEET WORD(L)		E57	Garcia L	Seremba, F	120
8	DILIGENT MONEY(L)		R72	Delgado J	Maldt, D	120
9	HEADLINE(L)		R85	Judice J	Rice, D	120
10	INTERNET BUBBLE		R84	Cabassa A	Pencheff, R	120

ALTERNATES

11	STONEY RIVER		S85	Buckley III P	Andres, P	120
12	SEMINOLE RENEGADE(L)		R89	Serrano A	Miller, R	120
13	CASINO WAGER(L)		R89	Yang C	Pittman, D	120
14	BAY HEY CHARLIE(L)		R89	Bernal O	Bennett, G	120

— 10-4alt-2exc —

Extra Races For Sunday, May 4, 2003

Race CX1 — ALLOWANCE

PURSE $20,200. (INCLUDES $1,500 FOA). FILLIES AND MARES THREE YEARS OLD AND UPWARD (CONDITION ELIGIBILITY) Three Year Olds 115 lbs.; Older 122 lbs. Non-winners of two races at a mile or over since March 4 allowed 2 lbs. Such a race since March 4 4 lbs. (Maiden, Claiming, And Starter Races Not Considered).

ONE MILE AND ONE-SIXTEENTH (TURF)

Race CX2 — ALLOWANCE

PURSE $17,800. (INCLUDES $1,500 FOA). THREE YEAR OLDS AND UPWARD WHICH HAVE NEVER WON THREE RACES Three Year Olds 117 lbs.; Older 122 lbs. Non-winners of two races since February 4 4 lbs. A race since February 4 4 lbs. (Maiden And Claiming Races Not Considered in weight allowances).

SIX FURLONGS

Race CX3 — ALLOWANCE

PURSE $17,000. (INCLUDES $1,500 FOA). FILLIES AND MARES THREE YEARS OLD AND UPWARD WHICH HAVE NEVER WON A RACE OTHER THAN MAIDEN, CLAIMING, OR STARTER OR WHICH HAVE NEVER WON TWO RACES Three Year Olds 117 lbs.; Older 122 lbs. Non-winners of a race since March 4 allowed 2 lbs. A race since February 4 4 lbs. (Maiden And Claiming Races Not Considered in weight allowances).

SIX FURLONGS

Race CX4 — CLAIMING

PURSE $7,300. FOUR YEAR OLDS AND UPWARD WHICH HAVE NOT WON A RACE SINCE FEBRUARY 4 Weight 122 lbs. Non-winners of a race since March 4 allowed 2 lbs. A race since February 4 4 lbs. CLAIMING PRICE $5,000 (Races Where Entered For $4,000

OFFICIAL TRACK PERSONNEL

The Clerk of Scales

At most tracks, the clerk of scales has complete control of the jockeys' room and all who work there, as well as all equipment. At the larger racetracks, he normally has a crew including an assistant clerk of scales, a supervisor of the jockey room, a color man who cares for and stores the racing colors, a number cloth and equipment custodian, security men and numerous valets.

It is the clerk's responsibility to ensure that the weight carried by the jockey is the weight assigned. He weighs all jockeys with their tack before and after the race. A jockey's weight includes his riding clothing, saddle and pad. Before the results of a race are declared official by the stewards, all jockeys must weigh in, in full view of the stewards and the public. If underweight after the race by more than two pounds, their mount may be disqualified.

The clerk of scales posts all overweights. He calls weight changes to the announcer, the jockey's room, the mutuels, *The Daily Racing Form*, stewards, and officials in full view of the stewards and the public. He does not allow a jockey to pass the scale at more than five pounds overweight except under conditions where the trainer may waive allowance previously claimed. The sex or age allowance generally cannot be waived. In most areas, two-year-old fillies are allowed three to five pounds. The clerk of scales is also responsible for providing the paymaster an accounting of riding fees due each jockey.

The CLOCKER

Clocker

The official timer hired by the racetrack to record timed workouts. All official work times are given to the racing office and the racing form, so that they can be posted publicly

Horse Identifier

Every horse entered in a race is positively identified to be the horse that appears on its registration certificate. Every horse which is racing at approved tracks must be tattooed on the inside of the upper lip with an official identification number. This number is placed on the horse's registration certificate and becomes part of its identifying features along with the natural markings and characteristics.

The Tatoo man (horse Identifier) checks to see that the horse matches his papers!

Each horse is definitely identified prior to his race by the official **track identifier** and thoroughly examined by the track veterinarian to assure that he is in fit physical racing condition. If there is any discrepancy in identification or a sign of any physical disability, the horse will be withdrawn, or scratched, from the race.

I'd like to share a story about Buddy Hatcher, the Track Identifier at Calder. He gives a dollar to the owner of each horse he tattoos and says, "I hope this is the first of many dollars your horse will earn." He is one of the track characters that brighten our lives on the backside. Can you imagine how many dollars he has given away?

**Respect all track personnel.
They work for you!**

Licenses

All persons actively involved in racing must be licensed. This includes racing officials, all track employees, jockeys, owners, trainers and their employees. Licenses are obtained from the racing commission office at the track. Anyone wishing to obtain a license must fill out an application supplied by the state racing commission and return it to the racing commission office at the track. A photograph and fingerprints are included for identification. The application is given to the stewards for review. In most cases, the stewards speak with the applicant or, in the case of a trainer, give a test.

Licenses must be held for each state in which the licensee races. The application procedure is repeated each year.

The Paddock Blacksmith

Most tracks have a paddock blacksmith. He not only keeps records of the types of shoes worn by each horse but also checks the shoes of every horse entered in the race before it leaves the paddock for the post, reporting to the stewards any improper or illegal shoeing. He is authorized to correct the shoeing of any horse, (at the request of the stewards) and can initiate a stewards scratch from a race. He is also available for last minute shoeing emergencies.

The Paddock Judge

Approximately 25 minutes before the race, the horses are taken to the paddock where they are saddled under the supervision of the paddock judge. The saddling is done by the trainer with assistance from the jockey's valet.

The paddock judge is in charge of the area where the horses are saddled for a race. He has control over the individuals who may be admitted into that area. He verifies the racing equipment of each horse and verifies the use of special equipment, such as blinkers. He signals the saddling of the horses in the paddock area, directs them to parade around the walking ring, and signals the jockeys when to mount. While they are in the walking ring, the public can view each horse from all sides and the state veterinarian can inspect them. If a horse is deemed unsound, the horse is scratched from the field and put on the veterinary list. The stewards are notified immediately as is the mutuel department. The paddock judge starts the parade to the post. If he is serving as a patrol judge at the same time, he leaves the paddock with the horses and proceeds to the tower or stand assigned to him.

Patrol Judges

Patrol judges supervise every race and assist the stewards in enforcing the rules and regulations. Patrol judges observe the races from elevated platforms situated at the clubhouse turn, finish line and the 1/2 and 1/4 poles at a typical mile track. Along the straightaway, generally two patrol judges are used, with one being stationed approximately at the halfway mark of the race and the other at the finish line. Their primary responsibility is to watch the race closely from their particular vantage point. They use binoculars to look for rule violations such as reckless riding, interferences, lack of jockey effort, and other practices which could affect the outcome of the race.

Viewing the race from their assigned stand, the patrol judges report findings to the stewards via intercom.

**The video tape patrol is so efficient,
some tracks are eliminating patrol judges.**

Placing Judges

Three placing judges assist the stewards in determining the order of finish of each race. The placing judges post the official finish after the race according to the photo finish camera. It is advisable to have three judges. As the horses cross the finish line, the judges write down the complete order of finish. They have a small board with numbers on it so they can post the order during the race and race fans can check the board if they lose track of their horses. The placing judges and stewards are aided in their decisions by photo-finish pictures if the finish is close.

Although the order of finish may be hardly perceptible by the spectators or even the stewards, the photo-finish pictures are accurate, and the placing judges and stewards can distinguish in fractions of inches the order of finish. Photo finish pictures are always posted in various places around the grandstand area in order for spectators to satisfy themselves about the finish of any race. The placing judges post the official finish after the race according to the photo finish camera.

When the finish of a race is close and a photo is called for, the word "photo" will flash on the tote board. One of the most unique systems ever conceived to provide the placing judges with absolute proof of the results of horse racing is the photo-finish camera. The camera system was developed in 1937 through the efforts of three key people: Bing Crosby, Buddy Fogelson and Bogart Rogers. With the photo-finish camera, the placing judges, in making close decisions, have as their ultimate reference a permanent photographic record of the finish of every race accurate to within 1/100th of a second.

It should be kept in mind that in any instance where the pictures furnished are not adequate or usable, the decision of the stewards will be final.

The Racing Secretary

The racing secretary has perhaps the hardest job in racing. His duties are many and important because he is directly responsible for the end result ... the horses competing on the track in races which he first created on paper.

Although the racing secretary is employed by the racing association or management, he has an unrelenting responsibility to:

1) The Public - Under the rules of racing, the racing secretary must provide the public with the best and most entertaining races he can provide with the horses available.

2) The Management - It is his duty to create a stakes program and write a condition book that will attract the best quality horses that are available.

3) The Owners and Trainers - When the racing secretary approves stalls for a stable of horses, he obligates himself to the owner and trainer of the horses because in accepting them, he implies they will fit into his scheduled program at the race meeting. He must be fair to them without compromising his responsibility to the public or management.

No single racing official can contribute more to the success or failure of a race meeting than the racing secretary. He must bear all of his obligations in mind at all times and uphold them, being dignified and impartial but firm in his attitude.

Bing Crosby, Buddy Fogelson and Bogart Rogers were key people in the development of photo-finish cameras.

The Starter

The starter takes charge of the horses once they leave the paddock and summons them to the starting gate. The horses and jockeys parade past the stands. Everyone can see them and make their final selection for wagering. Ponies may be used to lead a horse to the start.

Post time is the specified time horses are to enter the starting gate. It also notifies patrons of the time remaining for wagering. Following the parade, the starter may excuse horses because of injury or incorrigibility.

He gives the orders and takes the necessary measures to ensure a fair start. His goal for all the horses to have their four feet on the ground when the gate opens. Most starters stand on a platform slightly in front of the gate so they can see every horses.

The job of loading the horses into the gate can be dangerous. The dangers can be greatly reduced by thorough training and practice. The gate is towed to the various starting positions by a tractor-type truck and is pulled off the track after the start of the race. As a safeguard system, the gate truck is backed up by a regular tractor.

Along with actual loading of the horses, the crew is responsible for maintenance of the gate. The individual gates are operated by electromagnets and must be checked periodically as a precautionary measure. All moving parts must be lubricated on a weekly basis.

The Stewards

The stewards are equivalent to umpires or judges at the track. They have complete jurisdiction over the race meeting. Problems between individuals . . . owners, trainers, grooms . . . may be aired in front of them. Infractions of ground rules at the track, smoking under the shedrow, fighting, horses arriving late in the paddock for the race . . . are all aired before the stewards. The stewards may fine, suspend, or do both, depending on the severity of the problem. They may take purse money back, after the fact, if the medication tests show signs of overdoses or banned substances.

The stewards' most visual job, in relation to the public, is settling disputes in the actual races. If a jockey claims a foul or interference during the race, the stewards review the films and judge the incident. There are cameras all the way around the track. If there is an objection or inquiry, the stewards review the films. If they can't see the infraction on the film, they will not recognize that it happened. Film replays have improved their ability to discern infractions tremendously.

They report all suspensions and fines to the state racing commission and in turn to the Association of Racing Commissioners International so that offenders will be barred from taking part in all race meetings during the period of suspension.

The stewards have the most delicate position in racing. It requires a combination of attributes which one individual rarely possesses. In addition to integrity and knowledge of the sport, a steward must have some cognizance of the law, an ability to handle people and an understanding of psychology. Three stewards preside over the racing at all tracks, one of whom is a representative of the respective state racing commission. A board of three is appointed to provide a tie-breaking vote.

Stewards have complete jurisdiction over the race meet.

A Word With the Experts On -
STEWARDS
from *Handbook for Thoroughbred Owners of California*

**OFFICIAL INQUIRIES, OBJECTIONS, PROTESTS, AND COMPLAINTS
AND THE "STEWARDS LIST" "STARTERS LIST" AND "VETS LIST"**

In the back of the Office of the Racing Secretary is a group of three men or women, of varied dispositions and backgrounds, charged by the State with the supervision "in every particular" of the conduct of the race meeting – its attendants and management, its enclosures, the races themselves, and the behavior of everyone of its licensees (owners, trainers, veterinarians, jockeys and grooms). The actions they take to police racing become public knowledge, yet they remain isolated in aeries above the track, or in obscure offices "somewhere." Most fans think of Stewards only as invisible ogres who have often wrecked a good pari-mutuel ticket by setting down or disqualifying a winning horse for some "infraction." Owners, however, must regard them for what they are: Stewards have – and use -the authority to levy fines, issue penalties, suspend licenses, bar individuals from the track, and temporarily remove horses from racing.

Stewards might also be looked upon as the Circuit Court of the racetrack. Everyone, from grooms to competing stables to warring owner-partners, comes to them for the settlement of grievances, objections and financial complaints against one another. They are not the "final" court, however: any involved party wanting to appeal a matter decided by the Stewards can take its lawyers and go to the California Horse Racing Board for ultimate determination. As one veteran Steward put it, "It has been said that old-time licensees never dared ask for justice. Only mercy. Today, they not only deserve due process, they damn well better get it."

The Stewards' responsibilities, all of which involve ensuring the "absolute integrity" of the sport, settle out into fairly predictable (often prescribed) categories. Following is a list of those categories, and the issues that most commonly come up under each.

INQUIRIES:

These are the incidents everyone is familiar with – the ones which delay the posting of the "official" sign on the tote board and thereby the cashing of tickets and the owner's jog down to the Winner's Circle. The Inquiry is also one of the three ways in which an owner can lose that purse he could already "taste" (for the others, see "Protests" and "Medications").

An Inquiry can be called for by the Stewards themselves, by the Patrol Judges, by an owner or trainer of a horse in the running, or by a jockey.

The jockey may allege to either the 7/8ths turn judge or the Clerk of Scales that another

 **The Stewards are the referees for the track.**

jockey caused interference which affected the outcome of the race, or committed a whip violation. Although the Stewards have closely watched the race on TV monitors, are on walkie-talkies to their spotters (Patrol Judges) and though they have re-run the videotape of the race during the time the horses are returning to the finish line, they will hold up the "Official" declaration if a jockey "in the running'" alleges misconduct. Likewise, any owner or trainer can use the racetrack's Quick Lines (also called "Claim Foul Phones") to request an Inquiry and delay the final race result until the Stewards are "certain."

OBJECTIONS

These most often concern the eligibility of a certain horse for entry in a race, and are usually made by a competing stable.

In fact (other than the rare objections placed by racing officials), only owners or trainers with a horse in

the same race can file an objection to a competing horse. "Objections" to the entry of any horse in a race must be made no later than one hour before post time, and must be confirmed in writing. According to the rule book, "Grounds for Objection" are as follows:

A. That there has been a misstatement, error or omission in the entry under which a horse is to run.

B. That the horse which is entered to run is not the horse it is represented to be at the time of entry, or that the age is erroneously given.

C. That the horse is not qualified to enter under the conditions specified for the race, 'or that the allowances are improperly claimed or not entitled the horse, or that the weight to be carried is incorrect under the conditions of the race.

D. That the horse is owned in whole or in part by a person ineligible to participate in racing or otherwise ineligible to own a racehorse [as provided by CHRB licensing regulations].

E. That the horse was entered without regard to an existing lien [as provided/defined by the CHRB].

PROTESTS

Protests are usually made against a horse that has already run in a race, and must be submitted in writing and signed by the protestor within 72 hours of the completion of the race (excluding, of course, non-racing days). Again, Protests can be made only by owners, trainers and jockeys with a horse entered in the same race (or by racing officials). Protests are akin to "Inquiry" requests. They are filed on the following bases:

A. The order of finish as officially determined by the Stewards was incorrect due to oversight or errors in the numbers of horses which started the race.

B. A violation of the riding rules was committed during the race, and that such violation affected the order of finish.

C. That the jockey, trainer, or owner of a horse which started in the race was ineligible to participate in racing [as provided by the CHRB].

D. That the weight carried by a horse was improper, by reason of fraud or willful misconduct.

Stewards settle Objections and Protests.

E. That an unfair advantage was gained in violation of the Rules.

Pending the outcome of the investigation of a protest, the Stewards can withhold the distribution of a purse. If a purse has already been distributed and the Stewards ultimately vote to disqualify a horse, all monies and prizes awarded to the horse must be returned and redistributed! Furthermore, all fines imposed by the Stewards must be paid by the "guilty" party within 72 hours of being levied. (The fines are paid to the Paymaster of Purses, who keeps records of names and violations and forwards them, at the end of the meet, to the Secretary of the CHRB.)

MEDIATIONS

Believe it or not, the Stewards are most often called on for mediations between co-owners or partners. Where money or fame is concerned, even "friends" will war over whose silks the horse should race under, how much (or how little) the horse should be allowed to run for, or what percentage of the purse another owner is entitled to. The Stewards will have to examine such items as paid (and unpaid) bills, written or alleged agreements among partners, win-loss histories, Jockey Club Registrations - anything and everything that angry owners may bring to the table to make their cases. (The Stewards devoutly wish that co--owners and partners would put every detail of their arrangements into legal writing.)

COMPLAINTS

Complaints taken to the Stewards fall into two categories: "informal," in "Which anyone from a groom on up can walk in and complain of an unpaid bill, an "unfair" parking ticket, a dog running loose, or any conceivable infraction by another licensee (these are usually resolved with a phone call) - or formal complaints, which are submitted to the CHRB and referred to the Stewards for resolution. Formal complaints are usually made over financial issues, and involve the filing of official paperwork, which can, in turn, lead to a hearing. Furthermore, if they remain unresolved, they can land the "involved" horse on the Stewards List.

RACE CONDITION INTERPRETATIONS

These involve owners or trainers who are disputing with the Racing Secretary their horse's eligibility for a race (usually on questions of weights and "allowances"). PENALTIES: These are most often levied against Jockeys - for using illegal whips, for cruel or punishing behavior to a mount, for failure to maintain a straight course, for crossing-over without sufficient clearance, for "bumping", for being a "no-show" rider, for failing to make required weight, or even for arriving late to the Jockeys' Room. But the really serious penalties, for an owner, are the ones which involve trainers, and non-permitted medications.

STEWARDS LIST

Your horse (i.e., your investment) can be suspended from racing by being placed on the Stewards List for a number of reasons. One, as mentioned above, is an unresolved conflict among owners, a dispute over ownership, or even a financial dispute between owner(s) and trainer. Other grounds for a horse being placed on the Stewards List are: Lapse of a license (of anyone in your stable); the lack of a recent, timed work for a horse entered in any erratic or apparently uncontrollable behavior by

Stewards settle complaints.

your horse on the track, or an unduly poor performance (i.e., 30 lengths behind the pack) by your horse in a race.

Placement on the Stewards List for "poor performance" can (and must) be rectified by a demonstrated work by the horse in "decent" time.

Note: Unlike requirements for Vet's List removal [see below], the work required for Stewards List removal is not clearly defined. Although the work should be 5/8ths of a mile in a time of 1:03 or better, there is NO specific, qualifying time for a work mentioned in the CHRB rules. Apparently, any horse that officially gets onto the Clocker's work sheet that is, works at all and doesn't give a remarkably poor performance - can be removed from the Stewards List.

The lack of a recent, timed, "qualifying" work (obviously, this is also applicable to horses who have never raced), will prevent your horse from being eligible to enter in a race. This can be rectified by scheduling a work (timed by the official Clocker) which shall then be submitted to the Stewards. If a horse has not worked in over 30 days (up to 60 days), one work will be required; if the horse has not been worked, per the Clocker's work-sheet, in over 60 (up to 90) days, two timed works will be required" If the horse has not raced in 90 days or more, three timed workouts, recorded by the Clocker and reported to the Stewards, will be required before the horse can qualify for entry in a race.

TRANSFER OF OWNERSHIP

Once a horse has been registered with the Racing Secretary for an active race meet, and/ or is residing on the grounds of an active track, that horse's ownership cannot be transferred (except in the case of a claim) without notifying the Board of Stewards. The form the stewards will require is called "Report of Transfer of Ownership," [See Sample Forms & Charts, Figure 11] and before the transfer can be approved by the stewards, a formal, notarized bill of sale [See Sample Forms & Charts, Figure 12], signed by both the registered buyer and registered seller, must also be presented. [For details of the governing Business and Professions Code section regarding this issue, please see chapter on "Acquiring a Thoroughbred," last page.]

STARTER'S LIST

The Official Starter (who checks blinkers at the gate, witnesses the loading of horses and presses the button to start the race) may place on his List any horse which acted up in the gate or refused to load. Removal from the Starter's List can be accomplished when the horse's trainer is ready to demonstrate that the horse has been schooled to load and wait in the gate properly. Until that demonstration satisfies the Official Starter, however, the horse cannot be raced at any California track.

An Inquiry can be called for by the Stewards themselves, by their Patrol Judges, by an owner or trainer of a horse in the running, or by a jockey.

Stay off the Steward's List.

VETS LIST

As was described earlier in the handbook [see chapter entitled" Acquiring a Thoroughbred," section on Claiming], any horse who has failed to finish, or is observed by either the State or the Racing Veterinarian to be sore or bleeding from the nose post-race will be placed on the Vets List and barred from entry in a race for anywhere from a few days to six months. If the horse was placed on the Vets List prior to the race for observed "Sickness Requiring a Veterinary Scratch," the horse will be ineligible for entry in another race for five full days. If the horse is placed on the Vets List for "Injury Requiring a Veterinary Scratch" from a race, or injury observed post-race, the waiting time is a minimum of three full days, after which the State Vet must examine and "sign off" on the horse's recovery.

If the horse is placed on the Vets List due to observed "Unsoundness Requiring a Veterinary Scratch," or "Unsoundness Post-Race," the wait is five full days, and in addition, your horse cannot be removed from the Vets List until it has been worked -under observation of the State Vet or Racing Vet, by appointment only - at least 5/8ths of a mile in good time. Immediately after the work, the horse must also e blood-tested for drugs (both legal drugs at illegal thresholds and illegal drugs).

Certainly most troublesome of all, for the owner, is the issue of "bleeding" and the Vets List. Bleeding from the nose and larynx is, as we have discussed elsewhere in this handbook, not uncommon in thoroughbred racehorses under the stress of hard workouts or races. Bleeding may develop - and disappear- at any point in a horse's racing career. (Up to 70 or 80% of racehorses will exhibit "bleeding" during their careers.) Nevertheless, this is a legally defined and monitored affliction, for purposes of racing in the State of California, and must be attended to with prescribed measures. The first time your horse is observed (by the State Vet, the Racing Vet, the Stewards or their spotter) bleeding from one or both nostrils after a race, the horse will be placed on the Bleeders List. If the horse is then put on prophylactic medication for bleeding (with Lasix and/or Premarin), the Official Vet must be notified. If the horse then runs a race and is observed bleeding from one or both nostrils post-race, it will be put on the Vets List for 14 days.

After the prescribed wait, the animal's Soundness must be proved in a workout witnessed by either the State or Racing Veterinarian - appointment required - in which it must work 5/8ths of a mile in "good time" (1 :03 or better), and without signs of bleeding or coughing. If, after the work, the horse shows signs of possible bleeding (blood at the nose or coughing/wheezing), the State Vet will follow the horse back to its barn. Your trainer will page your vet to do an endoscopic examination of the nose and throat; the State Vet will personally look through the endoscope, and only then will the horse be removed from the Vet's List. If there was indeed blood as a result of the workout - OR if the horse is observed bleeding from one or both nostrils in a second race - it shall be placed on the Veterinarian's List for 30 days. If the horse bleeds post-race (or post-work) a third time, it will be prohibited from racing for six months (180 days). Removal from the Vets List in these cases will have to be demonstrated exactly as described above: by appointment, with a work-in-good-time, and with no signs of bleeding or coughing.

Keep your horse sound.

POST-RACE BLOOD AND URINE TESTS

If the blood test drawn by the State Vet after the race comes back from the state-appointed lab showing that the animal was contaminated by illegal drugs - or by an excess of "legal" drugs - it will be reported to the CHRB, be put on the Steward's List, and a Stewards' Inquiry will ensue. Even if the Stewards find "against" the horse's condition on the race day in question, the horse still may be raced during and after the inquiry period (for example, if it has been claimed, the new owner is not affected) but the former trainer will be penalized, and, if the horse finished in the money, the former owner will lose every bit of his or her purse winnings.

Note: The removal of a horse from any "list" can only be authorized by the entity (i.e., Vet, Steward, or Starter) on whose list the horse was placed.

California racetracks, by law, test all claimed horses (blood only), and take both blood and urine tests from 1.) the winners, 2.) the second 3.) from 9 other horses during the day, selected at random. The Stewards have a handler stationed near the Finish Line, and radio him as to which random horse should be brought to the receiving barn for post-race testing. (Any odds-on Favorite who finished poorly is likely to be selected as one of the "random" horses.) The tests are taken by the State Vet immediately after the race in the Receiving Barn (no stops along the way), and are sealed and signed in the presence of the trainer or the trainer's Representative.

California racetracks, by law, test all claimed horses (blood only) and take both blood and urine tests from) the winners, 2.) the second and third place finishers in a stakes race over $40,000 and 3.) from 9 other horses during the day, selected at random.

MEDICATION RULES AND REGULATIONS

Perhaps nothing is more vexatious to owners and Trainers than the slow work-in-progress that is the "Legal medication threshold" concept. Meetings of the Medication Committee of the CHRB regularly focus on the use of "non-therapeutic" drugs that could affect the outcome of a race, and the use of therapeutic drugs being administered for "non-therapeutic" uses (i.e., to make a horse run faster.) An abbreviated version of the CHRB's Current Medication Rules is printed in the Condition Book of every race meeting in every state, but the rules are revised often enough that trainers and owners should check them regularly and assiduously using the actual CHRB Rules and Regulations Code, copies of which are available at the CHRB Office. At present, California's Medication Rules are as follows:

I. Bleeders

A. Registration with the Official Veterinarian for first-time bleeders and out-of-state bleeders must be completed prior to entry time to be added to the California Bleeder List. Bleeder status must be declared at entry time.

B. Treatment with Lasix and/or Premarin, in a total dose not to exceed 5 ccs, is permitted up to 4 hours prior to post time.

Understand the rules and regulations of your track.

C. Yellow "Detention" stall sign must be posted at time of treatment.

II. Permitted Medication

One only of the following substances may be given no less than 24 hours prior to post time and must be reported to the Official Veterinarian by 10:30 a.m. of race day. The allowed levels in post-race test samples are indicated:

A. Phenylbutazone: 5 mcg.
B. Equiproxen: 5 mcg.
C. Banamine: 1 mcg.
D. Arguel: 1 mcg.

III. Other

All other substances are either improper or prohibited substances when found in a post-race test sample, and may not be given after entry time.

An important note: Under the "Universal Rules of Racing", trainers are responsible for the condition of horses in their care, and are presumed to know and understand all the rules of racing. It is, therefore, standard practice that the trainer is responsible for all prohibited substances found in a horse's system. The trainer may be penalized by fine and/or suspension (but it is the owner who will lose any purse involved). Note: a trainer may request a pre-race drug test to determine if any therapeutic medications remain in a horse scheduled to race (a common problem, for example, is the presence of procaine as a by-product of Penicillin treatment).

Your Responsibility With the Stewards

Mary Donato, Secretary to the Stewards at Calder gives the following advice to owners and trainers: "When dealing with the stewards it is of paramount importance to be honest. Once a steward catches you in a lie, it will be difficult for him to ever believe you again. Remember to always be polite, respectful and keep your emotions under control. Act professionally. When you have a question or when you are not completely confident about a situation **ask** the stewards. They would much rather help you avoid a problem than help you solve a problem."

Be Honest!

When you have a question,
Ask the Stewards!

Rules are made to help us all.

Track Bookkeeper

The track bookkeeper manages track disbursements. Keeping the expenses of stables, corporations, syndicates, jockey's fees, trainer's fees, and other track expenses can be a very complex job. .

Many thanks to Nellie Torrent, the bookkeeper at Calder and her assistant, Linda Johnson, for the following information: "Be aware that you pay sales tax on horses you claim. The bookkeeper will help you understand the amount of tax which depends on where and when you claim the horse. In Florida if the owner is the same as the breeder you do not pay tax. Example: Owner: Janet Del Castillo Breeder: Janet Del Castillo,

No tax. Owner: J Del Castillo & Nando Breeder: Janet Del Castillo, ½ tax. The breeder does not pay tax on the horse regardless of where the horse was born. When the horse is entered, the owner should get in touch with the bookkeeper and complete W9 form. In Florida we pay at least 1% from 5th place finisher to last place finisher. That is to provide funds to pay the jockey.

JOCKEY MOUNT FEES

Purse	Win	Second	Third	Unplaced
$3,500-$4,999	10%	$65	$55	$45
$5,000-$9,999	10%	$65	$55	$45
$10,000-$14,999	10%	$100	$60	$55
$15,000-$19,999	10%	$150	$90	$55
$20,000-$24,999	10%	5%	5%	$60
$25,000-$49,999	10%	5%	5%	$65
$50,000-$99,999	10%	5%	5%	$80
$100,000 and up	10%	5%	5%	$105

(These fees became effective on 8/29/2000 as agreed upon by FHBPA, and the Jockeys Guild.)

DIVISION OF PURSES

# of St.	First	Second	Third	Fourth	*Fifth-On
12	60%	18%	10%	4%	8%
11	60%	18%	10%	5%	7%
10	60%	18%	11%	5%	6%
9	60%	18%	12%	5%	5%
8	60%	19%	12%	5%	4%
7	60%	19%	13%	5%	3%
6	60%	20%	13%	5%	2%
5	60%	20%	13%	6%	1%

*Fifth-On divided 1% to each other starter.

Sample Purses and Fees

For stake races you must deposit money in your account prior to running. You have a nomination fee, an entry fee, and sometimes also a starting fee and jocks mount. Stake races do not pay after the fifth horse finisher. Also the purse varies betweeen a guaranteed or added stakes.

$50,000.00 guaranteed – The distribution will be:

1st 60% x $50,000.00 = $30.000.00
2nd 20% x $50,000.00 = $10,000.00
3rd 11% x $50,000.00 = $5,000.00
4th 6% x $50,000.00 = $3,000.00
5th 3% x $50,000.00 = $1,500.00
      Jocks Mount = $80.00

If it is a $50,000.00 added, the added money from the entry fees will become part of the purse increasing by the amount of those fees.

Understand all of your obligations and the worst case scenario in order to survive unscathed!

Horses born in Florida also get awarded extra purse money if they are registered Florida breds. When you see a purse of $23,000 (including $3,000.00 Florida Owners Award - FOA). If you are a Florida bred, you get 60% of $20,000 plus the $3,000. If not you only get 60% of the $20,000. This award only applies to the winner. If there is a dead-heat and both are registered Florida breds, each will get half the purse plus the $3,000 breeders award.

The first four finishers in every race are charged $3.00 for testing. A $25 fee is charged to your account for tattooing. Jockeys or owners who do not have a US Social Security Nnumber will have 30% deducted on their earnings.

You can apply for a 10% earnings deduction to cover your trainers percentage of the purse. It is a good idea to complete an appointment of agent that authorizes a licensed person to do transactions for you. Regarding partnerships, anyone listed as a partner can collect purses. The winner's purse may only be collected 72 hours after the race. Others may collect their purse the next day. However, you can use the purse immediately to claim a horse.

The best ways to put money in your account are:

> 1) Wire transfer
> 2) Cashier checks
> 3) Personal checks – which need 7 to 10 days for clearing.

To be eligible to claim:

> 1) You have a form for open claiming if you're never was an owner before to apply with the state, the director of racing. The T.R.P.B. Forms are available with the racing office.
> 2) Start a horse during the meet.

The Track Superintendent

It is the job of the track superintendent to maintain the racetrack surface. A racing surface is composed of a 10-to-12 inch firm base with a 3-to-3 1/2 inch cushion. Each of these layers is composed of sand and clay to varying degrees. Track conditions are rated as follows:

Fast (f): Footing at its best, dry and even.
Good (gd): Rated between fast and slow.
Slow (sl): Damp and clinging, between heavy and good.
Heavy (hy): A drying track, between muddy and slow.
Sloppy (sy): Condition immediately after a rain, usually has firm footing beneath its surface. Footing is splashy but even.
Muddy (m): Soft and wet.

Valets

The valet is a track employee who takes care of a jockey's equipment, sees to it that the correct silks are at his locker, that the rider has the proper weight in his lead pad, carries the saddle and equipment to the paddock, helps the trainer saddle the horse, meets the rider after the race, and carries the saddle and equipment back to the jockey's room.

Bookkeeping is complicated.

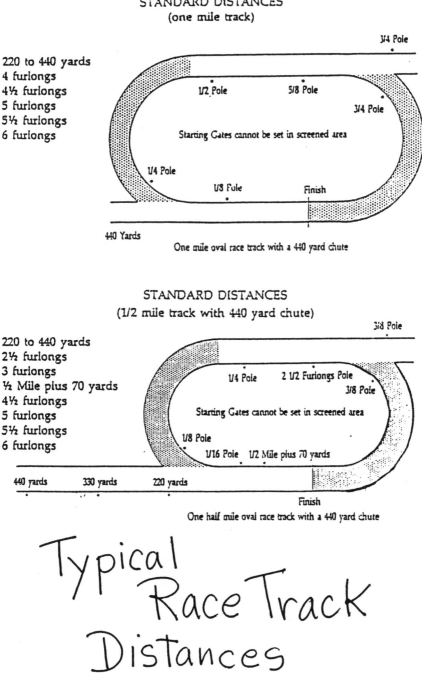

STANDARD DISTANCES
(one mile track)

220 to 440 yards
4 furlongs
4½ furlongs
5 furlongs
5½ furlongs
6 furlongs

1/4 Pole

1/2 Pole   5/8 Pole

3/4 Pole

Starting Gates cannot be set in screened area

1/4 Pole

1/8 Pole   Finish

440 Yards

One mile oval race track with a 440 yard chute

STANDARD DISTANCES
(1/2 mile track with 440 yard chute)

220 to 440 yards
2½ furlongs
3 furlongs
½ Mile plus 70 yards
4½ furlongs
5 furlongs
5½ furlongs
6 furlongs

3/8 Pole

1/4 Pole   2 1/2 Furlongs Pole

3/8 Pole

Starting Gates cannot be set in screened area

1/8 Pole

1/16 Pole   1/2 Mile plus 70 yards

440 yards   330 yards   220 yards

Finish

One half mile oval race track with a 440 yard chute

Typical Race Track Distances

How Do I Get My Racing Colors?

The Jockey Club has jurisdiction over racing colors. You must obtain approval of your colors from them. They will supply the necessary application forms and complete information. A page from the application form showing jacket designs is shown below.

The Jockey Club is there to help in many ways.

Racetrack Veterinarians - Private, Association and State

Be aware that no one on the backside except veterinarians may carry a syringe All non over the counter medication on the backside including Bute must have a vet's label and may only be administered under the direction of a veterinarian.

The Track or Association Vet

The **track** veterinarian is responsible for examining each horse to ensure that all entries are in "racing sound" condition. This includes pre-race morning examinations and close observation during the parade to the post, at the starting gate and during and after the race. In many tracks after the horses break from the gate he follows them around the track in his truck. This makes it possible from him to be on hand in case of accidents or breakdowns. After the race, he observes how the horses return, noting their condition. He notes any lameness or stress and puts such animals on the vet's list. These horses must do an acceptable official work before they can be removed from the vet's list or be permitted to race again.

He is responsible for the inspection of all horses registered with the racing secretary and for maintaining the veterinary list of all horses officially scratched from a race. He is also responsible for control of all communicable animal diseases, insect control and inhumane acts against horses including neglect in feeding, watering and care.

The State Vet

The commission veterinarian is in charge of all sample collections and must be available for stewards at scratch time and any time they desire identification of drugs or examination of a horse for tampering. He may not practice medicine on the racehorse; he may not wager nor may he sell drug supplies. It is his responsibility to study new medications and to disseminate this information to the practicing veterinarians and trainers. He supervises the collection of urine and blood samples in the test (spit) barn. All first and second place horses automatically go to the Spit Box. These horses are accompanied by an official from the time they leave the winner's circle until samples have been collected in the test barn. The Stewards may also randomly select animals for testing. Selected horses are treated in the same manner. The Spit Box is also where bleeder's certificates are issued by the state vet.

You want me to do what with that cup?

Only a vet may carry a syringe on the backside!

BACKSIDE PERSONNEL

The Authorized Agent

If you sign and notarize an authorized agent form, the person named on the form may conduct your horse business for you. Often, the trainer is the authorized agent for the owner. He may buy, sell, or claim a horse for you. He may take money out of your account or put it in. Needless to say, trust is paramount in this kind of relationship.

Farriers

Every track has a colony of farriers who understand the idiosyncrasies of the track and who should be able to guide you. Remember that changing styles of **certain** shoes is considered a change of equipment and must be OK'd by the stewards.

Jockeys

The jockey is another important member of the racing team. I do not like to hear disparaging remarks about them, or hear them referred to as pinheads, idiots, etc. Good jockeys do a difficult job well. Not only do they have a knack for knowing where to be when in a race, they can give the horse the courage and the desire to run. Great jockeys are artists. They take horses that are nervous, fractious and insecure, and mold them into willing partners of a racing team. Poor jockeys can lose the race with a fleeting instant of bad judgement.

Horses have completely changed their losing form when coupled with a sensitive, gifted rider. To win, a horse must want to run. A good jockey knows how to channel the horse's energies into that goal.

Of course, the great jockeys are usually the leading riders at major tracks. As small time players in the learning process of horse racing, you, as an owner and/or trainer, must strive to find the best jockey available. Don't expect a leading jockey to choose your untried two-year-old maiden, first time out. Understand that the jockey's agent is hustling to get his rider the best mount in any given race.

If the jockey hasn't been named on a better horse, he might try to pick up a ride on an unknown, on the theory that any horse can win. However, if the form on your horse is miserable, don't be offended if the jockey declines your mount. A well known jockey wants to ride the best horses to earn as much money as possible. The jockey won't want to risk his health, safety, and reputation on a horse that looks green, unpredictable or unsound.

Some of the jockeys at our local track are good friends. One year, I was running a bunch of "duds". I didn't even ask my regular jockeys to ride. They had much better chances on almost any other horse. I found a jockey who was an excellent rider, eager for experience and willing to work with quirky horses. He was learning the trade and willing to ride anything.

This does not imply that you settle for less than the best jockey you can find. It means that you should not take it personally if the jockey refuses to accept your mount until the horse shows some talent and is controllable. Remember, all jockeys charge the same for the ride, plus 10 percent of the purse, if they win.

Be sure to discuss the idiosyncrasies of your horse with the jockey. Share all the information on whether the horse likes to run in front, on the inside, the outside, etc. Then leave the running of the race to the jockey. Many trainers give very specific instructions as to where the horse should be every minute of the race. They become angry if the jockey doesn't

Be mature and realistic enough to understand the term "out run". It means that other horses in the race were faster than yours.

follow these instructions to the letter. My feeling is that trainers should discuss their goals for the horse, but allow the jockey to use his judgement in attaining them. Hopefully the jock has been on the horse in the morning for a breeze or two and knows enough to ride him confidently.

Also be sure to listen carefully to the jockey after the race. You must assume jockeys are the competent experts in race riding. As an owner, you have the right to accompany the trainer, horse and jockey after the race. At the moment of dismounting, your jockey makes the freshest and most informative comments about the horse and how he performed. The jockey will tell you about the horse. He knows whether the horse was frightened, intimidated, tired, fit, impressive, tried to bear out or in, if his teeth bothered him, if he was sore, lame, etc. You learn about your horse if you listen to your rider. I am offended by enraged trainers screaming at jockeys as they ride in to dismount after the race. This is an embarrassment to the Great Sport of Racing.

Many trainers joke that when the jockeys bring the horses back to the finish line after the race, they are frantically trying to come up with some excuse as to why the horse didn't win.

Respect the jockey and assume he is trying his best to win. If your jockey is blatantly not following your orders or if you see a pattern of riding that you find suspect, change jockeys. Be aware that there are jockeys that don't play by the rules. One usually hears about such things on the backside. Be all ears, but take all comments with a grain of salt.

As you learn more about the business, both on the frontside and the backside, you will be able to choose your jockey wisely. Try to understand all of your obligations and the worst case scenario in order to survive unscathed!

Great jockeys are gifted, instinctive riders.

A Word With the Experts On -
Jockeys
An Interview With Retired Jockey Rudy Turcott

1. What motivated you to become a jockey?

The love of horses. I always loved them and like most kids, I loved speed. The thrill of victory is another big thing. There is nothing like hearing 25,000 people cheering in the grandstands. I really wanted to be an athlete, but my size kept me out of football, basketball, etc. My brother had a lot to do with it. He was a top rider when I was in the 8th grade. Where else can a small highschool kid make that kind of money? Out of nine boys, 5 of us were jockeys. Maybe it was in our blood too.

2. What changes have you seen in spectators, sportsmanship, horses, training, breakdown, breeding and even jockeys?

In the mid sixties when I started there was no Off-track Betting or simulcast. There were huge crowds. The parking lots and grandstands were always full. People loved going to the races. It was exciting and horses were special. Nowadays horsemen see horses as numbers. They used to give the horses time off to rest. Now there are so many tracks the horses run year round. Used to be that New York ran March to December. Then they had four months off. If they were good maybe they came to Hialeah. That was the place to be. Now there are so many tracks and so many racing days, the horses run all the time.

Older families have died and the kids are not interested in racing. Now we have whiz kids for trainers. They aren't in for the long haul. This game isn't for people in short pants. You have to be business like. If you have a $5,000 animal, keep him where he can get a piece of the action. Owners always want to move them up to the big races. So they lose. Its better to keep them where they can win and pay some bills.

You don't see trainers like Ben Jones or Max Hersh anymore. The new people have no longevity. They jump in, make a big splash if they are lucky and get a good horse, and then they're out. There is no commitment. When there were less tracks, top horses used to run against each other. Those were real races.

Back then trainers didn't run as often. They had less horses and gave them individual attention. Now trainers work on numbers. Bet you if you asked some of the big trainers to show you a particular horse in their barns, they wouldn't be able to find him. Also now instead of individual farms and families, there are syndicates and horses are just numbers.

Now stakes horses aren't around very long. Up to the 70's horses ran 30 or 40 races. Now in 10 races their career is over. The tracks are better, drugs and vets are better, but trainers don't train - vets train with needles. If Hersh Jacobs had a sore horse he was turned out. Now they use drugs. Trainers like that are not horsemen, they're promoters. Most race trackers love horses, but some trainers and riders are in it for the money.

Meds are dangerous for jockeys. I got into a lot of trouble about my comments on Bute. I was half groggy when the reporters interviewed me in the hospital, so I told them that it was Bute that caused the break down. Boy were people mad, but a few years later, Bute was outlawed.

This game isn't for kids in short pants,

Years ago you had to be under contract with a trainer. You started from the ground up. And you only got to ride when the trainer said you were ready. There was no free lancing. The trainer ruled you. Nobody controls riders anymore. We used to come out between two guild riders. We weren't allowed to used a stick for the first five races or until the trainer felt you had control. Then you could only carry a whip with permission from the Stewards. They had to be sure you could control your horse and would not endanger anyone.

It used to be that a good rider could work a horse on the button no more than 1/5 or maximum 3/5ths off. It took years to learn that, to have control at all times, to be able to switch the stick from side to side. Now riders are like K-Mart Blue Lite Specials. Out of 100 riders maybe five will make it and only 1 or 2 for lifetime. Riders don't make the horse, the horse makes the rider.

One rider doesn't fit all horses.

We sure weren't prima donnas. We worked and learned to be tough. Now jockeys don't work around the barn. There weren't even any wheelbarrows allowed around the barn. Those things are dangerous. A fractious horse could hurt himself if he got tangled up in one.

Also there were very few women on the backside. Barbara Joe Ruben was the first woman rider I remember. Women are good with horses. They make good jockeys too.

And now they are breeding Thoroughbreds to look like Quarter horses with long legs. Lots of top bred horses look good on paper, but they can't run.

3. What brought about these changes?

Too much of everything. Too many tracks, too many trainers, too many horses and too much money involved.

4. What would be on a jockey's wish list of things to change.

Well you would think weight limits, but its self defeating. If they raise the weight limit for jockeys you would just end up with bigger guys starving themselves to meet the weight limit. In the old days you had to keep down to 105 to 108 lbs.

5. Do trainers and owners pay enough attention to the jockey's input?

Smart trainers don't give instructions to good riders, unless there is a strategy change. Good riders know what to do. When the gate opens, the game opens too and a good rider knows what he should do. I've seen a lot of horses beaten by instructions.

6. What are the major difficulties of a jockey's life?

The hardest thing was weight and knock on wood not too many injuries. Shoemaker and Day were lucky they never had weight problems.

7. What would you tell an aspiring jockey?

The most important thing to remember is to save money. Everybody loves you when you have lots of money to buy drinks and throw parties. But save that money, because nobody will be there for you when you're down. When the money stops the friends disappear.

There are lots of good riders out there who don't get a break. But once a rider is established he gets better horses and it just keeps growing. You have to start with the small meets and grow with your ability. Meanwhile, a jockey has to know how to handle himself. He needs to be a gentleman, courteous and professional. If he gets a big head, he'll be sorry. He needs to be professional.

**Riders don't make the horse,
the horse makes the rider.**

8. Is fear a problem?

Fear? When it becomes a factor, Hang it up! If you ever think of fear be careful! Quit!

9. What would you tell an aspiring owner?

Leave trainers alone. Don't tell him where to run or what equipment to use. He's the pro. Just be sure to find a good one. The stats don't matter. Look at how he handles his barn and horses.

10. What are your best memories, greatest joy and favorite horse?

Best day. December 2, 1969. Of eight races at Aqueduct, I won 6. I was the 3rd jockey in history to win 6. I also won the Canadian International Championship before I came to New York. The greatest joy? Coming down the stretch and hearing the crowd cheer you on. My favorite horse was Steel City. I rode him for four years until he broke down. We won 23 of 28 races, a lot of them were stakes. He also had personality. I cried real tears when I lost him.

11. What are your worst memories?

The worst day was at Pimlico. My horse broke a leg and the jockey behind me was killed. He was Bobby Pineda. We had been talking before the race. I found out about it in the hospital when I came too. That's when I made the comments about Bute.

12. Would you do it again?

Sure I'd do it all over, only I'd save some money and invest it. I quit because of weight. I had to take Lasix and diet pills which plus the drinking was no good. Also because I was injured 6 or 8 times. When the doctor said, "No more." I had 10,888 rides.

Rudy had 10,888 rides.
Congratulations!

The Jockey's Agent

This is usually the middleman between the jockey and the trainer. A jockey agent must be a real hustler. He should be up early in the morning and help his jockey get to all the morning works. While the jockey is riding one horse, his agent should advise the next trainer to prepare the next mount. Since so much work must be done in so little time at the track, it is imperative that a popular jockey have coordination between his commitments. If a jockey "hangs up" a trainer and misses riding the horse, it can throw the trainer's schedule off terribly.

A good agent keeps the trainer happy and the jock busy. If his jock is named on more than one horse in a race, he should follow-up and notify the trainer that he needs another rider. The agent must smooth feathers if he chooses one horse over another one. He wants his jock to ride the horse with the most chance of winning. However, sometimes he is committed to a big stable and is obligated to ride all of their horses, regardless of the chance to win. **Top jockeys can almost choose their mounts ... the others take what they can get.**

Agents scout riders in much the same way baseball or football scouts find players. They make trips to smaller tracks and try to find raw talent. Many riders come from Latin America. The agent may teach the rider how to shake hands, say, "Yes sir," and most importantly, "I understand" ... even when he doesn't. They often share an apartment, and the jock is molded and advised by his mentor agent. Certain agents are famous for developing talent. Many agents are retired from "real" jobs and have this as a second career. Since the agent's pay is a slice of what the jockey makes, he may need his pension to live on.

The Exercise Rider

Every track has exercise riders. They exercise horses most of the time. Generally large outfits have full time riders. They ride on all the horses every morning-possibly 6 or 7 days a week. Smaller outfits must use "free lance" help. These riders charge by the head. About $7 to $15, or even $20 a ride depending on how difficult the horse is and how much you want done with him. If your horse needs a lot of work at the gates for instance or if the horse is very dangerous or difficult it will cost more.

If everyone has the horses ready and tacked up, a smart rider can line up as many as ten or fifteen rides between 5:30 and 10:00 AM. As a ship-in person, you will find that there are riders who frequent the ship-in barn for the odd rides that show up. Its a good idea to keep phone numbers for riders, and call them to coordinate work on track days. Especially if you need two riders to work together. Track logistics are difficult. I often joke that I would love to own a rider that I could pull out of a closet when I needed him.

Galloping my own horses was an asset I didn't appreciate until I had to start depending on others. Understand that riders must put their steady jobs first and fit in odd rides later. Try to establish a rapport with a few riders. If you pay them promptly and well, they will look for you.

Listen!

If owner and trainer are philosophically in tune, they can work together

A Word With the Experts On -
Jockeys and Their Agents

by Greg Thompson

Every morning at about 5 AM or earlier a rare breed of people roam the tracks. They are truly the "businessmen" in racing. They have the dubious distinction of being called "jockey agents."

As a trainer or as an owner you are going to have to deal with a jockey agent in some form or fashion. These relationships are good ones for the most part, but due to the business nature of racing it can turn ugly quickly. An agent walks the shedrow of established trainers and checks out the training charts of the horses that must work that morning. Sometimes trainers will tell the agents a day ahead of time that a specific horse will work, but most trainers are "fly by the seat of their pants' kind of people and usually don't plan that far ahead of time. They struggle to keep horses sound. So what time they work also depends on the horse's health.

Most grooms and trainers are on the track at 5 AM. Trainers and grooms have many horses to get out, stalls to clean and horses to groom. This makes them demand that riders get to their barns early to get their horses out so they can finish all of their work as quickly as possible. If you are a one or two horse operation, you are most definitely going to be second fiddle when it comes to morning workouts, and even in the jockeys' choice of mounts. This is where the agent-trainer relationship becomes crucial. 'Haul-in' trainers need to depend on the reliability of the agent and the jock to show up at the appointed time.

First make it a habit to know your jockey's agent. The jockeys and agents are all listed in the condition books, and every entry clerk in the racing office is very familiar with who represents whom. Call the racing office and ask questions if you don't have a condition book. Get to know an exercise rider and write down his phone number. He should be willing to gallop horses out of the receiving barn or the barn where 'haul-ins' bring their horses in the morning.

Next we must know when to use an established jockey in the morning and in the races. Keep in mind that most riders don't mind getting on horses in the morning, if they are close to a race. Also remember that riders have a tough regimen of fighting their weight and are often crabby at 6 AM. The worst thing you could possibly do is to ask a jockey to gallop your horse in the morning. This is not acceptable on most racetracks and will make you look very "green".

Exercise riders gallop: Jockeys work horses and ride in races. Pulling a stunt like calling a jockey over the intercom to gallop in the morning, will make you look dumb in the eyes of the agents and jockeys. The jockeys want to ride "finished horses" ready to run. They don't want to gallop your unfit horses or do any work that an exercise rider could do. They may be willing to break them from the gates if they are ready to get the gate card so that they know how the horse acts.

The jockey does not want to be breaking your ill mannered untrained horses. Do not use a jockey for horses that are not familiar with the track. A jockey can't afford to get hurt fighting a young inexperienced horse. If the horse is rank in the morning the jock will assume he will be worse in the race when the adrenaline is really flowing.

Jockeys and agents are listed in the Condition Book.

A lot of two-year-olds fit into this mode. Being inexperienced is a trait all two-year-olds share. They may be fine at the farm but when shipped in, everything is new. Those first trips around the track should always be with an exercise rider. If you ride yourself, better yet as you can take all the time you need to let him get comfortable with the track.

Exercise riders should be used during the rigors of getting your youngster to its first race. Gate training, breaking from the gate, galloping, as well as most of the works and breezes should be done with an exercise rider. I would suggest not using a heavy rider. A young rider who is working towards getting an apprentice license could work well in this situation. It would be wise not to ask a jockey to work a young horse until a work or two before its first race.

Even with this general rule you should steer clear of the top riders for its first two starts, and you might even want to try an apprentice... although the combination of green horse and green rider is not advisable unless the rider is very talented and confident. You never know what will happen in the first couple of races with a two--year-old and believe me when I tell you - if you have a youngster that has run well in its first couple of starts and has behaved in the gates- you will be getting calls from some of the top agents to try to secure the mount for their riders.

Let's move to the next level of dealing with jockeys and their agents. In racing there is a term referred to as "being spun". That simply means that a jockey or his agent has decided to ride another horse instead of yours in the race at scratch time or even before. Trainers hate to be "spun" but here in lies the most blatant form of a double standard in the racing industry. Trainers, even top trainers, spin riders and pass it off without a conflict.

The reason for this is the racing world works in cycles. Good agents will come back around and allow their rider to pick up more mounts. How many times has a less known rider been replaced with a Pat Day and Jerry Baily of the game? More times than can be counted and nothing is really made of this fact. Turn this situation around where the jockeys spins the trainer and this is a tremendous conflict that has caused some trainers in isolated cases to throw locker boxes out in the shedrow in the heat of anger, promising to never use that rider or agent again.

The point is best expressed by a quote I once heard from a top east coast trainer Nick Zito: "I don't mind when riders choose to ride another mount instead of my horse, cause they are always wrong." With this line of thought I would urge trainers new to the game of racing not to worry when a jockey spins you. Your professionalism will show through if you just pick up the pieces and move on to find a jockey who wants the mount.

Let's face it, it would be better to get a jockey that doesn't have a mount in that race, than having a rider on your horse who thinks he could be on a better one! Due to the bottom line in racing and in the life, - the almighty dollar - riders and agents will ride what they perceive is the best horse in the race. And believe me they are wrong all the time.

Trainers want the best rider for their best chance to win, and jockeys want the best horses to have the best chance of winning. The better you understand this, the better you will deal with jockeys and their agents.

Some simple points to follow on using riders:

Top riders want and get top horses.

1. Be sure to call agents at least a day ahead of time and make sure to get an appointment time for a jockey to work your horse in the morning.

2. Be sure to call agents at entry time to see if their jockeys are open or have given the 'call' to someone else. The 'call' is the promise to ride a certain horse in the race.

3. If the agent says the jockey is open, ask the agent to make the entry for you and ask the agent if you have the 'call' for the race. This will cause the agent to be, most of the time, truthful with you. If he says he can't give you the 'call' that generally means he is hopefully waiting on another mount for his rider at entry time. Most agents who give you the call will not try to spin you. They fear that they will be reported to the stewards office and reprimanded when an angry trainer claims they broke their promise.

4. When calling an agent to find out if you can use their rider in a specific entry, consider who you would like to use if your primary rider already has a mount. Most of the agents are in or around the racing office during entry hours and the agent you are speaking with will probably also know or could find out quickly who is open in the particular race. Agents usually handle two riders and can also have one apprentice, so you might want to familiarize yourself with the agents' other riders.

Follow these points and stay away from committing people communication errors. As an ex-jockey agent I promise you an easier pursuit of the ultimate goal for everyone in racing: Winning!!!

Greg Thompson was a Jockey's agent. He still loves racing and the Backside. When he offered to share his experience with us I was delighted.

A good agent
Promotes his
Jockey!

**Establish a good relationship with
your jockey and his agent.**

Owners

As the owner of a racehorse, you have many responsibilities and should be aware of the following:

Horses must be registered in your correct name.

Fees must be paid or arrangements made with the trainer to pay all fees, such as entry fees, jockey mounts, tattooing, etc.

In most cases the owner must provide jockey silks. Colors are registered when the owner applies for a license in each and every state in which he will race.

If an owner changes trainers, he must notify the racing secretary and have the new trainer sign his name on said owner's registration.

The personnel of every stable must be registered.

After horses have been registered and owners listed with the racing secretary, no horse will be transferred (unless claimed at the meet) without permission of the stewards. The stewards will require a notarized bill of sale from the registered owner.

The purchase or transfer of any horse on the grounds at any track, whether by private sale, claiming, or public auction, does not guarantee the new owner a stall for such horse unless approved by the racing secretary and/or the stewards. The management has the right to allocate stalls only to those horses which fit the racing program and those horses which are healthy. Horses sold to any person or stable not registered for racing must be removed from the grounds within 24 hours unless approved by the racing secretary and/or the stewards.

Before a horse may be entered in a race, its owner must secure an owner's license from the racing commission. The stewards may grant a reasonable delay in the case of absentee owners.

Trainers

As the trainer of a race horse, you have many responsibilities and should be aware of the following:

No horse shall be qualified to start in any race unless he is in the hands of a licensed trainer.

No trainer shall practice his profession except under his own name.

A trainer shall attend his horse in the paddock and shall be present to supervise his saddling unless he has obtained the permission of a steward to send another licensed trainer as a substitute.

Each trainer shall register with the racing secretary every person in his employ.

A trainer is responsible for the condition of each horse trained by him.

A trainer shall not have in charge or under his supervision any horse owned, in whole or in part, by a disqualified person.

In some states when a trainer is to be absent for a period of more than two racing days from his stable or the grounds when his horses are racing, and his horses are entered or are to be entered, he must provide a licensed trainer to assume the complete responsibility of the horses he is entering or running. Such licensed trainer shall sign in the presence of the stewards a form furnished by the State Racing Commission accepting complete responsibility of the horses entered or running.

Only the trainer is authorized to withdraw the registration certificate from the racing secretary's office.

**If owner and trainer are philosophically in tune,
they can work together**

OBTAINING YOUR TRAINER'S LICENSE

You have been working with your horse, running him with a trainer and you feel comfortable and competent to go for your own trainer's license. Where do you start? Usually, there are three steps to obtaining your trainer's License.

1. The Barn Test
2. The Written Test
3. The Interview with the Stewards

Remember that each state has its own regulations. You can obtain local information from the stewards. The condition book at each track will also contain pertinent state information. It is imperative to learn the regulations of each state in which you plan to race and to be aware that these regulations can vary drastically from state to state..

The tests can be very difficult. The written portion may take up to five hours . You want to be well prepared. Put plenty of time aside for study. When your are ready, contact your local Horseman's Association or HBPA Office at the track. They will arrange for a qualified trainer to administer the "Barn Test", which is a review of your hands-on horsemanship. After you pass this test you must contact the Stewards to schedule your written test.

The Stewards will call you for your interview after you have passed the written test. Aside from your technical knowledge, they will want to determine your fiscal responsibility and your level of professionalism especially if you plan to train for outsiders.

Mary Donato, Secretary to the Stewards at Calder has the following advice for aspiring trainers: "Study the Condition Book, ask to see the rules in your racing jurisdiction. Know how to physically handle a horse. For the barn test, know how to saddle, bridle, bandage, groom, etc. Be prepared to obtain recommendations in writing from at least 3 trainers who are currently training and racing at the track where you will take your test, or from someone well known in the racing world.

You will have to take a written test. Know the common ailments of horses, how to treat them and the horse's anatomy. Know racing equipment; how it is used, why it is used, and when it is used. You must also know how to enter a horse, the conditions of a race, how to calculate weights and weight allowances.

Especially know that no one can represent you better than yourself and that the most difficult and valuable thing to achieve is a good reputation. It is also the easiest thing to lose."

The Barn Test

You may be asked to do any or all of the following:

Tack a young nervous horse. This would include exercise saddle; bridle; yoke; rings; blinkers; possibly a figure 8; and tongue tie. Your level of comfort and expertise handling a fractious horse in the stall will be evaluated. You may be asked to put on: a standing bandage, fleece wrapped with a polyester knit bandage with velcro fasteners; a polo bandage: a shipping bandage; vet wrap with or without cotton; and/or rundown bandages with a patch. You may also be asked to reassemble a figure eight that has been completely disassembled. Or you may be asked to clean a stall properly. The object of these requests (other than having a stall cleaned free) is to discern if you are able to handle the physical aspects of training.

Wow — Read every Thing!.

Study, study, study!

The Written Test

Many services sell samples of the written test. You will see ads for this service in the Classified sections of most racing publications. However, there is no guarantee that the sample questions will be used in the test you take. Remember this is a difficult test and you must be prepared. Each section may contain up to 200 questions. You also may be asked to identify the anatomical parts of the horse or the lower leg shown in a drawing. A few sample questions follow.

Equine Health:

State the normal resting pulse for a horse. (36-40 beats per minute.);

What degree angle is considered a club foot? (60 degrees or steeper.);

How many teeth does an adult male horse have? ((40);

What two tendons appear as one, until you raise the foot? (The flexor and superficial tendons.);

Can a horse breath through its mouth? (No.).

General Horsemanship:

When do most injuries occur? (In the morning, when exercising.);

What is the most important basic nutrient for a horse? (Water.);

What three negative effects does injection of cortisone cause? (Decalcification: degeneration of bone: and it stops all natural healing.);

Explain the position of the extensor tendon of the knee. (It attaches to the humerus and lies on the front of the forearm and goes over the knee.).

The Stewards:

What weight concession does an apprentice jockey usually get? (Check your state.):

If a horse has been laid up on a farm, approximately how many days would it take to condition the horse for a race? (90 to 120.); (Depends...)

Can a trainer have a registered stable name? No.

What is a starter allowance? (A race designed to allow former claimers to run in a non-claiming race.).

why blinkers?.

What is a figure 8 ?.

How many pounds off for a "bug"

Put together a bridle

Saddle a horse

Wrap a leg

Your most valuable asset is your reputation.
Keep it untarnished.

Pony Horses

Pony horses are not ponies. They "pony" racehorses. To pony a horse means that the pony rider exercises the racehorse, taking him on a lead rope at the side of the pony. The racehorse carries no weight. He is expected to move at the speed of the pony. This is done in the morning instead of galloping the horse. Racehorses can be so rambunctious that they want to run away with a rider. The trainer has such a horse ponied so that he won't burn up too much energy but will get exercise. Sometimes, when a racehorse is young and insecure, a pony rider will accompany the racehorse and rider to the track. The older horse steadies and comforts the young inexperienced animal. He may gallop at his side to get him going and then drop off as the racehorse gains confidence.

The pony is also very useful on race day. Many racehorses become over excited and ready to run when they see the track. The pony will accompany horse and rider and help control the racehorse as he warms up before the race. Some jockeys worry about the horse getting away from them in the warm up . . . and will not allow the horse to gallop unless accompanied by a pony and lead strap. After a few races, as the horse becomes accustomed to the routine of racing, the pony is no longer necessary. Some trainers always use a pony. Others never use one. It costs from $15 to $25 to hire a pony on race day.

If a horse gets away from a rider before the race and runs hard, the stewards may scratch him, on the grounds that the horse has already run his race and the betting public must be protected. That was frustrating for me. After hauling into the track to run, I wanted my horses to run. A mile gallop is a warm-up for most of my horses. If they got lose and ran a little, I still wanted them to race.

Older horses can become very professional and workmanlike. For the young and high strung animals, the pony and his experienced rider are a great asset.

Pony horses are not ponies. They "pony" racehorses.

RACING ENTITIES

Horse Racing Boards or Racing Commissions

These are government appointed bodies which act on behalf of the state, provincial or local governments to regulate the pari-mutuel horse (or other) racing within their jurisdiction.

State Racing Commissions

The various state racing commissions, by law, supervise the implementation of their rules and regulations regarding the operation of all racing within the state. The commission which governs each state is authorized by law to prescribe the rules of racing, grant the franchise for racetrack operations, determine how many tracks may operate within the state, limit the number of days of racing, approve purse schedules, pass the appointment of officials for meetings and supervise the strict licensing of all racetrack personnel. Licenses are issued only after thorough investigation. You must be licensed in each state you are going to race. State rules and regulations supersede breed registry or association rules.

State racing commissions are also responsible for testing each winning horse to see that no drugs which may have affected his condition were in his system. After every race, the winner and any other horse designated by the stewards are taken to the state racing commission's testing enclosure where urine, saliva and/or blood samples are taken. (The first three horses in stakes races normally are tested.) The state veterinarian seals, tags and delivers the specimens to the laboratory. Most labs are members of the Association of Official Racing Chemists. The labs run an extensive series of chemical tests on each sample to ensure that no drugs or prohibited medications appear which may have affected the racing condition and performance of the horse.

Although their problems and ways of dealing with them vary greatly from state to state, the commissions, through the Association of Racing Commissioners International, are able to act as one body on important issues and establish precedents concerning racing matters.

Please note that Florida is one of the few states that does not have a racing commission.

The Commission deals with Racings' problems!

Keep informed of the regulations of your racing jurisdiction.

TYPES OF RACES

STAKES RACES

These races offer the largest purses. They are races in which the purse consists of nomination, entrance and/or starting fees, plus money added by the track or sponsor. These races generally attract the highest quality horses.

Graded races are the premier stakes races, whereby a grade one (G1), grade two (G2) or grade three (G3), designate the class of horses participating. The size of purse, amount of added money and the historical significance of the race also are determining factors in the grade status. Grade one (G1) is the highest designation. Some stakes races are restricted to horses bred in a particular state, or to horses sired by participating stallions. Some restricted races are graded, whereby a grade one (RG1), grade two (RG2) or grade three (RG3) designate the class of horses participating.

HANDICAP RACES

These races feature better quality horses in which the Racing Secretary or Track Handicapper assigns weights designed to equalize the winning chances of entrants. The better horses get higher weights to enable a horse with a lesser record to have a chance at winning. The designation HDCP is utilized.

CLAIMING RACES

Claiming races are the most common, constituting approximately 70% of all races run. In these races, horses are entered for a specific price and can be purchased or "claimed" by any licensed owner at the track for that price. This tends to equalize the class or competition in these races. An owner who has a $25,000 horse is not going to put him in a race with a field of $5,000 claimers, for fear that someone would claim his horse at a greatly-reduced value. These races are designated by the claiming price (5000). A "C" in front of the claiming price in the past performance line means the horse was claimed in that race.

ALLOWANCE RACES

An allowance race is a non-claiming race for better quality or more lightly raced horses. These races generally offer higher purses than claiming races. Eligibility requirements and conditions are similar to those of claiming races, and weight allowances are given based on winnings and/or number or type of wins in a given time.

These races are designated by ALW plus the purse (ALW12500).

MAIDEN RACES

Maiden (MDN) races are limited to horses that have never won a race. There are two types of maiden races: "Maiden Special Weights" for better horses and "Maiden Claiming," which is designated by the claiming price (MD5000).

Getting in the right race can be a challenge

Mullikin Stu
We Love you!

A Word with Our Readers

Back Yard Race Horse
4th Edition

Stories We Had To Share

Racing is a difficult, humbling experience for most of us. It has great moments of glory and many agonies of defeat. Those who are in the business for the long run and do the right thing are the real everyday heroes in racing! Thanks to our readers for sharing their joys and foibles.

Letters
A Pat on the Back

I just had to take time to congratulate you on your mission and on your sound advice to readers. As a lifelong horseman myself, I have had the pleasure to sever as assistant trainer to such greats as Jack Van Berg and D. Wayne Lucas. I trained a public stable for nearly 18 years before becoming a track executive. I have also seen many examples of successful back yard trainers bringing in horses to beat the big boys.

As I learned from Van Berg, the master shipper if there ever was one, a trailer ride the morning of a race, if conducted properly, can be as easy on a horse as a jog around the track and just as invigorating. During my seven years on the eastern seaboard circuit, my peers from Fair Hill Training Center shipped all our horses in order to run - and we had an extremely high winning percentage everywhere we raced. And nearly any horse can become a good shipper if you load him up for short "pleasure trips" often enough.

An otherwise intelligent man - a friend of mine - scheduled an appointment with me the other day and asked me to tell him the best way to go about learning to be a trainer. Of course I told him to go to work for Van Berg or some other reputable trainer and then if possible to work for a series of such trainers. And when he asked me if there were any good books on the market he should read, I was happy to finally be able to say yes. I told him to buy a copy of The Back Yard Race Horse and to refer to it carefully and often.

Again congratulations on your outstanding work. Family involvement in racing is a great thing - both for the families and for the sport itself. My family was blessed with an All American Futurity winner way back in 1965 and it changed out lives for the better. Opportunities are out there - the tracks give away hundreds of thousands of dollars every day. The "little people" can get their share. That's one of the great things about racing!

Scott Wells

Scott, Thank you for your support. Since you have held many positions in racing and seen so much, I value your opinion.

Conversations From the Shedrow

Must share a conversation I overheard in the shedrow today. Two trainers were cooling out their horses and talking. The one was complaining about the races being cancelled due to snow, because he had spent over $250 to pre-race his horse and then didn't get to run. Then he started naming what he gave the horse. Two days out he gave bute, banamine and vetro (whatever that is) The day before the race he gave bute, Azium, depo, ESE, Theelan,

We all need a pat on the back.

Robaxin, ACTH, and glyco. Then he said the horse was a bad bleeder so on a race day, not only did he get Lasix, but also a double dose of Amicar, and four tubes of X-bleeder.

I almost had heart failure. He then wonders why his horse won't carry any weight and bleeds! There is no point saying anything. This fellow thinks I'm soft on my horses and not particularly bright. I guess that is why my horse has had a win, a third, a fourth, and a fifth in four starts. He has had both his horses for almost a year and only hit the board with a third once.

Name withheld by request

Edfitor's Note: What can I say?

News From Abroad

The Czech Republic - She Races Her Own Horse

I read your book last year before riding my horse Nox in his first start at six years old after a three year pause at home. Nox looks a lot like the picture of First Prediction on the cover of your book. He is also happiest in his field in the sunshine. Your book was a tremendous help in giving me the courage to prepare a horse at home to race against others that had been prepared at the track. As a three year old, Nox had started twice and finished last and next to last. This was to be my first race, at a mile and a half. At home I rode Nox out each morning, hosed his legs, groomed and fed him lunch, and then turned him out to spend every afternoon in his paddock until evening. I agree with your idea that a horse needs to feel like a horse even in training.

I heard jokes being made about my gray colt being too big to be athletic - 17.3 hands - or too slow, etc.... for three years everyone laughed at my backyard racehorse that had become my best friend. I did not care that he had finished last, he just was not ready at three. No one thought this big animal peacefully grazing could actually be a racehorse in training. Now at six he was working beautifully and I believed in him. So, I took Nox to the trainer to run him so that I would be in compliance with Jockey Club rules. The night before the race the trainer said, " It is too bad he is too pretty to be a good racehorse." He had also warned me that he was too big and I would never be able to push him strongly enough at the finish.

The trainer's skepticism became fuel for my determination. I believed in Nox and wanted to try to train and ride him in a race myself.

Race day was a dream come true. We started slowly, he is a big horse and I was aiming for steadiness rather than speed at the start. We ran steadily, as expected, dead last for the first time around the track. As we approached the 3/4 mile post I started to ask for a steady increase in speed and Nox responded in gradual increments. We began to gain on the field! The amount of dirt in our faces was horrible, so I took him around the outside. As we approached the final turn, I realized my horse was just starting his run, and the field was losing tempo. We came down the homestretch with only one horse in front of us, passed him and won by 3/4 length.

I was so exhausted that I nearly collapsed after we crossed the finish line. Everyone was shocked. At 15 to 1 odds in a field of 12 we had been the outsider. But the backyard racehorse surprised them all. Now all I hear are compliments for him and suddenly his size

He who laughs last...

does not seem to be a handicap! Thank you for writing such an informative book for all of us that are just starting to race.

With greetings from the Czech Republic.

Congratulations Mary! Mary is one determined lady. She lives in a castle in the Czech Republic.

News from Australia - She's Going for Her Dream

The common sense attitude in your book has made me feel that I can achieve my dreams. I live in Australia, have just turned thirty , and quite by accident have become the owner of a racehorse!

I grew up on a famous thoroughbred farm as a child but life being what it is separated me from my passion - horses. Fortunately, I have been reunited with them through my filly, Super Sonja.

Super Sonja is probably the ugliest, and most deformed animal imaginable, but she doesn't know or care. She loves to run! She lives in a small paddock and works on a six hundred meter sand track every other day tied behind a trotting sulky. She also does a couple of breezes a week. She is a dream horse to train with a great attitude.

For the sake of brevity, I am proud to report that Super Sonja ran forth in her first race against some good horses. She started as a 'bad investment' maligned by trainers and veterinarians, not to mention family. Now she is gaining notice, interest and offers!

Jeanine Coventon

Editor: Good for you too, Jeanine!

Malaysia - He's Going for His Trainer's License

My name is Deon Moh. I am a Malaysian Chinese. My country has 3 turf tracks and is about 20 hours by plane from California. I am 42 years old. My experience with horses began about nine months ago. It all started as a challenge. I believe that racehorses are like any athlete but my friends are trainers and owners of horses and they believe racehorses are run on drugs. In November 99, I became the owner of two ex-racehorses and start training them. Since I do not have any knowledge about horses, I start picking ideas from your book which is the first horse book I have read. After reading it I somehow have the idea that I should concentrate on nutrition and workout. So I started reading research material from the net and ordered more books. I joined the Horse Advisor net for support on technical questions.

To everybody's surprise, including myself, my horse Winmoh won a race. Winmoh had not been in his last race due to some skin problem. However, he now looked beautiful and everyone was very excited about Winmoh. His dapples gleamed and he was full of energy. So much energy Winmoh won the race without a single whip and was 3 lengths ahead of the favorite and 12 lengths from the 3rd horse. All the transformation took place with two months of good care.

Good loving care is essential.

I have proven that a racehorse does not have to run on drugs. Even if he is trained by a nobody like me, who has no prior experience. My next challenge was to maintain his condition for the next race which was expected in April 2000. However, it was postponed until May and finally cancelled indefinitely. My jockey was very impressed that we could maintain his condition for 3 months before returning the horse to the Amateur Racehorse Association.

I would like to learn more about training racehorses, because my family and I have fallen in love with horses. We love the response we receive from both of our horses when we are with them. The only way to continue now is to enter professional racing. Before I do, I want to be under a qualified professional trainer. I read every book on racehorses and spend a lot of time at the race track watching and studying the jockeys and trainers and their strategy in the race. I will be trying to get my official license.

Yours truly, Deon Moh

Editor: Deon is another source of inspiration.

Experiences In the Trenches

How Not to Get Your Track Experience

I tried to get my track experience at Delta Downs with a Quarter horse trainer. First he tested me in stalls. "You've done this before - right?" I answered, "A few times over the last twenty five years." Next he asked me to put a halter on, then a bridle, then a saddle. He was surprised to see they were all done correctly. So he allowed me to hotwalk a few. Hence forth, I was asked to put horses on the hotwalker, bathe them, clip them, load them, even to pull off shoes and paint their feet. He was amazed. One wonders where he found his previous employees.

One day he asked me if I could ride. "Well, I broke a few colts. Know a little bit about riding." This answer put me on a pony horse. He was further amazed when I stayed on and came back with the same horses I took out. He was so excited he asked me to ride some exercise horses. Now there is a vast difference between riding babies and riding fit horses in training. I mentioned this, but by now he thought I was Wonder Woman. Figuring I'd never get another chance to ride a real racehorse on the track, I decided to give it a shot.

The memory of the event makes my knees knock. He brings out a three-year-old filly and throws me up on this frothing beast. He's on the pony saying he is going to show me what to do. The filly trots sideways the entire way from the barn to the track. He tells me to take her to the middle of the track and keep her there. Then he stops. Wait a minute, I thought he was going with me. Now the filly and I are on the outside of

**There are all kinds at the track -
let's get the good people together.**

the track trying to get to the middle. Her steering wheel is not functional! Finally, as we reach the turn he yells, "Go ahead! Put her on the rail!" Great - more steering needed -at a gallop. I finally get her on the rail coming around the turn. By the way, since I don't have an exercise rider's license, we came out at 5:45 AM so we were all alone out there in the Dark!

The filly hit the top of the stretch in high gear. All I could hear was the roar of wind. I needed to slow her down. My previous experience kicked in, and I pulled back, got off the saddle in two point, and crouched down. My life was passing before my eyes. I wondered who would raise my child, not realizing that my body was telling the filly to run guts out while my mouth said, "Easy baby."

An eternity later about three strides from the finish line, I realized what I was doing. When she crossed it, she decelerated slightly and I stood up managing to stop her by the time we got back to the gap. By now I was calling myself every stupid imaginable name, expecting the trainer to chew me out and fire me on the spot. Instead he said, "Damn girl, why didn't you tell me you could ride?" The man was hopeless! The next day he expected me to ride again. I said, "Sorry, I'll stick to nice slow babies. No more fit horses for me. I may be stupid but I'm not suicidal!"

Although it was a thrill, I was never so terrified in my life. My respect for jockeys soared. By the way, the filly ran second three days later.   Name withheld by request

There is much to think about here. It is appalling that there are trainers willing to take such risks with untrained help. Fortunately nothing worse happened to her while she flew down the stretch. Every one needs guidance and help at the track but that was no way to learn to gallop. There is great danger involved when working with fit sound horses at high speed. Jockeys deserve respect for the difficult challenging job they do. It takes courage, strength and a very cool head to modify and direct the behavior of high strung horses.

A Family Affair

Our exposure has been brief, my husband and I have been bitten by the racing bug. I had given up on finding a way to share my love of horses with my husband . He is not a rider and I love endurance riding, which entails endless (fun) hours of riding. But I discovered to my delight that Ron loves the pageantry and atmosphere of the track, feeding carrots to the horses on the backside, flashing his owner's pass to the admittance people on the frontside, and talking to relatives about our racehorse!

Oh, the joys of racehorse ownership! His eyes no longer glaze over at the mention of Arab bloodlines. He now grabs copies of "Finish Line" out of my hands before I close the door. Our eight-year-old daughter is another enthusiast. Mt. Pleasant Meadows has a family oriented "country fair" atmosphere. Unfortunately, their marketing is poor and attendance is generally light. Perhaps, more families like mine, who race sound, healthy, sensibly trained horses could help.

So dreaming that we could own racehorses, we went in search of and found a trainer who would work with our ideas. We had known him before. He had been employed by our previous trainer until they parted ways because of differences on training methods. The final straw was the day the trainer told one of the pony riders to keep his horse cantering in the post

Keep it in the family.

34

parade because he limped at a walk!!! And I had sent my horse to this person! I went into this game very trusting and naive - but am learning fast.

This previous trainer and I did not part on good terms. As politely as I could, I told him that I was uncomfortable with the injuries, soreness, medicine, and medical procedures my horse had at his barn. He was unwilling or unable to work with me on an alternate training regime for my horse. He was not interested in an owner who didn't simply send the horse, pay the bills, show up on race day, and not ask too many questions.

The new trainer already trains following many of your principles and I'd like to give him a copy of your book. The more we spread and circulate your common horse sense approach, the better for the horses and the industry.

The Arabian industry is begging for new owners - people to get involved. My experience shows why they become involved and then just as quickly become uninvolved again!

You have touched many good points here... that your husband is now involved in the program... and that your horse is a family project.

I also feel for the trainer-he surely thinks he is doing the best he can to get the horses to races. His style did not suit your goals -you want a sound horse for another career if he is not fast. Some trainers feel pressured by owners to win at all costs. This allows little time for the healing process between hard works. The shortest route with the fastest results is medications. It would be hard to expect a trainer to change his style for you. He does what works for him. His attitude may be very appropriate for his other owners. Maybe they don't want to know anything except when the horse will run and when the horse will win. I know how difficult it is to have a horse ready for a race and then find him a little off on entry day. If it is a short meet, choosing to wait two weeks until he is right can be disastrous. The owner has expectations and may be upset if his horse doesn't run...after all...he is paying day money!

It is times like these that an informed and educated owner is the trainer's best asset. Such an owner can understand and help with these difficult decisions. Could your previous trainer have thought that the horse would run well when he is lame? You are better off with a trainer who wants to work with you because you want to be part of the complete program. The development of a race horse really takes more time than most people allow for... owners push trainers for answers and results too soon because the costs are so high. Trainers, knowing that the horse needs time and experience, push him forward and hope he won't crash. A pattern evolves. The horse runs well for a few races and then crashes-never to be seen again...or he'll be off a year or so and come back a lesser horse. It may take another two years for the horse to grow into his job only to find that after four year the owner has a healthy, fit, sound horse that is too slow to win more than a race or two! This horse will be useful and able to have another life. However, the costs of training will never be recuperated. That's why the program works for owners who like horses, and have a place to keep them during their "down" time. If an owner understands upfront how slim his chances are, he can still have a good time and end up with a sound horse for another life.

Let's keep good people involved.

THE ECONOMICS OF RACING HORSES

I had an unusual entry into the sport of thoroughbred racing. I owned a farm on which I was trying to establish some profitable enterprise. I tried cattle, goats and chickens for egg production. I found some success in several government programs and in timber and tobacco. Still, I had about 35 acres of well fenced, highly productive pasture complete with watering systems. Neighbors suggested breeding horses. I looked at Quarter horses, Tennessee Walking horses and Rocky Mountain horses. None of these breeds made financial sense to me. You might sell an average weanling for about $1,000 or an average yearling for about $1,500. Maybe you could sell a good looking two year old for $2,500 to $3,500. By the time you considered the cost of the mare, stud fee, feed and the vet bills, there was absolutely no money to be made.

Another neighbor offered to sell me a 12 year old thoroughbred mare who had won around $20,000 on the track. He had bred her to one of his stallions and was asking $800 for the mare plus $300 for a live foal. I did not believe I could go far wrong with an $800 mare . . . $1,200 in vet bills later she did not appear to be as sound an investment. She colicked in the pasture and lost her foal. I ended up giving her to the vet's younger sister.

Somehow this experience left me undaunted and I went to the Owners and Breeders' sale, where I bought two healthy fillies. I shipped them to Kentucky to be bred back. I keep pretty good books and I was surprised how fast breeding costs added up. It isn't just stud fees; boarding a mare while she is bred, vaccinations, feed and hay all cost money.

As I attended more and more auctions I began to realize that if I were patient, I could purchase better bred yearlings for less money than I could breed them. I could buy two-year-olds in training for less money than I could breed and break them. I could even claim horses for less money than I could breed, break and race train them. I began to think that maybe it was a better idea to buy horses of racing age.

Unfortunately, I could not afford to pay $50 per day to a professional trainer. That meant that I had to learn to race my horses myself. With this revelation, I began to collect any book or tape that I could find which related to racing Thoroughbreds. What I learned, was that there are very few books which actually described how a horse is trained to race. No one appeared willing to share what they knew about racing. The notable exception was Janet Del Castillo's *Back Yard Race Horse* (you don't know how lucky you are to have stumbled upon this book).

After reading *Back Yard Race Horse*, I attended one of the seminars at Janet's farm. It was wonderful and fun. Over a period of a year or so, Janet and I became friends. When I decided to get my trainer's license I bought a two-year-old in training and spent a part of the winter with Janet in Winter Haven, Florida. On the last day of the winter meet at Tampa Bay Downs I ran my first horse and activated my trainer's license.

Look at the economics carefully before you start.

Tampa Bay Downs closed. I had a fit horse that I wanted to race in Cincinnati. Janet had several fit horses, with nowhere to run for the next seven or eight months and this is where my real story begins...

Over the winter Janet had complained about the difficult competition at Tampa Bay Downs. She felt that more and more trainers with better and better horses were coming to Tampa Bay Downs to escape the cold harsh winters in the north. Was it so tough at Tampa Bay Downs? Was it really any easier to race anywhere else? Somehow I talked Janet into letting me race three of her horses along with mine just to see what would happen. It was a grand experiment. Could a new trainer (like you could be) bring four fit horses up from Florida, have any success and not lose a ton of money? Janet and I drove from Florida to Ohio each with our own trailer in a 24 hour marathon. Never again. In hindsight I will find a place to lay over if I make that trip. But we did it and somehow arrived safely.

The horses we brought to Cincinnati were: Winners Vision, a three-year-old maiden having raced only two times; Crafty Wolf, a three-year-old maiden who had raced about four times; What About Now, a five-year-old maiden who had raced about seven times and Hidden Glory, a six-year-old winner of one race who had raced nearly sixty five times.

My home track in Cincinnati is River Downs. River Downs is a lower level track but we do get a lot of Kentucky horses from across the river. Still, the competition is not too intense.

Janet stayed for the first week. It was nice to have the support since I had only entered and run one race in my life. We set the farm up to handle four horses. I had enough barn space and portable corral panels to set up four inside stalls. The stalls could also be moved outside on pleasant days or in the evening. I used two existing one acre paddocks up by the house for daily turnout. The routine for the entire summer was to keep the horses in the barn on hot sunny days. In the cooler evenings they were stalled in portable stalls outside or turned out in the paddocks to play. I rarely worked the horses in the paddocks and only on three occasions did I haul horses to River Downs in the morning for works. What I did was to race the horses... a lot. In fact with the exception of Crafty Wolf, everyone ran an average of once every twelve days for the four months of the meet.  To the Races!

Now for the exciting results...

Janet stayed in Cincinnati long enough to see each horse race it's first River Downs race. What About Now ran a fifth in her first race, just a nose from fourth place and fourth place money. This was encouraging and represented the best race that she had ever run. Winners Vision was very stiff and ran a poor first race. Crafty Wolf ran fourth. Hidden Glory ran a great race, closing strongly at the end to finish second by just a neck. The experiment seemed to be working. The horses were running well just a week or so after the long trip from Florida.

Through the rest of the summer of 2002, the horses ran competitively at the $5,000 claiming level but did not run so well when I tried them at the allowance or higher priced claiming level. Hidden Glory won two races and had a number of seconds and thirds. What

Establish a routine that works for you.

About Now had one second place finish and several thirds and fourths. Winner's Vision had a second and a third place finish. Crafty Wolf had two fourths but was laid up with a sore knee for most of the summer.

Total winnings for the summer were about $12,000 and it was a blast. There is nothing quite like running your own horse! I tend to be a little nervous and so I don't always enjoy the last few minutes before the race, but the excitement as the horses break out of the gates cannot be adequately described.

Twelve thousand dollars in winnings may sound like a lot of money but financially neither Janet or I got rich racing that summer. The reason that the horses did not make a lot of money is that racing is expensive! This is a short list of the expenses:

Farrier — each horse received new shoes once a month at a cost of $70. Each month I spent about $280 on horseshoes!

Vet — thankfully I only had a couple of minor injuries. I also had blood drawn for a couple of Coggins tests. I probably spent about $250 that summer on vet fees at the race track.

Gasoline — each race I drove about fifty miles each way from the farm to the track and back. Gas for the 100 mile round trip was almost $15.

Groom — a groom walks the horse over to the paddock to be saddled and cools them out after the race. Because I often went to the track alone, I needed to use a groom. Grooms averaged almost $40 per race.

Feed and Hay – each horse ate two scoops of grain and about a quarter bale of hay each day. I spent close to $10 each day just to feed the hungry little darlings.

As you can see, keeping Thoroughbreds really adds up! Actually it isn't that bad and if you have some pasture they can supplement their feed with grass. All you really need to do is win a race or two each year and everything works out.

The moral to the story is that it is difficult to make money racing Thoroughbreds, but you should be able to come close to breaking even if you do your own training. My advice to would-be trainers is to keep a close eye on the bottom line of your racing endeavor. Try to keep things inexpensive and flexible. I really like using corral panels to make outside (or inside) stalls. In the hottest part of summer I place them under trees or use a round patio umbrella to provide shade. I use buckets for water and for feed. I feed hay on the ground (although I also like hay nets which may waste less hay). Corral panels cost about $60 each and buckets cost about $6. For a little over $250 you can have a nice portable stall setup. When the grass is gone, just move the stall. The grass eventually grows back!

Be careful of your fixed expenses which include trucks, trailers, barns and the like. It is very easy and very tempting to buy lots of horse stuff. Just remember, not only do you have to pay for these things with purse money, but upkeep can become a major chore. I think it is best to keep a minimalist attitude.

Greg Verderber

Keep a minimalist attitude!

How do you make a small fortune in racing?
Start with a large one.

Vic and Sturmy

What seems a long time ago (3 years and some months) we fell into the magical and prestigious world of horse racing by way of a friend who had been in the racing business for sometime. Although we had experience with horses, we knew nothing about racehorses. On the advice of my friend, we decided the best way to get started was to claim a horse that was already running, trained and ready to win some races for us. Ha!

We did our homework for a month scoping out the cheap claiming races. Eventually we came across a magnificent black stallion with a good race record. He had been running allowance races up north and had earned nearly $100,000 in his three years of racing. We waited for his race ready for our claim. On the fateful day, we put in our claim $6,250. He won that race by about 8 lengths. He was magnificent.

Back at the barn everyone was excited and proud to have him in the barn. When we were inspecting him, we noticed he had a "knee." We were told this was common in racehorses, they all had some little problem - no big deal. We started spending time at the track in an effort to learn all about racing. Well, we didn't learn much that way; most of our questions were not completely answered. The practices seemed to be the exact opposite of everything we knew. We felt like complete idiots.

About two weeks later, our boy was ready to race again. Our friend/trainer had entered him in a race, so off we went to see him WIN???? Nope, when we got to the barn to check on him before the race, he was down in his stall looking colicky. Well, we might not have been racehorse trainers but we certainly knew when a horse was in pain. We watched him for a few minutes, decided he would have to be scratched from the race and called the vet. The horse spent the next four weeks in the hospital recuperating from surgery to repair a tear in his colon. After that he was shipped to our farm for another couple of months of rehab. And so we wait...

We knew things like this happen to horses. The day before Vic's surgery, we bravely claimed our next racehorse, Sturmovik. We had seen him in his last race and were impressed with him. At the time his record was 7 races, 3 wins, 1 second, and earnings of $13,000. It looked very impressive. He was a showy, fast little thing, built like a Quarter Horse. He was running in $5,000.00 claiming races and doing well. On paper it looked like a good claim.

The week after claiming Sturm, the trainer noticed heat and swelling on his right knee. A vet check and x-rays showed a chip in his knee. This meant surgery and about two months rehab. Sturm spent the rest of meet on the farm with Vic in rehab.

Five months and some $22,000 later it was time to start training for the upcoming Tampa meet. Time to find a rider, buy all the equipment and learn. Over the summer we parted ways with our trainer, so we decided to do it ourselves with Janet's help and guidance. The vet said that both horses were ready for training.

We all arrive at racing via our own route.

We started at the farm having a rider gallop the horses around the pastures. The horses seemed to be doing well. After two months of that it was time for the track. Our rider was instructed to back Vic to the wire and gallop for a mile. Back at the barn, our mentor, Janet noticed swelling in the knee. This was new. We called the vet who promptly took x-rays. This horse never showed pain or any lameness. The x-rays showed no less than six chips in and around the top of his knee. One was almost an inch in diameter. We took the x-rays

to two other vets. Not only were the chips a problem, but years of cortisone injections had damaged the carpal bones, cannon bone, ligaments and cartilage. It was obvious to the vets that this horse had been running with the chips for years. Previous trainers had masked the problems and continued to run him.

The vets voted 2 to 1 to retire him. If he kept running, the leg would soon break. This horse had started his career in graded stakes races at Belmont and very high priced allowance races. If I remember correctly he ran against Victory Gallop. It was a tragedy that a minor and relatively inexpensive surgery to remove a chip followed by a couple of months of rest to heal was not the treatment of choice for this horse.

We retired him and decided to use him for breeding. The first year we bred him to three mares. They didn't take. The next year we bought several cheap brood mares. Just as they were coming into season, we noticed Vic acting colicky. It was so severe he had to be put him down. The vet did a necropsy on her own because she was very fond of Vic. She discovered complications from the prior surgery. Our $6,250 claimer cost us $25,000 and a lot of heart ache.

Sturmy was a different story. He trained well and was soon ready for his first race. The question was where he should run. Some said that he was just a cheap claimer. We felt he was better than that. We put him in a starter allowance and that little guy made us proud. His first race back after a year he ran second. We were so happy, when he crossed the finish line. Our struggle with Vic and Sturm, trainers, getting our license, vets, farriers, stress, heartache, etc. vanished instantaneously.

Sturmy's next race wasn't so great. He ran 7th. That was OK we knew it wasn't his fault. He made up for it the next two races when he won both. He didn't get good reviews. Lots of people told us we were crazy, running him above his head, but he did it. He became a celebrity. Everyone asked about him, other trainers, riders always wanted to ride him, people we didn't even know would ask. We had several offers from people to buy him. What a season that was. He ran two more races that meet and got a six place and another first.

We turned him out for the summer and waited for the next Tampa meet. We had purchased two other horses at the end of the previous meet and spent the summer getting to know them. Then just before the meet opened we bought two more horses.

What a meet! We never won a race encountering every problem known to man. Although they were checked before we purchased them, the four new horses had various

The joy of winning makes it all worthwhile.

problems either mental or physical. (Beware when buying in KY). Still not discouraged we bought two more horses close to the end of the meet.

After our dismal Tampa meet we decided to go somewhere for the summer. The only place we could get stalls was in Nebraska. It was wonderful, not only did we get a good vacation in a delightful place, but the horses did well. We put Sturm in a stakes race where he ran second. One of the new horses got a first and a second. We had about given up on the other when she began to improve. By the end of the meet she had a third and with a bit more time might have done better. We had recovered from our disappointment at Tampa - a tough track. However, even with our wins, we had barely recovered our costs.

Three years down the road, a road with many ups and downs - emotional, physical, and definitely financial - we are three days short of the end of the 2002-2003 Tampa meet - another tough one. We finally got a win three weeks ago after 21 starts with six horses. Undaunted, we are preparing to go to Canterbury, Penn or River, - wherever we can get stalls.

Our advice - Learn all you can from every person, book, and magazine you can find and keep an open mind. Be prepared for more pit falls than mountain tops. You will face emotional and financial drains with no guarantees , so DO NOT spend more than you can afford to lose, and if you happen to make money - count your blessings.

Would we do it again? Who knows?

A Backward Backyard Tale

I can't remember how all this started. It has become a blur of memories and horses. There are always new horses and fresh ideas and always the dream of the golden pot at the end of a flaxen tail. All racehorse people are subject to fancy. If you are reading this you too are infected. It is inescapable if you have picked up this book because you have responded to a clever little ad of hand drawn horses peering up at you with big eyes and long graceful necks and the promise that you too can race horses from your backyard. Your curiosity will be your undoing.   ;)

I have always been involved in one way or another with horses; Jumpers, Hunters, Pony Clubbers and the like. I'm sure you have too to some degree. Well I was 40ish, out of shape, chain smoking, and on the way to a quick heart attack when I first picked up the same book you are now reading. Quick.........put it down; get a membership to the local gym. Save yourself while you can. Too late you say. Then read on and I will tell you my little race horse story.

I was a Real Estate Broker in Florida, relatively successful at my profession. Bored and fat. I was reading my Florida Horse Magazine and saw that innocuous little ad for the book *THE BACKYARD RACEHORSE*. It seemed like fun reading so I called this strange woman who talked to me for an hour or so. No one needs to sell a book so bad as to talk to a stranger for that long. I instantly liked her. You did too, admit it. Anyway before long I was sitting in a house in Winter Haven, FL with a bunch of woman talking horses, Racehorses! Then we were up in the dark loading a bunch of horses in a trailer and off to Tampa Bay Downs. Needless to say I thoroughly enjoyed the seminar and most of the people. When I left Winter Haven I was morphed into a horse saving, horse racing son-of-a-gun.

Within weeks I had rented a small farm and was back in the saddle. Riding again was my savior. I rode and rode and rode. My weight and health improved. Soon I wanted to get my license to train. I went to Tampa Bay Downs with Janet's help and met a Steward who processed my paperwork and gave me a test to take. I have taken many a test in my time and the prevailing method in the non-academic world is multiple-choice. Mine was not multiple-choice at all. Every question required a written answer. It seemed to me that some of the people taking the test were running out very quick while I was laboring. They had multiple choice tests! Why on earth would they want to discriminate against me?! I'm really a nice guy. Well

Horses can be addictive.

dummy it is because I am an outsider and so are you but I passed that test and the ensuing verbal grilling from the Steward. Now I thought I was ready to race!!!

I had a young gelding out of a mare of mine by a son of Secretariat. His name was Duke of Duchess. The day of his first race we shipped into the track and began the long wait. At about 11AM me and Duke were getting bored. I thought nothing would be better than to take him over to that pretty area of green grass and loosen him up with a short lunging session. I thought it better to have him move around rather than get stiff in the stall. This is what I might have done with my show hunter or jumper before a class if he was anxious or

on edge. Anyway we were merrily lunging, me and Duke, when all of a sudden strangers and security personnel arrived on the scene and started yelling at me to stop "jibbing" my horse.

I stopped but I couldn't figure out the problem. They must have been weird or something. What did they mean 'jibbing" my horse? I thought this must have been like an illegal drug or something. Who did they think they were anyway?

Rule # 1…….learn the track's rules and jargon. They are all different and many will *not* make sense to you but they make the rules and you are an outsider….repeat this sentence for at least the first year or until you win a race. They call the process of lunging, "gypin" your horse because anyone who can't afford a rider must be a gypsy.

Duke's race was the greatest. He saddled nicely, he handled the post parade nicely. I picked a girl to be his jockey. She was tough as nails and spoke with a nasal twang. Duke loaded in the gate and the bell rang!!! His first race and mine too!! Immediately he went to the front and the announcer yelled, "It's Duke of Duchess in the lead by a head!" Well………………that was the best he ever ran. He finished last but at least he got the call. Duke got a lot of first calls but he never got the purse. Finally I realized that Duke was never going to beat a fat man. Horse number 1 retired!!! Here I thought Duke was going to save me from the Real Estate world. Nuttin doin!!

Then there was Lady. She trained like a demon. I was sure she was at least an allowance quality horse. Of course by now I was getting more realistic. I had given up thinking that I had a "stakes" horse. I would let myself settle for an allowance horse. I was smarter and decided I would risk having her claimed by starting her at the bottom. This is a level of intelligence that comes when you realize you have spent tens of thousands of dollars and have no money in return. I love Lady and when I see her in the pasture today I get the urge to put her back in training. Well she never won nuttin but damn she could train.

Then there was High Johnson. Nada…Nuttin!

Then there was Aly. After several years of training I sent her to the track with a real trainer and she bowed a tendon.

Take nothing for granted.

Then there was Indy. IBID

Then there was Bennie. IBID

Finally I bought an unbroken two-year-old by a good but cheap sire. He was a small spooky black rat. I hated that horse. His name was Bill. Bill was the most aggravating horse I ever met. He cribbed. He bit. He kicked. He refused to eat. He never held any weight. He shied at the world. He was awful. I was depressed. He was the only horse to drop me in years but I persisted. This damn horse was going to race even if it killed me.

I got Bill to the races. His first race he stood in the gate and never came out. In his second race he ran out after the gates opened and trailed the field. In his third race he reared straight up in the gate and his jockey would never ride him again. As you can already tell when you spend several years getting one to the races that horse better damn well race 'cause you are not going to give up. Somebody has to win races!! At least 10 a day win at your track alone.

I always wanted to leave home for a short time and take some horses to a track like a real trainer. I took Bill to Hialeah and planned on staying a month. The last month of the meet was when all the good horses from up north had gone home and the good horses from Calder were waiting for their summer meet. If ever there was a chance to win anything it was at the end of the Hialeah meet.

Two races and he came in 7th and then 5th. Maybe he was improving. On the very last race of the last day, I entered Bill. You know what I am going to say. Yes, that ratty little horse jumped up and took the lead and never looked back. He won by 3 going away. My partner and I never screamed so loud in all our lives. Even track people thought we were nuts. Bill was a winner!! I was a winner!! We have the picture to prove it. The fact that I had spent a hundred thousand dollars to win $3,500.00 didn't matter a hoot. We are winners. We are winners. We are winners.

Bill's time in that race was pretty good. I had, of course, become an instant expert. For the rest of the summer I raced him way over his head. He only won one more race in his career.

I quit training with two wins in 73 races. Nearly two hundred thousand dollars in costs and about $15,000 in winnings. I had to go back to work. I never quit real estate but I didn't pay a lot of attention either. Money was a problem and I was addicted to race horses. God what a life!!!! I never had so much fun.

So read this little book and dream the dream, but listen to the author when she says, "Do not quit your day job!"

Just a little hint. Unless you are rich do not fool yourself into thinking you can make money with racehorses if you do it the way "they" tell you. The "correct" way will break you. Your costs with a trainer at the track will be $1,500 to $2,000 a month. When you shop for a

You _CAN_ be a winner!

trainer it will sound like less. It will not be less. When all is said and done it will always be more. You must come up with a way to train your horse for 25% of the normal cost. Drugs, grooms, exercise riders, supplements, vets, feed, hay, shoes, shipping…all these things add up. I see too many people with short budgets trying to play the game the same way as the wealthy owners.

If you get your training license you will be asked to train horses by people with no money looking for a cost sharing deal. Some times it looks tempting, but it is slow death. Do not make deals.

The way to stay ahead in the racing business is to use your head and ask your self, "How can I do this cheaper but not sacrifice the health or well being of the animal." You can do it cheaper and the horse will be better off!!!

If you were able to get your trainer's license then you are probably a pretty good horseman. If you don't have a farm you can find a place to board your horse. (Preferably with no kids around). This place will need a large safe place to gallop your horse. If your horse is difficult to gallop and spooky get rid of him. Find yourself a nice gelding. Easy horses are cheaper to deal with in almost all respects. Use good sense getting your horse fit. Racehorses break. Speed kills. Injuries are expensive. Take your time. The Backyard Racehorse has a good recipe for getting your horse fit. Let your horse be a horse. Turn him out as much as you can.

As your horse gets more and more fit he will begin to change mentally. Horses that are show-horse fit are not fit like racehorses. Horses that occasionally compete in combined training events are not fit in the same ways as racehorses. Racing fit is a level of fitness and a type of fitness you have not experienced. That is why you need a quiet gelding. Even he will get tough to handle. You don't need hormones getting in the way and putting your health at risk.

Take your horse to the track and get him used to the surroundings. Do this often. You can not simulate the track experience. If you can get a license to gallop your own horse at the track you will save money. Always hire a professional to breeze your horse. You will not be fit enough to "work" your horse unless you are riding 6-7 horses everyday. Since you only have time for one horse you will not be that fit!!

You say, "What if I ride 5-6 horses a day? Won't I be fit enough?" The answer is yes but you will have forgotten the first rule. Repeat after me. "Don't quit your day job."

Donald Brown
Real Estate Broker and Part Time Racehorse Trainer
hobay@bellsouth.net
or you can see my WEB SITE
www.HoeBay.com

Above all don't quit your day job!

Doing It His Way-
A Different Style of Training Suits This Previous Harness Trainer

My filly, Calar, continues to progress and is now doing 12-second furlong sprints and seems to LOVE to run, run, run! I have memorized your book and have applied the progressive principals gradually, and now have an athlete who can who can work seven or eight miles and leave the track with a smile on her face. In the early stages I worked her in the afternoon without other horses on the track. Now, she goes in with the other horses in the morning and what a change of attitude! She's hyper-alert, swells up to three times her size and wants to go, go, go!

I should point out that after I did my early stage backyard training, I transferred my filly to a training center nearby known as Spring Garden Ranch which is for Standardbred horses. I have trained Standardbreds for ten or

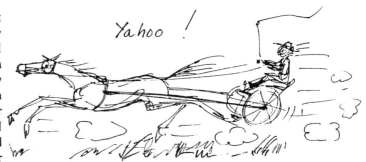

twelve years and become enamored with the notion of training a Thoroughbred. I had known that Standardbreds are used to prompters, running alongside, hooked to two-wheel carts. I opined that this could be done with a Thoroughbred as a training tactic. The advantages would be avoiding weight on the back as a yearling and a development of powerful driving hindquarters by pulling weight.

Of course, teaching a thoroughbred to pull a two-wheeled vehicle is not done overnight. With patience, persistence, and some adapted techniques, my filly became a natural.

I spent about five months doing slow work at my farm track which is really a wide trail through the woods. Occasionally I would encourage sprints and though they became wild rides which almost catapulted me from the cart which necessitated the use of a rigged seat belt. Calar eventually became too much for the farm track and was transferred a short ride down the road to the training center. Here was a full mile track inside of which was a half-mile track.

I began work on the mile track with a two-mile jog, then switched to the deeper half-mile track for galloping and speed spurts. A work out ended with a warmdown mile on the mile track. After becoming accustomed to the routine, we began furlong sprints. I recall that her first sprint was in twenty seconds, the equivalent of forty seconds for a quarter mile and terribly slow for a thoroughbred, but somewhat respectable for a Standardbred. My excitement mounted as she voluntarily reduced that time each time out.

When she dropped to fifteen second sprints, a real change occurred: she began to posture for the sprint, picked up her speed voluntarily and took hold. I know a 12-second

He flies through the air with the greatest of ease.

furlong may not seem like much to a jockey but to a driver in a cart hooked to a thoroughbred, it is like an explosion. Caler takes such a strong hold of the lines (reins) that I have difficulty controlling my stopwatch. Her speed increased so dramatically that I had to abandon the half mile track as she could not make the turns at full speed.

The time eventually came when she needed a rider and I asked an accomplished horsewoman to break her for riding. Caler had, or course, had the harness around her girth for six or seven months and I had slipped a pad and English saddle on her back from time to time. But I knew that a rider up on her back would be a different story.

We cinched her up for about ten minutes in a western saddle and walked her around for about ten minutes. Next the rider elongated the stirrup strap and put a foot in and slowly stood up. Calar rotated her eye to observe the action. The rider eased back down and we concluded that session. The second time out we went through the same procedure except this time the rider proclaimed that she thought Caler was ready for a full pull up and for the rider to be seated in the saddle. I nervously inquired if the rider was certain of this and as I did, recalled that the first time I put a harness around this filly, she exploded into a bucking and kicking explode that would have won a bronco high rider high points. Without hesitation, our rider pulled up, threw her leg over and settled in the saddle in one flowing motion. I held on for the expected explosion. It never came. Caler stood there rotating her eyes backward and up, obviously taking a long look at the rider. After a few minutes, I led her off and we walked around the quadrangle for about fifteen minutes. Half way through this period she stopped, took a deep breath and showed interest in munching grass. She has now been ridden several times without incident.

I was glad to see that the early training getting accustomed to the cart paid off for accepting the rider so easily. Now my filly is ready for the serious business of fast work with a rider.

It is my hope that the past few months of work pulling approximately 250 pounds at speed has developed powerful hind quarter muscles and developed front legs that will never know bucked shins. I recently had her examined by a race horse veterinarian who has declared her sound and without problems. You have seen her on video and declared her a "brick". Well, the brick is getting ready to fly. I will keep you updated on the next phase of conditioning. Thanks for sharing your knowledge, your enthusiasm, and warm spirit. Caler thanks you too!

Leo Salter, Florida

What a neat story! Leo did what he knew best adapting his skills to his goals. When he first called me and told me his horse was doing so many miles and at what speed, I asked him who was riding. Imagine my surprise and delight when he sheepishly admitted that actually the horse was doing this behind a cart! He said that he didn't ride but he had trained harness horses. His videos of the filly flying around the track at a full gallop with a cart are wonderful. On the off days Leo used "Mr. Bluejeans" to accustom the filly to weight.

Leo wanted to train a Thoroughbred and figured out a way to achieve his goals. He has a sound, fit three year old almost race ready and will be applying for his trainer's license soon. Keep us informed of Caler's progress, Leo. This story should inspire others to make variations on traditional training.

How can you get your horse to the track?

Making the Transition From Backyard to Backstretch
The Story of the First in the Series of My Greatest Humiliations.
(Or, I'd Like Another Chance to Make That First Impression)

The first horse I ever started was Donovan's Pride, a three year old first time starter in a maiden race at Fort Erie. My paddock groom from home didn't show up, so I had to wear the number vest and lead her over myself. She was tough to saddle and rank in the walking ring. I knew going in that she was flighty, but I figured that once she got on the track she would be good with the pony.

The jockey (the leading apprentice) became unnerved. As they turned to go the gate, she told the pony girl to take her back to the paddock. She wasn't going to ride this horse. I watched this unfold from the track apron and I hurried after them to the paddock. The jock jumped off and, without ever looking at me, peeled off my silks and tossed them to her valet. She disappeared into the female jock's room. I grabbed my silks from the valet and went into the jock's room with the clerk of scales.

"Anybody wanna ride this guy's horse?" he announced. You could hear the crickets chirp. No answer. Nobody made eye contact.

The phone by the scales rang, it was the stewards telling me not to bother looking, they were scratching me, putting my horse on the stewards list, the paddock list, and I got the feeling that they were going put me on a list too. I was humiliated. I was angry at the rider, angry at the stewards. I stalked off in a huff, threw the horse on the trailer (she was soon in season) and drove home where I sulked for two weeks. Then I started another horse.

The horse was Little Scarlet, another first time starter. I was determined not to be embarrassed again. I hired a well known paddock groom from Fort Erie that I knew from Florida. I contacted a local journeyman jockey who had a reputation for riding tough horses and he accepted the mount - reluctantly. The jocks had come to a consensus that I was a lunatic and my horses were dangerous broncos. They were only half right. Little Scarlet was an angel in the paddock and she did everything right. The paddock judge was literally right over my shoulder when I saddled her, watching my every move. I almost knocked him over when I stood up from cinching the overgirth. I could tell that the rider was nervous because out of the corner of my eye I saw him peeking out of the jock's room, waiting for the fireworks. Little Scarlet was so calm and collected that the jock broke off from the pony out of the post parade and she galloped to the post by herself. She broke from the gate like a quarter horse and finished a decent fourth to a Belmont ship-in. It was the quickest maiden six furlong event of the meet. The jock jumped off and begged to ride her back. I felt vindicated. The trackside weigh scale phone rang and it was the stewards. They still wanted to talk about Donovan's Pride. My presence was requested at a meeting the next week.

I knew that I'd made a mistake being aloof and not making contacts on the backside with the other horsemen and on the frontside with the racing officials. I'm not really a people person. I suffer from a poorly reasoned superiority complex. I thought that my trainer's license was the only credential that I needed to train horses. I know now that reputation and familiarity are crucial not just for success, but just to be able to compete. As a backyard trainer and owner, it's essential that you make a few friends, or acquaintances on the track who can vouch for

Always be cordial.

you when a jock's agent asks around to check you and your horse out or a paddock judge sees you forgot to put a tongue tie on.

I managed to convince the stewards in that meeting that I was a competent horseman and a responsible trainer, that Donovan's behavior was out of character and I would get her off of the "bad" lists. Unfortunately, Donovan got hurt in training before she could start again so I retired her and found her a good home as a hunter jumper. One of the stewards who was in that meeting still to this day greets me every single time at the top of his lungs, "Jordan Lay! How's our Donovan's Pride?" He never asks me about Little Scarlet.

I decided that I needed to run some horses that already knew their jobs, so I bought a mare, Five O' Tea, for $3,500 at the end of the Woodbine meet. She had brilliant speed but had tailed off in form. I found out why the next spring when I tried to run her. EPM. I spent a lot of money treating her and I got her back to run her best race in two years on the turf at Fort Erie but she just didn't have it anymore. I retired her from the track but rode her in a 2 1/4 mile steeplechase meet flat training race in Genneseo, NY. I needed another veteran runner.

I claimed Iron Prospect for $7,500. I wish this had been the first thing I'd done in the game. He had been protected in starter allowances and I'd been tracking him for over a year. He'd had 24 starts in the previous year. The day I claimed Iron he was 47-1 and just got beat by a head. His owner was dumbfounded when the security guard put the tag on his bridle. Nobody claims a 47-1 shot. I assured the man that he was going to a good home and while we waited for Iron to finish in the test barn he told me all of the horse's vices and virtues.

Iron Prospect had form and nearly everybody knew he was sound but an "in and outer". You never knew if he was going to show up on raceday. All of the jocks knew Iron Prospect. He was a piece of cake to ride, although he had a rep as a "deadhead" or "puller" in the morning. I was able to gallop him in a rubber bit at home and he was only tough on a couple of occasions. I even jumped him over a few small fences to keep him from getting bored. He loved it. He put on weight and looked great.

I ran Iron Prospect over his head a few times just to keep him fit and to get myself some starts at Woodbine and Fort Erie. Iron was flat and finished up the track. I dropped him back down in claiming price to $10,000 and he was better, but he still wasn't threatening. He wasn't really finishing with any desire.

There were only a few weeks left in the meet so I decided to drop him down to $5000 and try to get a win with him. When I shipped into Fort Erie I noticed a sign advertising an upcoming "Horsemen's Series" Races for horses at different levels. However, in order to be eligible they had to have made at least six starts in the current season at Fort Erie. The purses for these races were 2 1/2 times what a normal race would run for. They were like Mountaineer pots.

Your reputation is vital.
Hard to make and easy to lose.

Iron Prospect was getting beat by a lot of horses shipping down from Woodbine and by horses at Fort Erie that weren't sound enough to start six times and still be rolling. He would have a really good shot in that race under those conditions. I should have scratched Iron and waited for that race. Shoulda.

I thought I was being sneaky at best. At worst I really thought I was going to win the race that day and I'd be "out" on the horse. I thought no one would touch him and when he was 49-1 as the gate opened, I was relieved and confident. He'd been training so aggressively that I couldn't gallop him at home, I'd shipped into Woodbine to breeze him three days before the race.

Iron Prospect jumped out to a three length lead and I figured he wouldn't be headed. I was straightening my tie for the win picture when I noticed a riderless horse emerge from the pack and bear down on my dark bay win machine as they went into the far turn. My jockey tried desperately to fend off the loose horse, slashing at it with his whip. It was like the chariot scene in Ben Hur. The loose horse slammed Iron into the rail and Iron clipped his heels too. Somehow my jock stayed on and kept his irons but the damage was done. Iron still tried to rally on the turn and got back up to the leaders but he tired in the stretch and finished out of the money. Now it was my turn to be shocked when the security guard gave my groom the claimed tag and ordered us back to the paddock.

My rider later admitted that the guy who claimed Iron Prospect from me had asked him about the horse a few days before the race. He apologized but I haven't used him since. Of course Iron Prospect won that Horsemen's Series race and then kept going. He's won over $50,000 since he left my barn but he really accomplished a purpose for me, he introduced me to everyone at Fort Erie. Despite the chagrin I feel every time I see him run - now the Fort Erie guys don't think I'm just an incompetent moron, I'm just a sucker, and everybody at the track loves a sucker.

I flipped on the satellite racing channel the other day (three years later) just in time to see good old Iron Prospect make the lead turning for home at Fort Erie. I yelled for my wife to come watch him run.

"Why do you torture yourself?" she yelled back. He got beat by a head.

The moral of the story?
Don't brag about your horse.

A Word With My Children

Victoria Del Castillo
Jacki Hanks (cousin)
Nando Del Castillo
Alex Del Castillo

A Gallery of Children

Coming Home Again... With a Better Mental Attitude
Determination is as important as Physical Strength
in Training Racehorses
by Victoria Del Castillo

I could feel the hot tears form at the corners of my eyes. How could he do this to me again? Embarrassed, frustrated, and angry, I resigned myself to call my mother. Oh, how I hated appearing helpless, especially since I was a self-proclaimed know-it-all fourteen-year-old.

It was an early Saturday morning and Mullikin Stu, my smart ass quarter horse and I had spent the night with my 4-H pal Lisa and Quazaar, her mindful Arabian. We had stayed up late oiling our tack, gossiping, and braiding manes and tails in preparation for the county horse show the following day. It was a highly anticipated show since it was there that one qualified for the state level. That night I had prayed fervently that Mullikin would meet me half way and just get through the day without any major catastrophe. It's not that he is a flighty, reckless animal: just the opposite - he is contemplative, lazy to a fault, and possesses a deadly sixth sense - a keen ability to size someone up and know exactly how much he can get away with.

On this particular morning, Mullikin decided he was not going to load. An hour and a half had passed, in which we had tried every trick known to horse people including coaxing him with feed, placing a shank around his rump to pull him in, and of course, the ever popular, beating the heck out of him (just kidding): all to no avail. He simply refused.

No sooner had my mom arrived and slammed the door to her truck, when we all witnessed a sudden attitude change - his recognition of her and her determination was unmistakable - she shook her finger at him and said, "MULLIKIN" in a deep angry foreboding voice and he literally hopped into the trailer. My mother always has had a presence around horses that I can only define as complete confidence that the horse WILL OBEY. There is no question that she is in charge - even with very fractious and hysterical horses. She doesn't lose her temper with them, but she has a way of looking them in the eye, shanking if necessary, and generally winning if there is a confrontation. I'm afraid I tended to think negatively... that the horse wouldn't obey me... that he would humiliate me... that he would get his way... and he usually did. I suspect the horse was looking me in the eye with a calculated defiance... knowing he could outlast my insecure teenage wishy washiness.

Its been 11 years since that experience, yet the significance is all the more apparent now that I am riding young Thoroughbreds for my mom. Mullikin was an extreme case, but this example points out the importance of fulfilling one's role as the horse's master. It is all too easy for us to grow lazy in training and allow unacceptable behavior to continue under the guise of "a bad character trait" or "breeding" or "moodiness". These excuses are valid sometimes, but not generally. I have in the past, been tempted to quit rather than confront the problem. I have now taught myself that if there is a confrontation, I must win... otherwise the horse knows he can bully me. (Reminds me of my teenage years where I tried to balk, but mom generally out-bluffed me.)

Use your common sense.
Choose what will work for you!

Growing up, I focused on Mullikin showing hunter jumper and really did not pay much attention to how the Thoroughbreds were trained - remember - I already knew it all. But since I have been back this winter helping out, life and some age have humbled my attitude and I have been ripe for learning. In the few months I have been here, I have made several interesting observations about my mother's BYRH philosophy and my personal application of it with my showing background. My fundamental knowledge of horses has not escaped me even though it has been many years since I have been around them on a daily basis. I must credit the 4-H organization for this education and the discipline I learned through their programs which included the basics of hoof care, grooming, horse health, conformation, diet, equitation, and overall responsibility for the horses' welfare. Learning in a peer group was a lot more fun than listening to my mother.

When I bring the horse in from the field, I always check the legs!

Mulliken was an easy keep and had good legs and hooves. I rarely checked him for soundness since he never had problems and thus, I never understood the importance of it.

With a not so familiar horse, I learned the need to run my hands down the horse's legs every time I went to ride. Knowing that any puffiness or swelling meant, don't ride. Instead, review the kind of work you did last. Could that have been the cause of the stress? A little too much galloping too early? Or did he merely hit while frolicking in the pasture? Or is your fence broken anywhere? Process of elimination and common sense will guide you to a conclusion. If you monitor the legs each morning early - before the horse has moved around, you can observe the healing take place on its own. With some rest and turnout, you should see the swelling (wind puffs) go down in less than a week. If they don't, consult a vet.

My evolution into an adequate exercise rider has required me to modify my seat and hands. In showing, I was always concerned about the angle of my toe in relation to my knee, whether my wrists flowed into the reins in a straight line, whether my back was erect and whether I was on the correct diagonal. Those concerns were a luxury considering that I am now riding in an orange grove with a two-year-old who doesn't even know what a straight line is. The key has been to ride defensively. For me that entails complete leg contact with the horse, having one leg a bit forward - the other a bit back. Then if he ducks, props or whirls, I'm ready. I keep my rear tucked under with my heels down to absorb the shock of rearing and bucking. I work on maintaining a balanced seat. Finally, I must keep my hands in constant contact with the mouth - otherwise known as keeping the horse "on the bit". By tightening the reins and "taking a hold" you are telling the horse that it is time to work and run into the bit.

Know your horse.

Riding helmets were more decorative than anything else in the show ring. I hated the dorky type with the chin strap that Mom made me wear. Now I won't hop on a horse without one. Even though I feel my seat is solid, you never know when a shadow is going to cause your horse to wipe you off on a tree, which brings me to what I feel is the rider's most useful tool - mental attitude.

If I am really honest with myself, I recognize that I have changed very little from when I was fourteen. I am still incredibly lazy, moody, and selfish; I have just learned how to act like a mature adult and cover up those traits with some acceptable behavior. This is the key to mastering your emotions when training your horse. No matter how rotten I feel, I must remember that this horse is a blank slate, he does not have an "opinion" yet. How I treat him largely determines how he perceives humans and his willingness to work with us. People think that a Thoroughbred just naturally knows how to run in a race. Not so! He may be born with the ability to run but the supreme confidence and soundness of mind to perform in a race and trust his rider rests on these early experiences. We want to teach him to go forward boldly and the rider must use positive imagery throughout the exercise. As you are riding, watch him in your mind's eye, moving freely with no trepidation.

Yet there are times when no matter how prepared you are, you find yourself in the middle of a free fall not knowing exactly what happened except that you are on your way to earth's surface - fast. But forget about what you can't control and think about the other times when you are riding and you let your mind wander to your plans for the day, work, hunger pains, etc. **Bring yourself back to the task at hand!** You are training a young impressionable animal that needs guidance and focused direction. They remind me of little kindergartners who need constant attention and reinforcement of the positive choices they make and punishment for behavior that is unacceptable. Other times I imagine I am at a horse show and am being judged on how I steer my horse forward with encouragement and gentle urging yet still defensive in my seat.

Finally it is vital to allow a horse to be a horse first and then ask for speed and business - just as you wouldn't have a child work an adult job - we must not expect too much from our babies until they are more mature. Horses love to frolic, graze, and socialize: it is a sin against nature that some trainers keep them locked in a stall for months, even years, at a time. We must never lose sight of the basic needs of a horse, if we do, we stand to lose more than trips to the winner's's circle; we lose the essence of the horse - the free spirit and natural

Your horse will reflect the treatment he receives.

desire to perform for their rider. The increasing use of substances to "enhance" a horse's God-given talent will only render him broken down in the future. Racing records have not been broken since the turn of the century except where the surface condition of the track has been changed, further proving that these "advances" in treatment have not made for a better racehorse.

I have witnessed my mother train over 100 horses with the common sense methods and I see that they are truly the only way to ensure that the horse lives a quality life after racing. The love of the animal supersedes any desire to artificially modify his behavior. I am now enjoying riding future racehorses even though they challenge me both physically and mentally.

Mullikin, presently an aging curmudgeon who ponies our babies, reluctantly allows novice riders on his back now and then, still giving them a run for their money. He has been known to plant his feet and not budge if his rider does not ask him in a "convincing" manner. The legacy lives on in me and instead of Mom having to make her presence known when the rider yells for help, I stride up, shake my finger, lower my voice an octave, and grumble "**MULLIKIN!**" To my pleasant surprise, he looks at me out of the corner of his eye, heaves a big sigh and obediently acquiesces. I smile to myself. I know I've come a long way towards having the MENTAL DETERMINATION necessary to master a young horse's mind. I continue to learn and stretch my capacity to develop the personal best in every one of my equine students. Maybe Star Prediction (the one I'm riding now), will be the next big horse for us!

Mom's note: I had asked Victoria to write something with her insight since she was basically a 4-H pleasure horse rider while growing up. It was a joy to see that she has observed so much by just being here... you see... horse racing can be a family endeavor.

We are all waiting for the big one.

From the Blue Eagle Ranch in Nevada to Rancho Del Castillo in Florida...
More Than Geography Was Different!

by Jacki Hanks
(Janet's cousin!)

"What's the temperature there today? 20 degrees below? Come to sunny Florida! Ride race horses in the orange groves and cool them off in the lake!" Having been born and raised in a cattle ranch in central Nevada, this opportunity was too good to pass up! My sort of "marches to different drummer", cousin Janet, invited me to pack my boots and jeans and help out at her farm, Rancho Del Castillo.

I had started riding before I could walk and in the nineteen years I lived on the ranch, I had quite a few horses. Some good some not so good. I rode cutting horses (not just for fun...but to work the cattle), reining horses, did team roping (I was the heeler), and helped with all the ranch work. I never once had any doubt about riding thoroughbreds...I'd seen the Derby on TV and that stuff didn't look hard! Well, someone once said "live and learn", or was it "that which doesn't kill us, makes us stronger!"...no matter...both apply.

Bright and early the morning after I arrived, Janet took me to the tack room and gave me my equipment. She handed me a saddle pad, a bridle, a crop, a shank, and a tiny thing she dubbed "my saddle". I was sure this was an attempt at humor since I would never put something that slight under my beautiful 50 pound western saddle. What if I needed to rope something? It had no strings to tie a slicker on—and surely I was going to get caught in the rain sooner or later. It had no place for a back cinch or a breastplate and absolutely nothing to grab on to if the horse started to buck! Jane assured me it was no joke, handed me a helmet, and we were off.

There were about thirty horses at the farm in different stages of training. Quite a few were just barely two and were there to start the long gallops that would build the foundation for racing. The more mature horses were doing the speed interval training and/or racing. I was very surprised that two-year-olds were being handled - let alone ridden. At the ranch the foals are left alone until they're three or four.

I helped Janet break a few thoroughbreds and must say it was most educational. At her farm we made friends with the little darlings, patted them with a blanket, let them get familiar with a bridle and free round-penned them with weight until they were ready to be ridden. Then Janet would put me on them and of course, I would fall slap off because there was nothing to hang on to. (Just kidding!)

As a little "buckerette" I remember watching my dad break colts each spring. They were usually four by that time and had been browsing out on the desert. He would put one in the round corral and, in his own way, give it as much respect, attention, and love as Janet would, only he did it in about forty-five minutes. I'd sit on the fence and watch as he would snub the horse to the post in the center of the corral, tie its hind foot to its neck, saddle it, let it struggle until it stopped fighting, touch and handle it, and then get on and turn it loose. I don't know what would happen next because I'd have my head in my hands afraid to look. But dad always seemed to come out on top and had the horses working with him as a team in no time.

Live and learn.

When I was about twelve, I was breaking a four-year-old colt, and had done all of the groundwork. I just wasn't able to do that "actually getting on the horse" thing alone. Dad came to my aid, got his sturdy dependable workhorse, held my colt's head by wrapping the lead to his saddle horn. He led me out in the desert behind the house where water from the field flowed onto a dry alkali lakebed. The area was the size of a baseball diamond and filled with thick mud-clay that made "uptite" seem like grape jelly. We slogged to the middle of the pit, the mud seeming to suck the feet off of the horses. They sank up to their knees with each step. Dad assured me the horse would only be able to leap a time or two before he'd tire. That was okay with me…I could ride two or three jumps. Dad released the lead and he and his horse cautiously and quietly walked out of the mud to wait for the "easy tiring" of my mount.

The colt promptly tip toed out of the mud in the other direction, hit the hardpan of the lakebed and took off. I guess two or three more leaps is all I rode before crashing on my newly permed…not to be washed for three days hair…in the dirt! Dad was yelling, "You got him rode! You got him rode!", which wasn't so, but a kind thought on his part. He said later he knew I was in trouble but couldn't do anything about it…so he figured he'd yell happy thoughts.

My confidence level sank with that episode, and though he ponied me many more times, I would plead, quiver, and cry, if he attempted to turn me loose. One morning as we rode out, he said, "This horse WILL be ridden home today". My heart pounded and I was thinking I'd leave my saddle to my sister Kathi, and wished I'd told her not to ride a hoppity horse down the stairs, to tie the milk cow's hind foot low on the post, and NEVER TRUST GEESE! I knew I'd never survive the ride.

Dad pulled up on his horse when we were a distance from the ranch. He looked at me…I quivered and sniffed. "It's time to turn back!" I quivered and sniffed some more. Quivering and sniffing is highly underrated…because it worked! Dad traded horses with me. I got the pony horse and he got on the colt. I freed the colt's head and waited for the fireworks to begin. Nothing. Not so much as a wriggle from that rotten animal. They leisurely ambled towards home with dad flapping his arms and making chicken-like noises in attempt to have the horse spook or buck. That horse was too smart…he knew the jig was up…from that day on, I had a nice little horse to use during roundup.

I quickly found out that quivering and sniffing didn't work so well on Janet's farm…or on two-year-old thoroughbreds. I still try every now and again. Once the horses were broken on the ranch they were basically kind and manageable. I was surprised to see that isn't the case with these thoroughbreds. Their personality and experience are very different…some are high strung and seem to be looking for invisible horse-eaters in the bushes.

As I got stronger and more comfortable in the saddle, I rode faster, fitter horses. The thrill of riding a healthy sound race horse at top speed can only be compared to the thrill of seeing that same horse win at the track! I guess the fact that you can't pick your family is a good thing…because I still learn from that Florida branch of mine. When Janet needs me at the farm, she calls and gives me the plan of action. I look at her squinty eyes, and flashback to the "saddle" issue. But, I've been listening to her for over ten years and I'm still around so she must know something!

You've got to have heart.

… *and Jacki is still a great help!*

My Childhood Training Racehorses On the Farm
or It isn't Work if You Love Horses

by Nando Del Castillo

Dad had read that horse racing was the Sport of Kings, and he, being a king in his own right, said, "Why not have racehorses and win the Kentucky Derby". Sadly it did not work out quite that way. He eventually lost interest and life moved on, as it does. Mom could not shake the dream quite so easily.

Returning to the farm from a trip to Milan, Italy, with my wife and the first of 5 kids, I found mom finishing her training manual. That first edition was rough, in notebook form, but soon to become the book you are reading now. Tears came to my eyes as I read some of the stories. I had lived them. Oh, had I lived them.

I am the middle child. Take that for what it's worth. Mom and dad divorced when I was fifteen. Alex, my older brother, Victoria, my younger sister and I found ourselves alone with our mother at the farm. Mom decided to take this opportunity and make a go at training racehorses, and away we went. She had always taught life's lessons through lessons with the horses. They were our life. Not as in "Oh, you have horses – yeah!" More like, "We have horses. Yes." Yes, it's fun, and yes, it's lots of work. Some would say hard work. Others, like my mom, would say, "It's what I love, so how is that work?" I fell somewhere in the middle.

Learning to ride - the hard way.

I've been riding as long as I can remember. In Manassas, Virginia mom threw me on the back of a horse with Alex and lead us around the pasture on Uncle Stu's Farm - Stu Mullikin. You might know the place. The Battle of Bull Run was fought on the very spot where I first remember riding. Uncle Stu and Aunt Noreen Mullikin gave us our first two horses, Joy and her yearling filly, Sunkist. They were a house/horse warming gift when dad and mom bought the farm in 1973. Today that farm is Rancho Del Castillo. It was home when I was growing up.

Training horses is really not that difficult, if you know what you're doing. We did not. Sometimes, actually most of the time, we learned the hard way.

For example, when I was young (I can't remember my age) mom had a filly that needed to learn to run in a straight line. Keep in mind this was a rural Florida lake front property home to lots of little animals. They often popped up to see what was happening in their backyard. The filly, Jan-Del, (a tribute to Janet Del Castillo) continuously shied at one particular spot on the route. This particular day, she dumped me in the cushy reeds and soft muck, knocking the wind out of me. Mom grabbed the filly and asked if I was OK. I just stared unable to speak. "You're OK. Now get back on and push her through that spot Nando. You can't let her get away with bad behavior, or it will just get worse." My heart was pounding, but I couldn't say, "No."

We went back again, and again, the filly continued to shy at the same spot. Once I slipped to her neck, not as prepared as I should have been, and fell to the ground. I got up quickly, climbed back into the saddle and held on tighter. Eventually Jan-Del learned that

It helps to know what you are doing.

I was the boss and she must listen. I learned that lessons in horse training, as lessons in life, can be painful. They are one and the same.

We had two home breds, born on our farm. We broke and trained them, fed them carrots, laid with them in the pasture while they sun bathed, and frolicked with them in the morning dew. They seemed like plain old horses. Then we asked for speed and their breeding came through. Mom rode Hail the War. I rode Hail the Greek. He was the epitome of a thoroughbred.

Five or six days a week mom and I rode these guys through the grove. Exercising them, teaching them manners and all the lessons young horses must learn as they grow up. It was not unlike raising a kid, if you can relate to that. While we rode mom and I talked. We always had something to talk about - not necessarily horses. But when we talked the horses listened too. They were funny. Their ears rotated like, fancy, hairy radars. More often than not those ears would warn us of some little critter lurking in the bushes ready to pop up and investigate us. The problem was that the silly horses were one step behind their radar and would stop dead often sending me to the ground. Eventually I learned to talk the horses through whatever was lurking in the grove. It seemed as if the little critters had a meeting before we arrived, saying, "OK, you go first. I dumped them last time, it's your turn today."

Another problem were the dogs that lived on the far side of the orange grove. They would pounce out at the same spot every time. Often the horses would careen into trees. Hitting an orange tree at 25 m.p.h. on a horse is not fun for horse or rider - me in those days. Since this was our racetrack, and the other side of the fence was the dogs' home, the problem had to be solved. We learned to warn the horses. We would sing and say ridiculous things like "Watch out horsy there are dogs. They are going to jump out and try to frighten you.. But don't worry. It's OK. They're fenced-in. Let's ride on past them."

Much to our surprise, this ludicrous strategy helped. The horses listened to us and would continue through the chaos. Eventually the horses recognized their size and power and started looking for critters to squash. Mom insisted that these were wonderful adventures. These critters, dogs, cats, rabbits, birds, snakes, whatever came in our way helped prepare the horses for the track - from the bustle of the backside to the screaming crowds at the finish line. It reinforced her belief that a potentially negative situation can be seen in different light. She firmly believes that the glass is half full.

The sand we galloped through in the orange groves was called sugar sand in Florida. It was tough to run through, but soft. How do I know? From chasing horses that dumped me, trying to catch them before mom would know I'd been thrown again. If you think I fell too much to be a good rider, let me clarify that I come from the school that learning how to fall is a prerequisite to learning how to ride. You could call it the school of hard falls, and believe me you want to be a quick study.

During our arguments about who was the better rider (me), my sister, Victoria, insisted that I fell too much to be a good rider. My answer, "Yeah but I get back on." You see, I'm not afraid of any horse but I respect them all. I mention falling because it will happen. When training racehorses even the most experienced rider must concentrate on being prepared. Heck, maybe it'll even help you from beating yourself up.

 Talk to the animals.

Learning to Haul

We also learned to haul early. My dad had a small ranch in Lake Wales, Florida. I loved it and loved spending time there. Once my dad asked me to haul some cattle to the sale. He didn't have a truck or trailer, so I asked mom if I could borrow her only truck and trailer. The "Red Truck", as we called it, was a Ford F250 Diesel stick shift with white, galloping horses on the side panels. It ruand decorated with galloping white horses - quite the rig at the time.

"Be careful," mom told me as she gave her permission. I reminded her I'd been hauling horses for her for three years. "All right, just remember to load more weight in the front and over the axles."

"Yes, Mom."

"Check the trailer brakes."

"I will, Mom."

"Be careful."

"Yes, Mom."

"Have fun."

"Always." and off to market I went.

Two miles short of our destination, the trailer and truck jolted like an explosion. An overactive bull had escaped from his enclosure and caused a fight. The truck fishtailed. The trailer pulling it into the middle of the road. My heart raced. I was only going 35 m.p.h. but the road was narrow, cars were coming at me, and there were ditches full of water on both sides of the road.

"You know what to do Nando." I said to myself. I knew to accelerate and use the trailer brakes to stop - instead I panicked and tapped the truck brakes. The trailer pulled me around like the scrambler ride at the fair. A perfect 180 finishing in the right lane, stalled. When I could breathe, I put my foot on the clutch, started her up and drove off as if nothing had happened. The incident could have wrecked mom's rig, or worse killed someone, possibly me. The moral of the story - you can never be too careful and you never, EVER, know everything.

Unless. . . You're a mother.

As I tried to sneak into my room that night, mom only had to take one look at my face to ask, "WHAT happened, Nando?"

"Damn."

4-H Horse Camp or I loved the girls, and the horses were great too.

I was a teenager and, of course, knew everything about horses. After all, I trained racehorses.

Horse Camp, however, was the proper toes up, heels down, elbows in, posting school, you know the drill. Students wore riding pants, tall black boots, black helmets (helmets?) and carried pretty riding crops. Heck, I was used to tennis shoes, jeans, t-shirts and a stick grabbed from the tree I slid under. Nevertheless, I was a quick study, and learned to ride "properly". It was good because now I can look "proper" should there ever be a need. Young green thoroughbreds don't care what you look like on them. Your goal is to stay on and make them go where you want. According to mom, I rode like a cowboy and loved the thought of myself as a cowboy riding racehorses. Visualize it, floppy arms like the wings

You can never be too careful.

of an ostrich - flapping, but not quite flying. There is nothing better than racing through the trees, sitting high on a horse, with short stirrups that make your legs act like magical shock absorbers. You're almost floating until the horse makes an unexpected move that sends you tumbling. For the record, I now ride with long stirrups. They give you more balance and control on an uneasy 2 year-old.

Loading horses was fun - Unless you were careless, which was not permitted

Alex and I, both over 6 feet tall, relished the fact that mom often needed us to help load. We could literally lift a horse from behind into the trailer. Often at 5:30 in the morning wearing bath robes and tennis shoes and half asleep we would stand on either side of a horse, latch our arms together behind it's butt, lift the little jerk into the trailer, slam the door, and go back to bed and to sleep. Occasionally it wasn't that easy. (Not much is easy dealing with young thoroughbreds.) If the horse flipped back, we'd jump out of the way shaking our heads in the knowledge that we weren't going back to bed anytime soon.

Sparks from iron shoes on concrete in the darkness before dawn was entertainment in its own right. At the time, I thought it was cool. Sometimes we blindfolded the horses or lured them in with feed. We did whatever it took get the idiot horse in the trailer.

Eventually Alex and I grew up and left home. And yes, necessity and my mother of invention came into play. She figured out another way to get them into the trailer. But, you can read all about it in this book. . . surely she knows better than I.

Speaking of the Mother of Invention

On a visit home I saw a pair of blue jeans down by the lake. They were ordinary looking except they were full of sand, each leg tied at the bottom with hay strings. They were straddled on the top plank of the board fence. I looked at mom bewildered. She grinned and beamed saying, "My new way of breaking horses. You put 'Mr. Blue Jeans' (what a name!), in the saddle, tie him down, let him flop and round pen the horse until he gets tired. You get on him when he's broken. No more bucking horses and aching bones." Great idea. Necessity is the mother of invention.

However, cowboying and showing off in front of my girlfriends was more exciting.

A Typical Day at the Track or What Is Typical On a Day at the Track?

It was a hot Miami day. So hot that getting hosed down just rinsed you off before your next sweat bath. We were at Hialeah Race Track for a race that afternoon. Mom was dressed up wearing a pretty sundress, high heels and makeup. She was beautiful, ready for the win picture. She deserved to win that day. It was her day.

Our horse had run well the last time out and was sitting on a win. We had shipped in the day before and mom was going to be the owner today, not the groom. At the ripe old age of 15, I could handle anything and was proud of my ability to do so.

I lead the horse to the paddock. He was SWEATING. . White foam lathered his body from his rear hind quarters to his chest. I knew how he felt as I was wearing my Rancho Del Castillo hat and shirt, my Levi jeans and my laced leather work boots. Sweat was oozing from my pores. The leather shank was so slippery I'd tied a knot in the end to prevent it from slipping through my hands. People were crowded around the saddling area in their brightly colored clothes. Our horse was the favorite, which made me very nervous. Mom saw how I felt. She whispered reassuringly to me that she was there and everything

A day with horses is never typical.

would be OK. She started saddling him, smiling as she patted him and tightened the cinch. I was holding his head and jingling the shank in an effort to keep him calm.

Who was sweating more, me or the horse? Who could tell? Suddenly he reared straight up his front hooves flashing by either side of my head. As they came down, they scraped my chest. Mom grabbed him. She shanked him yelling, "Are you all right Nando?" I feebly muttered I was. She then uttered a few well directed profanities at the horse, he calmed down and was handed back to me. The jock was legged up in front of an awed crowd. Mom continued her ritual, casually walking beside the jockey giving him a pat on his leg and saying "Via Con Dios". She looked at me and smiled as she moved to stand with the other owners in the beautiful paddock.

That was my mom. That is my mom. Did it faze her? Who would know?

Did it faze me? Oh yeah.

Did we win? It didn't even matter. We were horse trainers. This was our life and our family.

Common Sense - I Have. Have I always? Maybe.

Or maybe I just learned it from being a knucklehead. Nevertheless I still use common sense today. Mom always said, "If you're going to do something, do it right the first time so you don't have to come back and do it again"

Duh! But think about that for a second. Who is going to come back and do it right the next time? That's right, most likely you. I learned that quickly and so will you. It's ingrained in me, no matter what I'm doing. Farm life is wonderful. Look at the lessons you learn without attending school. Although sometimes an expensive school would have been easier than the costly lessons we learned.

Sometimes I wonder why and how we ever did it, but we survived and can share it with you. Would I change a thing in my life? Back then, maybe. Today, no. I'm the person I am because I learned the hard way. You're being given some insight. Will you use it? I hope so. Will you learn the hard way? Sure. Will you be better for it? Definitely.

There ain't nothing like standing next to your mother while she jumps, yells and pounds on you as your horse comes from behind to win the race.

After finishing these few stories, seeing mom at Easter and going back to Tampa Bay Downs, memories flooded my mind. I miss it... I loved it... It will always be an important part of my life... and I hope yours.

I was very touched by Nando's stories. As a parent you never know how you are affecting your children in the process of raising them. It is gratifying to hear them say when they reach age thirty something, "You know, Mom, you were right."

Enjoy the book and remember: if you can think it, you can do it.

RIDERS- A FAMILY AFFAIR
MAKING DO MEANS USING YOUR KIDS!
(OR...I NEVER ASKED THEM TO DO ANYTHING I HADN'T DONE!)

by Alexander Del Castillo with comments by his mother

If you've read my Mom's book, you might recall a vignette involving me and a colt named Epidemic. The gist of the story was that my size, strength, and eighteen-year-old hubris were no match for that animal's brute power and single-mindedness. While it is true that the horse loped back to the barn riderless and I limped back with "pieces of a tree sticking from my clothes," I feel that some of the details of the events leading up to that very low point in my equestrian experience might prove enlightening or, at the very least, entertaining to the aspiring Backyard Trainer.

First of all, I was nineteen. I know that because I was back home after an academically unremarkable year and a half at Tulane and awaiting processing into the Navy. I was less than thrilled with my achievements (or rather lack of any) of late and chaffed at the prospect of living at home and working for my mother. Ironically, just about the only thing in which I took pride was my ability as a horseman. Mom, my brother Nando, Victoria my sister, and I had not yet come across the horse that was our match. We regularly trailered and broke horses upon which other experienced 'trainers' had long since quit. Occasionally one would come along and defy the collective abilities of my family and any of the girls who rode for my Mom. It was at this point that I was usually called upon to show the animal the way of virtue.

By the age of ten, it was clear that a combination of genes and nutrition had made my prospects of ever being a jockey somewhat less than bleak. Mine was a physiogamy more suited for carrying heavy loads or digging fence post holes (that, alas, is another story). Nonetheless, having pretty much grown up on horseback, I was a good rider and was from time to time tasked to break problem horses of some of their nastier habits. These habits included, but in no means were limited to, bolting, bucking, rearing all the way up and over in order to squish the hapless rider (another horse, another story), and just plain running away. This is the story about one who ran away.

I was big and strong and used it to my advantage, but never considered myself stronger than the horse. I was smarter than the horse, though only marginally so or I would not have mounted many of them. I used that small advantage along with my size and persistence to convince the animals that I was stronger and resistance was futile. The patient application of this philosophy over time enabled me to cure Mom's problem horses of their vices. Most of the time anyway. Epidemic was not your typical Thoroughbred. Whereas most of Mom's charges exhibited the graceful, long boned physiques that have characterized the breed since the time of Eclipse, Epidemic seemed born of an earlier, less gentile era. Muscle and sinew thrust out against taut skin that seemed barely able to contain the power of the animal. Half again as large as anything on the farm, the horse looked better suited for a knight clad in plate mail than a jockey in racing silks.

 **You never know when you'll meet your match.**

That morning Mother and I had a rather heated disagreement over who should clean some tack. I felt Nando, who had soiled it in the making of a Mountain Dew commercial, should share in the chore. Mom disagreed, saying that my pay as wrangler in the filming covered such things. I guessed the "star" couldn't sully himself with such drudgery. As if it wasn't bad enough that I had been relegated to saddling, and cooling my younger brother's mounts. Suffice to say, I was less than pleased with my ever-expanding job description (which incidentally, would involve fence post holes on at least one occasion), especially since I'd already been paid. Each additional job lowered what had been a very enticing hourly wage. But I digress...

Anyway, I was muttering and grumbling unprintables as I scrubbed the muck from a saddle when the sun went out. Or so it seemed. The local eclipse had been performed by Epidemic, who gazed curiously at me. I noted the unbroken ring of white around the animal's irises; eyes open too wide, as if constantly in a state of surprise. I've found that to be a common trait among many equine psycho cases. The horse was blithely unaware of my mother, who struggled vainly with his reins and hadn't yet noticed me or the fact that Epidemic had effortlessly draggged her some hundred feet from the wash racks to where I was working. As I watched her struggles, an evil smirk crept over my face, and I forgot whatever I might have just learned about Epidemic's mental state. Mother finally looked up, and noticing me, her face darkened for an instant before it settled into a pleasant, though somewhat strained continence and she said brightly, "Oh! Hi Alex, I see you've met Epidemic," as if none of the morning's unpleasantries had occurred. "He's got a bit of a mind of his own...," she continued as she straightened out the reins in her hands, regaining her composure and a modicum of control over the animal who, for the time being seemed content to munch on the grass at my feet, casting a wary eye on the convening humans. I decided to take the proffered olive branch, no good came from fighting with Mom. I could see where this was headed and wasn't particularly averse. Besides, it was an excuse to take a break from those cursed saddles.

"Big sonofagun, looks like, he should be pulling a beerwagon or something," I said. "Has he got any speed?" I asked. "Seems so, but he's rough, goes where and how he likes, the trees, the road, the usual hot blooded teenager stuff. But now the girls are afraid to ride him," she replied, continuing, "I was going to get Nando to take him for a few turns around the grove but I haven't seen him since he left to get those promo shots taken for the modeling people, so I guess I'll just have to give him a try. Can you give me a leg up, I'm not as flexible as I used to be." Sheesh, first the peace offering, then the dare, and finally, the coup de grace - guilt. Where do mothers learn to manipulate their progeny so? Of course I said, "Crimeny Mom, just give me the brain bucket and a leg up, I never was that flexible and whatchamajiggit here is as tall as me."

"Epidemic", she grunted, as I placed my left foot in the interlaced finger of her hands, jumped with my right and heaved my bulk over the animal's back. As I got situated, feet in stirrups, reins in hand and all that, Epidemic continued to chomp placidly at the bahia grass through his bit. The sudden addition of some 260 pounds to his back affected him not one iota. I noted this as I surveyed the view from my new perch. Mother's face

Horses are bigger - we must be smarter.

was cast in our shadow, and from it issued the same tired and dire warnings about the horse, the trees and the road which I usually got once she had succeeded in getting me in the saddle of one of her nut cases. Only this time, there seemed to be an edge in her voice. Maybe she was still mad at me from this morning and only being nice to get me to ride her monster. As I contemplated, my observation of the horse's unnatural strength went the way of the one about his eyes. I don't suppose it would have mattered if I had put together the signs I saw. Things would have turned out the same anyway.

So, with a "click click" of the tongue and a squeeze of the legs I set off to exercise Epidemic. Only he was having none of it. Not only was he having none of it, I don't think he was aware of any of it. Save for the sounds of chomping and the occasional jerk of head as the horse pulled at the grass, I might have been on top of a statue out in front of a library for all the response I was getting. Mom just smiled and said something about the horse living in its own world, apart from the rest of us. After two or three bouts of clicking and squeezing, and even a couple of kicks, it was clear that I wasn't even a nuisance to that beast. I heaved at the reins, intending to jerk the brute's head from the grass and get his attention. Nothing. In fact, he almost pulled me over his shoulder as he stretched to reach for more grass. Mom smiled on, mutely, thank God. Okay, it was time to augment the strength with the brains I was supposed to have. Sure the animal was strong, very strong, actually. But I knew how to apply my comparatively meager strength for the most effect. Again, I held no illusions about our relative strengths, but I figured I could probably use most of mine to at least make him aware of my presence. Making him do my bidding was another task entirely, and I chose not to contemplate how I intended to do that just yet. First things first.

I choked up on the left rein with both hands, settled my weight into my legs and feet and gave a mighty heave. Epidemic's head came up and around slowly and he regarded the strange troublesome creature on his back with his crazy, all around white eyes. I thought I saw a glint of comprehension before he turned his head forward, almost taking me with it before I had the good sense to relent, and started trotting off towards the road in front of our ranch that led to the grove where Mom exercised her horses. I gathered the reins and my composure, hoping to at least look like I was in some semblance of control, looking over my shoulder I caught a glimpse of Mother, who seemed to be smiling. Hands full of reins and mind full of the ride ahead, I smiled back, half triumphantly and half nervously, not stopping to consider the knowing look that framed Mom's grin, or its ramifications.

Mark Twain once wrote that if horses knew their strength, men would not ride. Having been acquainted with one who did (yet another horse and another story), I heartily agree with Mr. Twain's thesis. I do not think Epidemic knew his strength, not because he had been conned by clever riders like me (in fact he never was), but because he had never met his equal. To my knowledge, no man or artifact or object of nature ever came between that horse and his goal. Such was his strength that trees, fences, gates and, least of all, men were never obstacles or even factors in whatever passed for reasoning in his pea brain. Epidemic pretty much did as he pleased. Most of the time it pleased him to munch on the

 **Some horses have a mind of their own.**

grass in the pastures and sometimes it pleased him to run. The rider was of no consequence to the horse save in the rider's capacity to suggest to Epidemic that it might please him to run, as I had just done. I began to come to these realizations as Epidemic trotted ever faster along the shoulder of the road leading to the grove, under no guidance from me. Beneath me, tree like legs pistoned up and down from a barrel chest. Between the reins a neck as thick as my own body arched, holding a huge head whose I mouth I was beginning to suspect of being completely devoid of tactile nerve endings. In-as-much as I had, after great effort, some success in my ability to move Epidemic's head in the general direction in which I wanted to go, I began to form my riding strategy around that small advantage. It was a two-step plan:
1) Stay on horse.
2) Attempt to point horse in direction (i.e. away from trees) such that Step 1 remains possible.

After only one close encounter with the white board fence in front of the house (which, by the way, led to the aforementioned post hole digging later), I seemed to be executing my plan pretty well. Epidemic was strong, and not exactly Mr. Ed in the brains department, but at least he wasn't malicious, and like I said before, he did not really pay much attention to the rider one way or the other. Basically, I just turned his head in the direction I wanted to go and, bless his big heart, he usually followed it. The main flaw in my system was that though I could more or less control the horse's direction, I had not attempted to do so at above a trot and really had no empirical data on its feasibility at higher velocities. I also had not given a lot of consideration to stopping. As it was, steps 1 and 2 were keeping me pretty busy. I guess I figured if worst came to worst, Epidemic would eventually tire or get hungry. Worst would be a lot worse than I had anticipated.

Finally clear of the road and the fence, I pointed Epidemic down the row in the grove that served as the first straightaway of mother's exercise track. It ran slightly downhill towards the lake, was some thirty feet across and flanked by orange trees. Near the turn, the grove stopped and ample room was provided for a wide right turn into the next straightaway along the beach. I let Epidemic have his head, as they say, and he took it and his body away down the row so fast that I was almost left sitting in midair, sans horse. Fortunately I managed to grab a handful of mane and claw my way back into some semblance of a stable riding position. I glanced past my knee and saw hooves exploding through the loose sandy ground of the grove. I felt the horse's strides lengthening as he accelerated. Finally, looking up from the violence of those flashing hooves, past Epidemic's outstretched neck, bobbing head, and pinned ears, my path through the grove was an indistinct blur. The trees were green walls, their ripening fruit extruded into orange streaks by our ever increasing speed. In time with my mount's stride, I crept further forward, my head way up on his neck, my legs locked in a death grip starting just aft of his withers. I finally drew a breath past gritted teeth and looked through squinted eyes at the turn into the lakefront stretch as it drew nearer at an impossible rate. I thought to myself, "Yee-ha".

Here was the reason I continued to ride. Even though it involved so many chores and inconveniences, nothing gave me the rush that I got from steering over one thousand

Always leave a "ride" plan.
Be sure someone knows
where you are.

pounds of living, breathing flesh, blood and bone around the course. Later in life, I would feel the same way piloting my sailboat through heavy weather, the heaving sea beneath my feet and howling wind in my face. The thrill was not from mere speed or raw power (my motorcycle was three times faster with presumably one hundred odd times the power of the single beast I now rode) yet riding my bike at the edge of the envelope only struck me as stupid. Ironically, mother was concerned for my physical well being when I rode the Kawasaki, not so much with the horses. The only thrill on the bike was the artificial rush of going fast enough to scare the hell out of yourself. Anyone can twist the wick and hold on, the results are predictable and were made possible by someone else's understanding of thermodynamics and mechanics. The interaction between a horse and rider is more sublime; there is usually some art there, when it's good.

It was not going so good. "Yee-ha" begat "Whuh-oh" as Epidemic and I careened towards the turn. Oblivious of his rider, the horse was beginning to cheat into the turn, a fact made all the more poignant to me as leaves and branches slashed across my body, punctuated by the thumps of unripened fruit bouncing off my helmet and shoulder. I knew I had to take action lest I be scraped off by a bough. Cheating into the turn is natural for most horses, not just head cases, so I was mostly annoyed at the interruption of my reverie rather than apprehensive. I knew the usual counter, taking a little outside rein and cuing with my legs (inside knee forward, outside knee back), was a little too subtle for Epidemic, so I decided to go with Plan B, which had yet to fail me. Plan B, made possible by my size and strength, was to choke up on the outside rein, dig in with outside foot and haul the offender's head around and back towards the center of the course. A little heavy handed, to say the least, but those branches smarted. So I set my foot, got some rein and hauled around, all the while maintaining my balance as the horse tried to run out from under me and the trees tried to snatch me. But something was wrong, the pull was too easy and I suddenly was reeling from that same feeling one gets when he steps into an unexpected hole. I found myself twisted sideways on my mount, reins against my chest. I was barely hanging on, with my right hand buried in Epidemic's mane and my right knee hooked over his withers. The saddle had slipped and I was sliding down towards the same thundering hooves I had just been admiring.

"Should'a checked the cinch," I hissed through clenched teeth as I heaved myself back over the withers, saddle and, all at once proud of having recovered from my slip and annoyed at having made it in the first place. I ignored the fact that I had lost my right stirrup in the slip. Mom had taught us never to rely on them anyway and I had more pressing matters to attend to, the stirrup could wait. Buoyed by my recovery from my gaffe, I redoubled my efforts to regain control of the horse. Stirrups or not, I clenched my legs around him, dug my heels in and got a death grip on his mane with my right hand. Epidemic got the message, but the wrong one. I felt him dig in, stretch out and angle even tighter into the turn. The branches were getting thick now, and disconcertingly close, they bothered Epidemic not a whit. My revised plan was pretty simple; lean down and become one with the horse and hold on for dear life. It had worked in the past, eventually they all tired, or at least got hungry I thought/hoped. I figured as long as I stayed low enough, I'd make it through wherever the horse thought he could run. I neglected to consider the fact

Check your gear before you mount.

that this particular horse did not really think much, especially when it came to running. The beginning of the end came with a crack, as the top of my helmet struck an arm thick branch.

The horrible instant following the crack during which I was wondering how much of the crack was orange tree branch and how much was my neck was curtailed by my feeling of being knocked back and up. The horse was bouncing under my tailbone in a way that was completely unnatural and, for what it was worth, my sensation of it reassured me that my spinal cord was still intact. I saw a quick montage of images, tree, sky, tree, horse, earth, and then black as I struck the ground.

"Badadump, badadump, badadump," was what I heard as I regained my senses. Damn horse. The sound of Epidemic's hooves faded, leaving me listening to the pounding of my heart. "Well," I thought, "that's a good sign," as I began to take stock of my condition. Fingers and toes wiggled OK so I decided to try my eyes. I opened them and saw nothing. Shocked, I gasped, and got a mouthful of sand for my trouble. My head had been buried up to my shoulders in the soft sugar sand of the grove. Upon extracting my head and sitting back, I found I could both see and, with some effort, breathe. Looking back up the course, I surveyed the scene of my demise, noting the fresh tracks and broken branches. I sat near my apparent point of impact, at the apex of a confused furrow in the sand, some twenty feet from the nearest hoof prints. Except for the tuft of mane still clenched in my right hand, there was no other sign of Epidemic. Damn horse.

As I labored to trudge through the same viscous sand that Epidemic and I had so recently flown over, the galvanizing effect of my adrenaline started to wane and the pain began to make itself known. The usual stuff, neck, shoulders, back, was there, and though unpleasant, did not really bother me much. I'd been thrown before, that was the price one pays for miscues or inattention to a high-strung mount. You walk it off and get back on the horse like the old saying. This time there was a different kind of pain, really more anguish. If it had any physical manifestation at all, I would attribute to it a slight discomfort in the pit of my gut. It was not just the usual shame or embarrassment one felt after being bested by a horse. I came to realize that the uncertain, queasy feeling I was experiencing started when I first lost control of Epidemic and was made more acute by one fact I had worked so hard to deny, for if I would have accepted it, it would have meant conceding that I had no business being on that horse in the first place. The fact of the matter was, I was never in control of Epidemic. I had never been so impotent or inconsequential to a mount, and that shook me. It scared me. Fear was one feeling I was loath to ever feel around a horse. They sensed it in their riders and were thus emboldened. Sure, I'd been apprehensive before, about bucking or biting or being thrown, but I could usually counter those behaviors and carry on. I could do nothing of the sort with Epidemic. He would do as he pleased and I was like the saddle, just another minor bother. I shuddered to think of what might have happened if Epidemic had actually decided to cause me harm. Cognizant of, though not at all comfortable with my newly realized stature in the world of horses and men, I plodded on through the orange grove, wondering if I would indeed get back up on Epidemic. Damn horse.

Pay attention to your horse.

COMMENTS! You can see that my sonny boy should have been a fiction writer...surely it wasn't that bad to be careening through the woods with an uncontrollable steed. But there are lessons to be learned here. Keep rank horses in a confined area until you know you can handle them. Horses like Epidemic should only be handled by professionals and they may decide that this kind of horse is too dangerous to train. Safety must be your number one goal I would know better than to try and train a horse like that today. Then, we were younger and less experienced. Of course now that they are over twenty-one, my children may be planning to charge me with child abuse.

Seriously, all of the children have come back to me as adults and assured me that the experience of having to work together and keep the farm going prepared them for the real world. They learned responsibility early and shouldered it well. Feeding three times a day, rain or shine, walking colicky horses, mending fences, maintaining trucks and trailers, breaking and training the youngsters, being humiliated time and time again when we would lose-all of this went into the fabric of their childhood. It gave them a good perspective of life - you can't win them all. But when you do win, what a high! And they know from experience that you've got to be in the body of the race to have a shot at winning!

WHUH- OH!

Safety must always be your goal.

Jacki

Nando

ALEX

Victoria

The Children!

As We Say Good-bye ...

SAYING GOOD-BYE TO YOUR BACKYARD RACEHORSE

A WORD ABOUT EUTHANASIA

SAYING GOOD-BYE TO
YOUR BACKYARD RACEHORSE

by Caren Sanders, Haddock, GA

There comes a time in every horse owner's life when the difficult decision must be made to reduce the number of horses you own. Finding a new owner for your horse can be a very difficult, traumatic, and stressful process. I know from firsthand experience. You want the best home for the animal, the same type of love and care that you have provided. There are a number of methods that I have discovered that might be helpful.

The first part of the process is to acknowledge that you must find a new home for Buddy. This action can be the hardest part of anything you will do, specially if you have raised Buddy in your "back yard". Personal medical reasons, financial concerns, relocation to a new job, or just deciding that the horse business is not your cup of tea are but a few of the reasons you might have to say good-bye to your back yard racehorse.

Once you have made the decision to say good-bye, you will probably feel sad and come up with a thousand ways to avoid the dastardly deed. You'll even be prone to tears. These are all normal responses and it's best to get your feeling over and done with. Talk to your friends about what you are going to do. Hearing yourself say, "I have to find a new home for Buddy." will help you accept the reality of the task. And do your crying - this is no less a traumatic than a family member moving to a foreign country or the death of a family member. Just don't let your emotions take control.

The first person to talk to is your vet. If your vet is like mine, not only is he the provider of your horse care, he's also a trusted friend who tells it like it is. Your vet may know someone who is looking for a horse just like yours who will provide Buddy with a good and loving home.

If you need the money and can sell your horse, you might want to consider the auction route. There is a cost to this route if you use an agent to prep the horse and take the horse to auction. The down side is that you probably won't see the potential owner before the sale to size up whether Buddy will get a good home and if you sell Buddy without a minimum bid above the meat price, Buddy could be bought cheaply for meat.

On the other hand, if your horse is not viable for sale due to age, injury or breeding, you need to try the private sale route. This can be very frustrating since you will have people call to see your horse and never showup. But if you are worried about the care of your horse, you can size up people when they come to see the horse. If you have not talked about price, and don't like the people you are dealing with, you can always jack-up the price. I did this once when a man in a pickup truck and trailer pulled up at my door and asked if I had any horses for sale. I said none at a price that he was willing to pay and told him to get off my property. SO BEWARE - DON'T LET SOMEONE MAKE YOU AN OFFER YOU CAN'T REFUSE WHEN YOU ARE VULNERABLE.

What can you do with Buddy, if he has an injury that precludes him from being the dream three day eventing horse? Well, there are a number of really good alternatives.

Check with your local 4-H. You never know when the 4-H is looking for a horse for a project. Buddy might just fill the bill. The 4-H will probably not have the funds to buy

Look carefully for a new home.

the horse. Check with the IRS or your tax advisor to see if Buddy can be considered as a charitable contribution. If Buddy is sound and a gelding, but not very attractive in the eyes of prospective buyers, check out organizations that provide riding for the handicapped. Those that I've contacted don't want fillies, mares or stallions due to their temperament. The horses they accept get tons of love and are doing a good service to society (again check on charitable contribution status).

Contact police in large cities to see if they have an equine squad in need of horses. Often they will take the horse for a specified length of time to see if the horse will fit in the program. If it does not, the horse is returned to you.

There are people around who will take horses that are unwanted and find them homes. I contacted a woman some time back who had such a program. She was a 4-H official in her home state and would take horses if you pay pre-shipping vetting, shots, and provide transportation to her farm. I found her through an add in an equine magazine. I contacted the magazine to check out her credentials. As far as they knew, she was legitimate. She was going to be the last resort for my two fillies. I have recently seen some of her adds. She often describes a few of the horses that she has taken in and the new homes that she has found for them. You'd be surprised, but some of the mares have been sent to stallions in Lexington for breeding!!!

There is also the New York State Thoroughbred Retirement Farm which I believe only takes formerly raced geldings. The horses are cared for my inmates at an upstate New York prison. There are similar prison programs in other states.

Finally, there is donation to equestrian programs at colleges. I found this approach through a friend. The college had a four--year equine program and was looking for Thoroughbred mares to breed to Norwegian warm bloods. I paid for all pre-shipping, vet work and shipping. I signed their papers over to the college and was able to take a tax deduction for the value of the donation. There are certain guidelines relative to determining the value of the contribution. Check with the IRS or your tax advisor before entering into this deal.

I visited the college, was happy with the environment and off went the two fillies. Within 60 days of their arrival at the school, they were in foal. To locate colleges with equine programs, check the classified adds in magazines such as *Equus* and *the Blood Horse*. If you decide to go this route, choose a school that your can visit. Meet with the person in charge of the program. See the facilities and be sure in your own mind that you are happy with the situation. While I went with the first school I contacted because it was highly recommended and lived up to its billing, there are other schools outs there - shop around.

If your state university has an animal husbandry program or vet school, check with them to see if they need horses for study programs or student work. Don't forget to check websites about horses for sale or donations.

These are only a few ideas. It may take time to find a good home for your horse, but if you do, you'll feel more comfortable with this very difficult decision.

Someone out there will give your horse a good home.

A WORD ABOUT EUTHANASIA

Since we have discussed what to do with a horse that no longer fits your program, it is necessary to mention horses who have an illness or infirmity that impairs quality of life. My dear sweet First Prediction was starting to look poor. At home she had always managed to get along with her founder problems and I had vowed that when she was no longer able to eat and be comfortable I would relieve her from her pain. At home she could go into the lake and float when she wanted the weight off her feet. She started to lay down much more and even with abundant feed she was not keeping her weight. I went out and looked at her one day and I thought...my goodness...she looks so poor! I loaded her into the trailer and took her to the University Hospital at Gainesville to see if there was something that would give her relief from her feet that were constantly abscessing.

On my way to the hospital as I looked out my rear view mirror at the trailer, I saw her peek out her head and let the wind ruffle her mane...she loved to ride in the trailer. We had done over a hundred trips to the races together and she ran soundly in every one. I know she enjoyed the ride.

It tugged my heart to think it was a high fever and virus that crippled this noble mare and foundered her.

She recovered from the first bout of founder but had a relapse that she was not able to overcome. One look at the x rays showed that there was no bone left in her feet.

The vet, Dr. Ethell, said he didn't know how she was even walking at all. I was truly horrified when I saw how deteriorated her hoofs were. She was indeed walking on pure heart. After saying goodbye to her and asking her forgiveness for the suffering she must have had the last month or so, she was put down. My heart is heavy when I remember she is no longer in her pasture on the lake.

You know why horses are considered so noble? It is because they don't scream or complain-they just carry on.

First Prediction's feet don't hurt anymore.

Horses
are Noble!

AS
WE
SAY
GOOD-BYE

In the previous pages, I hope to have given to you the ESSENCE of my horse training methods. **You must adapt them to your circumstances and that which suits you. A trainer's role is to develop the PERSONAL BEST of each animal...without breaking him down in the process.** People think I'm naive when I say good training can be done without medications and chemical enhancements. If I had not had the joy of a somewhat talented horse, I might have followed the advice of so many. Use the stuff or be at a disadvantage. But I had a decent horse ... I kept her sound enough to run for more than four years and earn over $300,000. Though she was not brilliant, she was wonderfully game and useful. She ran over one hundred times, and she only had problems when I couldn't get enough races to keep her fit. She was eligible for very few races and needed to run every ten to fourteen days to be at her tightest. The joy of having a stakes class filly who never ran on medication, was never unsound, and who was turned out every day of her life to be a horse, has given me the courage to write this manual. I want others to have and achieve the same goals.

A few newspaper articles are included to give you an idea of what a game mare FIRST PREDICTION was.

Talented and truly gifted horses are few and far between. Most horses are lucky to win bottom of the barrel claiming races. But even this kind of racing can be fun ... and your horse may last many years. If you run off the farm, the expenses are minimal and the horse has a better chance of paying his way.

Enter the Racing Industry cautiously ... one horse at time ... and invest your money carefully. If you start out with a reasonably priced horse ... the horse doesn't know what he cost ... and follow this program, you can be successful. Be patient and do your homework well. Learn everything you can about the Anatomy and Physiology of the horse. Read, study, and attend instructional seminars. Always follow your instincts about your animal. Above all - use your common sense.

**Enter the business cautiously . . .
one horse at a time.**

Beware of trainers and veterinarians who want to "give your horse a little something" to help him when he has an injury . . . and thus keep him running when he should rest. Bute is fine occasionally. It helps a lot of horses "warm out" of certain aches and pains. Remember, injecting ankles and knees with cortisone, administering steroids and continuing to race is setting your horse up for breakdown. Read the vet bills from your trainer at the track. Learn the names of drugs that are legitimately helping your animal, and learn those which are painkillers given a day or two before a race. Banamine, Ketofen, steroids, etc., may "help" a horse get through a race, but are short term fixes that cause long term damage.

Some of you will feel my suggestions are impractical in the "real life" atmosphere of horse racing. So be it. **I am in this for the long run . . . for the long term good of the horse and racing. WE MUST CLEAN UP OUR OWN ACT OR IT WILL BE DONE FOR US.** What better way to improve our image than by example . . . by running sound, useful, horses year in and year out. Horses are not disposable items to be weeded through in search of the good horse. I must train each and every animal with the proper foundation. That takes time . . . time that owners are not willing to spend unless they understand and agree with the reasons. Believe me, they will spend time later, with chips in young joints, bowed tendons, etc. Spend it early or spend it late. My program allows you to raise and develop your animal easily, with no real pressure until the animal is mature and physically and mentally more able to withstand the rigors of racing.

Doesn't that make sense? A good foundation for horses (and children) is best done while they are young and growing. **What they become, once fit, healthy, and sound, will depend upon their inherent genetic ability . . . their own individual "gift" of speed. Understand that all the training and galloping and drugging in the world will not make a horse run faster than he is meant to run. Give him the necessary time to develop the guts to withstand his own speed.**

I have enjoyed having this dialogue with you. If any of you have been inspired to pursue the great sport of horse racing with an attitude of fair play, I have achieved my goal. **Each and everyone of you that starts racing sound, fit horses and wins, is a solid reinforcement that the little guy can win!** That's a great message for everyone. I hope our relationship doesn't end here. The *Backyard Racehorse Forum* is now on line at Yahoo keyword "groups:backyardracehorse messages". I would appreciate input from all of you out in the field. The names of trainers willing to work with our style of training can be found in the Forum. The forum is a network for backyard owners and trainers to share, to exchange ideas, and to encourage and support each other. Racing varies drastically from one end of the country to the other. Working together we can have a positive impact on racing and win races!

GOOD LUCK AND GOD BLESS YOU!

GLOSSARY

Firing?

BLISTER?

Maiden?

CRIBBING?

Sesamoiditis?

Bog Spavin?

DAM?

SiRE?

GLOSSARY

The following are terms common, sometimes unique, to the racetrack environment.

ACEY DEUCY - A style of riding in which the right stirrup is shorter than the left enabling the jockey to balance more easily on turns.

ACROSS THE BOARD - A method of wagering on a horse to win, place and show. If the horse wins, the player collects three ways.

ACTH - Adrenocorticotropic hormone. It stimulates the adrenal glands to produce their own steroids. If used over a long period of time, it will suppress the horse's own adrenal glands. It is very harmful long term. Make sure you know what is being given to your horse. The accumulation of all of these medications definitely affect the overall structure and health of your horse.

ACTION - Besides the meaning associated with wagering, this term is used to describe a horse's manner of moving.

ADDED MONEY - That money which is added to a purse by the racing association (track), or by sponsors, state-bred'" programs or other funds added to the money gathered by nomination, entry, sustaining and other fees coming from the horsemen.

ADDED WEIGHT-The racehorse is carrying more weight than the conditions of the race require (and that the program states)-usually because the jockey "failed to make weight."

AEROBIC - (With air.) The phase of training where your horse gallops within himself, comfortably and for miles without going into oxygen debt.

AGE - All racehorses have January I of the year they were born as their official birth date, regardless of their foaling date.

ALL OUT - Indicates that the running horse has extended itself to its utmost.

ALL-AGE RACE - A race for horses two years old and up.

ALLOWANCE RACE - A race where horses run without a claiming price. Every track has a limit on the price of claiming races. Allowance races are a step above the highest claiming races. In allowance races certain conditions (non-winners of two races in a lifetime, for example) are met. A good allowance horse is a very valuable commodity.

ALSO ELIGIBLE - An entered horse that will race only if a scratch occurs (at or prior to scratch time) in the body of the field.

ALSO-RAN - Used to describe a horse that did not finish in the money (first, second or third).

ANABOLIC STEROIDS - The steroids you hear so much about in human sports. They create more muscle mass on the animal and make fillies and geldings aggressive. They produce an "Arnold Schwartzenhorse" according to Dr. Ruth James. Long term use of this on fillies can impair their ability to reproduce. It is contraindicated in colts. Muscle can become hyper developed and tear itself from the bone.

ANAEROBIC - (Without air.) When the horse is galloping hard and is going into oxygen debt he is in an anaerobic state. He will be huffing and puffing after the run to repay the oxygen debt to his muscle. The further he can go before running out of oxygen, the better the race horse he will be.

ANHIDROSIS - A non-sweater. Horses with the inability to sweat.

ANTHELMINTIC - A drug for killing worms or parasites.

APPRENTICE - Rookie jockey who receives weight allowances.

APPRENTICE ALLOWANCE - The allowance or weight off allowed an apprentice jockey during his/her first year of riding. Uusually an apprentice or "bug" rider gets 10 lbs. off until his/her 35th winner. This gives younger, inexperienced riders a more even chance against older more experienced "journeyman" jockeys. This rule varies from state to state, and does not apply to Quarter Horse racing.

APRON - The (usually) paved area between the grand-stand and the racing surface.

ASSISTANT TRAINER - A person employed by a licensed trainer to assist and assume responsibility in the absence of that trainer in all the daily work, chores, saddling, etc. involved in the training of horses. Assistant trainers are required to be tested and licensed by state racing commissioners.

ARTHROCENTESIS - Puncture and aspiration of joint fluid.

ARTHROCHONDRITIS - Inflamed joint cartilage.

ARTHRODESIS - Surgically induced fusion of a joint.

AUSCULATION - The act of listening for sounds within the body, chiefly for determining the condition of the lungs, heart, pleura, abdomen, and intestines.

AUTHORIZED AGENT - A person licensed by the commission and appointed by a written instrument, signed and acknowledged before a notary public by the owner in whose behalf the agent will act.

AVERAGE-EARNINGS INDEX. (AEI) - A breeding statistic that compares racing earnings of a given stallion's (or mare's) foals to those of all other foals racing at that time. (An AEI of 1.00 is considered average; 2.00 is twice the average, etc.)

AZOTURIA - "Tying-up" (Monday Morning Sickness) - Severe painful cramping of large muscle masses, resulting in discoloration of the urine with the by-products of muscle destruction. Commonly triggered in fit horses who resume heavy exercise after a few days of rest without any reduction in grain ration. According to *The Merck Veterinary Manual, Seventh Edition* relates to excess total feed energy consumption.

"BABY RACE" - A race (as short as two furlongs) exclusively for two-year-olds.

BACK AT THE KNEE - An expression for a leg that appears to have a backward arc (with its center at the knee) when viewed from the side.

BACKSIDE - The stable and training area of a racetrack.

BACKSTRETCH - Straight or far-side of track between the turns; stable are.

BACK-UP TO THE WIRE - Take the horse in the wrong direction to the finish line.

"BAD DOER" - A horse with a poor appetite - a condition that may be due to nervousness or other (possibly stomach) problems.

BANDAGES - For horses, these come in two forms: I) Standing-used in the stall at rest, for therapeutic purposes, and 2) Racing-using Vet rap or ace type bandages for support of tendons and to prevent a horse from "running down" or burning his heels on the track surface as legs tire.

BASE-NARROW - The distance between the center lines of the limbs at their origin is greater than the center lines of the feet on the ground; will be broad-chested.

BASE-WIDE - Opposite of base-narrow.

"BAT" - Jargon for a jockey's whip (also known as a "crop" or "stick").

BAY - A horse color that consists of a brown coat (which can range from a yellow-tan to a bright auburn) and a black mane and tail. The muzzle and lower legs are always black, except where white markings are present.

BEAN - A firm bean shaped mass formed from dried secretions and urine salts in the pouch at the end of the penis of a male horse.

BEARING IN (OR OUT) - A horse that moves or lugs inward (to its left toward the inside rail) or outward while racing. May be due to weariness, infirmity, whip use by rider or rider's inability to control mount.

BELL - The signal sounded when the Official Starter opens the gates. (The term can also refer to a buzzer hit by a steward to mark the close of betting.)

BEST BET - Term used by track handicappers, tip sheets, selectors, etc., to signify the horse they feel most likely to win that day.

BETAMETHASONE - The generic name for one of the most potent corticosteroids. Regulates carbohydrate and protein use and acts as an anti-inflammatory.

BIT - The metal or rubber bar (attached to the bridle) that goes into a horse's mouth to give the rider "fine control" of the horse's head-movements and direction. Bits are of various designs, and are chosen according to the particular horse's racing "m.o."

BLACK - A horse color that is black, including the muzzle, flanks, mane, tail, and legs unless white markings are present.

BLACK TYPE - Used in a sale catalogue to designate a horse who has won or placed in a stakes. The name of a stakes winner is printed in boldface uppercase letters (i.e., **FIRST PREDICTION**), while the name of stakes-placed horse is in boldface upper- and lower-case letters (i.e. **First Prediction**).

BLANKET FINISH - Or photo-finish; in which two or more horses are very close at the finish (one can "throw a blanket over them"). Very common in American Quarter Horse racing.

BLAZE (A.K.A. STRIPE) - A term describing a large, white, vertical marking on a horse's face.

BLEEDER - A term used for horses suffering from Exercise-Induced Pulmonary Hemorrhaging, a predisposition to hemorrhaging from the nostrils either during a work, in a race or immediately following such exertion.

BLINKERS - A hood placed over a horse's head with cups sewn onto the eye openings. The cups prevent a horse from seeing anywhere but straight ahead, thus preventing distractions. The size of the cups are varied to allow a horse more or less peripheral vision.

BLISTER - A chemical ointment or liquid which, when applied to a limb, causes an acute inflammation. It is used to treat chronic conditions such as an osselet, ring bone, bowed tendon, etc. When a trainer says he is going to "blister" a particular area of the leg, it means he is going to apply a caustic chemical that will cause severe inflammation to the area. The theory is that the inflammatory reaction will bring increased blood supply to the area and hasten healing. Aggressive massages might do the same with a fraction of the trauma to the animal. Ask trusted vets what they think.

BLOW OUT - A very short (220 to 250 yard) workout at full speed. Used to put a horse on its toes before a race.

BOBBLE - A bad step out of the starting gate (often evidenced by the horse ducking its head or nearly going to its knees).

BOLT – When a horse swerves sharply from his lane or the regular course, also a runaway.

BOG SPAVIN - A chronic distention of the joint capsule of the hock that causes a swelling of the front-inside aspect of the hock joint.

BONE CHIPS - concussion can cause chips in the fetlock and knee joints. These injuries are most common in young racehorses asked to gallop at high speeds. Their immature ligaments and the fascia have not yet thickened enough to stand up to the force of concussion. Chips may also result from kicks. They can be surgically removed or they may just exist and not cause a problem. They are most likely to cause problems in areas of articulation.

BONE SPAVIN - Osteoarthritis or osteitis of the hock joint. Can be caused by conformation, concussion and mineral imbalance.

BOOK - Group of mares being bred to a stallion in a given year.

BOOKKEEPER - The person who manages track disbursements.

BOTTOM LINE - Of a horse's pedigree or bloodlines, which indicates the dam, grand dam, maternal grandsire, etc.

BOUNCE- A poor race run directly following a career- best or near-best performance.

BOWED TENDON - A traumatic injury to the flexor tendons behind the cannon bone as a result of severe strain in which there is tearing and stretching of tendon fibers. This gives a bowed appearance to the tendons externally. A Bow keeps a horse from ever running to his best ability.

BREAK MAIDEN - A term used in the case of either a jockey or a horse who wins a race for the first time. (Also known as "earning a diploma.")

BREAKAGE - That portion of the payoff to winning bettors that is retained by the association. In most North American racing jurisdictions payoffs are to the next lower dime (i.e., the computer calculates an actual payoff as being $4.47896 for $2.00, then the actual payoff will be $4.40 and the breakage is $.07896).

BREEDER - The breeder of an American Quarter Horse is considered to be the owner of the dam at the time of service, while the breeder of a Thoroughbred is the owner of the dam at the time of foaling.

BREEDERS' CUP - Thoroughbred racing's year-end championship, inaugurated in 1984. Known as Breeders' Cup Day, it consists of eight races, effective with the 1999 season, when the Filly and Mare Turf was run for the first time. Through 1998, it consisted of seven races. The event is conducted on one day at a different racetrack each year with purses and awards totaling $13 million. The races are the:

> $1 million Breeders' Cup Sprint, for 3-year-olds and up at six furlongs.
>
> $1 million Breeders' Cup Juvenile Fillies, for 2-year-old fillies at 1 1/16 miles.
>
> $2 million Breeders' Cup Distaff, for fillies and mares, 3-year-olds and up, at 1 1/8 miles
>
> $1 million Breeders' Cup Mile, for 3-year-olds and up at one mile on the turf.
>
> $1 million Bessemer Trust Breeders' Cup Juvenile, for 2-year-olds at 1 1/16 miles.
>
> $1 million Breeders' Cup Filly and Mare Turf, for fillies and mares, 3-year-olds and up, at 1 3/8 miles on the turf.
>
> $2 million Breeders' Cup Turf, for 3-year-olds and up, at 1 1/2 miles on the turf.
>
> $4 million Breeders' Cup Classic, for 3-year-olds and up, at 1 1/4 miles.

BREEZE - To encourage a horse to gallop out to his full speed, usually without whipping. That's saved for the "work".

BRIDLE - The headpiece, comprised of leather or nylon straps, to which both reins and bit are attached. (This is rider's basic means of controlling the racehorse.)

BROKE RIGHT OR BROKE LEFT - As the horse left the starting gate, it immediately and radically veered away from (indicating "right") or toward (indicating "left") the inside rail.

BROODMARE - A female horse that has been bred and is used to produce foals.

BUCKED SHIN - A painful swelling on the front surface of the cannon bone, associated with microscopic stress fracture or periostitis. Caused by concussion in young horses in which bones are not fully conditioned. Rest from training is important until soreness and inflammation have disappeared. Given appropriate sport-specific exercise, the cannon bone grows thicker and stronger with training. However cumulative overstressing or stresses in a new direction by higher speeds, can develop microfractures in the outer layer. The accompanying inflammation causes the horse pain.

BURR - A leather or rubber disc with protruding bristles. It is added to the bit to aid the rider in keeping the horse from running wide on turns.

BUGBOY - An apprentice jockey. (The moniker derives from the bug-like printer's mark which appears in the program next to the weight the horse will carry. Please see Chapter on "Jockeys" for full explanation of apprentices.)

BULLET WORK - The best time for the distance on the work tab for a given day at a track.

BULLRING - A racetrack with either a half-mile or 5/8ths mile oval.

BUTE (Butazolidin) - Trade name for Phenylbutazone, a frequently used nonsteroidal anti-inflammatory drug (NSAID). Recent studies have shown multiple side effects. See Medications, What They Are and What They Do.

BUY BACK - A horse put through public auction that did not reach his reserve and was retained by the consignor.

CALCIUM-PHOSPHORUS RATIO (CaP Ratio) - The dietary balance of these minerals; needs to be between 2:1 and 1:1 for normal bone and teeth formation..

CALF-KNEED or BACK AT THE KNEE - A conformational fault of the forelegs where the knee is seen to bend backwards when viewed from the side.

CAPILLARIES - Smallest of blood vessels; connect arteries with veins.

CAPILLARY REFILL TIME - The amount of time required for blood to return to the gums after application of pressure. One to two seconds is normal; slower refill time may indicate low blood pressure, shock or dehydration.

CAPPED HOCK - A swelling found at the point of the hock and caused by a bruise. It usually stems from kicking in horse vans or stalls.

CASLICK'S OPERATION - An operation to correct pneumovagina and/or windsucking that involves suturing the upper vulvar lips together. This is a minor procedure that eliminates "wind sucking", air being sucked into the vagina when a filly runs hard. A rider can hear it after a hard work or you may observe it while cooling a very hot filly. There is a soft fluttering noise like passing gas, but it is in rhythm with her breathing. This minor surgery eliminates one more excuse as to why a horse didn't run well. Although conformation may pre-dispose some fillies to wind sucking, most barns do it routinely.

CAST - A horse that has laid down or fallen and is unable to rise.

CAULKS - Small cleats on the back end of a horse shoe or racing plate. Used frequently when track becomes muddy to increase the grip, avoid slipping, and provide better footing.

CHALK - The horse who has the "chalk" is the most heavily bet horse in the race.

CHART - The "box score" of a race. The chart gives all the information of the running of a race including horses' positions during the race, official order of finish, wagering handle, payoffs, closing odds, owner, trainer, jockey, purse distribution, times, speed ratings and conditions of race.

CHEAP SPEED - A horse that can run the first two furlongs in 22 seconds, but then peters out and finishes the race poorly has "cheap speed". He has the mechanical ability to run 11 second furlongs - but lungs, structure, or something doesn't allow him to carry his speed the distance.

CHECKED - The pulling back or sudden slowing due to traffic problems during the running of a race.

CHESTNUT - 1) A horse color that may vary from a red-yellow to golden-yellow. The mane, tail, and legs are usually variations of the coat color, except where white markings are present. 2) A horny growth on the inside of a horse's leg that is used in identification.

CHOKE - This involves an obstruction of the esophagus. Signs of choke include green, frothy discharge from the nostrils, coughing, gagging, distress and evidence of abdominal pain. (From *the Horse* April 2002

CHUTE - Any "straightaway" extension on the racetrack (backstretch or homestretch)

CIRCUIT - Describes several racetracks with complementing racing dates, which form a circuit within a certain geographic area.

CLAIMER - Horse that consistently runs in claiming races.

CLAIMING BOX - The compartment usually found adjacent to the paddock where the claim sheet/card is dropped.

CLAIMING PRICE - The price for which a horse is running in a claiming race. .

CLAIMING RACES - Races that have evolved so that horses of equal ability may have a chance to win. A horse that is more talented than the rest of the field will stand the risk of being claimed if put in a race he can win easily. If he is put where he belongs, any horse in that particular race could be the winner. These races came about to give the public a fair chance at betting and to give less than great horses a place to run. Even if it is at the "bottom", they still have an opportunity to be useful for their owners and trainers. I don't like claiming races. If I put my horse where he can be useful, and he is, he may be claimed, and all my work is lost. Our dream is allowance horses that don't risk being claimed in every race. Unfortunately, good allowance horses are few and far between.

CLASS - A horse showing all the best qualities in breeding, conformation, ability and stamina.

CLASSIC - A term used to describe a race of traditional importance.

CLIMBING - Describes the action of a horse which lifts its front legs abnormally high as it gallops, causing it to run inefficiently.

CLOCKER - Person responsible for accurately timing the workouts of a horse. All workouts are taken during the morning training hours.

CLOSING - The time published by the organization after which nominations or entries will not be accepted for a race.

CLUBHOUSE TURN - Generally, the turn closest to the clubhouse.

"COGGINS" - This refers to a test, named after its inventor, which detects carriers of a disease known as E. I. A. (equine infectious anemia). A "negative Coggins" is always required for the interstate/international transport of any racehorse, but is not required for intrastate transport.

COGGINS TEST - A laboratory blood test for the presence of antibodies against the Equine Infectious Anemia (EIA) virus.

COLIC - A term used to describe any abdominal pain in the horse. Most often such pain is associated with digestive upsets.

COLORS - The jockey's silk or nylon jacket and cap provided by the owner.

COLT - A male horse under the age of five.

COMEBACK TO THE RIDER - Allowing the horse to choose his own pace when slowing down from high speed.

COMPARABLE INDEX (C.I.) - Indicates the average earnings or progeny produced from mares bred to one sire when these same mares are bred to other sires. (As in "A.E.I.", a "C. I." of 1.00 is average; 2.00 is twice average, and 0.50 is half the average.)

CONFORMATION - Term used to describe a racing animal's build, muscle and bone structure as they relate to racing.

CONDITION - The qualifications or eligibility rules for horses to be entered in a race.

CONDITION BOOK - The track publication for horsemen listing conditions of upcoming races.

CONNECTIONS - Persons identified with a racehorse -i.e., owner, trainer, rider and stable employees.

CONSIGNOR - The person who executes the consignment contract, offering a horse for sale through the auction.

CONTRACTED FEET - Abnormal contractions of the heel. Can be caused by improper shoeing or excessive dryness.

CORD- UP - A term used at the track to describe the tightening of the muscle along the spinal column that you see when a horse comes back from a strenuous work. It is not as severe as tie-up (Azoturia).

CORTICOSTEROIDS - Any of a number of hormonal steroid substances obtained from the cortex of the adrenal gland. Therapeutically they may be injected into joints to decrease inflammation. Rest is a must when used this way. If used systemically, many trainers believe they enhance the horse's overall performance and make him more aggressive. Beware of the ramifications of long term use.

COUPLED ENTRY - Two or more horses belonging to the same owner or trained by the same person. They run as an entry comprising a single betting unit. Their program number regardless of position would be 1 and 1A. A bet on one of these horses is a bet on both.

COVER - A single breeding of a mare to a stallion.

COW HOCKS - A conformation fault where the hocks are very close together while the lower portion of the rear legs are widely separated and toed out.

CRACKED HEELS (GREASED HEELS/SCRATCHES) - A weeping, moist dermatitis found on the back of the pastern and fetlock just above the quarters; often associated with poor stable hygiene.

CRIBBING (STUMPSUCKING) - An incurable vice or habit often learned by imitation. The cribber closes his teeth on any convenient surface (manger, gate, part of the stall partition, etc.), continuously extending his neck to swallow deep drafts of air with a grunting sound.

CROP - The group of foals sired by a stallion in a given season

CRYPTORCHID - A male horse in which one or both testicles are retained in the abdomen.

CUPPY - A description of a dirt track surface which is loose and dry, therefore tending to break away from the horses as they run.

CUPPY TRACK - A dry and loose racing surface which breaks away under a horse's hooves.

CURB - A hard swelling on back surface or rear cannon about four inches below the point of hock.

DAILY DOUBLE - A wager which one must select the winners of two races in succession.

DAM - A female parent (mother)

DAMSIRE (BROODMARE SIRE) – The sire of a broodmare.

DARK DAY - A day that the track is closed to racing.

DEAD HEAT - A tie occurring when the photo-finish camera shows two or more horses crossing the finish line simultaneously.

DEAD TRACK - A racing surface which lacks resiliency. Declared: (See "scratched".)

DEAD WEIGHT - Tack and lead slabs that bring the rider up to the horse's assigned weight.

DECLARATION- The act of withdrawing an entered horse from a race before the closing of overnight entries. A horse that has been withdrawn is said to have been declared.

DEEP STRETCH - The area very near the finish line of a race.

DEHYDRATION - The excessive loss of body fluids such as would occur in severe diarrhea.

DERBY - A stakes exclusively for three-year-olds.

DEXAMETHASONE - A generic name for a potent corticosteroid often used to control inflammation.

DISQUALIFICATION - Change in the order of finish by officials for an infraction of the rules.

DISTAFF-The female designation for racehorses.

DISTANCED - Well beaten, finishing a great distance behind the winner.

DMSO - (Dimethylsulfoxide.) An oxygen-free radical scavenger used as an anti-inflammatory. It is often mixed with other concoctions, such as steroids, because it opens the pores and allows the medications to be absorbed into the bloodstream.

DOGS - Rubber cones placed away from the inner rail on the turf course during morning workouts in order to prevent wear and tear on the main portion of the course. Also used on dirt tracks when they are muddy or sloppy.

DRAW - The method (an actual "live" drawing of lots) by which every horse's post position in every race is determined.

DRIFTING IN -The horse ran on a slight sideways course toward the rail. (Lugging In means the horse drifted radically toward the rail; Bearing In is the most severe version of this movement.)

DRIFTING OUT - The horse ran on a slight sideways course toward the outside of the field or track (Lugging Out means the horse drifted way off-course toward the outside of the track Again, Bearing Out is the most severe version of this activity.)

DRIVING-A horse under strong urging by the rider.

DROPDOWN-A horse meeting a lower class of rival that he had been running against.

DWELT- The horse failed to move quickly out of the starting gate and broke well behind the field. (In extreme cases, where the horse barely moves, this is termed "Left at Gate".)

EASED - A horse not allowed to continue in a race due to injury, poor conditioning or inability to compete.

E.I. P.H. - Exercise-induced pulmonary hemorrhage (the common term is "bleeding").

E. I. A. - The initials refer to "equine infectious anemia", a virus-carried disease that attacks the central nervous system, causing a dangerous reduction in the numbers of red blood cells and in the levels of hemoglobin. Survivors of the disease can become symptom less carriers - thus the "Coggins test" was developed to regularly monitor the blood of all active racehorses for the E.I.A. antibody.

EARMUFFS - A piece of equipment that covers a horse's ears to prevent it from being distracted by sounds.

ECLIPSE AWARDS - Thoroughbred racing's year-end awards, honoring the top horses and humans in several categories. The Eclipse Awards are presented by the National Thoroughbred Racing Association, *Daily Racing Form,* and the National Turf Writers Association. Eclipse Award winners are referred to as *champions.*

EDEMA - An abnormal collection of fluids in body tissue. Congestion. Most apparent in the legs.

ELECTROLYTES - Salts that maintain proper blood balance. These are usually found in a well balanced feed program. However, if a horse is over stressed, he may need short-term supplementation after hard races.

ELIGIBILITY - Current qualification to a stakes race or incentive program.

ENDORPHINS - Morphinelike proteins produced by nerve tissue to suppress pain and regulate emotional state.

ENDOSCOPE - A flexible tube with an optical attachment on the end, enabling the vet to inspect the horse internally. It is the instrument vets use when scoping a horse.

ENDOSCOPY (OR ENDOSCOPIC EXAMINATION) -Using a flexible tube (as small as a pencil, rarely larger than your little finger), a veterinarian will insert a two- to three-and-a-half-foot fibroscope through a horse's nostrils to inspect via fiberoptic cable with lights -the nasal passages, larynx, pharynx and sometimes even lungs of those horses either known to be, or suspected of being, "bleeders." (Please see Chapter on Stewards/ Vets Lists for "bleeder" explanations.)

ENGAGEMENT - Refers to a stakes nomination; also to a jockey's riding commitment.

ENTER - To enroll a horse in a race.

ENTRY CLERK-A track employee stationed in the racing secretary's office to take entries in person and collect those from the entry box.

ENTRY FEE-Money paid to enter a horse in a race.

ENTRY BOX-A locked box into which trainers drop entry forms.

ENTRY - A horse eligible to run in a race; also, two or more horses entered in the same race that have common ties of ownership, lease, or training.

EPIPHYSITIS - An abnormal enlargement of the epiphysis (the horizontal growth line at the end of long bones) in young horses. It is often called big knees because of an enlargement over the knees. Can be a component of osteochondrosis.

EQUINE INFECTIOUS ANEMIA (EIA swamp fever) - An extremely contagious infectious disease of horses. It occurs in acute, chronic or inapparent forms, characterized in the acute or chronic stage by intermittent fever, depression, progressive weakness, weight loss, edema and anemia. Persists in white blood cells of all infected horses for life. See Coggins Test.)

EQUIPMENT - Gear carried by horse and jockey in a race, such as whip or blinkers.

EXACTA - A wager in which the bettor must select the first -and second-place finishers in order.

EXERCISE RIDER - Rider who exercises horses in the morning training hours.

EXOTIC WAGER - Any wager that involves more than one horse; generally the pari-mutuel takeout is higher, and the mutuel payoffs are higher than straight wagers (i.e., Quinella, Daily Double and Trifecta).

EXTENDED - Indicates that a horse is running at top speed.

FADE IN THE LANE - Tire in the homestretch.

FALSE FAVORITE - A horse that is wagered down to favoritism when others would appear to out class him.

FARRIER - Blacksmith.

FAR TURN - The last turn on any racetrack before the horses enter the "homestretch" approaching the finish line.

FAST (TRACK) - Footing that is dry, even, and resilient.

FAULT - A weak point in the horse's conformation or character as a racer.

FAVORITE - An entrant that has the shortest odds on the tote board.

FEATURE - The best race on a card.

FIELD - The term has two meanings. One (the more common) designates the collective group of starters in a race; the other designates a group of horses running in a race as a single betting unit because there are more horses running than the pari-mutuel equipment can accommodate (the limit is 12). In the latter case, the mounts are termed "field horses," and the unit they comprise is the "pari-mutuel field". All the field horses will be numbered 12 (i.e., 12a, 12b, 12c), but they do not (necessarily) break from the gate in 12th position, or even side-by-side (their positions are drawn). The field horses are selected by the Racing Secretary alone, who selects up to three from a group of extra entries.

FIGURE EIGHT - A leather strap used to keep the horse's mouth closed and keep the tongue from being put over the bit.

FILLY - A female horse at the ages of two and three.

FIRING - The terrible custom of burning the front of the cannon bone, generally because of bucked shins. (See Setback Section.)

FIRM (COURSE) - A condition of a turf course corresponding to fast on a dirt track. A firm, resilient surface.

FIRST TURN - Bend in the track beyond the starting point; also, clubhouse turn.

FIT - Term commonly used to describe a horse in the peak of condition.

FLAK JACKET Similar to jackets worn by football quarterbacks, the jockey's flak jacket protects the ribs, kidneys and back.

FLATTEN OUT- To slow considerably; describes a very tired horse.

FLOAT - A heavy flat piece of equipment used to seal and remove water from the racetrack surface. To file down the sharp edges of a horse's teeth.

FLUNIXIN MEGLUMINE - The generic name for Banamine, a nonsteroidal anti-inflammatory pain reliever.

FOAL - A young horse of any sex in its first year of life.

FORGING - A fault in the gait in which the toe of the hind foot strikes the bottom of the front foot on the same side.

FOUL - An action by any horse or jockey that hinders or interferes with another horse or jockey during the running of a race.

FOUNDER - See laminitis.

FREE ROUNDPEN - A Backyard Racehorse term for exercising without a lunge line in an area no smaller than 100' x 100', never in a typical roundpen, which is too small and puts too much torque on the legs of a young racehorse. A buggy whip is used to keep the horse at the desired speed, usually a steady gallop.

FROG - The V-shaped, shock-absorbing pad on the bottom of a horse's foot.

FULL BROTHER/SISTER - Horses that have both the same sire and dam.

FURLONG: Eight of these make a mile. One is 220 yards.

FUROSEMIDE - A medication used in the treatment of bleeders, commonly known under the trade name Lasix. It acts as a diuretic, reducing pressure on the capillaries.

FUTURITY - A stakes race for two-year-olds in which owners must pay nominating money and sustaining payments.

GATE CARD - The official permission from the Starter, stating that your horse has been schooled and has broken from the gate in an acceptable manner.

GAIT - The characteristic footfall pattern of a horse in motion. Thoroughbreds have four natural gaits: walk, trot, canter and gallop. The gallop indicates the rapid, rolling gait used in racing and to work horses for stamina.

GAP- An opening in the rail near the racing surface where horses enter and leave the course.

GELDING - A castrated male horse of any age.

GET - Offspring of a male horse. Term used for the progeny of a sire.

GIRTH - The elastic and leather band, sometimes covered with sheepskin, that passes under a horse's belly and is connected to both sides of the saddle.

GOOD (TRACK) - A dirt track that is almost fast or a turf course slightly softer than firm.

GRADED RACE - A designation established in 1973 to classify select stakes races, at the request of European racing authorities, which had set up group races two years earlier. Capitalized when used in race title (the Grade I Kentucky Derby). See group race. The grade that may be given traditional handicap, stakes, or classic races by quality of horses and size or the purse, with Grade 1 being best, Grade 2 next best, and, Grade 3 next.

GRANDDAM - The mother of a horse's dam (also called the second dam).

GRANDSIRE - The father of a horse's sire, unless otherwise stated (see maternal grandsire).

GRAY - A horse color where the majority of the coat is a mixture of black and white hairs. The mane, tail, and legs may be either black or gray unless white markings are present. Starting with foals of 1993, the color classifications gray and roan were combined as roan or gray. See roan.

GROOM - The stable employee, employed by the trainer, who cares for horses. Performs daily chores such as grooming, bedding stalls, bandaging, feeding, tacking and race preparation.

GROUP RACE - Established in 1971 by racing organizations in Britain, France, Germany, and Italy to classify select stakes races outside North America. Collectively called pattern races. Equivalent to American graded races. Capitalized when used in race title (the Group 1 Epsom Derby). See graded race.

HALF BROTHER/SISTER - Horses out of the same dam but by different sires.

HALTER - Headgear used on horse when being handled, around barn or when being walked, when not using bridle, also, to claim a horse.

HAND - A unit of measurement (four inches) by which a horse's height is measured from the ground to the withers. A horse that stands 15 hands is five feet tall at the withers.

HANDICAP - A race in which the weights are assigned depending on a horse's past performance and present form. The racing secretary or handicapper assigns a range of weights which would theoretically cause horses to finish in a dead-heat.

HANDICAPPER - The racing secretary or other official who assigns weights, handicaps, and races. Also the journalist who handicaps for a day's racing card and reports his selections for the wagering public.

HANDICAPPING - Making selections by determining relative qualities of horses through their past performances and class.

HANDILY - Said of a horse winning a race easily. In a workout, a pace which is a bit slower than driving but faster than breezing.

HANDLE - The amount of money wagered on each race by the betting public.

HAND RIDE - Urging a horse with hands rather than using the whip.

HANG - A horse that hangs holds back to run with the horse next to him instead of passing and forging ahead.

"HAY-BURNER"- Jargon for a horse not earning enough in purses to pay for its upkeep.

HEAD - A margin between horses which describes one horse leading another by the length of his head.

HEAVY (TRACK) -Wettest possible condition of a turf course; not usually found in North America.

HIGH WEIGHT - The highest weight assigned or carried in a given race.

HOCK - A large joint just above the cannon bone in the rear leg. Corresponds to the level of the knee of the front leg.

HOMEBRED - A horse bred by his owner.

HOMESTRETCH - The straightaway between the end of the far turn and the finish line.

HOPPED- Jargon describing a horse on illegal stimulants.

HORSE - A stallion five years of age or older.

HORSE'S BIRTHDAY - All horses become one year or older on January 1 of each year for purposes of competition.

HORSING - A filly or mare in heat.

HOTWALKER - The person who cools out the horse after exercise. A mechanical device with four 40 foot arms. Commonly used on backside to cool horses after exercise.

IDENTIFICATION - Of horses, involves a system of recognition of several types of markings by the horse identifier. Markings are noted on animal's breed registry papers and usually includes from coat color, lip tattoos, hair whorls, cowlicks, white markings, night eyes, scars and brands.

INFIELD - The area within the inner racing surface.

IN HAND - Running a horse under moderate control, at less than top speed.

IN THE MONEY - A horse finishing first, second or third is "in the money" for the wagering public.

INQUIRY - The stewards immediate investigation into interference in the running of a race which may result in the disqualification of one or more horses.

INVITATIONAL - A race in which the field of competing horses is selected by inviting horse owners to enter specific horses.

INFRACTION: A violation of racing rules, usually by a jockey during a race.

INNER RAIL - The moveable pipe-fence which designates the "inside" (left-hand) boundary of a race's course.

IRONS - Stirrups or where the jockey puts his feet while riding.

JAIL - Signifying the 30 days after a horse has been claimed, in which it must run for a 25% higher claiming price than for what it was claimed. Some tracks may differ in their regulations.

JOCKEY - Professional rider; also, to maneuver a horse in a race.

JOCKEY AGENT - Person employed by a jockey to secure mounts.

JOCKEY'S RACE - Refers to a race whose outcome will probably hinge on strategic thinking by the riders.

JOINT CAPSULE - A sac-like membrane that encloses a joint space and secretes joint (synovial) fluid.

JOINT MOUSE - A small chip of bone enclosed in the joint space.

JOURNEYMAN - A licensed jockey who has completed his apprenticeship.

JUG - A mixture of fluids with vitamins and electrolytes (and who knows what). It is administered to horses by IV by vets at the racetrack.

JUVENILE - A two-year-old and the youngest age at which one can race.

LAMINITIS - A disturbance of the sensitive plates of soft tissue, or laminae, in the horse's foot which leads to breakdown and degeneration of the union between the horny and sensitive laminae. Acute laminitis refers to a disturbance with rapid onset and brief duration, while chronic laminitis is a persistent, long-term disturbance. In severe cases either one may result in founder and internal deformity of the hoof. According to The Merck Veterinary Manual, Seventh Edition, usually caused by ingestion of excess carbohydrates, grazing lush pastures, and excess exercise and concussion in an unfit horse. Can also be caused by colic, postparturient metritis, or administration of an excess of corticosteroid or other medications.

LANE - Homestretch. The track in front of grandstand before the finish line.

LASIX - A brand name drug for furosemide, a diuretic.

LAYUP - A period of time in which a racehorse is sent away from the racetrack to rest.

LEAD PAD - A piece of equipment under the saddle in which thin slabs of lead may be inserted to bring a rider's weight up to the weight assigned the horse in a specific race.

LEAD PONY - A horse used specifically to lead the racehorses from the paddock to the starting gate.

LENGTH - Unit of measurement in racing and charting terminology. One length is equal to the length of one horse. Five lengths are equal to the distance covered in one second at racing speed.

LISTED RACE -A stakes race just below a group race or graded race in quality.

LIVE WEIGHT - The weight of a jockey that a horse carries.

LUGGING IN - A term used to describe a horse which is pulling strongly to the inside or outside while running. (See Bearing in and out.)

MAIDEN - A horse that has never won a race. "To break the maiden" means to win his first race.

MAIDEN RACE - A race for non-winners.

MARE - A female horse five years of age or older.

MATCH - A challenge race between two horses.

MATERNAL GRANDSIRE - The sire of a horse's dam.

MATURITY - A stakes race for four-year-olds and up in which owners must pay nominating money and sustaining payments.

MEDICATION LIST - A list kept by the track veterinarian and posted at the track showing which horses have been treated with legally permitted medication, usually limited to Bute and Lasix.

MIDDLE DISTANCE - Usually indicates a course-length from 1 mile to 1 1/4 miles.

MINUS POOL - When a horse is so heavily played by bettors that after the deduction of the state tax and commissions, not enough money remains in the pool to payoff the legally prescribed minimum.

MIXED SALE - A sale consisting of varying types of horses, such as yearlings, broodmares, horses in training, etc.

MORNING GLORY - A horse known for phenomenal morning workout times, but is a disappointment when raced in the afternoons.

MORNING LINE - The approximate odds usually printed in the program and posted on the totalizator board prior to any wagering. The morning line is a prediction *of* how the wagering will *go* on a race.

MUDDER -A horse which races well on a muddy track.

MOUNT FEE - The flat fee earned by a jockey who has not finished in the top three where he might earn a percentage of the purse.   -

MUD CALKS AND "STICKERS" - These are cleat-like additions (calks) to "regular" horseshoes, or shoes with built-in extensions (stickers), which are used to give extra traction when the racing surface of the track is muddy, or "sloppy." Calks and stickers are monitored equipment and must be reported to the Paddock or Equipment Judge prior to the race. (Calks and stickers are usually not permitted in turf races.)

MUDDY (TRACK) -A condition of a racetrack that is wet but has no standing water.

MUTUEL POOL - The total amount wagered on a race in each ticket category. The total number of winning tickets in the win category share the entire pool equally after the takeout is deducted. The same is true of the Daily Double and other exotic pools. The place pool is divided into two parts and the show pool into three parts and divided among the holders of winning tickets on the horses involved.

NAME (OF A THOROUGHBRED) - Names of North American Thoroughbreds are registered by The Jockey Club. They can be no longer than 18 characters, including punctuation and spaces. The words the, and, by, for, in, are almost always lowercase (for example, Love You by Heart; Go for Wand) unless one of them is the first word in the name (e.g., The Deputy).

NAPROXIN - The generic name for a non-steroidal, non-psychotropic anti-inflammatory pain reliever.

NAVICULAR APPARATUS - The small boat-shaped bone and saclike bursa located behind the coffin joint in the hoof. Together they regulate the angle at which the deep digital flexor tendon and the coffin bone meet.

NAVICULAR DISEASE - Insidious and degenerative pathology of the navicular bone, bursa and deep flexor tendon, with both circulatory and mechanical (upright conformation of the forefoot) cause. It may occur when the force of concussion is concentrated on the heel area of the hoof. Normally, the navicular bone provides a smooth surface for the deep flexor tendon to bend across. Too much pounding results in inflammation and damage to the tendon sheath, the cartilage on the back of the navicular bone, the navicular bursa (which ordinarily helps lubricate the area) and the bone itself. A horse with navicular tends to dig a little hole for his toes and stand with his toes in the hole to take the weight off his heels. (With laminitis he stands with weight on his heels and his toes extended.)

NEAR SIDE - The left side of a horse (the side on which the rider mounts).

NECK - Unit of measurement the length of a horse's neck; a quarter of a length.

NEURECTOMY - An operation in which the sensory nerve is severed with the idea of permanently eliminating pain that arises from that area.

NERVED - A horse that has had an operation or manipulation in which the sensory nerve is blocked or severed to temporarily or permanently eliminate pain in that area.

NOSE - Smallest advantage by which a horse can win.

NOSEBAND - A leather strap that fits over a horse's nose and helps - secure the bridle. A "figure-eight" nose band goes over the nose and under the rings of the bit to help keep the horse's mouth closed. This keeps the tongue from sliding up over the bit and is used on horses that do not like having a tongue tie used.

OAKS - A stakes event for three-year-old fillies.

OBJECTION - A complaint filed by an owner, trainer, or jockey.

ODDS-ON - Odds of less than even money.

OFFICIAL - The designation given to the result of a race by the stewards when any occurrences that affected the actual order of finish have been decided in terms of pari-mutuel payoffs to winning bettors.

OFF SIDE - The right side of a horse.

OFF THE BOARD - Used to describe a horse that has finished worse than third.

OFF-TRACK BETTING - Wagering on horses at legalized wagering offices, usually run by the state or the tracks.

ON THE MUSCLE - Denotes a fit horse, well-conditioned.

ON THE BOARD - Terminology indicating that a horse finished first, second, third or fourth.

ON THE BIT - Indicates that the horse is eager to run. (A similar term is "in the bridle.")

OSSELETS - A swelling of the front part of the fetlock joint. The swelling may be due to arthritis of the fetlock joint or to a bony growth. According to *The Merck Veterinary Manual, Seventh Edition,* "It may progress to degenerative joint disease. The exciting cause is the strain and repeated trauma of hard training in young animals. It has come to be recognized as an occupational hazard of the young Thoroughbred."

OSTEOARTHRITIS - (degenerative joint disease), is the number one cause of early retirement in sport horses. Tracy Turner, DVM, attributes most front-foot injuries to changes in blood flow and the subsequent failure of the hydrostatic and hydraulic anticonvulsive mechanisms of the hoof - a combination that stresses the sensitive laminae and sole. "An area is traumatized because the blood flow has been decreased there." Turner explains., "The trauma creates inflammation, which then increases with repeated irritation." Eventually, if the condition continues, the affected structures will try to remodel.

OSTEOCHONDROSIS - A bone disease possibly caused by severe over feeding and/or too much calcium supplementation. May also be caused by overuse of drugs, especially steroids. Anti-inflammatory drugs are not indicated since they promote physical activity, and thus aggravate the condition.

OUTRIDER - The official (mounted on a pony) seen leading racehorses down the track to the starting gate. The Outrider is responsible for the safety of riders and horses during workouts and races. The Outrider must catch any "loose" (riderless) horses on the track, and help riders pull up out-of-control (runaway) horses, whether during workouts, during a race, or after a race. At morning workouts, this Official controls the flow of horses on and off the work-track, and is responsible for clearing the track twice each morning for refurbishing. (The Outrider also assists in loading into the van any unfortunate mounts who breaks down or is injured during workouts or races.)

OVERNIGHT - A race for which entries close 72 hours or less before post time for the first race on the day the race is to be run. Also, the mimeographed sheet available to horsemen at the racing secretary's office showing the entries for the following day.

OVER-REACHING - When the rear toe strikes the quarter of the front foot on the same side while the horse is in motion, another name for grabbing his quarters. This usually happens when a horse stumbles upon breaking out of the starting gate.

OVERWEIGHT - Pounds that a horse carries in excess of his officially assigned weight, because the jockey is too heavy.

OVERLAND - Jargon for racing wide throughout - outside of the other horses.

OVERLAY - A horse going off at a higher price than he appears to warrant based on his past performances.

OVERNIGHT RACE - A race in which entries close a specific number of hours (usually 48) before the running. This is as opposed to stakes races, for which entries and nominations close weeks and sometimes months in advance.

OWNER - The name recorded on the back of the foal certificate. In most states, one is not permitted to race with an application for transfer attached to the foal certificate.

PADDOCK - The area where the horses are saddled and viewed prior to a race. The paddock is always adjacent to the jockeys' quarters.

PADDLE - The tendency of a horse to toe-in while running, resulting in an inefficient gait.

PARI-MUTUEL - From French meaning "wager amongst us; the system for racetrack wagering that returns to winning bettors the amounts wagered by unsuccessful bettors, less takeout taxes to state, track and purse.

PAST PERFORMANCES - Information published by Daily Racing Form or the racetrack which gives information on a horse's most recent races and works for handicapping purposes.

PASTEBOARD TRACK - A lightning-fast racing surface.

PATROL JUDCE - The racing official placed at critical points around the track in stands or towers, who observes the running of the race and reports back to stewards as to any interference or careless riding.

PEDAL OSTEITIS is inflammation of the coffin bone, which causes pain deep inside the hoof. When x-rayed during the progressive phase of the condition, the coffin bone usually shows a loss of bone density, especially at the edges. Later, after inflammation subsides and healing begins, the bone's mass may increase.

PEDIGREE - Lineage or parentage.

PHENYLBUTAZONE - See Bute.

PHOTO FINISH - Indicative of a very close finish in which only careful viewing of the photo-finish picture can determine the order of finish.

PICK-THREE, PICK-SIX, PICK-NINE, ETC- Wagers in which the winners of all the included races must be selected.

PILL - Small numbered ball used in a blind draw to decide post positions.

PINHOOKER - A person who buys a racehorse with the specific intention of reselling it at a profit.

PLACE - A wager in which one collects if the horse finishes first or second.

PLACING JUDGE - The racing official in charge of the official placing or order of finish of horses during and after the running of a race through the viewing of the race, especially at the finish, and the viewing of the photo-finish strip with stewards. At some tracks the stewards also serve as placing judges.

PLATES - Jargon for horse shoes (aluminum or steel).

POLES - Markers around the track indicating the distance to the finish line.

PONY - The good old faithful horse, usually an Appaloosa, Paint or Quarter Horse that helps the young, inexperienced horse.

POPPED A SPLINT - When a lump suddenly appears on a leg. See Splint. According to *The Merck Veterinary Manual, Seventh Edition,* "A periostitis with production of new bone caused by trauma from concussion or injury, strain from excess training (especially in the immature horse), faulty conformation, or improper shoeing. Complete rest is indicated. Local use of steroids delays the consolidation process and is contraindicated. In Thoroughbred practice, it has been traditional to point-fire a splint, the aim being to accelerate the ossification of the interosseous ligament. However, in most cases irritant treatments are contraindicated."

POST - The starting point for the race.

POST PARADE - The time period prior to the race when the horses leave the paddock, come on the racetrack, and walk in front of the stands where they break off and jog to the starting gate. The duration of the post parade is usually 10 minutes.

POST POSITION - A horse's position in the starting gate from the inside rail outward, decided by a drawing at the close of entries prior to the race, with the approval of the starter.

POST TIME - The official time set by the stewards and the mutuel department at which a race will start and the horses are required to be at the post and ready to start.

PREFERENCE LIST - A system which makes entering a horse to race more fair; horses with the longest time since last racing or having a chance to race, have the higher preference for the next race entered.

PROGENY - The offspring of either a male or female horse.

PROGRAM - The general program published and sold by the racing association; also, includes all vital information on the day's racing card, including race number, conditions, distance, types of wagering, horses' names, numbers, jockeys and weights.

PROP - The action a horse takes when it stops moving by digging its front feet into the ground.

PROTEST - A written complaint signed by the protester against any horse which has started in a race, and shall be made to the Stewards within 48 hours after the running of the race.

PUBLIC TRAINER - One whose services are available to the public and who expects to train a number of horses from a number or owners.

PULL UP - The action of slowing or stopping a horse during or after a race or workout

PURSE - The prize monies offered in a race, generally made up of the added money based on handle and/or sponsor's contribution, and any nomination sustaining or entry fees.

QUARTER CRACK - A crack found in the wall of the hoof in the area of the quarter. It often runs from the bottom of the wall up to the coronet.

QUICK OFFICIAL - The posting of first, second, third and fourth-placing horses on the tote board at the finish of a race. If there was no photo finish and/or no timely complaints or objections filed with the Stewards by jockeys, owners or trainers of horses "in the running."

QUINELLA - Wager in which the first two finishers must be picked, but payoff is made no matter which wins and which runs second.

QUITTOR - A chronic purulent inflammation of the cartilage of the coffin bone that drains through tracts at the level of the coronet band.

"RABBIT" - A speed horse in a coupled entry with a come-from-behind stable mate. The "rabbit" is expected to set a fast pace to help the chances of its partner.

RACING BOARD/COMMISSION - A state-appointed body charged with the duty of regulating and supervising the conduct of racing in that state.

RACING PLATE - A type of horseshoe which is very light, made of aluminum, with a toe grab or cleat for better traction.

RACING SECRETARY - The person who puts together the Condition Book at the track.

RAIL RUNNER - A horse that prefers to run next to the inside rail

RAIL-A barrier, generally made of aluminum covered with a plastic shield, which forms the inside and outside perimeter of the racing surface.

RANK - A term describing a horse that refuses to "settle" under a jockey during a race, instead running in a head-strong manner without regard to pace.

RATED - To control the horse's speed.

REBUILD-DAY - A *Backyard Racehorse* term for days the horse is not saddled. He is turned out and given time to rest and rebuild from stresses. If he needs exercise, you can swim, roundpen, teach loading or any lessons he needs.

RECEIVING BARN - The horse hotel, so to speak, at the racetrack. The barn for ship-in horses.

REDLINE - A *Backyard Racehorse* term used frequently in this manual. It means that the horse is doing his ultimate best, trying his hardest, giving you all he's got, stressing every fiber of his body to his own personal best. This should really only be done under race circumstances. The horse will need time to rebuild from such a workout.

REFUSED - The horse would not break from the gate.

REGISTRATION CERTIFICATE - The document forwarded by the breed registry that certifies that the horse is duly registered.

RESTRICTED STAKES - A stakes race in which conditions limit the participants based upon certain criteria. The more common restricted stakes races are state-bred races and races written for horses purchased through or consigned to a certain sale.

RHINOPNEUMONITIS - A contagious disease caused by a virus of the herpes group, characterized by fever, mild upper respiratory infection and, in mares, abortion. May trigger an "abortion storm" in broodmare bands.

RIDDEN OUT - Winning a race without rider urging horse to do his utmost because he has a wide margin over the second-place horse. Describes a race run by a horse under mild urging (not as severe as "driving.")

RIDGLING - A male equine with one testicle.

RING BONE - A bony enlargement seen in front and on both sides of the pastern. If it is under the top of the hoof, it is called a low ring bone. If it is found halfway up the pastern, it is call a high ring bone. Caused by faulty conformation, improper shoeing, or repeated concussion through working on hard ground.

ROAN - A horse color in which the majority of the coat is a mixture of red and white hairs or brown and white hairs. The mane, tail, and legs may be black, chestnut, or roan unless white markings are present. Starting with foals of 1993, the color classifications gray and roan were combined as roan or gray. See gray.

ROARER - A horse with paralyzed vocal chords. The condition causes fluttering noise when the horse makes a quick move. It interferes with the horse's ability to race, especially in distance races.

ROGUE - An ill-tempered, hard-to-control horse.

ROUTE - A long race (one mile or more).

"ROUTER" - Refers to a horse, which performs well at longer distances.

RUN-OUT BIT - A special type of bit to prevent a horse from bearing in or out.

RUNDOWN BANDAGES (WRAPS) - Bandages on the hind legs, usually with a pad inside, to keep a horse from burning or scraping his heels or fetlocks when he races.

SADDLE - The thoroughbred racing saddle is a virtual scar of patent leather, weighing less than two pounds (the lightest saddle used on any horse).

SADDLE CLOTH (TOWEL) - Cloth under the saddle on which program numbers and sometimes horse's name are displayed. On many tracks, color coded as to position.

SADDLE PAD - A piece of foam rubber (or sometimes, sheepskin or felt) used as a base under the saddle.

SCALE OF WEIGHTS - Fixed weights to be carried by horses according to their age, sex, the race distance, and the time of year.

SCALPING - The toe of the front hoof hits the pastern of the rear foot on the same side, when the horse is in motion.

SCHOOL - To train a horse, especially at the gate, in the paddock and before a crowd, and otherwise teaching him racing practices.

SCHOOLING RACE - A pre-race which conforms to requirements adopted by the state racing commission.

SCOPING - Inserting a fiber optic tube through the nostril and down into the throat. Enables the vet to see breathing problems such as paralyzed flap, loose palate, entrapped epiglottis. This procedure may also confirm bleeding lungs and is an absolute necessity when purchasing a horse.

SCRATCH - The act of withdrawing an entered horse from a race after the closing of overnight entries.

SCRATCH TIME - The deadline established by the race office for horses to be scratched prior to the printing of the official program. Generally, races are drawn 72 to 48 hours before race day and scratch time will be 24 hours before race day; for stakes races, scratch time can be up to 15 minutes before post time.

SECOND CALL - The secondary mount of a jockey in a race in the event his primary mount is scratched.

SESAMOID BONES - The sesamoids are two pyramid-shaped bones found at the rear of the fetlock joint and act as a pulley for the flexor tendons. They are attached to the cannon bone and long pastern bone by ligaments and form the back of the fetlock joint, beneath the flexor tendons.

SESAMOIDITIS - The tearing of the sesamoidean ligaments due to the great stress placed on the fetlock during fast exercise. Also an arthritic condition or mineral deposits on the sesamoid bones.

SET - A group of horses being exercised together.

SEX ALLOWANCE - Fillies and mares, according to their age and time of year, are allowed to carry three to five pounds less when racing against males.

SHADOW ROLL - Sheepskin or cloth cylinder strapped across a horse's nose to bar its vision of the ground, preventing the horse from shying from shadows.

SHANK - The rope or strap attached to a halter or bridle by which a horse is led. (Also known as a "lead.")

SHEDROW - The aisle in front of stalls at the track barn. Stable area with barns and walkways under a roof.

SHOE BOIL - A soft swelling at the point of the elbow caused by bruising with a long-heeled shoe when the horse is lying down or by lack of sufficient bedding to prevent the elbow from being in contact with the hard floor of the stall.

SHOW - Third-place position at the finish. A wager in which one collects if horse finishes first, second or third.

SILKS - Jockey's racing shirt displaying the owner's colors.

SIMULCAST - A simultaneous live-television transmission of a race at other tracks, off-track betting offices, or other outlets for the pur-pose of wagering.

SIRE - A male parent; father.

SKIN PINCH TEST - Time test used to determine horse's hydration level. The longer it takes for a fold of skin on the horse's neck or shoulder to return to normal, the more dehydrated he is. One to two seconds signifies adequate hydration; six to 10 seconds represents severe dehydration.

SLOPPY (TRACK) - A racing strip that is saturated with water, with standing water visible.

SLOW (TRACK) A racing strip that is wet on both the surface and base.

SOCKS (OR STOCKINGS) - Solid white markings on a horse, which extend from the top of the hoof to the ankles or knees.

SOFT TRACK - Condition of a turf course with a large amount of moisture. Horses sink very deeply into it.

SOLE BRUISE - is the simplest concussion-related hoof injury. It is basically an inflammation of the sensitive tissues of the sole.

SOPHOMORE - A three-year-old horse.

SOUND - The condition of a horse that is free of lameness, injury or illness.

SPEEDY CUT - Occurs when the front foot hits the inside of the hock or the rear foot hits the outside of the front cannon bone. It is caused by poor conformation and/or poor shoeing.

SPIT BOX - The State Barn where the horses go to be tested for drugs.

SPIT THE BIT - A term referring to a tired horse that begins to run less aggressively, backing off on the "pull" a rider normally feels on the reins from an eager horse. Also used as a generic term for an exhausted horse.

SPLINTS - Bony enlargements occurring on the cannon or splint bones, characterized by swelling, heat and sometimes lameness. Most common in young, strenuously worked horses. See **POPPED A SPLINT**.

SPRINT - A short race - as short as 2 furlongs (see "Baby Race," written for 2-year-olds), but no longer than 7 1/2 furlongs (just under a mile).

SPRINTER - A horse than can run fast at 6 furlongs or less.

STAKES - Races that have paid entry fees. A horse's winnings will pay his entry into the Stakes. If he can't earn enough to pay his own way, he shouldn't be competing at that level. A horse that runs in Stakes is a better than the average allowance horse. Remember, the horse's winnings tell you how good he is.

STAKES PLACED - Finishing second or third in a stakes race.

STAKES PRODUCER - A mare that has produced at least one foal that finished first, second or third in a stakes race.

STALLMAN - Person in charge of putting horses in their assigned stalls in the receiving barn.

STALLION - A male horse that is used to breed mares.

STAR LIST - A list of horses posted in the racing secretary's office which are given credit because they have been excluded due to too many entries. The more stars a horse has, the more likely it is to be accepted as an entry in a race since preference is given according to the number of stars a horse has.

STARTER - The official in charge of starting the race and head of the gate crew. He gives the okay for the horse to get his gate card. No horse may start racing without an official gate card.

STARTER (HORSE) - A horse is recognized as a starter when the stall door of the starting gate opens in front of it at the time the official starter dispatches the horse in the race. When the stall door of the starting gate does not open in front of the horse due to mechanical failure, the horse is not considered a starter.

STARTER'S ALLOWANCE - An allowance or handicap race restricted to horses who have started for a specific claiming price.

STARTER'S LIST - A list of horses that cannot be raced or entered until they have been schooled in the gates and approved by the Starter. The official Track Starter maintains this list.

STAYER - A horse known to be capable of running long distances.

STEADIED - A horse being taken in hand by its rider, usually because of being in close quarters.

STEP UP- When a horse moves up in class to meet better competition (and higher possible purses).

STEWARD - Racetrack official who presides over the race meeting.

STEWARD'S LIST - A list of horses that perform poorly or have problems concerning their ownership, etc. They cannot be entered in a race until the matter is cleared by the Stewards. This list is maintained by the official track stewards.

STICK - The jockey's whip; bat.

STIRRUPS - Metal D-shaped rings into which a jockey places his or her feet. They can be raised or lowered depending on the jockey's preference. Also known as irons.

STRAIGHT WAGER - Win, place or show.

STRESS FRACTURES - Bones that haven't had sufficient opportunity to adapt may develop tiny stress fractures. In other cases, the bone may become excessively calcified where it has overreacted to the stress, leaving these areas brittle and weak. Either scenario puts a horse at risk for more sever fractures if he does not receive six weeks or more of rest. Cartilage within the joints grows thinner with exercise over time, but it also becomes denser and thus more resistant to concussive forces. But cartilage, too, can reach a point of no return in the breakdown-and-repair cycle. That's when the damage becomes progressive and irreparable, leading to osteoarthritis.

STRENGTH TURN - Bend of track into the final straightaway.

STRETCH - Final straightaway portion of the racetrack to the finish line.

STRETCH CALL - Position of horses at designated pole markers, dependent upon the length of the race.

STRETCH RUNNER - A horse that tends to run its fastest nearing the finish line.

STRONGYLES -Large strongyles are a common equine parasite sometimes known as "red or blood worms".

STUD BOOK - Registry and genealogical record of Thoroughbreds, maintained by the Jockey Club of the country in question. For example, The American Stud Book.

SUPERFICIAL FLEXOR TENDON - The outer tendon connecting the superficial muscles of the upper leg to the back of the pastern bones.

SUSPENSORY LIGAMENTS - The strip of fibrous tissue running from the upper cannon bone over the fetlock joint to the pastern bones. Supports the fetlock joint, preventing it from sinking to the ground.

"SWIPE" - Jargon for a groom.

TACK - All equipment (such as blinkers, saddle, bridles and bits) worn by a horse during a race.

TAKEN UP - A horse is pulled up sharply by its rider because of being in dangerously close quarters.

TAKEOUT - The percentage taken out of every dollar wager, and split between state, track and purses; generally, in pari-mutuel racing, the percentage taken out is usually between 15-20% for straight wagers and 20-25% for exotic wagers.

TATTOO - A form of identification in which racehorses are marked under the upper-lip with a letter/number combination, which is also reflected on the registration certificate.

THE JOCKEY CLUB - An organization dedicated to the improvement of Thoroughbred breeding and racing. Incorporated February 10, 1894, in New York City, The Jockey Club serves as North America's Thoroughbred registry, responsible for the maintenance of The American Stud Book, a register of all Thoroughbreds foaled in the United States, Puerto Rico, and Canada; and of all Thoroughbreds imported into those countries from jurisdictions that have a registry recognized by The Jockey Club and the International Stud Book Committee.

THOROUGHBRED - Technically, a thoroughbred must be able to trace its parentage back 250 years to one of the three "founding sires" of the breed: either the Darley Arabian, the Byerly Turk, or the Godolphin Arabian. The thoroughbred must also have satisfied the rules and requirements of The Jockey Club and the International Stud Book Committee. (Any other horse, regardless of parentage, is not considered a thoroughbred for purposes of racing and/ or breeding.)

THOROUGHPIN - Puffy swelling which appears on upper part of hock and in front of the large tendon.

THRUSH - A chronic, moist deterioration of the frog of the hoof. Most frequently seen in horses that stand in bedding soaked with urine and feces or mud, and whose feet do not receive regular attention.

TOE-IN – A conformation flaw in which the front of the foot rotates inward and looks pigeon-toed. It often causes the leg to swing outward during locomotion.

TOE-OUT - Conformation flaw in which the front of the foot is rotated outward. It often causes the leg to swing inward during locomotion.

TONGUE TIE - Strap or strip of cloth used to tie down a horse's tongue to prevent choking in a race or workout.

TOTEBOARD - A display board in the infield on which data is posted electronically, Data includes approximate odds, total amount wagered in each pool, track condition, post time, time of day, result of race, official and inquiry signs, running time of the race and the mutuel payoff prices after each race is declared official, as well as other pertinent information.

TOUT - To give or sell wagering advice; also, a person who does so.

TRACE MINERALS - Minerals found in small quantities in feedstuffs and required in small quantities by the body.

TRACK BIAS - A racing surface which favors a particular running style or post position. (For example, a track bias can favor either front-runners or closers, on horses running on the inside or outside.)

TRACK CONDITIONS:

 FAST - A track that is thoroughly dry and at its best. The footing is even.

 SLOPPY - During or immediately after a heavy rain, water has saturated the cushion and may form puddles. The base is still firm. Footing is splashy but even, and the running time remains fast.

 MUDDY - Water has soaked into the base and it is soft and wet. The footing is deep and slow.

 HEAVY-A drying track that is muddy and drying out, Footing is heavy and sticky.

 SLOW - Still wet, between heavy and good. Footing is heavy.

 GOOD - Rated between slow and fast. Moisture remains in the strip but footing is firm.

 FROZEN - The track surface is frozen solid and unable to be maintained.

TRACK RECORD - Fastest time at each distance recorded at a particular track.

TRAINER - The person who conditions and prepares horses for racing, with the absolute responsibility to ensure the physical condition and eligibility of the horse in accordance with the strict interpretation of the rules, regulations and laws of racing.

TRIAL - Race in which eligible horses compete to determine the finalists in a nomination race

TRIFECTA - A wager in which the first three finishers must be chosen in exact order.

TRIP - An individual horse's race, with reference to the difficulty - or lack of difficulty - the horse faced during competition (e.g., the horse was blocked, or the horse had an unobstructed run).

TRIPLE CROWN - Used generically to denote a series of three important races, but is always capitalized when referring to historical races for 3-year-olds: in the United States, the Kentucky Derby, Preakness Stakes, and Belmont Stakes; in England, the 2000 Guineas, Epsom Derby, and St. Leger Stakes; in Canada, the Queen's Plate, Prince of Wales Stakes, and Breeders' Stakes.

TURF - Term used for infield grass course on which some races are run.

TWO-YEAR-OLD - Every Thoroughbred becomes a "two-year-old" on January 1 of the second year following the date of its birth.

TYING-UP - See Azoturia.

UNDER WRAPS - Horse under stout restraint in a race or workout.

UNDERLAY - A horse racing at shorter odds than he should.

UNTRIED - A horse that has not yet raced or been tested for speed. (Also can refer to a stallion that has not yet been bred.)

UPSET PRICE - The minimum acceptable price to open the bidding on a horse offered for sale in the auction.

VALET - A track employee who takes care of a jockey's equipment.

VETERINARIAN'S LIST - A list maintained by the official racetrack vet of horses that may not be entered in a race until approved by the official racetrack vet.

VIDEO PATROL - The system by which video cameras are strategically placed around a racing oval in order to broadcast and record the running of each race from each possible angle.

WARM UP - A slow gallop or canter to the starting point of a race.

WASHY - Horse breaking out in a nervous sweat before a race.

WEANLING - A foal being weaned and until he becomes a yearling on January 1 of the following year.

WEIGH-IN - The procedure where the Clerk of Scales, prior to the race, checks the weights of jockeys and their riding equipment against the officially assigned weight for each horse in the race.

WEIGH-OUT - The procedure where the Clerk of Scales, after the race, checks the weights of jockey and their riding equipment against the officially assigned weight for each horse in the race.

WEIGHT-FOR-AGE - A fixed scale of weights to be carried by horses according to age, sex, distance of the race, and season of the year.

WEIGHTS - Indicates two designations - one of which is the "weight" a horse is assigned, given the race's conditions, the horse's age, etc. - and the other meaning the combined weight of the jockey and his gear (saddle, and any extra weights added to bring total "weight" up to a particular race's specified conditions).

WHEEL - A type of wager where one entrant is combined with every other entrant in the race; can be done with various types of wagers.

WHIP - Leather instrument with which a rider encourages his horse to increase his speed.

WHITE - A horse color, extremely rare, in which all the hairs are white. The horse's eyes are brown, not pink, as would be the case with an albino.

WIN - Type of wager in which one collects only if a horse wins the race.

WIND - The term used to indicate a horse's capacity for breath (which relates to its endurance).

WINDSUCKING - Occurs when a filly, while running hard, sucks wind in through the vagina. Even when cooling out, you may hear the intake and expelling of the air under her tail. It sounds like she is passing gas. It can be painful! It is usually caused by conformation where the tail is set high and the opening to the vagina is at a particular angle. It is easily remedied by a Caslick's operation (having the vet take a few stitches at the top of the entrance to the vagina).

WIRE - Finish line.

WITHERS - Area above the shoulder, where the neck meets the back.

WOLF TEETH - Extra teeth found just forward of the first upper molar. They must be extracted because they are tender and interfere with the bit of the bridle.

WORK - One step up from a breeze and a tad below a real race. This is the timed tryout on the racetrack that gives you an idea of your horse's true ability. When a horse is "worked" he is generally pushed to the limit, against another horse or alone. The rider will use the whip on him and ride him hard.

WORLD THOROUGHBRED CHAMPIONSHIP - A supporting brand for a Breeders' Cup that describes what the event has come to: A day of international races that largely determine Thoroughbred Racing's year-end Champions.

YEARLING - Every Thoroughbred becomes a "yearling" on January 1 of the first year following the date of its birth.

YIELDING - Condition of a turf course with a great deal of moisture. Horses sink into it noticeably.

Note - These terms are taken from *The Merck Veterinary Manual, Seventh Edition, EQUUS Magazine, The Daily Racing Form, How to Speak Thoroughbred, Veterinary Treatments & Medications for Horsemen,* and various other sources. Many thanks to them.

WINNER'S CIRCLE - Where we'd like to be.

Recommended Reading

Books, Magazines, References

Books
hold the
answers

Magazines
keep you
up to date

References
for infor-
mation
in the book

BOOKS and VIDEOS

My philosophy is to read everything possible about horses and racing. Some books stand out in my mind. Their authors show a great sensitivity to the horse. This is a list of a few that should help you. Several of these publications provided invaluable information in our research.

ADAMS' LAMENESS IN HORSES, by Ted S. Stashak, published by Lea & Febiger, Philadelphia, PA.

AINSLIE'S COMPLETE GUIDE TO THOROUGHBRED RACING, by Tom Ainslie. We understand that Ainslie's books are out of print. Look for them in used book stores.

BLESSED ARE THE BROODMARES, Second Edition, by M. Phyllis Lose, DVM. Published by Howell Book House, New York.

BLESSED ARE THE FOALS, Second Edition, by M. Phyllis Lose, DVM. Published by Howell Book House, New York.

THE BODY LANGUAGE OF HORSES, by Tom Ainslie and Bonnie Ledbetter.

COLOR ATLAS OF VETERINARY ANATOMY, published by J. B. Lippincott Company, Gower Medical Publishing.

CONDITIONING SPORT HORSES , by Hillary M. Clayton, published by Sport Horse Publications, Box 355 RPO, University Saskatoon, Saskatchewan, Canada 57N4J8.

CONSIDERING THE HORSE, by Mark Rashid, published by Johnson Printing, 1880 South 57th Court, Boulder, CO 80301.

DRUGS AND THE PERFORMANCE HORSE, by Thomas Tobin, published by Charles C. Thomas & Co.

EQUINE DRUGS AND VACCINES, by Eleanor M. Kellon, DVM, in consultation with Thomas Tobin, DVM, MRCVS, published by Breakthrough Publications.

EQUINE INJURY, THERAPY AND REHABILITATION, by Mary Bromiley, published by Blackwell Science, Cambridge, MA.

EQUINE MEDICINE AND SURGERY published by American Veterinary Publications.

THE FIT RACEHORSE II, by Tom Ivers, published by Equine Research.
HOW TO BE YOUR OWN VETERINARIAN (sometimes), by Ruth B. James, DVM,

Books hold the answers.

published by Alpine Press, PO Box 1930, Mills, WY 82644. You can order this book through Alpine Press for $19.95 plus $2.50 postage and handling.

HORSEMAN'S GUIDE TO LAMENESS, by Ted Stashak and Cherry Hill, published by Williams & Wilkins.

IMPRINT TRAINING OF THE NEWBORN FOAL, A 60 minute video by Robert M. Miller, DVM.

THE LAME HORSE - by James R. Rooney, DVM, Wilshire Book Co., 12015 Sherman Road, North Hollywood, CA 91605, Call 215-875-1711.

THE OVERNIGHT STABLING DIRECTORY - A list by state of farms that offer overnight stabling for horses and often have hook-ups for trailers. Some even have Bed and Breakfast accommodations. This publication is a must if you do long distance hauling. It is published yearly.

PROFESSIONAL GROOMING & CARE OF THE RAACEHORSE - by T.A. Landers, Published by Equine Research Inc. For more information contact Ted Landers at 516-352-2544 or on-line at hosstcher@aol.com.

RACEHORSES AT RISK - by Lennert Krook and George A. Maylin, published by the authors, Ithica, NY 14850.

RIDNG FOR THE REST OF US, A Practical Guide For Adult Riders - by Jessica Jahiel Contact her by email at prairienet.org/jjahiel.

RUN, BABY, RUN -What Every Owner, Breeder and Handicapper Should Know About Lasix In Racehorses - by Bill Heller, published by The Russell Meerdink Co.

SEABISCUIT, AN AMERICAN LEGEND - by Laura Hillenbrand Published by Random House, New York.

THE 5-MINUTE VETERINARY CONSULT - Equine - by Christopher M. Brown & Joseph J. Bertone Published by Lippincott Williams & Wilkins, A Wolters Kulwer Company

SELECTING RACEHORSES USING THE AIRFLOW FACTORS - A 90 minute video by Dr. W. Robert Cook, produced by The Russell Meerdink Company.

SPECIFICATIONS FOR SPEED IN THE RACEHORSE: THE AIRFLOW FACTORS - by Dr. W. Robert Cook, published by The Russell Meerdink Company.

There are many other fine books. Read as many as you can.

SPORTS MEDICINE FOR THE RACEHORSE - 2nd Edition - by William E. Jones, DVM, PhD, published by Veterinary Data, P.O. Box 1209, Wildomar, CA 92595.

TRAINING THOROUGHBRED HORSES - by Preston M. Burch, published by The Russell Meerdink Company.

TRAITS OF A WINNER - by Carl A. Nafzger, published by The Russell Meerdink Co.,

WILD RIDE- The Rise and Tragic Fall of Calumet Farm Inc. - by Ann Hagedorn Auerbach, Published by Henry Holt and Company, Inc.

WIN, PLACE AND SHOW - An Introduction to The Thrill of Thoroughbred Racing - by Betsey Berns, Published by The Daily Racing Form.

For hard-to-find equine and racing related publications contact The Russell Meerdink Co., Inc. Call them at 800-635-6499 to order a copy of their catalogue.

MAGAZINES

THE BLOODHORSE - Is the magazine of the Thoroughbred Owners and Breeders Association. It comes out weekly and keeps you informed about what is going on where in the Thoroughbred racing world. Call 800-582-5604 for subscriptions.

CALIFORNIA THOROUGHBRED BREEDERS ASSOCIATION - 201 Colorado Place, PO. Box 60018, Arcadia, CA 910666018. Call 626-445-7800

THE DAILY RACING FORM - Is the state of the art, best newspaper around to get a history and form on the horses running. The articles are current and there are daily editions at every major track every racing day. It is the best money you can spend to get racing information. Call 1 (609) 448-9100 for subscriptions.

EQUUS MAGAZINE - Provides excellent and well written articles. Many of them explain complex subjects in layman's terms. There are also good articles on equine sports physiology and training. Back issues are available by calling 301-977-3900 Ext. 100 or call 1 (303) 678-0439 for subscriptions.

the HORSE - Provides up-to date news, in-depth horse health articles and more. Contact them at 800-582-5604. Fax 859-276-6743

HORSE JOURNAL - Is advertising free and packed from first page to last with honest ratings and evaluations of tack, feeds, supplements, training techniques, horse care products and much more. Write to *Horse Journal* Subscription Services, PO Box 420234, Palm Coast, FL 32142.

THE HORSEMEN'S JOURNAL - Published by the National Horsemen's Benevolent & Protective Association. Contact them at 859-259-0451 or email racing@hpba.org.

THE FLORIDA HORSE - Is the voice of the Florida Thoroughbred Owners and Breeders Association. Call 1 (352) 732-8858 for subscriptions.

THE FINISH LINE - Provides complete information on Arabian racing. Call 352-620-8069 for subscriptions.

THE HOME STRETCH - The news from the Oklahoma Thoroughbred Association. Contact them at Fax 405-330-6206

THE HORSEPLAYER MAGAZINE - A bi-monthly four color publication that caters to racing fans nationwide. Often referred to as the *Time* or *Newsweek* for horsemen. Call 800-334-6560 for subscriptions.

MID-ATLANTIC THOROUGHBRED - News of the area. Call 401-252-2100

QUARTER RACING JOURNAL - A monthly publication dedicated to Quarter Horse racing. Call 806-376-4811 for subscriptions.

QUARTER WEEK - A bi-monthly publication dedicated to Quarter Horse racing. Call 714-826-4195 for subscriptions.

RACING NORTHEAST - The official publication of the Horsemen's Benevolent & Protective Associations in New England and New York, and the Massachusetts Thoroughbred Breeders Association. Call 800-672-2464 for subscriptions.

SPEED HORSE - RACING REPORT - A weekly tabloid for Quarter Horse racing. Call 405-573-1050.

THE THOROUGHBRED TIMES - An excellent magazine to keep you updated on what's going on in Thoroughbred racing. Subscription Dept. PO. Box 9090, Mission Viego, CA 92690-9090

Arabian, Appaloosa, Paint and Quarter Horses are raced throughout the country. Contact the Racing Division of the Breed Registry to receive more information about their publications.

Include magazines in your reading. They will keep you abreast of new developments in the industry.

REFERENCES

Over the years, I have made it a practice to save outstanding magazine articles for future reference. Some of these as well as the text from several books have been quoted throughout the manual. The following list will help you find and refer to this information. Many thanks to the publications for allowing these reprints.

Text from *A 10-point Plan for Equine Worm Control* - by Rupert P. Herd, MVSc, PhD, Department of Veterinary Preventive Medicine, College of Veterinary Medicine, Ohio State University, *Veterinary Medicine*, May 1995, is quoted in *Farm Layout and Friends - A visit from the Vet.*

Text from *A Hoof-care Primer* - by Emily Kilby and Celia Strain, *EQUUS Magazine,* 1995, Issue 219, (Reprinted with permission of Fleet Street Publishing Corporation) is quoted in *Legs, Bandages, and Shoeing.*

Text from *Balanced Hooves* - by Barbara Robbins, *EQUUS Magazine*, 1992, Issue 170, (Reprinted with permission of Fleet Street Publishing Corporation) is referred to in *Legs, Bandages, and Shoeing - The Duck Foot.*

Text from *Handbook For Thoroughbred Owners of California.*

Drawings appear in *Legs, Bandages, and Shoeing*, from *Hoof Balance and Lameness: Improper Toe Length, Hoof Angle, and Mediolateral Balance* - by Olin Balch, DVCM, PhD, Karl White, DVM, Doug Butler, PhD, CJF, FWCF and Sarah Metcalf, DVM, from the *Compendium of Continuing Education, Practical Veterinarian 17 610: 1276-1283, 1995.* Reproduced with permission.

Drawings and text from *Land Flat, Fly True- -* by Matthew P. Mackay-Smith, DVM, with Emily Kilby, *EQUUS Magazine,* 1994, Issue 197, (Reprinted with permission of Fleet Street Publishing Corporation) appear in *Legs, Bandages, and Shoeing.*

Alleviating Surface Transit Stress on Horses - by Sue Creiger, PhD, is referred to in *Hauling.*

The Fit Racehorse and *The Racehorse Owner's Manual* - by Tom Ivers, were referred to in *Training Aids - Heart Rate Monitor and Interval Training.*

Text from *A Marvel of Design* - by Karen Kopp Du Teil, *EQUUS Magazine,* 1992, Issue 180, (Reprinted with permission of Fleet Street Publishing Corporation) is quoted in *Training Aids - Heart Rate Monitor and Interval Training.*

Keep a file of your favorite articles for future reference.

The Compendium of Veterinary Products - published by North American Compendiums, Inc., Port Huron, MI, was a source of information for *Medications at the Racetrack.*

The Complete Guide to Prescription & Non-Prescription DRUGS, 1995 Edition - by H. Winter Griffith, M.D. published by The Body Press/Perigee Books, The Berkeley Publishing Group, 200 Madison Ave., New York, NY 10016, was a source of information for *Medications at the Racetrack.*

Text from *Good Steroids, Bad Steroids* - by Laura Hillenbrand, *EQUUS Magazine*, 1991, Issue 166, (Reprinted with permission of Fleet Street Publishing Corporation) is quoted in the *Medications at the Racetrack - Another Real Vet Bill.*

Text from *How to be Your Own Veterinarian (sometimes)* - by Ruth B. James, published by Alpine Press, Mills, WY, is quoted in the *Medications at the Racetrack - Common Medications at the Racetrack: What They Are and What They Do;* and *Basic Training.* You can order her book through Alpine Press, PO Box 1930, Mills, WY 82644, for $19.95 plus $2.50 postage and handling.

Text from *Professional Grooming & Care of the Racehorse* - By T.A. Landers, Published by Equine Research Inc. For more information contact Ted Landers at 516-352-2544 or on-line at hosstcher@aol.com.

Text from *Unlocking Sticky Stifles* - by Matthew Mackay-Smith, DVM, Medical Editor of *EQUUS Magazine*, 1992, Issue 180 (Reprinted with permission of Fleet Street Publishing Corporation) is quoted in the *Bag of Tricks* on *Sore Stifles/Locked Stifles*

Text from *The Merck Veterinary Manual, 7th Edition* is quoted in the *Glossary*; *Medications at the Racetrack;* and *Feeds - When and How to Feed.*

Text from *Run, Baby, Run-What every owner, breeder and handicapper should know about Lasix in Racehorses* - Bill Heller, published by The Russell Merdink Co.

Veterinary Treatments & Medications for Horsemen - published by Equine Research, Inc., PO Box 535547, Grand Prairie, TX 75053, was the source for various medical definitions in the Glossary.

Thank you to all those that contributed!

Don't forget videos. They are excellent learning tools.

Racing Organizations and Information

THE JOCKEY CLUB
AND RELATED ORGANIZATIONS

The Jockey Club

For more than a century The Jockey Club has pursued its goal as an organization dedicated to the improvement of Thoroughbred breeding and racing, earning recognition as an industry leader through its competence and technological expertise.

Responsibilities of The Jockey Club consist primarily of maintenance of *The American Stud Book* in a manner which ensures integrity of the breed in the United States of America, Canada and Puerto Rico. The Registry maintains *The American Stud Book* on a break-even basis.

The integration of new technologies into Registry procedures has improved the efficiency and cost effectiveness of Thoroughbred registration on several fronts. The switch from blood-typing to DNA typing for parentage verification, beginning with the foal crop of 2001, not only improves efficacy of parentage verification to about 99.9 per cent, but is less costly for breeders who no longer need to employ the services of a veterinarian to draw blood and, in many cases, use expensive overnight mail services.

Additionally, more than 13,000 owners and breeders utilize the convenience of the Internet-based *Jockey Club Interactive*™ to complete the requirements for foal registration, including submission of digital identification photos. The service is also used to name Thoroughbreds and is a major reason why acceptance of first choice name submissions has reached nearly 80 per cent. A special feature of the service allows breeders to nominate their foals to the Breeders' Cup program while at the same time completing the Live Foal Report or Foal Registration Application.

The Jockey Club Information Systems, Inc. (TJCIS)   http://home.jockeyclub.com

TJCIS, incorporated in 1989, is a wholly owned subsidiary of The Jockey Club Holdings, Inc. All profits from TJCIS activities are reinvested in the industry. They defray the overhead of the Registry, thereby helping to stabilize registration fees, and fund many industry projects which would otherwise lack financial support.

The company is an industry leader in the areas of technology and information services for owners, breeders, trainers and other industry professionals, continually using the latest technology to advance the services provided across its three divisions - Information Services, Cataloguing and Software Sales and Consulting.

In support of its role as the Official supplier of breeding and sales information to the National Thoroughbred Racing Association, and as part of a commitment to expand its already comprehensive database, TJCIS continues to augment international data content for *equineline.com* (profiled below). Detailed racing and breeding information from Australia and Argentina were integrated into the database in 2001, with similar records from Brazil added in early 2002. These additions provide further value to the catalogue-style pedigrees and race records available to *equineline.com* customers.

In addition, in a joint venture with the American Quarter Horse Association, TJCIS has added American Quarter Horse mare produce records to the menu of products available through the equineline Reports service.

The Cataloguing Division produced nearly 27,000 catalogue pages last year and, in a joint effort with leading sales companies, made complete sales catalogue information, including indexes, available on the Internet well before the printed catalogue was published.

The Software Sales and Consulting Division's popular Farm Management Software continues to set the standard for how leading farms maintain health and breeding records, and perform billing and accounts receivable.

www.tjcis.com

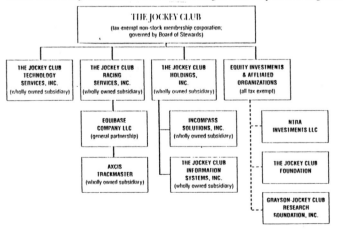

U.S. DEPT. OF AGRICULTURE - Animal & Plant Health Inspection Services:

Administrator	Washington, D.C.	(202) 720-3668
Veterinary Services	Washington, D.C.	(202) 720-5193
Animal Care (Horse Protection Act)	Hyattsville, MD	(301) 436-7586
Equine & Miscellaneous Diseases	Hyattsville, MD	(301) 436-5913

FOOD & DRUG ADMINISTRATION - Center for Veterinary Medicine:

Veterinary Equine Specialist	Rockville, MD	(301) 594-1740

INDUSTRY:

InCompass	Lexington, KY	(859) 296-3000
The Jockey Club New York	New York, NY	(212) 371-5970
The Jockey Club Lexington	Lexington, KY	(859) 224-2700
The Jockey Club Foundation	New York, NY	(212) 521-5305
The Jockey Club Information Systems, Inc.	Lexington, KY	(859) 224-2800
The Jockey Club Racing Services, Inc.	Lexington, KY	(859) 224-2860
The Jockey Club Technology Services, Inc.	Lexington, KY	(859) 224-2700

HORSE COUNCIL:

American Horse Council	Washington, D.C.	(202) 296-4031

RACING ORGANIZATIONS:

Association of Official Racing Chemists	Ottawa, ON	(613) 731-7137
Association of Racing Commissioners International	Lexington, KY	(859) 224-7070
Breeders' Cup Limited	Lexington, KY	(859) 223-5444
Equibase Company LLC	Lexington, KY	(859) 224-2860
Horsemen's Benevolent & Protective Association	Lexington, KY	(859) 259-0451
International Racing Bureau	Lexington, KY	(859) 223-3597
Jockeys' Guild	Lexington, KY	(859) 259-3211
National Museum of Racing & Hall of Fame	Saratoga Springs, NY	(518) 584-0400
National Steeplechase Association	Elkton, MD	(410) 392-0700
National Thoroughbred Racing Association	Lexington, KY	(859) 223-5444
National Thoroughbred Racing Association	New York, NY	(212) 907-9280
National Turf Writers Association	Frankfort, KY	(502) 875-4864
North American Pari-Mutuel Regulators Association	Meridian, IN	(888) 627-7250
Thoroughbred Horsemen's Associations, Inc.	Columbia, MD	(410) 740-4900
Thoroughbred Owners & Breeders Association	Lexington, KY	(859) 276-2291
Thoroughbred Racing Associations of North America	Fair Hill, MD	(410) 392-9200
Thoroughbred Racing Protective Bureau	Fair Hill, MD	(410) 398-2261
Triple Crown Productions	Louisville, KY	(502) 636-4405
Turf Publicists of America	New York, NY	(212) 521-5326
United Thoroughbred Trainers of America	Louisville,KY	(502) 893-0025

EQUINE HEALTH & RESEARCH:

American Association of Equine Practitioners	Lexington, KY	(859) 233-0147
American Veterinary Medical Association	Schaumburg, IL	(800) 248-2862
Grayson-Jockey Club Research Foundation	Lexington, KY	(859) 224-2850
Maxwell H. Gluck Equine Research Center	Lexington, KY	(859) 257-1531
Morris Animal Foundation	Englewood, CO	(303) 790-2345
University of California-Center for Equine Health	Davis, CA	(530) 752-6433

PUBLICATIONS:

The Backstretch	Louisville, KY	(502) 893-0025
The Blood-Horse	Lexington, KY	(859) 278-2361
The Daily Racing Form	New York, NY	(212) 366-7600
Thoroughbred Times	Lexington, KY	(859) 260-9800

State Organizations

ALABAMA

Birmingham Racing Commission	Birmingham	(205) 328-7223
Birmingham Race Course	Birmingham	(205) 838-7500
Alabama Horse Council	Morris	(334) 263-3407
Alabama Thoroughbred Association	Birmingham	(205) 877-8510

ARIZONA

Arizona Department of Racing	Phoenix	(602) 277-1704
Arizona Racing Commission	Phoenix	(602) 277-1704
Horsemen's Benevolent & Protective Association	Phoenix	(602) 942-3336
Apache County Fair	St. Johns	(602) 337-4364
Cochise County Fair	Douglas	(602) 364-7701
Coconino Fair	Flagstaff	(602) 774-5139
Graham County Fair	Safford	(602) 428-6240
Rillito Park	Tucson	(520) 293-5011
Santa Cruz County Fair	Sonoita	(602) 455-5553
Turf Paradise	Phoenix	(602) 942-1101
Yavapai Downs	Prescott	(602) 445-7820
Yuma County Fair	Yuma	(602) 726-4655
Arizona Thoroughbred Breeders Association	Phoenix	(602) 942-1310
Arizona State Horsemen's Association	Phoenix	(602) 867-6814
Race Track Industry Program	Tucson	(520) 621-5660

ARKANSAS

Arkansas State Racing Commission	Little Rock	(501) 682-1467
Horsemen's Benevolent & Protective Association	Hot Springs	(501) 623-7641
Oaklawn Park	Hot Springs	(501) 623-4411
Arkansas Thoroughbred Breeders' Association	Hot Springs	(501) 624-6328
Arkansas Breeders' Sales Co.	Hot Springs	(501) 624-6336
Arkansas Horse Council	Jasper	(870) 446-6226

CALIFORNIA

California Authority of Racing Fairs	Sacramento	(916) 927-7223
California Horse Racing Board	Sacramento	(916) 263-6000
California Assn. of Thoroughbred Racetracks, LLC	Sacramento	(916) 449-6820
California Thoroughbred Trainers	Arcadia	(626) 447-2145
Thoroughbred Owners of California	Arcadia	(626) 574-6620
Bay Meadows	San Mateo	(650) 574-7223
Del Mar	Del Mar	(858) 755-1141
Fairplex Park	Pomona	(909) 623-3111
Ferndale/Humboldt	Ferndale	(707) 786-9511
Fresno	Fresno ·	(559) 453-3247
Golden Gate Fields	Albany	(510) 559-7300
Hollywood Park	Inglewood	(310) 419-1500
Los Alamitos	Los Alamitos	(714) 751-3247
Oak Tree Racing Association	Arcadia	(626) 574-6345
Pleasanton/Alameda	Pleasanton	(510) 426-7600
Sacramento/Cal Expo	Sacramento	(916) 263-3279
Santa Anita Park	Arcadia	(626) 574-7223
Santa Rosa/Sonoma	Santa Rosa	(707) 545-4200
Solano/Vallejo	Vallejo	(707) 644-4401
Stockton/San Joaquin	Stockton	(209) 466-5041

CALIFORNIA *(continued)*

California Thoroughbred Breeders Association	Arcadia	(626) 445-7800
Barretts Equine Sales	Pomona	(909) 629-3099
California Thoroughbred Sales	Arcadia	(626) 445-7753
California State Horsemen's Association	Clovis	(559) 325-1055

COLORADO

Colorado Racing Commission	Lakewood	(303) 205-2990
Horsemen's Benevolent & Protective Association	Lafayette	(303) 688-9020
Arapahoe Park	Aurora	(303) 690-2400
Colorado Thoroughbred Breeders Association	Denver	(303) 294-0260
Colorado Horse Council	Boulder	(303) 449-6040

CONNECTICUT

Connecticut Division of Special Revenue	Newington	(203) 566-2756
Connecticut Horse Council	Durham	(860) 282-0468

DELAWARE

Delaware Thoroughbred Horsemen's Association	Stanton	(302) 994-2521
Delaware Thoroughbred Racing Commission	Wilmington	(302) 739-4811
Delaware Park	Stanton	(302) 994-2521
Delaware Equine Council	Harrington	(302) 697-4000

FLORIDA

Florida Division of Pari-Mutuel Wagering	Tallahassee	(850) 488-9130
Florida Pari-Mutuel Commission	Miami	(305) 470-5675
Horsemen's Benevolent & Protective Association	Opa Locka	(305) 625-4591
Horsemen's Benevolent & Protective Association	Oldsmar	(813) 855-4401
Calder Race Course - Tropical Park	Miami	(305) 625-1311
Gulfstream Park	Hallandale	(954) 454-7000
Hialeah Park	Hialeah	(305) 885-8000
Tampa Bay Downs	Oldsmar	(813) 855-4401
Fasig-Tipton Florida	Lexington, KY	(859) 255-1555
Florida Thoroughbred Breeders & Owners Association	Ocala	(352) 629-2160
Ocala Breeders' Sales Co.	Ocala	(352) 237-2154
Sunshine State Horse Council, Inc.	North Fort Myers	(941) 731-2999

GEORGIA

Georgia Thoroughbred Owners & Breeders Association	Buford	(770) **451-0409**
Georgia Horse Council	Conyers	(770) 922-3350

IDAHO

Horsemen's Benevolent & Protective Association	Meridian	(208) 888-4519
Idaho State Horse Racing Commission	Boise	(208) 884-7080
Cassia County Fair	Burley	(208) 678-7985
Eastern Idaho Fair	Blackfoot	(208) 785-2480
Gem County	Emmett	(208) 365-6144
Jerome County Fair	Jerome	(208) 324-7209
Les Bois Park	Boise	(208) 376-3991
Oneida County Fair	Fair Malad	(208) 766-2247
Pocatello Downs	Pocatello	(208) 234-0181
Rupert Fairgrounds	Rupert	(208) 436-4793
Sandy Downs - Teton Racing	Idaho Falls	(208) 529-8722
Idaho Thoroughbred Breeders Association	Boise	(208) 375-5930
Idaho Horse Council	Boise	(208) 323-8148

State Organizations

ILLINOIS

Horsemen's Benevolent & Protective Assn. (Illinois)	Caseyville	(618) 345-7724
Illinois Dept. of Agriculture - Horse Racing Programs	Springfield	(217) 782-4231
Illinois Racing Board	Chicago	(312) 814-2600
Illinois Thoroughbred Horsemen's Association	Stickney	(708) 652-2201
Arlington Park	Arlington Heights	(847) 255-4300
Fairmount Park	Collinsville	(618) 345-4300
Hawthorne Race Course	Stickney/Cicero	(708) 780-3700
Sportman's Park	Cicero	(773) 242-1121
Illinois Thoroughbred Breeders & Owners Foundation	Caseyville	(618) 344-3427
Illinois Thoroughbred Breeders & Owners Foundation Sales	Caseyville	(618) 344-3427
Horsemen's Council of Illinois	Springfield	(217) 585-1600

INDIANA

Horsemen's Benevolent & Protective Association	Guilford	(812) 576-2073
Indiana Horse Racing Commission	Indianapolis	(317) 233-3119
Hoosier Park	Anderson	(765) 642-7223
Indiana Thoroughbred Association, Inc.	Indianapolis	(317) 375-6406
Indiana Horse Council	.Indianapolis	(317) 692-7115

IOWA

Horsemen's Benevolent & Protective Association	Altoona	(515) 276-5533
Iowa Racing & Gaming Commission	Des Moines	(515) 281-7352
Iowa Horse Council	Des Moines	(515) 266-4734
Prairie Meadows	Altoona	(515) 967-1000
Iowa Thoroughbred Breeders & Owners Association	Altoona	(515) 957-3002

KANSAS

Horsemen's Benevolent & Protective Association	Zenda	(316) 243-6641
Kansas Racing Commission	Topeka	(785) 296-5800
Eureka Downs	Eureka	(316) 583-5528
The Woodlands	Kansas City	(913) 299-9797
Kansas Horse Council	Sabetha	(785) 284-0500
Kansas Thoroughbred Association	Fredonia	(316) 378-4772

KENTUCKY

Horsemen's Benevolent & Protective Association	Louisville	(502) 363-1077
Kentucky State Racing Commission	Lexington	(859) 246-2040
Bluegrass Downs	Paducah	(270) 444-7117
Churchill Downs	Louisville	(502) 636-4400
Ellis Park	Henderson	(812) 425-1456
Keeneland Association, Inc.	Lexington	(859) 254-3412
Kentucky Downs	Franklin	(502) 586-7778
Turfway Park LLC	Florence	(859) 371-0200
Kentucky Thoroughbred Association	Lexington	(859) 381-1414
Kentucky Thoroughbred Owners & Breeders	Lexington	(859) 259-1643
Fasig-Tipton Company, Inc.	Lexington	(859) 255-1555
Keeneland Association, Inc.	Lexington	(859) 254-3412
Lexington Breeders' Sales	Lexington	(859) 269-0695
Stallion Access/Fasig-Tipton	Lexington	(859) 255-1555

KENTUCKY *(continued)*

Kentucky Derby Museum	Louisville	(502) 637-1111
Kentucky Horse Park	Lexington	(859) 233-4303
University of Louisville Equine Administration Program	Louisville	(502) 852-7617
Kentucky Horse Council	Lexington	**(859) 367-0509**

LOUISIANA

Horsemen's Benevolent & Protective Association	New Orleans	(504) 945-1555
Louisiana State Racing Commission	New Orleans	(504) 483-4000
Delta Downs	Vinton	(318) 589-7441
Evangeline Downs	Lafayette	(337) 896-7223
Fair Grounds	New Orleans	(504) 944-5515
Louisiana Downs	Bossier City	(318) 742-5555
Louisiana Thoroughbred Breeders Association	New Orleans	(504) 943-7556
Breeders Sales Co. of Louisiana	New Orleans	(504) 947-4676
Fasig-Tipton Louisiana	Lexington, KY	(859) 255-1555
Louisiana Thoroughbred Breeders Sales Co.	Carencro	(337) 896-6152

MARYLAND

Maryland Million, Ltd.	Timonium	(410) 252-2100
Maryland Racing Commission	Baltimore	(410) 230-6330
Laurel Race Course	Laurel	(410) 792-7775
Marlboro	Upper Marlboro	(301) 952-4740
Pimlico Race Course	Baltimore	(410) 542-9400
Timonium	Timonium	(410) 252-0200
Maryland Horse Breeders Association	Timonium	(410) 252-2100
Maryland Horse Breeders Foundation	Timonium	(410) 252-2100
Maryland Thoroughbred Horsemen's Association	Baltimore	(410) 265-6842
Fasig-Tipton Midlantic, Inc.	Elkton	(410) 392-5555
Maryland Horse Council, Inc.	Timonium	(410) 489-7826

MASSACHUSETTS

Massachusetts State Racing Commission	Boston	(617) 727-2581
New England Thoroughbred Horsemen's Association	East Boston	(617) 567-3900
Northampton Fair	Northampton	(413) 584-2237
Suffolk Downs	East Boston	(617) 567-3900
Massachusetts Thoroughbred Breeders Association, Inc.	Boston	(617) 492-7217

MICHIGAN

Horsemen's Benevolent & Protective Association	Muskegon	(231) 798-2250
Michigan - Office of the Racing Commissioner	Livonia	(734) 462-2400
Great Lakes Downs	Muskegon	(616) 799-2400
Mount Pleasant Meadows	Mt. Pleasant	(517) 773-0012
Michigan Thoroughbred Owners & Breeders Assn.	Fenton	(810) 632-7771
Michigan Horse Council	Lansing	**(231) 821-2487**

MINNESOTA

Horsemen's Benevolent & Protective Association	Shakopee	(952) 496-6442
Minnesota Racing Commission	Shakopee	(952) 496-7950
Canterbury Park	Shakopee	(952) 445-7223
Minnesota Horse Council	Coon Rapids	(612) 576-1757
Minnesota Thoroughbred Association	Shakopee	(952) 496-3770

State Organizations

MINNESOTA *(continued)*
Minnesota Thoroughbred Association/Sales	Hamel	(612) 477-4829

MISSISSIPPI
Mississippi Thoroughbred Breeders & Owners Association	Madison	(601) 856-8293
Mississippi Horse Council	Tupelo	(601) 842-9346

MISSOURI
Missouri Horse Racing Commission	Jefferson City	(573) 751-2000
Missouri Equine Council	Republic	(417) 732-4062
Missouri Thoroughbred Owners & Breeders Association	Willard	(417) 742-2624

MONTANA
Horsemen's Benevolent & Protective Association	Billings	(406) 256-8364
State of Montana Board of Horse Racing	Helena	(406) 444-4287
Cow Capital Turf Club	Miles City	(406) 232-3758
Flathead Fairgrounds	Kalispell	(406) 756-5628
Great Falls	Great Falls	(406) 727-8900
Helena	Helena	(406) 443-7210
Marias Fair	Shelby	(406) 434-2692
Ravalli County Fairgrounds	Hamilton	(406) 363-3411
Western Montana Fair	Missoula	(406) 721-3247
Yellowstone Downs	Billings	(406) 254-8383

NEBRASKA
Horsemen's Benevolent & Protective Association	Grand Island	(308) 389-3073
Nebraska State Racing Commission	Lincoln	(402) 471-2577
Columbus	Columbus	(402) 564-0133
Fonner Park	Grand Island	(308) 382-4515
Horsemen's Park	Omaha	(402) 731-2900
Lincoln	Lincoln	(402) 474-5371
Nebraska Thoroughbred Breeders' Association	Grand Island	(308) 384-4683
Nebraska Horse Council	Denton	(402) 797-5865

NEVADA
Nevada Gaming Control Board	Las Vegas	**(702) 486-2000**

NEW HAMPSHIRE
New England Thoroughbred Horsemen's Association	East Boston, MA	(617) 567-3900
New Hampshire Pari-Mutuel Commission	Concord	(603) 271-2158
Rockingham Park	Salem	(603) 898-2311
New Hampshire Horse Council	New Ipswich	(603) 878-1694

NEW JERSEY
New Jersey Racing Commission	Trenton	(609) 292-0613
New Jersey Thoroughbred Horseman's Benevolent Assn.	Colt's Neck	(908) 389-0804
Atlantic City Racing Association	Atlantic City	(609) 641-2190
The Meadowlands	East Rutherford	(201) 935-8500
Monmouth Park	Oceanport	(732) 222-5100
Thoroughbred Breeders' Association of New Jersey	Long Branch,	**(732) 870-9718**
New Jersey Horse Council	Moorestown	(856) 231-0771

NEW MEXICO
New Mexico Racing Commission	Albuquerque	(505) 841-6400
The Downs at Albuquerque	Albuquerque	(505) 266-5555

NEW MEXICO *(continued)*

The Downs at Santa Fe	Santa Fe	(505) 471-3311
Ruidoso Downs	Ruidoso Downs	(505) 378-4431
SunRay Park	Farmington	(505) 326-4551
Sunland Park	Sunland Park	(505) 874-5200
New Mexico Horse Breeders' Association	Albuquerque	(505) 262-0224
Ruidoso Horse Sales Co.	Glencoe	(505) 653-4242
New Mexico Horse Council	Albuquerque	(505) 345-8959

NEW YORK

Horsemen's Benevolent & Protective Assn. (Finger Lakes)	Canandaigua	(716) 924-3004
Horsemen's Benevolent &Protective Assn. (New York)	Jamaica	(718) 641-4700
New York City Off-Track Betting Corp.	New York	(212) 704-5000
New York State Racing Commission	New York	(212) 219-4230
New York State Racing & Wagering Board	Albany	(518) 453-8460
New York State Regional OTB Corporations:		
Capital Regional OTB	Schenectady	(518) 370-5151
Catskill Regional OTB	Pomona	(914) 362-0400
Nassau County Regional OTB	Hempstead	(516) 292-8300
Suffolk Regional OTB	Hauppauge	(516) 853-1000
Western Regional OTB	Batavia	(716) 343-1423
Aqueduct	Queens	(718) 641-4700
Belmont	Elmont	(516) 488-6000
Finger Lakes	Farmington	(716) 924-3232
Saratoga	Saratoga Springs	(518) 584-6200
Genesee Valley Breeders Association	**Shortsville**	**(585) 289-8524**
New York State Thoroughbred Breeding & Dev. Fund Corp.	New York	(212) 465-0660
New York Thoroughbred Breeders	Saratoga Springs	(518) 587-0777
Fasig-Tipton New York	Elmont	(516) 328-1800
New York State'Horse Council	Webster	(716) 872-3178

NORTH CAROLINA

North Carolina Horse Council	Raleigh	(919) 821-1030
North Carolina Thoroughbred Breeders Association	Hillsborough	(919) **471-0131**

NORTH DAKOTA

North Dakota Racing Commission	Bismark	(701) 328-4290

OHIO

Horsemen's Benevolent & Protective Association	Grove City	(614) 875-1269
Ohio State Racing Commission	Columbus	(614) 466-2757
Beulah Park	Grove City	(614) 871-9600
River Downs	Cincinnati	(513) 232-8000
Thistledown	North Randall	(216) 662-8600
National Equine Sales	Springfield	(937) 324-5558
Ohio Thoroughbred Breeders & Owners	Cincinnati	(513) 574-5888
Ohio Horseman's Council	Miamisburg	(740) 385-0111

OKLAHOMA

Horsemen's Benevolent and Protective Association	Oklahoma City	(405) 427-8753
Oklahoma Horse Racing Commission	Oklahoma City	(405) 943-6472
Blue Ribbon Downs	Sallisaw	(918) 775-7771
Fair Meadows at Tulsa	Tulsa	(918) 743-7223

State Organizations

OKLAHOMA *(continued)*

Remington Park	Oklahoma City	(405) 424-1000
Will Rogers Downs	Claremore	(918) 341-4720
Oklahoma Horsemen's Association	Oklahoma City	(405) 843-8333
Oklahoma Thoroughbred Association	Oklahoma City	(405) 330-1008
Heritage Place Sales Company	Oklahoma City	(405) 682-4551
Oklahoma Horse Council	Tulsa	(918) 663-0471

OREGON

Horsemen's Benevolent & Protective Association	Portland	(503) 285-4941
Oregon Racing Commission	Portland	(503) 731-4052
Eastern Oregon Livestock Show	Union	(503) 562-5828
Grants Pass Downs	Grants Pass	(541) 476-6234
Harney County Fairgrounds	Burns	(503) 573-2326
Klamath County Fairgrounds	Klamath Falls	(541) 883-3796
Lone Oak Park/Salem	Salem	(503) 585-8237
Portland Meadows	Portland	(503) 285-9144
Oregon Horsemen's Association	Springfield	(541) 746-6564
Oregon Thoroughbred Breeders' Association	Portland	(503) 285-0658

PENNSYLVANIA

Horsemen's Benevolent & Protective Association	Grantville	(717) 469-2970
Pennsylvania State Horse Racing Commission	Harrisburg	(717) 787-1942
Pennsylvania Thoroughbred Horsemen's Association	Bensalem	(215) 638-2012
Penn National	Grantville	(717) 469-2211
Philadelphia Park	Bensalem	(215) 639-9000
Pennsylvania Horse Breeders' Association	Kennett Square	(610) 444-1050
Fasig-Tipton Midlantic	Kennett Square	(610) 444-9000
Pennsylvania Equine Council	Dallas	(888) 304-0281

PUERTO RICO

Puerto Rico Racing Sport Administration	San Juan	(787) 762-5210
El Comandante	San Juan	(787) 724-6060
Puerto Rico Thoroughbred Breeders Association	San Juan	(787) 725-8715

RHODE ISLAND

R.I. Dept. of Business Reg., Div. of Racing & Athletics	Providence	(401) 222-6541

SOUTH CAROLINA

South Carolina Department of Agriculture	Columbia	(803) 734-2210
Thoroughbred Association of South Carolina	Camden	(803) 432-4190
South Carolina Horsemen's Council	Columbia	(803) 734-2210

SOUTH DAKOTA

South Dakota Commission on Gaming	Pierre	(605) 773-6050
South Dakota Horse Council	Hayti	(605) 783-3832

TENNESSEE

Tennessee Thoroughbred Owners & Breeders Assn.	Nashville	(615) 254-3376
Tennessee Breeders Sales Co.	Nashville	(615) 373-8197
Tennessee Horse Council	College Grove	(615) 297-3200

TEXAS

Texas Horsemen's Partnership LLP	Austin	(512) 467-9799
Texas Racing Commission	Austin	(512) 833-6699
Gillespie County Downs	Fredericksburg	**(830) 997-2359**
Lone Star Park at Grand Prairie	Grand Prairie	(972) 263-7223
Retama Park	San Antonio	(210) 651-7000
Sam Houston Race Park	Houston	(281) 807-8700
Texas Thoroughbred Association	Austin	(512) 458-6133
Texas Thoroughbred Association Sales Co.	Austin	(512) 458-6133

VERMONT

Vermont Racing Commission	Rutland	(802) 786-5050

VIRGINIA

Virginia Racing Commission	New Kent	(804) 966-7400
Colonial Downs	New Kent	(804) 966-7223
Virginia Thoroughbred Association	Warrenton	(540) 347-4313
Virginia Horse Council	Richmond	(804) 754-8689

WASHINGTON

Horsemen's Benevolent & Protective Association	Auburn	(253) 804-6822
Washington Horse Racing Commission	Olympia	(360) 459-6462
Emerald Downs	Auburn	(253) 288-7000
Sun Downs	Kennewick	(509) 582-5434
Washington Thoroughbred Breeders Association	Auburn	(253) 288-7878
Washington State Horse Council	Port Orchard	(360) 769-8083

WEST VIRGINIA

Horsemen's Benevolent & Protective Assn. (Charles Town)	Charles Town	(304) 725-7001
Horsemen's Benevolent & Protective Assn. (Mountaineer)	New Cumberland	(304) 387-9772
West Virginia Racing Commission	Charleston	(304) 558-2150
Charles Town Races	Charles Town	(304) 725-7001
Mountaineer Park	Chester	(304) 387-2400
West Virginia Thoroughbred Breeders Association	Charles Town	(304) 725-5274
West Virginia Horse Council	Vienna	(304) 295-6363

WISCONSIN

Wisconsin Gaming Commission	Madison	(608) 264-6607
Wisconsin State Horse Council	Columbus	(920) 623-0393

WYOMING

Wyoming Pari-Mutuel Commission	Cheyenne	(307) 777-5887
Central Wyoming	Casper	(307) 235-5775
Energy Downs	Gillette	(307) 682-0552
Wyoming Downs	Evanston	(307) 789-0511
Wyoming Horse Council	Laramie	(307) 766-6855

Canadian Organizations

Canadian Thoroughbred Horse Society (National Office)	Rexdale, Ont.	(416) 675-1370
The Jockey Club of Canada	Rexdale, Ont.	(416) 675-7756
Racetracks of Canada	Mississauga, Ont.	(905) 821-7795

ALBERTA

Alberta Racing Commission	Calgary	(403) 297-6551
Northlands Park	Edmonton	(403) 471-7379
Stampede Park	Calgary	(403) 261-0214
Canadian Thoroughbred Horse Society (Alberta Division)	Calgary	(403) 229-3609

BRITISH COLUMBIA

British Columbia Racing Commission	Burnaby	(604) 660-7400
Horsemen's Benevolent & Protective Association	Vancouver	(604) 984-4311
Desert Park	Osoyoos	(250) 495-3232
Hastings Park	Vancouver	(604) 254-1631
Sandown Park	Sidney	(250) 386-2261
Canadian Thoroughbred Horse Society (B.C. Division)	Surrey	(604) 574-0145

MANITOBA

Horsemen's Benevolent & Protective Association (Western)	Winnipeg	(204) 832-4949
Manitoba Horse Racing Commission	Winnipeg	(204) 885-7770
Assiniboia Downs	Winnipeg	(204) 885-3330
Canadian Thoroughbred Horse Society (Manitoba Division)	Winnipeg	(204) 832-1702

ONTARIO

Horsemen's Benevolent & Protective Association (Eastern)	Rexdale	(416) 675-3805
Woodbine Entertainment Group	Rexdale	(416) 675-6110
Ontario Racing Commission	Toronto	(416) 327-0520
Fort Erie	Fort Erie	(905) 871-3200
Woodbine	Toronto	(416) 675-6110
Canadian Thoroughbred Horse Society (Ontario Division)	Rexdale	(416) 675-3602
Woodbine Sales	Rexdale	(416) 674-1460

QUEBEC

Quebec Racing Commission	Montreal	(514) 873-5000
Canadian Thoroughbred Horse Society (Quebec Division)	Lac Guindon	(450) 224-4020

SASKATCHEWAN

Saskatchewan Horse Racing Commission	Saskatoon	(306) 933-5999
Marquis Downs	Saskatoon	(306) 242-6100
Canadian Thoroughbred Horse Society (Saskatchewan Div.)	Saskatoon	(306) 374-7777

	Country Code	Telephone	Fax
AUSTRALIA			
Australian Jockey Club (Randwick)	(61)	2 9663 8400	2 9662 1447
Australian Racing Board	(61)	2 9313 8014	2 9697 9425
Australian Stud Book (Randwick)	(61)	2 9663 8411	2 9663 4718
Racing Services Bureau (Flemington)	(61)	3 9258 4721	3 9258 4715
Victoria Racing Club (Melbourne)	(61)	3 9258 4666	3 9258 4743
BRITAIN			
British Horseracing Board (London)	(44)	171396 0011	171935 3626
Tattersalls (Newmarket)	(44)	163866 5931	163866 0850
The Jockey Club (London)	(44)	171486 4921	171935 8703
Weatherbys (Wellingborough)	(44)	193344 0077	193344 0807
FRANCE			
France-Galop (Paris)	(33)	1 49 10 20 30	1 47 61 93 32
GERMANY			
Direktorium Fur Vollblutzucht und Rennen (Cologne)	(49)	221 7498 16	221 7498 64
HONG KONG			
Hong Kong Jockey Club (Happy Valley)	(852)	2966 8111	2577 9036
IRELAND			
Goffs Bloodstock Sales Ltd. (Kill)	(353)	45-877211	45-877119
Irish Horseracing Authority (Dublin)	(353)	1 289 2888	1 289 2019
Tattersalls (Ireland) Ltd. (Ratoath)	(353)	1 8256777	1 8256789
The Turf Club (The Curragh)	(353)	45-441599	45-441576
Weatherbys (Ireland) Ltd. (Naas)	(353)	45-879979	45-879671
ITALY			
Jockey Club Italiano (Rome)	(39)	6 58.33.09.25	6 58.33.09.21
JAPAN			
Japan Race Horse Registry (Tokyo)	(81)	3 3434 5315	3 3432 4668
Japan Racing Association (Tokyo)	(81)	3 3591 5251	3 3438 4893
Japan Racing Association (Stamford, CT)		(203) 973-0661	(203) 973-0665
National Association of Racing (Tokyo)	(81)	3 3583 6841	3 3585 0481
NEW ZEALAND			
New Zealand Racing Conference (Wellington)	(64)	4 385-3988	4 384-5867
SOUTH AFRICA			
The Jockey Club of South Africa (Turffontein)	(27)	11 683-9283	11 434-1636
UNITED ARAB EMIRATES			
Dubai World Cup (Dubai)	(971)	4 3322277	4 3322288
The Emirates Racing Association (Dubai)	(971)	4 3313311	4 3313322

American Paint Horse Association
Paint racing is on the fast track

The mission of the American Paint Horse Association is to collect, record and preserve the pedigrees of American Paint Horses and to stimulate and regulate all matters that pertain to the promotion, history, breeding and exhibition of the breed.

With its roots firmly grounded in American Quarter Horse and Thoroughbred bloodlines, the American Paint Horse is a formidable speed horse. Paints are generally considered to be sprinters - horses that run at distances ranging from 220 to 870 yards with 350 yards being the most common distance. Paint racers contend for nearly $4 million in purses each year on recognized pari-mutuel tracks.

APHA Racing Department
The Racing Department is responsible for recording race results, maintaining racing standings and overseeing the racing tattoo program. The department also furnishes information on the racing records of American Paints, and co-produces the bi-monthly APHA racing newsletter, *Paint Racing News*, with the Marketing and Communications Department. This newsletter is a free subscription with a membership to the American Paint Horse Association.

Champion Running Paint Horses are honored each year during the annual APHA Workshop, and a Register Of Merit (ROM) is awarded to Paint Horses who earn an official speed index of 80 or better. Superior awards are given to Paint Horses earning 50 or more points in racing.

For more information, contact the APHA Racing Department, P.O. Box 961023, Fort Worth, Texas 76161, or call (817) 222-6444. Visit the Paint racing Web site at http://www.apha.com/racing.

THOROUGHBRED OWNERS OF CALIFORNIA

The overall purpose of TOC is to provide effective leadership to the Thoroughbred industry in California.
It's goal is to serve as a voice for the broad interests of Thoroughbred owners and improve and increase the representation of horse owners in the day today activities of racing.

The TOC is the CHRB-recognized representative of owners and has taken a primary role in the California Horseracing Industry. Owners for too long have been ignored. TOC is now their recognized vehicle, and strives to protect the economic interests and investments of all horsemen and to gain public recognition of horseracing as a vital form of entertainment deserving of support, protection and preservation.

Its policy will be to work closely with all segments of this fragmented industry – to create coalitions as industry-wide policies are formulated, developed and implemented.

For more information call 626 574 6620, toll free, 800 994 9909 or www.topconline.com The Handbook for Thoroughbreds Owners Of California may be purchased through this office.

Many thanks To TOC for info shared from their _owners_ Handbook - it may be purchased from them directly and is full of information!

Arabian Jockey Club

10805 E. Bethany Dr. Aurora, CO 80014
303-696-4568 Fax 303-743-6246 e-mail ajc@arabianracing.org
Website www.arabianracing.org

Arabian racing was organized around 1959. Beginning in 1987, the Arabian Jockey Club is a national organization dedicated to the promotion, education and professional management of the Arabian racing industry. To ensure that opportunities for owners of Arabian horses continue, the AJC has developed a number of promotional and educational resources to help reach this goal.

. *The Original Racehorse* - This free educational video offers the racing newcomer
   a professional, evenhanded look at getting involved in the sport.
. *Arabian Race Source* - This online database gives users 24-hour access to over 30
   different racing reports that are pulled from the AJC's racing database from a
   personal-computer. The website is: www.tbearabsource.com
. *Arabian Racing Cup* - In 1996, the AJC began administering this breeders'
   incentive program. Nominators of Arabian Cup Sires, Broodmares and Runners
   reap the rewards of this lucrative program

For additional information, please contact the AJC.

Serving the Thoroughbred Industry for over 40 years. TOBA's mission is to improve the economics, integrity and pleasure of the sport on behalf of Thoroughbred owners and breeders.

* TOBA administers and manages the American Graded Stakes Committee.
* TOBA is a founding member of The National Thoroughbred Racing Association and holds a seat on the Board of Directors.
* TOBA Administers and manages The Greatest Game and is the only national organization that coordinates new prospective Thoroughbred owner educational programs, assisting the industry everywhere in recruiting and training new owners.
* TOBA publishes *The Blood-Horse* magazine.
* TOBA represents owners on the Racing Medication and Testing Consortium
* TOBA serves as a clearinghouse of industry information for owners and breeders, not only in North America, but worldwide.
* TOBA serves as a Communications network with its members throughout the world on issues and projects of vital significance in the industry.
* TOBA's International Equine Health Committee, monitors the outbreak and/or transmission of equine diseases throughout the world.
* TOBA created promotional projects such as Claiming Crown and America's Day at the Races.
* TOBA hosts the Annual National Awards Dinner, recognizing the efforts of our colleagues around the country who breed and own quality Thoroughbreds.
* TOBA represents the United States on the International Breeders' Secretariat, a forum that includes seventeen racing and breeding countries, which meet annually to discuss issues of global significance to the industry.
* TOBA supports the National Racing Compact.
* TOBA spearheaded the development of the Horse Industry Economic Impact Study, in order to identify and quantify domestic equine activity.
* TOBA represents the United States in the International Racing Owners Association (IROA).
* TOBA is a founding member of the Racing Medication and Testing Consortium, Inc.

P.O. Box 4367, Lexington, KY 40544-4367, (859) 276-2291, Fax (859) 276-2462 www.toba.org

P. O. Box 7065 * Louisville, KY 40257-0065
Phone (502) 893-0025 * Fax: (502) 893-0026
Toll Free: (800) 325-3487

United Thoroughbred Trainers *of* America. Inc., 45 years old in 2001, is an organization that exists to serve the interests of Thoroughbred trainers and Thoroughbred racing. Among its goals are: to elevate the standards of the vocation of professional training; to promote the sport of Thoroughbred racing and the ownership of Thoroughbred horses; and to work with track management, state Racing Commissions, the HBPA, Jockeys' Guild and all other racing bodies to protect the concerns of its members and to assist them In matters affecting the practice of their profession. UTTA offers reasonably priced workers' compensation and general liability.

The organization honors excellence in its field with an annual Outstanding Trainer award. Past recipients include Warren A. 'Jimmy' Croll, Claude R. 'Shug' McGaughey, H. Allen Jerkens and Frank L Brothers.

For Information on membership in UTTA and its benefits call (502) 893-0025 or (800) 325-3487.

AMERICAN QUARTER HORSE RACING

The AQHA Racing Department is the official record keeper for American Quarter Horse racing. They compile the results of recognized races from the United States, Canada and Mexico, maintain all official statistics, oversee the racing tattoo program and handle awards. The department also provides an extensive marketing and promotional program to assist tracks that race American Quarter Horses.

Some of AQHA's helpful materials available for potential racehorse owners:

"A Guide To Owning America's Fastest Athlete." This guide gives a new owner information on buying a horse at auction, claiming a racehorse, choosing a trainer and figuring costs, plus, interviews with American Quarter Horse owners. Free.

. *The Quarter Racing Journal.* An award-winning monthly magazine with accounts *of* major races, commentary from industry leaders, articles on racehorse health and management. profiles of notable owners. breeders, jockeys and trainers. and more. A one-year subscription is $25. To subscribe call the *Journal* Circulation Department at (806) 372-1192.

. "Owning America's Fastest Athlete" This 12-minute video explains acquiring a racing American Quarter Horse, choosing a trainer and the opportunities available in the industry. The video ends with the award-winning music video "Running Blood" by Michael Martin Murphy. $10.00.

To order the above materials, call the AQHA Racing Department at (806) 376-4888. ext. 357 or write AQHA. Racing Dept., P.O. Box 200, Amarillo, TX 79168.

APPALOOSA HORSE CLUB

President: Diane Rushing
Contact: Roger Klamfoth, CEO
P. O. Box 8403
2720 W. Pullman Rd.
Moscow, ID 83843-0903
208-882-5578 Fax: 208-882-8150
email: aphc@appaloosa.com
Appaloosa Journal

PACIFIC COAST QUARTER HORSE RACING ASSOCIATION

President: Dominic Alessio
Contact: Mike Fones, Bus. Mgr.
P. O. Box 919
Los Alamitos, CA 90720-0919
714-236-1755 Fax: 714-236-1761
email: pcqhra@earthlink.net
web address: www.pcqhra.org
PCQHRA Newsletter

What is the TRF?

Begun nearly two decades ago, the Thoroughbred Retirement Foundation provides lifelong haven to Thoroughbreds at TRF retirement farms in Connecticut, Florida, Illinois, Kentucky, New Jersey, New York, Pennsylvania, Vermont and Virginia. Registered Thoroughbreds with a racing record, free from contagious or communicable diseases, and for which private retirement is unavailable or unsuitable, are eligible for the Thoroughbred Retirement Foundation.

No horses are sold and none are ridden, unless suitable for our adoption program. The horses, in turn, continue to earn their keep as vital partners in the TRF's pioneering vocational training program for adult and juvenile offenders. Indeed, the TRF has become a model for humane efforts nationwide.

These accomplishments would not have been possible without the support and commitment of concerned individuals nationwide. But the job is not complete. To continue our dual rescue mission, more than ever, we need your help. Can we count on you? Tax-deductible donations, large or small, will be gratefully accepted.

Yes, I want to help.

Here is my "winning" tax deductible contribution of $ _____
(Please make checks payable to the Thoroughbred Retirement Foundation.)

Name _____

Address _____

City _____ State _____ Zip _____

Please mail checks to:
Thoroughbred Retirement Foundation
Suite 351, 450 Shrewsbury Plaza, Shrewsbury, NJ 07702

All contributors will receive RENEWS, the TRF newsletter.
The TRF is a registered 501(c)3 nonprofit organization.
Your gift is tax-deductible.

Visit our website: www.trfinc.org

A copy of the Foundation's latest annual report may be obtained, upon request, from the organization or from the Office of the Attorney General, Charities Bureau, 120 Broadway, New York, NY 10271.

THOROUGHBRED RETIREMENT FOUNDATION

... offering renewed hope to all involved.

We are thrilled when powerful thoroughbreds round the turn into the stretch, pounding towards the finish line. It's a heart-catching moment when anything still seems possible.

For too many of these horses, though, the possibilities will end when they've run their last race. Their finish then will be as certain as it is tragic—a trip to the slaughterhouse.

They deserve better from us.

That's why, eighteen years ago, the Thoroughbred Retirement Foundation (TRF) was born. Today, racehorses no longer able to run due to age or infirmity are finding haven at TRF farms in New York, Maryland, Kentucky, Connecticut, Illinois, Virginia, Vermont, Florida, and New Jersey.

Racing fans will remember such TRF pensioners as Creme de la Fete, who won 40 of his 151 starts—more than the legendary John Henry; the champion New York sprinter H.T. Willis, who courageously finished his last race despite broken sesamoids; Banker's Jet, a multiple stakes winner of $680,000, but abandoned and near death from starvation when we found him, his protruding ribs casting dark shadows across his shabby coat.

Juvenile offenders in the TRF vocational program at the Charles Hickey, J. School in Maryland have given the horses a big-hearted welcome. Through caring for these magnificent but needy animals, the youths are discovering within themselves feelings of love and responsibility and a sense of purpose that will help them to resurrect their own troubled lives.

At our home in Wallkill (N.Y.) State Correctional Facility, these horses and their stablemates have thrived under the loving attention of inmates who are learning horse care skills in the TRF's state-accredited vocational training course. It's been called "the best rehabilitative program in the system." In November 1999, TRF duplicated this program in Lexington, Kentucky. Our facility in Ocala, Florida will open in May 2000. This expansion will double the number of Thoroughbred Racehorses finding a haven through the TRF.

At TRF, everyone wins.

This is like the United Way — They help support groups around the country!

TRANQUILITY FARM

BOARD OF DIRECTORS
Priscilla Clark, President
Gary Biszantz, Vice President
John Russell, Secretary
Trudy McCaffery, Treasurer

NTRA CHARITIES

P.O. Box 210 Tehachapi CA 93581
661-823-0307 Fax 661-822-7072
email: info@tranquilityfarmtbs.org
www.tranquilityfarmtbs.org

United Pegasus Foundation –
A 501 (c) Non-Profit Organization
120 First Avenue, Arcadia, CA 91009
www.unitedpegasus.com Phone: (626) 279-1306

unitedpegasus@yahoo.com

There are many good local organizations fo Race Horse Retirement - these are a few - Go on the "net" To find out more!

ORDER FORM

Backyard Racehorse
3708 Crystal Beach Road
Winter Haven, Florida 33880
Tel 1 (863) 299-8448 FAX 1 (863) 294-9401

SEND TO:

_____

_____

_____

Telephone:_____

Backyard Racehorse - $35.00 per copy

Number of Copies: ____ x $35.00 = _____

Florida Residents add 6%   _____

Shipping - Priority Mail $7.00

Total Enclosed   _____

For information regarding The Backyard Race Horse Newsletter, or seminars at Rancho Del Castillo or in your area, contact Prediction Publications at the above address.

Drop me a Line!

I am interested in The Newsletter   _____

I am interested in Seminars   _____

*Ft. Lauderdale Lynes
Pompano - Sun
July 21, 1985*   7/21

Dave Joseph

■ HORSE RACING

'Prediction' making fond memories for trainer and charity

There are fond memories, Janet DelCastillo says, but not many of victory.

Between bushtrack racing and bad breeding, DelCastillo, 40, has had little luck and fewer winners with the thoroughbreds she has trained.

After eight years, she can't recall any of her horses as "noteworthy. It seems they've always been bottom-of-the-line claimers."

In Winter Haven, where DelCastillo lives with her three children, the locals don't care a lot about horse racing. In February they turn their attention to the Boston Red Sox, headquartered there for spring training. The rest of the year Winter Haven is known as the home of Cypress Gardens.

But DelCastillo may yet change the way they think. In the middle of Winter Haven, on 12 acres, DelCastillo has what seems to be a legitimate stakes horse in First Prediction.

The horse has been in the money six of her 10 races, and in her last start finished second in a division of Calder's Gloxinia Stakes.

DelCastillo isn't the only one profiting from First Prediction's success. The Florida Horsemen's Children's Home in Ocala for "problem" boys and girls shares.

When Ed MacClellan of the children's home offered to sell DelCastillo the filly and another horse in March for a bargain-basement $5,000, DelCastillo didn't have the money.

"I was helping them with artwork at the school, and Ed asked if I wanted the two," DelCastillo said.

The horses had been donated to the school, and "he said that I could pay him when I had the money."

When First Prediction began earning some purse money, DelCastillo didn't forget. Now, every time First Prediction earns a check, the children's home gets a donation.

DelCastillo's odyssey began 10 years ago. Born and reared in San Francisco, she trained polo ponies until she joined the Peace Corps and went to Colombia, where she met her husband.

After living in Buffalo and Staten Island, the DelCastillos moved to Winter Haven and started racing horses.

"One day my husband said that we should get some race horses, so we got a few mares and we bred them," DelCastillo said.

"We raced [quarter horses] at Pompano, then we got thoroughbreds. But after putting around $16,000 into the horses we were lucky if they were running in $2,500 races at Tampa [Bay Downs]."

Finally, along came First Prediction, a 3-year-old by On To Glory-Around The Bend.

First Prediction is not a large filly, but she has showed enough to be considered a runner.

After breaking her maiden at Tampa Bay Downs in March, the filly has continued to improve.

After running respectably in two allowance races at Hialeah, the filly moved to Calder and finished second to C'Mon Liz in the Gloxinia two weeks ago.

Appearing to weaken after C'Mon Liz passed her entering the stretch over Calder's turf coure, First Prediction made a run at the victor in the closing yards to place.

In lieu of a track, DelCastillo has used her back yard. She builds her horses up with slow five-mile gallops through orange groves

"It's really more like a trail," mostly heavy sand, which DelCastillo says builds up stamina.

"I think it's like a child," she said. "If you expose a horse to a lot of things, then it's only a question of speed. I think my training builds up a horse and makes it a stronger piece of equipment."

After building up the endurance and then testing her horses with intervals of speed workouts, she swims them in a mile lake behind her house, "sometimes two times a day if it's hot."

The rest of the time, DelCastillo quarters her horses in her eight-stall barn as little as possible.

"I think a horse needs sun and vitamin D," she said.

"Sure, mine have a few problems with some cuts and nicks they get on our fences, and their coats always look bleached, but their bodies are much more solid, and I've never had any tendon problems because of the long, slow foundation."

The foundation has been laid for Saturday's $50,000 Office Queen Stakes for 3-year-old fillies over Calder's 1 1/16-mile turf course.

"I really think we've got a chance," DelCastillo said. "All I've ever really wanted all these years was a horse I could throw in the van to race that I wasn't afraid was going to get claimed.

"I've waited a lifetime for this, and I may not get another chance."

So Friday Janet DelCastillo will van First Prediction the 4½ hours from Winter Haven to Miami in hope of winning the Office Queen.

There will be a lot of people pulling for DelCastillo, but none more than the boys and girls at the Florida Horsemen's Children's Home.

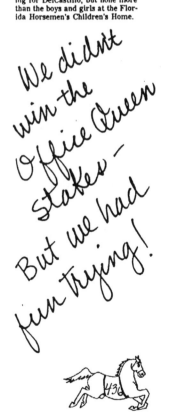

We didn't win the Office Queen Stakes — But we had fun trying!

Can nice girls finish first?
Calder race tells the story

By LUTHER EVANS
Herald Turf Writer

First Prediction held only a head advantage over charging Truly when they reached the eighth pole in Saturday's $47,650 Black Velvet Handicap before 9,884 fans at Calder.

On which filly would you have bet your money at that point?

Truly was the 2.20-1 favorite. She is is a daughter of the great stallion In Reality, bred by the eminently successful Frances A. Genter. She is trained by Frank Gomez, Calder's all-time-leading winner of stakes with 58. She was being ridden by Jose Velez Jr., Calder's 1985 riding champion with 109 winners.

First Prediction went off as a 15.30-1 long shot. She is a daughter of On to Glory and was bred by Paul Marriott, who culled her from his yearlings as being too small and gave her to the Florida Horsemen Childrens' Home in Citra, Fla. Later, Janet Del Castillo bought her on credit as part of a two-filly package for $5,000.

The primary training of First Prediction consists of Del Castillo, admittedly "a large woman," galloping her through a Winter Haven orange grove and also swimming the filly in a nearby lake. Saturday, First Prediction was being ridden as usual by Benny Green, a nice guy who has to scuffle to make a living ... unfortunate for a jockey with his ability.

At the sixteenth pole, First Prediction and Truly had swept past front-runner Merry Cathy and C'mon Liz and still were at each other's throats. Now, by all logic, you would have bet on Truly. Right?

Wrong.

First Prediction, under a super ride by Green, refused to yield more than a few inches in the drive and outgamed Truly by a nose to earn her first stakes victory.

"I knew she had the guts to do it," said Del Castillo said.

But the first female owner-trainer to win a Calder stakes this season didn't come down to earth to analyze 4-year-old First Prediction's unexpected added-money triumph until 10 minutes after it had been accomplished. She had rushed onto the track, leaping high with every other stride, to hug Green and his mount before they got to the winner's circle. And all the time, she was whooping in sheer ecstacy.

Del Castillo was entitled. When Ed McClellan, the children's home director, decided that the home couldn't care for the fillies and offered to sell them to her, she tried to say no. "I was in the middle of a divorce, had four kids, and no money," she said. "But I couldn't resist buying them, if on credit."

The other filly never panned out, but before Saturday, First Prediction had earned $94,241 in 35 starts with a 6-8-7 record. And that had allowed Del Castillo to, pay off the $5,000 debt last year. But she didn't stop there. Since then, every time First Prediction earns a check, the home gets a donation from her. The next contribution will be the biggest — First Prediction collected $29,790 in the Black Velvet.

First Prediction carried 114 pounds over the mile and 70 yards in 1:45 3/5 and paid $32.60, $10.20 and $5.20. Truly returned $3.60 and $2.60 and Hail The Lady $3.60.

End of an improbable — but heartwarming — report on a horse race.

23 in Desert Vixen

The six-furlong Desert Vixen, the opening test in the fifth annual Florida Stallion Stakes series, headlines the card at Calder today. It has been split into two divisions because of 23 entries.

Twelve 2-year-old fillies will compete in the first division and 11 in the second.

Ocali Gal, Rapturous and My Nicole are expected to be among contenders in the first division.

Allaise, a winner at Belmont Park, and Calder victors Blues Court and Jill Of All Trades head the second division.

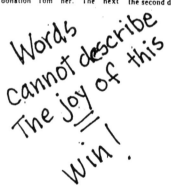

Words Cannot describe The joy of this Win!

At Calder, 'Prediction' turns dream to reality

By DAVE JOSEPH
Racing Writer

MIAMI — Against all odds, dreams can still come true. Just ask Janet Del-Castillo.

Two years ago while visiting the Florida Horsemen's Children's Home in Citra, DelCastillo bought two horses on loan from the home's administrator Ed MacClellan for $5,000. One, an On To Glory filly named First Prediction, had been donated by breeder Paul Marriott so the home's neglected children could ride her for recreational purposes and later breed her, not to become a stakes-winning filly at Calder Race Course.

"I remember having no money at the time," DelCastillo recalled. "I didn't even know if I would be able to keep my farm (in Winter Haven) at that point. But a voice from heaven said, 'Take a shot.' I figured once she started winning I could pay the $5,000 off."

That's how sure DelCastillo was that First Prediction would not only become a winner, but a stakes winner. Some called her a dreamer, but DelCastillo wouldn't give in.

On her Winter Haven farm, she trained First Prediction through sandy trails of orange groves and took her for swims every day in a lake behind her farm.

Despite everyone telling her that she had wasted her money — that you couldn't expect to win when you ship in overnight from a tiny farm to a major racetrack — DelCastillo dreamed on. And Saturday at Calder, her dream came true.

Racing third down the backstretch, First Prediction and jockey Benjamin Green came driving down the middle of the stretch to nose out Frances A. Genter's Truly to win the $47,650 Black Velvet Handicap.

A 1½-1 longshot, 4-year-old First Prediction took the lead just past the eighth pole and held game while favorite Truly and jockey Jose Velez Jr., battled with her neck-and-neck to the wire. First Prediction covered the mile and 70 yards in 1:45 3/5.

First Prediction was second in an allowance race Aug. 15 at Calder. Instead of preparing her for the Black Velvet by galloping her as she usually does through the groves, DelCastillo prepped the filly with daily swims on the farm. During the day, DelCastillo turns First Prediction out in a pasture.

"It's a dream come true," said DelCastillo, who danced for joy in the winner's circle after the race. "Today she

SEE **CALDER** / 14C

CALDER

FROM **PAGE 1C**

First Prediction turns dream to reality at Calder

just wouldn't give up.

"Everyone always told me you wouldn't ship a horse in like this and win. But in this particular case, it's all worked."

DelCastillo's good fortune has also helped the children's home. After First Prediction's prior victories — she has won seven races and placed in 22 of 36 — DelCastillo has donated $1,000 to the home. "And you can bet they'll be getting another check tonight," she said.

Breaking fifth in the nine-horse field, Green moved First Prediction up along the rail around the first turn and settled into third going down the backstretch behind C'Mon Liz and Merry Cathy. It was an unusual move, because First Prediction's best running style is usually to close from well off the pace.

"I was closer than I expected to be today," Green said. "But she was running strong so I let her run."

While C'Mon Liz was setting fractions of 24, :48 2 5, First Prediction continued inching closer to the front. By the time Green hit the 3/8th pole, First Prediction was full of run, as was Truly, closing from sixth.

"As we came around the 3/8th pole she was picking up horses and they weren't really moving away from her too much," Green said. "She just kept on going."

Two-wide entering the stretch, First Prediction took the lead from Merry Cathy at the eighth pole. A neck behind on the outside Truly was closing. But First Prediction would not give in. The filly continued on strongly in the last sixteenth and to the wire.

"I am so glad she is a legitimate horse," DelCastillo said. "I am so glad."

So is the Florida horsemen's Children's Home.

First Prediction paid $32.60, $10.20 and $5.20. Truly paid $3.60 and $2.60 and Hail The Lady, who closed from eighth, returned $3.60 to show.

DelCastillo

Commoner almost dethrones royalty

By LUTHER EVANS
Herald Turf Writer

First Prediction, a racing commoner who works out in a Winter Haven orange grove, almost put the squeeze on aristocratic Fragrant Princess in Calder's $52,030 New Year Handicap before 12,267 fans Thursday.

First Prediction, purchased in a two-horse package for a mere $5,000 from the Florida Horsemen Children's School near Ocala two years ago, charged between horses in the final furlong but just missed catching winner Fragrant Princess by a head. But her rally from last place in the early going did enable her to finish one length ahead of Greentree Stable's Perfect Point, who had been expected by many to deprive Harper Stables' Fragrant Princess of her third consecutive victory.

Trainer Luis Olivares sprinted down from the fourth floor just in time to make the winner's circle. "I told you to expect me here because I was here after Powder Break won the La Prevoyante last Jan. 1," he said. "I like to start every year in a big way. And I think my Flying Pidgeon will win the W.L. McKnight Handicap at 1 1/2 miles on Wednesday, closing day."

Olivares has gone on from such January success to earn the title as South Florida's outstanding trainer of the past two winter seasons. "I believe that three is an even better number," he said.

Fragrant Princess carried 116 pounds over the nine furlongs in 1:55 and paid $8.60, $5 and $4.60. First Prediction (113 pounds) returned $6 and $3.60. Regal Prin-

third-place Regal Princess.

Julio Pezua, who rode First Prediction for the first time for trainer Janet Del Castillo, thought that jockey Heriberto Valdivieso had allowed Fragrant Princess to drift in and shut off his gray mount late in the drive. Stewards studied race films and decided that the winner had been clear when she lugged in and did not force Pezua to check the runner-up.

It was a good horse race. And it probably would have been even better except for heavy early-morning rain bringing five scratches after the 1 1/4-mile test had been taken off the turf course. Included among the defectors was cess, whom trainer Jose "Pepe" Mendez had sharp enough to lead most of the way under Walter Guerra, paid $3.80.

Fragrant Princess disposed of Regal Princess and Donna's Dolly inside the eighth pole and seemed to have matters in hand when First Prediction began her powerful bid that made the finish exciting.

There is financial parity today between Fragrant Princess, a 4-year-old Diplomat Way filly, and First Prediction, a 5-year-old On To Glory mare. Fragrant Princess' $34,150 purse increased her earnings to $163,531. First Prediction's $9,050 second-place money increased her winnings to $152,464.

And who, you may ask, is nervy enough to get aboard First Prediction and gallop her through an orange grove? Owner-trainer Janet Del Castillo, that's who.

The Jan. 1 crowd wagered $1,722,256.

This was amusing!

The story covered the horse that lost more than the horse that Won!

Tale of Gift Horse And Home for Kids

Lew Zagnit / *TAMPA BAY*

OLDSMAR, Fla.—You take a horse with a broken leg, add a trainer, a divorcee trying to make it on her own, and tie in a home for dependent children, and what have you got? No, not a remake of "Annie Meets National Velvet." You have the Gold Coup—Janet del Castillo—Florida Horsemen's Children Home story, which is being played out at this meeting. You can catch the latest installment of this real life melodrama on Saturday, when del Castillo runs Gold Coup in a $5,000 claiming race here.

Now a little background on the cast.

"The Florida Horsemen's Children's Home offers long-term residential care for neglected and dependent children; children from families with problems or whose parents are divorced," explained director Ed Mac-Clellan, when contacted by phone at the Florida facility.

MacClellan had for 12 years served as the director of the Rodeheaver Home, a boys ranch in Putnam. Thus he was an obvious selection when people within the horse industry here, particularly Joe Durkin of the Florida Horse Magazine, decided there was a need for a similar facility in Marion County.

"We started raising money four years ago, and George Steinbrenner, through his New York Yankee Foundation, gave us a grant for one half of the land purchase. We raised the other half by donations. We do not receive any government funds. We are supported entirely by donations.

"We turned 1-year-old in November," said MacClellan. "We have one cottage for 12 kids, 60 acres of land, and 15 head of horses. Our staff consists of one set of cottage parents and a relief set of cottage parents, one of whom doubles as a secretary. We also have a thrift store in Ocala.

"We have paddocks for the horses, but no barns, but we are trying to raise funds to build barns."

Part of the support the horsemen contribute comes in the form of horses who are donated for the children to take care of or, if possible, are sold to race, which is how del Castillo became involved.

A couple of years ago, she paid $5,000 for two thoroughbreds who had been donated to the home. One of them just recently broke his maiden, but the other one turned out to be a pretty good runner. He name is First Prediction, and the 5-year-old On to Glory mare just went over the $170,000 mark in earnings with a second in an allowance race at Hialeah last Saturday.

First Prediction, who was donated by breeder Paul Marriott, has been a steady and useful campaigner partly by design, and possibly partly due to a mistake by del Castillo, who took out her trainer's license three years ago after she and her husband were divorced.

"I think part of the reason she's so strong," said del Castillo, the mother of three teenaged children, "is that I never start my horses until they're 3-years-old. And, when I was galloping First Prediction around the orange grove I thought I was going three miles a day, but I was actually going closer to five and a half.

"She was the first one I got from the children's home. They've gotten wonderful support from the horse community, certainly from Clayton O'Quinn, and Helmuth Schmidt. I've worked with them the most at picking up the horses that were donated, trying them out and either getting rid of them, or trying to run them. And Gold Coup, who was donated by Evelyn Poole, was the first one good enough to run in the childrens home's name.

"I got him sometime in the middle of last summer "continued del Castillo, who spent time serving in the peace corps." He had a fractured cannon bone, and was very body sore. The first thing I did was bring him home, geld him, and turn him out. Then I started long slow gallops. I tried him a few times in Miami, but I think he was just tuning up, and he's gotten better since. He's been on the board or won every race he's been in since."

Gold Coup is owned in partnership with the children's home, (even through the children, who are of course minors, are not allowed at the track due to state law) and del Castillo's mother and stepfather. Thus half the money the 5-year-old Gold Stage gelding makes, which totals about $4,000 so far, goes to support the home.

And the best thing about this story is there's no happy ending, just a happy continuation.

C. V. B. Cushman Dead; Rode In '30 Carolina Cup

RANCHO PALOS VERDES, Cal.—Charles V. B. Cushman, who rode in the inaugural running of the Carolina Cup Steeplechase in 1930, died here on January 13 at the age of 84, it was learned Thursday. He was one of four generations of the Cushman family to participate as amateur and professional riders.

Mr. Cushman, whose grandson, John, won the Carolina Cup in 1982 aboard Quiet Bay, operated Eastland Farm Stable and campaigned stakes winners. In 1928 he paid a then record yearling price of $75,000 for New Broom, a Whisk Broom II colt.

He is survived by his widow, Elizabeth; two sons, two daughters, 14 grandchildren and eight great-grandchildren.

Leading Filly and Mare Earners

(Includes horses who have started at least once in North America. Lifetime earnings of horses who have raced in foreign countries are included through the date of last start in North America.)

(Includes Racing of January 18)

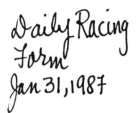

This was another horse I got from the Children's Home

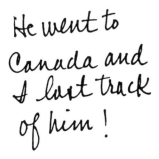

He went to Canada and I lost track of him!

Daily Racing Form Jan 31, 1987

Art Grace

Horse racing

Gulfstream announcer and his memorable goof

Grace

I have listened to a lot of track announcers (Hialeah's Tom Durkin, a notable exception) mangle a lot of pronunciations, but my recent favorite is the most notable, by Gulfstream's Ross Morton.

As far as I know, there is only one way to pronounce "Benigna." It has to rhyme with fine. Unless it is Morton's interpretation of the 4-year-old filly Benign Begum.

When she ran at Gulfstream the first time on March 20, I thought I must have been fantasizing when I heard Morton refer to her, throughout the seven-furlong race, as, so help me, "Benigan Begum." (He also mispronounced "Begum," but that's understandable.)

Nah, it couldn't be. I decided to wait until Benign Begum ran back in order to make sure I had not been hallucinating. She finally showed up again in the first race last Sunday. And sure enough,

Morton called her "Benigan Begum" with every rundown as the field plodded its way through the mile and a sixteenth.

I think I'll go out for dinner tonight ... for a hamburger and fries at that popular restaurant on 163rd street. You know the one I'm referring to: Benigan's.

* * *

Apparently, I am not the only race track person to have been smitten by Patty Smyth's new solo album, and especially the title song, "Never Enough," Janet Del Castillo, a very nice lady who owns and trains First Prediction, has decided that "never enough" is the way to handle her horse. A more appropriate theme would be "enough is enough."

First Prediction, a 5-year-old mare, has been one of my favorites for a long time. She is, or rather was, a stone closer who made a big run virtually every time.

I liked her a lot when Bennie Green was riding her at Calder last year and positively loved her when Julio Pezua got the mount beginning Jan. 1 this year. It was a perfect marriage, a closer with a

great finishing rider.

She just missed in the New Year's Handicap at Calder, at 7-1, and won at 8-1 at Hialeah nine days later. She then finished second in the Bal Harbour and third, beaten a neck and a nose to Anka Germania and Chaldea, in the Columbiana. Next time out she closed big again to finish second in the Key Largo.

At that point she had to be considered an iron horse. She already had run five times in six weeks in 1987 after a very rigorous campaign in 1986.

She was back in one week later at Tampa Bay and finally the regimen caught up with her. She finished fifth, beaten 14½ lengths.

Undiscouraged, DelCastillo vanned her back to Hialeah for the Black Helen two weeks later. First Prediction never got out of a gallop, finishing 11th.

I got the message loud and clear two weeks later at Gulfstream when First Prediction turned back to seven furlongs and finished a weak fifth. When she failed to fire going short I knew the romance was over between us.

When she showed up still again, just eight days later in the Suwanee River Handicap, I wasn't about to bet on her. She finished fifth.

Surely Del Castillo would give her a rest now? Yeah, three whole days. Four days later First Prediction was in the Rampart Handicap, in good but not in spirit. She was last all the way, finishing 16 lengths behind the next to last horse.

First Prediction is nominated for Saturday's mile-and-a-half Orchid Handicap and next Wednesday's seven-furlong allowance feature at a mile and a sixteenth on the grass. Unless 20 races in 29 weeks prove a mile debilitating, I'm sure she will be able to make the Orchid and Old Hat.

I went through the same depressing experience with another personal favorite, Command Attention, owned and trained by Nathan Kelly. Command Attention hasn't been around much lately this year.

The 9-year-old gelding was running in

stakes races two years ago. I will never forget the afternoon in October, 1985, when he won an allowance race on grass at Calder by a nose and paid $59.80.

How sad it was to see him running for a $5,000 claiming price at Tampa last December, finishing seventh, 15 lengths behind Spindle City.

He raced only 16 times last year because he had to laid up from July to December. But if he could make it to the paddock he didn't miss any dances in previous four years. He ran only nine times as a 2-year-old and only 13 times at 3. But from 1982 through 1985, he maintained a twice-a-month schedule without buckling.

If he was a cat I'd take him home and let him enjoy the good life.

First Prediction already has matched Command Attention's busiest year — 27 starts in 1983. She equalled that total last year and is well on her to surpassing it this year.

More's the pity. Horses are not machines, but sometimes they are treated as though they were.

Art Grace

Horse racing

Del Castillo has a right to feel wonderful

April 17, 1987

Grace

In this column, yesterday, I excoriated owner-trainer Janet Del Castillo for what I considered poor, and possibly abusive, management of her horse First Prediction.

After running extremely well against top competition all winter, the 5-year-old mare appeared to have been ground down by an exhausting schedule — 20 races in 28 weeks.

I was moved to voice my displeasure when First Prediction ran three times in 12 days at Gulfstream, twice in major stakes, and had run five very poor races in a row. Immediately before going off form, First Prediction had finished third, beaten a neck and a nose, to top fillies Anka Germania and Chaldea in the Columbiana at Hialeah Feb. 1 and two weeks later came from last to finish second to Singular Bequest in the Key Largo.

Then came five terrible races, three in the Rampart Handicap April 5. But there are two sides to most stories and Miss Del Castillo surely was entitled to present a defense. She came to see me yesterday and did so, an hour before First Prediction ran again in the ninth race which, to Janet's discomfiture, had been switched from grass to dirt.

"I know it looks terrible on paper," she said. "All people see is that she ran on March 24 and April 1 and April 5. What they don't realize is that I can't ever work this mare like a normal horse.

"Every time I try to work her, she ties up (suffer severe cramping.) If I let that happen, it takes two months to get her ready to run again. So I never work her. She has to get her exercise by running and to stay off her she has to run at least every 10 to 14 days. If she's off longer than that I have to start from scratch again.

"If I ever felt she had a physical problem, if she ever went off her feed, I'd stop on her immediately. She's like a part of my family ... she's in our yard. She's like a part of my family ... she's in our yard. Del Castillo lives in Winter Haven) when she's not running. I could never abuse her. She's absolutely sound.

"She's been running poorly, but I've been trying to get her back into her rhythm. I know it looks bad when she runs in a tough race like the Rampart with only three days rest. What they'd never understand is that I needed that race to get her back to optimum form. Not many people use a $125,000 15-horse field into the first turn. She didn't have a chance.

"She's been acting just fine: I expect she'll run well today. If it hadn't been taken off the grass I'd really like her ... to. She downhole seem to like the dirt. But I still expect her to run even better.

"After what you wrote in the paper today, I hope the people don't throw rocks at me when I go to the paddock. If she runs bad again, I'd consider resting her until Calder opens (in six weeks), which would mean it would take me four races to get her ready again. That's something I can't really afford to do.

"If I had to choose yesterday to lambaste Miss Del Castillo, at least my timing was exquisite. First Prediction was so utterly worn out that she came from next to last on the backstretch and wore down the front-running Bereavement in the last 50 yards to win the mile and a sixteenth allowance feature by a length. Julio Pezua, of course, rode her flawlessly.

"After the race, Miss Del Castillo could not resist rushing to the press box and tell me, "I told you so."

"Well, indeed she had. Practically everyone except Janet had agreed with my criticism, but I'm the only one who went public with it. She had a right to rub it in. It was the least she could do.

"I feel wonderful, it's such a relief to know I wasn't wrong," she said. "For a while I was starting to doubt myself.

"Before the race Janet had felt First Prediction could not run well on dirt 'except for Calder (which has a unique racing strip). She was running super on grass down here, then I made the mistake of running her at (Hialeah). Tampa (seven days after the Key Largo at Hialeah).

"She didn't like the track and didn't fire (finishing a bad fifth). When she ran back in the Black Helen it was against killers and she was widest of all in a 15-horse field into the first turn. She didn't have a chance.

"At that point, I had to try and get her back into her rhythm. I ran her seven furlongs and she did close ground. But she couldn't handle those fractions: 22.4 and change. 1:10. And she didn't like the dirt. But only place to run her next was the grass stake at Gulfstream (Suwanee River) and the fractions were so slow she couldn't make up ground.

"With a horse like her, who comes from way out of it, things have to break right (a realistic early pace by the speed horses) for her to run well. But I felt she needed that race, and one more, to reach her level of competence.

"The reason I ran her back four days later (in the $125,000 Rampart Handicap) is that I got suckered into it. Just before the entries closed, they called me and said only four horses were entered. It turned out to be seven.

"I told Pezua not to abuse her if she didn't have a shot. The pace was slow again and he realized there was no fun to train her in front of everybody in the afternoons. She has to get her works in her races. She doesn't do well in a stall.

"I have her in a normal environment at Winter Haven, in cycle with nature. She's out in the pasture every day, in the sunshine, not locked in a stall. She swims every day. That's it.

"A horse can't talk to you; you have to go by your perceptions. I can tell you she hasn't gotten sour in two years; she's never refused to eat up. She's like a working man who puts on his hard hat and goes to work every day. Another day, another dollar."

"If the race sets up right (with early speed) she'll be there. If it doesn't, she won't. If I can run her with no more than 10 to 14 days between races, I don't have to be concerned about not working her. If it's 20 days I fall two races behind with her.

"It's tough when I have to keep running her in stakes but it's the only way to keep her in her rhythm.

"Most people have no idea how tough this game can be. They've never had to load a hysterical 2-year-old filly on a van at 5 in the morning and take her to Tampa to work."

First Prediction ran 19 times in 1985, 24 times last year, and already has run 11 times this year. She has finished in the money in 32 of those 54 starts, winning nine. She went over the $200,000 mark in earnings with a $13,200 winner's purse yesterday.

While I still have reservations with Miss Del Castillo's handling of First Prediction, she aced me in straight sets yesterday and the overall results have been good.

Last year at Hialeah First Prediction ran twice in five days and finished second both times. She ran at Calder Aug. 2, 15 and 23 and won twice and finished second once.

Before the slump hit late in February this year the mare ran eight times in 2½ months and every race was a corker. After her performance yesterday, I doubt she ever will break down. Her career will end when the iron starts to rust.

Racing *Daily* Form

Copyright © 1987 by Daily Racing Form, Inc. All rights reserved

VOL. 17. No. 130   HIGHTSTOWN, N.J., SUNDAY, MAY 10, 1987   PRICE $2.00

Fieldy Heads Gulf's Very One

HEADLINES and Front Page on Racing FORM! Guess WHO WON?

"..Not Fieldy!

By WILLIAM C. PHILLIPS

GULFSTREAM PARK, Hallandale, Fla.—Arriola and Seltzer's Fieldy, an Irish-bred 4-year-old who dead-heated for win with Fama in a division of the Grade III Suwannee River Handicap on turf April 1 and then was unplaced in the Grade II Orchid 'Cap on grass April 18, heads a field of 11 fillies and mares entered for the inaugural running of the $62,700 The Very One Handicap, which features a Mother's Day card here Sunday.

The race will be decided at a mile on the turf for a winner's prize of $37,620.

Craig Perret will return from the North to ride Fieldy at topweight of 115 pounds.

Janet del Castillo's First Prediction, a winner of her last two starts, is next in the weights at 114, with leading jockey Julio Pezua back in the saddle.

The field is completed by J. Robert Harris Jr.'s Thirty Zip, 113, Earlie Fires; J. C. Dudley's Tri Argo, 112, Robert Lester; Barbara Hunter's Duckweed, 111, Jose Velez Jr.; Mike J. Doyle and Sherry Farm's Miss Enchanted, 111, Steve Gaffalione; Southlake Stable's Lady of the North, 110, Pezua on another call; Dana S. Bray Jr.'s Evening Bid, 110, Santiago Soto; Buckram Oak Farm's Royal Infatuation, 110, Constantino Hernandez; Joanne and R. Thornton's Tuscadoon, 108, Mike Lee, and Mrs. Henry D. Paxson's Lustrous Reason, 108, James Reed.

Fieldy showed her class in France as a 2-year-old by winning the Group I Marcel Boussac at Longchamp. She was off form for three other races in France as a 3-year-old, but trainer Steve W. Young reports that whatever her problem

was, it no longer exists. His statement is supported by her two winning races and a close second in her United States race this year. Fieldy was not a factor in the Orchid, but that race was at a mile and a half, and Young described the race as "an experiment" to see whether she could handle the distance.

"She couldn't," he said, "but the mile will suit her fine."

First Prediction has gained a large following on the story how she was a yearling purchase from an orphanage home near Ocala and is trained by her owner in an orange grove next to a lake in Winter Haven. The attractive 5-year-old gray mare by Or to Glory has come from off the pace for a number of top efforts on the turf, including a third in a three-way photo finish at Hialeah this past winter with Anka Germania and Chaldea in the Grade III Columbiana Handicap, and a rousing two and one-half length tally on the grass her last start, beating Truly.

Larry Geiger has found Thirty Zip performs best when her races are spaced a month apart and this event fits the schedule perfectly. She was fourth behind the crack filly Life at the Top in the Grade III Rampart Handicap that was run on the main track on April 5. Three weeks before that, she finished strongly at a mile on the turf and just missed catching Small Virtue in a division of the Joe Namath Handicap.

The 4-year-old Tri Jet filly also ran well on the grass at Calder last fall when third behind Anka Germania and Slew's Exceller in the Calder Breeders' Cup Handicap.

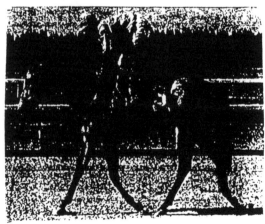

Prominent

First Prediction seeks third straight Florida win Sunday.

HORSE RACING

Photo/JIM RAFTERY

Thirty Zip (2) doesn't have enough zip to catch Julio Pezua and First Prediction Sunday.

First Prediction has enough gas to capture third straight victory

By FRAN LaBELLE
Staff Writer

HALLANDALE — The photos had been taken, horse and jockey dutifully kissed and Janet Del Castillo was about to answer any questions about First Prediction's 2½-length victory in Sunday's $62,700 Very One Handicap at Gulfstream.

"Do you think we can tell her how we ran out of gas on the turnpike now?," said her son, Alex.

"Don't tell me any more," Del Castillo said.

As it turns out, Alex and his brother, Hernando, ran out of gas near the Pompano Beach exit of the turnpike Friday while shipping in First Prediction for Sunday's 1-mile turf test for older fillies and mares. After a 20-minute wait, the van was back on the road.

Fortunately, Del Castillo left the driving to Julio Pezua Sunday. This time, no one ran out of gas.

Pezua, whose victory was his second of the day and increased his record season's total to 75, got something extra from First Prediction in the stretch to get by J.R. Harris Jr.'s Thirty Zip. It was First Prediction's third straight victory, and it came before a Mother's Day crowd of 10,752.

"I had to lay up closer to the pace than usual because the race was only a flat mile," said Pezua, who stayed fourth behind Tri Argo, favored Fieldy and Tuscadoon until the stretch. "I saved all the ground I could and was able to get through inside. My horse made the lead in the stretch, but then the [Thirty Zip] went by here. When my horse saw that, she dug in and went ahead to win the race."

Del Castillo said her main worry was that the early fractions of :23 4/5, :41 1/5 and 1:11 1/5 would mean Pezua would have to use his mount earlier than he would like.

"It was a wild race," said Del Castillo, whose charge turned in a winning time of 1:35 1/5 for her second stakes victory. "But First Prediction's been knocking at the door. She's a game little thing, and God bless Pezua. He knew enough to keep her close."

First Prediction, a 5-year-old daughter of On To Glory-Around The Bend by Hagley, returned $7.80, $4.20 and $3.00.

It is also thought that Del Castillo will use part of the winner's purse of $37,620 to gas all of her vehicles.

NOTES: Pezua has been named on another stakes contender. He will ride Easter Mary for trainer **Sonny Hine** in Wednesday's $41,195 Honey Fox Stakes for 3-year-old fillies at a mile and a sixteenth... Gulfstream will offer simulcasting of the Preakness next Saturday.

Breeding Business: Romance and Glory

Racing Form 5/19/87

Bill Giauque / *FLORIDA*

OCALA, Fla.—Imagine, just to test your business sense, a smallish, late, gray 2-year-old filly. Consider also the parentage of this filly. She came into this world as the daughter of a modest but successful Florida sire and a more or less undistinguished dam.

Further imagine that the breeder, a man of means, donated the filly to a home for children, who, for one reason or another, need supervision from other than their parents.

The supervisor of this home, unable to get an offer of more than $500 for the filly and another horse of similar origin and condition, finally sells the horses to a woman trainer for $5,000, to be paid whenever.

The new owner runs her horse operation with her three children. She is in the middle of a divorce, trains her horses in an orange grove and ships from the farm to the track to race, a four-and-a-half-hour trip, if the traffic is light.

Based on this scenario, would you predict success for the principals involved? If you said yes, you have the business sense of the man who bought a share in John Henry, the heart of a Hollywood movie producer and your address is the Magic Kingdom ... but you are right.

The stakes-winning filly, First Prediction, has earned owner-trainer Janet Del Castillo more than $200,000. She paid the Florida Horsemen's Children's Home for the two horses long ago, and according to Children's Home president Ed Mac Clellan, Del Castillo sends a check for $1,000 every time First Prediction wins a race. Not only that but breeder Paul Marriot got his tax writeoff for the donation, and he continues to receive Florida breeders' awards every time the filly wins.

"The most anybody offered was $500 apiece," MacClellan recalled. "I knew they were worth more than that, so I sold the package (to Del Castillo) for $5,000, but she didn't have to pay anything up front."

On the buying end of the transaction, Del Castillo remembered, "Ed McClellan called me, said he had two horses for sale. One was a May filly 14-months old. The Florida Horsemen's Children's Home didn't even have fences up yet. In the middle of trying to say, 'No,' this voice from above said. 'Shut up and take the horses'."

Because Del Castillo trains her horses long and slowly in the deep sand of the nearby orange grove, First Prediction was not rushed to the track at 2. Still, her training performance did not give rise to any burst of confidence in the trainer.

"She absolutely trained like a very, very ordinary horse," said the Winter Haven trainer. "I would never have said this one is going to be great. In fact, I offered another trainer a half-interest in her for $2,500. He didn't have any money, either."

Two years ago in February after First Prediction rolled up a couple of seconds and a third, an agent offered $25,000 for the filly. "When you get a horse for $2,500, and someone offers you $25,000, that is a lot of money," the owner said. "I went to the kids and everyone said, 'Oh, Mom, don't sell the filly'."

After the daughter of On to Glory broke her maiden at Tampa Bay Downs, Del Castillo snipped to South Florida for a crack at the big time.

"I was so stupid I didn't know you couldn't ship in and win," the unorthodox trainer said. "But she was fit and had a tremendous stretch run to win a $25,000 claiming race.

"I was going to put her back in a $35,000 claimer, but Roger McElhiney told me not to run for $35,000 or she'd get claimed. First Prediction ran third in an allowance race, and afterward someone offered me $50,000 so she probably would have been claimed away at the lower price. Every time I was going to lose her someone always helped me."

In all First Prediction has started 59 times with 11 wins and 14 seconds and earnings of more than $250,000.

In the latest chapter of this movie-like story, the gray filly defeated Thirty Zip in a thrilling stretch run in The Very One Handicap. "She was passed by Thirty Zip in deep stretch, and she came again to win," said Del Castillo with excitement still in her voice.

The owner's three helpers and children are Alex, 19; Hernando, 18; and Victoria, 15. The Very One Handicap was the first time the boys had been allowed to transport a horse five hours down the Florida Turnpike for a race. They made the trip the night before the race.

"In the winner's circle, my son turned to me and said he ran out of gas on the turnpike," Del Castillo revealed. "The gas gauge was not working right. Here the poor little filly is coming down to run in one of the biggest races of her life, and she is stuck on the side of the Turnpike."

First Prediction has given the woman from Winter Haven credibility and a belief in dreams.

"You must not ever forget," she explained, "there is serendipity in life. Getting this wonderful horse is the greatest thing that ever happened to me. She has made so much that it would be awful not to remember."

And the checks continue to arrive at the Florida Horsemen's Children's Home.

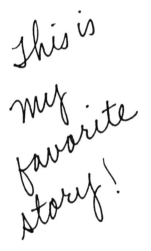

This is my favorite story!

URF AUTHORITY

Daily For

Daily Racing Form, Inc. All rights reserved.

WEDNESDAY, MAY 20, 1987

'Prediction' Risks Skein In Gulf 'Cap

By WILLIAM C. PHILLIPS

GULFSTREAM PARK, Hallandale, Fla.—Janet del Castillo's First Prediction, who has become a favorite of Florida racing fans, seeks her fourth straight triumph in the second running of the $39,620 Candy Eclair Handicap here Wednesday. Six fillies and mares are entered to compete at a mile and a sixteenth for a winner's purse of $23,772.

The public has become enraptured with First Prediction's background: a yearling purchase from a home for orphans and wayward children near Ocala, trained in her owner's orange grove next to a lake in Winter Haven, and brought to the racetrack for her afternoon engagements in a van driven by Castillo.

The fans have been impressed, too, by Del Castillo's display of joyful emotions after she has saddled her mare for a winning race, and the apparent comaradarie she shares with Julio Pezua, the mare's regular rider this season.

First Prediction began her skein by beating Bereavement by a length in a mile and a sixteenth allowance race on April 16. She defeated Truly by two and a half lengths in a mile race on the grass May 1, and outgamed Thirty Zip by a nose in a dramatic stretch duel to capture The Very One Handicap at a mile on the turf nine days later.

A winner of 11 races in a career of 59 races, accruing $255,520 in purses, the 5-year-old gray daughter of On to Glory will carry 115 pounds.

Mr. and Mrs. Cleo Hall's 4-year-old Judy's Red Shoes, a multiple stakes winner, whose earnings total $269,349, is topweighted at 116 pounds. Santiago Soto will ride.

Ross Heritage Farm & Baird's Lady Vernalee, a winner of three straight, including the Sweetest Chant and Lady in Waiting handicaps, will carry 114 and Robert Lester will ride.

The field is completed by Frances A. Genter's Truly, 114, Jose Velez Jr.; R. & J. Thornton's Tuscadoon, 108, Mike Lee, and C. & E. R. Dixon's Warm and Soft, 107, Norberto J. Palavencino.

This will be the first race for Judy's Red Shoes since she was third in a division of the Joe Namath Handicap here at a mile on the grass March 15. She was the winner of a mile and a furlong overnight race on dirt in three starts at Hialeah this winter and won seven of 19 outings last season.

Lady Vernalee has been raced as a sprinter but the 4-year-old Hold Your Peace filly's recent performances have been so strong the stable decided to give her a shot at the longer distance. Tuscadoon is the only rival in this race with the speed to challenge her early, and if Lady Vernalee steals off to a long lead she could be hard to catch.

Santiago Soto
Has Mount in Gulf 'Cap

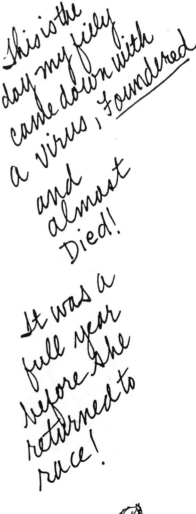

This is the day my filly came down with a virus, Foundered and almost Died!

It was a full year before she returned to race!

Nine Clash at Gulf In F-M Turf Event

By WILLIAM C. PHILLIPS

GULFSTREAM PARK, Hallandale, Fla.—Cynthia Phipps' For Kicks, who was a good third behind a pair of stakes-winning rivals on the turf in her only race at the meeting, will be solidly supported in the wide-open betting field of nine older fillies and mares named to compete at a mile on the turf in the allowance feature here Thursday.

For Kicks was the pacesetter in a mile and a sixteenth race on the grass the opening day of the meeting, January 8, and held on gamely in the drive to be third behind Without Feathers and Vana Turns. Both of those fillies won on the grass in their next starts.

For Kicks was still a maiden and she tired after showing speed and finished unplaced when she first tried the grass in the third start of her career at Belmont Park last spring. The 4-year-old Topsider filly since then has won four of six races at distances from seven furlongs to a mile and a sixteenth on the dirt at Belmont Park, Aqueduct and Calder. She is trained by Angel Penna Jr. and is to be ridden by Jorge Chavez at 119 pounds.

She is opposed by Holly Ricon's Ana T., 122, Earlie Fires; D. E. Hager 2d's Stop and Smile, 119, no rider; and six contenders who are each to carry 115 pounds. They are M. Miller's Luckie's Girl, Jorge Duarte; Stanley M. Ersoff's Miss K. L. Taylor, Doug Valiente; Janet del Castillo's First Prediction, no rider; Firmanento Farm's Kalerre, also Valiente; T. Asbury's Bug Bug, no rider, and

Big Bucks Racing Stable's Lost Weekend, no rider.

Two of the rivals to For Kicks have shown speed on the grass at the meeting and can be expected to challenge her for the early lead.

Stop and Smile came back after tiring in her first start to lead from the start and to widen her margin to better than two lengths over a good allowance field in a mile and a sixteenth race on January 19. Incidentally, she was the first to win on the turf at Gulfstream this winter by leading from the start. The 6-year-old daughter of Libres Rib appeared to be overmatched in the first division of Saturday's Grade III Suwannee River and dropped back after showing early speed to finish last.

This will be the fifth race for First Prediction since she resumed racing in the fall. The 7-year-old On to Glory mare is a stretch runner and the class of the field going back a couple of years when she won two stakes on grass over this course.

Bug Bug was in front into the stretch run of a mile and a sixteenth race captured by the stakes filly Orange Motif on grass here on January 29. She lost by a little more than four lengths and finished fifth. The 4-year-old Ginistrelli filly similarly held the early lead in the Atlantic City Oaks on turf last summer at Atlantic City and in the Tropical Park Oaks at Calder in the spring.

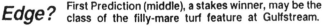

Edge?   First Prediction (middle), a stakes winner, may be the class of the filly-mare turf feature at Gulfstream.

Mixing oranges and horses

Dick Evans

On the Money

The dew glistens atop the oranges as the sun rises. Suddenly, the birds stop chirping and the ground starts to shake. From around the bend come three thundering thoroughbreds in a race down the narrow lanes between the rows of heavenly laden trees.

For three miles, the horses maneuver the tight curves and straightaways through the groves around Winter Haven, Fla. Then, it's everyone in the lake for a cool dip.

Del Castillo

Is this anyway to train thoroughbreds?

According to Janet Del Castillo, it's the best way.

"I raise them like I raised my three children, by using good old fashioned common sense," said Del Castillo, 43, a former Peace Corps volunteer who began training thoroughbreds fulltime four years ago. "I allow them to be horses, to do what comes natural. I put them in their natural environment so that they can frolic together, eat grass and definitely talk to each other.

"I tell them that I'll give them two weeks of devotion on the farm if they will give me two minutes of devotion on the horse track."

Del Castillo realizes most trainers and many owners laughed at her unorthodox training methods. "I would say the first couple years I was like the Country Bumpkin coming to the big city. I had no money at all and had to do everything myself.

"I know some veteran trainers were laughing and snickering. But I didn't care. When I was in the Peace Corps in Colombia, I taught the poor natives that they had to make do with what they had. I was in the same boat. I didn't look for excuses."

On her 14-acre farm outside Winter Haven, she built barns, a mini-paddock and make-shift starting gates. She did it all — training the horses, riding them, feeding them, swimming them, bathing them and doctoring them like her own children — with the help of her three children.

In 1976, all the hard work started to pay off. First Prediction, a $2,500 castoff who had been given to a children's home in Central Florida, proved that Del Castillo's methods worked during a Cinderella racing career that produced $270,000 in earnings. "First Prediction saved my farm, she was a heavenly gift,"
said Del Castillo. "When I was first galloping First Prediction through the orange groves, I thought I was going three miles a day, but I was actually going closer to 5½ miles."

Little wonder First Prediction went on to become known as the "Iron Maiden" with more than 70 career starts.

Make no mistake, Del Castillo trains her eight to 14 thoroughbreds each year to run forever.

"I like to have a solid foundation in my horses before I take them to a race track," said Del Castillo, who was born in Oregon but raised in San Francisco where she worked with polo ponies before joining the Peace Corps. "By working them three miles through heavy sand, up and down hills and around tight turns, I am building a racing machine. I don't believe in drugs, so when my horses reach a point where they want to tear through the three-mile course, then I know they're ready to go to the race track."

That presents another problem, getting them to the tracks in South Florida. And, often, it's not to race, but just to get work out of a real starting gate. "I don't mind the drive down," she says of the 220-mile trip. "It's something that has to be done."

It can seem a short trip home if her horse wins. "Nothing beats winning, nothing." It can be a very long trip home if her horse loses, or maybe doesn't even get into the race.

But the long and short of it is that Del Castillo believes in her method.

"I train a lot of young fillies, and some are hyper and delicate and tend to tie up or get nervous when they run. But when they are home, they are with their friends and can talk and play together. It's not their natural life style to be cooped up at a track 24 hours a day. God meant for them to graze and to be moving all the time. I know it may sound silly, but I think it's important to let horses be horses."

Asked if she would like to become a conventional-type trainer, Del Castillo was quick with an emphatic "NO."

"But I would," she added, "like for owners to have enough confidence in me and my training methods to let me have their horses from age 18 months to 2½ for what I think is solid progressive type training. I also would love for an owner come to me and say, 'Here is $20,-000 or $30,000, go out and buy me a good horse.'"

There is one point to her training methods that can not be overlooked. Even if her horses do not make the grade on race tracks, they do as family horses/pets. "They are raised in such a placid setting, they can do something else other than be race horses. So I always try to find them a nice home," she said.

And there is a personal benefit that would make her reluctant to trade places even with Hall of Fame trainer Woody Stephens.

"The best part of the day is working the horses," she said. "Tearing through orange groves is a fantastic ride through nature. It's thrilling, a natural high without doing drugs."

SEPTEMBER 1988
THE MIAMI HERALD

Del Castillo's training style unorthodox

By Lisa A. Hammond
The Ledger

EAGLE LAKE — Most racehorses learn to run during one mile jaunts within the confines of a racetrack. Janet Del Castillo's thoroughbreds train by galloping for three miles in the deep sand of an orange grove on her Rancho Del Castillo.

Her methods, including swimming the horses in Eagle Lake, are considered unorthodox.

"People feel sorry for me when I have to train on the farm and not at the track, but I wouldn't trade them," she said.

Her horses negotiate the sharp turns of the orange grove which, she says, makes the gradual curves of the race track a breeze.

"People say the sand will bow the horses' tendons, but my horses are very sound. Galloping through the deep sand and up the hills strengthens all of their muscles, and going around the sharp turns makes them surefooted," Del Castillo said.

The grove and ranch are located off of State Road 540 on Crystal Beach Road.

"I love the orange grove," she said. "To be able to support my family doing this is just heavenly."

She often treats herself to an orange plucked off a tree after she rides.

Del Castillo, 43, is a tall, stocky woman, who radiates strength. She has shoulder-length brown hair with a few streaks of gray. She seems very motherly and kind, especially to the horses, which she strokes with her large hands and calls her "little babies."

She began by training polo ponies when she was in high school.

"I started cleaning stalls so I would be allowed to gallop the polo ponies," she said.

Later her uncle, who owned a quarter horse ranch in Virginia, got her family involved with quarter horses, which she took to the Green Swamp for match races.

Her association with thoroughbreds began when her ex-husband, Dr. Hernando Del Castillo, acquired some.

"I watched how the trainer trained these horses and I couldn't believe that the horses could run. I think they really damage them structurally," she said. "I think they need a better foundation, which is why I train the way I do.

"I want to put guts in them," she said.

Trainer Dwaine Glenn of K-ville said Del Castillo's practices are based on a sound theory.

"Anytime you run a horse in deep sand like that, you're going to leg them up real well," Glenn said. "It's an endurance program — it does help them. I see nothing wrong with it."

Glenn said more orthodox methods are often used because the trainers don't have the facilities to train the horses any other way.

Del Castillo's horses do not get drugs, liniments, or leg wraps, all common practices in horse racing.

"If a 2-year-old needs leg wraps, he shouldn't be training," she said.

She has been training thoroughbreds for about 10 years and says experience has been a great teacher.

"I used to gallop them all the time," she said. "But I learned that no matter how fit they are, they won't run any faster than God will allow them to run. They won't run faster than their natural ability."

The proof, of course, is in the race results, and Del Castillo's evidence is First Prediction, a horse she refers to as "sweetness and light."

First Prediction, owned and trained by Del Castillo, is a 7-year-old gray mare who has won two stakes races. Only 3 percent of thoroughbreds ever win a stakes race.

"She is a dream come true. People wait for years for a stakes horse, and I never knew what I had," Del Castillo said. She bought the delicate mare, which is gray with dark flecks, from a children's home for $2,500. First Prediction has won more than $270,000.

First Prediction has displayed heart, a racehorse's most elusive quality, in both her racing style and in coming back from injuries.

"One time she started at 26 lengths behind, and ended up losing by three lengths," Del Castillo said.

"She had a bone chip in her knee from being kicked in the pasture, and then she got a virus and foundered (an inflammation of the tissue that attaches foot to hoof)," Del Castillo said. "People said she would never race again."

First Prediction's rehabilitation took place in Eagle Lake. Del Castillo would attach a long lead to the horse's halter and stand on a dock while the horse paddled around

Janet Del Castillo, right, and Vicki Portlock, an exercise girl, run some horses through an orange grove on Del Castillo's ranch near Eagle Lake.

in the lake. Swimming exercised the horse without straining her sore feet and legs.

"She loves to swim now. Sometimes she'll lay over on her side and just float," Del Castillo said.

First Prediction returned to dry land to win several races at Gulfstream Park, including a stakes race, the Very One Handicap, which took place on Mother's Day of 1988. Del Castillo said that race was especially meaningful to her.

"She is really my baby, and it was wonderful to win a stake on Mother's Day," she said.

First Prediction now is trained almost exclusively by swimming because galloping causes her muscles to "tie up." The small, sprightly mare, who looks more like a pet than a racehorse, has won 12 races in her long career, including a $30,000 allowance race on Feb. 21 at Gulfstream.

She races most often at Gulfstream, Calder and Hialeah, where she is viewed as an underdog.

"Whenever I haul this horse down to Miami, they think she's a pony horse," Del Castillo said.

Del Castillo uses a chart to keep track of the 12 to 15 horses she trains. Assistant Eric Low, two exercise riders, and Del Castillo's children, Nando, 20, and Victoria, 17, help out at the ranch.

Most of the other horses Del Castillo trains run in claiming races at Tampa Bay Downs.

"First Prediction is the only big-league horse I've had," she said.

Lisa Hammond was an intern for The Ledger during the winter months. She is a student at Northwestern University in Evanston, Ill.

a nice Background story !

First Prediction Tops F-M Feature On Grass at Gulf

By WILLIAM C. PHILLIPS

GULFSTREAM PARK, Hallandale, Fla.—First Prediction, a dappled gray 5-year-old who is owned and trained by Janet del Castillo, will attract the most attention when 10 fillies and mares go postward in the mile allowance feature on the turf here Friday. Another four are listed as also eligibles.

Del Castillo, who trains her horses under the orange trees at Winter Haven in the central part of the state and vans them to the track to race, entered her stakes-winning earner of $204,700 to carry 122 pounds. The mare will be piloted by her regular rider, Julio Pezua.

First Prediction, who obviously thrives on the unorthodox method of training, closed with characteristic speed in the final run and won a mile and a sixteenth race by a length last out on April 16. The race was transferred from the grass to the main track.

But she is also adept on the grass. This past winter at Hialeah she got up approaching the wire for a neck victory over Christmas Dancer, who will be one of her main rivals on Friday. She was beaten by the same short margin in a three-way photo with Anka Germania and Chaldea over the Hialeah turf course in a division of the Grade III Columbiana Handicap, and in her last start at that meeting she took second behind Singular Bequest on the grass in the Key Largo.

The others who drew into the field are J.S. Carrion's Christmas Dancer, 117, Earlie Fires; Dr. Keith C. Wold's Opera Diva, 122, Robert Lester; Cam M. Gambolatti's Stuttering Sarah, 122, no rider; Gladys Ross' Frau Agustina, 115, no rider; W.P. Sise's Lycka Dancer, 119, apprentice Jorge Milian; Gray and Yingling's Betsy Mack, 115, Robert Breen; Horse Haven's Social Occasion, 108, apprentice Jorge Santos; Virginia K. Payson's Imprudent Love, 117, Lester, and Frances A. Gen-

||||||||||||||||||||||||||||||||||||||||||||||||||||||||||||||

Special Kentucky Derby Edition on Saturday

Saturday's issue of Daily Racing Form will be the annual Kentucky Derby Edition, featuring complete Past Performances of all the entrants, including latest workouts, plus special articles on their owners, trainers, jockeys, Pedigree Profiles and many other features about the race and the people associated with it.

Included in Saturday's issue with the Past Performances will be a graded handicap, probable odds, expert selections, a handicapping analysis of the race and consensus.

||||||||||||||||||||||||||||||||||||||||||||||||||||||||||||||

ter's Truly, 117, Jose Velez Jr.

The also eligibles are Wimborne Farm's Grande Couture, coupled as an entry with Imprudent Love, 115, Earlie Fires; Knoll Lane Farm's Tea for Top, 119, Mile Gonzalez; Peter Barbarino's Lucky Touch, 117, no rider, and Hardesty and Walden's Bereavement, 117, Fires.

Christmas Dancer, third and fourth in a couple of other turf races at Hialeah, comes off a sharp second to True Chompion at a mile on the grass here March 22. She held a daylight lead before she was overtaken by First Prediction in their previous meeting at Hialeah and she has the speed to either take the lead or be near the pace in this event. She is a 5-year-old daughter of Sovereign Dancer and trained by J. Bert Sonnier.

This will be the first race for Truly since the 5-year-old In Reality mare was second behind Algenib in a race taken off the turf and run at seven furlongs on a sloppy track March 24. She won four of 16 races in 1986, including the Impatiens and Vizcaya handicaps and lost the Black Velvet Handicap on the main track there to First Prediction by a nose in August

Florida

First Prediction Makes Grade

A View From Florida
Tampa Bay

Training in the Orange Groves

Imagine this scenario, if you will:

You're sitting on a beautiful bass lake in central Florida, casting artificial worms and crank baits against the cattails while in search of that trophy largemouth. The lake is all but deserted.

You're 90 miles from Ocala, 50 miles from Tampa Bay Downs and more than 200 miles from Miami. The furthest thing from your mind is horses and horse racing.

But suddenly you hear a sound, a familiar sound you've heard a hundred times before. It starts as just a murmur, but in a matter of moments it grows louder and more distinct.

It's the sound of horse's hooves, and from the pattern of the sound, it's obvious these horses are working. You look around for a training track, for some sign of a racing strip, but all you see are orange trees.

After some investigation you find out that you had indeed heard race horses at work and that those charges came from the Rancho Del Castillo, a unique training facility located high on a hill overlooking Eagle Lake and the surrounding rolling landscape of central Florida.

The story of Rancho Del Castillo and it's master, Janet Del Castillo is one well worth repeating.

JANET DEL CASTILLO
An off-beat trainer

From the Peace Corps to the Race Track

It seems that many years ago a young Peace Corps volunteer found herself in the wilds of Columbia. While working with the natives there, she met a doctor who she later married. The couple eventually settled in Winter Haven. The husband wanted some race horses so they went into business the usual way, by contacting a trainer and buying some stock.

"To make a long story short," continues Janet Del Castillo, "the horses were soon beat up and injured from racing and wound up on the farm here. My husband wanted to get rid of them but I persisted, stalling him for a time.

"After he went to work I would work with the horses, learning as I went along. I snuck them over to the track to work once they were recovered, hurrying back before my husband got home."

Although the marrriage failed to survive, Del Castillo's interest and love for thoroughbreds not only lived, it blossomed. Using training methods and philosophies considered radical and outlandish by many of her peers, Del Castillo went about training and developing horses the way she wanted to, with only a modicum of success.

Then along came First Prediction. "I got her from the Children's Home, believe it or not," the trainer recalled. "They had two fillies they couldn't keep and I took them both for $5,000 on the cuff."

That modest purchase went on to become a top stakes and handicap distaffer for Del Castillo, earning more than $260,000 during her career and recently came back from a bout with founder to race again with top grass company at Gulfstream Park.

Developing Sound, Healthy Horses

And where did the pounding hooves come from?

"I gallop my horses through an orange grove," Del Castillo explained. "It's exactly one mile around, with a half mile stretch where we cluck 'em and let them work."

Del Castillo calls her training style the "Montessori school of horse training" and her horses are permitted to develop at their own individual pace. She doesn't race horses at two and admits it takes her charges several races to acclimate themselves to racing once their careers start.

"Because I'm here on the farm I can take my time with my horses. I don't believe in pushing young horses and I believe the results speak for themselves. I rarely use medications, hardly ever have a horse on Lasix and I don't believe I've ever had a horse of mine bow a tendon.

"Here at the farm they're allowed to graze in the paddocks, we swim them in the lake after training and we do everything to give them a natural environment.

"I substitute time, patience and healing powers Mother Nature has given the horse over speed, medications and shortcuts. I know one thing: I develop sound, healthy race horses. We may train in the groves but it's training all the same."

—————————— **Doug McCoy**

Doug McCoy is RACING ACTION's Tampa Bay correspondent.

This is the tale of a woman and a horse.

It is also the tale of good things coming to those who do things, "my way" and the "hard way."

Best of all, it is the story of charity, the good side of horse racing, the nice people involved and their rewards.

The woman raised in San Francisco during the 1950s always loved horses. She cared for and trained polo ponies in Northern California while growing up. She joined the Peace Corps in the mid-1960's, served in the poverty of South America doing whatever she could.

In fact, it was while there that she met her husband and aided him delivering babies by candlelight in Columbia. Her name is Janet Del Castillo.

The horse is a mare. A gray mare foaled in 1982 by On To Glory out of the Hagley mare Around The Bend. She was just

JANET DE CASTILLO
Trains in groves

another one of the yearlings in breeder Paul Marriott's large operation and when the herd was culled, her destiny was to be donated as a yearling to the Florida Children's Home in Cintra, Florida. Her name is First Prediction.

Dr. Hernando Del Castillo and his family returned to the United States and bought a farm, Rancho Del Castillo, in Winter Haven, Florida and went into the thoroughbred business with the expectations of raising a champion. Janet took out a trainer's license but there were no champions.

"When the horses (they were) just cheap claimers) did not win the Kentucky Derby right away, my husband lost interest in racing," she said. "But we had over $25,000 invested and I didn't want to give up just like that."

Then she got a break.

While working at the Florida Children's Home, still helping others, she spotted a gray yearling filly that she thought might have some ability on the race track and invested in her and took her back to her farm in Winter Haven. The filly was First Prediction.

First Prediction's road to success has not been traditional, unconventional would be more apt.

"I can train horses in an orange grove," Janet said, "and have them as fit as any that train at the race track."

First Prediction's success story on the track is just as unbelievable. She could really be called the "Iron Mare," for in nearly 60 starts, she has earned over $250,000 and done it the hard way—on the rubber-based strip at Calder, the main tracks at Gulfstream and Hialeah, and the grass courses of all three South Florida race tracks.

Her most recent string of wins began in an even more bizarre manner. It seems Gulfstream Racing Secretary Tommy Trotter was having a tough time filling the Rampart Handicap because no one wanted to challenge Wayne Lukas' Life At The Top and Woody Stephens' I'm Sweets. He approached Del Castillo, and though she had another race in mind for First Prediction, she said that she would be there.

When we questioned her on why she accepted this spot she responded, "Did you ever hear of a trainer using a handicap race as a tightener for an allowance race?"

Unfortunately, everything did not go right, as First Prediction did not reach a contending position for her patented late charge and trailed throughout.

But 11 days later, she made the six-hour van trip from Winter Haven down to Gulfstream and won an allowance race.

Then on Mother's Day, after a lengthy van trip, First Prediction—under the brilliant handling of Julio Perua—was up to win The Very One Handicap by a nose at one mile on the turf.

As First Prediction came back to the winner's circle, hundreds of fans circled around and cheered the winning horse, jockey and owner in a display of emotion most befitting the holiday.

Oh yes, in a story with a happy ending such as this, what began as a charitable venture continues on that way. That's because Janet Del Castillo makes a donation to the Florida Children's Home after every win.

—————————— **Derk Ackerman**

Racing Action Contributing Writer

Peace Corps Service In Trainer's Past

By Graham Ross

OLDSMAR — The first thing that Tampa Bay Downs trainer Janet Del Castillo projects is a free spirit. She is a happy soul but one with a sense of adventure — a trait perhaps first noted on Nov. 18, 1963, when she left her San Francisco upbringing on a trip to Kansas City as a Peace Corps volunteer.

Four days later President John F. Kennedy was shot, and a lot of dreams died for a lot of other children of the '60s, but Del Castillo was one of those who kept the flame burning — serving honorably in the most rural areas of Colombia, dependent on villagers for all human contact and existence itself.

"You learned to depend on others — and they on you — for everything that kept us all alive. If you didn't learn to speak the language you didn't eat, so you learned quickly, but you also learned to deal with things at their simplest level," Del Castillo now recalls. "Basicaly it was the 'in-order-to-make-lemonade-you-start-with-lemons' kind of lesson in life repeated throughout the two years I was there.

"But I also learned not to be so quick to judge other people's way of doing things while I was in Colombia. You'd start to build a roof on a hut and the villagers would tell you to wait until the moon was right — and if you resisted the temptation to scoff, you could learn that sap flows better when the moon is right, and would help hold the roof in place."

But while in Colombia Del Castillo met and married a doc-

tor, returned to this country, and mostly through her husband's initiative, became involved with thoroughbreds at their farm in Winter Haven. When the marriage failed, Del Castillo became a horse trainer by default, using training methods as unorthodox as her Peace Corps past and her life with the villagers.

"I take my horses on three-mile gallops through the orange groves overlooking Eagle Lake," Del Castillo offers, as one of her training exercises, and I find that the middle mile is the hardest. That middle mile pretty much tells me a lot about each horse — whether or not they are going to want to go that third mile"

Mercedes Won In Beam Stakes

OLDSMAR — Florida Derby winner Mercedes Won, owned locally by Oldsmar resident Christopher Spencer, came out of his third-place finish in the Tampa Bay Derby "better than he went into it," according to Spencer, and will be in northern Kentucky for a planned next engagement in the upcoming Jim Beam Stakes at Turfway Park on Saturday, April 1.

"He came back bouncing," Spencer said of Mercedes Won following the Tampa Bay Derby on March 19. "he just had too much to overcome. It would have been nice to win one in front of the home folks, but that's racing luck and it wasn't meant to be."

Spencer plans to remain in northern Kentucky area until after the Jim Beam.

Another somewhat unusual training regimen — swimming her horse in Eagle Lake after training—led to an unusual experience for one of her three children, who range in age from 21 to 17 years old. "My kids always helped with the training of the horses from the time they were 14. They did everything. No matter what, they pitched in," Del Castillo now recalls.

"For some reason, my son always wanted to be one of those smiling, happy kids you always see on television commercials for soft drinks, and I've always tried to teach my kids the power of imagery: the ability to make things come true by thinking positively about them and working to make them happen.

"One day a television camera crew came to town, and ended up filming a Mountain Dew commercial at our farm, with my son riding one of our horses around Eagle Lake towing a water skier in the lake itself. It was a great commercial, and a dream come true for my son."

And what of her own dreams — this child of Camelot — beyond the usual fantasies of horse trainers? "I'd like to have my cartoon strip, that I call 'Mulliken Stu,' become syndicated," Del Castillo says. "It's centered around thoroughbreds being raised on our farm by kids, and the idea is to present the world of thoroughbreds as a fun thing, full of family involvement, not as a threat to families.

"That's how we all need to project thoroughbred racing —

showing its health and its basic communication with nature," Del Castillo concluded.

She explained all that following:

Trainer Janet Del Castillo shows a condition book to one of her thoroughbreds running at Tampa Bay Downs.

Photo by Bob Cicero

a day when she had no horses entered and no real reason to make the hour-long drive from her farm to the race course, other than to help promote the sport Tampa Bay Downs' Saturday which she initially inherited by default.

'Horses need to romp on grass. They need each other's company.'

It's a strictly down-home operation

Del Castillo believes in her methods despite skeptics

By TOM AINSLIE

JANET DEL CASTILLO

In a 14-acre orange grove on the sandy shore of Eagle Lake, near Winter Haven, Fla., a non-conformist named Janet Del Castillo raises, schools and trains thoroughbreds for the racing wars.

Even as these racing her horses live at home, 60 miles from Tampa Bay Downs, 220 miles from the eastern Florida tracks. They van to the track on race day. That evening they come home to recuperate in grassy paddocks, swim in the lake and gallop every few days on the trails among the orange trees.

It is important to Del Castillo, a horse-lover, that horses need to romp on grass. They need each other's company. Individual confinement to racetrack stalls for 23 hours a day is unnatural.

She does not race 2-year-o'k. She asks no horse for speed until he is almost 3. Her horses race on food and water, unmedicated.

These methods arouse skepticism, but her horses dispel it. They win their share above a horse's usual indoor-outdoor race. They last for season after season. She never pays more than $2,500 for a yearling. But she has won stakes.

Her best buy was First Prediction, a 2-year-old filly that had been donated to a children's home where Janet was a volunteer worker. The tiny gray was by On to Glory, a half-brother to Ruffian. Janet and Buckfinder in a six-year career, she compiled in more than 13 stakes and earning $312,000 novel but not new. Before racing

was urbanized in enclosed stadiums, horses trained at home. Some harness races, quarter horses and thoroughbreds still do. What sets thoroughbred apart is the essence of bounden duty to advance an idea that might benefit fellow horsefolk, the breed and racing itself.

To encourage experimentation by others, she is writing an instruction manual called, "The Backyard Racehorse." She also conducts seminars. She recently regaled a two-day gathering of enthusiastic horsefolk at the New Jersey farm of a friend and fellow owner-trainer Ann Cain. She was interviewed there.

"Thousands of Americans already have horses on their own property," said Janet. "Not only thoroughbreds, but horses of all kinds—pleasure horses, cutting horses, draft horses, you name it. When these horse-lovers learn how gratifying it is to school and care for a racehorse and hard care practical it is to our sport. Master of fact, we already have.

Obviously, not everyone with a horse has enough acreage for serious conditioning. But many do, says Del Castillo, and others have access to useful trails, hills and bridle paths. If shipping back and forth between home and track is not feasible, horses properly schooled at home are welcome in the trackside stable of good trainers. And can return home for furloughs.

"Before its first start, a horse needs to be at the track a few times to become acclimated to the environment and accustomed to the producing speed on a dirt oval," Del

Castillo points out. "But, before and after those workouts and all the races that follow, home is the best place to keep the horse."

As the reader may have surmised, these ideas come from no shrinking violet. Janet Helene Mulgannon Del Castillo is a strapping, strong-minded individual who speaks her mind. She is a 40-something, with three grown children and a divorce from three family name behind her.

She grew up in San Francisco, where her father was a Federal narcotics agent. She became horse-happy at an early age, walking and rubbing polo ponies. While an art major at San Francisco State, she opted for real life, joined the Peace Corps and spent two years of privation in a Colombian village. She nursed the sick, struggled to establish rudimentary sanitation and warned of the beauty and generosity of the poor family and the lake and the Kentucky...

She returned home and married the young Colombian doctor whom she had assisted in the village. He revived her interest in horses when he decided to buy an inexpensive yearling and win the Kentucky Derby, then that failed, he dropped the project. But she was hooked and has racehorses ever since.

All right now. What exactly are the advantages of "backyard" schooling and conditioning? And what does it take to develop winners who go the track only to race?

"The purpose of training," says Janet Del Castillo, "is to fulfill a horse's potential without breaking him down. At home you give your

horses the natural environment in which their bodies and spirits thrive. Frolicking and grazing with each other makes them more resilient, makes them happier.

"But the main factor is the severe disadvantage of trying to strengthen equine bone, muscle and speed in a track. Conditioning is a cycle of stress-recovery-stress-recovery. As a track, the horse stressed by a hard race or workout is confined to a stall, sometimes with pain-killing medication, and walked under the lead of one who may then stay confined again to strain himself at high speed. That program, combined with the frequent after-effect of medication, can hasten the onset of physical problems. But a horse naturally from routine trauma, free to walk and jog his way through the discomfort.

Another major advantage is the economical. The inexpensive shipping to and from the track is far less than the cost of keeping a horse in training there. And there is in the joy of having your horse around and knowing that no other arrangement could be more constructive.

As to the Know-how, she describes it as low for horses plus a horse can turf commonsense than command sense. Start of the excursion that begins before age 2. At her own place, Del Castillo has cut a trail that winds up and down gallop young horses slow... for three miles every three or four years at a year, monitoring their reactions. After that winds starts turns). She approaches her most difficult animals, ready for racing, rugged

JANET DEL CASTILLO has been training in Florida from her home base.

Horses Benefit from Fruits of Her Labor

JANET DEL CASTILLO of Winter Haven, Florida has bucked the odds when it comes to training Thoroughbreds.

Most trainers run their horses at the closest racetrack. Not Janet. She works her horses in the orange groves on the family farm.

"It's the perfect environment for them to build up muscle and stamina," Janet says. "Galloping through the deep sand and up the rolling hills of the groves gives strength to all their muscles."

Makes sense especially when you consider Janet got the idea from raising her own children. "I thought about raising strong, healthy kids and applied the same thinking to horses. The best place for them to develop and grow is right in their own backyard!"

Horsing Around

At the farm, the horses are turned out early in the morning and given the freedom to frolic in the pasture.

Janet only works them every 3 or 4 days, and often includes a swim in a nearby lake as part of the routine. "I found that it's good therapy, especially if a horse has an injury."

To support her claim, she points out one of her Thoroughbreds that had a bone chip in its knee and suffered from inflammation. "People said she'd never race again," Janet recalls.

She took the horse to the lake, attached a long lead rope to the halter and let the horse paddle around, getting exercise without straining the injury.

"She really loves to go

> *"Sometimes she'll lay on her side and float in the water!"*

GALLOPING GROVES. Janet Del Castillo chooses to train her Thoroughbreds at home instead of at the racetrack. She runs them through the orange groves on the family's Winter Haven, Florida farm.

to the lake and swim now," Janet affirms. "Sometimes she'll actually roll over on her side and just float!"

Proof's in Pace

When her horses aren't floating or frisking in the orange groves, they're often winning races. "First Prediction", a gray mare Janet bought on credit in 1984, is a prime example.

A Florida breeder had donated First Prediction and another filly to a children's home where Janet was a volunteer. The director of the home decided that he couldn't house the horses and asked Janet if she was interested in them.

The other filly turned out to be best suited for pleasure riding. But First Prediction went on to win dozens of races, earning over $300,000. Not bad for a "backyard" horse!

"My horses get to run free and act like horses every day, and I think that gives them an edge," Janet informs. "There are many ways to train Thoroughbreds, but I think my 'backyard regimen' will soon become more popular with other trainers."

No doubt. Why buck a winning trend?

EQUUS
Jan, 1991

THE FILE

The Road Less Traveled

Racehorse trainer Janet Del Castillo
says at-home conditioning is the best route
to the winner's circle.

By Laura Hillenbrand

Janet Del Castillo's multiple stakes winner First Prediction thrived under her owner's unconventional "backyard race training" regimen. Del Castillo (right), conditioned the mare through swimming and long gallops on her farm.

From the moment she first visited a racetrack backstretch, Janet Del Castillo was uneasy about the physical and mental demands placed on conventionally trained racehorses. Kept in their stalls 23 hours a day, pushed to destructive speeds early in their lives and oftentimes plied with medication to add a competitive edge, most equine athletes are not allowed enough time to "be horses" in Del Castillo's view.

Nonetheless, it wasn't until the former polo pony trainer faced a tricky personal dilemma that she discovered that a completely different training style was feasible—and profitable.

In 1985 a divorce left Del Castillo with three children to raise on her own and a barn full of racehorses to train. Complicating matters was the fact that her home, an orange farm located in Winter Haven, Florida, was a 4½-hour drive from the nearest racetrack. But she solved her problems by drawing on her experience as a Peace Corps volunteer and the maxim she had once taught to others.

"In the Peace Corps, my mission was to teach people to look at their problems and cope with their problems with what they have," she says. "If you have lemons, make lemonade."

In surveying her lemons—a 14-acre orange grove and small barn miles from the nearest racetrack—it occurred to Del Castillo that her horses might train just as well, or even better, on the heavy sand trails between her orange trees. Then, to the scorn of many trainers, owners and journalists, she packed up her horses, shipped them to her farm and began making lemonade. With the help of her children, she galloped her horses into condition on the meandering trails of her orange groves and swam them in a nearby lake, ferrying them to the track only for races and occasional timed workouts.

More than a decade later, a brilliant, multiple-stakes-winning mare and a matchless record of training sound, durable horses have silenced the naysayers. And Del Castillo is spreading the word about her concept of a "backyard racehorse."

Del Castillo's offbeat training approach does not consist of simply keeping racehorses on the farm. Blending practical experience with common sense, her program is designed to engender the endurance, strength and physical maturity needed to withstand the breakneck speeds of racing.

"Horses have a capacity to do more than what is good for them," she explains. "On the track, [trainers] go straight to speed. The horses start pulling themselves apart. That's damage you can't undo. You have to allow them a certain amount of growth time." Thus, Del Castillo's horses are not raced or asked for speed drills before they are three years old. Instead, the trainer uses swimming and long gallops at graduated distances and weights to give them the "substructure to allow them to hold up to their own speed." And, once horses are fit, Del Castillo gallops them only every three to four days. "All you have to do is keep their wheels greased," she says.

The trainer also takes a commonsense approach to her horses' stabling arrangements. Unlike track-dwelling athletes, who are usually out of their stalls only for training or racing, Del Castillo's horses are turned out for much of the day, an arrangement that allows them to stretch, graze and socialize at will. "I try to inhibit the horse as little as possible," she says. "Horses are very social animals. When they are emotionally undernourished, they develop

I didn't have a book when this article came out – I got many calls from readers!

neurotic habits to cope with it."

"People think a horse has to be jumping out of his stall and acting like an idiot to be a good runner. Those things don't go hand in hand," she continues. "My horses are relaxed, but when they go to the racetrack, they know what they're there for."

While one set of unusual circumstances spurred the development of Del Castillo's unique training approach, another led to her greatest triumphs—as well as the long-awaited vindication of her methods.

In 1984, a Florida breeder donated two Thoroughbred fillies as pleasure-horse prospects to a children's home where Del Castillo was a volunteer. The home's director soon determined that he could not house the fillies, and asked Del Castillo if she was interested in them. Although in such a precarious financial position that she feared losing her home, Del Castillo saw enough potential in the fillies to buy them, on credit, for the bargain-basement price of $5,000.

One of the fillies did indeed prove to be best suited to life as a riding hack, but the other, a little gray named First Prediction, thrived on the backyard training regimen and became Del Castillo's most accomplished runner.

First Prediction, who won several stakes races and earned more than $300,000, almost single-handedly put her trainer on the map and proved the legitimacy of her once-maligned training approach. Dubbed the "Iron Maiden," the mare was phenomenally sound, racing more than 100 times between ages three and eight, while sometimes competing as often as three times in two weeks.

So far, First Prediction is the only stakes-class campaigner to emerge from Del Castillo's barn, but the trainer has also had notable success with her less celebrated charges. Although she has been able to afford only obscurely bred runners, almost every one of her horses has made it to the winner's circle during its racing career—an extraordinary statistic for any racing stable.

In addition, Del Castillo has managed to avoid the soundness troubles that frequently plague racing operations. She reports, for example, that none of her horses has a tendon problem, an affliction common among conventionally trained runners. And, although she does use medication when necessary, such instances are rare. "I try to combine common sense and medical know-how," says Del Castillo, "The horses I train last."

Currently at work on a backyard training manual, Del Castillo is also planning a series of seminars for those interested in learning more about her philosophy and techniques.

While admitting that backyard training is not for just anyone with a horse, barn and pasture, Del Castillo believes that her program can bring much-needed new blood to racing. "I'm trying to appeal to competent horsepeople. I want to encourage racing to be a positive force," she says. "People have illusions that only the rich and the criminals are involved, but there are many, many people like me in the sport."

A strong selling point is the comparative cost of backyard training as opposed to conventional race training. On-track training can cost as much as $100 per day, Del Castillo says, while training a racehorse at home costs no more than keeping a pleasure horse. Plus, she points out, racehorses normally spend months at the track, running up bills before they are even old enough to have their talent gauged. In contrast, her program calls for a horse to be shipped to a professional trainer at the track only when the animal is ready to begin speed training and racing. If a horse turns out to be a poor racing prospect, he has cost his owner far less than a conventionally prepared horse would have, Del Castillo says, and his relaxed upbringing will make him an excellent pleasure horse.

Basically, the trainer says, she wants to share some of the enjoyment she has derived from racing. Looking out the window of her home, Del Castillo's eyes rest on her Cinderella horse, First Prediction, now in foal to Preakness winner Gate Dancer. "The joy I've had with this you could never buy." ■

Laura Hillenbrand, BestSelling author of Seabiscut wrote this article in 1991 ! What an Honor!

EQUUS
Magazine
Nov '93
HORSE
TRENDS

"Restoring
a
Tarnished
Image"

A Voice In The Wilderness

Janet Del Castillo is on a mission. She's a Thoroughbred trainer who believes that the flagging industry can be revitalized by returning the focus of the sport to the welfare of the animal athlete. The current American way of keeping racehorses "incarcerated" 23 hours a day, of undertraining them and then using legal, painkilling drugs to control body soreness is a recipe for the horses' eventual self-destruction, she says.

Del Castillo trains her stable on the home farm in Winter Haven, Florida, conditioning the runners with gallops through the orange groves and swimming them in the pond, and ships to regional tracks on race days. She shares her do-it-yourself training principles and practices in booklet and seminar forms under the title "Backyard Racehorse."

She also writes letters to the movers and shakers of the Thoroughbred industry, letters that have gotten no positive response but which have, with uncanny accuracy, foretold rude awakenings to come. From a letter dated December 3, 1992 to the Animal Welfare Committee of the American Association of Equine Practitioners (AAEP):

"The spectacle of horses snapping their legs in front of the grandstand and jockeys going down on them is not good. The standard comment when breakdown occurs is that it is a tough business...high speed...fast horses...accidents happen. That is true; however, we know that if we look at the history of the majority of the horses that break down, we see warnings all along the way. The vet bills tell a story of a horse with problems. Potent painkillers used when the horse runs, injections of cortisone in knees and ankles, an abundance of short- and long-term steroids given persistently over a period of time—these are not indications of a fit and healthy racehorse."

In September 1992, Del Castillo wrote to the head of the Arizona Race Track Industry Program, hoping she might be included in the annual symposium. She wasn't, but her calls for better owner relations, reduced dependence on drugs, more rational conditioning and greater fair play and honesty in the industry are just now being uttered by some of the recognized leaders.

"I am fully aware of the pressures put to the trainers and vets by the owners and tracks," she wrote in her letter to the AAEP Animal Welfare Committee. "I realize that everyone is struggling to survive, but the decisions made for short-term gain are long-term disaster. From within the industry, we must encourage change."

"Backyard" trainer Janet Del Castillo and First Prediction, the castoff filly who ran 100 races, some in stakes company, and earned over $300,000 while being conditioned on the home farm.

Karen Del Castillo

Racehorse Trainer Makes Name as Speaker

BILLIE ELLIS

The world doesn't stand still, and neither does Janet DelCastillo.

For a number of years, Janet has been training racehorses at her farm, Ranchero DelCastillo on Crystal Beach Road, and has made quite a name for herself. She even wrote a book, "Backyard Racehorse-The Training Manual," with Lois Schwartz. Now she is facing other challenges as a sought-after featured speaker at seminars and conventions.

"Training racehorses is my real job," Janet said. "But I have managed to also incorporate teaching, writing and speaking in that field to my other endeavor. Having had a varied life experience, I enjoy doing motivational speeches that can be tailored to the groups' needs.

The basic message is: One person can make a difference and achieve his dreams. The little guy can win with persistence and determination. "Adversity," she said, can make you stronger — if you know how to use it!" The underlying theme in all of Janet's talks is that the individual can make a difference; personal responsibility and capability are alive and well. "You can be ethical and survive in the '90s," she said.

"I'm getting into the convention market," she said, "to try to help us back to reality. I try to bring us back to the point of reference of what is important to us. Like how to raise a moral child in an amoral world."

Her desire to share her hard-...

earned knowledge with others and the desire to improve the racing industry from within have led to a career in writing and speaking. She has published various articles, written and illustrated comic strips that have appeared here and in South America, and is now a professional speaker. The third edition of "Backyard Racehorse" has just come out, and Janet has a full schedule of seminars to wedge in between her training duties.

Public speaking isn't new to Janet. She has had lots of experience and is piling up more of it because of the demand. She gives exciting talks based on her own experiences and her strong belief that you can win by working hard and playing by the rules.

From delivering babies by candlelight at the age of 19 while in the Peace Corps, to galloping through orange groves training her horses, Janet has led a life full of excitement and challenge. She has held steadfastly to her belief that the little guy can win. Hard-work and tenacity do pay off in her opinion.

Janet DelCastillo, a former Peace Corps worker, an author and a successful racehorse trainer, has added motivational speaking to her resume.

A former student in the art school at San Francisco State University, she joined the Peace Corps in 1963 and found herself in a rural part of Colombia, South America. She spent the next two years as the only American in a small rural village. She barely had time to ask the village what she could do for them before being sent off in a dugout canoe to inoculate neighboring villagers against an outbreak of smallpox. Later she was involved in combating malaria, rescuing an insane woman ned to a stake, and trying to teach the villagers basic hygiene - all providing insight that made her the woman she is today.

After 18 years of marriage to a physician, divorce forced her to confront the realities of making a living in the "real" world. She was left with the responsibility of raising three teen-age children, a barn full of racehorses and a

small farm to manage.

Janet has had many years of teaching and public speaking experience. She has run the gamut of public speaking situations from working and teaching young women from San Francisco's inner city, through her Peace Corps volunteering, on to designing and implementing a health program for the Florida State Medical Auxiliary. Her personal warmth and vivacious personality make her a favorite with every audience.

Her favorite subject matter is horses, a subject she knows well. She broke and galloped her own horses for years, both at the track and in the orange groves around her farm, and she took her first horse out of the gates personally. She has observed and learned from every horse that has been through her farm. Her practical hands-on experience and her complete honesty make her a valuable adviser to

owners and trainers.

Janet's offbeat training program does not consist simply of keeping racehorses on the farm. It blends practical experience with common sense and is designed to enhance the endurance, strength and physical maturity horses need to withstand the breakneck speeds of racing.

In addition to speaking at various seminars and conventions, she even holds one at her home. These are five day seminar.

An update on Janet's children: The oldest son, Alex, 29, a graduate of the Naval Academy, is stationed in Japan. Nando, 27, is an international model based in Miami, and Victoria, 24, works in real estate in New York City, and enjoys auditioning on Broadway.

Janet DelCastillo is a versatile lady and one well worth knowing.

HIGH SCHOOL REUNION

The Winter Haven High School graduating class of 1942 had a great reunion, according to all

ORDER FORM

Backyard Racehorse
3708 Crystal Beach Road
Winter Haven, Florida 33880
Tel 1 (863) 299-8448 FAX 1 (863) 294-9401

SEND TO:

_____

_____

_____

Telephone:_____

Backyard Racehorse - $35.00 per copy

Number of Copies: ___ x $ 35.00 = _____

Florida Residents add 6%   _____

Shipping - Priority Mail $ 7.00

Total Enclosed   _____

For information regarding The Backyard Race Horse Newsletter,
or seminars at Rancho Del Castillo or in your area, contact
Prediction Publications at the above address.

I am interested in The Newsletter   _____

I am interested in Seminars   _____

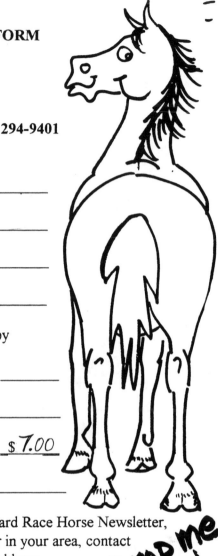

Drop me a Line!